THE

HISTORY

OF THE

REFORMATION IN SWEDEN.

By L. A. ANJOU,

COUNCILLOR TO THE KING OF SWEDEN

TRANSLATED FROM THE SWEDISH

BY

HENRY M. MASON, D. D.

New-York:

SHELDON & COMPANY,

No. 115 Nassau-Street.

1859.

CONTENTS.

BOOK I.

CHAPTER I.

CHAPTER II.

CHAPTER III.

CHAPTER IV.

CHAPTER V.

CHAPTER VI.

CHAPTER VII.

CHAPTER VIII.

CHAPTER IX.

CHAPTER X.

CHAPTER XI.

BOOK III.

CHAPTER I.

CHAPTER II.

CHAPTER III.

CHAPTER IV.

CHAPTER V.

CHAPTER VI.

CHAPTER VII.

CHAPTER VIII.

APPENDICES.

THE HISTORY

OF THE

ECCLESIASTICAL REFORMATION

IN SWEDEN.

CHAPTER I.

THE SWEDISH CHURCH TO THE YEAR 1520.

1.—EPISCOPAL SEES.

The first stream of the light of Christianity, as far as we can discern, falls over our fatherland at the same time in which our history advances into day. That Ansgarius, who came from the monastery of Corbey, in France, here preached the Gospel in the year 829, is the first incident that occurs in the annals of Sweden, with full historic certainty. But if this is beyond all doubt, we are still in doubt in what part of our fatherland he made his appearance; and with this rising of the sun it is still wrapped in the mist of morning what people heard of him the word of life. For nearly six-and-thirty years after his first coming, venerable missionaries watched and worked over the tender plant. Some time after his first visit, he returned, in his old age, to keep it alive, since, of the teachers he meanwhile sent to Sweden, at least one had already become a blood-witness for the new faith; as archbishop of Hamburgh, and afterward of Bremen, he had charged himself with the conversion of the North.

The erection of the archbishopric of Hamburgh, in 834, its confirmation by the pope in 835, and the union of the see with Bremen, in 858, had for their object the Christianizing of the North. The archbishop of Bremen had this mission under his care, until its primacy over the Swedish church was transferred from Bremen to the archbishopric of Lund, created in the year 1103. At length the archbishop of Upsal and the Swedish church publicly refused to acknowledge the bishop of Lund as their primate; and the Swedish ecclesiastical provinces, through their own archbishop, stood in immediate connection with the Roman chair.

For more than three hundred years after the first efforts of Ansgarius for the conversion of the Swedes, and for more than a century after Christianity, in consequence of the baptism of king Olof Skötkonung, began to be more generally known by the Swedish people, the Swedish was a missionary church. The country was visited by teachers, at first from France, afterward chiefly from England, whose distinguished missionaries began to turn their attention to the North, when their former fields of labor in the Netherlands, Switzerland, and Germany, had well nigh fully received the seed-corn of God's holy word.

These teachers traversed the regions to which either opportunity or the hope of success called them. We are informed by Adam, of Bremen, that about the year 1070, there was found in Sweden, because of the late planting of Christianity, no episcopal see with defined boundaries; but that any bishop, approved by the king or people, built churches in common with others, travelled over the land, converted to Christianity as many as he could, and ruled them during his life, without the jealousy of another.

In the twelfth century, for the first time, the Swedish church was brought into a close agreement with the general institutions of the Western church; and from being a missionary field, became a complete member of the ecclesiastical communion of Western Europe. This condition of things was perfected, and the structure completed, in 1248; when, through the decree of a council held in Skening, the law of clerical celibacy was brought into practice in Sweden, and the whole legislation of the Roman church was more widely recognized and considered as a pattern. To present to the reader a clear picture of the church whose emendation was the work and honor of the sixteenth century, it is necessary, even in this general outline, to explain her condition anterior to the commencement of the Reformation. The present Sweden contains within its borders the two cities which, during the middle ages, from the twelfth century, were centres, the one, Upsala, for the church of Sweden, and the other, Lund, for the church of Denmark. A picture of the church's outward condition must present the two metropolitan sees; and also the episcopal sees which were subject to Upsala, and embraced in that ecclesiastical province.

The see of Upsala first presents itself, with clearness for historic purposes, in the time of king Erik the saint. He had raised to this see the Englishman Henrik, who is reported to have come to Sweden with his countryman, Nicholas Breakspear.* Henrik, who is wont to be considered the fourth bishop of Upsala, was, through a similarity of pious tastes, united in close friendship with king Erik. The king and the bishop labored mutually for the establishment of the Swedish church, and mutually to promote the conversion of the Finns.

A few years after their death, an archbishopric was created at Upsala. The confirmation brief of pope Alexander

* Cardinal of Alba; afterward pope, under the title of Adrian IV.

III., dated August 5, 1164, for Stephen the first archbishop, places him below the archbishop of Lund. As Stephen, according to the pope's grant and command, was consecrated to his office by archbishop Eskil, of Lund; so, without doubt, were the successors of the one to receive consecration, and to show duty and obedience to the successors of the other, as primate.

The immediate successors of Stephen received consecration to the archbisopric of Upsala from the archbishop of Lund. But an effort was soon made to be released from this obligation, which seemed derogatory to the Swedish people. It was sometimes even denied that the obligation ever existed; and the Roman chair upheld or permitted the case, according as ignorance of the true state of things, or the interest of the times, influenced the matter.

It is said that Nicholas Ragvaldi, bishop of Wexio, representative of the kingdoms of the North at the council of Basle, and in the name of Erik XIII., effected the Swedish church's independence of the primate of Lund. It may be added of this remarkable man, that, on his entrance into the council, he arrested attention by his speech on the origin of the Goths from Scandinavia; a speech which showed the right of Nicholas, as envoy of the Gothic kings, to take the first place among the legates of princes. He was afterward sent, by a commission of the council, to establish a peace between the king of France and the duke of Burgundy. In the year 1438 he was elected, and at Basle confirmed and consecrated, as archbishop of Upsala; with firmness contended for the Swedish church's independence of the temporal power in the election of bishops; as archbishop, after his return, laid the foundation at Stacket of that unfortunate castle, and in 1440 bartered it with the crown. Not a word, however, of the independence of which we have spoken, occurs in the records of the council; and we are left in doubt of the passage of such a decree. In our day we see that, in Sweden, this claim of the primate would be improper.

Some years after the appearance of Nicholas at Basle, it happened, at the Scandinavian council of Kalmar, that Tuve, archbishop of Lund, permitted his archiepiscopal cross to be borne before him. This right belonged to a metropolitan only in his province. The archbishop of Upsala, the Nicholas we have mentioned, was not in Kalmar; but his suffragans, the bishops of Linkoping, Strängness, and Wexio, considered him injured, because Tuve, by the use of the cross in this place, seemed "to show that he wished to press either his pre-eminence or right of primacy within the province of Upsala." The protestors, together with the lagman or judge, Bengt Jonsson, and the castellan of Stockholm, Magnus Gren, publicly and solemnly, in an express action noted and witnessed, appealed to the privileges and immemorial prescription of the church of Upsala. In vain had archbishop Tuve declared, that, solely for the honor of God, and from respect to king Christopher, who was present at the council, had he employed his cross, but that he thereby by no means wished to signify any pre-eminence in the Swedish ecclesiastical provinces, and that he would readily permit the archbishop of Upsala to bear the cross before him in the ecclesiastical province of Lund. The legal protest was, nevertheless, in right of their archbishop, recorded by the cautious Swedish bishops.

A like scene occurred again at Kalmar, in 1482, at a council where were present the archbishops of Upsala and Lund, Jacob Ulfsson and John Broksdorp, who, besides other merits, were each men of mark, and active in laying the foundation of the first universities in their fatherland at Upsala and Köpenham. John, like Tuve, permitted his archiepiscopal cross to be borne before him. Jacob Ulfsson protested, proceeded by two messengers to forbid the attempt of the prelate of Lund, and even laid his complaint before pope Sixtus IV.

The relations, however, were in process of time considerably changed. John Bengtsson, the dean of Upsala, was called, after the death of Nils Ragvaldsson, in 1448, to the archbishopric. His procurators were sent to seek confirmation from that pope, for whom a strong party in Germany declared itself. There was no question of seeking this confirmation in Lund. One of the messengers hastened before the others to Basle; the others to Rome, to pope Nicholas V., who wrote to John Bengtsson, that if he would reject and denounce the council of Basle, and acknowledge Nicholas as pope and Christ's representative, to whom belong confirmation and investiture in office, the election should be approved, and John in all else experience the pope's favor. The archbishop, who had been consecrated at Upsala, on the confirmation of the council of Basle, allowed himself to be consecrated anew after he obtained the confirmation of Nicholas. The reward of this compliance was received in 1455, when pope Calixtus III. called him primate of Sweden, a title which thus belonged at the same time to two archbishops.

With John Bengtsson, who was connected with the most influential families of the land, and portioned it among his time-servers and partisans, began, with increasing vehemence, even in Sweden, the effort to match the visible church's strength with that of the state.. This false extension of the church's power, which culminated in the contests between the popes and emperors, had chiefly shown itself in Western Europe, and had for some time occasioned the archbishops of Lund to reach the highest point of rivalry with the kings of Denmark. Jacob Ulfsson, successor to archbishop John Bengtsson, was nominated at Rome, though the chapter of Upsala elected another, Thord, who, however, died before the return from Italy of Jacob, who was living there when the nomination occurred, and who possessed his dignities the unusually long period of nearly forty-five years.* He experienced, in 1497, the revenge of the elder Sten Sture in the sack and plundering of the archiepiscopal garden at Upsala, and in other outrages done to the persons of churchmen and the property of the church; for which Sture was excommunicated by him. But Ulfsson was to a great degree protected, partly by his own skill, partly by the quieter state of the times, from the storm which obliged his predecessor, at last, in order to escape the wrath of king Charles VIII., to seek refuge in Oeland. There he died; and prepared for his next successor the mournful lot of bringing upon himself a more determined hate than ever any Swedish man experienced from his countrymen.

This was the well known Gustavus Trolle, whom Jacob Ulfsson proposed as his successor. He had studied at foreign universities, especially at Cologne, and resided at Rome; when, in 1513, he became dean of Linkoping, and May 25th, 1515, archbishop of Upsala, with the right of retaining the deanery of Linkoping. He hastened home to Upsala to strengthen, by the weight of his office, the party in his native land to which he and his father, the senator Erik Trolle, belonged. But already had the union with Denmark begun to show the fruit which, in some few years, was fully ripened; for the struggle to preserve this union was, in the eyes of many, treason against the fatherland. The noble and placable regent, Sten Sture, had determined to solicit the pope's confirmation of the election, which raised to the chair of Upsala the son of the man who was in rivalry with himself for the regency. His innate mildness did not permit him to foresee the character of that passion of party hate, which, in the confusion of the times, disconcerts men,

* He was consecrated at Rome in 1470, laid down his office in 1514, and retired to a monastery of the Carthusians, where he died in 1522. His body was removed to Upsala in 1526.

and confounds every noble suffrage of their hearts. From the moment the archbishop again trod the soil of his fatherland, was he the declared open foe of the regent. All the advances Sture took for a reconciliation, were rejected with contempt and ridicule. The defiant prelate regarded neither the pope's advice to him, nor that of the clergy, not to begin an open strife with the temporal powers, but to aim at promoting peace. In vain did sundry of the bishops, the former archbishop Jacob Ulfsson (now in a monastery), and the chapter and burgesses of Stockholm, exhort him to moderation. After Trolle had declined to appear at the diet of Sodertelje in 1516, where he had been called, the regent was obliged to attempt by force to put a restraint upon him, and undertook to besiege him in his castle of Stacket, St. Erik's castle, in which the archbishop had shut himself up. At the diet of Arboga, the estates, Jan. 7, 1517, decreed that Trolle should be degraded from his office, and that Sture was not worthy of *his* office if he allowed such treason to be unpunished. It was desired that the pope should be applied to for another archbishop, and Jacob Ulfsson was imprisoned on suspicion of having part in the machinations of Trolle.

In vain was an effort made to effect a reconciliation in a diet at Stockholm, in the end of November of the same year. The archbishop, who was there under a safe conduct, declared himself unwilling to acknowledge the estates for his judge. He wished to prove his innocence before the holy father at Rome, who intrusted him with both the spiritual and temporal sword, by which he hoped to maintain the allegiance he swore the royal house of Denmark, and added that *he* would be more ready for treason who seduced them from that allegiance. Still more provoked by this insolence, the estates pronounced Trolle guilty of high treason, as one who rose in opposition to the lawful authority of his native land; and decreed that he should be degraded from his office, and that his castle of Stacket, which had been from its foundation prejudicial to the kingdom, should be razed to the ground.

The archbishop, whom the defeat of the Danes at Dufvena deprived of all hope of relief, was obliged, soon after his return from the diet at Stockholm, to give up his castle, which, as every one who had held possession of it had used it as a stronghold of power, was in the following year levelled to the ground. Trolle himself, who, on the arrival of the Danish succours at the rocks of Stockholm, had inconsiderately and unworthily declared that he now "would make his blessing in the kingdom, over its peasantry, with his sharp spears," was rescued with difficulty from the rage of the people, and was shut up in the convent of the grey friars. He then resigned his office into the hands of pope Leo X., because the estates refused to pay tithes as long as he held the episcopal chair, with an oath vowed to God they never more would acknowledge him as archbishop, or take the sacrament at his hands, and required his solemn promise never more to resume the crosier. At the diet of Arboga, in December, 1518, he renewed his abdication, and obtained a permission to maintain himself on his father's property at Ekholm in Upland.

In the last named diet, the judgment of degradation pronounced upon Trolle by the estates, was approved by Arcimbold, the papal legate. The judgment was, nevertheless, contrary to the rule and law of the church; and Arcimbold was found not more disposed to it for Sture's sake. It was also already settled that the contest between Sture and Trolle was at an end. Pope Leo X., who had already, in 1514, excommunicated, or threatened to excommunicate, Sten Sture for his unkindness to the queen mother Christina,* commissioned, in 1517, Berger, archbishop of Lund,

* Mother of Christian II., to whom Sture refused to give up her widow's seat at Orebro.

"as primate of Sweden and legate of the Apostolic see," and the bishop of Roskild, to inquire into the charges which king Christian brought against Sture; such as his outrage toward archbishop Trolle and the church's property, the imprisonment of Jacob Ulfsson, the withdrawal of the revenues of Upsala which were due to Trolle, and the support given to the injustice of his countrymen who were traitors. Berger, on May 30, 1517, put in force the excommunication against the regent and his adherents, declared Sture unworthy to hold office, and his descendants in the second degree incapacitated from having places or benefices within the diocese in which the archbishop was besieged. This excommunication was renewed and sharpened in 1519. Sture and his adherents were mulcted for the sum of a hundred thousand ducats if they did not, within a given time, place Trolle in full freedom, leave the church and castle at Upsala in as good condition, or better, than before, and restore or make compensation for the church's property which had been destroyed.

So rose the mightiest prelates of the North, the arch bishops of Upsala and Lund, and the resigned archbishop Jacob Ulfsson, with the united strength of their own and the pope's authority, to oppress the cause, which, in Sweden, was all the more embraced and accepted as that of freedom and the fatherland. Events verified the expression which was used in 1497, by the elder Sten Sture, that "bishops should not have fortresses, but seats in their churches;" and they prepared the minds of the people for the measures adopted at Westeras, in 1527, to avert for the future what the kingdom had felt, that "bishops, and the privileges of the church, had been used for means of power."

But still the matter was not brought to completion. King Christian's chance of war soon roused again Gustavus Trolle, who, on the ground that his degradation was illegal and extorted, resumed his office, became the king's firmest supporter, and, to outward appearance at least, the occasion of the massacre at Stockholm, in 1520, whose remembrance the changes of the three hundred following years have not sufficed to blot from the hearts of the Swedish people. The archbishop made his appearance there as complainant, and the pretence for the massacre was the persecution he suffered, and the violence done the church's domains by Sture and his followers. As the king's revenge went no further than Trolle's purpose against the men, who now were considered and treated as being under the church's bann, so has the memory of that prelate become indissolubly connected with Christian's cruel tyranny. The death of two bishops on the same occasion, without lawful judgment by a spiritual court, was to punish one evil by another.*

When, upon the breaking out of the war of freedom, the fortune of Christian began to decline, Gustavus Trolle was forced to fly from his country, where his degradation was held valid, though the Romish church still considered him as legal archbishop of Upsala. He never ventured back to Sweden, although summoned under a safe conduct given by king Gustavus I. What he had to expect, he could foresee. The mere report that king Gustavus designed to reconcile himself with Trolle, roused the threat of the Dalecarlians, that they would renounce fealty and homage to the king if he became reconciled to that traitor to his country. Together with the counts of Denmark, Trolle appeared,

* Thus were all those branded as "Bannmen," or excommunicated, who had been against the archbishops, and consented that Stacket should be demolished. But king Christian accounted none for Bannmen who did him homage as king. Nor were bishop Vincentius and bishop Matts so considered, when they, with the archbishop, crowned him. Bishop Hans Brask saved afterward his life by reference to the protest which he secretly put under his seal, with the judgment. He had attached a piece of paper on which he had written the words, "This I was necessitated and constrained to do."

with weapon in hand, to sustain the cause, on the success of which depended a change in his own condition. He was nominated by count Christopher to the see of Odensee, and conquered it by force. But wounded in battle at Fyen, in 1535, he was carried as a prisoner to Sleswick, where he died. Soon after, and there probably, the letter reached him, in which Gustavus desired him to return to Sweden. Previously the pope had abandoned him.

The archbishopric of Upsala embraced of old, beside its present provinces, the whole of Norrland. Even Jemtland and Herjdalen, though under the crown of Norway, was subject of old to the church of Upsala.

Of the suffragans of Upsala, the foremost was the bishop of Linkoping, to whose see even the present sees of Kalmar and Gottland, and the whole fief of Jonkoping, or the whole of Smaland, except Varend, which is peculiar, paid obedience. There was doubt, when the Swedish archbishopric was to be erected, whether it should be placed at Upsala or Linkoping.

From the first part of the twelfth century, the bishops of Linkoping began to present a regular succession, shining through many personally eminent men, and by the respect acquired from the favor of many kings, and its accumulated wealth. Among these,

> " That bright examples might be given,
> Of men who gained their strength from heaven,"

appears, in the first rank, bishop Henrik, of Upsala, who became a martyr for the extension of the gospel on the eastern coast of our eastern sea. In the fourteenth century the honors of a saint were gained by bishop Nicholas Herman for his pious life and the miracles at his tomb.

The bishops of Linkoping soon became powerful in the state; but especially has Kettil Wase, bishop from 1459 to 1465, and cotemporary with archbishop John Bengtsson

Oxenstjerna, made himself more remarkable for his administration, and the manner in which he used the temporal sword against the king of his country, than for any merit toward his church. On the death of his successor, Henry Tideman, in 1500, who is commended for his care of his see, Dr. Hemming Gad, eminent for his learning, eloquence, and policy, was, in 1502, elected bishop. In 1478 he was sent by Sten Sture, the elder, to Rome, and remained there probably more than twelve years, as representative of the regent in the Roman court. He is said to have been mathematician and chamberlain to pope Alexander VI. In a man who remained near the Roman see in the most vicious days of the popes Sixtus V., Alexander VI., and Innocent VIII., we cannot expect to find a spiritual mind; but his participation in the momentous public affairs of his native land, his eloquence, and his death by Christian, that worthy hangman of cruelty, have preserved his name in the annals of his country. Afterward, in 1512, he visited the diocese of Linkoping, into which he never was consecrated. The resistance of the Danish king, and especially the circumstance that the pope promised the see to cardinal Jacob Arborensis, were impediments that could not be overcome.

Hans Brask,* born in 1464, at Linkoping, of which his father was burgomaster, was consecrated bishop of that see in 1513. He was educated at Skara, became a master at Grifswald, in 1488, and in his travels remained seven years, from 1499 to 1506, at Rome. After being made canon of Linkoping, he became, at the age of forty-one, dean of the same; and in his forty-ninth year was made its bishop.

Bishop Brask was one of those men who, without depth or comprehensiveness of mind, have a tolerably sharp judgment, while their imagination and vivacity ripen it to imme-

* He held his first mass at Linkoping, on December 8, 1513, when, as the rhyme chronicle observes, a furious storm raged over East-Gothland.

diate action. They shun every doubt of the existing right of discipline, because this doubt maims healthy action, and disturbs the soul's joy in doing and suffering on clear conscientious grounds, and for clear conscientious aims. They are thus champions in the contests of church and state, in such wise, that their immovable firmness will not permit the good which has been tried to be lost through whim and passion; but they restrain, by stubborn resistance, the novelty which is to prove and purify itself in the progress of controversy.

It was this species of activity which places Brask foremost among the opposers of ecclesiastical reform in Sweden. Jurisprudence had been his study; and even the old lawyers of Rome were not unknown to him. But his epistolary correspondence, which is yet preserved, shows that he had not the freedom of thought and the ease which are wont to be exhibited in such lighter forms of communication.

For his rejection of the church's reform, he had the one fundamental maxim, that the truth of the Roman church was a closed case. To doubt of this was itself a crime.

His view of civil society is disclosed in the following expressions from his letter to Peter Benedict, on September 3, 1524:* "We talk strongly of the kingdom's freedom, and meanwhile do not consider where it is to be found; while the church and nobles in other kingdoms which are hereditary,

* The quoted passage is taken from a commission to Peter, who was on a journey abroad, to apprise Brask of the church's condition in foreign lands, of the people's right to determine taxes, the temporal privileges of princes in respect to the church's tenants, of the duties of bishops to the crown, &c. In conclusion, to prove the multitudinous cares of Brask, it is said, that Peter is advised to learn the Italian, and especially the French tongue; "for it grieves us to neglect," as he says, "to be informed of the mode of making salt, the refining of gold and silver, the difference between the precious stones, the art of the apothecary, and the prices of book printing at Paris, and how to procure the newest books on jurisprudence, and in particular the Inamorata of Charlemagne and the Orlando." These the bishop wished to translate for the sake of soldiers. He sent books to read to Thure Johnson, to bishop Magnus of Skara, and to Margaret, the sister of king Gustavus.

not only enjoy their ancient liberties, but have more than we here at any time have found. In other lands, bishops have whole tracts, castles, and towns; here a man may not have a house where, if it so pleased him, he could turn a pair of oxen. * * * The freedom of our kingdom depends upon the church and nobles; because the peasantry will always make their yearly tax, board, and day's work, alike, when they enjoy nothing but freedom; because the revenues of the crown must not be diminished; and because, if the church and nobles do not enjoy their old privileges in their tenants, there is here no freedom to take, but their property is laid waste for the numerous house tenants. And thus the church and clergy become first ruined, and then doubtless the crown; if they are helpless who should protect it when it is pressed."

To the support and success of his resistance to the reformation, two obstacles presented themselves, furnished by his position and his own obligations. The one was the disturbances caused by king Christian and archbishop Trolle.* Brask loved the freedom of his country, in the sense we have just seen him explain this freedom. This love obliged him to take part with the cause of the deliverer, Gustavus I., while the obligation weakened him in his opposition to the men who enjoyed that king's favor, and in his opposition to the king himself. The other obstacle, though not affecting him alone, but the condition of the church, whose champion he became, was the want of moral purity and strength in action. It was this jesuitical seed, which long grew in the

* On the journey to Denmark, after the massacre of Stockholm, Christian passed Christmas with bishop Brask; how welcome a guest, surrounded as he was by those worthy of the hangman and the gallows, may be supposed. The king showed his gratitude, when, on his return home, he allowed the abbot, and twelve monks of the monastery of Nydala, to be drowned. During the summer of 1520, the bishop's estate at Linkoping was besieged by the burghers of Wadsten, who were provoked that the bishop subscribed the reconciliation which was agreed to, on the 27th of February, between him and the king.

old church, in which learned men, through the violence of the times, had become scarce, that determined bishop Brask to substitute compliance for open opposition; as he did in the case of Trolle's doom of degradation, in 1517, and at Westeras, ten years after. There was a want of moral strength, when, in 1527, he gave up all opposition and fled the country.

The bishopric of Skara, to which Vermland and Dalsland belonged, dates its origin from the time of Sigfrid, who baptized king Olof Skötkonung, as appears from its list of bishops and the first bounds of the diocese. The regions of country from which the kingdom of Christ first made its advances in Sweden, have at least the praise of having at once publicly embraced Christianity, and in the first century after king Olof's baptism they became its firmest support. Of the many bishops accredited for zeal and ability, mention only may be made of Brynolf, the first of that name, who died in 1317, eminent for his learning, eloquence, and canonization. At the close of the middle ages, the bishops of the see of Skara were of less importance in the state than those of Upsala, Linkoping, and Abo.

In the year 1520 the diocese became vacant by the death of bishop Vincentius, at the massacre of Stockholm. In his place Christian intruded his own chancellor and favorite, master Didrik Slagok, to whom he soon after gave the bishopric of Lund. That he was so far canonically elected, as the choice of the chapter by compulsion of the king could make him, is probable; but after his nomination he never came to Skara; and when he died, in 1522, the see again was for some time vacant.

In the region where the plant of Christianity was first watered, the diocese of Strängness, which grew out of the blood of the martyrs Eskil and Bothvid, according to our legends, attained its present condition at the close of the twelfth century. Among the older bishops, is commended Thomas, the contemporary of Englebrecht, on whom he wrote a beautiful elegy; nor should we forget Conrad Roggo, doctor of law at Perugia, learned, pious, and active, who died in 1501. His successor, Matthias Gregersson, who first received and introduced into the service of the church Olaus Petri, on his return from Wittenberg, became master at Greifswald in 1489, then doctor of moral jurisprudence, dean of Strängness in 1495, count palatine at Rome in 1500, and the year after, bishop of Strängness. On the degradation of Trolle, he appears to have been proposed for the archbishopric of Upsala. He was put to death at the massacre of Stockholm. His death roused the strongest indignation, as he had been active for the recognition of king Christian in Sweden. On the occasion of his being beheaded, it was for the first time made known that this man, of unblemished reputation in transacting the most important matters of his church and country, wore next his body, in the practice of self-mortification, a rough haircloth shirt.

As he had done in the case of Didrik Slagok, at Skara, Christian introduced John Bellenake into the see of Strängness. But without executing anything in his diocese, he was obliged, in 1521, to fly to Denmark; and the see, notwithstanding his election, again became vacant.

St. David is said to have set out from England for Sweden, to find martyrdom in a country where, as his attendants told him, the three nephews of St. Sigfrid had suffered the same. But when he could not find martyrdom in Värend, he went to Westmanland, and is accounted the first bishop of Westeras. Long afterward, at the same time with Strängness, this see was put into form, and its limits marked out. These limits are still the same. In the year 1501, Otto Svinhufvud was elected bishop of Westeras. He was among the friends of king Christian, and appeared, with Gustav Trolle, in 1520, as complainant against Sten Sture and his adherents, because during the war they had imprisoned the bishop as well-affected to the Danes, and had pillaged his estate at Westeras. It is reported, that to this bishop is attached the sad distinction of having made out the list of the men to be beheaded. Together with Trolle, he was at once accuser and judge. At the breaking out of Gustavus Ericson's war of deliverance, he took refuge in the castle of Stockholm, during the siege of which, in 1522, he there died.

The see of Wexio, like that of Skara, dates its origin from the time of St. Sigfrid. Within its limits, at least in the beginning of the sixteenth century, Varend alone was inclu ded; but its list of bishops runs back to the twelfth. In the year 1495, the episcopal chair of Wexio was seized by Ingemar Persson, and held by him till his death, in 1530. He could not be less than sixty-five years old at his death, perhaps older. The energetic Brask, who never depended upon his concurrence in opposing the reformation of the church, made excuse for him in 1523, as advanced in life and sickly. bishop Ingemar was the only one of the Swedish bishops who, maintaining the post he had previously received, lived beyond the disruption of the old and new state of things for ten years after the death of the younger Sture. His age, together with a quiet and complaisant disposition, may have been the cause of his taking no measures for staying the first advances of the principles of the reformation. In the first years, after 1520, he was called to the diets, but had withdrawn himself from the decisive measures that were in progress. He was representative, however, at Westeras in 1527, and at Orebro in 1529, and approved the decrees there adopted.

Through the crusade which was undertaken by king Erik the saint, and his friend the bishop of Upsala, St. Henrik, was begun the conquest of territory to the crown of Sweden, and the foundation of the church whose episcopal seat was ultimately placed at Abo. From the year 1200, proceeds its regular list of bishops. Many men of note filled this see. Among them was Hemming, who died in 1367, and who obtained the honors of a saint. From the position of this diocese its bishops were less involved in intestine troubles. The missionary work, going on in Finland and the neighborhood of Russia, gave them commonly enough to do. These missions were of much consequence in the relations of Finland to Sweden; but they had much to suffer from the neighborhood of Russia. Arvid Kurck, consecrated bishop of Abo, in 1511, was thereby often placed in difficulties. After the outrages of Christian the cruel, the bishop soon declared himself for Gustavus Ericson, but was obliged to fly to Sweden from apprehension of Sverin Norby. During his flight, he was overtaken by a storm and drowned, in the summer of 1522, near Oregrund; but not before the storm of the Reformation sufficed to prove his spirit. In the bishoprics now named, Sweden, as it then existed, was included in respect to its spiritual administration. Of the provinces afterward acquired, the fief of Bohus was subject to the bishop of Opslo, in Norway. Halland and Blekinge constituted the archbishopric of Lund.

Erected in the year 1103, afterward freed from subjection to the archbishop of Bremen, and itself endowed with the primacy over the Swedish church (a prerogative, however, which ultimately became a mere title), occupied by remarkable men, though often more suited to bear the temporal than the spiritual sword; now fighting the battles of its king, now prescribing terms to those who wished to wear the crown of Denmark, the archbishopric of Lund was the mightiest and most splendid of the North. The last who held it, while yet it remained in its full strength, was Birger Gunnarsson, who became its bishop in 1497, and who, like many bishops his cotemporaries, was master at Greifswald. He it was who, through the excommunication of Sten Sture, the younger, and his adherents, carried to a last excess the papal authority committed to him. This excommunication was the last known act of an archbishop of Lund, which concerned the Swedish church. The primacy expired with a curse upon its tongue.

King Christian's violent temper and conduct caused him to become one of those scourges of God, which execute his punishments of doom upon the old, and introduce a new order of things, by shaking and removing the established foundations. After the death of archbishop Birger, on the 10th day of December, 1519, he endeavored, by passing over Ake Sparre, whom the chapter elected as successor, to introduce into the archiepiscopate of Lund, first Ake Skotborg, withdrawn when he would not comply with the king's demand to deliver up Bornholm to the crown, and who died at Cologne in 1551, then Didrik Slagok, sacrificed by Christian as an expiation for the massacre of Stockholm, in 1522, and ultimately John Wese, who, in 1523, fled the country with the king, declined the office, because he heard the people were unwilling a stranger should occupy the archbishopric, and afterward became bishop of Kostnitz. Ake Sparre took possession of the see till 1553, without being consecrated or confirmed at Rome, and then voluntarily resigned his dignity.

2.—CANONS AND CATHEDRALS.

The papal legate, cardinal William, of Sabina, who came to Sweden for the purpose of regulating the affairs of the church, and held a council at Skeninge in 1248, had directed that, in every cathedral in which there was no chapter, a prelate and at least five canons should be created, to whom it should belong, in an occurring vacancy, to elect a bishop. This had now become the canonical election in the Roman church, from which election laymen were altogether excluded; although the approbation of kings never ceased to be respected. The confirmation of the election remained in the metropolitan, the primate, and at last in the pope.

This ordinance for the Swedish church was appproved at

the request of the Swedish clergy by pope Innocent III.; and, on the contrary, was disapproved when the practice became prevalent in Sweden for bishops to be appointed by the power of the kings and nobility, and the people's call.

Chapters had already begun to be formed by the existence of monk collegians, or the so-called regular canons. About the year 1190, archbishop Peter, of Upsala, gave, for the maintenance of the canons, all the tithes of Balinge and Vaksala; to the bishops, the revenues derived from Aby, in Vaksala; and a hundred yards of cloth the year the archbishop visited his converts in Helsingland; while all the property and income the canons already legally possessed were confirmed to them. Secular canons (*canonici seculares*), or such as were not bound by any monkish rule, had begun to be established. The bishop of Skara obtained permission, in 1220, to provide his church with regular, or, if this could not be done, with secular canons. The bishop of Linköping received, 1232, a license from pope Gregory IX. to establish canons in his diocese, where such ecclesiastics from time immemorial were not found.

At Upsala, archbishop Jarler (from 1236–1255), in whose time the council of Skeninge was held, began to establish secular canons. At first they were four in number, but that was increased by degrees. The strength of the chapter in numbers contributed in no small measure to the cathedral's glory and honor.

To these canons belonged the election of the bishop. Through them the bishop's regimen and oversight in the management of his see were exercised; and in an occurring vacancy, the management became the duty of the chapter or society of canons. They were obliged to be present at divine service in the cathedral at canonical hours; although they are often complained of for their negligence in this particular. In conclusion, different canons had certain different duties; especially the prelate or provost, who, as the name imports, had precedence of the rest. These dignitaries were called by titles now lost in the Swedish church; the *præpositus*, or provost, who was to attend to the ordering of divine service, and when the bishop declined their performance, to administer such priestly functions as belonged to the bishop, except such as required episcopal consecration; the *archdeacon*, who had ward of the church's property and maintenance of the poor, but was gradually raised to a very high degree of influence in the chapter and diocese; the *decanus* who watched over order and propriety within the chapter, and among the clergy of the cathedral; the *cantor*, who specially presided over the music of the church; the *scholasticus* who kept or had inspection of the cathedral school. There was also a confessor generalis or penitentiarius, the father confessor, to whom the more difficult cases requiring confession and absolution could be referred from the clergy of the diocese; but as this seemed not agreeable to certain prebends, it became only a bishop's commission. Certain privileges and immunities were granted them by the bishops; and in Sweden there did not, perhaps, fail, what occurred elsewhere, that the canons, on an election of bishops, consulted their interests by a preconcerted bargain with the man for whom they shaped their suffrages. The cardinals of Rome set the example on this path.

In propriety, each canon must remain in the place he took when he entered the chapter. But this prescription does not appear to have been observed, at least not in Upsala. And for the higher dignities within the chapter, this was not the common practice. That a man should hold canonries in several cathedrals at a time, was permitted; as a bishop could, in another diocese than his own, hold the canonry he possessed there before his nomination to be a bishop.

The revenues of the canons were in part derived from the prebendal churches in the diocese; partly from tithes, when the bishops assigned portions of their own tithes, or when the tithes of the poor were transferred to the chapter; partly from the gifts of individuals, and legacies of goods and money.

They were appointed by election of the bishop and the chapter. Yet it seems the king had the right of appointment to particular dignities; and this was even reserved to the bishops.

Besides these canons, there were in the cathedrals, vicariæ, or simple prebends (simplices præbendæ, whose possessors were called prœbendati), established by gifts or legacies on a vow made at the church in special seasons of the year, or from the wish to have masses for given objects, such most commonly as for the souls of the dead, and the souls of founders and their relatives. But the masses were sometimes in honor of the holy Trinity or the virgin Mary, or particular saints, or for the safety of travellers, and the like. These prœbendæ simplices, whose possessors were not members of the chapter, were supported from a sum of money once for all given to the church, from presents of goods and fields, from fixed yearly revenues from lands exempt from taxes, and kindred resources. For these many masses, the churches had also many altars; the number of which depended upon the call for their use. The clergy were called altarists, who, for a certain price, performed the mass at certain altars, with the exception of settled prebends.

Not only the cathedrals, but other large churches of the towns, had prebends; yet merely as special establishments. Thus the churches of St. Nicholas, St. Henrik, St. Christopher, St. John at Stockholm, had many prebends. The prebendaries, at least some, were appointed by the burgomaster and council. The church of the city of Kalmar had also many prebendaries; and those at the church of Lodose were called prœbendati and altaristæ. The same may be said of Wadstena.

Except in the smaller churches there were required for

the solemnization of divine service, basket boys, for whose maintenance sometimes a special rate or tax was laid. They were scholars of the cathedral school, and were brought up there for the service of the church.

We are not enabled to give an accurate and full enumeration of the provosts, canons, and vicariæ, which belonged to each of the old seven cathedrals of Sweden. The metropolitan church of Upsala had, according to a schedule which cannot be older than the year 1531, five dignitaries: the provost, the dean, the archdeacon, the scholasticus and cantor; thirteen canons and twenty simple prebends. An old record assigns to this church, about the year 1500, at the same time, a provost, archdeacon, dean, and at least seventeen canons, or altogether, at least twenty. One or more of the canonries had, in 1527, ceased, from a return to the estates of the original donors of the incomes which had been appropriated to those offices.

The diocese of Linkoping vied with that of Upsala in the number of its establishments and its riches. It is reported to have had not less than twenty-four canons; among whom, as is likely, were the same dignitaries as at Upsala, with fifteen simple prebends. The registry of Linkoping for the year 1543, counts, however, merely nineteen canons and twelve simple prebends.

Of the church of Skara, we cannot give the number of dignitaries. We may, however, assume that in this church were to be found a præpositus or provost, archdeacon, and dean; since, in certain records, we find these dignitaries even at Strängness, Westeras, and Wexio. How many canons and simple prebends belonged to each of them we cannot, with certainty, tell, except that the registry of Strängness counts, besides its dignitaries, twelve prebends; and that Wexio, besides its canons, had, in the year 1527, ten cross bearers of the clergy.

For Abo there are given twelve canons, with but two dignitaries, though an indefinitely large number of simple preb ends. Lund, the metropolitan church of Denmark, far exceeded the sees of Sweden in the number of her canons and simple prebends. It had, at the period of the Reformation, four dignitaries—a provost, dean, archbishop, and cantorium; thirty canons and forty vicars.

The hierarchy was specially represented through these offices and establishments, which, around the bishop, the shepherd of the see in the apostle's chair, labored for the welfare of the diocese, and building up of the parish clergy, who were yet for the most part limited to a training in church usages, and outward demeanor in its offices, and an acquaintance in ecclesiastical services. They were, in particular, habituated to the solemnities proper in the divine service of the cathedral. This structure was the visible image of the strength and riches of the hierarchy, and of the attitude of the church. It was considered as the stock and stay of the parish churches in the diocese, within whose circuit was the bishop's throne, encompassed by dignitaries and canons, and other priests apart from the position of laymen. Around the altars of the church was a clergy, who, like the parish priest, according to the hierarchical idea, represented the bishop, and took charge of the parish churches as imperfect establishments for the performance of divine service, which, in the cathedral, was celebrated on the canonical seasons; the church sounding and glittering with pomp, with many masses, with its numerous crosses and altars. At the cathedral, the hierarchy, in a word, appeared as representing the church on earth. Laymen were not necessary for public worship. Even if these were absent, the church still celebrated, by the offering of the flesh of Christ in the holy communion, by the praises of God and the saints, and by intercessions and prayers, the victory of the atoning sacrifice, and the union of the church on earth with that in heaven.

A splendid cathedral structure was the glory of the hierarchy; and the cathedrals, which still stand in the old sees, were all, though often reconstructed after suffering damage by fire, or enlarged beyond their first dimensions, completed before the Reformation. The oldest of those that are certainly known to be old, is that of Lund, consecrated in 1145. The age of the cathedral at Wexio, is unknown. That at Skara was consecrated in about the year 1150; that at Westeras, in 1271; that at Strängness, in 1291; and that at Abo in 1300, or near it. The present cathedral of Upsala was consecrated in 1435. The time of the consecration of that at Linkoping is not with certainty known. Its completion took place about the year 1490. Most of them had been worked on for centuries.

3.—THE CHURCH'S WEALTH AND OUTWARD POWER.

Even the kingdom which is not of this world, when it advances into external organization, requires that which is necessary to the stability of every constitution of human society, and to render it independent of fluctuating caprice. God's word needs not the aid of men, or of worldly things; but men themselves stand in need of giving a true defence against their own inconstancy, their own wilfulness, their own passions. This is humanity's ennobled, voluntary offering, whereby, in order to insure firmly the preaching of the word and the practice of divine worship, the proclaimers of the word are protected from the temptation of preaching it with an eye to man's favor, whereby the proclaiming of the word itself is secured, even should a time-serving complaisance make men for a while unwilling to hear.

But it is the part of human folly, by excess, to frustrate what is good. An excess in what is good in itself, runs on, till the ruin which follows must be checked or amended. The church has no less to beware of having too much, than of having nothing of worldly things. They who enjoy the advantage of the church's goods, must take care, that the church looks not solely to the kingdom of this world.

The Western church had already begun to yield to this temptation, when Christianity was first preached in Sweden. She was already deeply sunk, when she stretched her remaining power over the Swedish people. The wealth which the needs of the church called forth had, by the accumulated benefactions of centuries, made her an earthly power.

After the church became fully established in its external form, the Swedish people paid tithes, of which the parish priest had a third; which is still assigned to the clergy out of the corn produce, and, besides this, out of the root and pod fruits, and the domestic cattle. The church, the bishop, and the poor, divided the remainder; either so that each had a third, or in unequal proportions, as might be customary in different places. The application of the tithes, called tithes for the poor, was made by the bishop, sometimes as a contribution to hospitals, to the support of poor scholars, to the building of cathedrals, and lastly to the canons.

After the kings began with zeal to embrace Christianity, their spirit engaged them to build churches, according to the fashion which the habits of the times required, and to enrich them with gifts and money. They, as well as private persons, were animated thereto, by the belief in the meritoriousness of such liberality. From the year 1200, the property of the church became, through each king's renewed assurance of such exemption, free from tribute to the crown, and in like manner the fines and suits of the tenants of these estates followed the condition of those to whom the estates belonged.

To give an accurate account of the number and sum total of the lands and rents which, in the year 1520, were in the church's possession; of what belonged to the bishop, the cathedral, and other churches, with their priests, canons, and prebends, is, on many accounts, difficult or impossible, and would not for us be of particular interest. But when we find how many endowments and grants belong to the church of Upsala; and that, under control of the bishop of Linkoping, were more than six hundred greater or less estates and benefices; and that, in Finland and Sweden, the estates and manors which the cathedral of Abo and its head possessed, amounted to more than four hundred, we may form a somewhat accurate idea of the riches of the church in Sweden.

Besides large landed estates, each bishop had a fortified castle. The archbishop, before Stacket was destroyed, had a strong palace at Upsala; the bishop of Linkoping one at Norsborg; of Skara, at Lecko; of Strängness, at Tynnelso; of Westeras, at Granso; of Wexio, at Kronoberg; of Abo, at Kusto.

As senators, the bishops had also investitures of the crown. In this manner did the archbishop of Upsala, about the year 1500, hold Westerbotten, Oeland, the fief of Stacket, thetown of Upsala, and Nordmarken, in Westgothland.

A report of the military service of all the untaxable lands and investitures, rendered at the diet of Stockholm, in 1526, leaves us, if we have rightly understood it, a sufficient acquaintance with the bishop's revenues, in proportion to the other nobles and fief-holders within the kingdom. The knights, bishops, and nobles, were obliged, for every four hundred marks rent, to maintain six able-bodied men. The archbishop was to keep fifty men; the bishop of Linkoping, thirty-six; of Skara, thirty; of Strängness, twenty; of Westeras, ten; of Wexio, ten. Among the occupants of the laylands exempt from taxes, or fiefs, the highest number given is twenty-four; another has fourteen; two have twelve; one ten; and the rest under that number. The number of men to be raised amounts to the sum of 441; of whom 156 were to be raised by the bishops, though the domestic revenue of the bishop of Westeras was already considerably diminished. When each ton or sixteen barrels of rye and corn was valued at sixteen marks, of the return in rye and corn, 3,333 barrels were reckoned to the archbishop of Upsala; 2,400 to the bishop of Linkoping; 2,000 to Skara; 1,333 to Strängness, and 666 to the respective bishops of Westeras and Wexio. To all this should further be added, the *special bishop's tithes*, the suits, the tributes from priests and parishioners at visitations, and many other sources of income, not to be classed under the denomination of lands exempt from taxes and investitures of the crown.

We do not positively assert, but have reason to believe, that from 1522 the newly-consecrated bishops did not receive the investitures of which we have spoken. Bishop Brask, in 1524, delivered up the district of Gullberg. Their chief possessions then consisted in the lands exempt from taxes; and if, to the goods and estates which appertained to the support of the bishop's table, we add the goods belonging to churches and canons, the domestic incomes of the priests, and their glebes, the report of king Gustavus, in 1527, "that the crown and nobility together hardly had here in the kingdom a third part of what the priests, monks, churches, and monasteries had," will not appear too much exaggerated.

The unequal wealth of the sees at this time, appears from the circumstance, that in the diet of the same year, the clergy took upon themselves to raise a tax of 15,000 marks for the whole country; which was so proportioned, that the clergy of the diocese of Upsala were to pay 4,000; of Linkoping, 2,500; of Abo, 3,000; of Skara, 2,000; of Westeras, 1,000; and of Wexio, 500 marks.

The question naturally arises, when we reflect upon the large incomes of the bishops, how were those incomes employed? The employment of them depended, in a great measure, upon the constitutional temperament of the occupant of the see. The customs of the times and current ideas presented many unavoidable demands and difficult temptations. The latter part of the middle ages was fond of pomp and state, and required them as emblems of might and power. The bishops yielded, for the most part, to this passion, and surrounded themselves with a court, as did the grandees and feudal lords. The temptation grew stronger, as the apprehension of the invisible church retired from view. The disorder and mutability of the times, the spirit of self-revenge which often defied the laws, and to which, among men that only submitted murmuringly to the church's firmness, the bishops must be peculiarly exposed, obliged them to be surrounded with a life-guard. A law of the country allowed the archbishop to ride over the king's land with forty, and his suffragan bishops with thirty followers, and not more. How large a train the bishops might have in their official journeys within their sees, was not expressly determined by law, but it thence became soon necessary to fix the impost on which the priests and parishioners might relieve themselves from the exactions the bishops might otherwise make. In the year 1527, the archbishop elect, John Magnus, was to have had on his visitation of the diocese a train of two hundred persons. Bishop Otto Svinhufvud, of Westeras (who died in 1522), is said never to have traveled with less than sixty courtiers; and in 1527, bishop Brask, of Linkoping, had forty armed men with him at the diet of Westeras. Besides this, the fortified castles and the bishop's court were furnished with a garrison sufficient for their defence.

That these incomes were, however, sometimes applied to the claims of Christianity, in conformity to the purpose of the charities bestowed for that object, and which in the later centuries were encouraged, cannot be denied. The piety of many bishops, and their liberality for the promotion of a higher condition of religion, have left sufficient evidence.

It is natural that the church should possess, in the civil community, a strong influence. This was not merely a consequence of the energy of Christianity, and the superior character which belonged to the men of the church, of whom a bishop or other dignitary was always the king's chancellor. But the bishops and prelates had, in an indefinite number, a seat in the councils of the kingdom, and took among the *lords of the council* the first place. To the council, the archbishop was self-summoned. Between the legislation of the church and state there was sometimes a contest.

The temporal power of the church was in continual increase, when she did not herself lose or dissipate her property and dependencies. By purchase, by mortgages, by gifts and legacies, which the principles of the times encouraged, her possessions perpetually rose in extent and value. In respect to testamentary devises, the church had the maxim, that every one could of his fortune give the church a principal part, or, as was the mode of expression, that he who had one heir, could make Christ the other; he who had two heirs, could make Christ the third. But on the side of the civil society it became necessary to limit this maxim still further; and after many different ordinances in various provincial codes, and manifold contests between the clergy and people, it became a law of the land, in the time of king Christopher, that without consent of the heir no man should, for the good of his soul, give more than a tenth of the patrimony; but of acquired property he might give as much as he pleased.

Concerning the patrimony of the clergy, respecting which there were various decrees in the provincial codes, it was ordered in a provincial council at Arboga, in 1474, as also in a like council at Soderkoping, that the clergy could freely dispose of their property; but if they died without a legal testament, their goods and chattels should be divided into three parts—one of which should belong to the poor, particularly scholars; another to the heirs; and the third, with consent of the bishop and chapter, was employed for the soul of the deceased. The patrimony of a native devolved, half to the king, half to the good of the deceased man's soul. In the patrimony of the clergy, the bishop had the same right as the king.

A source of revenue for the bishops was the fines which, in many cases of trespass, fell to them. As long as society was not wholly Christianized, the church's legislation and administration of justice, were wholly independent of the civil law. But after the civil law began to avenge the breach of morality and good order, which before it had disregarded, legislation and the administration of justice were exercised by both the church and the state; and the guilty were amerced in fines to both the king and the bishop. The sergeant of the district sued for the breach, and collected the fines which the law assigned to the bishop. This sergeant was sometimes the district provost, sometimes a member of the chapter, sometimes a man specially appointed. The law of the land enumerates the cases when the fines fell to the bishop; such as affiance, marriage, excommunication, usury, and disrespect to holy days, and all matters which could be regarded as properly belonging to the church's legislation. There naturally belonged to the bishop all fines adjudged by the spiritual court before which a priest could be impeached. Beside these, there followed, usually with investiture, the right of collecting within the fief even all the king's fines. In conclusion, it may be observed, that the grants to the church were not always settled on the cathedral and bishop, but on certain canons or prebends, on parish churches, or on the tables of the clergy, on hospitals, and monasteries, and corporations.

4.—MONASTERIES.

THE first missionaries of Christianity to Sweden were monks. How many afterward came hither, or how they lived; whether any societies of monks existed, other than the regular canons, who belonged to some cathedral, is not known. As far as is known with certainty, the twelfth century saw the commencement of monastic institutions within the land.

At this time, when the Christian church also began to gain stability, the rule of St. Benedict, which, at that time, in its main features, was the pattern for the monasteries of the West, had, after many reforms, acquired special regard through the improvements made at the monastery of Citeaux ; and this order, called Cistercians, became renowned in St. Bernard, the abbot of Clairvaux. To him, king Swerker and his consort made application to send monks to Sweden, who came in 1144, and first settled in Alvastra and Warnhem.

Some time after, in the beginning of the thirteenth century, when in Southern and Western Europe the then existing frame of the church did not satisfy the hunger and thirst after God's word, and the life which comes of God, and occasioned many (partly real, partly fancied) disorders, the monastic institution assumed a new aspect, according to the spirit of the times. Preaching and the care of souls became the chief object ; and there was now intercourse with the people. For, the monks, before they were called to the missionary work and the offices of the church, lived for the most part solitary, in their cloisters ; and their influence was exerted through the example of their lives, and the schools within the convent, where the youth were received and instructed. These were supported out of the incomes which the monasteries had from their property. The monasteries were called rent cloisters. Those who went about to preach the word, and hear confessions, lived on the alms given them ; because, according to the example of Christ's disciples, they were to carry nothing with them, and the laborer is worthy of his hire. Out of these alms the monasteries, as well as their inhabitants, were maintained ; and they even thus became rich. The monasteries were termed alms-cloisters; the monks alms-monks, or brethren of the bag. Their efficiency was of very wide extent. From the pope they had obtained permission to erect moveable altars; and they often possessed, in the parish, their own house and domicil. But when their superior activity awakened the ill will of the parish priests, their freedom of preaching was restrained; and at a provincial diet at Arboga, in 1474, their moveable altars were prohibited, and they were ordered, within half a year, to give up the domicils they owned outside their monasteries, and which commonly were situated in the towns.

The Dominicans and Franciscans, the genuine begging orders, settled themselves in Sweden in the first half of the thirteenth century.

The monastic institution soon spread over the middle and southern parts of Sweden, through the munificence of the kings and private individuals; a munificence called forth by the spirit of the age, by the desire to participate in the good deeds of the monks, and to receive the benefit of the indulgences which were communicated in return for gifts.

At the commencement of the sixteenth century there stood, within our fatherland, without taking into account the schemes commenced but not completed, or those abandoned, or those of which there is no certainty, the following monasteries:

In the diocese of Upsala, the begging monks had especially diffused themselves. The Dominicans had, at Sigtuna, their oldest and most considerable monastery, whose prior appears to have been often provincial over Sweden, Denmark, and Norway. The last prior and vicar-general of the order in Sweden was Martin Skytte, afterward protestant bishop of Abo. The order had also establishments in Stockholm. The Franciscans had monasteries in Upsala, and at Stockholm, the popular monastery on a holm called after them, the holm of grey monks, and a convent for nuns, called the order of St. Clare, founded by Magnus Ladulas, at Norrmalm, where his daughter was subsequently abbess. At Enkoping also, there was founded a monastery of this order.

Of the rent cloisters, the Cistercian nuns had, within this see, Skokloster and Malaren, devoted to an abbess and twelve pure maids.

When we pass to the see of Linkoping, there first meets us the monastery of Wadsten, by St. Bridas or Bridget, who founded the rule for the order of our Saviour, of which this was the chief seat, and the sanctity of whose daughters of St. Catherine was the most memorable in the North. St. Bridget, extraordinarily respected and honored as a saint, raised the importance of the monastic institution among the Swedish people; and a contribution was ordered by king Albrect, to be paid it by every Swedish peasant. At its consecration, in 1384, were installed forty-six virgins and sixteen brothers. The establishment was estimated for sixty sisters and twenty brothers; but this number could hardly have been filled. Beside the site at Wadsten, it had possessions in all the old provinces of Sweden below the valley of the river.

There were, moreover, establishments belonging to the Cistercian order in the same see—the magnificent and rich Alvastra, the family burial-place of the kings of Sweden. Four hundred and thirty-eight peasants gave scot and tribute to the monastery. Nydala, in Smaland, was contemporaneous with Alvastra, and was as richly endowed. It experienced one of Christian the cruel's last acts of violence, when, in 1521, he left Sweden. He caused to be drowned, in the moat of the convent, the abbot and eleven monks. Bishop Brask consecrated a new abbot. There were convents for nuns of the same order at Wreta, known for its king's graves, and at Askaby, both amply endowed. Askaby had seventy-eight farms in East Gothland. In the year

1462, this convent was tenanted by an abbess and nineteen sisters.

The Dominicans had, in this see, two considerable monasteries at Skeninge, and two at Kalmar, and a convent for monks, and one for nuns, in each town. Both of those for nuns were, in 1504, removed to Skeninge. The order of the Franciscans had monasteries at Linkoping, Soderkoping, and Jonkoping.

In the diocese of Skara, the Cistercians had two rich and considerable establishments: the monastery at Warnhem, the burial-place of king Inge, and of the royal family of St. Erik, and a convent for nuns at Gudhem. Of the begging orders, the Dominicans had a monastery at Skara and at Lodose; the Franciscans only at Skara.

The diocese of Strängness had monasteries of more orders than any other in old Sweden. To the Cistercians belonged the monastery of Juleta or Saba, whose last abbot was consecrated in 1522, by bishop Brask. The Dominicans had also a monastery on the spot where, according to the legends, St. Eskil suffered martyrdom; the Franciscans one at Nykoping. The Johannists, the brothers of St. Anthony, were respectively seated at Eskilstuna and Ramundaboda. The Carthusians had their sole monastery at Mariefred, founded by archbishop Jacob Ulfsson and the bishop of Strängness, Konrad Roggos, at the suggestion of Sten Sture the elder, in 1491; and it was consecrated in 1504, the day before Sture's burial there, by Jacob Ulfsson, who there also spent most of his time after he had laid down his office. This was, of the Swedish monasteries, the last founded and the first suppressed. The Carmelites had a monastery at Orebro, remarkable from the tradition, that the brothers Olaus and Laurentius Petri there had their characters formed.

In Westeras stood, after 1486, the monastery of Husaby or Gudberga, belonging to the Cistercians, and another at

Koping, of the same order. The Dominicans had, at Westeras, a monastery, whose last prior was made dean of the chapter at that place by king Gustavus. One of its last monks was promoted to be bishop of the see. At Arboga the Franciscans had a rich monastery.

The see of Wexio had in its capital a monastery of grey friars. In the diocese of Abo, St. Bridget's order, or the monastery at Wadsten had, at Nodendal, its sole family within the present Sweden. It was established "specially for preaching, confession, and the grant of indulgences, as there to be had more pure than in other orders." The Cistercians and Dominicans also had establishments in this see.

To complete our view, should be added the monasteries which lay within the provinces that, at the time of the Reformation, belonged to Denmark and Norway, and had not disappeared at the change made in the Swedish church.

Gotland, which lay in the diocese of Linkoping, had two rich Cistercian establishments: the monastery of Gudvalla extended beyond the wall of Wisby; and a convent for nuns, with a monastery for black, and another for grey friars, within the town.

The rich and widely-extended diocese of Lund had a great many monasteries. The Benedictines, older than the Cistercians, had one at Lund, and nunneries at Bosjo and Boringe. Beside a monastery at Lund, the monks of Cluni had establishments at Herrevad in Skane, and at Aes in Halland. The Augustinians were seated at Dalby; the Carmelites in Landskrona; the Premonstratenses in Bekaskog; the Dominicans in Lund, and many other places.

In the fief of Bohus, under the see of Opslo, lay the cloister of the Premonstratenses, at Draksmark. The Augustinians were seated at Kastelle; the Franciscans in Kongelf; the last named being but little known.

Of a different description from the monastic institutions

were the guilds or brotherhoods, which, during the latter part of the middle ages, were counted in great numbers; so that not only every town had many, but also in the country parishes were they to be found. They were sometimes for priests, sometimes for laymen, and most often were made up of both. They were properly societies within the civil com monwealth, directing their views to a mutual protection and aid in council and support, and to mutual pleasure and cheerfulness. But they belonged to the church, in respect of being named after the Saviour, or the Virgin Mary, or one of the saints, under whose patronage they put themselves, and of having masses together, and for the souls of their deceased members. They had also their large property in common.

In conclusion might here at least be mentioned pious establishments, holy houses and hospitals, formed into a brotherhood at a time when security was not to be had from the sole protection of the law. Such was the union for aid of the sick and the poor formed into a brotherhood, at Upsala, which appointed two clergymen and a layman to attend to that duty. To these unions also belonged considerable wealth.

5.—CHARACTER AND MORAL CONDITION.

The differing opinions which have been pronounced, in respect to the character and morality of the Swedish people, when, on the one hand, the middle ages are accused, and on the other king Gustavus is condemned, incite us, in order to present the reform of the church in its true light, to devote a brief examination to what the condition of things was, at the time the Reformation began.

The message of Christ which first went forth to contend with and vanquish paganism around the shores of the Mediterranean, and within the limits of the Roman empire, had developed itself in a high grade of culture. From failure, however, in that precept of love which requires the effort to ennoble *all* men, it harbored deeply in its bosom stolidity and ignorance. In the course of its development, there had arisen an internal canker which began its ruinous work, and brought into the hearts of men principles of skepticism and irreligion, requiring for fallen humanity a fresh manifestation of the truth.

Christianity, in its collision with science and the form of civil society, must regulate its course accordingly. It must either exhibit its vitality in bloom and fruit, or surrender its claim to be for a lost world the power of a new birth. Individuals may and ought to accommodate themselves to established relations, as long as these do not interrupt their inward life in God; but it is natural that *if* new views, new laws and practices, influence the spiritual life of individuals, they should advance into the framework and civilization of human society, and that, too, in proportion as they strike deeper and broader their roots in the hearts of the people.

The contest of Christianity with Greek and Roman paganism, resulted in the benefit of an extended chain of ideas, and in a settled frame of society. But while these were based upon an obedience to the church, and grew out of the seed of the Divine word, they also partook of the spirit of that which had been fought and vanquished. They imbibed something of the characteristics of the soil on which they reposed. These characteristics disappeared in proportion as the church displayed her excellence; and the laws and ordinances which in the first ages rescued the church from a relapse into paganism, could only preserve their sanction by a living principle within the church, and by an authority which promoted unbounded submission. When Christianity was introduced into a nation, if it had, like Athens, Alexandria, and Rome, all the pantheism and polytheism of paganism, its science and popular belief stood proportionably in need of being rooted out. The preaching of the gospel in the northern parts of Europe, brought along with it the patriarchal authority of Rome, and the weapons, though lessened in strength, of the Grecian learning, the Latin tongue, and the Roman dominion.

The living spirit of the church, the Holy Ghost, could still give a victory over the world; and the piety and self-sacrifice of the missionaries, which opened the path for Christianity in our own and adjacent lands, merit our esteem and gratitude. But when their labors had prepared the way of the Gospel and givens trength to the power of the hierarchy—when it was no longer a question whether Christianity should be embraced—the people were ready not only to accept what was conformable with Scripture, but whatever was strange or new, and above their comprehension or general culture. This could only be received through a *blind* faith, such as the church permitted; declaring that for the individual it was only necessary to believe what the church believes, but that she was not obliged to make herself or another clearly understand that truth. To render it clear, there must be a previous inoculation in the old Greek and Roman literature. This basis, however, of their own system, had, within the church's hierarchy itself, become enervated and obsolete; and the church had advanced not so much in opposition to paganism, as to the church's own declarations, and in the prevalence of principles which those declarations, with their practical effects, were designed to exclude.

The faith which was preached among this people was not the simple world-vanquishing faith which was sown among those who constituted the first Christian church. The apostles of what was taught were not merely the apostles of Christ; they were the apostles not less of Rome. The question was not concerning the Holy Scripture, but of the whole doctrine of Rome. Our people had not begun with the beginning of Christianity. Their advancement in knowledge, the arts, and frame of society, was the search after the foundation; a return, not a going on to something beyond. They missed and regretted in *their* historic life the beginning of Christianity. Their search was anxious, of long duration, and foreboding. The reward of search came through the newly awakened, recent acquaintance with the service of Greek and Roman literature. The opposition between Christianity and paganism became clearer. The spiritual culture, when it became strong enough to investigate the Holy volume, and the early annals of the church; when it desired to embrace Christianity in its *life-giving truth*, resulted in a revival of the true spirit of the gospel, in the Reformation, and in Protestantism.

That the Reformation passed successfully and specially through those lands which first became Christianized after the papacy grew strong, either less stirred or retreating in regions where the church was established during the first centuries, seems to indicate, that Christian truth and Christian life struck a deeper root in the latter, and therefore less needed a thorough alteration, while the former stood in need of acquiring the truth which had never been communicated to them. But the strength of the hierarchy was the greater the nearer to its centre; and its influence was less effective in remoter regions, where there was begun the resuscitation of the Christian life. The hierarchy, however, did not at first determine to stifle this life; but carefully watched it, and, in watching, stood in the way of its development. In Southern Europe the hierarchy had, through its own false aggrandizement, withdrawn the life of faith from its original purity; but the Reformation was there comparatively weak, because its necessity was less acknowledged; and till another opportunity, men remained content with such a degree of improvement in the church, as was produced by the deeper reforming action in the North. As in the thirteenth century, the intervention of begging friars, so now a new form of the monastic institution stepped in to check the progress of amendment in the church. When the North of Europe, turning from the papal church to Christianity, withdrew from the Roman chair, the South was saved to it by the order of the Jesuits.

When the faith of Christianity was introduced into Sweden, the frame of it, which was entirely foreign to the life and tone of its people, did not win acceptance. Here, however, as elsewhere, was established the almost exclusive church, and it spread its influence even to those who did not acknowledge a direct obedience. But we are justified in the assertion, that the spiritual power, combinedly exercised by the ecclesiastical and civil society in our fatherland, spread more slowly than in countries to the south of us, from which it was hither exported.

The means by which it spread were partly through our journeys to foreign lands, partly through early teaching and training.

During the whole of the middle ages, Sweden stood in very near connection with Southern Europe. The business of the church, and, according to the ideas and habits of the times, the piety of individuals, called many to Rome. There, princes, and even bishops, had Swedish representatives. There, the house of St. Bridget, appertaining to the monastery of Wadsten, gave entertainment and maintenance to such monks of Wadsten as should seek a habitation in the capital of Western Christendom. There, many, shortly before the Reformation, remained for some years; and among them, those who, in Sweden, were its active agents, as Laurentius Andreæ, or its hinderance, as Hans Brask. But not only was Rome the capital and seat of resort for those who sought improvement, or those who, by a stay in a foreign land, were necessarily subject to the effects of the culture and education they received there. Pilgrimages drew many to the South and East, and in return, brought also many foreigners to the native land of St. Bridget, and the monastic establishment renowned for her piety. Monasteries, too, of the same order, in various lands, furthered an easy exchange of both people and manners; and the universities invited into their bosoms such as sought a higher grade of instruction. There were scarce any of the universities of Italy, France, and especially Germany, which lay nearer to us, in which were not to be found some Swedes. Many remained there to take upon them the office of teachers. Many returned home after a protracted stay abroad, and could not but have imbibed the manners and ideas of the lands where they had received their education. When the celebrated bishop of Skara, St. Brynolf, who died in 1317, returned to his native country, after eighteen years' residence in the renowned school of learning at Paris, must he not have imbibed, in spirit and character, and brought home with him, whatever such a stay and such a place were likely to create?

From the twelfth, but especially the thirteenth century, the process continued, for preserving, spreading, and increasing the tone and discipline which had entered with Christianity. In that direction moved the schools established in monasteries, the cathedrals in various towns, the statutes and rules of chapters, and the university of Upsala.

The monastic schools were properly nothing else than preparative patterns for the literary occupations of the tenants of those establishments. Their principal purpose was not the teaching of children. The pursuit of learning depended upon the character of the rules of the order. The rule of the Benedictines promoted attention to letters, while among the Cistercians it was restrained. Those descendants of St. Bernard, who owned so many and rich establishments in the land, are said, at the time of the Reformation, to have sunk so low that, in the year 1525, a translation of the New Testament into Swedish was divided among the cathedrals and several monastic orders; Alvastra and Warnhem, of the Cistercian order, not having a man competent to take part in the important work, notwithstanding their noble descent and their rich litany. The decline of this order, in respect to a very high degree of culture, is, of itself, a reasonable justification of its being suppressed; though neither at the time was there found in these monks any other high characteristic.

The purpose of the begging orders, not only to separate themselves from the world, but to labor for the promotion of truth and virtue, induced a necessary regard to the interests of learning. These orders were the fruits of a time which, on the one hand, experienced the evil of the church's mere worldly condition through wealth and the temptations of pleasure; on the other, more or less felt the insecure position which the church had, in the faith to be propagated by *knowledge* among an intelligent people. The people stood in need of the church's learning, to be established in the truth.

The preaching monks paid particular attention to their studies. The monasteries, such as those of the Franciscans, had readers to instruct the brothers in theology, and in various assigned general studies, which were attended by those of other monasteries of the same rule. This course of general literature, the studium generale, for Dacia, embracing Sweden, Denmark, and Norway, was, at least for some time, established at Skeninge. They were likewise obliged to send some of the brothers to Paris.

The many, who, out of this monastic order, were active during the Reformation of the Swedish church, as Martin Skyte, afterward bishop of Abo, Henrick of Westeras, subsequently bishop of that see, Claudius Hwit, who from the monastery of Kalmar went to Wittenberg, to convert or to confound Martin Luther, are a proof that among the Dominicans science was still regarded.

In what proportion the monastic schools were attended by those who did not purpose to renounce a secular life, we are not able to ascertain. It is certain, however, that at least in many instances, boys were received into the monasteries to be educated, as were girls by the nuns. But this was not always the case; and certainly, the reception was limited to the children of the higher ranks, who could pay for them. It does not appear that anything like a corps of teachers was established in such monasteries.

The cathedral schools were of two kinds. One was for the training up of the cathedral basket boys, who, beside their service as singers in divine worship, received a preparation to enter, at a mature age, the order of the clergy. The other was for the purpose of imparting a higher theological education, and was placed under the care of a dignitary who, by the name of scholasticus, was to be found in every cathedral.

In many large towns were to be found schools which were put under the church's immediate ward, and that of certain learned men; or, as at Stockholm, in charge of the council and burgesses of the city.

As in other parts of Europe, here also, the requisition of an advanced science among the dignitaries and canons of the cathedrals became more and more a matter of concern; as it also was, that these places should be reserved for native born men. At the provincial synod of Arboga, it was resolved, that, under like circumstances, native men of talents and *graduates*, should be preferred to others in filling benefices and dignities. Examinations at the cathedral preceded the conferring of prebends on young men who, by means of the incomes from them, pursued and completed their studies abroad.

At the time of the Reformation, we find among the bishops and members of the cathedral many magistrates and physicians. These, who very commonly resided many years in foreign schools, had acquired a high degree of cultivation; but they were required to produce, in writing, evidence of their zeal and industry, and of the grade of scholarship they possessed on their return home.

We are to presume, that the higher culture was found among the higher clergy, and a less degree of it among the lower; in like manner, among the monks, ignorance was no less to be discerned than the intelligence for which many among them were remarkable.

From the year 1477, when the university of Upsala was solemnly dedicated and opened, after long-considered plans and resolutions, Sweden also had her own high educational establishment. In 1480, lectures were delivered there, by the learned Erik Olaus. But this establishment of it neither came to a completion, nor indeed to any special efficiency. It was more nominal than of real advantage. It had no endowments. Neither of rents, nor of gifts to it, have we the slightest information. It was kept up by the cathedral of Upsala, from whose canons and prebendaries it doubtless had its teachers; and if it had any help from other sources, they were but casual. There was no division of academical duties; and Swedes, who sought a high grade of literature, went still, as before, to foreign universities or high schools.

How long the new establishment continued to give any sign of life, is uncertain. In the year 1498, when king John forbade Danes to go to foreign universities, before they had studied three years at Kopenham, he made the university of Upsala an exception to the prohibition. The founder of the university of Upsala was chiefly archbishop Jacob Ulfsson, in connection with the regent of the kingdom, Sten Sture. They and the other members of the council, as was declared in letters of privilege, at Strängness, on July 2, 1477, had not, "on account of other matters relating to the kingdom, time and opportunity to reflect upon and determine the measures for supporting a collegiate course of studies," as they would gladly do. It appears that the time and opportunity came not; except as the archbishop alone, with his chapter's concurrence, had taken care to keep up the high school. After Jacob Ulfsson had, in 1514, resigned his see, there is found no trace of the existence of a high school; and amid the confusion which specially centred around Gustav Trolle and his chapter, it was vain to hope for stability to such an institution, dependent upon their ability or good will.

We must consequently presume, that, at the beginning of the Reformation, Sweden had no university in active operation.

For the general improvement and cultivation of the people, there were no means provided but through the influence of the cure of souls and the public worship. In the year 1441, archbishop Nicholas Ragvaldi and his suffragans decreed, at the provincial council of Soderkoping, that the Lord's Prayer, the Hail Mary, and the Creed, should be translated into the mother-tongue; and on Sundays and holy days, be recited by the rectors of churches, in the audience of the people. This, as a common rule for the Swedish church, was less than what sixteen years before the eminent bishop of Linkoping, Nicholas Hermanni, enjoined upon the clergy of his diocese: that they should preface their preaching with the Lord's Prayer and Apostles' Creed, the Hail Mary, the ten commandments, and the seven works of mercy. But this shows that a hundred years before the Reformation there was a care for the people's instruction in faith, and at the same time how circumscribed was that instruction.

If, among the great mass of the people, little or no literary intelligence is found—if the instruction in Christianity which was imparted was of narrow compass—we cannot draw the certain inference that the extremest degree of stolidity and ignorance prevailed. Energy in preserving, propagating, and impressing on the people's minds, that traditional knowledge, which works in the heart of society, and which finds its field, as now in Sweden, in the house, family, district, and province, furnishes resources which supply the lack of learning. But the church, which had herself declined from Christian purity, was little likely to engage in *innoculating* the life of the people with a living spirit of Christianity, as she did engage in the effort to annihilate its strength and effects. She had adopted as a maxim, not to leave the Scriptures in every man's hand, and therefore excluded laymen from the fountain of truth, which became a stranger even to the clergy themselves. It was the error and ruin of the hierarchy to wish to keep the Scriptures to themselves, and to permit truth to enter merely as a preceptive part of the education of the individual mind, but without watering the church's garden by an immediate and direct overflow. It must follow, that the life of the garden withered away, that faith was converted into legal morality, love into the constraint of obedience, the worship of God into outward display. The church, in such a condition, could present neither to priests nor people the appearance of a living body and form. When such was the state of things, the Christian life and spirit of the church suffered more injury, through the forms that stifled them, than could be compensated by the benefit of the church's government and direction. The protesters against the meretricious character of the church, who, especially from the twelfth century, stood forward in various parts of Western Europe, did not make their appearance, it is probable, in Sweden, as they did not in the north of Germany, before the beginning of the sixteenth century. To what degree the decrees of Swedish provincial synods, in preventing the ban of excommunication against those who denied being under the pope or church of Rome, were caused by the views to which we have alluded, is unknown. Our annals do not mention the popular opinion on the subject. Nor is it known to us if any influence was exerted by the teaching of Heyno, pastor of St. Olof, in Wisby; that after the Dominicans and Franciscans began to hear confession there had been no true shepherd in God's church; that he commits mortal sin who hears mass of wicked priests; that the priest who sins wilfully cannot forgive the sins of others; and that monks were the deceivers of the people. But this, as well as the account we have of a peasant named Hemming, who, in 1442, appeared at Wadsten as the messenger of the virgin Mary, and who proclaimed before the monks of Wadsten some unacceptable articles against the saints and the rule of St. Bridget, seems to prove that the entire indifference to such subjects which is apt to be attributed where there is no book learning, did not exist in the church of Sweden.

The witnesses which remain to us concerning the moral condition of the clergy, are not unexceptionable. It is as unsafe to judge of the general character of times gone by, from some insulated cases, as to judge of a people's or country's manners and customs by what we learn of an individual. We must judge the Reformation by the times that preceded. But the church, which, in its high places, was represented by Jans Bengtsson and Gustav Trolle, could have no claims to an exalted estimation. The morality of individuals must, in a degree, be judged according to the character of the times, and here, from the year 1248, present themselves the continually repeated complaints of transgressions against the law of celibacy. The decrees of councils furnish evidence of these complaints, and that notwithstanding the bishops having laid a tax on the priests for permission to keep concubines, the sons of priests sometimes obtained permission to enter the sacerdotal ranks; while the public tribunals confirm the last wills of priests in regard to their "property and sons." The charge on the morality of the priests may be considered pretty well established when so much can be presented on one point, and the breach of the law in this respect gives us no reason to presume perfection in another.

We do not need, in order to magnify the merits of the Reformation, to paint the precedent times altogether in black. But, we add, that when one, in our day, declared that an increased immorality among the clergy was the fruit of the Reformation, the assertion is refuted by what we find in the preceding century. It amounts to a degree of wickedness that constitutes a more than sufficient apology; though our advices on the subject are in some particulars defective, and the times immediately succeeding the Reformation could not escape the confusion which follows upon every rupture of human relations.

Concerning the general morality of the people, we hear the echo, in 1412, when the council of Arboga was held, of complaints of the lewdness, rapes, rapine, murders, usury, contempt of penance and the Lord's Supper, and a mock religion, which satisfied itself with mere outward forms, that sufficiently indicate the spirit of the age. The judgment so passed is not to be considered as the ordinary condemnation of the mere casual exceptions to good order. In like manner, the care which the Swedish church, in the middle ages, gave to the interests of the soul was not calculated to accomplish the transformation of a heathenish people into a Christian. Its righteousness of the law could not restrain and check the natural pride of the heart, or only so long as compulsion rendered necessary a specious submission. This compulsion kept pace with the papal hierarchy, and necessitated more than once, both nobles and people, with weapons in their hands, to protect their human and Christian rights against bishops and priests. The difference between things and persons was well understood; but he of the people who cursed the church's head as the cause of the kingdom's disasters could not await the church's order, being already more accurately acquainted than her learned men with the difference between God's holy will and law, and that hierarchy which affected to hold the keys of heaven in their hand.

A deeper inward improvement, if it was not on the side of popish Christianity, could, with great difficulty, be introduced among our forefathers. Heathenism, therefore, in fact remained, only modified by a Christian form of public worship, or a form of Christian superstition. Alms-deeds, as the chief of good works, atoned for all sins. "With man," it was said, "when he flits from this life, follows all that in mercy he has given to works of piety." Men forgot the motive on which alms should be given; and found the meritoriousness in the mere alms-giving itself. Of such alms-giving the church enjoyed the revenue, and her huckstering in indulgences was, as is well known, the chief cause of the Reformation in Germany. Even in Sweden the Reformation was prompted and the way made ready by this pardon-mongering. Although this had not here the same intimate connection with reform as in Saxony, it is yet proper to inquire in what way, even in Sweden, the sale of indulgences contributed to make the need of a reformation sensibly felt.

CHAPTER II.

OF THE SALE OF INDULGENCES, AND THE PAPAL LEGATE, J. C. ARCIMBOLD.

POPE LEO X., of whom Paul Sarpi, a writer of the Roman church, but no friend to papal domination, had said, that of all the qualities which should adorn a pope he wanted but two—theological culture and any disposition to goodness—was advised, soon after his being seated in the chair of Rome, to employ, in his need of money, that drag-net which had so long been a rich source of revenue to Rome.

The sale of indulgences had been, from the thirteenth century especially, the means employed for replenishing the papal treasury. Indulgences, which remitted the church's penance, under which any one had fallen, had a very extensive significance and expiatory power. Christ, it was said, had commuted eternal into temporary pains, which men must suffer in this life, or in purgatory, if before death they were not reached, or were neglected. The doing of penance in the church partook of the nature of suffering and fulfilling the punishment, and had a value in being voluntarily undergone, and on the supposition of a penitent mind; a supposition which was but seldom considered of no importance. But on the strength of Christ's and the saint's merits the church could remit this penance, or change it from the doing of penance by the individual to his execution of a like work, which should be for the common benefit and advantage of the church. From the inexhaustible spiritual treasure of the merits of Christ and the saints was distributed grace to those who stood in need, so that through their participation of it might be collected a temporal tribute for the church's benefit.

The crusades were undertaken by men who, by this military service, fulfilled all the church's requisition of penance. Many churches were built out of the money collected from the sale of indulgences; the sum corresponding to the penance to be done, which otherwise might occupy a certain time for its accomplishment. The customary price for building a church was a fourteen days' indulgence, or a remittal of a fourteen days' penance. This was the highest kind of indulgence a bishop could grant. But the consummate power of the pope enabled him to extend the indulgence to a longer time. It was given by him for a hundred years, for a thousand; yea, for eternity.

For the sale of indulgences there was always a good object assigned. Most commonly the money was spent on worldly, not seldom on selfish and criminal purposes. The pretended spiritual purpose was a cloak, and the same mockery was shown which pope Innocent VIII.'s chamberlain offered in behalf of his master's exaction of money for the pardon of murder: "God willeth not the death of a sinner but that he should *refund*, or pay a tax, and live."

The mode of collecting the returns for indulgences was formed into a regular money market. The sale was farmed to certain persons, either according to a prescribed ratio of the profits to be made, or for a given sum at once to be paid into the papal treasury. The nobles, at least in the fifteenth century, took opportunity to share with the church. The pardon-mongers were obliged to purchase in any country the license to sell indulgences, or to bind themselves, on certain conditions, to divide the profits with the nobles of that country.

The Scandinavian North was not neglected in this traffic, even if there was not there quite so much extortion as in Germany, which was most harassed by tribute to Rome.

Such was the report, in 1460, of one Marinus de Fregero, the papal commissioner of indulgences, among other places, for Norway and the kingdom of the Goths. The reason assigned, was the protection of Christian truth against the Turks. In the year 1489, Raymond Paraldus, had, on the same excuse, a similar commission for Sweden, Denmark, and Norway.

Pope Julius II. began the sale of indulgences for the building of St. Peter's church. Leo X. carried on the traffic upon the same pretext. Purchasers were absolved from all the sins and misdemeanors they committed, from every penalty they incurred, from ban and interdict; and even in all the cases in which the pope alone could absolve, they were reinstated in the innocence and purity with which they were invested at their baptism; and leaving the world, the gate of paradise would immediately open to them. The pope desired, through indulgences, to give Christians an opportunity for good works, especially the building of St. Peter's; but as all could not go to Rome to put their alms in the coffer, he had, as Christ sent his apostles into all the world, sent his embassadors into the countries of Christendom.

An agency was, in 1514, committed for many countries, among them the province of Upsala, to John Angelus Arcimbold, doctor of law, dean of Arcisate, papal prothonotary and referendary. The accurate Sarpi is, however, mistaken, in his history of the council of Trent, when he intimates Arcimbold to have been at this time a bishop; but he is less mistaken, perhaps, in his severe judgment, when he says that Arcimbold, in taking upon himself the bishop's office, had put off none of the qualities which belong to a consummate Genoese chapman. Arcimbold was by birth of Milan, became, after he had been the agent for indulgences, bishop of

Novara, in 1525; held the archbishopric of Milan, the chief see of Italy, in 1550; and died in 1555.

In September, 1516, Leo X. executed for Arcimbold a brief in which, it is said, that, as the apostolic chamber stood in need of resources for the building of St. Peter's, his powers were prolonged over the northern kingdoms, the ecclesiastical province of Upsala, and the bishopric of Meissen for two years, and for other countries, one year. When the pope, moreover, not without grief, perceived that, in the province of Upsala, discord existed between certain prelates and nobles and communities, through instigation of that sower of weeds, the devil—so that war was kindled to the great satisfaction of infidels and foes of Christ's truth, and to the injury of the Christian community—he sent Arcimbold to heal the rupture, and execute other business as embassador of the apostolic see, as well as to be the angel of peace, with the authority belonging to a legate à latere. He began, within a month after the reception of this brief, his journey thither, and endeavored to establish peace and harmony, for which purpose he was to employ ban and interdict.

This appointment was given at the commencement of the dispute between Sten Sture, the younger, and Gustav Trolle. It seems that the excommunication of Sten Sture either had not been carried into effect, in 1514, or been revoked; since no mention is made of it, and Arcimbold, moreover, was furnished with the pope's recommendation to Sten Sture, dated September 6, 1516.

In the year 1516, Arcimbold was at Lubeck, and there carried on his traffic with profit. The following year he came to Köpenham, accompanied by his brother, Antonello, and many followers, and obtained, on the payment of 1,100 Rhenish guilders, permission from king Christian II. to sell indulgences in his kingdom. He set up his cross and chest of indulgences in all the churches of Köpenham. In time he had the good fortune so much to win the confidence of the king, that he hoped, through that monarch's co-operation to advance his views on Sweden, whither, as legate, he was preparing to take his departure. The king laid open his plans before him, and named to him the Swedes upon whom he relied. In January, 1515, the legate sent his agent, Didrik Slagok, to Sweden, with an overture for a suspension of arms between the two kingdoms, till April 23d, during which period peace might possibly be established.

In the month of March, 1518, came Arcimbold to Sweden, and pursued his journey through the land to Upsala, where, in the house of St. Barbara, near the cathedral, he opened his traffic. He came here soon after Gustav Trolle gave up his castle and renounced his office. All this had happened before archbishop Birger of Lund, who also received the pope's commission to watch the proceedings in Sweden, excommunicated, or, as is more correct, threatened to excommunicate, Sture and his adherents. Arcimbold's commission appeared to the Swedes a possible means, through the intervention of Rome, of gaining strength in the contest with Denmark. The legate, previously entangled and pledged to the interests of Christian II., and obligated to resent the sentence against Trolle, as an illegal act, was won over by the attentions of Sture and his friends, by their permission, without interference, to make the most of his lucrative traffic, by costly presents, and, as is supposed, by the alluring prospect that, if the pope could be induced to approve the deposition of Trolle, himself would be elected archbishop of Sweden. He arrived from Strängness, at Stockholm, on Friday, the 12th of November; was visited by Sture's wife, and all the nobles, and clergy, who, from his lodgings in the convent of grey friars, conducted him to the cathedral and again home, and he immediately set up his cross and oblation coffer. Soon after, he followed the regent to the diet of Arboga, in December of the same year, and there confirmed the sentence upon archbishop Trolle, and advised him to reconcile himself to the measure.

In time Arcimbold, either himself or by his agents, had extended the imaginary blessings of his merchandise of indulgences over Sweden and Norway, and gathered considerable profits, partly in ready money, partly in iron and butter, of which he purchased large quantities, that by their sale in other countries he might still further increase his gains. Many persons followed in the track of his example. He put into use his brief for the sale of indulgences at the nunnery of Askaby, on the 4th of April, 1518; at the monastery of Wadsten on May 15; confirmed September 17, the tithe system established by bishop Brask of Linköping, gave, on the same day, to that bishop the right to absolve those who injured clerks, so that they should not be obliged to go to Rome; confirmed the privileges of the city of Stockholm; directed, in behalf of the pope, that bishops only and men of the ecclesiastical order should be judges in cases of tithes; and forbade kings, queens, nobles, or other lay persons, at all to meddle therewith, on pain of excommunication and a fine of 500 guilders; issued, on December 19th, a decree against violence to churchmen or their property; and on the following day established the time when the feast of St. Nicholas, a former bishop of Linkoping, should be observed, together with many like acts.

In a letter of January 2, 1519, the legate informed pope Leo X. of the state of affairs in Sweden, of the diet of Arboga, and the sentence pronounced against Trolle, and promised, on his return, soon to render a more exact account. But neither Christian, nor Trolle, could be satisfied with Arcimbold's proceedings. Both hastened to lay before the pope complaints of his deceitfulness.

The king, whose fury was probably increased by his disappointment in the war of 1518, was not of a mind patiently to await the spiritual trial and sentence, on the conduct of the legate. He accused him of participation in the Swedish schemes of rebellion, and ordered the people and merchandise which belonged to Arcimbold to be seized. A monk of Gothland, who preached indulgences, was put to death ; and a vessel, loaded with iron and butter, was seized at the island of Severin Norby ; and another, with a similar cargo, was stopped at Köpenham ; where, also, Antonello Arcimbold was put in prison ; and the profits of the indulgences he had brought with him, in cash, were taken from him, amounting, at the lowest computation, to twenty thousand ducats.

When the legate himself, on his homeward journey from Sweden, came to archbishop Birger, at Lund, information reached him of the king's stern remonstrances, of a summons to give an account of his conduct, and of the collections he had made, and of his stopping in Lund. But he did not consider it expedient to put himself in the fierce king's hands. After that, he wrote a long letter to the king, in which he endeavors to excuse himself; desires that the goods seized should be restored, together with his brother, "half his soul and heart ;" and promises that, as soon as Antonello reached Lubeck, he would remit to the king one thousand Rhenish guilders. He then returned to the borders of Sweden ; stopped at Calmar, and thence passed on to Lubeck.

In all probability, a new act of excommunication was passed, in the spring or summer of 1519, upon Sture and his adherents. A papal brief, of May 13, 1520, mentions one as already issued by archbishop Birger and bishop Lage Urne, of Roskild ; but after Trolle's imprisonment, and the destruction of Stacket, since it would only have been enforced while the archbishop was not at liberty, or restored to the church of Upsala, or while the castle remained unbuilt, either of a like strength or greater than the former one. This excommunication cannot be the same with that which the author Hvitfeldt regards as executed by Birger alone in 1517; or, what is more likely, this last is a mere fable, since it neither supposes Stacket to be destroyed, nor speaks of the one hundred thousand ducats—half to the pope, half to the church of Upsala, and a compensation for the lost goods—wherewith, according to the papal brief just mentioned, Sture and his adherents were threatened, as the result of the episcopal excommunication. But this excommunication, by Birger and Lage Urne, was not promulged before Arcimbold's journey to Sweden; so that it cannot be that in the course of the year 1518, while the papal legate resided in Sweden, with extensive powers and a multiform commission, affecting the contests between the chief men of the church and state in that country. It could not again have occurred in the short interval between the surrender of Stacket and the coming of Arcimbold. The thing had then been done; and Arcimbold would not willingly reverse the church's sentence, once passed. That the excommunication was published in 1519, is expressly mentioned by Olaus and Laurentius Petri, with the remark of the former, that "the Swedes regarded such excommunication as of no account."

But the pope was troubled on account of the legate, his brother, and the tribute they had left behind. In a letter, on August 26th, 1519, he wrote to Christian, that Arcimbold, who had been recalled to Rome to give an account of his trust, had, on the king's complaint, declared that one of Arcimbold's servants had, through false pretences, deceived the king. The pope had charged the archbishop of Lund to enter upon an investigation of the legate's conduct, and he should be punished if found guilty. Meanwhile the king was to give up his brother, and servants, and the tribute collected for St. Peter's church; and the money and merchandise for the papal treasury might be sent to a commercial house in Antwerp. On the same day with the above-mentioned letter, the archbishop of Lund received a commission to investigate the proceedings of Arcimbold, and to induce the king to give up the goods held back.

The suit against Arcimbold, if ever begun, was probably interrupted by the death of Birger, the other cares of the see of Rome, and Christian's conduct. His brother Antonello was at length liberated; but of the tribute derived from the last traffic in indulgences in Sweden, little or nothing flowed into the papal treasury. Most of it fell to the share of Christian the cruel, and furnished him new means, with Swedish money, to promote his warlike preparations against the Swedes. Of these preparations, the bloody fruits, when Christian came forward as the church's avenger, hastened the breach through which a new order of things, within the church and commonalty, found entrance. Through this traffic of indulgences, Sweden acquired, on an entirely different basis than human cunning and selfish calculation, though with the loss of some of her noblest sons, a freedom from spiritual and social bondage.

At the time when the first bitter fruits of the disorders in our fatherland were developed, there came from Wittenberg a Swedish youth, who had there been a witness of the mischievous consequences which, in Germany, followed the merchandise of indulgences.

CHAPTER III.

OLAUS PETRI.

Of the smith Peter Olofsson, of Orebro, and his wife, Christna Larsdotter, were born two sons: Olof, in the year 1497, and Lars, in 1499. Their father died in 1521. The mother afterward lived a widow for four-and-twenty years; enriched, amid cares and joys, by the zeal and conduct of her children; a witness of the disappointments of the elder, of the eminence of both. She saw, at her death, in 1545, the one as shepherd of the chief church of Stockholm, the other as archbishop of Sweden.

In the Roman church, whose law respecting the celibacy of her clergy does not allow them to leave a legitimate issue, the dedication of a son to that office is regarded as an offering to God on the part of the parent. Whether it were such a motive, or the desire of improvement, according to the ideas of the times, that induced the parents of Olof and Lars, who were well disposed for study, to devote their sons to the offices of the church and literature, we do not venture to decide.

The opportunity of acquiring the elements of learning was afforded by the site of their patrimony, in the neighborhood of the monastery of the Carmelites.

This order, which counted its own descent from the prophet Elisha, came originally from the monastery on mount Carmel, in Palestine; a hill, from remote times, the abode of Eremites, who, in memory of the prophets Elisha and Elijah, there established their seat. The order was translated, in the thirteenth century, to western Europe, where, in the year 1245, it held of the pope the privileges of a begging order, for the redemption of the holy land. They came to the North slowly, and few in numbers. In the year 1407 was founded a monastery at Landskrona. In old Sweden the only monastery was at Orebro; probably founded in 1418. It was here termed the brethren of the Virgin Mary.

In this monastery, it is said, the brothers Petri had their first rudiments of education. The Carmelites prided themselves in their zeal for letters; though it is not certain that they merited the claim. How far Olof availed himself of the opportunities he had in his native country, for literary instruction, is uncertain; although it appears that he went to Strängness, where, it is to be presumed, that his character was more fully developed.

At the age of nineteen, Olof, the elder, left Sweden, to finish his studies in a foreign university. He chose that of Wittenberg, as not remote, and celebrated for its learned men.

The university of Wittenberg was dedicated in 1502, after the stars had been consulted, and the horoscope of the new institution settled. The elector of Saxony endeavored to assemble there men eminent for their learning and skill in teaching. The unsteadiness and confusion of the times kept the young institution in restraint. The controversy of the Dominicans against Reuchlin, and the attendant war respecting mental culture, which the authors and language of old Greece and Rome had begun to call forth, roused all minds, and increased the ferment which portended, in the church and realms of science, tempestuous clouds. But Wittenburg was not opposed to the cause of Reuchlin. Spalatin, the elector's chaplain, held with Reuchlin a correspondence by letters. Staupitz, provincial of the Augustinian order, and the friend as well as favorer of Luther, had studied, at the same time with Reuchlin, at the university of Tubingen. The ardent Carlstadt, one of Wittenberg's most famous scholars, and afterward renowned in the history of the Reformation, was Reuchlin's zealous admirer.

In the year 1510, Martin Luther was called to take a professor's chair at Wittenberg; and he soon gained it a high degree of respect. The influence or persuasions of Luther, it is said, induced Olof to go to Wittenberg, instead of Rome, whither the piety of former times, and the renown of that city, together with the prospect of a retreat and support in the house of St. Bridget, there established, had first drawn his attention, and directed his steps. But the origin of this tradition is unknown, and may resemble similar reports, after Luther, in 1517, become world-renowned. It was, upon the contrary, very customary, after schools of rank were opened in places nearer than Italy or France, for Swedes to attend these, in preference to such as were more remote. Olaus Petri was not the first, nor the last Swede, who studied at Wittenberg. Olof came to Wittenberg, and was matriculated at the university, in 1516. Among the students from Sweden, were Olaus Phase, of the diocese of Strängness; Olaus Brunes, and Dyro de Handolau, of Linkoping. In the year 1517, on the 10th day of February, Olaus Petri was promoted to the degree of master of philosophy.*

The three years Olof spent in Germany, for the most part, if not constantly at Wittenberg, were fruitful in the acquisition of knowledge and mental vigor. He stood in connection with the man who, in a short time, became, during his own and for succeeding centuries, the foremost man in the history of human progress. He was present in Wittenberg when Luther posted up his ninety-five theses; the results of which, through Olof's own exertions, changed the condition of church and state in Sweden. He was an ear and eye witness of the first disturbances, at the very spot where the fer-

* An eminent writer assigns reasons for the opinion that *Laurentius* Petri was not a student at Wittenberg.

ment first began. He had also, though for a shorter time, an opportunity of hearing the famous lectures which the young Melancthon, born in the same year with Olof, and Luther's truest and dearest friend, and the second man of the Reformation, began to deliver at Wittenberg, in the autumn of 1518. The spirit of Olof, however, was more allied to Luther's than to that of Melancthon.

Olof had thus stood, in relation to men and circumstances, the memory and impression of which could never be effaced from his soul. He had received this impression and this memory, in an ardent and youthful soul, burning with love for truth and right; with a zeal and courage boldly to proclaim that truth, and resuscitate it to a life-giving energy. This love, this zeal, and this courage, attended him during the whole of his earthly career. But the excess to which he carried these virtues too often colored them with the appearance of faults. His courage always continued to resemble a young man's rashness. He never learned to restrain and control himself; but, a man of fifty years, he still needed the force of necessity, to keep the fire of his nature within proper limits.

The compass and depth of his knowledge cannot be accurately determined. They were not small; but the men, who have to pass through a school of life like that of Olof, cannot be measured according to the rules of books and reading. A luminous and clear understanding, and a power of eloquence, applied with an exact suitableness to the circumstances which called it forth, were the supports of his mental activity.

That internal conflict of soul, which fitted Luther for his high vocation, Olof does not appear to have experienced. But of how many such champions for spiritual freedom, in the sixteenth century, have we to make report? Is not Luther, in this respect, alone? All minds of a higher cast, experience, in a greater or less degree, sympathy and pain for the maladies of the times in which they live. They feel a joy in their amendment. But, whenever there is a great breaking up in the life of humanity, it is not unusual that *one man* experiences, in all its depth and bitterness, this pain, in which is the death of the old and birth of the new. What he suffers he suffers for all. The experience of all times, repeats, in however low a point of view by comparison, the experience of humanity through the suffering of Jesus Christ, the Son of God, for us all.

Olof returned to his fatherland in 1519, after about three years' stay in Germany. On his return he presented himself to his bishop, the before-mentioned Matts Gregersson of Strängness. He held the canonry of the cathedral of that see, and was ordained at Michaelmas, September 29, 1520, as deacon of the bishop, who, when he lost his life in the massacre of Stockholm, left to the church a greater legacy than he himself expected. Olof had won the bishop's confidence. He had become his chancellor; and, being in this capacity near the bishop's person, was witness to his efforts to have homage rendered to Christian, and was even employed in the negotiations. That his own life, or that of his brother, was in danger at that sorrowful event, the massacre of Stockholm, is doubtful. Neither of them, in their accounts of it, speaks of the circumstance; and there is no other source known to me of that danger having been incurred, than a supposed letter of Laurentius to king Erik XIV.

CHAPTER IV.

THE FIRST ACCOUNTS OF THE MOVEMENTS AT WITTENBERG—LAURENTIUS ANDREÆ—OLAUS PETRI AT STRANGNESS—KING GUSTAVUS I.—JOHN MAGNUS.

(UNTIL AND AT THE DIET AT STRANGNESS IN 1523.)

The constant intercourse with Germany, maintained by the coming hither of German merchants and soldiers, by the return of Swedes from foreign universities, and by the trade carried on between the chief Swedish commercial towns, and the German citizens, would not allow of the transactions at Wittenberg and other parts of Germany in 1517, and the following years to remain in darkness, and unknown among us.

The people, who, in defiance of the papal menace of the church's law and the ban of the pope, had already, in a diet, declared his archbishop unworthy of office; who, with weapons in hand, conquered and destroyed the castle of St. Erik, his patron saint; who, with the profits of his indulgences, but furnished to his foes the means of war; and who prepared a bloody revenge for his aims and his traffic, in order that they might regain the freedom of their native land; a people like this could not be indifferent to the doubt awakened by the monk of Germany, whether indulgences were lawful in the use, or to the abhorrence of their misuse; if it may not rather be said, that by their actions, they had ventured further against Rome than he had yet ventured. Steps and measures were already taken and means provided for giving security to those measures against the Roman hierarchy, to which, as a consequence, the transactions in Germany must lead.

The earliest written information of Luther's advances against the sale of indulgences came from Rome, but were penned by a Swedish hand. The monastery of Wadsten always had one of the brothers residing in its house at Rome, who had charge of the house, and was the embassador of the order to the papal chair. Petrus Magni, who, in 1499, when he was rector of the school at Wadsten, and chaplain of St. Peter's church in that town, had been ordaiued as priest of the order, was sent, in 1508, to Rome; and he appears to have remained there till his return home to become bishop of Westeras. In a letter to "the abbess, father confessor, and all the beloved brothers and sisters in God" at Wadsten, dated September 30th, 1518, he replies, among other things, to the requests of the monastery, that he would procure of the pope the privilege of more indulgences, with their accompaniments, for the use of the officials of the cloisters. "A doctor," he says, "of the order of St. Augustin, in Germany, has written, the present year, many conclusions against indulgences, and widely circulated them; and sent them even here to the pope. If the pope had him, he would burn him; but he has supporters. Another doctor here, in Rome, has written, at the pope's command, a reply;* and where he thought to loose the knot he has only tied it. An account of the matter accompanies this letter to you. I have read how indulgences first began, and it is slippery ground. Repentance is the surest way, and in that will I hope to die." The openly declared disesteem of Petri for indulgences, is a proof of what men ventured, even in Rome, to think of the case.

* Silvester Prierias. His dialogue on the presumptuous conclusions of M. Luther appeared in December, 1517. He appeals to the pope's supremacy, as the ground for issuing indulgences. He declares "that man to be a heretic, who does not confidently repose upon the Roman church and the pope of Rome, as the unerring foundation of truth; from which even the Holy Scriptures derive their authority and regard."

In the year 1520, Laurentius Andreæ was the archdeacon of Strängness; for his knowledge, his temper, and talents in business, a man of high esteem. He was probably born at Strängness, and about the year 1480. Of his earlier life we know no more than that he became a master of arts, and was some time in Rome. John Magnus, the archbishop, who fled from Sweden, speaks of him with all the bitterness with which a passionate man judges an adversary, in contending with whom he has been a loser. He censures especially his violent behavior at Rome, where he became associated "with subtle men, and whence he brought home nothing but a stolidity combined with a singular malignity." Rome, in the days of Alexander VI., who in times past was the most vicious of all the popes, and in the days of Julius II. also, was no good school for a young man; but the subsequent life of Laurentius furnishes ample reason to reverse the sentence of John, and to attribute to Laurentius qualities and virtues correspondent to the admitted vigor he displayed. We find in him a calm and grave man, but at the same time we find firmness and resolution, and a prudent, calculating spirit. In another work which he has written, the same adversary bears witness to the piety of Laurentius, though he says it was "more as pretence than reality," and reproaches him for "an insatiable appetite for honor and applause and novelty."* What John further reports of Laurentius Andreæ's rage at being passed by in the choice of a bishop for Strängness, may be dismissed, since nobler motives are found to vindicate his subsequent proceedings. It proves, however, his influence in the chapter, as well as his colleague's distrust of his principles, or the fruits of his superior predominance. It merits remark, that the writings of John were, after his death, published by his brother Olaus

* "A man, religious more in appearance than reality, but extravagantly fond of glory, praise, and novelty, and enraged because he was not elected into the place of the deceased bishop."

Magnus, who was the colleague of Laurentius in the cathedral of Strängness, or its prœpositus, a part of the time Laurentius was its archdeacon.

That Lars, who received, though we know not where, the degree of master of arts, had an extensive mental cultivation, is manifest from his letters and writings.

After the death of bishop Matts Gregersson, king Christian, contrary to the will of the chapter, to whom canonical law gave the election of a bishop, wished to introduce into the see of Strängness John Bellenake (the bald-headed), one of his advisers in the massacre. Having a little before despotically deprived him of the see of Odense, in Fyen, he now wished to place him in Strängness. He was obliged to fly from the country in 1521, and it is doubtful if he could be possessed of the see. The most important man of the chapter, even with a bishop, and still more in a vacancy, was the archdeacon. He was the "bishop's eye," to assist him in the care of the clergy, in business, and in the general affairs of the diocese. He exercised, in no inconsiderable degree, the bishop's power of pronouncing sentence; and had, at least in many sees, a part in the government and administration of the church's property. This office was now held at Strängness, by Laurentius Andreæ; and could, in these times of confusion, be of the utmost importance. The archdeacon was the foremost man of the diocese.

Master Olof had begun, at Strängness, to read portions from the Old and New Testaments, for those of the prebends and basket-boys who wished to hear him. The archdeacon soon began to be attentive to his instruction, approved of it, and was the cause of the school being intrusted to Olof. This patronage, and Olof's legal right in his new vocation openly to give instruction, increased the number and interest of the hearers. This was the first commencement of the improved teaching propagated in Sweden.

That Olof did not conceal the insight into truth to

which he had himself attained, appears both from his own course and from the attention which the spread of the doctrine from Strängness began to awaken in the land.

When, in the autumn of 1521, master Olof, with his brother Lars, came to Orebro to attend their father's funeral, they wished to exclude from its celebration the Carmelite monks, who, in the will of the deceased, were remembered with a legacy, on condition of having masses for his soul. Their mother, upon this, refused to go in, and showed both her piety and sense when, to the question of her sons, if she understood the Latin mass of the monks, she answered, "I do not understand them, but then I hear them, and I pray God in my heart that he will deign to hear their prayer, and I doubt not but he will." These words completely express the Roman church's idea of the layman's relation to the church, and of performing mass during public worship in an unknown tongue. Yet she yielded to the will of her sons, to the great scandal of the Carmelites. They were destined to suffer from the freedom of speech of these young men. In a letter, dated Nov. 30, 1521, Magnus Birgersson, confessor general of the Carmelite convent, arraigned master Olof before doctor Nils, the dean of the chapter of Strängness. The deacon Olaus Petri, and his brother Laurentius, had been at their father's funeral, "and spoke many opprobrious things against God and his holy name, to the great scandal of us the brethren and all Christians, and have said, that they would change the church's holy state and law, which our forefathers have so inviolably kept. They have turned away contemptuously with many blasphemous words, us brethren of the convent, from holy rites over their father's dead body, entirely contrary to their good father's command, who for his poor soul ordered masses, and therefor for our support gave his land east of the town; in evidence of which he left a letter, still in possession of his ungodly sons (whom may God graciously convert), so that it will never be of any advantage to us brothers. God help us. They have also spoken in opprobrious terms against the pope, and said they despised his power, as has been done by the heretical monk Luther of Rome (?), of whom they spoke in strong terms, and exalted him in the eyes of the people, as is remembered by many who treated us with ridicule and scorn. But we are willing so to suffer for God's sake, who suffered for us and our sins. Dear doctor Nils, to you belongs the care of these things, and the terror of the church's law against this deacon Olaus Petri, who has been the occasion of so much confusion." It is not known whether this accusation was attended with any evil consequences to master Olof.

What doctrines were specially presented by Olof in his lectures, or in what relation they stood to the existing church, we are not informed. A specimen, however, we have in the notes which the above-mentioned doctor Nils made of sundry dangerous declarations, which Olof from time to time advanced, in the course of his preaching at Strängness, and which notes, with Nils's refutation, came, in 1523, into the hands of bishop Brask. They may be quoted, as a proof of what was either *considered* as the boldest of Olof's declarations, or as a proof of what he was then making the subject of his meditations. In the former case we contemplate the stand-point of the Swedish church, at that time; in the latter case, to some extent, Olof's own position.

Master Olof's errors were as follows:

1. In the authentic Scriptures it is not found that St. Anna was the mother of the promised virgin Mary. Doctor Nils appeals thereon to the church's gloss upon the Bible and the church's liturgy; concerning Master Olof's appeal to authentic Scripture, he does not express his mind.

2. Joseph, who was betrothed to the promised virgin, was not an old, but a young man. Nils, in reply, appeals to the church's testimony in her hymns and legends; and he does

not appear to reflect that, respecting the validity of even this testimony, there will arise a controversy.

3. Olof had said, "No one has here preached the truth for you before me." Against this presumptuous declaration, Nils objects the modest reply, that the question may be determined by direct proof; St. Eskil had here (in Sodermanland) suffered martyrdom, because he here preached the catholic truth.

The ground on which this expression of Olof rested, was dangerous, and decided the character and genius of protestantism. It might thence be concluded, that now, for the first time, truth was opened to the world; or that now, for the first time, it stood forth in a light which allowed men to apprehend its real nature, and thus transform the doctrines of faith into human assurance. By master Olof the declaration was made from an historical point of view; so that he thereby intended to signify, that the church was already lost, when Christianity was first preached in Sweden. But even this supposition involves a degree of rashness and arrogance, since it implies that the Christian truth, and life in the church, might at some time be entirely stifled.

4. No monk should beg; because it is said in Deuteronomy xv. (according to the Vulgate), "There shall be no poor or begging person among you." Doctor Nils replies to this, that the passage quoted should be interpreted of the Jews; and refers, for the justification of begging monks, to the writings of Thomas Aquinas.

5. No one ought to put his trust in man, nor in the promised virgin, nor in any saint, but in God alone. According to Jeremiah xvii., "cursed is he who trusteth in man." This point, which involves one of the weightiest controversies between the Roman and Protestant churches, because it is connected with the doctrine of the relation of man's nature to God's grace, was answered by Doctor Nils, in regard to the quoted passage, by remarking, that it is spoken of Zedekiah

and his people, who trusted in the king of Egypt and mistrusted the help of God. But to trust in man, in such a manner as to put the chief trust in God, is no error. He here also refers to Thomas Aquinas.

6. The vocation of the preacher is the highest in the church of God, and is of more consequence than the mass; "it is considered," he says, "of little consequence, compared to the mass." Doctor Nils regards this position to merit no further reply than this, that the consecration of the body and blood of Christ is the highest and holiest action in the church of God; and he again refers to Thomas Aquinas.

As in each of the other points, so here, also, had master Olof predecessors within the Roman church itself. So spoke, in the thirteenth century, a Dominican, or general of the order of preachers, Humbert de Romanis, who asserted that preaching was before all else. Christ had only once celebrated the mass, did not hear confession, seldom administered the sacraments, but often preached. As laymen understood preaching, but not the mass celebrated in Latin, so God would more clearly and openly bless the former than the latter. An order of precedence does not, however, express the protestant sense of the various acts which, in public worship, aim to awaken, invigorate, and promote, the spiritual life of man.

7. The brotherhood of the psaltery of the virgin ought not to be allowed; because they have no warrant in Scripture. To this doctor Nils answers, that where two or three are gathered together in His name, Christ will be in the midst of them; and that, if a righteous man's prayer availeth much, so must the prayers of many, united in a brotherhood, avail much more.

Master Olof's appeal solely to the Scriptures, proves that he followed, with steady step, the protestant development. His disapproval of the brotherhood of the psaltery of the virgin, was a direct blow to the circle around him. The celebrated deceased bishop, Conrad Roggo, about twenty years before the preaching of master Olof, and a little before his own death, introduced, with allowance of the pope, in 1470, the fraternity of the psaltery of the blessed virgin. Six priests of the chapel of St. Eskil were to celebrate mass daily, from Easter to the end of the ecclesiastical year, with the exception of Saturday and Sunday; singing the psalter, to the praise of the holy virgin, and imploring her protection. This psalter gained the title of the psaltery of Mary; for the psalter itself was altered, and applied to her honor; the first psalm, for example, being made to read, "Blessed is the man who loves thy name, O virgin Mary! thy grace shall strengthen his soul."

8. Confession should be made by every one before God alone, and not before the priest. Doctor Nils admits that this could be permitted in case of necessity, but not else. Man needs spiritual medicine in order to be blessed; but this he cannot give himself; he knows not if he has a true repentance for sin; he needs, therefore, to make known his sins to the priest, who is put in the place of Christ. Confession before a priest is valid, by divine right; silent confession, before God, has merely a natural right. The pope himself cannot excuse from confession, for he cannot abrogate a divine right.

We find in these notes from the sermons of Olaus Petri, at Strängness, the propositions, which exhibit many of the points of doctrine, on which turned the controversy between the Roman church and protestants. They were, for the most part, protests against the abuses which, within three centuries, had crept into the western church, and there became, or were said to have become, established by law. At the fourth council of Lateran, in 1215, whose decisions, however, were in legal form received, as the church's conciliar decrees, auricular confession was declared necessary. At the same council, the doctrine of transubstantiation, as already commonly entertained, was taught and enforced within the church. The year after, the pope gave an act of confirmation to one of the most conspicuous of the orders of begging monks; and the worship of the virgin Mary, and the saints, of which there were traces even in the fourth century, was, at the close of the middle ages, in a state of continual advance.

But the condition of the church, with the improvement of which the ecclesiastical Reformation in Sweden began, did not escape master Olof's attention and censure. In July of 1523, bishop Brask received, from the chapter of Upsala, advices of how widely the Lutheran heresy began to spread all around, within the church of Strängness, by means of a certain Olaus Petri; of whom Brask appears, this year, for the first time, to have had any knowledge. There would be especial danger to the holy Roman church's power, and the church's privileges, in the attempt to return the church, as now existing, to her first state of poverty, and her other primitive characteristics; though, beyond contradiction, she had long lived in poverty, through her own choice. She had certainly taken the temporal goods which were bestowed upon her. The heretic who then rose up had still more fired the laity, who already showed themselves hostilely affected to the church. It was now again pretended, that the church, by renouncing her worldly possessions, should be brought to a conformity with the church of primitive times. This would be only to give support to heresy.

The zeal of Olof had not yet encountered the man who, for a time, was to stand forth as the most faithful and the strongest champion, in Sweden, of the old religion. Brask had already, with an observant eye, followed the course of Lutheranism in Germany. In February of 1523, he writes of having heard that the Lutheran heresy was on the decline; on the 7th of May following, of the mention of a man in Strängness, who wrought scandal and schism by his sermons in favor of the Lutheran ferment. He calls God to witness, that he was deeply concerned that there was no superior officer in the church who would watch over its peace. He circulated pope Leo X.'s brief of August 23d, 1518, to cardinal Gaeta, against Luther. A letter which, on March 7th, 1523, Brask wrote to master John Magnus, then at Rome, contains the bitterest complaints, and the blackest picture of the Swedish church's condition. "The kingdom," he says, "is shaken by war; and men can enjoy no peace or quiet. Whereas it was hoped, through the recognition of king Christian II., to gain peace and harmony in the kingdom, we have experienced the sternest disappointment. The heaviest weight of the war has fallen on the church, whose property and persons are ruined. This might patiently be borne, if there were any compensation; but it cannot be regarded with indifference, that the church can obtain no other return than hate for love. If an attempt is made to recover the lost property of the church, we are charged with avarice and the love of contention; but if a layman has an eye to the church's possessions or to her persons, the profoundest meanness takes the place of justice, where she or her officers are concerned. There was none to comfort the church of Abo, which has lost her castle, her richest jewels, and her shepherd, who perished by shipwreck. Bishop Otto of Westeras had died the previous summer, at the siege of Stockholm, and left his church wasted by foes and in poverty. The clergy of Strängness, three times plundered in one year, mourned over the sufferings of their see. The church of Skara, burnt by its foes, lamented and expected further cause for lamentation over its desolation, and its stern necessities. It needed not to speak of the church of Upsala; which has undergone ineffable sufferings. The bishop of Wexio, a man stricken in years, and full of infirmities, placed on the hostile frontiers, was in daily dread of captivity. Kalmar was possessed by enemies, and had become so commonly a prey by indecent guests and other burdens, that its property, which before was a curse to the monks, was now more so to the priests. If complaint was made of plundered tithes, of disorderly occupants of glebes, of intrusions upon the rights of the clergy, it was said, that censure fell upon the landsman, who did less mischief to the church, more than upon her enemies, who left her nothing. With all this co-operated certain spiritual evils which must be passed over, that were the result of the infection of Lutheran principles. For these principles had brought many laymen to the opinion, that the church was made for the civil community, and that therefore all that the church owned should belong to this community."

Occasion will hereafter occur to speak of various points of these complaints of Bishop Brask. His fear of the Lutheran heresy was justified, not merely by advices from Strängness, but by the effects of it he experienced in his own diocese, where Severin Norby's power was the support of the heresy. It was this circumstance probably, and the news he received from Germany, which induced Brask, soon after the raising of the siege of Kalmar, to thank the prior of the Dominicans in that city, while congratulating him on his escape from the Danes, for his opposition to Lutheranism, and to send him the bulls of the universities of Louvain and Cologne, with the heresies of Olaus Petri.

Although the more liberal principles began in many places to take root, it was from Strängness, the centre of reformation in our fatherland, that the seed of the new dogmas was sown over Sweden. Archdeacon Laurentius Andreæ was won over to the cause of the Reformation, and became the disciple of his younger colleague, Olof.

At Whitsuntide, near the close of May, 1523, was opened the diet of Strängness; which, for Sweden's and the church's future, was of so great consequence, as resulting in the coronation of Gustavus Wasa as king. Bishop Brask was not present. He excused himself on account of sickness, but sent his chancellor with his seal. Of the king's election, he says not a word in the letters written before and during the diet; either not having heard that it was in question, or, as is more likely, from the rest of his conduct, being too discreet to say anything beforehand. But, at this point, make their appearance in Swedish church history, two men of singular importance, King Gustavus I., and the papal legate, John Magnus.

It may, with certainty, be assumed that Gustavus Wasa, during the nearly eight months he stayed at Lubeck, between the years 1519 and 1520, had heard of the proceedings within the church, of which the effects were soon felt over the whole of the German dominions. But it is not known how much attention, amid the solicitude for his own safety and the welfare of his native country, he could bestow upon this subject; or what leisure his mind could have, after his return to Sweden, amid the first three years of care, anxiety, and strife, to preserve or refresh the impression he had received—an impression, which could never be effaced from his soul—an impression imbibed at the court of the younger Sten Sture, and in the wars against king Christian and archbishop Trolle, in which, before his being carried off to Denmark, he took an active part—an impression which the massacre of Stockholm, where he lost father, brother-in-law, and many relatives, must have acutely deepened in his mind—an impression which was no less kept alive by his subsequent battles for freedom. This impression was a deep and inappeasable hate of the Roman hierarchy. He appears from that time never to have put confidence in a man who belonged to it. But that on this hate he grounded any plans for Sweden's future, when it was yet a question whether Sweden should have a future, is not probable.

But then, when hope and quiet began to return, and Gustavus was seated on Sweden's throne, he could not, while staying at Strängness, fail to hear mentioned the new dogmas there preached. He also heard master Olof's disciples preach, and found in them the vindicators of the same views to which he was himself inclined. Laurentius Andreæ, whom he summoned to acquaint him with the positions of the new teaching, opened to him the reasons of Luther's line of conduct, the papal error, the hierarchy's unjustifiable claims, and the unlawfulness, according to holy scripture, of its worldly power and dominion. To arrive at the truth, the king procured information from Germany; and as this corresponded with what master Lars communicated to him, "he readily adopted the same views, and made daily progress therein."

All the advices we have from and of this period unite in assuring us that King Gustavus became, through Laurentius Andreæ, decided in adopting the principles of the Reformation, and was entirely won to them. In what degree a lively spiritual sensibility operated on the king's mind, as it was gradual, and for some time resulted in no open declaration, it is scarce possible to determine; while it would be unjust to deny him all pious emotions as the groundwork of his line of action. One thought, one determination, one fixed purpose, filled his soul and fired his firm heart: to establish the freedom and independence of his native land, and secure the throne to which God, amid great perils, and by a wonderful providence, had elevated him. This object mingled with all his thoughts, and influenced his whole life. The freedom of Sweden and establishment of her church, his own kingly dignity, and the stirrings of piety in his heart, were fused together as his motives to action; and although statesmanship and policy caused him to throw his weight into the scale against the church's external might,—these can, with little justice, be offered as the chief or only motives in his movements for the church's reformation, which, it may be affirmed, he undertook from purely spiritual reasons.

It is very usual to attribute to King Gustavus either great

praise or great censure for having, by his will or by his power, forced on the Reformation in the Swedish church in which he made use of men who were his willing agents. A closer view into the life and disposition of Gustavus brings to light, in connection with the testimony of history, the falsity of this opinion. The king was irritable and quick of temper, but, like all men of that disposition, pliable, and easily led by those who understood how to win his confidence. In combination with their influence and vigor, he threw into the scale the weight of his royal power and authority; but even this with great forbearance, and only so far as he saw to be required by the occurring changes, and the fitness for them of his people. The will of an absolute prince had not suffered the work so long to progress, and left it, after well nigh forty years, unfinished and incomplete; had not begun a reform which needed two of the ages of man for its completion; had not given his work a slow development, that, for the first time, the third part of a century after, his fourth successor on the Swedish throne might then put the seal of perfection. But that the improvement of the church was indifferent to him, except as a means of gaining and keeping her wealth, is an accusation which the following pages will refute. We shall not, however, intentionally conceal the king's defects, which, according to our conviction, do not diminish his greatness and his merits toward the church and fatherland.

At the diet of Strängness, commences a brighter prospect for the Reformation of the church in Sweden; and there dawns a hope for the stability of its temporal strength. At the same diet, makes his appearance, John Magnus, the papal legate, sent hither to regulate the affairs of the church.

The massacre of Stockholm must have awakened at Rome, the more attention and concern, as the abominable act was committed on the pretext of vindicating the church's wrongs, and on the ground of her commission. King Christian's other arbitrary acts; his alarming treatment of the episcopal sees; his equivocal leaning to a reformation; his offer to Luther of a refuge in Denmark when his life was jeoparded in Germany; his church laws, and other of his proceedings, could not but awaken doubts. He had engaged the chapter of Lund, by putting aside Ake Sparre, to give the crosier to George Skotborg, the king's secretary; but when this man, whom Christian expected readily to surrender Bornholm when put in the archiepiscopal chair, refused to resign his office, the attempt was made, though in vain, to force the chapter to elect Didrik Slagok. The papal chair was not decidedly favorable to Christian, who, partly to avoid the threatening consequence of the measures by which he had given offence to the church, and partly to get confirmed his nomination of the bishop he wished, sent, in the years 1520 and 1521, several embassadors to Rome. He obtained the promise of Didrik's confirmation, in virtue of the supremacy by which the pope, during the later periods of the middle ages, found himself able to annul the election of the chapters, and to appoint bishops independently of them.

But the loud complaints of the Swedes, in the pope's name, averted the act of violence, and the general abhorrence it awakened, together with the church's danger, did not allow pope Leo X. to seem indifferent. In September, 1521, there came to Köpenham, John Francis de Potentia, from Naples, a Franciscan monk, as legate of the pope. The investigation made, resulted in the legate's condemnation of what had passed at Stockholm, and the sentence that had been executed. Didrik Slagok was made the sin-offering for the king's offences against the church. After a trial by torture, this man, who from a low origin, and a beginning of little promise, had been elevated to the place, which in the Scandinavian North, was next the king's throne, was hanged and burnt, on January 24th, 1522, in the market-place of Köpenham.

In Sweden there had long been desired, as a necessity, the intervention of a legate. Against the blood-thirsty king himself men anxiously awaited the restraining justice of the highest moral guardian of order. The sentence which punished the official tools could not, in the eyes of the sufferers, expiate the crime, and gave only occasion to increased discontent. But, at Rome, there had already appeared, unexpected and uncalled, an advocate for his countrymen, the Swedish people.

This man was John Magnus. Born in the year 1488, at Linkoping, of which his father was a burgher, he had, at the age of sixteen, after receiving instruction at home, and an examination before the bishops and chapters of Linkoping and Skara, become canon of both these churches. He afterward went to the universities of Louvain and Cologne, and was, at the former, a pupil of the then professor, the learned and pious Adrian of Utrecht, afterward pope Adrian VI. He was subsequently sent by Sten Sture, the younger, to Rome, to attend to the affairs of the regent and his native country, and he there employed the opportunities which offered for his own improvement. After the death of Sture, he withdrew to Perugia, where he occupied the chair of theology. But when the news of the massacre of Stockholm reached his ears, he hastened back to Rome, and appeared before Leo X., in the name of the Swedish people and of justice, demanding vengeance for the cruel deed. He had thus been the means of procuring the mission of the above-named legate. But as the issue of this mission did not prove satisfactory, John considered his self-imposed duty not completed.

Leo X. died, December 1st, 1521, and left in full flame the fire which his course had not so much enkindled as given occasion to break forth. To him succeeded, February 2d, 1522, the emperor Charles V.'s former preceptor, Adrian, a man, according to the opinion held of him, "too good in those times to be a pope," and the last of the few men born out of Italy who wore the triple crown. He was not a friend of the new views, but he concealed neither from himself nor others, that the dissoluteness of the hierarchy was the root of the church's disasters. "You may say," he writes, in his directions to his legate, at the German diet of Nuremberg, in 1522, "that we confess that God has sent this persecution (the Lutheran heresy) for the sins of men, and chiefly for those of the clergy. The Scriptures show, that the sins of the people flow from the sins of the priests. We know that vices, for many years, have crept into this holy chair, abuses into holy things, transgressions of the laws, perversions in all. It is, therefore, not surprising that maladies press from the head to the members, from the popes to the inferior prelates. We, prelates and churchmen, have all gone, each one his own way. For a long time none have done good, no not one. Therefore must we all give praise and honor to God, and humble our souls. May every one see in what he has fallen, and recover himself, rather than be scourged of the displeasure and indignation of God."

This man could not be deaf to the complaints of the Swedish people. He determined to send to Sweden as legate of the apostolic see his former pupil, John Magnus, the zealous for his fatherland and its church. The legate immediately commenced his journey, provided with the necessary letters of commission, and sundry directions of the pope to the bishop of Linkoping, to whom the pope declares his satisfaction at the pious zeal he had manifested for the pure truth, and especially for the extirpation of the monstrous dogmas of Martin Luther, which had begun to spread over these regions. Adrian exhorts him to persevere; apprizes him that he has determined to send to Sweden John Magnus, his notary and chamberlain, in whose truth, learning, and probity, he had the utmost confidence, to extirpate the Lutheran delusion, to strengthen the hearts of the faithful, and in general have a care of affairs appertaining to the faith. Brask was admonished to be aiding and assisting the legate, and to regard him with the same confidence as if the pope himself was heard speaking.

John, who had also a commission to effect a reconciliation between king Sigismund of Poland, and Albrekt, grand master or duke of Prussia, but found them already reconciled; hastened to take ship at Dantzic, then the usual port of passage for Sweden; landed at Stegeborg, and arrived after three days' journey at Strängness, without having time to communicate with Brask, who, through real or pretended sickness, was absent from the diet, and, as appears from his correspondence, was then staying at Norsholm or Linkoping. The legate came to Strängness the day after, or at least soon after the 6th of June; that day of election when Gustavus Wasa was crowned king of the Swedes and Goths. He was received in Sweden with the customary solemnities.

It soon appeared that the purpose of the legate's coming was not understood, and there was discontent at the plenary power with which he was invested. A fresh investigation of archbishop Trolle's conduct, an amelioration of the church's excessive powers, as well as a commission to examine into king Christian's proceedings, had been expected; but the legate was only anxious or authorized, in the first place, to root out the Lutheran heresy.

The legate himself could not but see that he could do nothing toward this object in the disordered condition of the Swedish church, under an archbishop sentenced by the diet as a traitor to his country, and now in exile; while, except the inactive Ingemar of Wexio, she had only a single consecrated bishop, and was in a state of desolation from a war that had dissipated the strength of both church and state. John, as well as the king, perceived that he must return to give an account to the pope of the condition of the Swedish church and obtain more ample powers. Already had the estates and the senate written, on the 12th of June, a letter to the pope, which was prepared to be carried by the legate, and which shows the state of things. "The legate," they said, "had presented the subjects which he had to deliver on the part of the pope, respecting the welfare of the kingdom and church of Sweden. He had, in a convincing manner, engaged them to enter into the views of his holiness; that they desired, as much as they could, to promote and maintain the honor and stability of the apostolic chair. The legate *had assured them that the pope was disposed to reform the Christian church*, and they were in hope he would have a care that such bishops were chosen in Sweden as far more promoted peace and harmony among their fellow-citizens, than the seditious Gustavus Trolle had done in the times lately passed. This archbishop had so misused his episcopal rank to produce war and discord, that it would seem of the singular grace of God, the respect for the church was not wholly and entirely lost among them. They had exhibited proof of his bad conduct and loose habits, before the legate, who would lay a true report before the pope; and because Trolle had *abdicated his office*, and gone over to their foe, king Christian of Denmark, *they had unanimously and forever banished him.* His holiness was called on especially to look to the interest of the tottering church of Upsala, on whose eminence and worth well nigh the whole of the Northern church's welfare depended. It had, of late years, suffered many losses, and could not be saved, unless a new archbishop, by great prudence and the king's confidence and favor, could reinstate it in its former privileges. In this they were desirous to co-operate as soon as they found the pope disposed to exert himself for its re-establishment. Many errors had, during the disorders and confusions in the kingdom, crept into the faith, and could not easily be removed; therefore they prayed that the embassador of his holiness, John Magnus, already appointed a bishop in their land, might return to them, furnished with full authority by the holy see, and with the laudable prudence they had found in him, to make the necessary regulations for the outward discipline of the church, and for the conservation of the faith."

It is little probable that this letter, delivered to the legate, ever came to Rome. John remained three whole years in Sweden, and the relation of things was soon very materially changed. But the document exhibits the opinions and views which in Sweden were commonly entertained. Cases were here put according to their importance, in another fashion than that by which it was customary to judge them at Rome. The abdication of Trolle was first considered, of which the pope was put in mind, that he himself abdicated his office, and was obliged to go into exile. Then, if his doom of abdication by the estates, in 1517, was considered a nullity, it was acknowledged there was a trespass against the existing law of the church; but his removal from the archiepiscopal chair of Upsala was, and remained, the primary condition of Sweden's return to obedience. The confirmation of the election of bishops and their consecration, was expected or recognized; but that the usual, and in later times continually increased imposts, should go from the land into the papal chancery, was not to be thought of. In the third place, after discipline should be restored to the church, attention was to be paid to the extirpation of errors; but these were only indefinitely mentioned, and seem to have been considered as the means of engaging the pope to compliance in other points. A severance from the Roman chair was not then thought of; but with self-confidence and the consciousness of strength, as in a strife for freedom, it was as little thought that there should be submission to all that came from Rome.

CHAPTER V.

LAURENTIUS ANDREÆ, THE KING'S CHANCELLOR—JOHN MAGNUS ELECTED ARCHBISHOP—PROCEEDINGS AT ROME IN RESPECT TO THE ELECTION AND CONFIRMATION OF BISHOPS TILL THE YEAR 1527.

LAURENTIUS ANDREÆ won the confidence of the king during his stay at Strängness, in 1523. After the diet held in that place, he was called to be the king's chancellor; an office which, for the three hundred years it was found in Sweden, was held by churchmen, either at the time bishops or afterward made such. Known and tried fitness must have gained him this post, on which he entered in the course of this summer. Thus was the most prominent of the friends of ecclesiastical freedom placed in immediate connection with the king, and obtained in his councils the strongest influence. He took a place, also, at least not later than in 1526, among the senators of the kingdom, and held, in connection with the archdeaconship of Strängness, the presidency of the chapter of Upsala, after the flight of Sven Eriksson, who took his departure with Gustavus Trolle, and who lived to the year 1532.

The influence of Laurentius with Gustavus I. commenced at the same time with the appearance of John Magnus as papal legate in Sweden. The point of time was momentous, and the business of the legate in the highest degree intricate and important. How should he reconcile the pope's reluctance to give up the unworthy Trolle, with the settled, decided determination of his countrymen not again to receive him as archbishop of Sweden? How should he be able, by filling the vacant sees, to protect the supremacy of Rome and her interests? If the newly-elected king was so fortunate as to defend, and on his head to seat the crown stretched out to him, would he be found, amid the storms of human strife and the menaced defection from Rome, to be an obedient son of the church? *Which of them would win his ear and mind, the skillful and confident Laurentius Andreæ, and the indefatigable and undaunted herald of the new faith, Olaus Petri, or the temporizing policy of the legate, or the old interests on an unaltered basis, with Brask for their sponsor?* There was, amid all casualties and as opposed to the more liberal views, the possibility of again raising the old bulwark of the church's constitution, broken and impaired by the indiscretion and imprudence of its apologists.

Was John Magnus the right man, in an hour so decisive, to be a leader in the church's cause? Integrity, moderation, and a well-intentioned mind, are the qualities necessary for him who has undertaken the critical problem it was now the part of John to solve. But he had also two defects, and these among the most fatal for a man in his position—irresolution and vanity; and in addition to these, what is common with many, in times of revolution, a temporizing disposition.

It was, perhaps, vanity which tempted John to hasten to Strängness without having met Brask and consulted with him on the affairs of the church. It seems as if he did not wish to share with any one the honor of reconciling the existing contentions. Bishop Brask laments that he did not meet with the legate, who seems, in his haste, not even to have delivered the pope's letter to him. He had learned, so he writes on the 15th of July, that the legate had concluded to take his departure without their meeting together to consult on the affairs of the Swedish kingdom and church, and rooting out the Lutheran heresy. This heresy was a source to him of pain upon pain. He suffered from sickness, but still more from the spread of heresy through a master Olof of Strängness. Olof's errors, a copy of which was communicated to the legate, had become so openly promulgated that he could not with honor and conscience leave them without investigation and correction. He might add to his troubles the heads of the chapters who were attached to the pope. Inquisition ought to be appointed in all the dioceses, to watch over the purity of the faith. The legate should also see that there should be brought before a spiritual tribunal, the complaints made against churchmen. There was danger that what happened yesterday might happen on the morrow. The church's privileges had been seized, on the plea that there was no justice in the spiritual courts. The legate should labor to recover to the church the immunities she had enjoyed for more than three hundred years, and which the king, when he was called at Wadsten to the administration of the government, promised to preserve. It would also be important to protect the church in case of a large assessment by the king. Such was the language and such the views of Brask.

But the legate procrastinated, and did nothing of all that to which Brask prompted him. He was satisfied on his part with wishes, ideas, consultations. He speaks, in his letter, written at this time, of being able to effect *what had long been passing in his mind*, in regard to the advancement of truth and the church; "but the unhappy state of the times, operated against his devout wishes and strenuous endeavors." The king promised him to sustain the church's immunities; declared himself averse to the maltreatment of the peasantry of the church by his subordinates; had avouched his dissatisfaction with the extortions which times of necessity had occasioned, and promised that his attention would be directed, when the kingdom was restored to quiet, to have the forced loans refunded. The king had also obligated himself to check the Lutheran heresy; but had begged the legate, with caution and gentleness, not with bulls, to execute his commission in this respect, as otherwise, the whole Swedish church would be put in commotion. John was aware that the sterner modes of the church intervention had in other lands kindled an unquenchable fire. He negotiated with the men of Strängness, and had their promise to refrain from new doctrines, and in writing to attack no one, if themselves were not drawn into controversy by others. "Your grace," he writes complacently to Brask, on August 1st, 1523, "may be assured that my coming to Sweden has not been without its fruits. I may soon leave it. I came here. I examined the sore, the more effectually to heal it." He should return the following summer, or get the direction of the affairs of the Swedish church to be left in the hands of Brask.

Soon after this, the business of the legate became so entangled, that he could neither depart nor effect anything. Five of the old episcopal sees of Sweden, were contemporaneously in need of consecrated shepherds. Skara and Strängness, vacant by the murder of their incumbents in 1520, were again so when Didrik Slagok, and John Bellenake, intruded by Christian, were obliged, with the declining fortunes of that king, surreptitiously to leave the land. The disasters of the times caused two other vacancies, by the death of Otto of Westeras, and Arvid of Abo. In the year 1522, thoughts were entertained of placing new bishops in the sees. For Upsala was elected, or at least proposed, master Knut, chancellor of the regent, and the propositus of Westeras. For Skara, Christian's preference being disregarded, and the chapter disapproving its previous forced election, Magnus Haraldsson, archdeacon there, was chosen. For Strängness, the propositus of the chapter, Magnus Sommar. For Westeras, he that was deacon there, the dangerous Per or Peter Sunnanvader, who now returned, and was absolved from accountability. Abo, which was held by the followers of Christian, could not be provided for. But Upsala and Westeras were soon again declared vacant by king Gustavus, when master Knut and Peter Sunnanvader, were deposed in September, 1523, for their turbulent machinations. The king, as soon as sure proofs of the treason of Sunnanvader were in his hands, had hastened to Westeras, placed this proof before the chapter, and declared the elected bishop unworthy of the office; and soon after declared the same of provost Knut. He also desired the chapter immediately to proceed to a new election, of which, the legate preparing for his departure, might procure confirmation at Rome. As the canons were at a loss where to find a suitable man, the king proposed the administrator of the house of St. Bridget at Rome, Petrus Magni, who was accordingly elected. The pope confirmed this election, and after having been consecrated at Rome, he came home, in the year 1524, and took his seat in the senate of the diet—the last bishop, who, by virtue of his office, there had a seat and voice, as he was the last Roman catholic bishop who was consecrated to his office, before the Reformation took place in 1527.

In September, 1523, the legate undertook the purposed return to Rome, which he had contemplated ever since his arrival. The king now wrote to the pope, and "declared the delight which the coming of the legate had given him and all his people, and lamented that the envoy could not effect the perfect re-establishment of the Swedish church, the cause of which was the tottering condition of the cathedral churches, which had now, for some years, been without bishops. The appointment of these was, above all, consequential; and after this took place at Rome, and the legate returned with full powers, the king would aid him in all matters that concerned the church's dignity and Christian truth, according to the determination of the bishops to extirpate all heresy, to bring the schismatical Russians to the unity of the church, and Lapland to the faith of Christ. The legate had urged the king to have pity of the church's privileges. For these the king had contended against king Christian, the church's most ferocious foe. He would not now let them suffer any wrong; *if only the apostolic chair appointed such bishops as were content within their limits, and had a care for peace and harmony among the king's subjects—such as so vindicated the church's privileges, that they did no harm to the crown.* The king desired not this, to restrain the free appointment of bishops by his holiness, who by his holy manners had already improved the church, but to knit the firm alliance, which at this period was so necessary, between spiritual men and men of the world. The legate knew who were the men acceptable to the king, and useful to the church, and therefore suitable for bishops. The king had conceived such confidence in the legate, he wished the pope to intrust to him the reformation of the church."

It is impossible not to be struck with the open and free, the firm and dignified mode of address in this letter of the king. Adrian VI. had, through his own uprightness here, as in Germany, called forth this candor. Men immediately laid hold on his promise of reform. This letter is also the first known act subscribed on the king's order by Laurentius Andreæ, as Gustavus's chancellor. Immediately on his entrance into the service of his majesty, he prepares a draft of the programme of the recess of Westeras in 1527.

The letter of the king was given on September 10, 1523. A few days later, September 14, the king wrote again to the pope, and requested confirmation of the bishops' election The provost and chapter had solicited the king, to write to the pope in behalf of the men who had been canonically elected as bishops. All these were then enumerated, but first John Magnus, as elected to the see of Upsala. Abo alone is announced, as unable from the tumults of war, to proceed to the election of a bishop. All those elected were acceptable to the king, and he therefore requested confirmation for them, and that as soon as possible. But he also asked *his holiness to remit the taxes paid to the apostolic chamber*, because those churches were reduced to the utmost poverty, and plundered, and the bishops elect had applied and must daily apply their income against the foes of the privileges of the church. By this liberality the apostolic chair would win great interest in the king and the kingdom, and the former to great obsequiousness.

On the same day this was written at Stockholm, died, at Rome, the man to whom it was addressed, Adrian VI. In November, Clement VII., cousin-german to Leo X., succeeded to the papal dignity; and with him came the old policy of Rome, to yield nothing. There was now no more question of reform; and what might be hoped from the pious and well-meaning Adrian, it were vain to expect from Clement.

But even in pope Adrian had Sweden been mistaken, when entertaining the ardent wish to be entirely delivered from archbishop Trolle. The Roman chair had not approved of Trolle's deposition. The chapter of Upsala now elected his successor; probably regarding the former sentence upon him to be fully ratified by what had occurred in 1520, in the outrage at Stockholm. This election, perhaps, took place between the 10th and 14th of September, as in the above-mentioned letter. There is no mention of a wish to have the legate as archbishop. John stood prepared to take his departure for Rome, to obtain confirmation for himself and the others. The king had fitted out a ship to transport him to Germany; when at the moment he was about to embark, there came a letter which changed the relation of things. The pope wrote, and enjoined, under threat of the church's correction, that the banished archbishop should be again received in Sweden and into his office. Was this a mere respect for the church's laws, disregarded in the treatment which Trolle received, or moreover a colored and apologetic view of his conduct founded upon the report of John Francis de Potentia, when legate? or was it through the influence of the emperor Charles V., who might suppose that by Trolle's reinstatement, a way might be opened for his own brother-in-law's recall to his reconciled kingdom? or was it to furnish, although he was already provided for, the same bait for John Magnus, as for Arcimbold, in the hope of being raised to Trolle's place, if he was got rid of? or what other motive originated this unexpected letter? These are questions we are the less able to answer, as the letter is only known to us by the king's reply. The surprise, regret, and indignation, which were expressed upon the favor shown to Trolle by the pope, were a sufficiently clear indication of what was to follow. Among other things it is said, in the king's answer: "We have not been able to receive this communication otherwise, than as if your holiness had ordered us to interrupt or annihilate the peace of our church and fatherland, which, with our own and the blood of ours, we had gained. Harsh to the kingdom and the Swedish church, was the Danish king Christian, who cruelly murdered bishops and nobles, but no less harshly would the apostolic see act, in regard to our quiet, if it intruded, to the disturbance of our commonwealth, this archbishop, the close ally and most cruel accomplice of Christian. We had long waited, holy father, to see what the pope of Rome would do against the aforenamed king Christian, for his sacrilegious slaughter of bishops; and now the apostolic see takes this bishop, the foremost co-operator in the godless murder, under its protection, and wishes again to place him on the pinnacle of the Swedish church, whose liberties he has thrown to the ground. It were a grief to us, that the apostolic see should not avenge the godless murder of the bishops. But, still less can we endure that this archbishop should return to Sweden, who is not only unworthy of the priesthood, but of life itself. We acknowledge ourselves to hold in such high reverence the holy Roman church, that we would willingly offer our blood and life for it; but this act of severity, which threatens our commonwealth with such disasters, we shall endeavor to arrest, with our blood, if so required, and will show, if it be necessary, in the face of all Christian princes, how justifiably we have resisted such an outrage. Well did the afore-named envoy, John Magnus, endeavor to convince us, that never did such a brief emanate from the apostolic see, but that it was dictated and concocted by some illy-disposed men, who sought occasion for scandal; and we have given some credit to what he says, for the honor of the apostolic see. But in consequence of this news, our intention to send him to your holiness has become changed, until we find out what your holiness will do in the case of the afore-mentioned archbishop, for our weal and the quiet of our subjects. As soon as we ascertain this, we shall either, according to your holiness' pleasure, effectually aid this embassador in all the points of Christian faith, or give him liberty to leave us, in order to announce *in what manner, as a consequence of the tardiness of the apostolic see, the Swedish church shall be reformed by our royal authority.* God is our witness, how ardently we wish the church herself, through the authority of your holiness, and the decrees of the fathers, to be placed on a better footing, since *it is altogether necessary, and the sooner the better, that a Reformation should take place in her spiritual and temporal condition.*

The cause of Gustavus Trolle was irremediably lost in Sweden. The diet of Soderkoping, in October, 1523, again declared him the foe of the country, until he could make atonement to the king and kingdom; and the estates approved the election of John Magnus as his successor. Trolle had written to bishop Brask, who was then at Soderkoping, to try and effect his restoration; but received from this, in other cases, so prudent man, a harsh answer, which did honor to Brask's patriotic heart. Trolle had, on so many accounts, made himself odious in his native land, that Brask advises him to make no further attempts to return, but have recourse to God, who disposes the destinies of men. Brask wished to partake the welfare, and resemble the other inhabitants of the kingdom; and because he determined to live and die for the freedom of the kingdom, he requests the archbishop not to incur any further pains and expense in writing to him.

It appears, at this time, to have been considered, that the archiepiscopal chair was not vacant, till a spiritual sentence confirmed the deposition of Trolle. In the month of October such a sentence was pronounced by the legate, and Trolle declared unworthy of his office. Perhaps, also, the legate was willing to take into account, the vacancy in the Roman see, after the death of Adrian. But if the archiepiscopal chair, not legally vacant before, became so only after this sentence, then the previous election of John was invalid. Wherefore the king called together the chapter of Upsala, where, on November 23, John was again unanimously made archbishop.

Olaus Magnus, the brother of the elected archbishop, is said to have gone to Rome, at the close of the year 1523, on his own and the king's business. But his business with Clement VII. was not successful. Against the confirmation of John as archbishop, there stood in the way, that the pope had not yet examined the charges against Trolle, and either was, or pretended to be, ignorant of the sentence pronounced against him by the legate, during the previous autumn, or the sentence was not approved. But he gave directions, May 6, 1524, to John Magnus, to whom, as its dean, the chapter of Upsala committed the management of the see, to proceed therewith until the case of the banished Trolle was finished. Petrus Magni immediately obtained the see of

Westeras, for which he obligated himself to pay a sum of money, for the discharge of which, he was, after his return home, forced to provide the means by great economy. But against the papal approbation, as well of John as of the other elected bishops, operated the before-mentioned declaration of the king, prohibiting them from engaging to pay imposts into the Roman chancery. This was, for the money-coveting Rome, a too alarming and sensible reform, and was highly disapproved. The confirmation and consecration of the proposed individuals were, however, promised; and the pope was ready, it was said, out of his own money, to pay the requisite fees to the officers of the Roman courts, were it not, that, just at this time, in the beginning of his pontificate, the greatest need of money pressed upon him, and the Roman see was altogether bare, and indebted to a considerable amount.

Against Magnus Haraldsson, elect of Skara, there stood also an objection of another kind. The above named papal legate, John Francis de Potentia, had, when, in the years 1521 and 1522, he was at Köpenham, cast his eyes upon the see of Skara, which became vacant through his own sentence upon Slagok, had obtained the promise of it from pope Adrian, and had been elected. This was not relished in Sweden, where there was an aversion to foreign bishops. In 1524, Laurentius Campegia, at that time the papal legate in Germany, had written to king Gustavus, and recommended the cause of Francis, but was answered, that the king would not allow of foreigners being bishops, as long as suitable men could be found at home; that the see of Skara had suffered too much from the murder of Vincentius to allow of a bishop being intruded against the will of the parties concerned, and that Francis, by his remissness and by his justly suspected conduct in his commission, had lost all confidence.

As a consequence of king Gustavus's system of taxation,

in the autumn of 1523, and the demands of the Roman chair, disapproved in Rome itself, measures of reform within the Swedish church were already begun. To the requisition of the king, that such bishops should be named as vindicated the church's privileges without injury to the crown, Rome gave no answer. The other two demands, that the election of bishops in the place of Trolle banished, and John Francis de Potentia not recognized, though nominated by the pope, should be approved, and that no money for an act of confirmation should be paid to the Roman chancery, were, through love of procrastination, virtually refused.

The primitive statutes of the church, at least from the sixth century, forbade those who were consecrated to a holy office to pay anything to the consecrator; and this was done to prevent simony. But to those who assisted at the consecration, he who was consecrated might give a compensation, though not exceeding a year's income of the benefice he held. In the western church, however, the abbots, bishops, archbishops and others, began to receive these *annates* out of such benefices as they bestowed. When the powers of the church became accumulated in the hands of the popes, they gave away, for the benefit of the church, the right of receiving the first year's income of such offices as, falling vacant, were subject to their obedience. Instances could be multiplied. Boniface VIII., granted annates to pay the debts of prelates. The need which the popes had of money was especially felt during the schism from 1378 to 1415, when many popes divided the revenues, and it was increased by multifarious losses and by waste. These incomes, therefore, not seldom increased by exactions, were forced either directly into the Roman treasury, or went as fees to the multitudinous officials of the papal chancery. If there was a wish for the dissolution, or the change of the Swedish church's relations to the see of Rome, nothing could be more desirable or welcome than the refusal of the pope, without a fee, to confirm the elected bishops in their secs. On the one hand, the resistance of the old church against any novelty injurious to it was thereby weakened. Not only were the duties of the office neglected and confused, but ordination and confirmation—those sacraments which a bishop only could perform—could be received only from the few consecrated bishops, especially Brask, either at their homes, or by journeys undertaken at the request of another diocese; or he that was not consecrated must have by his side some man consecrated by a bishop to perform the office which he, the unconsecrated, could not. But a greater source of lamentation was the loss of influence and respect; as it appeared how insecure and unstable was their position, when an election by the chapter, if not approved by the pope, was to be recalled, and of no validity; neither did Brask forbear to complain of this uncertainty, and John Magnus joined in the chorus. The king, too, declared his dissatisfaction with this treatment, which was greatly to be desired by him if he had already resolved on a reformation. But it appears that he and his counsellors looked for, or pretended to look for a reform, more after the spirit of Adrian VI. than the Lutheran. The recess of Westeras had begun to rise in its views, but not the council of Upsala. By degrees it was found out that Rome set a mark of heresy on every doctrine which was not in entire conformity with the old abuses.

On the other hand, the demand of fees, in money, for confirming the election of bishops, gave the aspect of meanness to the cause of Rome, in the eyes of the people. There had long been complaint of the extortions of Rome, and dissatisfaction was now more current than ever. After the refusal given by pope Clement, in 1524, to the king's request for a remission of these fees, was received, the subject became one of the points for deliberation at the diet of Wadsten, in October, 1524. Among the articles proposed was one "concerning the coronation of our gracious lord, * * * and since the bishops for that purpose are few, what measures shall be adopted; as *the pope will not engage in the consecration of the good lords elect, unless they purchase it of him.*" The resolution which it is likely was passed to renew negotiations with Rome is not on record; but it is evident the case was under consideration. The question had, previously to this diet, been started, whether they should wait for confirmation from Rome, or whether the legate, then in Sweden, had not, in this respect, the ability to put in use the papal right. It was also a principal subject of concern, whether the authority of the legate ceased, in its full extent, with the life of Adrian. In that case, must the hopes of John Magnus himself for support at Rome, in restoring the Swedish church, have fallen with this pope to the ground. But, if his authority had any abiding strength, he had not the right of appointing to offices, the bestowing of which was reserved to the pope alone.

The difficulty with Rome occasioned an examination into the ancient customs of the church, respecting the confirmation of the election of bishops. It had belonged to the metropolitan of the ecclesiastical province.* But when the papal supremacy swallowed up all other power within the church, the confirmation of the election of bishops was also reserved to the pope. We dive not, in Sweden, into investigations and scrutiny of this matter, only so far as bishop Brask was a participator in it; in whose acquaintance with canonical law may be reposed the highest confidence. He affirmed, with respect to the confirmation of bishops, that he and his two predecessors, from 1459, Kettil Wase and Henry Tideman, received confirmation in Rome, but that all the rest, here at home, received it from the metropolitan. Even he, otherwise so Romishly inclined, finds it probable,

* In 1299, the chapter of Westeras requested, that the archbishop of Upsala would, by his *metropolitical authority*, confirm its elected bishop, Nils Ketilsson.

"the case was so from the beginning." But a return was now not possible; since the metropolitan see itself was vacant, at least was so considered in Sweden.

Brask was afraid that they would break the church's unity, if they did not take the advice of their mother. He desired that the apostolic see might at least fill up their numbers, and urges dispatch in the act of confirmation.

It appears as if the elected bishops were in doubt, whether to procure confirmation from Rome, on such conditions as they could, or rely on the firm will of the king to save them from the consequences. Nothing. however, can positively be affirmed. Possibly they were undecided, or of different opinions among themselves. This hesitation and difference of opinion peep forth from a letter of Brask's, dated March 10, 1525, to master Erik, bishop elect of Abo. "It would be agreeable," he says, "to obtain some information, however stale, of your negotiation on the subject of confirmation, in which you might not appear separated from the unity of the catholic church and the Christian faith. But if my brother, *like some others*, goes with the times, I fear that the Swedish church is lost—which may God avert in our days. The church has few protectors, but many aggressors. But, if these few, who ought to resist such aggressors, have not confirmation, or some sure footing, they cannot, wanting security themselves in their position, give security to the church. The idea of separation, and some Lutherans, are the root of the deception. I counsel, rather to obey God than men, and in time, to procure authority for .office, that another may not win for himself your blessing. For we must not doubt if the ship of Peter shall endure, however shaken by the storms of heresy."

Counsel was sought, even from abroad, in these momentous difficulties; at least such is found given by the dean of the chapter of Lubeck, John Brand, and by a canon of the same, John Roden. They advise the elected bishops to make representation at Rome of their fears, on account of the king's stern prohibition of the payment of annates, of their own obedience to the Roman see, of the spread of the Lutheran heresy over the land, of their proximity to the Russian schismatics, all of which would rouse the pope not to refuse confirmation.

In the year 1526, it appears to have been seriously proposed that the bishops should be consecrated, and enter upon the full exercise of their office, without confirmation by ecclesiastical authority. Bishop Brask, who, all the time, so earnestly pressed the confirmation and consecration of his colleagues, now advised delay. They could not now, he thought, be consecrated without danger of a schism; when this danger ceased, the assent must be redeemed, and money be paid for it. Advices from Rome had given him hope of a yielding on the part of the pope; and the letter he received, assured him that he would be shown any degree of favor whatever, who would make resistance to the Lutheran heresy. The pope was apprized of the condition of the Swedish church, as was well known; and that it was not the fault of the bishops that confirmation from him was not sought. The mark might possibly be gained without danger to the body and the soul, and the whole church. * * Especially was it advisable, that Magnus Haraldsson, elect of Skara, should avoid being consecrated, before the dispute respecting the episcopal staff, between him and John F. de Potentia, became settled; since it would be of evil consequençe, and in opposition to apostolic order, to be consecrated for a church for which another was already consecrated. Brask apprehended that if confirmation were not obtained, Sweden would have bishops separated from unity with the Roman church. But, "if we in this time of the persecution of the Christian faith, become severed from the Roman church and ecclesiastical unity, I see not how far we shall fall and hang our heads."

In this cause, the pardon-monger, John Arcimbold, once more makes his appearance, in the history of the Swedish church. To him, who was then bishop of Novara, had Magnus Haraldsson applied for aid in persuading the apostolic chair to confirm his election. Arcimbold answers on September 30, 1526, that the appointment was made out for Magnus to carry on the diocese of Skara; but that the final adjustment of the case of John F. de Potentia, who had returned from an embassage to Russia, was waited for, the pope intending to provide him with another benefice when he took from him that of Skara. At all events Magnus might be sure of the diocese of Skara. He should, therefore, as soon as possible, send the money to pay the fees of his commission.

Thus, at the end of the year 1526, the case stood at the same point. But at this time men had begun to weary of the trafficking at Rome in the offices of bishops.

CHAPTER VI.

OF THE ASSESSMENT OF THE CHURCH, TILL THE YEAR 1527.

At the time the negotiations were carried on, respecting the remission of the fees to Rome, for the nomination of elected bishops, it was said that the Swedish church was impoverished by the losses and expenses it incurred during the war of deliverance against king Christian the cruel. This war was said to have been carried on for deliverance of the church from unworthy oppression, and, therefore, the church could not avoid a participation in the heavy costs of that war.

It was an especial maxim of the papal church, that the wealth and revenues of the church, in personal property and dues, were entirely separated from the civil purposes of the community and its system of taxation. They were destined to purposes irrespective of the calls and necessities of the state; and the foe of the existing constitution of the state, was a foe also of the church, only so far as he hindered the latter in the operations for what was evidently divine truth, and for peace with God and mutual peace among men. But this maxim was as indefinite and vacillating as the claims of the papacy itself; and not only in the church of each country was the love of fatherland too powerful to permit this maxim to strongly operate, but the church would often furnish pay for the soldiers who fought for that country. Its defenders also had a difficulty in distinguishing the true interests of the church, and the real welfare of fatherland, from the oblique views and agencies which were inspired by a carnal spirit and civil partisanship. Party disputes between fellow-citizens were often called disputes of the church; and the church was obliged to suffer in its property and to pay for illusory benefits. The church could not, during times of confusion and violence, preserve, in the face of its outward wealth, its sanctity untouched. Human strife knows no distinction between cause and persons; has no leisure to compare the innocence of office with the defects of those who hold it; and necessity, when outward violence is current, knows no difference between the property of friends and foes.

More than once, in Sweden, had the church experienced the fury of the foes of its privileges. The capture and destruction of Stacket were in point. The elder Sten Sture had, in his contests with archbishop Jacob Ulfsson, taken and pillaged the episcopal pleasance at Upsala; and the adherents of Sture were obliged to take considerable supplies from the church. During the war against Christian II., the church was levied on by both friends and foes. Christian himself showed no meekness in regard to the church's possessions. In his plans of reform, he had in view, to draw to the crown the investitures of the church. Bishop John Bellenake, placed by him in Strängness, was compelled to give up the castle of Tynnelso, which was re-conquered by Gustavus Wasa, who kept it with consent of the administrator of the kingdom, till 1523, when it was voluntarily restored, as a pledge of compensation for all the losses the bishop might have suffered.

Unnumbered casual pillages by foes, had the church undergone in the year 1522; a willing tribute, however, to carry on the war of freedom. This tribute had, at least in most of the dioceses, proceeded from the property of the cathedrals, and monasteries, and from taxes on the clerical holders of benefices. In the year 1523, when payment was made for the admitted assistance of Lubeck in the war, the king was obliged, with consent of the estates of the kingdom, to procure a loan of the churches and monasteries. Whatever could best be spared from their jewels, moveables, and cash, was to be brought to the king, for which a receipt in proof of the loan was given, with a promise of future payment. This loan was taken while the ambassador of Lubeck was still in Sweden waiting for payment. What was thus collected in indefinite sums, might be an offset against certain taxes. The king had also heard that bishop Brask had money upon deposit in Lubeck, and of this he requested an advance. The bishop denied that the money was his. A contribution was also required from the domestic supplies of the bishop. The requisition, as usual, awakened Brask's displeasure. Even the mode of collecting the taxes, sometimes produced dissatisfaction. Thus, the king had required from the bishop of Skara, for nearly half the churches of his see, four hundred marks of silver, but laid on the other half an impost whose amount was unknown to the bishop, collected by two laymen, as the churches were attached to their investitures. A contribution had previously been made by the clergy and churches of the diocese, and now there was the requisition from them of two hundred oxen. A like assessment was made on nearly all the clergy and churches of the kingdom, and a like dissatisfaction was commonly expressed. Bishops Brask and Haraldsson poured out bitter complaints. The discontent of Per Sunnavader proceeded to action, and the church's grievances were at least the pretence for those rebellious plots, which occasioned his own and master Knut's deposition and flight to Norway.

At the commencement of the year 1524, when king Gustavus was desirous of raising men and arms for an expedition against Gothland, which, however, miscarried, he made application to the bishops to obtain money. The bishops elect of Upsala, Strängness, and Abo, pledged themselves, "because the pacification of the kingdom and church depended on the successful issue of this expedition," to contribute according to their own and the ability of their churches, and to supply whatever might still be found in the private repositories of the churches. Even Brask and Magnus Haraldsson, not indeed without murmurs, though they had before warmly advised the expedition, gave their contributions, and the monasteries bore their share.

The complaint that the monasteries were stripped, was not just. Their contributions were for the most part, free-will offerings. They were shown, after 1527, to have still the greatest part of their property left them; and twenty years later, Peutinger and Norman estimated that there remained in the coffers of the churches, far larger rents than they now voluntarily offered for the benefit of fatherland.

The king often declared his dissatisfaction, in the slowness and meanness, with which they made their contributions, at least from the diocese of Linkoping, whose reluctance he, not without reason, attributed to the unwillingness and tardy movements of bishop Brask.

For the two years succeeding 1524, the churches appear to have been exempted from contributions in silver and cash. But, on the other hand, a new assessment took place in the year 1525, by which all the chnrch tithes, in the whole kingdom were appropriated to the maintenance of the war of the people, with the exception of what was required for the purchase of wax, wine, and the consecrated wafer. On Sunday, January 1, 1525, a contribution was made of the tithes that came in the foregoing autumn. On a Sunday in January the following year, there was offered two parts of all the tithes "of that winter," to pay the debt to Lubeck. On both occasions this tribute was said to be made in order to spare the country people. In August of 1526, two parts of all the tithes were granted, and a contribution from all the clergy of the diocese, to the amount of 15,000 marks. This contribution was given in place of a proposed tax of 25,000 marks, which would have taken up two thirds of the incomes of the clergy. The prelates at the diet then in session, said, that half the incomes of the clergy scarcely amounted to that sum; but that it was preferable, on many accounts, to give a round sum, than to have nice questions started on the conditions of a loan. The bishops were also, like the knights and nobles, to give an escuage for all the revenues which were derived from the investitures of the crown, or the lands called fralse, that is to say, exempt by law from taxes. The tithes were collected by men appointed by the chapter, in connection with officials appointed by the crown.

The pastors of churches were the most spared. No tribute was laid on their valuation. But they suffered much from the entertainment given to wayfarers, common in that age, and which was peculiarly felt as a burden, when the land was being trampled under the foot of war. The king once sent thirty sailors to the diocese of Linkoping, to be maintained by the bishop and his clergy. The burdens laid upon the bishops, fell mediately on the parish priests, who were not unfrequently obliged to assist the bishop in sustaining them.

From the incomes of the canons, it is said, the king, at this time, derived nothing for the crown, except that they also were obliged to take their part in the general assessment of the church and clergy. Another case arose, when the brethren of the hospital at Soderkoping started the question, whether the tithes should not be restored to them, which had gone to the chapter of Linkoping. These tithes had been granted the hospital, during the building of the church; but in the time of the younger Sture, had been adjudged to the chapter. The king wished a new investigation to be instituted; and meanwhile sequestered the tithes.

Besides the escuage, undertaken in 1526, the bishops were compelled to make another levy. As yet the king had not taken general cognizance of the incomes of the bishops. But with the five dioceses, which had yet no independent occupants, he was able to deal with some freedom. Imposts, in such a case, were not to be laid, with a consideration of how much the king was to divide with the elected bishops. Before his election as king, he restored Tynnelso, for the domestic support of the bishop of Strängness; but, on the contrary, he retained from Westeras, Gronso, which was retaken by the enemy. Tynnelso was restored, in 1523, as we have said, before the king's election. When Petrus Magni came home, in 1524, the king had come to another way of thinking; in which we fancy may be detected the influence of Laurentius Andreæ. Gronso, it is said, had come from the crown to the cathedral of Westeras, and they had held it sufficiently long to be fully compensated for all accruing expenses. The king was blamed, because Petrus Magni was put upon a retrenched establishment. The king declared, that he did not so much curtail his income, but that he observed the bishop husbanded his means to pay his debt to Rome, "when he bought his see of the pope." They who were dissatisfied with the bishop's parsimony, seemed to themselves to apprehend what a real bishop is. "The scripture," writes the king, "says that they are the people's servants for the gospel's sake. He comes better provided to take care of them who has few courtiers than he who has many."

The officers of the king often did violence to the property of the church, sometimes of necessity, sometimes, perhaps, from ill will. But that this was done with consent of their lord is not mentioned. The monasteries had to pay their portion of the often-mentioned loan of money in cash. The monastery of Wadsten, in the beginning of 1524, gave up a portion of the silver which was offered by the people at the shrine of St. Catharine. But some weeks after, the king sent his chaplain to Wadsten, with the request, that the remainder of this money should be sent him. If the abbess wished a fief of the crown, in pledge of repayment, it would be granted her.

In the year 1524, the question was introduced, at the diet of Wadsten, whether it was not advisable, that the horses of the war of the people should be quartered on the monasteries, which had few persons to maintain. The resolution, it appears, was not then entertained; but at Stockholm, in the year 1525, it was determined that the king should, that summer, have his horses in the lodges of all monasteries. The case was an unusual one in Sweden. It had come from abroad, through monasteries, to which princes had resorted with numerous retinues, to pass away the days of fasting or other holy seasons. In Denmark, at least, king John began to lay this burden on the monasteries, and king Christian II., had wished to import the same practice into Sweden. It became the first sore in the reign of Gustavus I., as it had been unhappily projected by Christian. Against this use of monastic lodges, Brask made his remonstrances, which were forcibly answered by the king. It is true, that through these lodgments, the service of God was interrupted, if there were no such service but to feed a multitude of hypocrites and liars; but the service of God consists rather in sympathizing in the interests and the deprivations suffered by the kingdom and its inhabitants. If the crown had not given wealth to found churches and monasteries, the spiritual nobles would have had no ability for the service and tribute they were called to pay.

The demand of these tributes, and the accuracy with which the interests and rights of the crown were protected and observed, are attributed to Laurentius Andreæ. He was the king's counsellor, of whom complaint was often heard, from those who were offended at the measures adopted.

He had, at once, from the first, won the king's confidence. As early as March, 1524, when bishop Brask, in a letter to John Magnus, mentions the king's dissatisfaction with the bishop's declaration respecting the tithes of the hospital at Soderkoping, he adds, that he trusted he did not deserve blame, except so far as seemed good to master Lars, the man, who, with the good God's permission, governed everything. We shall soon come to speak of the maxims of master Lars, in regard to the wealth of the church, and offer new proof of the dissatisfaction awakened against him, among the friends of the old order of things.

The tributes and taxes, which were now demanded from the persons and property of the church, were not new and unheard of, with the exception, perhaps, of the use of the monastic lodges. They are not, therefore, to be wholly regarded as the fruits of the new views, although these furnished new reasons and apologies for them. In making a comparison with former times, it will be sufficient to cite only a single case—that which occurred in the reign of king Albrekt. As reported in the chronicle of Olaus Petri, all the tenants of the church were obliged twice to pay money to buy horses. The king took half of the church tithes, in four successive years; for one year, half of all the rents of the priests, bishops and churches. He borrowed of all parish priests and their churches, moneys which never were returned, and ultimately demanded that every third house of all the tenants of the church should be given to the crown, to help its enfeebled income.

CHAPTER VII.

OF THE CONTINUED PREACHING OF THE GOSPEL, WITH THE ACCOMPANYING INCIDENTS AND CONSEQUENCES, TO THE DIET OF WESTERAS IN 1527.

We return to the narrative of the progress and spread of gospel truth in our fatherland, of its combats, and its success. No ordinance was passed for or against the new views during this year; and the influence exerted by writers on either side, is, for the first time, manifested in the year 1527. We have thus far occupied our attention with the times immediately preceding the diet of Westeras, in order to give a picture of the movements within the Swedish church, before the first firm step was taken for a thorough reform.

It has already been mentioned in what manner the attention of king Gustavus, when he was called at Strängness to the throne of Sweden, was attracted to the new teaching, and that he soon after made the man his chancellor, who became the foremost support of its propagation.

Olaus Petri either accompanied his patron to Stockholm, or went there at a later period, at the latest, in the spring of 1524. He was free from his duties at Strängness, and was appointed, during the occurring changes of the magistracy at Stockholm, to be secretary of its council. At the same time master Michael Langerbeen was appointed by the king to be pastor of the church in Stockholm. He also had studied at Wittenberg, had lately come home, and was inclined to the principles of the Reformation. Olof, who was not in the priesthood, was appointed as deacon to preach in the city church.

This was the commencement of the preaching of the pure word of God in Stockholm, and it opened a more extensive field for those who most actively labored for the church's reform.

The church of St. Nicholas, at Stockholm, or as it was then commonly called, the city church (stads kyrka), because it was the only parish church, proper, to which the rest, as chapels or monastic churches, were subordinate, was now occupied by two of Luther's disciples, Langerbeen and Olof. Of the former we have nothing special to relate. Probably his opinions and his line of action were less determined, and he was overshadowed by the more energetic, bolder, and more eloquent Olof. He often preached in the city church, and was called by a name, derived from the form of the pulpit he used, master Olof of the basket.

Who procured his commission to preach in this church is not clear. It is probable that the burghers of Stockholm themselves wished to hear him, from his known activity and the fame of his preaching, and that the request was still further superinduced by the conviction entertained of his freedom of speech in regard to the old teaching of the church. This presumption becomes fortified, when we consider that the proceedings in Germany could not be unfamiliar to this community, and that Stockholm was not under the immediate influence of the bishop's residence, and of the chapter seated there.

That the new preacher and his pulpit roused attention, cannot be attributed to the novelty of preaching. It had never ceased during the middle ages, if here and there it was rarely practised. It was a duty of the bishops, which they might execute through others. Nor were the canons and parish priests exempted from that duty, and pulpits were common. That deacons, to which grade Olof still belonged, should preach, was allowed, at least not forbidden, and the common pulpit of the church was filled by them. This pulpit (the ambo), usually stood in the choir of the church. Perhaps that he might be better heard, a pulpit more like what we now commonly have in our churches, was erected for Olof; and as one like it had not been there before, beside the dissatisfaction given the papists, it gave occasion to some sneers.

All were not content with the new doctrines. Olof was sometimes interrupted in his preaching, by having stones cast at him, with other insults. But the attachment of many, and the protection he had of the king, so that no ecclesiastical authority had yet condemned him, made it practicable for him to continue his course, till, by degrees, all violent opposition ceased of itself.

The tenor of the doctrine he now promulgated, is, in its details, not known. No writings, at this time, of his are to be found, from which we can have assurance of the platform on which he now stood. The main points of his opinions we shall hereafter examine. But, that his opinions were not mature, that he was not fully established in his knowledge of the truth, appears from the circumstance, that not long after his removal to Stockholm, he fell into the same errors, through which, two years earlier, many of his former teachers at Wittenberg became infatuated.

It seems to appertain to men in general, that every attempt at reform, which is to be attended by a loosening of the bond which united the civil or ecclesiastical community, results, in the first place, in anarchy or disorder in the struggle for freedom. The desire of independence in man's nature, engenders the attempt to shake off all outward bonds, until the inevitable law of order and concord, as a restrainer and avenger, curbs the haughty spirit.

Such an attempt was presented, at the commencement of Lutheran protestantism, on the appearance of the anabaptists upon the scene. Within the church, the tie of human laws and ordinances was to be torn asunder. God's word alone was to be the light and leader of the way. Man had this word in the Holy Scriptures; of this man was sure. But the thread of monkish indulgences could no longer be followed. The Holy Scriptures alone were the watchword of freedom. But why should the Spirit of God speak in the Holy Scriptures, and speak immediately now no more? Are not the Scriptures, in truth, the curb which checks the divine free work of the Spirit in and over the hearts of men? Is it not the immediate work of the Spirit, that we are able to see the existing weakness and defects of society? Does it not belong to this insight into the fullness and maturity of humanity, *now* to go forward without leading strings? Before these questions of the tempter Satan, the anabaptists fell, as many did before and after them. To them, they thought, the spirit of God revealed himself. This alone should govern men. Outward order was but shackles to men. Baptism in infancy, was an involuntary, and therefore a void obligation. It was a fruitless and empty offering.

Upon their appearance at Wittenberg, Carlstadt became their zealous adherent. Melancthon was vacillating and doubtful. The breaking of images, and other acts of disorder, attended their progress. Luther, himself, was, for a moment, at a loss; but soon, from their fruits, satisfied of their false professions, he determined to check their proceedings.

In the year 1520, when king Gustavus passed the summer and part of the autumn in Southern Sweden, at a conference with the king of Denmark, in Malmo, attended by Laurentius Andreæ, there came to Stockholm, in a vessel from Holland, some of the anabaptists. Among them the chief were Melchior Rink and B. Knipperdolling, the former a leather-dresser, the latter a shopkeeper. These men began to promulgate their doctrines of spiritual freedom, of the immediate revelations of the Holy Ghost, of the abhorrence of popery, of the heavenly kingdom, which was to go forth in light and salvation, as soon as the papal power, with all its idolatry and outward pomp, should be overthrown. Rink undertook, without being requested to do so, to preach in the church of St. John, on the book of the Revelations. His and Knipperdolling's proceedings, called forth more preachers, chiefly mechanics. They preached in churches and chapels, in the suburbs of towns, in the churches of the monasteries, and in the island of the grey friars; or, where they were not permitted to use the churches, they preached in the open air. The swarm was soon in full career. Not only among those who comprehended the views of the German preachers; but among others the evil was at work. The churches and monasteries were attacked. The images of the saints were mutilated around the market-places and in all the streets. Altars and organs became a wreck. The work of destruction was universal, except where it was practicable to put some limits to its progress.

Master Langerbeen and master Olof did not, indeed, participate in this outburst, but "thought that good might come of it," "togo det för godt." They were so taken by surprise that they did not, till it was too late, take measures to protect their flock and recall it to its senses. There was here, as in Wittenberg, an exemplification, though happily incomplete, of the disorders, confusions, and tumults, which distinguished the appearance in 1533, of the anabaptists, at Munster in Germany. They wished to appear carrying on the work of the Spirit, while practising the works of violence. The papists and priests, it was said, had put a lie in the place of truth. Now light had come, though apparently in deeds of darkness. The few adherents of these new views, who retained their senses, doubted if this disorder was indeed the undoubted mark of evangelical freedom. The papists continued to condemn all novelty, and attributed to the preachers, who were said to enjoy the king's protection, the blame of all the disturbance. The king himself was accused of favoring the tumults. The peasantry about Stockholm, witnessed with abhorrence, the indignities done to whatever they had been accustomed to regard as sacred; and their dissatisfaction was near breaking out into an insurrection.

King Gustavus hastened to return to Stockholm, in order to appease the tumults. Vehement reproaches were brought against Langerbeen and Olof, as not having put obstacles in the way of the outbreak. The leaders of the anabaptists were imprisoned, and had well nigh paid the forfeit of their lives; but the king allowed himself to yield to the intercessions and petitions made in their behalf, and deemed it sufficient to banish them from Sweden, to which they were forbidden to return, on the penalty of death. This disappointment did not stay the riots of Rink and Knipperdolling. The punishment of death, which they here with difficulty escaped, came home to them, in the tumults in which they participated at Munster, on their return to Germany. How far the impression made by these brigands of the Reformation, or the reports concerning them, may have contributed to maintain or strengthen an unfavorable opinion of the new teaching during the succeeding years, cannot be estimated. But it is a reason for not estimating this influence too high, that no mention is made of it in the private correspondence of Brask, in which the principal occurrences of these years are spoken of or discussed. This bishop, if the case had awakened deep or extensive interest, would not have failed to cite it as a proof of the perniciousness of the new doctrine. For the city, which was its theatre, the mischief done by the anabaptists could bear no other fruit, than what is common in such cases, to strengthen the aver sion to anything new in minds deeply rooted in partiality to the old order of things. But, it also gave vigor to the new teachers; because it modified and gave discretion to their advance, and, on the return of order, after the storm permitted, allowed an adjustment between the old and new. It permitted that something should be attributed to the temper of violent spirits, and diminished still more the numbers of the lukewarm, or entirely removed all sanction for errors which merited to be scorned and trampled under foot.

From this time the Reformation advanced in Stockholm with rapid steps. We cannot accurately follow them, because sources of information are wanting. But the hints, which here and there are disclosed in public archives, manifest how far this city was in advance of other parts of the kingdom. The new doctrines were preached there openly, and without hinderance; psalms, in the Swedish language, were used in divine service. Monasteries and guilds were allowed to remain, but with diminished respect. The two monasteries of begging friars especially felt the change, from the evident disinclination of the people to give them alms.

Laurentius Andreæ was, by his absence, protected from the danger of being infatuated by the error of the anabaptists. The quiet sense, which enabled him to understand the problem of the Reformation, while at the same time he took into view the church's connection with the state, will scarcely allow of his being reproached with those errors. His desires centred in the advancement of the peace and welfare of the commonwealth, and the terms on which the church's faith might be secured. His ideas of the visible church, and other points that were now in dispute, had, on February 14, 1524, before the events in Stockholm, been expressed in a letter to the brethren of Wadsten. When the king, for the weal of the kingdom and the conquest of Gothland, asked a loan of money from the monastery of Wadsten, some of the monks, former friends of Laurentius, solicited his protection, and recommendation to the king in behalf of their establishment. They regarded this demand of the king as a felony of holy things. "Therein," answers master Lars, "they were mistaken in calling it a felony of holy things, to use for the benefit of one's neighbor the money belonging to the church, or, to adopt their own words, dedicated to God. They understood not their own language. For, when they called it the church's money, they pronounced it the money of the people. It had become common to use the term 'church' for the prelates or the clergy, or sometimes for the material edifice. But in the Holy Scriptures, it is spoken only of men, and especially of the community of believers. Therefore, when we speak of the church's money, what do we speak of but the people's money. Such were the contributions of which mention is made in the Acts of the Apostles and epistles of Paul, out of which widows and the poor were maintained, and the administration of which belonged to the deacons or ministers, apart from the apostles, who were to give attendance to the word of God, and not be hindered by such worldly things. But we, who are successors of the apostles, have abandoned God's word, and use his church's, that is to say the people's money, as if it were our own. It were well, if we so used it as the deacons did, in helping the necessities of our poor neighbors. But we keep it to adorn the walls of temples, or to build the shrines of saints, or for the host, or for other purposes, which, perhaps, are forbidden of God, or nowhere commanded in the Holy Scriptures. Moreover, we consider ourselves to act piously when we lean upon a reed, and plead custom and the decrees of the pope, *which are in no wise to be observed when they militate against the Holy Scriptures.* We priests steal this money, in the name of God, from the people, and make free use of it, as if we were not its stewards but its owners. We call the place of assembling for the faithful the house of God, not because God dwells in houses made by hands, but because the faithful are wont there to come together to learn the things of God, especially God's word. Therefore, as the house is for the men, the money is for the men. It is consequently impious, when the people are in danger, for any one to think he ought to spare the church's money, and let his poor neighbor, whom Christ commanded us to love, and for whom he died, be so far oppressed as to suffer hunger and thirst. Has God, then, more care of stocks and stones than of men? Would to God, that we clergy had a like concern for our neighbor's salvation as we have care for money. What godless piety, when the wealth of the church is rather bestowed on stately, yea, sometimes extravagant structures, than on the necessities of the faithful! Otherwise acted the old Jewish kings, Joash and Hezekiah, of whom the one sent to Hazael, king of Syria, all that he could find in the treasury of the temple, to induce him to withdraw from Jerusalem; the other broke up the vessels in the temple of the Lord and the golden shields he had himself fixed there, to give them to the king of Assyria. Neither of these is blamed in scripture for having thus, for their subjects, bought what is surely the most precious of all things, peace. Now, a most Christian prince who does likewise, is called a felon of holy things. In what deep hidden meaning could they well call it a felony of sacred things, to give this holy money to God's holy temple?" Master Lars adds, that he could write more on this theme, did not the other business of the king prevent him.

In conclusion, he desires, in the same letter, to let the brethren of Wadsten know, that the king, when in Wadsten, heard with dissatisfaction some one declare that a "less catholic teaching" was spread over the kingdom. The king's pleasure was, that they should refrain from such vain speeches, lest the people should be misled by them. They should prove all, and hold fast that which is good. If, therefore, in some of the new books, either of Martin Luther or of others, they found strange doctrine, they should not cast them away before carefully reading them through, and critically examining them. If they found anything at war with the truth, they also might write books and confute such doctrine *through the Holy Scriptures.* Thus, teachers might test what was right, and the truth be conformably promulgated from the pulpit, and not according to one-sided views. He doubted not, that some among them were competent to this. "For, although little comes to my knowledge of the doctrine called Martin Luther's, yet, from the little I have seen, I have discovered, that he cannot be confuted by us simple men, because he is protected, not by the weapons of St. Bridget or any other, but by the weapons of the divine scriptures. We must take care, if even we have truth, that we do not, illy armed or entirely unarmed, advance against the well armed, and thus make manifest our own simplicity."

This letter of a prelate of the church, is in the main a declaration of the general principles of protestantism. Regard for the Holy Scriptures, independence of traditions, the idea of the church as the society of the faithful, who are all alike accounted members of it; these, with more, are the outlines of what is signified or expressed in that letter. Its writer had thrown down this gauntlet of defiance in the diocese which was almost the only one where the ecclesiastical power still remained in its strength, and in a monastery which, of all those in the North, was most respected, and which stood in constant communication with Rome, whose chair it regarded as the mirror of sanctity.

Laurentius Andreæ was a man of action; and his activity was directed by the principles of the Reformation. But nothing he had written had he yet put to press, nor had Olaus Petri carried his instruction beyond what he could communicate from the chair, the pulpit, or through personal intercourse. The influence of the activity of these two men must thus have been defective in depth and compass. But the minds of men were at this time inflammable. The attempt at reformation had loosened many bonds; and it was a moment, in Western Europe, when men talked of reform, even if they could not clearly determine wherein it ought to consist; and when even those who were friends of the old order of things, urged reform, though the old attachments made them irresolute, in comparison with the often headlong zealots for a change.

A century had rolled away since the demand for reform had been the watchword of almost the whole of the western church, even in its ecclesiastical councils. This cry had abated, but was never put to silence, till it was again loudly raised through Luther.

At such times the ideas of uneasy minds hover around a name, a word, often without further apprehension of its significance than that it is connected with deliverance from the old constraint. It acts as a skeleton-key of argument, which is to dissolve an enchantment. So was it with many Lutherans, who knew little more of Luther than that he defied the pope and the priests. But not merely were such common challenges of freedom now at work in Sweden. We have seen how master Lars showed what he thought and wished. Travellers from Sweden, or strangers who had been in Germany, could accurately describe the condition of things in that country. The writings of Luther and others, against the papacy, its doctrines and constitution, were circulated and read with avidity. They were welcome in monasteries, among the burghers of towns, among the pastors of churches, among knights and nobles. We find traces of Lutheranism even there, where the reformers, in the peculiar meaning of that term, could not operate. With the exception of Stockholm, the see of Linkoping was perhaps most exposed to the infection. The great commercial towns of Soderkoping and Kalmar, lay exposed to foreign influence. So too with Wisby, though at first it was defended from Lutheranism, by the regard felt for its bishop. The war, which for a time centred in these parts, also operated against the power of the church. Bishop Brask complains, that all around Kalmar, the Lutherans spread erroneous opinions, and enervated church discipline. He had been informed that the brethren of the hospital at Soderkoping had concluded to send two of their number to Germany, to finish their studies there, and that one of them in his preaching, had declared himself favorable to the Lutheran errors. The bishop, therefore, strictly forbade the prior to allow them to leave the limits of Sweden without the king's and the bishop's consent, because so many parts of Germany were infected with that heresy. But if their going out of the country was necessary, they must previously appear in person before the bishop. Berendt Von Melen, who had the investiture of Kalmar, was advised by the bishop not to suffer priests to unite in marriage persons who were nearer of kin than the fourth or fifth degree, according to church law and established custom; "notwithstanding many of Luther's party countenanced such and many other evils *which were complained of as very common.*" A Dominican monk who collected alms in the neighborhood of Skenninge, had, in the presence of many, said that he gave what was collected, to the monastery and St. Olof the devil.

Nor were the walls of Wadsten itself, a shelter from trouble. The brethren of this monastery, sent the above-quoted letter of master Lars, to their bishop, to ask his counsel and aid. The spark had kindled. Within their cloister, often before the theatre of strife and discord, had appeared a disposition to freer opinions, and many turned to the side where it was believed the favor and grace of the king would meet them. In the case of the Lutheran heresy, they dreaded more the human than the divine majesty. The bishop, who thought he saw in the letter of master Lars, much that was not seemly in a good prelate, counselled them not to allow themselves to be drawn from the true foundation of truth, though an angel from heaven preached any other. Religion depended more upon the simplicity of truth, than on the subtle and swollen words of worldly science. He wished them to bear in mind, what canonical law established respecting obedience, the church's unity, the church's order, and the church's property.

But he was himself excited, by all he had learned, to stronger measures and courses of action. Two years before, in 1522, he had publicly, by a notice at the entrances and doors of churches, and by proclamations from the pulpits of all towns, forbidden to buy, sell, receive, spread, or read, the writings which emanated from the Lutheran heresy, until a council of the church had examined their contents. To the town of Soderkoping, the bishop, on June 3d, 1524, wrote that he daily learned that many men from abroad, both merchants and others, brought into the diocese these heretical doctrines and books, and seduced Swedes not better informed than to abandon holy Christian truth and obedience. He, therefore, would implore them not to postpone truth to such false doctrines. The burgomaster and council ought, if any one was faulty in this respect, to take bail for his person, and sequester his property, till the king and spiritual judges had pronounced a decision on his person and goods, according to the equity of the church and of the civil law.

The prohibition was repeated, on Easter Even of 1525, and was now affixed to the doors of *all* the churches and convents within the diocese. The bishop was persuaded that the Lutheran heresy would be arrested. God would not always be angry with his people. Its errors were enumerated. The friends of this heresy condemned the mass, despised the sacraments of the church, disapproved the holy estate of single life, and would open the doors of the convents, that monks and nuns might freely leave them, and enter into wedlock. They overthrew the images of Christ and the saints, and forbade as godless the worship of the Virgin. They wanted to make the estate of the church odious to the laity. They recognized, in the civil power, the right to break and alter the ordinances of the church, and to gain a freedom which they called Christian, but which might better be called Lutheran, yea, Luciferan. They despised the judgments and laws of the church and state. They declared the merit of good works, purgatory, confession, penance, fasts, canonical times, invocation of saints, prayers for the dead, and indulgences, to be but the devices of men. Laymen, priests, and monks, were infected with these errors, spoke of Lutheranism as of the gospel itself, and were ready to defend the doctrine of their chief, because they knew nothing of it, or at least, did not understand it. All, therefore, ought to beseech God to protect his church, to warn people and priests against these errors, and attend to the church's doctrine, customs, and ordinances.

In conlusion, Brask continued diligently to watch the proceedings in Germany, expressed his hopes when he thought he perceived the heresy to be on the decline, and published such refutations of it as he deemed most likely to effect the object.

He addressed king Gustavus, on May 21, 1524, assuring him of the loyalty in which he was bound to him, but beseeching him, for the king's own sake, and for the sake of the kingdom, that he would not further the purchase and sale of Luther's books in the kingdom, or allow Luther's disciples support and protection, before a council of the church should determine what should be renounced or adopted. "The Germans have received no faith for our sake; neither should we reject any for theirs." This letter was a covert complaint against the king's chancellor. But the king did not leave his servant without protection. He replied that he did not perceive how he could forbid the writings of Luther, when he had not yet found them condemned by impartial judges. Writings against Luther were imported into the country. It was but justice that men should have cognizance of both sides. None of Luther's disciples had asked aid or protection from the king. But if it were so, the bishop ought to know that the king was bound, in his sovereignty, to protect every subject. If the bishop wished, in a lawful way, to address or reprimand any who were under the king's protection, he would find the king offer no impediment.

It is remarkable that neither this answer, nor many ex pressions and actions still more decisive, led Brask to despair of the king. During the three years and more, he passed at home, and in the exercise of his office, he ceased not to warn, to advise, to complain, and to remonstrate, with king Gustavus himself, and his friends. But, the hope of better times, though lessened, was not abandoned by him. As late as 1526, he writes, that he had hopes of the king, "whose heart is in the hand of God, who is able of a Saul to make a Paul," if only evil counsellors were put away from the king.

The friends within the land in whom Brask most trusted, and to whom he could open his heart, were the high steward of the kingdom, Thure Jonsson, and the bishop elect of Skara, Mans Haraldsson. The latter was a good papist, though dissatisfied with the difficulties which arose to his obtaining the see, and straitened in his energies by the uncertainty of his position. He approximated to Brask, and rarely undertook anything without consulting him. Brask made him his deputy at the diet held during this year not being present there in person; and set his seal to no decree without concert with the bishop elect of Skara. Mans, too, closely watched the progress of events. When he received some heretical books from master Sven, canon of Skara, then engaged in the king's chancery, and in 1529, elected to the see of Skara, and which books were sent to the king from Rome, he left them with Bishop Brask, and to the information that the king caused them to be sent, adds this prayer: "May God forgive those who sent such books to a stiff-necked people, hard of heart."

To these men, a respect for the church's law and constitution, was the first and imperative duty of a Christian man. Canon law soon appeared to be their bible. The rules of canon law, and the schoolmen, were to them what proofs from the Holy Scriptures were to the Lutherans. So acted Dr. Nils, of Strängness, and so bishop Brask.

When some scholars from Upland, as Rasmus Ludvigsson relates, came on a certain occasion to bishop Brask, he asked them what the Lutherans taught. They answered, "The pope is anti-christ, and the prelates followers of anti-christ." "Then," said the bishop, "it is not long since the administrator, Sten Sture, placed me at his right hand, and now I shall be proclaimed an anti-christ." He proceeded to inquire on what these new teachers relied. The scholars answered, they relied on Paul. On this the bishop rose up from his seat and exclaimed, "Better had Paul been burnt, than that he should be where we may suppose." *

This is the very expression it is declared that he used. It is not unlikely, though the words were not meant to apply to St. Paul in particular. According to the views of the Roman church, which supposes its developments to be under the immediate teaching of the Holy Ghost, a return to the pure and simple teaching of the apostles must be a heresy, and the apostles themselves must appear as heretics when they stand forth to protest against these developments.

* When, before bishop Ogmund of Skalholt, a certain priest was accused of heresy, he was asked, on what he built his heresy. He replied, "On the words of St. Paul." The bishop rejoined, "Paul was a teacher for the heathen, not for us."

Bishop Brask issued out threats of excommunication and interdicts within his diocese, but without success even there, when an order of the king that compulsive measures should not be employed rendered the bishop's blows impotent. Neither was he from the first supported in his zeal. Nowhere could threats and interdict be issued except in the diocese of Linkoping, nor there with the same force and authority as aforetime. We are in want of information how the chapters of the several sees were affected toward the cause of the Reformation. That the chapter of Upsala was attached to the cause of the papacy is clear enough, although it had suffered much in the contests of its bishops with the administrators and the kings, from the time of John Bengtsson, and had thence learned caution. The differences of opinion in the chapter of Strängness may furnish a presumption of a like condition of things among the rest. Seldom or never does a case arise among men, however founded on right, but that it is neglected or betrayed by some of those who ought to be its protection.

John Magnus could certainly, as papal legate, if else able after the death of pope Adrian, to take cognizance of its concerns, be possessed of the power to take the necessary measures for quieting the church. But he was fettered not only by his own natural want of decision, but by his election as archbishop, and his uncertain position as long as the pope did not approve the deposition of Trolle. As long, too, as a man attached to the Reformation stood near the king in the enjoyment of his full confidence, Magnus might not have thought it advisable, by rigid measures, which would have proved empty, to expose his real want of power.

In 1523, Olaus Petri, with others, had received a summons, and been warned by him to desist from preaching the gospel. But we do not find that he did anything more.

The disorder and commotion in the Swedish church must not, however, be represented as at this time such, that the old order was lost, and its preservation set at naught. We have already spoken of the signs which, in the year 1524, foreboded the storm. But, in general, the community of church and state, proceeded in the order of law, according to the old institutions and customs. The rites of public worship went on uninterruptedly; the discipline of the church was maintained; the chapters examined the candidates for the different grades of office, and the bishops made visitations of their sees. Bishop Brask gave forty days' indulgence to all such as would aid the abbot of Nydala to collect the rents, which were wont to be paid to the convent from the district of Smaland, but of which, after the massacres of Christian the cruel, the returns were more slowly rendered by the peasantry. In the year 1525 was printed, at Upsala, a collection of the decrees of the council of the ecclesiastical province of Upsala, which had been issued in 1440, during the life of archbishop Nicholas Ragvaldi; at the same time there was published, at Upsala, a popish mass book, and a manual of prayer at Soderkoping. As the so called year of jubilee was approaching, in which every pilgrim to the shrines of St. Peter and St. Paul at Rome, obtains a full indulgence, Clement VII. issued beforehand a bull. In this bull, it was made known, that, in consideration of the great distance from Rome, the war, and other hinderances, the jubilee would be observed in Sweden, by whoever confessed his sins to any father confessor that might be chosen, which father had the power to release the person confessing from all sins, and from all, except the four cardinal vows, provided, that, after confession, he fasted on Wednesday, Friday, and Saturday, repeated on these days five paternosters and ave Marias, in memory of the sufferings of Christ and the five wounds; giving also, according to his ability, alms to the poor, and receiving the eucharist the following Sunday.

The papal chair remitted all money dues of this year of jubilee, a remission very acceptable to bishop Brask. "They who favored heresy," he said, "pretended that indulgences were a bribe for good works, and a mere means of getting money for the pope. They were now confuted; since the pope gave this indulgence for nothing, and since he who received it was excited to fast, give alms, and, as far as human infirmity admits, be worthily prepared for the reception of the Lord's supper."

Since the time, when Arcimbold was engaged here, in his office of pardon monger, what a change had six years wrought for Rome! Then the grace of indulgence was sold for money, now it was given for nothing, if anybody would take it.

The end of the year 1524, was memorable for the first public disputation between the contending parties. When king Gustavus held his Christmas festivities at Upsala, at his request, and that of many of his council, this disputation was held in presence of the chapter, between Olaus Petri and doctor Peter Galle. This man, an intimate friend of bishop Brask, was scholasticus of the chapter, or, as he calls himself, professor of theology at Upsala. He died in 1537, or the year after. He must have been considered the most skillful champion of the land, to defend, by pen and tongue, the Roman church, as he was more than once summoned to that duty. He was a learned man, but in disposition he was still and quiet. His name was Galle, but he was without gall.

The disputation involved the most momentous tenets, in which the papists and Lutherans differed from each other. It was carried on with much vehemence, and Olof was the superior, in that he proved his propositions from holy scripture.

This report of the disputation may be relied on, for the thing itself has strong probability. It corresponded with the king's course of conduct, not to declare himself for either side, but to allow the champions to measure their strength, and by that means to gain more certain information. This must also have been a contest very agreeable to the wishes of Olof, and those like minded, for the contest was itself a victory, and was the means of attracting attention to their doctrines. It is the usual difference between the friends of the old and the new views, and marks their respective merits and defects, that the former rely upon the cause to defend them, the latter upon themselves to defend the cause. What Rasmus Ludvigsson reports of Brask's dissatisfaction with the archbishop's permitting this disputation, and thus drawing things already settled in the church into a fresh investigation, is very much in agreement with that bishop's principles. But our oldest sources of information are, in this case, not altogether clear. Tegel reports the case, but is undoubtedly mistaken, when he makes the twelve questions put forth in 1526, to be a fruit of this disputation. Messenius furnishes us the same substance of debate, but gives the wrong year, when, as does the oldest witness, Rasmus Ludvigsson, he refers the matter to 1525, in which year the king passed his Christmas not in Upsala but Wadsten.

In the year following, 1525, there was again a disputation respecting the truth at the diet of Westeras. We know no more of it, than that John Magnus, according to his own report, with energy and success, placed himself in opposition to the new teachers.

The beginning of the year 1525, was made full of significance by the marriage, on Septuagesima Sunday (February 12), of Olaus Petri, who, "being a deacon, thus rebelled against papal usage, and put at defiance the existing laws of the church." He wanted not precedents, since the marriage of clergymen had taken place in Germany as early as 1522, though he had not the example of his master; since Luther was not married till June, 1525, some months later than Olof. The case was a thunderclap of scandal, although somewhat softened by his not having yet taken priest's orders. The bishop of Linkoping could scarcely credit the report when it reached his ears, and was reluctant that the heads of the church should leave the case without avenging it. He mourned over it to his friends, and wrote the same day to the king and the archbishop. He urged the latter, by his sense of duty, to put a stop to the delusion, and if it was necessary, to call on the king for aid. To the king he represented, that this marriage of a man belonging to the spiritual estate, and who was in the metropolis of the kingdom, was a topic of conversation throughout the land. Much irregularity would be the result, as the law did not recognize the inheritance of the children of priests. The Greek church did not permit those who were already in the clerical state to marry, although she permitted those already married to be, on certain conditions, ordained. The marriage of master Olof, therefore, was not legitimate wedlock or the conjugal state, but he would, according to the church's rule, be under a curse for such an act. The king, therefore, should aid in punishing this offence, as was the duty of a Christian prince.

John Magnus was, as usual, still and quiet. The king again declared, that he was ignorant of Olof's marriage, till it had already taken place, nor when it occurred had he been at Stockholm but in Upsala. He had already summoned master Olof, and desired him to say how he would justify his action, so contrary to old usages. Master Olof answered, he would justify it by the law of God, before equitable judges, who would take into account, whether the law of God should not take precedence of human law. "Such being his answer," continues the king, "that he entirely submits to be judged thereby, we cannot refuse him. If he cannot defend and justify himself, we leave him to the consequences." It seemed to him strange, that a man, who belonged to the spiritual estate, should, according to the law of the pope, be excommunicated for marriage, which God had not forbidden, and yet not be for breaches of the sixth commandment.

It appears that the predictions of the ill will and troubles to be raised by Olof's marriage were not verified. Clerical celibacy was, with difficulty, after its introduction in 1248, enforced, at least with strictness, within the Swedish church. The dissatisfaction of the people at first with the restriction itself, and afterward with its loose observance, diminished the dissatisfaction when it was thrown aside. It was so common for the priests to live in commerce with women, though not sanctioned and blessed by the church, that the supplement of the church's blessings could not be scandalous in the eyes of those who were living in no nearer conformity to the church's teachings and laws. Concubinage was so common, that fines for the mistresses of priests and their bastards, were no inconsiderable sources of revenue to the bishops.

King Gustavus, who strictly maintained his purpose to restrain the abuses of the old order of things, and check the forwardness of the new, took, during this year, a step which advanced the improvement in the church's faith and teaching. The Lutherans constantly appealed to the Holy Scriptures, as the witness against the doctrines and constitution of the church, as then existing. The popishly affected clergy were exceptionable judges in the dispute. The appeal must be to the people. But to form a judgment they must have a knowledge of the word of God, on which the men of the new views avouched themselves to stand. The Bible must be made accessible in the mother-tongue, in order to determine the controversy. The common people demanded such a translation. But the wish to open to the hearts of men the healthful streams of the divine word, for comfort and consolation, was compatible with Roman catholic, though not with papistic belief; since no general council had confirmed the policy adopted in 1229, of forbidding the laity to possess or read the Bible in their mother-tongue. Translations already existed before the Lutheran Reformation.

There was, however, at this time, no translation of the Holy Scriptures to be found in the Swedish tongue. Portions had been translated, but not the whole, and these portions were very rarely in the hands of the people. The translation which doctor Matthias, father confessor of St. Bridget's, made, was so scarce, that bishop Brask, in 1525, knew of it only by report.

In the year 1522, came out Luther's translation of the New Testament. Two years after came out the Danish translation, which is attributed to the burgomaster of Malmo, Hans Mickelsen, who was a fugitive with king Christian. This is said to have called to mind the need of having the precious possession in the Swedish tongue.

King Gustavus made application on the subject to the archbishop elect, and desired that the prelates of the church would provide a translation of the New Testament in Swedish. The king alleged, as a reason, that almost all nations had the New Testament, indeed the whole of the sacred volume, in their own language. The times were such, that, in consequence of the many disputes respecting the sacred writings, it was necessary to lay them open before all Christian people and congregations, that pious and well-informed Christians might render an intelligent judgment, in order to quiet the existing divisions. The king had with sorrow learned, "what even I," says John Magnus, "must, alas! acknowledge to be true," that the clergy were so ill educated, that very few of them could preach God's word to the people. Some could not correctly read the Holy Scriptures, still less expound them; and for such it was undoubtedly useful to have the Bible in their own language. By this means, foolish and indiscreet persons were deprived of an occasion for interpreting the Scriptures, as had often been attempted by such, in monasteries and other places. "His majesty declared that we were shepherds, and obligated, by every consideration, through learned and sufficient men, to feed the sheep of Christ with the word of God; and that, if we refused to take upon us this work, he could not see how we deserved the name of shepherds, when we not only did not feed the sheep, but grudged them pasture ground."

These reasons of the king are enumerated by the archbishop, in his letter from Stockholm, dated on Trinity Sunday, June 4th, 1525, to the bishops, chapters, and some monasteries. He adds that he could have no objection, but promised, with the assistance of many of the bishops, to fulfil the wishes of the king. And because all those who were called shepherds, were obligated to this work, at least all to whom God had given that grace, he had, after consultation with the king, apportioned the New Testament among the chapters, and some learned men in the convents. He had also, by the king's permission, advised them all immediately to undertake the translation of the parts respectively assigned to them. As soon as the archbishop returned home from Germany, one or more of each chapter was to appear at Upsala, where he summoned all his fellow-laborers to meet, on the 10th of September of that year, so that each might give, in presence of the rest, an account of his work, and according to their combined judgment, a complete translation be produced and approved.

The parts were so distributed, that the chapter of Upsala was to translate the gospel according to St. Matthew, and the epistle of St. Paul to the Romans; of Linkoping, the gospel of Mark and both the epistles to the Corinthians; of Skara, the gospel of St. Luke and the epistle to the Galatians; of Strängness, the gospel of St. John and the epistle to the Ephesians; of Westeras, the acts of the apostles; of Wexio, the epistles to the Philippians and the Colossians; of

Abo, the epistles to the Thessalonians and Timothy. To the vicar of the Dominicans and his brethren, were assigned the epistles to Titus and the Hebrews; to the minister of the Minorites and his brethren, the epistles of Jude and James; to the brethren of Wadsten, the epistles of Peter and John; and to the prior of the Carthusians and his brethren, the book of the Revelations.

We know no other country, where, at this time, the church had a proposal so high and consequential, as that now made by the king to the church of Sweden. What would have been the future of the Swedish church; what of our fatherland; had the spiritual estate, with united hearts and hands, arisen to accomplish the momentous undertaking, with one voice, to speak in our tongue, the wonderful works of God? There had not been an immediate separation from the Roman church. There had been a collision and a struggle, whose consequences we may not venture to estimate.

It was not the illegality in itself of the measure, but his opinion of its utility, which again called out bishop Brask in opposition. The archbishop was now out of the way of his reproaches, and he turned to Dr. Galle of Upsala. He was in the highest degree astonished, that the archbishop, without consultation with the heads of the church and its chapters, should "enter into this labyrinth." So many translations into the mother-tongue, had but bred so many heresies. This it was which led to the revolt from the church of the Beguines, and the poor men of Lyons. The Scriptures might be interpreted, or explained, in a fourfold manner. They could not, therefore, without much danger to souls, be explained in a literal sense. The letter killeth, but the spirit giveth life. Such a translation could not benefit laymen who were not book learned, for they could not then read it; while among those acquainted with books, both of the clergy and laity, there were few who did not understand the naked text, at this time, as well as hitherto, though it was now maintained otherwise, in scorn of the clergy. If the translation now proposed were rejected, as containing Lutheran heresy; or, if any new errors were found in it, or arose from it, the Swedish church would thus have the appearance of favoring heresy. He had seen the gospels for the year, translated into Danish. These which, from similarity of the language, might easily be understood, could be easily made accessible by the facilities of the press, and thus, all that was needed, be gained without danger to the Swedish church. He designed, moreover, to look after the translation of doctor Matthias.

The meeting appointed did not take place till September, 1525, probably because John Magnus did not, till then, return from Lybeck. At Wadsten, on Sunday, January 11, 1526, when most of the bishops were present, there was a hasty decision made of the case. The chapter of Linkoping was even ready with its contribution; and on January 23d, master Erik, cantor of the chapter, was sent to Upsala. "Many," writes bishop Brask to the archbishop, "were of one mind, that delay in the work would be safest, and he should think so, were it not for the carefulness of the trans lator (probably the aforesaid master Erik) and the maturity of preparation of the theological faculty at Upsala, to whom he was willing to commit all. He hoped the case would be directed by the Holy Ghost."

Here all traces of the progress and termination of the work are lost. Whether it was thought best to put off the work, or whether there could not be had an agreement in a common translation, or whether the workmen were not ready with their parts, is unknown to us. There soon after occurred hinderances to the carrying on of the work. In the year 1526, there reached Stockholm, a translation of the New Testament, composed in the spirit of protestantism.

It is singular, that in regard to a work of this compass and importance, there should be wanting an accurate account of its authors. That their names have not come down to us, is the less surprising, as the evident object is, to appear unconnected with the party strifes respecting the doctrine and constitution of the church, while the names of the translators would have stamped it as a party production. But during and after the times when it came out, general opinion has not fixed upon its authors. No contemporaneous witnesses are to be found; and later ones are divided in attributing this undertaking to Laurentius Andreæ, or Olaus Petri, or both; some giving reasons in favor of one or other of these men, probably no better founded, than because at this time, no other than these two can be found, from whom to expect such a work. That with these men, the sponsors of the new direction things were taking, the translation had its origin, there is no reason to doubt. But when we, with most authors, are disposed to assume that Laurentius Andreæ was its genuine author, we acknowledge that we have no other reason for this assumption than that the translation betrays a consistency and *maturity*, which, *in a work of this sort*, is not to be expected from one of Olof's age. We regard it, however, as highly probable, that in this matter the two friends consulted together, and worked in concert.

What relation this enterprise had to the challenge made to the heads of the church, to provide a translation, cannot be certified on historic testimony. But, when the provision was made by the same men, who, in matters that concerned the church, were the king's counsellors and prompters, the work may be considered as the result of that challenge, and as itself a challenge to rivalry. Either in the year 1526, the work had been already put to press, or master Lars, who, as a prelate, was included in the king's challenge to the church, took, himself, the work in hand. The proposition made the church, to take in hand, by her principal men, this great work of the church, was in keeping with the king's usual course, not to pass by these men in any thing, in which their co-operation could be reasonably counted on. Their rejection was a judgment of the Roman church upon itself.

The prompt accomplishment of the task was, for the friends of the new order of things, much easier than for those of Rome. These latter were embarrassed by doubts, not only whether the work should be taken in hand, but how. They, on the other hand, who had no need to conform their opinions and modes of expression to an abstruse and difficult system of theology, could, with surer step, greater confidence, and brisker progress, carry the work for ward.

Lars, or whoever was the translator, had also in Luther a predecessor and leader, in whom he could place dependence. This relation to Luther's versions was not mentioned, as, in all public measures, steps, and proclamations, which related to the reform of the church in king Gustavus' time, the words Luther and Lutherans were avoided. But the Swedish translator was far from being a slavish follower. He differs in many places, omits the disputed word *all*, which Luther inserts, Rom. iii. 28, and inserts 1 John, v. 7, which Luther leaves out, and these are but examples. He declares that he had consulted many books and many treatises of learned men. The depreciation of the epistle of St. James, which he allowed to be preceded by Luther's condemnatory preface, he regarded in conformity with Luther's judgment. He even introduced, though with caution and some alterations, those marginal notes, partly to make clear the protestant sense, and partly to explain the words which are to be found in Luther's translation.

In the preface, the translator states that he undertook this work for poor simple priests, who knew but little Latin, and were unskilled in the Scriptures, and that other Christian men who could read might have at least the text, as given by the evangelists and apostles. It had been required, says this preface, that priests should read Latin; why then does Paul, enumerating the qualifications of priests, 1 Tim. iii., not reckon among them the knowledge of Latin? As in centuries gone by, among various peoples of Christendom, missionaries established their work of conversion by a translation of the Bible, for which purpose they were obliged to construct an alphabet, so now, in Sweden, the deliverance from the yoke of a foreign church, dates its commencement from a translation of the New Testament. This was the first work published at the time of the breaking up of principles; and it was considered as a work for the future of the church, the first-born and foundation of the new order. But it was also destined to begin the deliverance of the *Swedish language* from a foreign domination by which it was oppressed at the close of the middle ages. What struggles were required for this object, appears from a catalogue of words, with which the translator thought it necessary to preface his work. The writings of the reformers that afterward came out, and the translation of the whole Bible, fifteen years later, well nigh completed this deliverance.

The cause of Swedish progress and freedom, has, therefore, for all time, been married to the truths of protestantism.

Nearly at the same time with the New Testament, there was made a translation into Swedish, of the Psalter, and some small portions of the Old Testament; but these were never printed.

A Swedish translation of the New Testament, in the spirit of Rome, was made "with learning and fidelity," by a canon of Linkoping, Petrus Benedicti, who had there corrected (as he said) more than a thousand places, falsified in the translation of 1526. His work, to which he was prompted by John Magnus, and in which he made use of the writings of the learned men of his church, was never printed; and it is probable has not been preserved. It was written at a somewhat later period, and not on Swedish ground. Its author, Petrus, was staying this year, before 1527, at Rome, and probably never returned to his native country, which was soon abandoned by his friends and patrons, John Magnus and Brask, but employed himself in this occupation, during his voluntary expatriation, with hope of better days. The expatriated archbishop, whom he served as chaplain, could not, from want of funds, procure the translation to be printed.

Over the popish church hovered a threatening cloud. The king became, as the enemies of the Reformation said, more and more a captive to those who were about him, and favored the new principles. Much was hoped from a change of counsellors; but still Laurentius Andreæ stood, as he had done ten years before, the foremost man in his confidence, and the attempts at his removal, had only resulted, as one might say, in passing from the fire-pan into the fire. The seditions in the kingdom, a fruit of the anxiety which agitated all minds, and loosened the ties of obedience, conduced to give the king a mistrust of the church. The dissatisfaction of the clergy sought aid in the credulity of the people, and the consequence was, that the strong hand, which in the ferment of men's minds held the commonalty in check, was laid heavily also on the men of the church, who sometimes were, and more often were suspected of being, instigators of rebellion.

Already, in 1523, had the newly-elected bishop of Westeras, Per Sunnanvader, begun to write seditious letters; tempted by his love for the house of Sture, and discontent with the taxes laid on the church, but perhaps still more seduced by his naturally adventurous spirit. The king, hereupon, did no more than recall his approbation of the election of Per to the see of Westeras, and deprive Knut, the former chancellor and designed archbishop, of all hope of the metropolitan dignity, as being proved guilty of the like seditious practices. These men retired to Dalecarlia, where, together with the brother of the chapter, master Jacob, who was also pastor of Mora, they fomented rebellion. It was among the complaints made, that the king broke his oath of coronation, because he imposed in an unchristian manner taxes upon churches, monasteries, priests and monks; took the valuables which were given and consecrated to the service of God, the offering to the shrines of saints and holy women, and scattered them uselessly over the kingdom, took all the Swedish money from the churches, and in its place substituted valueless money, called *kleppings*, which he himself rejected, and appropriated the church's titles, which no Christian prince before him had done. For these, his cruel acts, would the wrath and vengeance of God, as natural results, come upon the kingdom.

When, afterward, Per Sunnanvader and Knut or Canute, fled to the archbishop of Trondhem, they were claimed, on the ground of the treaty of Malino with the Swedish government. After a long negotiation and assurance, given by king Gustavus, "that they should be tried by proper judges, and suffer and undergo what justice required," master Knut was sent home, in 1526, and tried, not before a spiritual tribunal, but before senators of the kingdom. On the trial sat the bishop of Linkoping, the bishops elect of Upsala, Skara and Strängness, with the provost, Goran Roos, of Upsala; and it cannot be supposed that these, had they found illegality in the conduct of the suit, would have failed to pass their comments. Even Brask admits that there were grave offences committed, yet he hoped in the possibility of an accommodation. To the intercession of the court the king answered, that such cases were not so readily to be pardoned.

Knut was condemned, on August 9, 1526. Soon after, Per Sunnanvader was brought home a prisoner from Norway. Both were carried in an ignominious manner around the gates of Stockholm, clothed in tattered habiliments, Per with a crown of straw, Knut with a mitre of birch bark on his head. Per was condemned at Upsala, in the large hall of the archiepiscopal close, by a court, consisting of many temporal nobles, besides the bishop of Westeras, the elect of Strängness, and the chapter of Upsala, headed by its provost, Goran Thuresson. The spiritual nobles protested afterward against the competency of this court. It was said that churchmen had approved a sentence upon spiritual persons, passed by the senators of the kingdom, but not where laymen participated without the senate. The protest had no effect. Per was executed at Upsala, during the time of its fair, on February 18th, and Knut at Stockholm, on the 21st of the same month, 1527. The severity of the punishment, and its public ignominy, were before unheard of, but acted as a significant warning to those of the spiritual estates. The temporal power would no more regard consecration to a holy office when crimes were to be punished. Among the participators in the seditious plots, were Robert, vicar of the Dominicans, a Norwegian, prior of the convent at Westeras, and many monks of that city, among whom, besides the prior, were many of the brethren of the convent, also Norwegians. The monks had been sent from thence to Dalecarlia, to foment dissatisfaction. King Gustavus deposed Robert, put in his place Martin Skytte, as vicar general, and one Nils Andreæ, as prior of Westeras; and ordered Robert and other foreigners in the Dominican convent, to leave the country before the feast of St. John the Baptist. When the king heard that great disorder existed in the Franciscan monastery of Arboga, he sent there one of his attendants, Lars Sommar, a lawyer, and directed him, in concert with the bugomaster and council of the town, to nominate a guardian for the monastery, and take an inventory of its jewels and wealth.

The king showed an arbitrariness, which spared neither

the spiritual persons, nor the freedom of spiritual establishments, whenever they stood in the way of the freedom and security of the land. Nor did he refuse, though with caution, not violently to interfere with the administration of the church, to afford his protection whenever solicited by individuals. The daughter of a citizen of Wadsten, whose father, against her wishes, had placed her in a convent, had, by a private message, begged the king's protection, as he stopped in 1524 in that city. He wrote to the bishop, that he ought not to devote her, and if he did it against her will, it appeared to the king irrational and deserving of punishment by him and every good man. What respect the bishop paid the king's remonstrance and recommendation is not known. With great firmness the king, three years later, treated the notorious case of Olof Tyste. This man had been affianced to a girl, who soon after was consecrated a nun by bishop Brask, "not only," as the king says to him, "against the law of God, but also, *as we are instructed*, against what ye call the law of the church." She was taken by her lover from the convent, whereupon the bishop excommunicated them. Olof Tyste applied himself to the king, who expressed his surprise that the bishop did not better acquaint himself with the case before making her a nun, declared the excommunication unrighteous, and prayed the bishop to remove it, at least till more of the church's prelates had met together, and examined into this and other matters.

Many tenants of convents already sought occasion to leave them. The new principles had loosened the bond of monastic discipline, when they declared life-long vows to be of no force, and that the service of God could be more worthily performed, and in a manner more acceptable to him, by an active attention to duties without a separation from the world. The monks, especially, were exhorted and stirred up to labor for the propagation of the gospel; this was the highest and most important, before which all other vows ought to give way. This consideration determined many, for whom the cells of a cloister had become too cramped. As early as 1524, consultations were held at the monastery of Wadsten, with regard to the conversion of the Lapps and others. Brask would have checked their zeal, by the remark, that it was of more moment to aim at the conversion of those belonging to their own order who had fallen away. The king himself participated in the good work. In 1525, he gave the charge to one of the brethren of Wadsten, "as king's commissioner, to bring the people of Lapland to the worship of God."

In the following spring another monk of Wadsten took his departure for Lapland, "with the king's good will and leave," to promote the faith of God, and if it should prove advisable, there to establish a school "for the children of the Laplanders, and other good men throughout the land." He was furnished with a passport from the king. At the close of 1526, the king's protection and favor were granted a Franciscan monk of Arboga, who, for reasons which he was willing to lay before such men as the king might appoint, desired to renounce his cloister and his order.

From king Gustavus' own words, rather than from known records, we have the means of ascertaining the methods taken to prevent gifts and legacies to spiritual establishments. At the town-house at Stockholm, the king made "a long discourse," in presence of the council, respecting the prebends and monks of Stockholm; how they said that the king wished to introduce a new faith into the land, because he wished to put a stop to their covetousness, that they should no longer engross to themselves so much wealth, to the injury of the crown and nobility, as had now for a long time been done.

This form of expression, then uttered, became, two years after, the law of the kingdom. But before that time action was taken by the king in the suppression of the monastery of Mariefred or Gripsholm. The administrator, Sten Sture the younger, founded it with certain hereditary property, by consent of king Gustavus' father, who, through his mother, the sister of Sture, was the heir. The law required, that if any one, for the benefit of his soul, wished to give of hereditary property to a church or monastery, the gift was binding with consent of the heir; otherwise, tithes only could be given of such kind of possessions. But Gustavus I. declared that his father was forced to seal this settlement; was, with menaces and compulsion, crowded out of his inheritance and rights, and moreover, gave his consent, on condition, that if the cloister, for any reason, should not continue, Gripsholm was to return to the right heirs. The king, arbitrarily, offered the monks in exchange the Cistercian convent of Juleta or Saba, in Sodermanland, because there was in it a small number and very few brethren, and they could, therefore, there very well be fed, agreeably to the course of life to which they were accustomed. The reasons of the king's dissatisfaction are no further known. But the Carthusians did not find it advisable to accept the offer, because, from the objections the Cistercians would raise, they perceived they would be unable to obtain undisturbed possession. They proposed that each should provide for himself among his friends, or accept whatever the king saw fit, as they had no other resource, and added that few of them remained to perform masses or serve God in any other manner for their maintenance in food and clothes. Those who withdrew were to be supplied by the king with clothes and money, in compensation of which, he was to retain certain funds of the convent taken in pledge. A council of the kingdom adjudged the convent to the king, at the diet of Wadsten, and the bishop of Strängness witnessed the deed of resignation given by the monks. In the spring, the convent was evacuated by the monks, and afterward their butler, Erik, received from the king the charge of its property. He received, as soon as the agreement with the Carthusians was closed, an order to transmit to Stockholm the chest of silver which stood there in custody, yet so secretly, that the brothers were to know nothing of it, and he was to restore to the owners the evidences of pledge which were left with the monastery, and take a sum of money for such restored evidences. The property of Sten Sture and his wife was removed from Gripsholm to the neighboring church of Kjernbo in Sodermanland, and finally from thence, by duke Charles, in king John III.'s time, to the cathedral of Strängness.

That Gustavus, in this case, went beyond strict justice will not be denied; and his enemies saw a judgment from on high, in the events which made this place of Gripsholm a mournful witness of the fraternal hatred of his sons.

The king had, of old, the right, on the occurrence of a vacancy among the prelates of the chapter, to present to the bishop the man whom he wished to promote. This right was sometimes exercised by Gustavus, at this period, to pay the incomes of those who were the officers of his chancery. Thus the income of the dean of Linkoping was received by the king's clerk, John, until it was in 1526 restored to its former possessor, the elect of Abo, in consideration of his services to the kingdom.

The strength which the new principles acquired by their continued progress, and the king's manifest inclination toward them, at last waked John Magnus from the slumber into which, as is common to weak minds, he had been lulled, by the hope that time would cure the evil, and give his irresolution the color of judicious calculation. He had, the previous year, resolved upon a visitation of his diocese, assisted in the work, which could only be performed by a consecrated bishop, by one Vincentius, a Franciscan monk, consecrated to the see of Gada, as titular bishop. But he, especially displayed his state, when, in the winter of 1525–'6, he travelled with a train of two hundred persons, and had even some nobles in his service. Beside the consecration of churches and their furniture, he was now hot against the Lutheran heresy, and exacted, with severity, fines from the clergy for their concubines and bastards, a severity which was remarked upon by the other bishops of the kingdom. From Ljusdal, in Helsingland, John wrote, on February 20, 1526, to the archbishop, Olof Engelbrektsson, of Tronhem in Norway. He informs him that, according to what he had before told him, he designed to be in Jemtland in the month of March, and begs an interview there with Olof, in order to renew their old acquaintance, and "consult together on the affairs of the northern kingdoms and the Christian churches."

Whether the two bishops really met, is unknown to us. But the knowledge of John's connection with the man, who, by his protection of Per Sunnanvader and his accomplices, lay under suspicion of the king, increased the monarch's dissatisfaction at the archbishop's conduct during his visitation. He summoned him to return home, and asked if Christ commanded his disciples to appear with such pomp to the world, or concerned himself with such vanities.

The king's more enlighted principles were shocked at such abuses, which gave the more scandal, as proceeding from the heads of the church. And it must have particularly irritated him, that the archbishop warned the people strenuously against the Lutheran doctrines, and sowed the seeds of hatred to it among them. Neither for John himself, after he manifested his dislike of the men that promoted the principles of reform, nor for his office, as it hitherto existed, have we further room in the history of that ecclesiastical change for the better, which was ripened in 1526, by king Gustavus and his chancellor.

In the spring of 1526, the plans for this object were disclosed, not merely in those encroachments upon the privileges of the church, to which we have before referred, but in the effort to establish more comprehensive principles and a change, founded on the consent and approbation of the people.

The king had summoned the peasantry of Upland to Upsala, on May 18th, being the feast of St. Erik. He came there himself at the head of an army of two thousand horsemen, and no inconsiderable number of foot soldiers. On the heights of old Upsala, he addressed, or, as it is said, held conference with the peasantry, on the true faith and worship of God and on state affairs. At his side, upon horseback, was his chancellor, Laurentius Andreæ. The archbishop was not present. The king complained, among other things, that here in the kingdom were too many lazy and unprofitable priests, and convents full crammed with monks, all of whom were nothing but vermin, who consumed the best fruits of the land. He asked, therefore, the peasantry if they did not approve his making an example of such. Those who were learned and competent to preach he would support in a creditable manner. But the other unprofitable priests might well be obliged to feed themselves by the sweat of their brows, as God had commanded. In their stead he would put schoolmasters and scholars, who would educate and foster the youth in Christian learning and good habits, or poor, sick, halt, blind, and lame men, who would thus have necessary food and subsistence. The peasantry shouted, and replied, that they would keep their monks and not have them turned out, even if they should have to feed and support them. They then began to complain that it was the intention to prohibit the Latin masses and other parts of the old faith. The sin of all these new things was to be attributed to the chancellor. He induced the king to disturb the privileges of the church. They demanded, with increased arrogance and fury, the king's leave to drive the chancellor out of the city. "Do ye know him?" asked the king smiling. "We know him not," replied the peasants, "but if we had him here upon the ground, we should certainly learn to know him." Laurentius Andreæ being present, was an ear-witness of these expressions.

This parley shows, that as yet the people were not ripe for any change in the church, although in Upland the preaching of the gospel, taken in the wider sense, was more diffused and unimpeded than in the southern parts of the kingdom. It also appeared how general was the impression that Laurentius Andreæ was the man who influenced the king to principles and acts opposed to the old discipline.*

This transaction, with the king's open declarations, and his attempt to win the peasantry to a reform in the church, awakened strong solicitude. "We have no remarkable tidings from Upland," writes bishop Brask, on the 16th of July, to Thure Jonsson, "except the conference at the feast of St. Erik, of which every one has enough to say. May God dispose all things for the best!"

King Gustavus's disappointment at the result of the attempt on the peasantry, vented itself in his treatment of the archbishop elect and the chapter of Upsala. On his return to the city, from the parley at old Upsala, he nominated John Magnus a mock earl, and placed on his head a garland of flowers, which he wore on his ride home. This is thought to have been done to depreciate the archbishop in the eyes of the people. But it is doubtful whether it is not merely the report of later times. John himself does not

* On a certain occasion, the year after these events, the peasants petitioned the king for the Latin mass. He called his chaplains and told them to curse the people in Latin. He then bade the people answer for themselves. They replied: "We don't understand what is said; how then can we answer?" The king replied: "What do you want then with Latin masses. Ye don't understand them."

mention such an act of degradation, though, if it were so, he surely would not have forborne to consider it a part of the martyrdom which his whole life appears to have been, from the time he was elected to the crosier of Upsala.

At Whitsuntide (May 20th), he is represented as having undergone a humiliation. John was desirous, on this occasion, to exhibit the dignity and riches of his office. The king was displeased, both with the sumptuousness and extravagance of the entertainment, which himself could not have provided "in half a year," and at the haughtiness with which his host, seated on one of the two elevated dais, turned to the king, seated on the other, and said, "Our grace drinks to your grace." The king answered, "Our grace and your grace have not room under the same roof," and with these words he left the table. When, on the same visit to Upsala, Gustavus was present with the chapter, he asked doctor Galle, whence the church derived her privileges and freedom? Galle answered, that the holy church had them from Christian emperors, kings, and princes; nobles and commoners had also given goods and property to churches and monasteries for the support of persons who should attend on the worship of God. These gifts, the temporal sovereigns had made sure, by their letters of donation, so that the grants might be inviolable and eternal. The king further inquired, whether kings and princes might not, in the chances of time, recall these privileges, whenever inconsiderately given, being deceived by the preaching of monks and priests, and the idea of souls being delivered out of purgatory, which had no authority from Holy Scripture? To this, doctor Galle made no answer. Even the archbishop, to whom the king put the same question, remained mute, because he marked the king's anger rising. But the provost Goran Thuresson Roos, began with zeal to defend these privileges. What princes had once granted and assured to the benefit of the church, their successors could not recall, without God's highest displeasure and everlasting condemnation. Finally the king bade him corroborate his assertion by proof from holy writ, and he might then enjoy it for himself; he denied not that they who industriously wrought in the church, to promote the honor of God, should have sufficient support, but the others, "lazy bellies," who could do nothing but unprofitable bawling in churches and convents, were deserving of nothing. When it came to proof from Scripture, even the provost was silent.

John Magnus, who began to take a more independent position in regard to the king, is suspected of having been at work for the preservation of his church, by secret machinations. There were reasons for believing that he sought to form foreign alliances, to the injury of the king and kingdom. He was therefore summoned to Stockholm, and there placed in custody, in the convent of grey monks. He was soon, however, set at liberty, and left the kingdom forever, in October of the same year. Different reasons are assigned for his departure. Either, as is said by John himself, after the resolution to put him to death was abandoned, the king banished him; or he was employed in a commission to ask for the hand of Hedvig, the Polish princess, though the king afterward refused his assent to the negotiations of John; or he feigned some public commission as a pretext for leaving the country, and of his own accord made this overture in Poland. That John desired now to leave Sweden, his subsequent conduct proves; that the king was pleased with his being out of the way, seems not to be doubted. But, under what specious plea he left his post, is not clear.

He set out on his journey with whatever things of value and books he could collect together. His vessel was lost on the rocky isle of Stockholm; upon which, after he had returned a while to the city, he called together the priests of Roslag in the church of Soderby, and pleading that the ship was lost on which he had embarked with his effects, on a foreign mission; by the king's order, requested of them a subsidy, which, on his return should be repaid. The priests loaned him what they had themselves, or could borrow from their friends. The repayment was made at the same time that the borrower returned.

From Dantzic, where he stayed, or at least obtained his chief means of support, he endeavored to obtain from the pope confirmation and consecration for himself and the other bishops elect. God, he said, displayed his wrath to him for the punishment of his sins, or as a probation to the bishops elect, whom, forsaken by God, the popes of Rome had also forsaken, although at the pope's command he was brought into these troubles. He would take his oath, and give his written obligation, to pay for three years after his consecration, annates to the Roman see. He declared his unwillingness on several accounts to return to Sweden, unless invested with sufficient authority to sustain the church, preferring to exchange his fatherland for banishment, his episcopal office for private life. To the pope he wrote that he could not venture back to his own country, without having received the archiepiscopal pallium. He solicited the recommendation of bishop Henrik, of Lubeck, and his chapter, who, as well as the burgomaster and council of that city, (where the Lutherans had many followers) petitioned pope Clement VII. in his behalf. The king of Poland, its primate and bishops, did the same at his request.

During these transactions, tidings reached him of the diet of Westeras. He had obtained information from Sweden, he writes, which being too true, showed that difficulties presented themselves, not less than if Christianity were anew to be established.

On this quarter thus died all hope for the banished man. The star of hope, for even his return to Rome, was for a moment eclipsed.

The wonderful counsel of God, through which he makes

the prudence of men folly, exhibits itself most remarkably in the revolutions of human affairs. Such revolutions did the years 1526 and 1527 witness, in the events occurring in Southern Europe, which extended itself also to Sweden. On the 23d of March of the former year, the emperor Charles V. wrote from Spain to many of the German princes, that he designed to solicit the pope to concert with him on the best and surest means of rooting out the Lutheran heresy, and to visit Germany in order to commence there the operations agreed upon. At the diet of Spires was also announced by Ferdinand, on August 3d, the firm determination of the emperor to maintain and carry into execution the edict passed at Worms, five years before, against the Lutheran heresy. But pope Clement VII., having become dissatisfied with the emperor's movements against his schemes, to weaken that prince's power in Italy, had now arranged a holy league against him. The emperor immediately recalled his rigorous orders against the German protestants; was disposed to let the edict of Worms remain unexecuted; proposed to the protestant princes a compact for a common expedition against the Turk or the pope; on the 27th of August framed the decree for the calling together of an ecclesiastical council, either general or for Germany; and, till the controversies were terminated there, each of the estates of the empire was to settle the affairs of the church, as might be justified before God and the emperor.

Two days later, was drowned at Mohacz, in his flight from the Turkish sultan Soliman II., Lewis, king of the Hungarians and Bohemians, who had willed his crown to Ferdinand, the rigid and zealous popish brother of the emperor Charles. He abandoned the concerns of Germany to attend to this rich but uncertain inheritance.

Amid these disorders, the pope is supposed to have been in alliance with the sultan of the Turks. King Gustavus failed not to remind the pope's friend Brask, of this unworthy proceeding. "It strikes us," writes the king to him on November 9, 1526, "that the pope is he who most departs from Christian fidelity, in giving himself to the Turk, who now is all powerful over the whole of Hungary, and is close to Germany, and has eminent means for extending his power over Christendom, where he has support from the pope, who ought to be first and most his foe." The bishop, on this, declared to Thure Jonsson: "To-day our gracious lord has written us, that the pope holds with the Turk, and we cannot conceive how that can be, surrounded as he is with difficulties on all sides. If it be so, the holy Christian faith or church, can in nothing be bettered. He has done, *as if he wished to go in the way of others who, for such causes, have been deposed. And there is thus left no sure ground for opposing the Lutheran or any other heresy.*" The suspicion of Clement's conduct, provoked Brask to accept the principles of the councils of Constance and Basil, to which his mind naturally leaned. He replied to the king in much the same strain as that in which he had written to Thure Jonsson; but added, "it is no wonder the Turk attacks Christendom, when he hears that the new doctrines are in favor."

The mind of the emperor was embittered against the pope. Charles spoke and acted as a foe of the papacy would have done. He declared to the pope his astonishment that the vicegerent of Christ could dare to shed blood for the sake of worldly possessions. This was contrary to the teaching of the gospel. Ferdinand received a commission to have recruits raised in Germany. He directed it should be given out that the army was to march against the Turks. Every one well understood what Turks he meant.

At the close of the year 1526, Clement having previously shut himself up in the castle of St. Angelo, in consequence of the riots in the city of Rome, the German troops of the emperor broke into Italy. In conjunction with the soldiery of that country, who were in arms against the pope, and in defiance of the emperor's suspension of arms with that spiritual prince, they stormed Rome on the 6th of May, 1527. "It is the judgment of God," said Brask, when he heard of the differences between the pope and the Cæsar. The judgment was now fulfilled.

While the elect, but banished archbishop of Upsala, was preparing to solicit the pope more earnestly than ever for aid and protection, the pope himself, a prisoner in the capital of Christendom, stood in need of his own and his friend's intercessions and prayers.

We must here make a short digression to follow the two last Roman archbishops of Sweden, the brothers John and Olaus Magnus, to the end of their career. John remained some years in Poland, where he was maintained by the alms of the king and bishops. In 1533, after a protestant archbishop had been for two years seated in the chair of Upsala, he obtained, by an advised journey to Rome, confirmation from the pope, and was consecrated for the church and province of Upsala, Gustavus Trolle being previously declared by the pope to be deprived of his office, and John himself having now no more annates to give. He was also made the pope's legate to Sweden, to recover the Swedish church to apostolic and catholic unity. But this was now too late. For some time, immediately after he left Sweden, king Gustavus had frequently summoned him to return, but he refused to leave his darling ease. He now wrote in vain to the king and chapter of Upsala. The bond between him and fatherland was dissolved. The king had forbidden correspondence with him.

In 1537, he was called again from Poland to Italy, to the contemplated council at Mantua, where he had a vote to support the papal party. The council was postponed, and he stayed some time in Venice, supported by its archbishop. At last, having in contemplation to return to Poland, he was, instead, invited to Rome by pope Paul IV., and was there quartered in a hospital. After long-continued entreaties, he obtained at last a better harbor, but in vain solicited the covetous pope for a settled income. Some years passed in empty requests and futile hopes, when the college of cardinals allowed him an annuity, which he received till the time of his death. Yet it is said that during his unwearied begging applications to the pope, his poverty had six attendants. He died in the year 1544, and was buried in the church of St. Peter at Rome, at the expense of the pope, who then first extended to him a helping hand.

Fourteen years later, 1558, was laid to rest by his side his brother Olaus, who, after his embassy to Rome in 1523, never again returned to the Swedish soil. He faithfully shared his brother's misfortunes, and after the death of that brother, was nominated and consecrated archbishop of Upsala and primate of Sweden. After him the archiepiscopal title of Upsala ceased to be considered even in name Roman catholic.

Both brothers ameliorated their exile, and kept alive the memory of their fatherland, by historic works. In Dantzic John composed his history of the metropolitan church of Upsala, brought down to his brother's death by Olof, and published at Rome in 1560, after the death of both. In Venice John compiled his praiseworthy history of the kings of the Goths and Swedes, which Olof first published at Rome in 1554. A year after came out, also at Rome, Olof's history of the northern people, their habits and customs.

Olof also made vain attempts to reconcile himself to king Gustavus. In 1554 he sent him the lately published history of John, which, in some copies, probably those designed for Sweden, has, in place of the dedication to the pope, a similar one to the sons of king Gustavus. He complains, in a letter to the king, of May 1st, 1554, that for eleven years, since his appointment to the bishopric of Upsala, he had not received a farthing, not a word by letter, nor an instruction from the king, which grieved him more than all else. "That the king built a castle at Upsala and Wadsten, might," says Olof, "be useful, in case any of his sons became archbishops, or any of his female descendants wished quietly to serve God in the convent at Wadsten." The king's answer was a mixture of seriousness and pleasantry. Gustavus regarded, at this time, both the reformed church and his own throne as too well established to be annoyed or agitated by the letter of the poor man. The books, he said, when he could overlook and examine them, he would recompense according to their merit. The castle at Upsala he had caused to be built, to restrain the superstitious and indecent outrages of priests. The castle of Wadsten would certainly be erected, that his successors might there live in peace. But, as St. Bridget had prophesied that the last mass before the day of judgment would be held in Wadsten, and that Rome herself should come to Wadsten on that occasion, and as to this end it ought to be adorned, he would, on the part of the young ladies of that convent, beg Olof, as their guardian, to come to their help with a hundred thousand ducats, to be taken as a loan from the worthy mesdames of St. Bridget's at Rome, from the holy doctor, brother Peter, and that pious holy man, Marten Skinnare, who allowed no good deeds to be unrewarded, as they showed at Lagloskoping and Susenborg.

But we return to the position and fate of the Swedish church in the year 1526. After his arrival in Dantzic, John Magnus wrote to Brask, and intrusted to him the care of the diocese of Upsala, in whatever required episcopal acts. This duty he took upon him, but appears not to have been satisfied with John's leaving the kingdom. The only comfort he received from John's two letters was, to learn that he had found a safe harbor, while the Swedish church was shaken by the storm. Of the condition of the Swedish church he did not wish to write, as it could afford no consolation.

It is not surprising that bishop Brask felt his courage sink and his dissatisfaction increase under the many vexations which now accumulated around him. The pope neglected the welfare of the Swedish church, and exposed, by an unwise entanglement in worldly affairs, the strength and dignity of his office. The king now treated him with more disrespect, and an extreme, sometimes an unreasonable degree of suspicion. The temporal sword which, according to the doctrine of Gregory VII. and Innocent III., was committed to the successors of St. Peter, threatened to turn itself against that church. The man who came hither in the name of the pope, to give the Swedish church order and discipline, had brought dismay by his remissness and indiscretion, and at length deserted his charge. Of the shepherds of the sees, more than half were not acknowledged at Rome, and acknowledged by the government of the country only for the sake of quiet. In full power there stood on this man's side but two bishops, and in strength and will to exercise that power he stood alone. Ingomar of Wexio, was an inactive spectator of the times, and a yea and nay man in his resolves. Peter of Westeras—already, in 1517, a skeptic in the church's doctrine of indulgences, and ten years later indifferent to the church's riches, partly, it seems, from dissatisfaction with the old church, partly, it may be, from age and weakened vigor—was little interested. The protest against the sentence on Per Sunnanvader, and a later protest, in 1531, are almost the only striking acts of his life. It is singular that John Magnus intrusted the care of the see of Upsala to Brask, and not to the nearest neighbor, which was Peter.

How far other men, besides the king, could now venture against the church, was shown by Arvid the Westgoth, who, in 1525, obtained Kalmar, More, and Oeland, in investiture. He took the tithes of the bishop in Oeland, violently quartered on the clergy and tenants of the bishop, carried off the bishop's oxen and horses, levied his fines, imprisoned priests, dissolved marriages, allowed those to go to church who for adultery and other offences had been excommunicated, and committed many other outrages. It was the threatening precursor of the dissolution of the church's discipline, which many times and in many places followed the Reformation, wherever it was carried on with any degree of vehemence. Brask wrote and complained, admonished Arvid, and begged his wife's mediation. Arvid, who pretended to have a commission for what he did, denies, in a letter to the bishop, having done anything unlawful, and begs the prelate not to put in use with him any Romish tactics. "May God put an end here to this," exclaimed the bishop, in a letter to Thure Jonsson, "otherwise we shall evidently be obliged to give up all, according to the desires of those who have long coveted it."

The disagreement between king Gustavus and bishop Brask, proceeded to greater lengths, and was more earnestly pursued on the part of the former, after John Magnus left the country. The bishop desired, from the press he had established at Soderkoping, to circulate over Sweden a translation of some of the German emperor's decrees against the doctrine of Luther, and also the letter against Luther by duke George of Saxony. On the 10th of November, 1526, the king wrote and declared his disapprobation of such an attempt. It was not certain that these edicts were not supposititious. The king seemed to himself to find their circulation, as well as of George's letter, opposed to his own jurisdiction, as he had not so seriously decided as they had done against the doctrine of Luther. The king, therefore, enjoined him to refrain from the promulgation of these writings. "And let there be sent hither," continues the king, "some learned men of your church, who with, reason and demonstration of the Scriptures, can prove that here another teaching than that of the holy gospel is bruited and preached. They shall be heard with forbearance and with all favor, may set forth their positions, and where it can be proved that any unchristian doctrine is preached, we will willingly see that they are punished who cannot render a reason." The bishop exculpated himself. He had no intention of offending the king, and desired him to place no confidence in those who, without being authorized, carried the bishop's message. The challenge to a disputation with the priests at Stockholm, he had communicated to his clergy, and they had all declared themselves to harbor no doubt of the Christian truth which hitherto had been held in Christendom.

The course of Brask was watched with great suspicion. While they were still lying in press, the king had learned his intention to publish the above-named writings. The bishop complains that his letters were intercepted. The letter to Upsala, in which he censures the new teaching, had come to the king's knowledge, who also suspected that more such were written to many parts of the kingdom. It had been said, what, however, the bishop denied to be true, that after his printing press in Soderkoping was prohibited, because it did mischief in Stockholm, he caused refutations of Lutheranism to be printed at Kopenham. The king, therefore, at last, on February 2, 1527, forbade him to let anything go abroad among the simple-minded people, before the king had seen it and investigated the character of its teaching.

The question often before agitated, of a religious conference for the settlement of disputes, was, it appears, now taken up in earnest. Dissatisfaction had been expressed through many parts of the land, to the effect, that the king was desirous of introducing a new faith. This the king regarded as the more unjust, because he offered that a strict examination should be instituted into the teaching and preaching called new. He now declared his determination to call together the most learned and eminent men in the land, to investigate what was most true, which should be the base of an unalterable concord. He therefore directed bishop Brask to propose the time and place for such a conference.

The letter of the king to this effect, bears date January 2, 1527. Fourteen days after, it was answered by Brask, evading the question of a religious conference. Such new doctrines had been before examined in many ecclesiastical councils, and no intelligent man could desire further to dispute upon them, contrary to the decrees of all Christendom. But if the king wished, in the course of the summer, for a provincial council, and to call together the church's prelates and chapters, to consider of these and other matters, the bishop would in this, proceed according to the royal pleasure.

Bishop Brask shunned and feared a disputation on the articles of the faith. He regarded it as dangerous for the disputant, *who, perhaps might himself be wavering in the faith*, and so commit a sin in its defence; and he regarded it as dangerous for the hearers. These might be confirmed in the faith, if strong defenders were found; but the simple and weak in faith might easily become still weaker, when they perceived that faith to be called in question, of which they never doubted because they never heard of any deviation from it. Hence had the canon law forbidden laymen, publicly or privately, to dispute on the faith. He would prefer that the king should give up the idea of a provincial council, under which form he supposed king Gustavus designed matters of faith to be examined; but if the king could not be induced to change his purpose, one need not be frightened, knowing that patience has its perfect work. It would be proper, however, that such a case should be managed and carried on by men of the same rank and condition, doctor against doctor, knight against knight, king against king.

The king of England had already trod on that path. Such is the tenor of Brask's letter to doctor Galle.

The reports disseminated through the land of an approaching change within the church, became more and more the topic of all men's thoughts and conversation. The minds of men were the more disturbed as they were the more perplexed and uncertain. In many parts were proclaimed the hitherto almost unheard-of sentiments, respecting the overthrow of the papacy, the spiritual thraldom, the unfitness and incompetency of the priests and monks to be guides in the way of salvation, and many more topics of the like kind. But the new teachers preached many crude ideas, little else than a denial of what had hitherto been reverenced as truth. In other parts where these new teachers were unable to penetrate, there came alarming reports that the king was attached to a new faith, and they excited the greater alarm, that men wist not what this new faith meant. Many priests who possessed the confidence of the people, represented the case as dangerous to the existence of Christianity. From Upsala such reports were spread over all the archdiocese.

During the disturbances, in Dalecarlia, in the years 1524 and 1525, complaints were rife against the king, for injuries done to the property of the church, though nothing was said of the introduction of a new faith. But in the year 1526, inquiries on this subject became more lively. Early in the spring, John Magnus had written to the king, of having heard that in Norway, where the news of the king's apprehended defection was probably carried by Sunnanvader and Knut, prayers were offered up that the king might remain firm in the faith. "It is well prayed," replied the king, "although, perhaps, the most of them know but little of what the true Christian faith is."

The dissolution of the monastery at Gripsholm, had excited such interest throughout the land, that Gustavus found it necessary to issue a proclamation on the subject through many provinces of the kingdom.

There soon followed, occasioned by the above mentioned reports, letters from the king respecting the new faith, as it was termed, to Helsingland, dated on the 26th of May, 1526; to East Gothland on January 7th, and to West Gothland, on February 22d, of the following year.

They are all in the main points, of one and the same tenor, and clearly show how much was done beforehand for the subsequent transactions at Westeras. It was complained that the king protected and favored in Upland certain preachers, who taught another faith than that we have learned from Christ and his apostles. This was not true. The king desired to die a Christian man, as his father and forefathers were before him. Dissensions had in other Christian lands arisen from the circumstance, that some prominent men were desirous of exercising the vices which had grown up within Christendom, to the oppression and injury of many. And here also, in this kingdom, had some begun to press forward to the same mark. But the lordliness and avarice of the heads of the church were obstinately opposed to every change; an opposition prejudicial to the public weal and the good of the people. The heads of the church, the pope, the bishops, and their allies, had committed unbecoming outrages, and thus put the kingdom in danger. They had for selfish purposes oppressed the laity. So when any one owed them anything, they withheld from him the holy sacrament, against the laws of God and all equity. This the king wished not to permit, but that like other good men they should recover their debts by law, and at the assize of the proper lord. In like manner it was an objectionable thing with regard to the breach of holy days, that, if any one shoots a bird or takes a dish of fish, he must pay a fine to the priest on behalf of the bishop. God had not forbidden this, provided it is not done during divine service, when a man ought to be hearing the word of God. It was an objectionable thing that priests offending against laymen had privileges above others. There would be better reason in their having only equal justice. It was also objectionable, that, if a priest beats a layman he is not excommunicated, but the layman is if he beats a priest. God had here made no distinction, but equally commanded priests to live in concord, love, and harmony, with laymen, as these with priests. It was objectionable that when a priest dies without having made a will, the poor heirs lost their right, and the bishop, though not of kin, took the inheritance. So also when the king wished to watch over and guard the interests of the crown, and not permit them, as hitherto, to draw the property of the crown to themselves, or receive the king's fines, they said the king wished to introduce a new faith and the doctrines of Luther. The king had expected that from all Christendom a general diet would be assembled on the subject of these disorders, but as this had not yet taken place, he would call together a council of the kingdom, and the most prominent men of the whole realm, and by their counsel and consent, under the help of God, ordain what, between God and his conscience, he found to be right.

The king, on May 18th, 1527, puts forth a kindred defence, in answer to the complaints of the Dalecarlians, among which was that of Lutheranism being introduced into the land, and of the kind of preaching in Stockholm, as well as of the Swedish psalms and hymns. The king knew not of any other Lutheranism, than his having ordered to be preached the word of God and his holy gospel, that the priests might not deceive the poor peasantry and people with fables for their own avaricious ends, and trample upon nobles and princes. A swarm of priests and monks called this Lutheranism, and a new faith. The censure of the practice in Stockholm of Swedish psalms and hymns, surprised him, as "over the whole kingdom in parish churches, it was usual to sing in Swedish and so praise God." It was as well this should be done in our own mother-tongue, as in Latin, which was not understood.

At last, but to no purpose, pope Clement VII., began in 1526, to think of the flock in Sweden, which was well nigh being lost to Rome. Probably the urgent negotiations respecting the consecration of the bishops elect, recalled this flock to the forgetful heart of the chief shepherd. On September 19th of this year, he wrote a letter to the bishops of Linkoping and Westeras, in Rome's usual sharp and extravagant style. Through the repeated complaints of many, it had come to his ears, that some priests and clerks, and even monastic folk, whose life and faith ought to be an example to others, had so forgotten their duty and station, as to receive the godless and condemned doctrines of Luther. The pope had learned that they publicly entered into illicit marriage; that the service of the holy mass was either altogether changed, or wholly neglected and abandoned; that the holy eucharist, without reverence, was received under both kinds; that Christians of both sexes went to the holy communion without penance, without confession, without contrition; that the sacrament of baptism was administered without holy unction, holy oil, and consecrated water, not in churches, but in worldly and indecent places; and that extreme unction was given in contrariety to the church's order and the decrees of the fathers and councils, and was even refused to those who desired it. It was chiefly those to whom the souls of the faithful were intrusted, that seduced them, and incited them to follow the standard and dominion of Satan. It was the duty of the bishops, even if it were requisite with the aid of the temporal arm, to thrust these unworthy ministers of the altar from the sanctuary, and for that purpose to address themselves to the king and nobility of the kingdom. In conclusion, the pope addresses his letter to the king, princes, knights, and all nobles, admonishing them to turn their regards, power, and influence, to support the honor of God's holy name, that, by their exertions, with those of the bishops, the faith of Christ might be purified from these abominable errors.

Historic information is wanting, to corroborate each point of complaint in the pope's letter; although it is probable that such expressions were the emanations of an unwise zeal. But there is no evidence that the papal letter, which came to Sweden in December, 1526, was published there, or communicated to the king and council. Either the bishops found it most advisable to delay its publication, the rather as from Clement's relations with the emperor Charles V. and with Sweden, they might foresee how useless it would be, or the king had forbidden its promulgation; and we turn to the complaints made by Brask to his friends.

In the soul of bishop Brask, faith maintained a contest in behalf of the old church; and firm confidence was mingled with deep dissatisfaction and mistrustful dejection. "Be not uneasy," he writes, on January 22, 1527, to doctor Peter Galle, of Upsala, "knowing that faith has its perfect work. We have determined, according to the exhortation of the gospel, to fear Him who can cast the soul into hell. You have your prayers, your address to the Lord God, to St. Erik and other patrons of the kingdom, and nothing shall finally harm, because it is of the church a peculiarity, that she then triumphs when she appears oppressed. For the gates of hell shall not prevail against her."

On December 11th, 1526, he wrote to Peter Benedict at Rome: "Your longing for cares, tumults and confusions, must hasten you hither; and you must not leave your patience behind. We are in hope that it is to us instead of our purgatory; better here than in future, now than hereafter. The Swedish church is in the worst condition, and will be so as long as God pleases. The poorest peasant in Sweden is in a better condition than she, for he enjoys law and justice, his proper privileges, and the old good customs of the kingdom. I shall, as far as lies in my power, willingly carry into execution, the papal brief, with consent of the king, which I hope to obtain, since his heart is in His hand and depends on His pleasure, who is always able to make a Saul to be a Paul, by removing evil counsellors." "If the Lord doth not shorten these days," he wrote on the 20th of March, 1527, "we can look for nothing but daily enmity, or await the dissolution of the flesh, when the goodness of God so determines." On occasion of the insurrection of the Dalesmen, in 1527, he exclaims: "God forgive those who have brewed all these evils with their new gospel, which Luther has dragged from the bench, according to the expression of duke George's letter."*

In the midst of these sorrows, hopes, and remonstrances of the bishop, came to him the summons of king Gustavus to the diet of Westeras. Surprised that the place of meeting was changed from Soderkoping to Westeras, and uneasy for the quiet of East Gothland, he wrote, on May 23, 1527, to his friend, the administrator, Thure Jonsson, "We will certainly drag ourselves up to this diet, though we know what will thence befall us."

The important change in the shifting scene, was now about to take place. Gustavus determined to hazard all upon the diet he had summoned on the very confines of the insurgent Dalesmen. A month after, the 23d of May, worse had befallen the bishop than he even foreboded.

* Petrus Benedict was the bishop's agent at Rome, where he resided in the house of St. Bridget. The bishop paid yearly for his agent's support there, to the abbess of Wadsten, the sum of a hundred marks.

CHAPTER VIII.

WRITINGS CONCERNING THE REFORMATION, BEFORE THE DIET OF WESTERAS IN 1527. THE ANSWER OF OLAUS PETRI TO PAULUS ELIÆ. THE ANSWERS TO THE TWELVE QUESTIONS.

UNTIL the year 1527, there appeared in Sweden, with the exception of the translation of the New Testament, no writings designed to win public opinion to a change in the teaching and discipline of the church. The spirit and condition of the times demanded the use of this instrument, less than immediate energy in word and action. For those who desired further instruction, there were in circulation, from Germany and Denmark, works for and against the Reformation.

It was such a consideration that called forth the first of the two Swedish works, composed before the diet of Westeras; although we cannot with certainty say that even these were in general circulation. They are to be received as representing the predominant views of the contending parties, so as to give a clear idea of the material points of the controversy.

At this time there lived at Köpenham a Carmelite monk named Paulus Eliæ, come from Holland, born in Warberg, and therefore a subject of Denmark, though on the mother's side, of a Swedish family. When he speaks of master Sven of Skara as his teacher, he seems to intimate that for some time he had the benefit of education in Sweden, where, it is likely, West Gothland was the home of his mother's family, though he does not enter into particulars. He belonged to the Carmelite monastery at Helsingor, and removed to that of the Danish Carmelites erected into a college, and as bachelor in theology, lectured in the university of Köpenham, after king Christian II., on that condition, had transferred to the monastery of Helsingor the hospital of St. Gorau, at Köpenham. He soon took hold of the principles of the Reformation, read and approved the smaller treatises which first emanated from Luther, but afterward stopped short, or rather went back, when the Reformation appeared to him to go too far, and acquired, through this defection, which was sometimes attributed to not very creditable motives, the nickname of Paul Turncoat. In the year 1526, he opened the campaign against Luther, in a letter to the knight Tyge Krabbe. This letter was circulated through Sweden by the enemies of the Reformation, and a copy of it fell into the hands of master Olof.

Olaus Petri was requested to reply to this letter, as it might have an injurious influence upon those who were not experienced in the Holy Scriptures. His "Answer to an unchristian letter, which a lying monk called Paulus Eliæ has put forth against the Holy Gospel, which is now, by God's grace come to light," bears date March 28, 1527. In this, his first production, Olaus Petri comes out in sound, vigorous, and noble language, but with little mercy against his adversary, and with a clearness, depth, and compass of thought, which, from the commencement, appoints him that marked position among the learned men of the Swedish church, which posterity has continued to assign him. The grateful disciple defends his teacher against Paul's attack. The latter, had in his letter, which is only known through Olof's answer, presented a multitude of accusations: as that Luther and his followers were the cause of the anarchy which had entered into church and state, and displayed itself in the war of the peasants then raging in Germany;

that they rejected good works and the books of the learned, and even portions of the New Testament; desired, from abuses which possibly existed within the church, to remove the usages that were good and wholesome; denied the freedom of man's will; discarded the sacraments of the church; sought to deprive priests of all their incomes; threw discredit on the poverty of monks; abolished festivals; with other charges of the like description. Olaus answers every point according to its importance, with greater or less prolixity, and retorts upon the popish church the charges which his adversary wished to cast upon Luther and his followers. A careful study of the Holy Scriptures and of the fathers of the church, is apparent in this work of the reformer. From the writings of Luther, which had hitherto appeared, he quotes nothing; but yet displays an accurate knowledge of them. He was far removed from the blind worship of Luther which had beome so common. Paulus Eliæ had blamed Luther for asserting at different times, that the church had been in error for three hundred, for a thousand, for thirteen hundred years. Olaus does not undertake, in this respect, a defence of Luther, but remarks: "He is but a man as we are, and may be mistaken as well as we. But he counsels us to follow the Scriptures. Let us see that what he says corresponds with the Scriptures, then let us follow him, otherwise not." Then, with an air of persuasion, he draws the distinction between the commandment of God and the commandments and ordinances of men, and shows how the latter, by little and little, prevailed, and how a good practice often degenerated into an abuse. He adds, as a defender of the Reformation: "our fathers have confessedly changed good into evil, why should we not confessedly have changed evil into good?"

Although the church reform in Sweden was, in respect to doctrine, now approaching maturity, we must direct our attention to another nearly contemporaneous production,

"An answer to twelve questions on several points, in which the evangelical and papal doctrines do not agree, and a refutation of the answer given by doctor Peter Galle to these questions. Olaus Petri. Stockholm, 1527."

"King Gustavus had," says Olaus, in the preface to this production of his pen, "laid to heart the differences which existed respecting matters of faith, and made inquiries from both parties, in order to find wherein that difference was most to be found. He had at length become satisfied, that if there was a dissonance in many particulars, there were twelve points in which there could be no concord. The king put these points into the form of twelve questions, sent them to some men of both parties, and begged to have their answers and arguments on the same." Olof supposes the purpose of the king to have been to call together some learned men and prelates of the church, to set them upon proving and settling these questions, and by this means to quiet the disputes.

Who were the learned men named to answer the questions is not known. The chief, however, were the two leading champions of the war, Peter Galle and Olaus Petri. To doctor Galle the king sent the questions, on December 4th, 1526, with the request, that by Christmas eve he would return his written answer. The king supposed Galle obligated to give his answer: "Because you are a doctor of the Holy Scriptures, and have to that end devoted your studies, that you might be able to teach us laymen those points, which for us to know is necessary to our salvation."

The questions delivered to Galle were but ten. More were at first not on the list, but the other two, respecting the monastic life and the sacrament of the altar, soon came, that they too might at the same time be answered. After master Olof returned the king his answers, he was asked if he were prepared to sustain and defend them, should any one appear in opposition? He declared himself ready and willing so to do, and twice made a journey to Upsala to meet doctor Galle, and had, in presence of the king and council and others, challenged him to the contest. But the latter had excused himself from further disputation. Olof, therefore, prepared a new set of answers, and sent them to him to see if he could find any further objections. Olof was the more incited to do this, as the friends of Galle declared he had gained the victory, and no one would now venture to attack or reply to him. At this point, when Olof had the advantage of the last word, the questions came out in print. The 14th day of May is the date of the printed copies.

The significance and importance of these answers, which might be considered as containing the confession of faith of both parties, and as an evidence of the position and spirit of the leaders when the reform of the church commenced in Sweden, demand of us, as to their substance and quality a closer investigation.

The first question was: "*If we may abandon* (withdraw from) *the teaching of holy men and the church's usages and customs, when they have not the word of God with them?*"

Doctor Galle divides his answer to this question into two parts. On the first, whether we may fall away from the teaching of holy men, he remarks, that the Holy Scriptures have sometimes so high and deep a meaning that they cannot be understood, unless interpreted according to the mind of the Holy Ghost. So speaks Peter of the things hard to be understood in the epistles of Paul. (2 Peter iii. 10.) So the eunuch could not understand the 53d chapter of Isaiah, until Philip was sent to him by the Holy Ghost. (Acts viii.) Holy men who interpreted the Scriptures, have had the inspiration of the Holy Ghost. (2 Pet. i. 21.) God has dealt out divers gifts of grace, some apostles, some the interpretation of Scripture. (1 Cor. xii.) Now after that holy men of the church have taught and interpreted the Holy Scriptures, not according to their own will but inspiration of the Holy Ghost; to fall away from the teaching of holy men is to fall away from God and the Holy Ghost, who has spoken through these men.

In regard to the other point, of falling away from the church's usages and customs, which are not founded on the word of God, doctor Galle remarks, that such church usages as are reasonable *and are not at variance with the Scriptures*, and have been a long time held by our fathers, holy and learned men, who were more experienced in the Scriptures than we, ought to be kept. The apostles had ordained much that is not found in Scripture. (1 Cor. xi. 34; 3 John 13; Acts xvi. and xvii.) Augustin also writes, that in all matters of the church, which are not mentioned in Scripture, the customs and practices of the fathers should be esteemed as law.

Master Olof makes answer: The word of God cannot be altered. If, then, teachers, and so the usages of the church, carry with them the word of God, there should be no departure from them; for by not doing so respect would be paid to the word of God. But if they have not God's word with them there may be a departure; for otherwise there would be no difference between God's word and man's word, from which it would follow that God and man were equal, because their word was equal. There is no doubt that holy men, as Ambrose, Augustin, Jerome, and others, were full of the Holy Ghost; "but it must be known to every one who reads their books that the Holy Ghost did not always direct them when they wrote, since they often, of human infirmity, wrote in contradiction to each other, often in contradiction to themselves, if not to the word of God itself." *But their writings were to be read with judgment*, with careful heed how they kept close to the Scriptures.

That the Scriptures are sometimes difficult, does not proceed from their being in themselves obscure, but from our blindness and ignorance, and want of skill. "It is not the fault of the sun that they who have weak eyes cannot look up to him. He is clear enough in himself, and has no need of being enlightened and clarified." *Teachers should interpret the Scripture by the Scriptures; the Scripture which appears dark and obscure by that which is plain and obvious.* When it is said (2 Pet. i. 20) that no Scripture is of any private interpretation, but that holy men spake as they were moved by the Holy Ghost, it follows that they who give themselves to the Scriptures can interpret them. This comes to pass when Scripture is interpreted by Scripture.

Certainly the apostles had ordained much in the churches which is not found in the Scripture; but no one can say what that was, with the exception of some particulars. We have no need to know it, for had there been the need it would have been penned in Holy Writ.

Some practices are in use from the apostles' times; as the mode of keeping the Lord's day, celebrating Easter and the feast of Pentecost, with some others; but on these things our salvation does not depend. Other things have been changed, as the prohibition to eat blood, that there was no difference between presbyter and bishop. In days of old, when a priest committed open wickedness he was deposed and considered no more a priest, but now it is said that he can be allowed no more to execute his office, but that he is still a priest. The bishop or priest who cumbered himself with worldly cares was deposed from his office. This now takes place no more. They who gave money to become bishop or priest were degraded, as were those who took money to bestow the office, but now no man becomes a bishop without giving money to the pope. Pope Marcellus ordained twenty-five men at Rome, who were called cardinals, their office there to baptize those who embraced Christianity and to bury the dead: "now there is such a change made in the buriers of the dead and the baptizers, that they are kings and princes."

The second question was: "*If our Lord Jesus Christ is found to have bestowed on priests, bishops, popes, any power or dominion over mankind, other than that of proclaiming his word and will; and ought there to be any other priests than they who do so?*"

His answer to the former part of the question, doctor Galle rests upon the words of Christ to Peter (1 Matt. xviii.): "If thy brother sin against thee," &c. Where it is said: "If he will not hear thee tell it to the church," doctor Galle inserts, "tell it to the *heads of the church.*" According to this commandment of Christ, the doctor regards spiritual power to have been given to popes, bishops, and priests, over all those who are disobedient to God's commandment, and over all matters consequential to the church's welfare. This position he fortifies from Tit. iii., 10. 1 Cor. v. 5, 11.

The question, if there should be other priests than those who proclaim the word of God, doctor Galle answers in the affirmative. 1. Because Paul, in his epistle to the Romans (i. 12), and in other places, speaks of manifold spiritual offices, as apostles, prophets and the like. 2. Because the priest's office is to pray for the people. So in the Old Testament, according to the prophet Joel (ii. 17); and what is true under the old is still more true under the new dispensation. Christ had also commanded (Luke xviii. 1) always to pray and not to be weary, which Bede interprets thus: always to pray, that is to read or sing the seven horæ canonicæ of the church, and this interpretation the royal psalmist fortifies. (Ps. cxix., clxiv.) 3. Because the highest office of the priest is to consecrate the body of our Lord, and to offer Him for men according to the apostle. (Heb. v. 1.)

Master Olof replies, that Christ taught that His kingdom is not of this world. He was obedient to the existing powers, and so were his apostles. If the popes, bishops, and priests, are now followers of Christ and the apostles, they cannot have worldly dominion. They should feed the flock of Christ, feed them with the word of God, for no other food profits them. To proclaim the word of God is the business of a priest, as to forge is the business of a smith. The priests are ever called in Scripture expounders of the word, and the Scriptures know nothing of any other priests than those who preach the word of God.

Galle incurs the severe censure of his critic, for his manner of expounding the Scripture. When it is said, "tell the church," it is made wholly different, "tell the heads of the church." These words are not said to St. Peter alone, but to every one of the apostles, and afterward to every Christian man. Galle also confounds spiritual and worldly power. All know that bishops and priests receive from Christ himself, in trust, the spiritual sword, *which is the word of God.*

Olof further remarks, on Galle's answer, that the corporeal or legal priesthood of the Old Testament, denoted the spiritual priesthood of the new, in which priesthood every Christian man is included. The command always to pray, also includes all men. The prayer we are always to make is not with the mouth. It is an affectionate longing, a desire and wish of the heart, to which our needs compel us. Did the words of Christ mean that priests should read or sing the seven horæ canonicæ, they could never sleep or do anything else. The words of Bede are also by Galle misinterpreted. Bede declares, "They are said always to pray and not to faint, who, at the appointed times (the canonical hours), do not fail to pray, or also, all that a righteous man does or speaks, according to the will of God, ought to be reckoned as prayer." Why are the words of David quoted for the praise of God seven times a day, and not of Daniel (Dan. vi.), who prayed three times a day? It is nowhere found in Scripture that Christ commanded priests to consecrate his body and blood, but he has strongly commanded them to preach. "We may be saved without ever partaking the Lord's Supper, but we can never be saved unless we are taught by God's word on what we shall rest our faith, and be thus made spiritually partakers of Christ, who is the Word of God." The passage in Heb. v. 1, is spoken of the high priest, who was a type of Christ.

The third question was: "*Whether their law, commandments, or ordinances, be so obligatory, that they sin who do the contrary?*"

Galle: If the commandments of the heads of the church are righteous, and draw men to salvation, they are truly our Lord's commandments (Prov. viii. 15). As God continuously works (John v. 17) to retain all creatures in their natural existence, and does not create them anew, so Christ upholds the church, not so as to found a new church, but to uphold that already founded. So is it with the seed sown in the earth, which grows with time and does not immediately appear full ripened to perfection. The church is developed by degrees, so that Almighty God constantly gives timely and often new impulses to the hearts of those who are her heads, in order to govern his holy church. Therefore their commandments may be the impulses of God, though they are called the ordinances of men. But if they were merely the commandments of men, they should be obeyed when they are given in the church, which God has intrusted to men. To this effect are cited Luke x. 16; Mat. xxiii. 3; Heb. xiii. 17. If also the heads of the church, our fathers, came together in the unity of the Holy Ghost, and established certain commandments, then were these to be regarded more as the ordinances of the Holy Ghost than of men. For Christ said: "Where two or three are gathered together in my name, there am I in the midst of them." Their commandments and ordinances, therefore, are so obligatory that they sin who do the contrary.

Olof: That alone is sin which is contrary to the commandment of God. If bishops and priests could thus bind men in sin, there would be no difference between the commandments of God and the ordinances of men. But it has been proved under the first article that we can withdraw from or forsake the teaching of men.

After refuting the other answers of Galle, and his interpretation of the passages quoted from the Bible, he turns to the momentous tenet of continual impulse or inspiration and the church's progressive development. Did God give always new impulses or inspiration to the hearts of the church's officers, there would follow an awkward rule in Christianity, and the Holy Scriptures would have been given in vain; for what need would we have of such old writings, having always a new inspiration and teaching by the prelates, which are equally of God as are the Scriptures, which we have of the apostles and prophets. It will also follow, that the longer Christianity stands, the better and more complete it will be; so that now it will be much better and more complete than it was in the times of the apostles, and those immediately succeeding, and that the prelates in our times will have a fuller teaching than Christ himself or his apostles had—inasmuch as the tree is better when it is grown than when it is small. What became of the prediction of Christ and his apostles, that charity should be burnt up and faith be scarcely found upon earth? And how, if progressive inspiration be received as true, shall we act, in case the prelates are opposed to each other? How shall we know which is right? "I think doctor Peter must confess that party to be in the right, which best agrees with the Holy Scripture."

The fathers came often together, but not always in the Holy Ghost. This appears from the history of many ecclesiastical councils, especially within the last three or four hundred years. One council had often been in opposition to another. There is, therefore, but loose ground for building on their ordinances.

The fourth question was: "*Whether they have power to separate any one from God, as a member cut off from God's church, and to make him a member of the devil?*"

Doctor Galle to this question only replies, that in answer to a former one it has already been shown, from Mat. xviii., that popes, bishops, and priests, have spiritual power.

Master Olof, on the contrary, declares, that, as the church of God is a spiritual church in the Holy Ghost, so that he who has not the Holy Ghost belongs not to this church, bishops and priests cannot take the Holy Ghost from a member of the church, and make those who are children of God children of the devil.

When with the word of God one Christian comforts another who wishes to repent and amend, he looses him from sins, not by his own might, but by the might of the word of God, which he brings to him. In like manner, when he reproves another with God's word, and the person reproved will not change his mind, repent and amend, he binds his sin upon him. The word of God binds him. Every Christian can use this power. But the wisest and most judicious are chosen to exercise it. It is a spiritual power; extends so far that he who will not change his mind or repent may be cast out of the Christian church, "so as not to partake with other Christian men of the precious body and blood of Christ, and none shall have intercourse with him. Thus is he also corporeally bound by an outward punishment, that he may repent, and submit, and amend." In support of this answer on the right of excommunication in the church, reference is made to Mat. xviii.; 1 Cor. v.; 2 Cor. xiii. "Doctor Galle," says Olof, "might have had a better answer than he has given to this question from his own master of the sentences, Peter Lombard."

The fifth question was: "*Whether the dominion now set up by the pope and his party, is for or against Christ?*"

In his answer to this question, the champion of the papal dominion shows a special want of decision. The question was evidently framed to receive an unevasive answer, and doctor Galle shows he does not know what proper answer to make. Yet it seems to him that Christ (Luke xxii.), when He commands the chief of his disciples to be as the servant of the others, did not forbid dominion, but the pride and severity which unchristian lords practice toward their subjects. Hence St. Paul writes, that "He who desireth the authority of a bishop, desireth a good and gentle office." Had Christ forbidden his apostles and their successors all dominion, St. Gregory, who was powerful and rich, and yet meek, mild, and benevolent, would be condemned for disobedience, and so would many other popes, bishops, prelates and priests with him, who yet will be saved. For twelve hundred years or more, from the time of St. Silvester, had emperors and kings, lords and princes, held the pope as their own and the head of Christendom, as the officer of Christ and successor of St. Peter, and reverenced the church of Rome. The pope, therefore, called them his beloved sons. Wherever this relation was broken, it had taken place through the intervention of enemies. He could not, therefore, find that the dominion of the pope and heads of the church was against Christ, when it was properly exercised to the praise and honor of God and the salvation of Christian men. To the spiritual or ecclesiastical body belongs the spiritual office of teaching and the authority which Christ committed to the popes, who are the successors of St. Peter, since he said to St. Peter alone, 'Feed my sheep.'

In answer to the question, master Olof alleges, that Christ commanded his disciples and their successors to go and preach the gospel, and forbade them to be kings and princes; hence he concludes, that such a dominion is against Christ, is anti-christian.

But doctor Galle, in his answer to this momentous question, had too much exposed his weak side, not to be hit by the cut of his adversary. With respect to the passage in 1 Tim. iii. 1, Olof with reason asks him, who taught him grammar, when he makes the episcopate or office of a bishop the same as the dominion of a bishop, and work (opus) to mean the same as office.

Master Olof then combats the singular proof offered by Galle from the example of Gregory and others. "Heaven and earth may pass away, but the word of God remains sure, though the example not only of Gregory and other popes and bishops, equally sure, though the whole world and all creatures stood in opposition. Who has taught him that the word of God must give way to the acts and examples of weak men? I thought that the actions of men should be judged as right or wrong according to the word of God, and not that the word of God should be judged according to the actions of men." To Galle's remark, that the dominion of the pope and others had stood for twelve hundred years or more, Olof replies: "The words of God which say that the office of a bishop is not a dominion, are still older than twelve hundred years, although the dominion now upheld by the pope and bishops, is not as old as doctor Peter says. Neither does the strength of its position depend upon how old a thing it is, as upon how right it is. The devil is old, and yet he is not the better for it. The longer an unrighteous dominion lasts, the worse it is. Through the privileges granted by emperors and princes, the pope has acquired the means of lifting himself above them; and it is well nigh come to pass, that they must fall down and kiss his feet. The pope with his crew has left off to feed the flock of Christ, and has for many hundred years milked, shorn and slaughtered them, and shown himself to to be a wolf and not a good shepherd. May God forgive it."

The sixth question was: "*Whether there be any other service of God than to keep His commandments. Are human devices of the same type, God not having enjoined them?*"

Doctor Galle answers, that there is no other service of God than to keep his commandments. What men are to do for salvation is comprised in the ten commandments. There also is to be found the worship of God; the inward, which is Christian faith, and which, consisting in trust in God's mercy and the love of him above all things, is contained in the first commandment. The outward worship of God, which is to evince the soul's inward godliness, consists in praying with the mouth, singing or reading the seven horæ canonicæ, going to church, hearing mass and preaching, falling on the knees, smiting the breast, taking holy water, burning a candle and the like, and is, with the duty of keeping Sunday holy, to be found in the third commandment.

It was expected of master Olof, that he, like his adversary, would regard the necessary manifestation of the inward in the outward worship of God. But he addresses himself instead, to oppose the merit of adding the latter to the former. He remarks, that all the commandments which relate to outward acts have their completion in love to our neighbor. "For as God is a Spirit, and will be worshiped and loved in the spirit, he commands no corporeal service of us, but he expects this of us in regard to our neighbor; so that when we do good to our neighbor, we keep God's commandment and serve him. Thus, whatever we do in his name, for the welfare of our neighbor, is accounted as the worship of God—as are the works which men do for wife and children, and children for their parents." He reproves Galle for including in God's commandments what does not belong to them, as reading and singing the canonical hours, using holy water, and the like.

The seventh question was: "*Whether men can be saved on account of their merits, or of God's mere grace and mercy?*"

In the answer to this question, Galle and Olof were in greater concord than in any other. Doctor Peter alleges that God makes man capable of good works through His grace, by which He moves the free will of man, and for these good works gives him a reward, which thus is obtained of God's mercy and pity. Master Olof comes, on the basis of many passages of Scripture (Rom. vi. 23; Eph. ii. 8), to the same conclusion, that salvation cannot be gained through our service or merit, because then in vain did Christ suffer death. When men gain reward for good works, they gain it because God himself bestows it on their free heart and will. God who gives His favor to good works, gives also the good heart and will for such works.

It is remarkable, that master Olof, in this answer, does not aim to develope the relation between faith and good works. He had just before, in his answer to Paulus Eliæ, with clearness and truth treated of that topic. Perhaps he wished, from his agreement with Galle, to give the more force to the consequences he saw could be thence derived. Would doctor Peter, he says, consider what follows, he would perceive what becomes of indulgence, monastic vows, masses, and the like, "and this conclusion strikes down all the pretensions of the priests."

The eighth question was: "*Whether the monastic life has any firm foundation in Scripture?*"

Galle answers: "Samuel gathered together the prophets, their sons and disciples. That they lived in a monastic life, in poverty, obedience and purity, is proved from their doing nothing but praise and serve God. Elijah and Elisha assembled also such godly men on the hill of Carmel." From the book of the Acts (ii.) it appears, that when the faith began to be preached in Jerusalem, "many men of a pure life from all countries" were there. The words of Christ (Mat. xix. 12, 21; xvi. 24) have led many to the three vows on which the monastic life is founded. These vows remove the three hindrances to salvation; the desire of the flesh is removed by purity of life, the desire of the eye or covetousness by poverty, pride of life by obedience. The monastic life "helps man to his salvation, and is a short cut to the kingdom of heaven." It belongs to the evangelical counsels, which, in Scriptures, are over and above the commandments. It is surprising that any one can doubt this, when the monastic life is found existing for more than a thousand years. St. Gregory, St. Jerome and many others, lived in cloisters.

Olof had an easy task in refuting his adversary. The prophets did not live in cloisters. They had wives (2 Kings iv.), and monks to be their followers ought to be married. The passages quoted from Scripture were wrongly interpreted. "He who has grace, is in the right way to salvation. He who has it not, is in the wrong way, though he made ten journeys in a cloister." And "none can say, that the monastic life is founded in Scripture, because holy men have lived in cloisters." It was then a different thing to live in a cloister from what it is now.

In Scripture there is not a syllable concerning the monastic life when the true meaning of Scripture is given. That meaning and its development are furnished by Olof. No monks are to be found in the apostles' time. More than two hundred years elapsed from the commencement of the church, when first began the monastic institution. Monks lived then in deserts and supported themselves by their labor. They began afterward to unite in monasteries, for which St. Basil wrote rules. These cloisters were then schools, and the monks were laymen, and could quit this kind of life whenever they pleased. Then came St. Benedict, and began to found cloisters in Italy, and give new rules. But in time men gave to cloisters goods and chattels, so that their occupants began to live on their rents, and laziness and ease, more than the exercise of piety, were the motives which enticed many into cloisters. Thus, at length, about the twelfth century after Christ, arose the four mendicant orders, the Dominicans and Grey monks, the Augustinians and Carmelites, who neither worked for their support, nor lived on their rents, but begged; whereof came much roguery and lying into the world.

The ninth question was: "*Whether any one has or has had authority to ordain in the sacrament of bread and wine, otherwise than Christ himself has ordained?*"

No one has authority, replies doctor Galle, to alter the sacrament in what Christ himself has ordained, that is to say, the nature itself of the sacrament, the wine of the vineyard, and the bread of wheat, and words of consecration over the bread and wine. Other things, such as the quality of the bread, the mixing of wine with water, the gestures and dress of the priest, and the like, the church regulates, because she has a tradition of them through the Holy Ghost, from the apostles and their successors.

With Galle, master Olof also denies that the institution of Christ can by any man be changed. But when Christ has ordained in this sacrament, that we should eat his body and drink his blood, Olof inquires how the pope and bishops can refuse laymen participation in the blood of Christ, contrary to his appointment and the church's practice, observed for many hundred years? Christ instituted not the sacrament for laymen otherwise than for clergymen. Nor has Christ ordained the sacrament as a sacrifice. He has not said, "Take and sacrifice," but "Take, eat and drink." Christ has once offered himself for sins. If we offer him anew, we crucify him anew. But if the Eucharist or Supper of the Lord is not a sacrifice, "doctor Peter may see on what ground prebendaries are instituted, and what is their use, if the mass is not a sacrifice."

The tenth question was: "*Whether any revelations, said to have been made, are to be the rule of our conduct, other than those declared in Holy Writ?*"

Doctor Galle, for the solution of this question, resorts to the writings of Dionysius the Areopagite. It is the law and providence of God, that the lowest order of intelligences, for the sake of the elect, that is to say, for God's everlasting glory, should, till the day of judgment, be drawn to the highest order, by the intermediate order, the order of angels. The lowest order of angels is under the supervision of the highest, and men under that of the angels. Thus in all God's government of His creatures, providence and order are maintained; so that Almighty God governs the lower by the higher, and thus come to pass many revelations of God's secret judgments and determinations. Men ought, therefore, to rule their conduct by them. They must, however, be shown to proceed from God and the good spirit, for the devil can transform himself into an angel of light.

Galle then alleges some proofs of these revelations. In particular, he brings forward two striking cases, which occurred through the spirit of St. Jerome, after his death. But Olof regards the narrative of these revelations, contained among the writings of Augustin, to be supposititious, and later examination, even by Roman theologians, has ratified his judgment.

In conclusion, Olof retorts, that the truth of God is so completely communicated to men in the Holy Scripture, that they need no more for salvation. To seek for further revelations is to run into the snares and wiles of the devil. It might be that some revelations were true, which were not found in Holy Scripture. But it was safer to neglect some that were true, than to be misled by the false.

The eleventh question was: "*What proof is found in Scripture for purgatory?*"

"This question," replies doctor Peter, "seeks a difficulty where none is, a knot in a rush where there is no knot. For all nations, languages and men, who have reason, confess with the holy church, that there is a purgatory." It is proved from Scripture, Mat. xii. 32; 2 Macc. xii. 44. The sin which is forgiven in the other world, is not forgiven in heaven, for in heaven there is no sin, nor in hell, for in hell there is no forgiveness—therefore in purgatory. It is still further proved from the teachings of holy men, for proof of which assertion, Gregory of Nyssa and Augustin are quoted, and it is proved from the practice of the church since the apostles' times, of which evidences are produced. The church's prayers and masses for the dead, to deliver them from pain, are a proof.

Master Olof again replies, that in Scripture nothing is taught respecting purgatory. Mat. xii. 32 is cleared by Mark iii., in which passage it appears that a distinction is not made between the sins forgiven in this life, and those forgiven in the life to come, but that is merely a phrase, to express that the sin against the Holy Ghost is never forgiven. The narrative respecting Judas Maccabæus, is not to be relied on. The book in which it is contained is not considered a part of Holy Scripture. The Scriptures seem to testify against purgatory, for, if there were a purgatory, the death of Christ has not done enough, does not suffice for all sins. But, upon the contrary, it is said in Scripture, that he who believes hath everlasting life, and is a beloved child of God; faith makes pure the heart, and in death all sinful desires are cast down. Now they have unspeakably greater torments who are in the pains of purgatory, than those who are in the world, whence it follows, that we ought to leave those who here in the world suffer grief and anguish, and day and night strive to help those who are in purgatory, "and indeed follow the mad behavior of some among us." If there were such pains after death, Christ has imperfectly taught us charity, since reckoning up so many works of charity, he omits to mention the acts and prayers by which we might alleviate to the dead the pains of purgatory.

But revelations, the opinions of teachers or doctors, and the usage of the church, Olof regards as uncertain witnesses, where the Holy Scripture does not hold out the light of its instruction.

He considers himself, however, not able, with full certainty, to deny that there is a purgatory. "Not that we positively," he says, "deny a purgatory. But this I say, that it cannot be proved from Scripture. I leave it in the hands of God. He knows best how it is with the dead. It is enough to be feared, that our own bellies and our covetousness are more concerned in defending purgatory than the charity we have to the souls that are therein. Purgatory is very profitable to us. It is a part of us."

The twelfth question was: "*Whether we are to venerate, worship or pray to the saints, and whether the saints are our defenders, protectors, patrons, mediators or proposers of terms of capitulation before God?*"

Galle finds this a subject that admits of no doubt. The church, which is directed by the Holy Ghost, into which Christ, who is its head, daily infuses his grace, keeps the festivals of saints, so that she may praise God in his saints. Holy men ought to be worshiped, though not with the worship that belongs to Christ, his holy cross, crown, thorns, and whatever else is peculiar to him; nor yet to be worshiped as if they had the power to create or give God's grace, but because they have the grace of God, and the peace of the kingdom of heaven, and are our helpers and mediators before God. God can indeed hear and grant our prayers without them. But if he heard the prayer of one who prayed, for the sake of Abraham, Isaac, and Jacob, who were then in limbo, much more does he hear the prayers for us of those who are now in everlasting joy.

Master Olof admits, that, although the Holy Scriptures do not command us to worship saints, neither do they forbid us, provided there is no such honor given as that which belongs to God alone, and that we may praise and bless God in all his creatures, so even in his saints, that is in all Christian men living and dead. We praise God in his saints, when we thank and honor God for the grace and mercy he has showed in his saints. But that the saints are mediators between God and us, is contrary to the Scriptures, which teach that Christ alone is our mediator. It can well be, that they pray for us, but this we know not, and we need not know, for in that case it would have been written.

That Galle should esteem the cross, crown and thorns of Christ worthy of higher honor than the saints, Olof thinks to be an indiscretion. "Shall a beam of wood and a piece of iron be worthy of more honor than the highly favored virgin Mary, mother of God, and the other saints of God?"

We have been somewhat prolix in the examination of these questions, and the different answers given to them. But the questions themselves show more clearly than anything else, the nature of the contest, and how the armed champions of the different views stood toward each other in that decisive hour. Protestantism undeniably had, apart from the strength of truth, the more skillful advocate on its side. Galle comes forward with a want of elasticity, and with lukewarmness, the consequence of his reluctance for the controversy, probably, too, of his age, but certainly also in many of the questions, as in the fifth, of his own doubts. He seems to have wavered, not willing openly to betray his cause, but too honest to speak with vigor against his conviction. He threw forward the naked points of defence, that they might pass for what they could.

But the papacy had at this time, if we deduct the men of mediocrity, who when great principles are at stake do more harm than good, only a small number of defenders, and they illy weaponed. The waxing fury of the onset called forth by degrees a stronger, and for the times more adequate defence. But it was fifteen years later, before the Roman church could attempt to recover what it now soon lost in Sweden.

On the other hand, the men of the new times already showed very well what they wanted, and took their measures with acuteness and as men under a deep conviction. The king was won to the principles of church reform. It was now a subject of interest, to try whether the constitution of the Swedish church and kingdom could be altered to a nearer conformity with these principles. Upon this trial king Gustavus was willing to hazard the crown he held in his hand. It could not indeed be seated on his head, before the change was happily accomplished, which it was seen involved the possibility of maintaining it there.

BOOK II.

CHAPTER I.

THE DIET OE WESTERAS IN 1527—THE TREATY AND ORDINANCES OF WESTERAS.

THE summons which king Gustavus issued to the estates of the kingdom, to meet him at Soderkoping in the beginning of the month of June, 1527, foreboded important and vexatious deliberations. The king declared himself in doubt, if he could longer be able to retain the administration of a kingdom overwhelmed with such disorders. In conformity to his previously announced determination, the disturbances within the church should be examined into. The bishops were charged to bring along with them two or three or more of the most learned men of the chapter, in order that agreement might be made upon the differences respecting faith which had arisen here as elsewhere, and which if not harmoniously settled might bring danger and ruin to the kingdom. Besides the nobles, bishops, and canons, were summoned a burgomaster and member of council from every market town, and six of the principal men from every district. The assembly had the character of a council both of the kingdom and of the church. Parish priests were not summoned.

The summons to the diet was issued in Eastertide, 1527. About fourteen days later the king was induced, by the disturbances among the Dalesmen, to remove the place of meeting to Westeras, and the opening of the diet was put off from Whitsuntide to the 16th of June, being Trinity Sunday. As present at the diet, are reckoned 129 nobles, or persons exempt from taxes; 32 representatives of market towns, among whom, however, were not found deputies from Stockholm (though named in the proceedings), Kalmar, Upsala and other towns; 105 farmers; 14 mountaineers or miners. The church was represented by the bishops Hans Brask of Linkoping, and Petrus Magni of Westeras, the bishops elect, Magnus Haraldi of Skara, and Magnus Sommar of Strängness, two chapter men, doctor Peter Galle and master Henrick Sledorm, as representing the church of Upsala, two as representing the bishop aud chapter of Wexio, and the chapters of some other bishops, then present. The dioceses of Abo and Finland had no representatives, although they were summoned.

It may well be imagined with what strained emotions the men who belonged to the different parties in the church would there meet. For the Romishly disposed the prospects were threatening. Round about the land no help was to be accounted of. The grand duke of Russia, the natural foe of the papal church, could not become its supporter. The question of war or peace with this neighbor was to be a subject of discussion at the diet. Denmark and Norway were in the hand of king Frederick, inclined to Lutheranism. If he had not yet taken any open steps to a change within the church, yet were the duchies of Sleswig and Holstein already reformed, and the doctrines of Luther daily gained strength in Denmark, while the city of Malino in Scania, had declared itself for them. In the north of Germany, the powerful electorate of Saxony was reformed according to the Lutheran tenets. The landgrave of Hesse held in October, 1526, a church council, in which was to be a disputation on articles of faith, but the champions of the papal faith declined to appear when they learned the con-

9

ditions, that no other proofs were to be offered than those from the Holy Scriptures. The grand master of the German order of knighthood, the Teutonic, had revolted, changed East Prussia, which belonged to the order, into a hereditary dukedom, and married the daughter of Frederick, king of Denmark. Above all moved onward the doctrine of Luther, and in many cases, nothing but the strong arm of temporal power prevented an open declaration.

The foremost and mightiest of the princes of Europe, the emperor Charles V., was the declared foe of the head of the Western church, the pope, and in open war with him. Of this prince no active aid could be expected. At the time the diet of Westeras was opened, tidings must have reached Sweden that Rome was conquered, and the pope in prison, and how the army which, sword in hand, entered the city regarded as the capital of Christendom, had mockingly in its license proclaimed Luther pope. How the Cæsar designed to deal with the affairs of the church, could not with certainty be foreseen. The breach between the emperor and pope was so sudden and unexpected, that it might be predicted, at a time which defied all ecclesiastical authority, that a reconciliation could not be effected without some detriment to the existing church.

What thoughts the condition of things in Sweden must have given the friends of Rome, has been sufficiently shown in the foregoing book.

But those favorably disposed to Lutheranism, had not any sure expectations of quitting the struggle with the laurels of victory. The dissatisfaction of the Dalecarlians, resulting from the king's attempt at Upsala, in the spring of 1526, to win over the peasantry of Upland, and the influence among the nobles and in Gothland of the men attached to the papacy, such as the bishop of Linkoping, the bishop elect of Skara, the administrator Thure Jonsson and others, might give strength to the principles opposed to the Refor mation, and turn the decrees of the diet in a direction inimical to the supposed heresy, and favorable to its suppression. On the proceedings of this day, depended, not only the fate, the culmination of the star of the new teaching, but the liberty and life of its proclaimers.

The result was uncertain, but of inconceivable importance; of more importance indeed, than most of those who were members of that assembly were aware. It was for our fatherland one of those moments, in which the judgment of God determines the future of centuries in the destinies of a people. The question was not merely of outward independence and welfare, but of spiritual freedom, and of the direction in which the popular mind should be trained, not merely for the present age, but for successive generations.

Some days after the coming together of the estates, king Gustavus showed his determination to lower the importance of the bishops. At an entertainment, which, on the 20th of June, he gave to the deputies of the people, he caused the civil members of the council, and the principal temporal nobles, to take, at the repast, the highest places. These had previously, both at the council table and in society, always belonged to the bishops, even in preference to the administrators, when the kingdom was governed by such. Now, the seats next to the nobles of the second class were assigned to them and the canons.

This omen warned the prelates to prepare themselves for the measures to be pursued, in respect to the project, which, in the deliberations of the diet, was to be brought forward. They assembled the following day, in the church of St. Ægidius, with closed doors. The question arose, what course they were to pursue, should the king and estates purpose to abridge their power and wealth. The bishop of Westeras, Petrus Magni, and Magnus Sommar, bishop elect of Strängness, declared themselves in this respect to be as poor or as rich as the king would have them; they had little to collect, and therefore little to give up. Bishop Brask of Linkoping, who did not flinch from his confidence in the establishment of the old order, and its returning victory, answered them with passion, that they were madmen if they so acted. If the king by violence would take anything, he must, but by their yea and good will he ought to get nothing. Thus only could they answer for it to the pope. Many kings and princes had formerly undertaken what Gustavus now wished to do, but they had been branded with the thunderclaps of the holy fathers, which are interdict and excommunication, so that churchmen got their own again. But were they to fall away from the pope, who was their ultimate refuge, life, anchor, and protection, they would have fire and stripes on all sides, excommunication from Rome, and little better than slavery here at home.

The irresolute were drawn over to the opinions of the more firm, and men paused at a measure which had too much resemblance to bishop Brask's course in the case of archbishop Trolle, at the diet of Stockholm in 1517, for them not to be aware of his schemes. Those present offered protests against any decree which could import violence or wrong to the church, revolt from the pope, or favor to the Lutheran heresy. These protests were found, fifteen years after, in the cathedral of Westeras.

Had Brask been equally rigid and strong in open and unreserved opposition to every reduction of what he called the freedom or privileges of the church, as he was in his belief of the final victory of the papal cause, the Reformation in Sweden would probably have required severer struggles and the victory been dearer bought.

The estates were assembled for the deliberations of the diet in the great hall or dining-room of the Dominican convent. The king's chancellor, the archdeacon Laurentius Andreæ, read the king's address to the estates. In this, mention was made of the government of the kingdom and its difficulties, and of the unjust accusations against the king, among which were enumerated those that related to the church and faith.

These accusations were: 1. That the monasteries were used as quarters for the troops. The necessities of the kingdom were the occasion of this act. When God should give the kingdom security and peace, the king would not impose this burden.

2. That the king plunders churches and monasteries. The aid derived from this source, was applied to the ease of the people, by advice and consent of the council of the kingdom. This was not unreasonable, since this wealth belonged to the people, who jointly bestowed it.

3. That the king pulls down churches and monasteries. This was not true. Agreeably to the request of the citizens of Stockholm, he had not allowed the churches in the suburbs of that city to be thrown down, although they interfered with the siege of that place. The monastery of Gripsholm was the king's inheritance and property, had been built against his father's consent, and certainly had not been a monastery, if Sten Sture had had children of his own.

4. That the king introduces a new faith into the land. The king was falsely accused of this "by the heads of the church and their dependants." The king had, with many learned men, both within and without the land, become convinced that the crown, nobles, and people, were in many ways cheated and oppressed by the men of the church, who raised themselves to be masters, humiliated the princes, nobles and people of the country, and by their own self-devised forms of worship, by mortgages, sales and other contrivances, heaped up riches, so that the crown and nobles had scarce a third part of what the priests, monks, churches, and cloisters, had. What was said of meat being eaten on

Friday, of the contempt of the Virgin Mary and the like, was a mere and manifest lie. They had, as all were aware, in times past provoked the lords and princes of the land, and some of them were now minded to do the same.

The king would confess that he allowed the pure word of God and the gospel to be preached, as our Lord himself had commanded. He had offered that the preachers should argue the truth of their doctrines, but the prelates of the church had refused, saying they would abide by the old customs, right or wrong. He had now some of these preachers present, and wished their doctrines to be examined in presence of all, that the party which had right on its side might receive the support of all, and all such dissensions be done away.

5. That the king wished to have no priests in the land. This was an infamous lie. The king desired to die as a Christian man, and was well aware that this could not be without teachers and priests of the chnrch, to proclaim the word of God. These he would support because they were worthy of it, provided they fully performed their work. But, of the others who did not preach and did no service, the king wished to hear the advice of the estates how to deal with them, "as in Scripture it is not found that there is any need of such."

The evils which the king reported, and of which he demanded redress from the estates, were comprehended in the answers to them under the four following heads:

1. The usually disturbed state of the kingdom, from the many insurrections and plots.

2. That the income of the crown was so impaired, that the dignity belonging to royalty could not be maintained.

3. That the nobles were reduced, and always obliged to beg help from the crown, because the greater part of their wealth was swallowed up by churches, monasteries, prebends and the like.

4. That the king was accused of introducing a new faith into the land.

With the report of these abuses, the king put forward a project for their redress. The superfluous wealth of the church should be restored to the crown, nobles and people; the bishops should give up their castles; appeals to Rome should be forbidden; confirmation of the episcopal office should not be purchased from there, with other like methods of redress.

After the reading of the king's exposition, he turned himself, according to the order he lately established, first to Thure Jonsson, as the foremost of the nobles, in order to learn, through his voice, the opinions of the nobles respecting the proposed project. But the high steward begged the king to allow them some time for reflection, and left directions with bishop Brask, who now declared, that they who were of the ecclesiastical estate had promised and sworn to the most holy father, that without his consent and good will they would undertake nothing in regard to doctrine or any other spiritual matters. They acknowledged themselves to owe obedience and bounden duty to the king, so far as was not inconsistent with the decrees which the pope or a general council prescribed to them. But of the property of holy church they could give up nothing. The extortions and superstitions which bad priests or monks, with commendation or leave of their superiors, continued, must be put down, and those be punished who practised them.

The king turned to the council and nobles, and asked them if they esteemed this to be a proper answer. Thure Jonsson and his allies replied, that they could not but agree with the bishop's opinion, though he had not made a full answer to all the articles. Then Gustavus declared, that he could no longer be their king. He was blamed for every act of necessity. He must redress, and bear all the grievances of the kingdom, while it was designed to put over him monks and priests, and all sorts of creatures of the pope. On such conditions would not the worst spirit in hell be willing to be their king, and still less any man. They might take into consideration to redeem his personal estate, and reimburse him what from his own means he had spent for the kingdom. Hereafter he should abandon his fatherland. Upon this, tears burst from the eyes of the king, and he left the assembly.

After his departure, the chancellor invited the estates to consider what counsel they would adopt, whether to close with the terms of Gustavus, or seek another head. But no one ventured to utter his thoughts aloud. After a whispering parley, the timorous and fearful were in doubt what to do, and were divided in opinion; but Thure Jonsson who on going home struck a stroke on his drum, murmuring said, at the same time acknowledging the importance of this day's work for fatherland, that come what would, no one should make him a pagan or heretic for that year.

When they came together the next day, there reigned in the assembly perplexity and a Babylonish confusion. The people first cried out, that the council and nobles must soon come to a determination, and already began to declare, that when right and equity were taken into account king Gustavus had done nothing amiss; that if the council of the kingdom did not soon provide a remedy they would do so themselves, though, perhaps, not to the satisfaction of all. Still Brask and Thure Jonsson did not give up all for lost. The chancellor, Laurentius Andreæ, wished to speak, but being king Gustavus's man, was silenced by Thure Jonsson.

Then stood up the bishop elect of Strängness, Magnus Sommar, from whose sentiments and words both the parties were in hope of stay and support. He was in favor of the Roman church, yet without approving its abuses and worldly pomp.

The bishop made signs for silence, begged leave of high

and low that he might speak, and that they would vouchsafe to hear him patiently. They were, he said, in the utmost danger. He besought them, by the death of our Lord, to reflect upon what would be best. Children and old men might alike perceive, what would come of abandoning king Gustavus, and crowning a new king. He thanked Thure Jonsson for his good intent to protect churchmen, but feared that they might thence receive more harm than good. Rather than be so protected, as to bring ruin on the kingdom, they would bide their time as they could. The kingdom was beginning now to recover itself. If they lost the head they now had, its enemies would not long leave it in peace.

These expressions found an echo in many hearts, although, as is not unusual in moments of agitation, the most part did not venture first to utter them. Now, many of the nobility rose, many of the other estates thanked the bishop for his speech, and declared themselves openly for king Gustavus. It was now remembered, that the differences with the king were occasioned by matters of faith, and that the king demanded a reformation of the church. The awakening spirit reminded them of the king's offer, to let the proclaimers of the faith, pretended by its opposers to be new, stand forth to answer for their doctrines. Olaus Petri, who followed king Gustavus to Westeras, was called forward, and in opposition to him, his old adversary, the representative of Upsala at the diet, Peter Galle. They were each true to their principles, in the choice of the language in which they wished to carry on the controversy. Olaus, who desired to appeal to the sense and judgment of the people, spoke in Swedish. Peter, as advocate for a church which forbade laymen to meddle with controversies of faith, made use of the Latin tongue. After speaking an hour, he was obliged to yield to the clamor for him to speak in Swedish. The disputation lasted long, and closed the meeting for that day.

On the third day, the burgers and farmers began, with murmurs and grumbling, to require the council to put an end to the confusion. Many of the nobles, among them Maus Bynteson, who previously adhered to Thure Jonsson, desired a reconciliation with king Gustavus. At last, Thure Jonsson himself gave way and joined them, but with the declaration, that the king would never be able to win or force him into Lutheranism. After the estates had agreed to comply with the king's demands, Laurentius Andreæ and Olaus Petri, who, during these days, were spending a cheerful life in the castle of Westeras, were sent to him to solicit him to resume the government of the kingdom. After many refusals and renewed entreaties, he promised at length to present himself, the day following, before the assembled diet.

On the following day, therefore, June 24, 1527, the conclusion was arrived at, which at once altered the condition of the Swedish church. This conclusion, in part, fixed the relations of the church to the civil community and the royal authority, and in part related to the arrangements within the church. The former, which constituted the decrees peculiarly proper to the diet, were called the Treaty of Westeras, the latter the Ordinantia of Westeras. Their importance demands that we devote to them a closer examination.

1.—TREATY OF WESTERAS.

To the exposition of the king, distinct and separate replies were given by the nobles, with and without consultation together, by the market towns and boroughs, and by the farmers. The council of the diet or senators issued out a common determination with the diet.

This takes up, in the order given above, the defects and abuses which the king alleged to be found, and the means for their redress.

1. "To remedy the first abuse," license, insurrections and plots, all promised, on their word and honor, to punish those who were the cause of such rumors, troubles, and ruin, and that they themselves would be true to the king.

2. In regard to the insufficiency of the income of the crown, it was determinined that, whereas the rents which the bishops, cathedrals, canons, and cloisters, had, came from the inhabitants of the kingdom, and from grant of those who were then masters of them, the income of the crown should be again augmented from those rents.

For diminishing the incomes of the bishops, there was also assigned the reason, that the church thereby became a worldly power, or, as it said, the bishops were for the time being too mighty, so that they often set themselves up against the lords of the land, brought loss to the kingdom, and deprived many good men of life and goods, as happened in the time of archbishop Trolle and many times before his day. The estates therefore agreed for themselves and their successors, in order that the kingdom might henceforth be out of danger, to the two following prudential measures, which together might be the means of strengthening the crown:

(*a.*) The bishops should thereafter not ride with more men than the king permitted, and what accrued by this deduction in their collection of taxes should be applied to augment the incomes of the crown. This might be managed by their compounding with the king for a certain sum of ready money, which they must pay down to the crown.

(*b.*) The bishops should assign over to the king the castles and fastnesses which they possessed.

On the former point it may, by way of illustration, be remarked, that, by a law of the land, in the chapter concerning the king, "the archbishop might ride over the king's land with forty horses, a suffragan bishop with thirty, but not more." In this respect, the then existing law had given the bishops a prescriptive privilege; but the ordinance now passed was an unlimited right in the king, to restrain this privilege of the bishops as he might find necessary for the income of the crown and compatible with the security of the kingdom.

The pomp of the bishops was a burden to the land at the time of their visitations, during which the parish priests were to provide sustenance, and when a church was to be consecrated the parishioners were obliged to pay a tax. The excesses of the bishops in this respect induced the council of Arboga, in 1423, to put a stop to their ostentation, of which John Magnus had lately exhibited a proof. King Gustavus also often called the attention of the clergy and people to the relief they experienced from the reduction of the number of attendants on the bishops at their visitations.

Whether there should be such a thorough-going change, as that the office of bishop should be abolished, and the ancient constitution of the church founded upon it should be shaken, there was not one to propose as a question of debate. To account for this we may suppose there was a disposition on the one hand, in carrying through a change within the church, to avoid the necessity to which the German Reformation was reduced, of doing without bishops, whereby the church's government, both theoretically and practically, was placed in the power of princes, and on the other hand, to avoid the theory of the presbyterian form of government, which the Swiss Reformation adopted. This disposition and proclivity were a peculiarity, through which the Swedish church took from the beginning a principle of development, removed alike from the sacrifice of that independence, which followed upon the advance of Lutheranism in Germany, where Luther soon began to ordain priests, and from the too hostile attitude to the civil community and power which the Calvinistic reformed church, like the papistic, assumed.

The reformers of Germany did not at first contemplate the rise of occurrences, which should compel the church to do without the episcopal constitution. The reformers of the Swedish church thought of nothing less than of placing the constitution of the church on new foundations. The conservation of the episcopal office was presupposed. Laurentius Petri declares, in the explanation he wrote of the treaty of Westeras, probably not long after the treaty was made: "The office of a bishop is of necessity as well as that of king, though the former can be exercised at less expense than the latter, for the office of a bishop is carried on by the word of God, not by force. * * * Therefore as both these offices ought to be maintained by the people, something is taken from that which is abundantly provided, and transferred to that which is less so, and thus both are provided for, and each takes care of his own office."

When the estates of the kingdom, in 1527, exercised their right of settling the incomes of the episcopal office, in a letter of the council of the kingdom to the inhabitants of the land, dated June 24, 1527, it was added, that none should pervert the meaning of their order for money to be had from the bishops, as it was their intention to maintain and support that office. "We truly desire," says the letter, "that there should be bishops, but not so powerful as to endanger the kingdom. Their riches ought to be diminished when they have illy acquired them, some by extortion and self-advised modes of worship, which God has never commanded, some by their craft and evil devices."

With respect to the castles and fastnesses of the bishops, it is simply said in the decrees, that they must be delivered up to the king, but in the letter of the council it is added, that the king may take them, till the castles of the crown be rebuilt, the reason being given that the castles of the crown were partly decayed, partly in ruins. The opinion of the nobles agrees with the letter of the council. The burghers, and men of the market towns, propose that the bishops should relinquish their fortified castles to the king, till those of the crown be rebuilt. The farmers express themselves to the effect of relinquishing the castles as a loan to the crown: "they agree that the king may take them as a loan, and use them till the kingdom can come to a better condition, and the people, who are so exhausted, recover themselves again."

It appears as if it were not seen that there was a necessity for the security of the kingdom against a too powerful hierarchy, to take from the bishops their castles and fortifications. But, at the diet of Strängness, in 1529, king Gustavus declares, that their transfer to the king was necessary, because they were often a protection for rebels, adding, however, that they must be in possession of the crown at least till its own were rebuilt. Laurentius Petri gives the same reason, and any restitution of them was never afterward proposed, probably because a strict inquiry would have had a similar result.

The rents of the cathedrals and canons were, according to the treaty, to be dealt with in the same manner as those of the bishops. "When it was deliberated, what was required for their support, it was concluded that the king might help himself to what was superflous in their rents."

This conclusion was in expression conformable to the answer of the nobles. The citizens and men from the hills, declared on the whole of this question, merely in general terms, that in regard to the rents of the crown and nobles, as the churches and cloisters had lowered, so they must augment them. The farmers still more avoided a decided answer. They said that they left the question of improving the incomes of the crown to the king and council, and were willing to acquiesce in what those should determine.

Of the canons, Laurentius Petri, in his exposition of the

treaty, expressed himself in correspondence with the general views in matters relating to the king. The office was not so necessary as that of the bishops. It was instituted to strengthen the bishop in his office, and for the purpose of superintending with him the affairs of the diocese. The office of a bishop rests on the word of God; canons are only useful as they are learned and experienced in the Scriptures. There was no need of so many as formerly. They should give attention chiefly to the word of God, and not so much to the administration of justice, trials and jurisdiction. Canons were designed merely for masses, celebrations, and the like, and arose from man's device and not from God's word.

In regard to the rents of the cloisters, it was decided, that as, in the cloisters supported by rents, there had been for a long time a feeble regimen, because they had weak administrators, and as the buildings were decayed and the property wasted, the king be, therefore, empowered to place over each of them a knight, who should allow their tenants an honest support, and keep the cloister in repair. Out of the surplus rents, he was to do service to the king, in the manner his majesty saw fit. The bishops should neither, by quartering on them nor by fines, burden the tenantry of the cloisters, nor themselves meddle with them. When the consecration of one of these monasteries took place, the bishops were not to come there with a larger train than was allowed to men of their order.

This decree is, like the former, in full agreement with the opinion of the nobles, in which, however, nothing is mentioned of the decay of the cloisters and the weak administrators. The train of the bishops on their visits to monasteries, it was proposed by the nobles, should be limited to six or eight persons. The nobles also propose, that the prebends of cloisters should be treated like other prebends, and hospitals in like manners provided the sick were there maintained, "especially those who were injured in defence of the kingdom." *

The farmers passed their resolution that the cloisters should keep open house, but on condition that good men were sent there, "who should conduct themselves without noise or roguery, enjoy what these poor men had to give them, do no violence to those living about the convent, and in no manner interrupt divine service there."

The king's declaration on the treaty, at the diet of Sträng-ness, in 1529, furnishes a further reason for the arrangement now effected, and for the disesteem into which the rent-cloisters had fallen. The cloisters, he says, were so decayed, that where formerly there were forty or fifty brothers, there were now but four or six, while the rents were as large as ever. This was the occasion of a libidinous life, and justified for the public good, a watch over the surplus rents.

The measures adopted for transferring the convents to the uses above mentioned, or at least the surplus of the rents to the king, would naturally be followed by their complete decadence. Laurentius Petri also remarks in his explanation, that in this matter there was the less difficulty, because the existence of the conventual system was built on a sandy foundation, and could well be dispensed with by all.

3. To redress the third abuse, the poverty of the nobility, it was agreed that the king and nobility might appropriate all the chattels given, sold, or mortgaged to the churches, monasteries, and prebends, after the time king Charles Canuteson inventoried the same; provided that the goods bought or in mortgage, might be redeemed according to the longer or shorter time that had elapsed. No one should take his own, till he had proved his claim before twelve men, in the presence of witnesses. The lands on which rents had been paid, should be returned to the legal claimants, how long

* This is probably the first essay in Sweden toward the establishment of a house for invalids.

soever in pledge, with the exception, in Norland, of so much of the land as was necessary to the decent support of a priest.

The decree was in conformity with the expressed sentiments of the nobles, except a stronger requirement respecting the lands that were to be redeemed, and some slight variations respecting the lands in Norland.

The ecclesiastical law book from which we quote, because though specially meant for Upland, it was generally adopted, provides, (chap 2), that the glebe on which the parsonage shall be built, shall consist of a mark of land for the church of a district, and half a mark for every twelfth church. The glebe shall be free from taxes. The farmers are to pay tax for the church land. If the church requires more land, it shall pay full taxes, unless the king gave it as land free from tax.

In respect to the support for the table of the priest, the meaning of the treaty was obscure and defective. Laurentius Petri, in his explanation, gives a determinate sense which is not there found, but yet appears to have been practically followed. When the treaty allows the restoration of property from the church and prebends, master Lars would have it understood of the establishments which have no foundation in Scripture. But it was not the meaning of the treaty, that the goods should be taken again, which were given for maintenance in hospitals and the like; for in the word of God it is required of us, "to help the poor as well as help parish priests." Nor was it the meaning of the treaty, that the support of their table should be taken from the priests. An exception was made in Norland, because it was known that the support there was derived from lands that paid rent. It would be well for the practice in Norland to be extended over the whole land. But still less did the treaty design, that the lands not subject to rent should be restored. The final reason for his explanation, Lars finds in the common maxim, that in this, as in all laws, we are to look to the intention of the law, and when that is known we are to interpret the words accordingly.

The whole decree, which in this third point was ratified by the treaty of Westeras, relative to the Swedish church, and which was alike made applicable in all lands where the Reformation prevailed, called forth here from the popish party accusations of a breach of faith, since it violated the sanctity of the will of the dead. The popish church, therefore, preserves her claim to restitution. She must have this claim if she will not allow that unrighteous possessions are in the control of the community or their representatives. The claim cannot be made good, where the changes of centuries make it impossible to find the property in the hands of those amenable to restoration. So rest the claims.

Protestantism defends the decree, and justifies it on two grounds. The first reason for a change in the property of the church rests on the principles of Christianity itself. Those testamentary grants which conveyed property to the church, were in a great degree based on error and superstition. The intention and purpose were at war with the truths of Christianity. The church, which did not allow of masses for the souls of the dead, because these masses were a noxious superstition, and which did not recognize the value of alms for the alleviation of the pains of purgatory, and which did not recognize gifts to ecclesiastical establishments to be absolutely a good work, could not allow to stand within her borders, in full strength, a constitution or state of things which had a superstitious or delusive foundation. Even without regard to the right or the wrong, it was unavoidable, that when the order of things to which these establishments appertained, ceased to exist, there should be no longer place for them.

But who was the lawful heir to the property which could

no longer be applied to the purposes for which it was given?

The only valid course to be pursued was, that the gift, or thing sold or pledged, in the two latter cases according to an equitable redemption, should go back to the giver or seller, to be left to their free disposal. These, or the proprietors of their rights, according to the communal law of inheritance, acquired the right of birth or redemption, which right again, according to the same law, where there was no legal heir, fell to the community of the borough. The inheritance became lapsed.

In the last named case, another view of the subject presents itself. The gifts were bestowed with a pious design, for pious purposes. This purpose could, in the manner the givers immediately designed, be no longer obtained. But it was possible to employ the gifts, in the spiritual changes of the times, in a manner most nearly corresponding to the intention of the givers. We therefore find, both within and without our fatherland, the wealth bestowed on a vanishing faith, transferred, either by resignation to the community, or by the course of events, to the church which conquered that faith. So, in the empire of Rome, the Christian church received the patrimony of paganism.

For recalling its property from the church, there was still another reason, on the part of the state. The community, with respect to the basis on which it seemed to rest, had lost its stability. The excess of the church's wealth occasioned a correspondent weakness in the crown and nobility. These gifts were not legal if they weakened the basis of society; the state must possess the right of enforcing the sanctity of the condition of its own stability; the church must submit to that change in the possession and use of its wealth, which restored the lost equilibrium. During the two previous centuries, but especially after the bishops obtained worldly power which induced them, either for a cause, or from party passion, to oppose the king, and exercised this power, as did John Bengtsson Oxenstjerna and Ketil Vase, a change had been urged and kept in view throughout Sweden. The diet of Westeras carried into execution what, nearly eighty years before, king Charles VIII. desired, and in 1453 and 1454, attempted to carry through.

When the treaty of Westeras only declared, that the pure word of God might be preached in the land, but did not decide which of the contending parties was right—when it only pre-supposed that the church had, or claimed for itself, the truth—it did not commit itself by a transfer of the church's property to the upholding or promotion of superstition and error. It treated of and decided only the question of the inevitable necessity there was for putting the state and civil condition of the country in order. But certainly the decree silently implied the supposition, that this wealth was for the church dispensable, only so, however, that she became poorer, not so that the objects of its establishments and appointments should wholly disappear.

The restitution to the heir, of property exempt from taxes, was limited to the period after the inquisition of king Charles VIII. Whatever was from that period given to religious establishments, was considered within the memory of man, and the heir could reclaim it if the givers them selves were not living. But the older establishments were to remain undisturbed, and there was the strong reason for not taking from the church what it was allowed to retain under the former inquisition, that other principles were not professed than those prevalent in king Charles' time.

But the taxable land was also another point for consideration, the church claiming exemption from taxes for all its property. The giving away of such lands was an embezzlement of the rights of the crown and people. The individual giver, when giving the property to the church, withdrew it from taxes to the crown, and thereby laid a great burden on his fellow-citizens. On the contrary, from the necessary equipments for war, the lands exempt from taxes were not excused, and this was, besides, a personal service.

The treaty of Westeras, places the decree solely upon the ground of the necessities of the state. Laurentius Petri, also, in his explanation, takes the view, that if there were no outwardly constraining motive, the property ought to be left with the church, but be more fitly employed. There being no demands made on the property of the nobility, was occasioned by the conviction of their poverty. Had this not been the case, it would have been necessary to consider how best to deal with this property. The gifts to the church were doubtless made with a good intention; givers purposed to serve God and his good pleasure, although they did not properly understand what the pleasure of God is. In the measure adopted, the good intention was carried into effect, not indeed in the manner thought of by the givers, but according to the word of God now better understood.

4. With respect to the accusation against the king, of introducing a new faith into the land, both parties had, in compliance with the wish of the estates, disputed in their presence. And as the estates learned neither from the disputation nor from the preachers who were considered proclaimers of the new faith, anything else than that the latter had good reasons, and taught nothing but God's word, the estates engaged, that each, in his place, would seek to quiet the clamor raised in this respect against the king, and would assist in punishing those who caused it. "*And they prayed all, that God's word might everywhere in the kingdom be purely preached.*"

The several opinions of the estates as given, were: of the nobles, that as the king offered that the preachers of the new faith should stand forth to answer for their doctrine, it was to be observed, if their adversaries would not or could not convict them of error, that they had not reason on their side who spread the report of a new faith being introduced. Wherefore, each of the nobles pledged himself to quiet this rumor, and desired " the pure word of God to be preached everywhere according to God's command, and not doubtful tales, human devices, and fables, as hitherto had been too much the case, and that the good old Christian customs should be countenanced." The men of the market towns and of the hills, said this subject of the new faith was beyond their understanding; but they wished to know in what lay the difference, which party had the right, and had willingly listened to a disputation thereof, and desired that what is right might be preached. The farmers or peasants acknowledged that many idle reports had been spread among them respecting the new faith or learning as it was called, but as it surpassed their small understanding they referred the case to those good men who are highly learned and well experienced in the Scriptures, bishops, prelates, and others, to critically investigate what was right or wrong. At the same time they would earnestly beg of the king to allow those whom this matter most concerned, to meet in their presence, that they might be properly instructed in what was right and Christian.

These answers of the respective estates do not make mention of the disputation which had already taken place between doctor Peter and master Olof. The decree in common, both speaks of its having already taken place, and " consents," that the king should let it take place. It seems from this, as if there had been another conference on the subject of the faith, although it is not mentioned by the chroniclers. This is the more probable, as that previous conference and disputation acquired, in all likelihood, during the confusions of the time, less importance, and was less remarkable.

The decree of the diet on this fourth point, was a recognition of the truth of the evangelical doctrines, and a requirement that they should be promulgated over the whole kingdom. But it was an eminent characteristic of the Reformation of the Swedish church, that it did not place the new and old order of things in sharp collision with each other. The name *Lutheran*, which in Denmark, at the diet of Odense, was as freely used as that of catholic, was for a long time not employed in the public transactions in Sweden. The change effected, never lost in the minds of the Swedish people, its property and quality of a *reformation*. It was not a new faith. It was the old truth of Christianity, which came forth purified from error. Only on the part of error boasting itself to be the original Christianity, could truth be branded as a new faith. "Many bad customs," says Lars Petri, "had arisen through those who ought to have preached the word of God, and when it *again began* to be preached, it seemed to many extraordinary, and they called it a new faith."

That the pure word of God ought to be preached, was here assumed as a confessed case, and not the most inveterate adherent of the papal church could plead anything against this position of the Swedish church. But it was not declared by those adherents, that this word of God was only found in the Holy Scriptures, and that its preaching should by degrees cleanse away the corruptions which had crept into the church. The preached word was not wanting in efficiency, as long as oral tradition was nowhere in the church recognized and established as independent of the Scriptures, and of equal validity for settling the Christian faith. But this came to pass for the Roman church, when, from 1564, the decrees of the Council of Trent gave to tradition a distinct and conclusive authority. Hence, Laurentius Petri, closes his explanation of this point of the treaty, with the following weighty sentiments, his programme for the order of reform in the Swedish church: "In proportion as we experience the gospel to be preached, we experience all that follows from the preaching of the gospel. All the changes, therefore, are valid which are made in accordance with the sense and meaning of the gospel, and when it is preached the people become rightly and completely instructed."

The estates gave no obscure declaration that they regarded the preachers who were declared to be heretics by the hierarchy, to be preachers of the word of God. Who should now determine between the contending parties? This right was left to none; but the ordinantia intrusted the king with power, not to prescribe dogmas of faith, but yet so far to interfere in the direction of the church, that the hinderances might be removed out of the way which could obstruct the preaching of God's word.

2.—THE ORDINANTIA OF WESTERAS.

Many enactments, which in part were a necessary consequence of the treaty, in part were considered necessary improvements in the church, were comprised in certain decrees, which are here termed *ordinantia*. It contains twenty articles, which for more easy examination we shall consider under certain general heads. The most important are those which relate to the power intrusted to the king in the affairs of the church.

1. The king's title to an inspection of the official conduct of the bishops, and his right of nominating to ecclesiastical offices.

The first article declares: "The bishops are to make provision for the parish churches when they become vacant. But where they provide clergy who are unfit, manslayers, drinkers, or those who cannot or will not preach the word of God, the king may inquire for those who are fit, have power to drive out those who are unfit, and provide the church with those who are fit."

ART. 20. "The prelacies, canonries and prebendaries, shall not be filled, unless the king is asked, or unless by one who is satisfactory to the king."

ART. 19. "The bishop may ordain no one to be a priest but one who can preach to the people the word of God."

To comprehend this and the following enactments, we must compare them with the condition of things which previously existed in our fatherland. We limit ourselves to the most necessary points of the church law prevalent in Sweden, derived from the general canon law.

The right of bishops to appoint priests to a benefice was ancient. The bishop was, however, obliged to respect the will of the parishioners, or his who had the right of patronage to the parish church, even as the king's will, if it was the king's benefice. The bishop was also to inquire into the capacity of the presentee.

In certain cases, at least if the bishop refused to consecrate their churches, the law gave the peasants the right to complain of the bishop to the king. But the oversight now conferred on the king left the emendation of the church in the king's hand, as it was not settled what was to be understood by the preaching of the word of God. For nominations to the episcopal office there was no responsibility, but the king could immediately exercise his power and reject the man opposed to the views of the king. The king could not remove a priest from his office, but, as all promotion in the priesthood depended entirely upon him, there was a restraint thus laid upon ordination of priests by bishops.

The high species of episcopacy thus intrusted to the king within the church, might become both dangerous and humiliating if abused. Laurentius Petri, an ecclesiastic, desired, therefore, to have it regarded as a mere temporary exigency, because the bishops at that time were not well disposed to the evangelical principles and the word of God. "But when we have true and Christian bishops there is then no need of this article, but the bishops may then have their rights as of old."

The king's right of nomination to prelacies, was in part merely a ratification of what already existed. But it was extended, at least so far that to no such office could any nomination thereafter be made without the king's knowledge and consent.

It is remarkable, that of the appointment of bishops nothing was determined. The king appears to have proposed to the estates, to put a stop to the practice of the bishops to seek confirmation to their office from Rome, and send their gifts, imposts, and purchase moneys for the purpose. The men from the hills requested, in their opinions at the time of the treaty, that this custom of bishops asking confirmation from Rome should be abolished. In the decree itself, however, there is no mention made of the subject. It appears to have been taken for granted, although it was not thought advisable explicitly to say, that all the pope's influence in the church should disappear. The old practice, therefore, was tacitly continued, although not always acted on by Gustavus, that the chapter elected, and the king confirmed the election.

2. The king's rights in respect to the property of the church. The third and fourth articles of the ordinantia, repeated the decree of the treaty respecting the rents of bishops, cathedrals, and canons. There is only the addition of the mode in which the reduction shall take place. Catalogues of all the rents from tributes, tithes, moneys, butter, iron and the like, were to be furnished the king, who was to determine how much should be retained.

3. The king's right to try or receive suits against transgressors of the church law.

An account was to be given to the king of the fines for seduction after a promise of marriage (art. 5), and for suits in marriage causes generally (art. 6). Fines for adultery and fornication were paid to the king (art. 17). The priests were to pay fines to the king like other men (art. 10).

The eighth article prescribes that as the treaty decided that the king should receive all suits and not the bishop, so the provosts should thereafter travel about and prosecute the suits which the bishops were wont to manage, and should give an account to the king of the moneys received. Of this there is no mention made in the decree signed by the estates. But in a letter of the council it is declared, "*According to the proverb, that 'a man is burdened who is under two masters,'* we agree, that they who are found guilty of a breach of the holy days and other offences, pay fines from this time to the king and not to the bishop." To the same effect is the opinion of the nobles.

The two masters, of which complaint is here made, was a natural consequence of the efforts of the Roman hierarchy to acquire temporal power. Instead of being a leaven to pervade and renew the life of the civil community, the church placed herself without or by the side of the state with her own outward legislation. As long as the temporal power was kept in subjection, as long as the community was theocratically governed in the spirit of the Old Testament, the opposition between the church and the state could not disappear. The ecclesiastics stood apart from the civil law, and laymen were, as Christians, under another law than as citizens. Thence, the highest condition was to escape from a life in the world. The priest is better, more perfect than the layman, the monk than the priest. Protestantism removes these sharp distinctions. The perfection of man is, unpolluted by the world to labor for the purification of the world, the civil community is not estranged from the aims of the church, the legislation of the church becomes that of the state, what is criminal or wrong in the one is so in the other community. There is no need of "two masters," because the law of the kingdom avenges what in the view of the church is evil.

It is here presupposed, that the citizens of the state are not divided as members of different churches. In Sweden it was not supposed possible; and the decree that the fines which it was a trouble to the bishops to impose, should be transferred to the king, was an acknowledgment of the sanctity of the state through its incorporation with the church, the former taking upon itself to watch over the moral regulations which the latter established.

The provosts obtained a commission to receive these suits; but when they had not sufficient authority to call them in, the king, a year after the change, caused the bishops to receive and account for the suits, which fell under the class of cases belonging to episcopal jurisdiction. Others were to be received by country stewards and fiefsmen, and were no longer called bishop's suits, but were classed with king's suits. So was wiped out the very memory of "two masters."

4. Diminished and prohibited suits, and other sources of income.

Fees for marriages and churching of women, burials and the like, were to be charged according to a law of the church and not above the legal sum (art. 7). Work in harvest time, and when there were shoals of fishes, or if "a man shoots a bird in the forest," was not to be accounted a breach of holy day (art. 9). If a man lie with his sweetheart, he shall not be punished for it after there has been between them a right marriage before God, and he shall not be separated from her. If he desert her, he shall be punished according to law. The custom ought to be abolished, that when a priest dies the bishop takes his goods, to the injury of the lawful heirs. Sick people shall not be constrained by the priests to make a will against their own free will.

What is here enacted respecting breach of holy days, Laurentius Petri vindicates, on the ground that even a law of the pope, who was wont to be strict, permitted work in harvest and fish seasons. The Swedish chapter of church law, before the Reformation, makes no such exception. The condition which the king previously made, that divine service was not to be neglected, is wanting in the ordinantia, but appears in the king's manifesto for direction of the country stewards and fiefsmen in the king's suits.

In respect to married persons, it may be remarked, that betrothal took place according to the law of the land, the bidding of banns and the wedding, according to the rites of the church. This point was thus an acknowledgment of the civil marriage, although certainly under requirement that the church's benediction should follow.

Of the enactment respecting the legacies of priests, king Gustavus, who anxiously guarded the rights of the crown, soon gave his own explanation. As the possessions of the priests were collected out of the rents received from the peasantry of the crown, it was fit the legacies hitherto given by the priests to the bishop should now be given to the crown. This did not become law, but probably was the view the king took in his often-occurring claim to the inheritance of rich priests.

Of the more than twenty cases in which fines were paid to the bishop, two were suppressed, in the rest of them the fines were paid to the king. But, as in many of them, the king previously received the suits, so their amount was not diminished, but mingled with the others. The chapter on church law required the dead body of one guilty of an assault to be consecrated by the priest in the house of the dead, and not in the churchyard. The king decided, that "the dead body should be held innocent."

5. Enactments respecting matters reserved for the judgment of the bishops.

Open and public confessions were put upon the same footing as heretofore. The bishop and his officers were, however, to exercise the power of excommunication with greater caution than had been done (art. 5). Of marriage cases the bishop should have the management, as knowing what true marriage is according to God's law, and whether separation ought to be allowed or not (art. 6). If any one had a complaint against a priest in a spiritual case, as that he did not truly fulfill his office, did not preach the word of God, or the like, the complaint should be laid before the bishop, and be judged by him (art. 10).

According to the king's manifesto, in 1528, the priests should be answerable, and pay a fine to the bishop, in cases which affected their office, and "for their women." This last-named case was probably placed among spiritual cases, partly because the question of the concubines of priests affected their morality, partly because the marriage of priests was either recognized by the general laws, or it was not thought advisable now to decide upon the subject.

6. The equality of priests and laymen in the eye of the law.

In temporal or civil cases, such as trespasses, affrays, assaults, breach of bargains, the priest, as well for himself as the church, should seek his remedy at assize or by legal warrant, and pay a fine to the king like any other man (art. 10). The Lord's Supper should not be refused to any one on account of debt to the priest or church (art. 16). Where a priest and layman strike each other, the one shall no more be under ban or interdict than the other, since God has forbidden the one as well as the other to strike, but each must pay a fine according to the law of the land (art. 11). The priest is not to give legacies otherwise than according to the book of laws, like other husbands (art. 13).

7. Of clerical benefices, schools, and monasteries.

Where the benefices are weak, if occasion calls for it, two may be united into one, yet so that the word of God be not hindered, still less be not preached (art. 2).

This detail of the enactments is quoted from Laurentius Petri's explanation of the ordinantia. By the junction of benefices, the parishioners were able better to maintain the church and priests. Thereby was removed the necessity for those gifts, which for that purpose must heretofore be bestowed and, if they were now recalled, yet was provision made for the support of the church and priests. The difficulty of providing the churches with evangelical preachers, might, perhaps, have contributed to the desire to lessen their number.

In respect to schools, it was prescribed, that "after this day the gospel shall there be read among other lessons, because they are, to be sure, Christian schools."

The treaty placed the wealth arising from the rents of the cloisters under management. The ordinantia (art. 12) forbids that their tenants be allowed to go out begging. The mendicant monks proper, "as in truth they are found to circulate throughout the land much deceit and lying," are placed under inspection of the king's country stewards. A monk shall be allowed, for collecting alms, no longer time than five weeks at the feast of Olof, in summer, and five weeks at Candlemas, in winter, and shall take a letter of the country steward when he goes out, and present himself to him when he returns (art. 12). The limitation of time allowed them to collect alms for the cloister, limited also the possibility of their working on the minds of the people.

After the decree was passed, which was contained in the treaty, it remained to obtain the approbation of the bishops present at Westeras. This was given on the 24th of June. After they had quoted in their declaration the king's complaint of the great and often misused power of the bishops, they add their consent in the following words: "Thus, since it is admitted and agreed by all, we cannot, and will not say to the contrary, *but let it so be, especially* that the suspicion may be removed that the bishops, by their power and their castles, would endanger the king and kingdom, and let us have peace, how rich or how poor soever his grace will have us to be."

This declaration was so conceived, that under a possible alteration of circumstances, it permitted the bishops again to resume the authority now laid down. But from this ambiguity, which, no doubt, originated in the influence of the bishop of Linkoping, we are not to conclude that the hierarchy of the Swedish church were altogether opposed to reform as far as in 1527 it had been carried. When it is considered that the bishop of Westeras, and bishop elect of Strängness, at the opening of the diet, in the very terms of this declaration, expressed themselves unwilling to oppose a reduction of the wealth of the church; that bishop Magnus Sommar was the man who, by his speech to the hesitating and discordant estates, produced unity in their decree to comply with the king's demands; that the foremost counsellor and guide of the king in these proceedings was archdeacon Laurentius Andreæ, who himself held a prelacy in the church; that the most important and influential preacher of the reformers was a canon in one of the cathedrals of the kingdom; when, in addition, there is taken into consideration the undeniable abuse many prelates made of their power, how spiritual power becomes the instrument of party strife, it will be seen how little reason there is to represent the intervention of king Gustavus as an outrage to the church, against the will of both the clergy and laity. Seldom or never has a change in the ecclesiastical or civil community won a contemporaneous, undivided approbation. Still less could the rupture in Sweden in 1527 win it. But that the king had, among both priests and laymen, a sufficiently strong support and countenance, that among both he had with him the stronger party, the annals manifest, as do the success and establishment of the cause.

The most fugitive glance at the treaty shows how great was the advantage derived to the nobles and knights from the decree. The recovery of the property exempt from taxes, and the grant of monasteries to the knights, might allure minds which were not more strongly rooted than these showed themselves to be in reverence for the church. The first overture proceeded not from the nobles, but from churchmen, and the opposition was, at the beginning of the diet, strongest among the nobles, and a bishop was the man who undertook to conquer that opposition.

Upon the altered position of the bishops followed the cessation of their dignity as members of the council. It was a necessary consequence of those views of the episcopal office which lay at the base of the treaty and ordinantia. It is also reported, though it cannot be fully proved, that they themselves desired a release from this dignity and duty, which the reduction of their incomes that now took place did not allow them to maintain. It is probable that they as willingly laid these honors down as let them be taken from them.

We will not omit to observe, what is sufficiently apparent in itself, that in the decree of Westeras regarding the incomes and wealth, the change affected the highest posts in the church, the bishops and canons. The position of the parish priests, in respect to their incomes, remained wholly untouched; the reduction did not extend to their salaries.

The diet of Westeras was a commencement whose progress could not be discerned. It was not the destruction of the old church, because its principles were not so settled, that place could not be found in it for the new order of things, notwithstanding the exception that this new order was an insurrection against the papacy. But the chains which bound the faith, life and efficiency of the western church, the friends of a reform had for some time been shaking. Many among those who were disposed to the old times, first made the observation after the council of Orebro, in 1529, that a new order of things had indeed begun.

CHAPTER II.

THE OPERATION OF THE SECOND AND THIRD POINTS OF THE TREATY OF WESTERAS.

It behooves us now to show how the decree concerning the reduction of the church's wealth was carried into execution. We shall consider the subject in the connection of its several parts, without confining ourselves to any certain time, except that the account to be made of the goods of the bishops and canons was limited to the year 1544, when a change took place to be hereafter mentioned and discussed.

As soon as the consent of the bishops present at Westeras was given to the treaty, king Gustavus immediately went to the diet to demand of them their castles. The castle of Gronso, belonging to the church of Westeras, he already had in his hands, as has been before told. That of St. Erik at Stacket, the fortress of the archbishop, was some time previous destroyed, and the departure of John Magnus had left the king in the free use of the incomes and property of the archbishopric. The king now asked Magnus Sommar for Tynnelso, subject to the church of Strängness, which castle he had once won from the Danes, but had restored. The bishop declared, without hesitation, his willingness to give up this, and all of his incomes or property that the king should desire. The king then turned to Magnus Haraldsson of Skara, of whom he asked Lecko, and of him too obtained "a most pleasing answer." Now came the turn of bishop Brask, of whom the king demanded Munkeboda. The bishop "puffed, and blowed, and stammered, and was reluctant to pledge himself." Then stood up Thure Jonsson and begged for his friend, that he might be allowed to hold the castle during his lifetime. But the king not only refused the request, but immediately required of the bishop forty armed men then present, which were to be transferred to the king's service. The bishop was allowed to retain only two followers. He was besides required to put the castle in repair, and was forbidden to leave Westeras without the king's permission, which was not given him before the king's people were able to garrison Munkeboda.

This castle, according to the treaty, was to belong to the crown. For the employment of the other property on which the king obtained the right of raising money, there appears to have been adopted a settled principle, though not publicly announced, and not strictly observed. So many cases, however, occur, that we may regard the maxim as settled, and the deviations from it as occasional exceptions. All the rents and tithes, which, as superfluous, passed, according to the treaty, and were used for the increase of the revenues of the crown, were employed for the public advantage and transferred to the customs and general system of taxation. The vacated revenues of the prebends were used for two purposes—partly for the support of those who labored in the king's chancery, partly to maintain those studying in the German universities, who aimed to perfect themselves in any branch of human knowledge. They were thus used for acquisition of a learned education, or for payment of the almost only posts in the community for which, out of the church, high acquirements were requisite, and which of old were held by churchmen, who were maintained by their prebends. The rents of the cloisters were considered as crown goods, and *were granted in fee*, according to the custom of the times, to the knights. The mendicant cloisters which were generally situated in towns, were appropriated to hospitals or transferred to some such purposes.

In conformity with the decree of the diet, the king made different agreements with each bishop, chapter or cloister. The bishops and chapters themselves received, in the usual manner, their incomes, and remitted the portion agreed on to the king. The agreements were either renewed every year, or were made for an indefinite time. This continued until the year 1544.

Some examples may be produced, how the reduction, imimmediately after 1527, was undertaken and carried into execution.

From Westeras the king retired to his newly-acquired castle of Tynnelso, where, on July 4th, 1527, it was ordered that the tenants of the bishop's residence at Strängness were, with Sela and Salabo, to be attached to the crown under Tynnelso. The other tenants, wlth their rents, obligation to lodge and board, and fines, the bishop was to retain, together with the tithes of the districts of Rekarne, Oppunda, Akers and Selbo.

The same day a copy of the treaty and ordinantia was sent to the chapter of Upsala, with an admonition to conduct itself in conformity. The incomes of the archbishopric were already administered by the king. How it was ordered with respect to the chapters and cathedrals of Upsala, Strängness and Westeras, is not known. For Abo, whose bishop elect, Erik, had obtained permission to relinquish this office and retire to the deanery of Linkoping, it was ordered, from Stockholm, July 7th, that provost Hans should, till further opportunity, manage the establishment, but John Westgote have the care of the episcopal grounds, tithes and tenants, with responsibility to the king. With bishop Brask it was settled at Wadsten, August 2d, that he should yearly give the king fifteen hundred Danish marks, one and a half tons of butter, one and a half tons of honey, and on his part receive all incomes from Norsholm and the peasants who there were day laborers.

The king then went to Skara, and there agreed, August 24th, with bishop Magnus, that he should give one thousand Danish marks, and four baskets of salmon, and on his part hold all belonging to the benefices, except Lecko and the day-laborers of Kallandso. The town of Skara also, and the fines falling due there, were to appertain as revenues to the bishop, except certain imposts. The cathedral of Skara obligated itself to a certain yearly payment.

The king returned again this year to East Gothland, and entered into an agreement at Linkoping with the chapter there. It throws light on what took place with the chapters in general.

Six prelates and canons, beside the bishop, should remain in the cathedral, with the best prebends, and keep ten priests to bear crosses, the bishop two, the provost two, the archdeacon two, the four canons each one. The chapter itself was permitted to fix terms for the non-resident canons, except doctor John, master Olof and Anders Algotsson, who were in the service of the king and kingdom. The king should have control of the prebends becoming vacant. The country priests could become canons, but without separate incomes from the cathedrals. Vacant benefices in the land should be offered and opened to the canons and prebendaries of Linkoping, until those residing in the cathedral were reduced to the number just mentioned. The cathedral and chapter were allowed to hold the goods and rents they now had, except what, according to the treaty, was legally recovered from them, and to pay jointly to the crown eight hundred Danish marks. Of that sum, there should be a correspondent reduction when the number of prebends was reduced. The money, which under the name of Roman tax, was wont to go to the papal chancery, should, instead, be paid to the crown. Of proctors, the chapter should have the appointment, on condition that useless investitures were abolished, that two chaplains were retained for morning service, and that the schoolmaster was properly maintained.

At Linkoping arrangements were made the same day for Wexio, that there should be there four canons, with the best prebends, and six cross-bearing priests, and a school. The rest should be maintained by benefices in the neighborhood falling vacant. The bishop, cathedral and chapter should jointly every year give the crown two tons of butter, which amount should be diminished in proportion as their numbers diminished. They were allowed to hold all the goods which, according to the treaty, they were not obliged to surrender. The bishop moreover should hold the town of Wexio and all its incomes, upon payment of one hundred marks Danish.

The agreements, though often renewed and altered, continued for the most part to rest on the same basis, till 1544. When the number of canons and prebends was diminished, which appears soon to have taken place—when their position in succeeding times could not be particularly agreeable, and a removal to priestly benefices in the land more advantageous—the houses belonging to their office in the towns, which fell to the crown, were either sold for their benefit or used for other purposes. As several country priests possessed prebends and canonries in Skara, the king considered them to be contented with their benefices, and in 1533, declared his pleasure to be to receive the rents of these prebends. In 1529 the king appropriated a multitude of houses in Stockholm, belonging partly to the prebends, partly to the corporation already dissolved, to the support of preaching, and of schools in Stockholm. Now, for the first time, Stockholm obtained preaching without rectors.

Beside that the king, in his journey through the kingdom, in every place entered into these agreements, he sent about certain men to every cathedral, who were to examine and take into custody the records, by which the wealth of the ecclesiastical establishment might be ascertained.

Of the rents of the monasteries, the king took immediately the management. It was not always taken as the treaty directed, to leave them in investiture with the knights, but sometimes arrangements were made with the cloisters, as with the bishops and chapters, for a certain yearly payment, or proctors were appointed, who should for the benefit of the crown give an account of the taxes and expenses. The last mentioned expedient was often adopted with nunneries. The nuns of St. Bernard in Sko, were ordered, on October 30, 1527, to apply to Laurentius Andreæ for a proctor to the cloister. Peter Svenske was, on September 1, 1527, appointed administrator of the cloister in Skeninge, because there was a profuse expenditure, as the cloister had more chaplains and took in more girls to support and instruct than was necessary. The abbess of Wadsten was required to pay three hundred Danish marks. The like agreements of a yearly payment were concluded with the abbots of Alvastra and Varnhem, and the abbesses of Wreta, Askaby and others, which monasteries afterward became investitures.

In consequence of the profuse expenditure of the means of the cloisters, the increased difficulties attending the admission of new monks and nuns, the widely spread change in principles which created a disinclination or contempt for conventual life, one cloister after another disappeared, so that for the greater portion of them the time cannot be given when the last mass was held, or the last conventual vow vanished from within their walls. The crown, which became heir general to the property not restored to particular persons, had already taken possession of it, and when, at last, nothing was left of the monks and nuns, it was a matter of small importance.

Of the monks, many became parish priests, others returned to a secular life. Of the nuns, many went forth into the world, married, or gave themselves up to a loose life, which was adduced by the papists as a reproach of the consequence attendant on the dissolution of cloisters; by the protestants, on the other hand, as proof of the little modesty and religious stability acquired in monastic life.

When the number of monks and nuns was in any place diminished, the remainder were removed from the different cloisters, to one which became the common home of those who, from age and sickness or want of friends to take care of them, would not or could not again return into the world. But few or no proofs are found that the tenants of cloisters were anywhere hunted with violence from their sanctuary. Yet it may well be imagined, that selfish fiefsmen and country stewards, either with undisguised rapacity, or under the cloak of protestant zeal, by their treatment of these forlorn objects of their care, compelled them to abandon the cloisters.

As the decree was not to abolish monasteries, but to take care of their property, the principle in effect followed, that none were to be forced to renounce the monastic vow or live from under its influence. In modern times, on the suppression of monasteries in Roman catholic countries, a certain yearly support has been assigned to each tenant of them, but with expulsion from the cloisters, which were put into possession of the state. The same took place in Sweden, in 1526, when Gripsholm was recovered by king Gustavus, but so that each monk got at once a round sum. After the diet of Westeras there appear very few instances of the like.

What tenderness was shown in the suppression alike of convents for monks and nuns, appears from the conduct of the king toward the above-named eminent cloister of Skeninge. The prioress, in the year 1529, was allowed to resume the management of a part of the property on hand, in consideration of a yearly sum. Two years after, the king saw fit that the nuns should remove to Wadsten or Wreta, and the goods were stored there. But the nuns remained in their cloister, because they were disinclined to unite themselves with another order. In 1544, the question of their removal to Wadsten was again raised. The nuns still refused to go there, and declared that they preferred the life of peasants. The king thought this unadvisable, because he feared they might spread disaffection among the people. He again offered them instead the convent of Wreta.

The cloister of Askaby was, in 1520, united to Wreta under the same abbess. The cloister to which bishop Brask, in 1516, gave property on condition of having masses, vigils and other ceremonies performed for his deceased friends, was burnt down in the year 1537, the year before the death of the exiled bishop, and was never rebuilt.

Some few cloisters that produced rents, remained beyond the times of king Gustavus. So Sko had a cloister standing in 1566, Wadsten and Nadendal, in 1595. The nuns of the latter, implored the king, in 1530, to be allowed to retain their incomes, and obtained his promise for their keeping at present the goods which appertained to the crown, but the king could not hinder the restoration of the rest contrary to the treaty of Westeras. The monastery of Wadsten, the most important establishment of the papal church, was continued, though with a languishing life. Its wealth was considerably diminished. No more monastic vows were taken there. No bishop was found who wished or ventured to consecrate young women to such a life. In 1541 this cloister, formerly so rich, gained permission to collect alms. In 1544, the king issued a letter of permission for the monks and nuns who wished it, to leave the cloister and enter the marriage state. This permission is said to have been given at the request of many of its tenants, who wished to return to a secular life. Soon after, a brother of the cloister ceased to be found, and it scarcely possessed a father confessor. Its diary, one of the most important documents the middle ages has left us, becomes laconic and cautious from the beginning of king Gustavus's time, and the record ceases at the year 1545. Yet there were still eighteen sisters left in the cloister in the beginning of king John's reign, when, for a short time, it appears to have been again in bloom, until the stronger protestantism of Charles annihilated, on its suppression, in 1595, the last monastic establishment in Sweden.

More expeditiously than those which were supported by rents, the mendicant cloisters were suppressed. The time for gathering alms was limited by the ordinantia of Westeras, and the new principles diminished the number of generous hands. Once the king extended the time for begging. Thus, the brothers of St. Anthony in Ramundaboda, obtained a prolongation of time for twelve weeks in winter and eight in summer, because they were obliged to entertain wayfarers in the forest.

The first mendicant cloister which was surrendered by its tenants, was the oft-mentioned convent of the Franciscans in Stockholm. This was evacuated by the monks in 1527, either they disapproving their vows, or the unkindness of the people forcing them to the measure. The same year, the nuns were removed from the cloister of St. Clair, which was pulled down. In 1531 a cloister was turned into a hospital, "as the monastic life was fast vanishing away, while the Scripture commands us to take care of the poor and sick." This hospital, whose incomes are joined with another in Stockholm to support a certain number of rooms for the sick, was placed under the inspection of the burgomaster and council of the city. The nuns who were left, if sufficiently healthy and strong, were to attend on the poor and sick. The same regulation was adopted in other towns, of uniting hospitals and placing them under the care of the burgomaster and council.

The convent of grey monks in Jonkoping was changed to a hospital in 1529; that of the black monks in Enkoping, in 1530, with privilege to both of begging for the hospital, as they had before done for the convent. The property of the black brothers in Skeninge, was transferred to a hospital.

The more full information of Olaus Petri acquaints us, that the suppression of the cloister of the black brothers in Stockholm may be considered an exemplification of the course pursued, when the cloister was not turned into a hospital. On December 5, 1528, the prior, Peter Oxen, the readers, Lars and Enger, and the brother Olof, appeared in the town house of Stockholm, and represented to the council that many, in both town and country, declined giving them any support. They were therefore under a necessity of leaving their convent, and providing for themselves as well as they could. They would first explain their necessities to the burgomaster and council, and then solicit their good advice. They had already laid them before the king, and he had acknowledged that they had good reason for leaving the cloister, as it would not be well for them to starve there. Some good men there were willing to help them, but not enough to provide them food. They would add, that master Olof, the illustrious secretary of the council, had, the day before, been in the cloister, at the king's command, and found that the monks had neither malt, meal, nor bread. Ale they had for two or three weeks, of flesh and fish a month's provision, of money the prior had but one mark, and owed thirty. The monks had within the last two years supported themselves rather than been supported by the convent. If they could not live in the convent the good men of the council ought not to compel them to stay there. If they could be supported there they might be content to stay, otherwise they ought to have permission to support themselves. The same day, the king sent master Laurentius Andreæ, master Olof, the chamberlain, and master Olof Petri to the cloister, who removed and carried to the castle the jewels and valuables, and distributed the remainder, the mass-dresses and the like, among the monks, for clothing.

As this cloister was not turned into a hospital, neither was that of the grey monks in Wexio, which, in 1530, was given up. Gudmund Spegel, præpositus of Wexio, whom the king made a prebend of the cathedral there, received also a grant of all the books left by the monks. The cattle around the convent he was to distribute among the poor. The ecclesiastical robes he was to give to poor country churches in the neighborhood. He was to sell the houses in the town belonging to the cloister, and account to the king for the money.

The Dominicans in Skara, to whom an extension of time for collecting alms had been allowed, had concealed, in 1530, one of the brothers adjudged to be banished from the land. Provoked by this act, the king recalled the permission he had granted, and directs the bishop elect of Skara, master Sven, to advise with the lagman and others, whether the cloister should not be suppressed on account of its disorders, and the monks who were unwilling to leave it be removed to Sigtuna.

Immediately after the diet of Westeras, commenced, as directed by the treaty, the general restoration of property granted by individuals to ecclesiastical establishments. There was no establishment in the land which did not thus lose more or less of its possessions and property. Many were thus wholly stripped. When it was attempted to extend the claim for restoration to hospitals, alms-houses and houses for the sick, the king interfered, and on January 25, 1528, forbade such an extension. To take back such gifts, was in opposition to the command of God, who has committed to us the care of the worthy poor. Such was not the meaning of the diet of Westeras nor of the king.

The inquisition made by king Charles Canuteson limited the restoration of property exempt from taxes. Sometimes, indeed, king Gustavus permitted goods given before that time to be restored, when the heir had well served the king and kingdom, and the property itself been given so short a time before that inquisition, as to be accounted within the memory of man. But in respect to such goods as the treaty appears to have intended to remain in the church's undisturbed possession, the king took the ground, that they should be applied to increase the rents of the crown, after the clergy, churches, and monasteries, had received the necessary maintenance.

The king deemed it necessary to prevent the new inquisition from operating further back than was contemplated, and he perceived there was much caution requisite, that the property of the ecclesiastical establishments might not be wrested from them without reason, and in disregard of the legal form prescribed by the treaty. More than once did he remonstrate and complain of attempts of this sort. In a letter to the nobility of East Gothland, dated February 28, 1539, he professes, with some bitterness, that he had expected the men who held the king's fiefs to aid him in protecting and advancing evangelical doctrine. But they look through their fingers, and let it get on as well as it could. "To take the goods, lands, houses and other property from churches, cloisters, and prebends, they were ready and willing enough, and in this respect all men were Christian and evangelical."

The reduction proceeded during almost the whole of king Gustavus's reign. In its later years, questions more often arose as to the true heirs entitled to this property. Gustavus Wasa himself was particularly attentive to his own rights, as belonging to one of the richest families in the land, and by his domestic relations, in many cases, a joint heir with others. He laid claim, as an individual, to considerable property, which devolved to the church before 1453. King Erik XIV., reclaimed this for the crown in 1563, but in 1566, took it back as an inheritance and as his own. After the dethronement of Erik and the disinheritance of his sons, the remaining sons and grandsons of king Gustavus contended for this inheritance, which was at the time assigned to the house of Wasa, but though to be divided only among the sons, was often disputed for by many of the nobility. These last were conciliated by Gustavus Adolphus, into whose hand, after the death of the dukes John and Charles Philip, and after Sigismund and his successors lost their right of inheritance in Sweden, the whole property devolved. That prince's generous grants and gifts to the university of Upsala, atoned, in the eyes of men, for what in his forefather's claim to his personal advantage was considered a stretch of power and a selfish proceeding.

The number of farms and homesteads, which, by this reduction, were taken from the church, has not been accurately computed. But it has been estimated at thirteen to twenty thousand, and more. That which had been for five hundred years, but chiefly in the last century, bestowed for the building up of the visible church, was, for the most part, now taken back, when it was seen, that the overflowing bounty tempted churchmen from their duty and proper functions, and became, for the descendants of the donors, a heavy burden instead of a blessing.

It was a work of thirty years to break down the structure which rested on a false basis, and bring to light the true structure of the church, which reposes on the word of the living God, and this is everlasting.

CHAPTER III.

FLIGHT OF BISHOP BRASK—CONSECRATION OF THE BISHOPS ELECT—WRITINGS OF THE REFORMERS DURING THE YEAR 1528.

Bishop Brask, of Linkoping, for a long time contended almost alone for maintaining the papacy within the Swedish church. He had for some time confessed his courage and his strength to be shaken, and unable to find any support within the land, and Rome herself incapable of bestowing her thoughts on the distant church of Sweden. After the diet of Westeras, therefore, he began to feel still more tempted, as before expressed, "to give up all for lost," and make all smooth. Bend and succumb to the new order of things he could not, without being false to his convictions and his duty. There was little security to him, or to his usual expedients, in any attempt to protect himself by private protestations and exceptions against the strong hand which now grasped the sceptre of Sweden. But, to suffer and endure in his own person for the church's sake, demanded a stronger faith than the popish spirit of the time was capable of infusing into the hearts of men. The kingdom of the pope was a kingdom of this world, in which circumstances allowed of changes to be made.

At Westeras bishop Brask was called on to give the king sureties for his good behavior. But when king Gustavus, in the beginning of August, 1527, came to East Gothland, and was there entertained as a guest by the bishop, who appeared perfectly reconciled to the new order of things, the king engaged to relinquish these sureties, and declared in a letter he caused to be published, that he withdrew all the suspicion and dissatisfaction he might have entertained against the bishop. He gave him also permission to make a visitation in Gothland, from which the bishop had been deterred by the war against Denmark and Sven Norby, and when he would have undertaken it in 1526, by the king's prohibition. The king not only now permitted him to take the journey, but furnished him with a letter of recommendation to the Danish governor of the castle of Wiborg.

The favor with which he seemed again to visit bishop Brask, did not prevent the king from openly declaring, on the same day he gave the letter, that he had appointed him, in conformity with the ordinantia of Westeras, John Petri, canon of Linkoping, as his procurator. This officer was to see that the bishop, in the appointment of parish priests, provided the churches with men competent to preach the word of God; was to accompany the bishop in his visitations through the diocese, there himself to preach God's word, and to protect the priests against tyranny and oppression, as also, in the king's behalf, to inspect all cases of clerical breach of the sixth commandment.

As soon as the king left East Gothland, the bishop went from Soderkoping to Gothland. He there conducted himself, according to some accounts, with much severity against the Lutherans, whose preachers were driven from Wisby. On the recall of them by the citizens immediately after, he again went on board his vessel, prayed that any wind might blow except that toward Sweden, and steered for Dantzic. The king suspected him of having carried off a large sum of money, which the bishop knew to be laid up in the cathedral of Linkoping. Gustavus, who was thus circumvented by the bishop, was much provoked.

Bishop Brask landed at Dantzic in the beginning of September. From that place he wrote to the king, that he had been weather-driven there, and designed there to spend the winter, that he might have the benefit of skilful physicians. In another letter, which came into the kingdom, he more clearly makes known his views.

It appears that the king soon obtained information of the bishop's flight, and on the 9th of October, directs master John, whom he had placed near the bishop, as we have above narrated, to make diligent inquisition respecting the bishop's goods and chattels. He was also ordered to collect the episcopal tithes, which, by the agreement of August 2d, the bishop himself was allowed to collect, and if the bishop had imposed any new intolerable taxes on his clergy the grievance was to be abated. On the 25th of December, the king makes known to the diocese, that, by a letter from the bishop, he had been informed of his departure to Dantzic; that, through other letters from the bishop to Sweden, it had come to light that he plotted rebellion and insurrections, and that his flight was designed to secure himself from the consequences of the many complaints alleged against him. The king exhorts the diocese to peace and quiet, and to continue to collect the episcopal tithes, which should not be withheld, as appertaining to Christianity and the office of a bishop.

A certain knowledge of the time of Brask's departure from Gothland, and his first letter from Dantzic to Sweden, would repel the suspicion that the measures now adopted by the king, and not merely the bishop's previous dissatisfaction, drove him from the land. We have nowhere found that Brask complained of any particular grievance as having been now inflicted upon him. Complaints, both from the bishop and against him, were not wanting, and it was in consequence of this, that the king, on January 25, 1528, issued his summons under a safe conduct, commanding him to return before Whitsuntide of that year, either to justify himself or answer the charges against him.

Brask did not return, but from Dantzic sent a pastoral letter to his diocese. In this document, dated September 29, 1528, he promises to come back after settling his business abroad. He denies all participation in the insurrection of the Dalesmen. He desired, as on his part he assured the king, to live and die as a good Swede and Christian man. He exhorts his flock not to be seduced by letters, or books, or Lutheran preaching, to swerve from Christianity or the Christian customs which they had received, and which their fathers and forefathers held before them, that they might thus escape the plagues, bloodshedding, untimely deaths and famine, with which the wrath of God, on account of the Lutheran doctrines, had afflicted other lands.

Both to the king and diocese he afterward wrote often, with the admonition to renounce heresy and return to the faith of their fathers. From the former he received an answer, probably in the year 1533, in a portion of which the learned argument bears witness to the aiding pen of Laurentius Andreæ. Severe, but to the point, is the reproach against the bishop for having abandoned his flock. "Formerly good men were reluctant to undertake the episcopal office, but, when once they had entered on it, they would willingly die for it, and would not be separated from their sheep, till driven from them. It is not so with you, but you have done quite the contrary. You pressed into the office, and without necessity or compulsion have fled from it. As long as the case was such, that you could milk, shear and slay the flock, you were right at hand. But when the word of God came, and said that you should feed the flock of Christ, and not shear and slay them, then you fled. How you have made your case better, let every good man judge. When we now saw that you, and many such, forsook the flock of Christ, we did what our office required, sent others, good men, instead, who would be at hand, and in this we had the law both of the pope and of the Cæsar to agree with us."

In Dantzic, the place of flight for disaffected Swedes, Brask met with John Magnus. Neither of them had, by the methods each thought the most suitable, been able to put a stop to the church's reform. They were, after the appearance of Gustavus on the scene for the deliverance of the church and fatherland, the first among Swedes who saw fit to fly from their country, because there was no room for their activity in the new order of things. Bishop Brask saw his country never more again. He remained for a time in the cloister of Olof, at Dantzic, and passed the rest of his life, the hope of a return becoming more and more remote, in the Cistercian cloister of Landa, in the archbishopric of Gnesen, where he closed his days, on July 30th, 1539, or more probably a year sooner.

Nothing could more contribute to further the preaching of the gospel, and the consequent changes, than the flight of John Magnus and Hans Brask. The favorers of the old faith were abandoned by those who should have supported and led them, and if the breach could only be stopped by the sacrifice of martyrs for the popish faith, it could not be expected their numbers should be accounted of, when the flock was deserted by its chief shepherds.

The events of the year 1528, also showed how far all hinderances both to begin and prepare the new order of things, were removed.

Without further waiting for confirmation from Rome or any metropolis, the year began with the consecration of the bishops of Skara and Strängness, elected in 1522. To these was now added Martin Skytte, the bishop elect of Abo, a Dominican monk, and vicar-general of the order in Sweden. He is said to have been won to the cause of church reform during his foreign journey, and for this inclination to have acquired the confidence of king Gustavus. Not only the freedom and security which had been won for the land, but the impatience of the people, urged the king to hasten forward the consecration, which indeed must precede, if the king's own coronation was to be performed according to ancient practice. The bishops elect, at least Magnus of Strängness, were in doubt and hesitated. *But the king left them only the choice between consecration or abdication*, in which latter case he would endeavor to find some other for the office.

The three bishops were consecrated in the cathedral of Strängness, on the 5th of January, 1528, by bishop Petrus Magni of Westeras. He was himself consecrated at Rome, according to the popish ritual. It was wished not to break the old order of the church, although the unfounded pretensions of the Roman bishop were set aside. By this cautious proceeding, the so-called apostolic succession was secured to the bishops of the Swedish protestant church, by the laying on of hands by an already consecrated bishop. This succession may be defined to be the continuance of the line of bishops in the church, in an unbroken chain from the apostles and those who, by the laying on of their hands, were first ordained bishops of the church. If the consecration of the bishops consecrated in the year 1528, was not canonical, that is, in conformity with a law of the church which directed it to be performed by three or two bishops, yet had this a meet apology as a case of necessity. In the absence of the bishop of Wexio, no more ordainers could be procured, provided bishop Vincentius, who was then, it is probable, either in Sweden or Finland, is not asked for. Petrus Magni for some time refused to perform this office, because the elect were not confirmed by the pope. Laurentius Andreæ could not induce him to consent, till he had given a promise that the newly consecrated bishops should themselves seek this confirmation, and make an apology for Peter at the Roman chair.

Eight days after, the king's coronation took place in Upsala, at which the newly consecrated bishops officiated.

It created remark, and soon after objections, that the relations of the church having been settled when the king placed the crown on his head as the estates had desired, he omitted the oath customary at a coronation, to protect the holy church and her people.

The remark and dissatisfaction of the popishly disposed, certainly called forth the sermon which Olaus Petri made upon the occasion. It was an exhortation to the king and his subjects. The former was admonished, among other things, to watch over the pure doctrines of God within the land. "As the king ought to punish his stewards and officers, when they abuse their trust, so ought he to have oversight of the bishops and priests in his land, when they are neglectful of what is committed to them, that is, when they do not faithfully make known the word of God, as they ought to do. Yea rather, he ought to punish them, since from their mismanagement follows the greater hurt, in proportion as the soul is better than the body." On the duties of subjects it is said: "As it is to the injury of many men that the king should misuse his power, so is it to the injury and ruin of many, that a part should withhold the obedience they owe to their king, and of the default of which—may God amend it—we have had too much evidence in Sweden. But him who has been at the root of this we have taken in hand. Doubtless they who have withdrawn their obedience to the powers that be, under pretence of privileges and liberty, and have adopted a new rule for themselves, had nothing to gain by the king. This is evidently contrary to what St. Paul says, that every man shall be in subjection to the powers that be; he excepts no one, pope, prelate, or bishop."

Thus was consecrated the new reign, with an open rejection of the former position of the church. From that day the Swedish throne rests on a protestant basis.

The liberty of teaching, which was granted at Westeras the previous year, was used, in 1528, by the reformers, especially Olaus Petri, to settle and confirm the principles of those who leaned to the Reformation, by a multitude of small treatises. Many such productions on various subjects, by Olaus Petri, came out in the course of the year, and one from the pen of Laurentius Andreæ.

The first of Olof's writings was again called forth by the Danish Carmelite monk, Paulus Eliæ. The questions of king Gustavus being circulated, had also fallen into his hands. He published, in 1528, an answer furnished with a preface and appendix, after he had read the answers of Peter Galle and Olof, being of opinion that neither of these had given the right reply, "because the one could not, and the other would not." They were also deemed by Paul to have each been obstinate in opinion, and not to have done justice to the parts they were to perform. He was yet to learn how little availed a temporizing policy.

Paulus Eliæ, who frequently quotes the predictions of St. Bridget now about to be fulfilled, and who attempts to flatter the king, by declaring that he did not believe his sovereign to have proposed the questions with any evil design, but for the purpose of making known and pointing out the heresy, closes his tract or answer, with twelve questions put to the king, manifestly referring to the decree of Westeras. The general tenor of these twelve questions may be comprised in the one, whether that constitution of the church and its hierarchal power, cannot and ought not to subsist, with which the civil constitution and royal power can rightly possess its due stability, in other words, whether that ecclesiastial regimen ought not to endure which is best consistent with the civil regimen?

It was this question which called forth the answer of Olaus Petri, dated May 27th, 1528, in which, with strength and clearness, and in a manner hardly expected in dealing with his adversary, he beats down his positions. As Olof, a few years before, had with youthful presumption announced, that no one before him preached the truth in Sweden, the following expressions in his treatise merit observation, as an evidence of his meaning, and how entirely he was attached to that conservatism which is a striking feature in the Reformation of the Swedish church. "You have never proved that St. Ansgarius and St. Sigfrid taught us to believe, that bishops and prelates were to lay aside their proper office in order to rule castles, lands, and cities, to tax us with their indulgences, to oppress us with their self-derived bans, interdicts, and the like. First prove that they brought such a faith into the land, and then that we have deviated from the faith they brought us. These good men brought us the holy gospel of Christ, the pure and precious word of God, and showed themselves faithful according to the grace which God gave them, and taught us that we should firmly abide by God's promise and word, put our dependence on the death and pains of Christ, who has made atonement for us to his Father in heaven whom we had offended, and who has gained for us everlasting life. On this should we believe, and place our trust, and in this faith have mutual brotherly love and do good to one another. This is the faith those men brought here."

We will not repeat the positions, which, from Olof's answer have been sufficiently apparent, but cannot omit the following particular, which witnesses Olof's modesty and sound judgment, alike. Paulus Eliæ had expressed a doubt of the truth of protestantism, inasmuch as its power to improve the life and conversation had not been manifested. To this Olof made an answer which was not needed in outward defence, while the truth of the church was confined to doctrinal controversy. "You say, also, that you yet see great sinners among those who have fallen off from the church of Rome, and the governors appointed by Jesus Christ in the land. I acknowledge there are such sinners among us. The old Adam rebels and draws us to act against the commandments of God, whether we will or not. But the case between us depends not on this point. We dispute not which party has the more or fewer sinners. We dispute which party has the true doctrine. *We defend our doctrine and not our sinners.* The saints, Peter, Paul, John, and the other apostles, were sinners, as themselves confess, though I do not compare our life with theirs, yet they had true doctrine."

Soon after appeared, on the 12th of June, this treatise of Olof, under the motto: "A good shepherd giveth his life for the sheep;" and another also of his: "A Christian admonition to the clergy meeting at the next clerical councils of Upsala, Strängness, and Westeras, wherein is set forth what the clergy owe to the laity, and what the laity to the clergy." It is said to be the duty of priests to the laity to preach the word of God, to administer the sacraments, and by their good lives to set a good example; of the laity to the priests, to be obedient, to judge their failings with tenderness, and afford them a proper maintenance. The purport of the writings of the reformers was to inculcate that rents and tithes were given for preaching and not for reading, for singing, for masses, and baptizing, all which without preaching was unprofitable. It was a snare to the soul to receive tithes without preaching. Priests who could not do this, should have assistants, for above all there should be preaching. These expressions corresponded with the ordinantia of Westeras, and were a prognostic of the decree passed the year following at the council of Orebro.

But this treatise of Olof was also designed to obviate one of the consequences of the treaty of Westeras; as the people began to refuse payment of taxes to the clergy. The priests had, says Olof, previously abused the Scriptures to tax laymen, and force them to give more than they ought. Now, in their turn, laymen abused the Scriptures to give their clergy less than they ought, or nothing at all. "The one desired, on authority of the Scriptures, to have all, the other, on the same authority, to give nothing." Olof wished, therefore, to show what the Scriptures truly taught and commanded in this respect.

A few months after the diet of Westeras, it became necessary to inculcate in the minds of the people, that duties and payments should be made to the clergy, according to the old customs and usages, except where the treaty had made a change. In August, 1527, the king was obliged to warn the people against a perversion of the treaty and ordinantia to anarchy and selfishness. In the beginning of 1528, these admonitions were renewed, and from time to time, during almost the whole of king Gustavus's reign, and with increased earnestness. In a letter to some of the provinces of the kingdom, in 1534, it is said, that the king had not abrogated such dues to priests; else would the office of bishop have been abolished. If this admonition did not avail, *they would not be allowed the privileges of Easter as they now enjoyed them.* This was a threat to restore the usages abrogated at Westeras in 1527, and repel from the Lord's Supper those who refused to pay their dues to the clergy.

Two months later than the work last mentioned, Olof was ready, August 14th, with another: "A small book on the sacraments, what they are, and how they may properly be administered, many unchristian appendages being with good reason laid aside." This production is, of all those which appeared in the course of the year, the most comprehensive and the most deeply involving a doctrinal change. It treats of the nature of a sacrament, of baptism, of the forgiveness of sins, of confession, of the distinction between plain and mystical language in Scripture, of auricular confession, of absolution, penance, and vows, of indulgences, of the election and consecration of priests, and how practised in apostolic times, of confirmation, extreme unction, marriage, and the prohibited degrees, of the Lord's

Supper, and how far Christ made in this sacrament a difference between priests and laymen, of the carrying the body of Christ in procession, of masses as a sacrifice, of the spiritual priesthood of all Christians, of masses and prayers for the dead, of true prayer, and of purgatory. The views of Olof in all these particulars may be learned and understood from his answers to the questions, and from the present existing confession and usages of our church.

In the same month with this book, appeared also Olof's "Instructions respecting marriage." Olof had for some time, as he says, had it in contemplation to put in print something on the subject of marriage, but for the sake of weak brethren had deferred his design. But as a knowledge of the truth began to be now more widely spread, "so that innumerable many now embrace the gospel of Christ, who were at first firmly opposed to it," he would no longer procrastinate. Under three heads, that marriage is ordained of God, is permitted to all, and can be forbidden by none, Olof presents an exhortation to bishops and prelates to grant freedom of marriage to the priests under their jurisdiction, and thus put a stop to the licentiousness which then existed and had been common among them.

In the zeal which led Olof, in 1528, to set forth general principles, by writings which rapidly succeeded each other, the conventual life was a topic not to be neglected. A small volume, therefore, came out in November. Its purport was apparent from its motto: "They shall proceed no further, for their folly shall be manifest to all men."

Not only as a controversial writing, but as a picture of the times, this treatise is of great value. After some notices of the origin of the cloistral life, and of the different orders, with their badges, the author enters upon an examination of the three vows, which he finds in part contradictory to the command of God, in part binding upon all men. A special chapter is bestowed upon the mendicant monks.* In fourteen points are developed the injuries brought on Christianity by the cloistral life, from which emanated divisions and schisms, seduction of children in disobedience to their parents, the enticement of people from faith and reliance on Christ, and the evil example which followed from the practice of begging. The hideous occurrences in Switzerland, in 1507, when four Dominican monks, agreeably to a pretended revelation of the Virgin Mary, bored through the hands, feet, and side of a brother of their cloister, are not forgotten in his picture of the evils consequent upon the conventual life.

The admonition given to the tenants of convents to go back into civil life, and the sooner the better, and to all those who had children, friends or relations, to aid them in such a purpose, was, in a word, the very end that the king and Laurentius Andreæ, in their treatment of monasteries, had in view.

The list of Olof's writings during this year, closing on December 18th, concludes with the words: "Of God's word and man's ordinances, which in spiritual things are the rule of life for the soul." This treatise, which purposes to lay for the teachers of the Reformation a religious philosophical foundation, merits a particular attention. It was by no means desired to have a rupture with the faith and discipline of the church, but to guard against the abuse of them. God's everlasting wisdom and counsel, it is here declared, in which his inscrutable providence makes itself known, is his word, in whom all his will and purpose are contained, through whom also he has created all things. For all that he has created, he has created as from eternity

* "When the devil was let loose after a thousand years, mentioned by St. John, he waked up the begging orders, so that God has suffered the world to be plagued with the mendicant monks, as, in the Old Testament, he plagued Egypt with frogs and grasshoppers."

he determined to create it. Thus, God's wisdom, decree, and counsel, are called in Scripture God's word, God's Son, God's heart, God's mind, God's arm. No one knows the Father but the Son. He who shall know the Father has of necessity God's word and wisdom. He who has this wisdom and science has everlasting life. Thus everlasting life comes from God's word. But where the Father and Son are, there also is the Holy Ghost, for He is the love wherewith the Father loves the Son. There love is, where he is diffused and manifested, as God in all creatures has manifested his love.

As long as men had this word, they had truth and life, but when they turned away from him they came to lies and death. But when God willed to recover men he willed that his inward word, which he has in his heart, should become man, and so be declared in the outward word, of which men shall be enabled to conceive the meaning, and from which they derive life and truth. But if the Holy Ghost does not infuse into the hearts of men the outward word, it cannot be comprehended or understood. *The outward word is contained in the Bible.* To this nothing can be added and from it nothing subtracted. For it is impossible that the word of God, which is his eternal wisdom, and the reason of sinful man should be of equal value: for through Adam's sin man is fallen from God, who is wisdom, unto vanity and foolishness. His thoughts are not equivalent to the word of God, therefore they cannot be added thereto, unless we would mingle truth with lies. All that is not founded on Holy Scripture is the commandment of men, and is no rule of action for the soul. It is said that the Holy Ghost directs the church, and protects it from error, but it must first be declared what the church is, "for the ordinances of men have given us the benefit of not knowing what the church is." If thereby is meant the society of men who have the Holy Ghost there can be no mistake, but if, as is common, be thereby meant the pope, cardinals, bishops, prelates and all ecclesiastics, this church, which is corporeal, has, in many of its parts, been in error. The crafty devices of men are now, for the most part, made to be the worship of God. . The fathers of the church, councils, tradition, are of value only if they have the Scriptures with them.

To the year 1528, must be assigned one of Olof's productions: "A short introduction to the Holy Scriptures," which develops sundry points, as what the law, gospel, and faith of Christ, are.

But Olof labored at the same time to gain an opportunity for having divine service in the Swedish tongue. It is probable that, in the course of this year, first made their appearance, the psalms in Swedish, which, with additions, became the basis of the present psalm book of the Swedish church. At this time, also, mention is made of the postils, which, for the aid and direction of the clergy, Olof translated from the German, and which, in 1530, came out complete, with the addition of a short catechism.

In recording the protestant productions of the year 1528, we cannot omit a short treatise by Laurentius Andreæ, the only one with certainty known to be his: "A brief instruction on faith and good works." Its purport is to show the injustice of their reproaches, who say that good works are rejected and made of no account, when faith is exalted as that through which alone we are justified. That is not the case. We are obligated to do good works, but we are not to place our dependence on them. "Good works make no man good, but on the other hand, a good man does good works."

This review exhibits the compass and indefatigable zeal of Olaus Petri as an author, during the year which followed the diet of Westeras. The soil was opened and prepared to receive the seed, and the men of truth neglected it not. Including the coronation sermon, there appeared within the year at least nine larger or smaller productions from the pen of Olof. This activity would be still more surprising, did we not consider, that the previous year gave him opportunity for quiet preparation, and that these writings were in a measure translated or compiled. We do not regard it as worth while to examine into the relative labor he bestowed on each of them. This fancy for searching out the foreign origin of every Swedish book is of little consequence, when we are concerned with the opinions and efficacy connected with these writings.

The general views contained in them were of a protestant complexion, and there is no question that Olaus Petri and Laurentius Andreæ were mighty men in the principles common to protestants, and in their mother tongue, being in a great degree its framers, so that it may well be supposed they showed a spirit of independence in their explanation of those principles. While these writings were being spread it the land, king Gustavus issued his directions to the clergy to make themselves acquainted with the word of God out of certain portions of the Holy Scripture, and to promulgate them among their hearers.

The following year bore the fruit of this seed corn of the word, and serious efforts were also employed to stop its growth.

CHAPTER IV.

THE COUNCIL OF OREBRO IN 1529—DISSATISFACTION—FLIGHT OF BISHOP MAGNUS OF SKARA.

On the 25th of November, 1528, king Gustavus issued a summons for an ecclesastical council to be opened at Orebro, at Candlemas, February 2d, 1529. The prelates and learned men of the church were to assemble, to determine on what was necessary for the improvement of the church and unity in her usages.

At this council, Laurentius Andreæ, archdeacon of Upsala, acted as president, "in behalf and right of the archbishopric," and as plenary envoy of king Gustavus. That the presidency was assigned to the archiepiscopal see gave the council the legal form of a provincial synod, although certainly not because the council was held during a vacancy of that see or the voluntary absence of its occupants. That the king had his envoy at the council was not uncommon, but it was uncommon that the envoy and president of the council should be one and the same person.

There were present at the council three bishops, Magnus Haraldsson of Skara, Magnus Sommar of Strängness, and Petrus Magni of Westeras. The representatives or deputies from the two other bishops to be found in the land, Ingemar of Wexio, and Martin Skytte of Abo, are not named. The diocese of Abo was now, as often before, not at all represented.

The list of the chapters, parish priests and monastic

orders, named as present or represented, is as follows: From Upsala two clergymen, canons, and John Kokemastere, pastor of the church in Stockholm, with Olaus Petri, secretary of the council of that city. From Linkoping, one prelate, the cantor Erik Magni, the same who was chosen by bishop Brask and the chapter of Linkoping to take part in the translation of the New Testament, two canons, of whom Thorer Magni was one, with the pastors of the churches in Soderkoping, Skeninge and Wadsten. From Skara, two prelates, the provost Sven Jacobi, soon after made bishop of that see, and the archdeacon Magnus Arnberni, with two canons and the pastor of Lodose. From Strängness, four canons, of whom two were besides pastors of Nykoping and Kumla, with the pastor of Orebro. From Westeras, three canons, of whom two were also pastors of Fellingbro and Leksand, and to these were added the preachers of Westeras and Arboga, with the pastor of Rattvik. From Wexio, two canons, one of whom was the Gudmund Spegel mentioned in a former page. The monkish orders were represented by the vicar and two brethren of the Dominicans, a confessor and two brothers from the cloister of Wadsten, with a custos and a brother from the Minorites. The names thus counted, were therefore, in amount, three bishops, nineteen canons, of whom four held prelacies, eleven pastors of sundry the chief parishes of the sees, among whom some were canons, three preachers, among whom Olaus Petri was numbered, and eight monks. There were also many other clergymen present at the council, although of their names and titles we have no information. Among the names of the forty men who took part in the council of Orebro, the thirty, bishops, canons and monks, men of standing in the church, who were deeply interested in the direction which church reform began now to take, may serve to illustrate the quality and character of the council, a circumstance of the greater consequence, as, with the exception of the decree there passed, information is wanting of the course pursued by an assembly so important to the church's future.

The proceedings were neither diffused nor of long continuance. The council met on February 2d, and its decree was passed February 7th, five days after. The work of a century is without verbosity summed up in a decree.

The decree now framed at Orebro, may be divided into three heads. 1. Of the preaching of God's word. 2. Of the church constitution and discipline. 3. Of church usages.

In regard to the preaching of God's word, the members of the council confessed themselves bound by their office to propagate, spread, and advance it. They would, therefore, provide that over the whole kingdom, in all its churches, the word should be preached purely and without molestation. The bishops obligated themselves to pay special attention that the parish priests within their dioceses, *with the hazard else of losing their benefices*, should either preach God's pure word, or if they could not do so, allow it to be done by others "versed in the Holy Scriptures." By this last expression, it was more plainly than at Westeras declared, that in the Holy Scriptures alone the word of God was to be found. To promote an acquaintance with the Scriptures there should daily be had a lection of some portions of them, "with a good and true explanation." This Bible illustration should be frequented by the parish priests, in order "to become learned in the word of God." There was also to be in cathedral schools a daily reading of the Scriptures. On such occasions, the priests who were cross-bearers, and the candidates for the priesthood, were always or sometimes to be present, that the Holy Scriptures might be read in their ears. The times of the cathedral service were to be so regulated, that there might be leisure for this. The bishops were to take heed, that for the scholars there should be books of the New Testament in Latin, and that learned men should be appointed as pastors of churches in towns, to whom the priests in the neighborhood might resort for instruction in the word of God, and who should travel about and preach in country congregations. To furnish opportunity for more general instruction, and probably also to produce an effect on the occupants of monasteries, it was ordered, that, in the churches belonging to monasteries situated in towns, there should be preaching only in the afternoon, so that there might be a better attendance on the preaching in the town church during the morning. Priests were forbidden mutually to recriminate each other in the pulpit. If any found fault with the preaching of another, he should give him his opinion in private, that scandal among the people might not be the result of an opposite course. The Lord's prayer, the creed, the hail Mary, were to be repeated before every sermon, "for the benefit of young and simple people," as also the ten commandments once or twice a month. All preachers were to begin and end their sermons in the same manner.

The second division contains, under seven articles, directions relating to the discipline and order of the church.

1. The first treats of scholars going about in parishes to collect alms, a subject on which canons were often passed in the councils of the Swedish church during the middle ages. Thus, for example, it was decreed at the provincial council of Arboga, in 1412, that priests should confine the scholars found in the houses of the country people beyond the appointed time, and were to transfer their collections to the nearest schoolmaster, for the use of his poor pupils. In the diocese of Abo, this going about in parishes to collect alms, was, in 1489, prohibited, and the clergy of the chapter were requested to receive what "the friends of God" were willing to give, and this the chapter was to apportion according to merit. The reason assigned was, that the scholars, by long journeys through the country, neglected their

studies, practised manifold artifices among the people, preached to simple persons in a false and unreasonable manner respecting indulgences, and were guilty of other improper practices.

On similar grounds the decree was passed at Orebro, that scholars should not long be allowed to collect alms about the country, to prevent their spreading lies among the people for their own selfish views, and that the priests of the parishes where they were sent, should have an eye over them.

2. The second article says: "As the law of the pope forbids some to enter into marriage whom God has not forbidden, it is determined to dispense with this law, for honest reasons, provided scandal be avoided as far as possible." This point was one of the few plain protests against popery, which had been yet openly uttered in Sweden. From what was done at Westeras it appears that the right of dispensation was given to the bishops and chapters. But that there was no renunciation of the pope's law, but merely a dispensation from it, is another proof of the caution used in the measures adopted.

3. As the bond of previously existing laws was now loosened, the penitentiaries of cathedrals were allowed the right of taking such a course with offenders, as they deemed most advisable, "and they might use any degree of severity with murderers and other heinous transgressors, as the worldly sword appears to be idle, and has not the force it ought to have."

4. The cloisters, which, in 1527, were, as to their outward discipline, placed in the hands of the king, were now, as to their spiritual relations, placed under the care of the bishops. The monks, it is declared, shall be under obedience to the bishops, especially in matters that appertain to the preaching of the gospel.

5. The number of saints' days shall, by each bishop in his diocese, be diminished as circumstances admit. The

reason given was, that there were more saints' days than necessary, that they gave occasion to many sins, and were injurious to the body politic. "The peculiar high festivals of our Lord, of the Virgin Mary, of the apostles, and the days of patron saints," were to be kept.

In conclusion, it was decreed that where there were many parish churches in the same town, they should be placed under the control of one pastor, and that bishops should not, without weighty cause, give commissions for begging.

The third division treats of the true explanation of church ceremonies. The council did not enter into an examination of the truth of the doctrine of confession, but laid it down as a maxim, that the words of the Bible, now released from bondage, should accompany and explain what was truth upon the subject. It aimed to assist the erring eyes of the sons of the church, to recall the worship of God, which stood in outward ordinances, to a worship of Him in spirit and in truth. The outward usages of the church, which now existed and expressed the life of piety, were not suddenly and violently to be removed; they were on the contrary to furnish a text for the preaching of the truth.

We present this part of the council's decree in its own words: "As many abuses and erroneous views have been entertained respecting the customary ceremonies, we here give an account of some of them, and explain their true purpose. First: consecrated water is not used for the sake of taking away sins, for that the blood of Christ alone effects; but it shall be borne in mind that we are baptized and sprinkled with the blood of Christ. Images are used, not for the purpose of courtesying and bowing down to, but for a remembrance of Christ and holy men. The palm branch is not consecrated, not used, that men should take comfort in it, but in memory that the people strewed palm branches in the way of Christ, when he entered Jerusalem. Candlemas lights are not used for any special worship of God, not given as possessing any special power, but in memory that the true light, Jesus Christ, was offered in the temple. Anointing, or chrism, is not used for any power it possesses, but to be an outward sign of an inward unction, which is effected by the Holy Ghost. The ringing of bells is only used that the people may be called together. Church structures are kept up, not for any peculiar sanctity in themselves for the worship of God, but that men may meet together there, and learn God's word. God dwells not in houses built by men's hands. Consecrated churches, consecrated salt, meat, and the like, are not in themselves any the better, but they are consecrated to remind us that such things should not be abused by us; so that the calling of God's name over them, is to improve us, not the thing consecrated. So should the people be taught, that they should rather give the poor lights than place them before images. Fast days are kept, not as a special worship done to God, but to tame our lustful bodies. Saints' days are observed, that men may have a time to hear God's word, and rest from their toils, not as a special worship done to God. The people shall be taught that the ceremonies of Good Friday and Easter, are only in remembrance of Christ. It is also necessary that the people be instructed with regard to pilgrimages, that, although such was scarcely their origin, their meaning is that the people should go where they can gain better instruction than at home; so that pilgrimages are for the sake of good doctrine, and not for an especial worship done to God, or to obtain indulgence which can be obtained in all places, for God is as much in one place as another. The like instruction shall be given the people beforehand, who will then not seek for it abroad."

That besides the subjects which the decree of the council contains, others also were either discussed, or through the decree became established, will appear from what follows.

It will be evidenced from these, no less than from the open measures adopted and published, that, for the first time, after the council of Orebro, the favorers of the old church discipline began to dread that it was to be shaken to the foundation. So little was commonly foreboded of the consequences of the diet of Westeras, held somewhat more than half a year before, or so commonly admitted was the necessity of the reforms there adopted, or so sure were men of the views which would be current at Orebro, that the result of that council awakened astonishment in many of the friends of the papacy. It seems to have been expected, that after the necessary improvements in the condition of the church were allowed and confirmed at Westeras, the order would now be, to adopt restraining measures against heresy. Thus, the diary of the cloister of Wadsten, mentions that three of the brethren had, on the 26th of January, gone, by command of the king, to the council of Orebro *against the Lutherans*, and had, on February 12, returned "*in consternation.*"

The council of Orebro also held the middle path of caution, which distinguishes the reformation of the Swedish church, in almost all its progress. It was, therefore. natural, that both parties, who went to the extreme on either side, both the zealous protestants and stubborn papists, should be dissatisfied. The former thought far too little done, far too great a concession to error to have been made; the latter, now first having opened their eyes, began to perceive where the current of the times was leading them.

The dissatisfaction exploded on the one side, though in a movement of less consequence, in the city of Stockholm, which was full of German protestants; on the other side, in insurrections throughout many provinces of the kingdom.

When the representative of Stockholm at the council returned home, he found the German merchants of the city, and a German preacher, named Tileman, who seems to have been either invited or favored by Laurentius Andreæ, pouring out reproaches against the council for having fallen away from the Gospel, and returned to the old opinions because it allowed images, holy water, palms, and other practices to be continued. In vain did Olaus Petri and others offer the apology, that circumstances did not permit this council to go further, "that one must travel softly with the people of this land," and that all that was allowed might well be borne with, and was not contrary to the word of God. Tileman preached openly against this toleration. The king and master Lars were absent; but the governor of the castle, and burgomaster of Stockholm, now less crest-fallen than during the disturbance of the anabaptists five years before, forbade Tileman to preach before the coming home of the king, and, though soon setting them at liberty, imprisoned the most turbulent of the Germans.

In an opposite direction, were the insurrections which occurred in this year in many other places. Of very little importance were the attempts of Goran, Thuresson provost of Upsala, who raised commotions in Roslagen and Helsingland. More menacing was the insurrection provoked about the same time in West Gothland, by Thure Jonsson Roos, father of provost Goran, and by bishop Magnus of Skara; the object of the bishops, nobles, and priests engaged in it, being to bring back the old order of things, by the election of another king. In Smaland, not in Warend, the diocese of bishop Ingemar, but in the district under the jurisdiction of the see of Linkoping, the revolt assumed the character of a dissatisfaction with the changes made in the church. At a later period, after the insurrection was stifled, king Gustavus complains of the provost and chapter of Linkoping, as having taken part in it; although this conduct of theirs does not correspond to the commission previously given them by the king to negotiate with the men of Smaland.

There is no reason to be assigned for the supposition, that the spirit of the insurrection, although fed by the disorders of long continuance throughout the kingdom, presented the condition of the church merely as a cloak for the leaders' ambition and thirst of revenge. The letter which was published in the name of the burgomaster and council of Jonkoping and the people of Smaland, exhibited a deep insight into the true position of the case, when it declared that it would be too late to stop the reformation of the church, if active measures and timely precautions were not adopted. The danger was delineated in striking colors, and with the common exaggeration, which makes a particular instance current as a general rule. It was known to all, what an unchristian regimen came into this poor kingdom by means of the Lutheran heresy, so that it would be altogether ruined if no good counsel were found, *if timely and immediate preventives were not used.* Otherwise, they might all become heathens and damned. In Upland, and, indeed, the whole kingdom, the cloisters were either laid in ruins, or the jewels and property, the pictures and images, yea, and the very tiles from the shattered buildings, were carried off. Bishops, prelates, monks, and priests, were expelled from their homes, that the king might come at their goods and tithes; heretics and recreant runaway monks were placed as pastors in towns and all over the land. The king had eaten meat in Lent, and even induced others to do so. He had also broken his royal oath. The mass was neglected or abolished in Sweden. Many, in Stockholm and all over the land, made a laughing-stock of the mass, of the saints and their images. How the sacraments were debased and depraved, and the good old Christian customs contemned, *is evident from the books which the king permitted the last winter to be published on the sacraments.* They had punished Gottfrid Sure, who obtained the cloister of Nydala in investiture from the king, and they invited others to deal in the same manner with robbers of the sanctuary. In the published letters, the insurgents lay all the blame on the king. But, by those whom king Gustavus employed to negotiate with them—either it was really so, or they put in the mouth of the insurgents their own convictions and their own personal spite—he was informed, that the fury of the rebels was directed against Laurentius Andreæ and master Olof, with others devoted to evangelical principles. In East Gothland there was discontent with the teachers, who from Upland were scattered over the country, and whatever was preached or printed was said to be done with the king's knowledge and consent. Laurentius Andreæ, in particular, was blamed for all the ill will the people harbored against the king. He had used some violence in his treatment of the cloisters and in other respects, and was the first to advise the removal of the jewels and other chattels of those establishments, shutting them up that no masses might be said within their walls. This he had done in Skeninge. They, therefore, propose to the king, to sacrifice this counsellor to appease the anger of the people. It were better that he alone should be punished, than that many others should suffer for his sake.

This proposal did not induce king Gustavus to withdraw his confidence from the man who guided his counsels and resolves in the affairs of the church. The insurrection was quelled in the course of some weeks, after he had approved the agreement, which in his behalf, the knights Holger Karlsson and Mans Johansson, the chapter of Linkoping, and the burgomasters and council of the towns of East Gothland, with the envoys of some districts, had signed with the disaffected. He pledged himself, not to suffer any heresy to be introduced into the kingdom or be there countenanced, not to allow the preaching of any unchristian doctrine inconsistent with the pure word of God and ancient Christian customs. He wished to abide by what was done at Westeras, and by what, with the people's full approbation, the treaty contains.

The king could, without double dealing in word or act, accept these terms, since it was yet undetermined what was heresy or pure doctrine, and since on both sides it was admitted, that the pure word of God was the fountain of truth. We cannot forbear to present in a compendium the declaration he laid before the estates of the kingdom at the diet of Strängness, after the disturbances were quieted.

The king went into a copious defence of the treaty of Westeras, which he declared it to be his wish should remain unaltered. It was the condition on which he took the Swedish crown. It would be contrary to his wishes, if any other doctrine were preached in the kingdom than the pure word of God and the gospel, the preaching of which the people themselves solicited at the diet of Westeras. He was yet desirous that learned men in the kingdom should meet together and investigate the subject. Complaint was made of his having broken his oath, because he did not protect the churchmen, but he well knew that it was the duty of a king to punish the bad and countenance the good, and when he did this he fulfilled his oath, "*to protect and uphold the church and churchmen, that is to say, his Christian subjects, since the holy church is no other than the congregation of Christian men and Christian women.*" Would any one desire to interpret his kingly oath as confined to bishops, prelates, and priests, and consider it broken, when the power of these was diminished? then let it be recollected, that this diminution was made with consent of the council and estates of the kingdom. Their power had become noxious, and to protect it was to oppress the church. The bishops had not been driven away by the king, but by their own unquiet tempers, nor could this be attributed to the new teaching, since long before its appearance, lords and princes had contended with bishops. Churches and monasteries he had put under contribution, but it was done with consent of the diet. Monasteries he had not laid in ruins; but their occupants, discontented with the curtailment of their privileges and selfishness, which took effect at Westeras, had themselves run away. Only some monks, plotters of rebellion in Upland, had the king expelled. So much holiness was not attached to monastic life as some supposed. Their jewels and chattels, rather than they should squander them, he had taken to pay the debts of the kingdom and to support students. The performance of masses in Sweden he had neither advised nor prohibited. Whether any had blasphemed the saints, he could not say. If, in the writings put to press, there was anything contrary to God's word, it was not by his will and order. If the king ate meat on a fast day, it was to the injury of no one; it was allowed in many other countries, and in Rome meat was sold during the whole of Lent. The marriage of monks and priests it was not in his power to prohibit, because they said they had the word of God in their favor. They must answer for themselves.

The knight Thure Jonsson, and Magnus, bishop elect of Skara, with whom bishop Brask, as long as he remained at Linkoping, carried on an intimate correspondence by letters, had been the heads of the rebellion in West Gothland, and by its unsuccessful issue, were obliged to fly to the borders of Denmark. From Halmstad the bishop issued a protest against the treaty of Westeras. The approbation of the bishops to this treaty was declared by him to be merely an acknowledgment that the king and temporal estates so decree; but suppose the approbation real, it was extorted, and therefore without validity; hence, he now appealed to the judgment of the pope and church of Rome, the Cæsar, and all Christian princes in the approaching general council. From

Halmstad both these men wrote, that they could not return home under the king's letter of safe conduct offered them, because in that letter mention was made of the treaty of Westeras, which they could not approve, the rather as they had heard that the princes and lords of Germany were assembled at Spire, to condemn and punish Lutheranism and its allies. Both, together with archbishop Gustav Trolle, soon after took part in Christian II.'s war, marched into Norway, and, by letters, endeavored to raise new disturbances in their fatherland, although now to no purpose. Thure Jonsson was assassinated in Kongelf, the two bishops were carried captive into Denmark. They betook themselves to Mecklenberg. Magnus, who more than once wrote a letter of admonition to the Swedes, and, in 1543, of exhortation to them to dethrone the heretical king, passed his last years in a cloister near Rostock, and about the year 1560 there died.

Bishop Magnus and Thure Jonsson appear, from the above mentioned answer, to have hoped that the decree of the German diet of Spire would effect a revolution which might operate on the Swedish church. This diet, so remarkable in the history of the German Reformation, was opened in March, 1529. The Swedish diet of Westeras, in 1527, was preceded by the German at Spire, in 1526, where religious freedom was accorded the evangelical party, and by a reconciliation between the emperor and pope. But this reconciliation was employed to suppress religious freedom in Germany, and in 1529, it gave rise to an attempt in Sweden to put a stop to the progress of the Reformation. On the 15th of March, it was declared, on behalf of the emperor Charles V., before the estates again met at Spire, that, as the religious freedom, granted three years before, had produced many disorders, it was now withdrawn, by the power and authority of the Cæsar. Thus, on the same day when rebellious hands sought to pluck the crown from the head of king Gustavus, because he was said to favor the pretended heresy, the estates of Germany, in contradiction of the former decree, resolved that the further spread of evangelical doctrine shonld not be allowed. This occurred on 6th and 7th of April. On the 19th of that month, king Ferdinand, as representing the Cæsar, confirmed the decree. On the same day, the evangelical part of the estates promulgated that *protest* against the decree which has become world renowned, and given name to the confessors of the truth.

The disturbances in Dalecarlia, which were occasioned by the proclamation of a tax on bells, and had little connection with disputes of faith, were provoked by the menaced plundering of churches, and at once were arrested by the simultaneous attempt of Christi an to recover his lost kingdom. At the council of Upsala, in 1530, it was resolved that, for the payment of the foreign debt, the second largest bell of every church, chapel, and cloister, in towns, should be taken. This tax which was laid without opposition, was extended, the year after, to the country churches, but with a right to parishes, by payment of copper, or by money, to release their bells. If there was but one bell, it was to remain, but to be released at half its valuation. A ransom was to be paid, not only for the bells, but for some of the products of the glebe, except what was needed for wine and wax; and what was not indispensable of the contents of the chests of the church, was to be delivered up. The discontent among the Dalesmen, to which the imprudence or ill will of Petri of Westeras, appears to have contributed, exploded in an attack upon the collectors of the taxes. The disturbance was fomented by some priests, among whom was Her Ewert, of the copper district, who, as pastor of Leksand, took part in the council of Orebro. There came out also, the usual accompaniments of a storm, insurrectionary letters from Gustav Trolle and others, in the camp of Christian II. These persons wrote to the nobles of West Gothland, that the holy father of Rome declared that no faith was to be kept with Gustavus Eriksson, who had usurped the throne of Christian. To the Dalesmen, they wrote, that homage to Christian would be attended by many advantages, and, what was of the utmost consequence, by the friendship and favor of the holy father, the pope of Rome, and by communion with the holy Catholic church, from which Swedes, by reason of the Lutheran teaching, were at that time excluded.

The Dalesmen complained, in regard to questions of faith, merely in general terms, of the change of good Christian customs, but in particular of the use of the mass in Swedish, which they would neither bear nor permit. This charge against the mass in Swedish, touched the city of Stockholm, where, at least from the year 1529, the mass had been performed in the mother-tongue; and an answer was given by that city, which had been chosen by the king to mediate with the Dalesmen. The king, it is said, in the letter of the city to these Dalecarlians, had put constraint on no one, but allowed learned men to discuss the case. Not men, but the pure word of God, had induced the city to introduce the mass in Swedish. It was more to edification that men should hear any good thing in their own mother-tongue, which it was shameful in us to despise, more than the people of Germany, Liffland, Denmark, and other countries, despised theirs. As the Dalesmen were probably but ill informed of the true state of the case in Stockholm, they were invited to send thither some envoys, one or two from each parish, the expenses of whose journey, both going and coming, would be defrayed by the city, to satisfy themselves that the usages adopted in that city were not so wicked and unchristian as was represented. At the same time the mass in Swedish was printed, and this itself was answer to the accusations.

The issue of this disturbance was, as regarded church reform, that it corrected the elasticity of the Dalesmen, as also that of Christian II., who now came forward as the champion of the Roman church, and who henceforth ceased to hinder the development of the new life of church and state.

CHAPTER V.

PROVISION FOR HAVING THE GOSPEL PREACHED—CHURCH-MANUAL AND MASS-BOOK IN THE SWEDISH LANGUAGE

The most impartant result of the decree passed at Orebro, was the advancement of the knowledge and preaching of God's word. In order to give it energy, the king sent one or two learned and approved men to each diocese, to preach in the cathedrals, or to establish cathedral schools. They were commended to the care and attention of the bishops and canons. It is said, that at this time men were invited for this purpose from the schools of Germany, as were the brothers Henick and Marianus, who had Strängness assigned them as the scene of their operations. To Skara, was sent a certain Mans Mansson, who, some time before, read lectures in Stockholm upon the gospels. But he was not welcome in Skara, where he seems to have arrived soon after the council of Orebro, and, therefore, just at the time of the insurrectionary ferment in West Gothland. When he entered the school, the pupils encountered him with stones and missiles, so that he was obliged to save himself by flight, and when he saw that he was not safe in Skara nor in West Gothland, he betook himself to Wadsten. The behavior of the scholars was an indication of the feelings with which the bishop returned from Orebro.

The ancient Christian church, did not read in her divine service the word of God without the accompaniment of an exposition, as appears from the homilies yet extant from the hands of many of the fathers of the church. But, after preaching became through the sacrificial worship of the middle ages only an occasional part of divine service, it was also in the Swedish church much neglected. It was natural that the Reformation, which again called the word of God into the light of day, should endeavor to elevate this word and the explanation of it to its proper place in divine service. The duty required of every parish priest, either by himself or an assistant, to preach the pure word of God, went not immediately into full operation, partly because of the disinclination of one or another of the bishops to enter heartily into the measure, partly from the influence of habit, but chiefly from the impossibility of procuring a sufficient number of competent preachers on whom reliance could be placed.

The indefatigable Olaus Petri, in performance of his promise given a year before, endeavored to relieve the difficulty, by complete postils for the direction and assistance of preachers. "It has been a great oversight," he says in his preface, "that we have not practised our clergy in God's word, before sending them out as priests of churches. Nor has the word of God been used in schools as it should have been, and as some provincial councils in this kingdom in former times commanded, but, which may God amend, has been neglected. It has thus come to pass, that, as soon as any one has knowledge enough to read or sing a mass, he is immediately good enough to become priest of a church, though he knows nothing of the word of God, on which his office chiefly depends. God grant we may yet find a cure for this.

In addition to exhorting priests diligently to read God's word, Olaus also proposes a method to render the people acquainted with the contents of the New Testament translated into Swedish. It was a long time since it could be presupposed of every member of the church, that he had the ability to read for himself the holy books, and also be added, that they were to be found in his own possession. But Olof, on the contrary, advises that the parish priests, "who have the New Testament in Swedish," read a portion every holiday in divine service, so that the people might hear the whole gospel from one end to the other.

At the end of the postils, are added directions how the priests ought to end their preaching with prayer and admonition, and a catechism freely translated from the larger catechism of Luther.

The decision of the prelates and heads of the church respecting the publication of the postils, was one of those measures concerted at Orebro, which are not mentioned in the acts of the council as subscribed. An important work of a similar kind, with which Olof was ready, soon after the council, or in April, 1529, was a church-manual in the Swedish language. It was not now first composed. The holy exercises prescribed in this manual, were already in use at Stockholm. It was published as a pattern, which might be followed and used, if found serviceable and convenient. It was a subject of deliberation at Orebro, that there ought to be a ritual of baptism in the Swedish language, and that there should be published an instruction for the sick, to prepare them for death. Olof, therefore, took occasion to add some other parts, and he was in hope that his work would be found more in agreement with the Holy Scripture than the Latin manual. It was absurd that the language understood by the people, should not be used in the holy actions of the church.

In this manual the most common practices of the church were contained, especially with respect to baptism, but exorcism by salt put into the mouth of the child was rejected, "because salt is one of the pure creatures of God."

Two years later than the manual, when dissatisfaction was expressed, during the insurrection of the Dalesmen, at the introduction of the mass in Swedish, master Olof published a little work, upon the reasons why the *mass* ought to be in the mother tongue understood by the people. At the same time appeared the Swedish mass as it is now holden in Stockholm, with the reasons why it is now so held.

This order of the mass, in 1531, is the most important change which took place in the church. Not only were laid aside many practices and usages, genuflections, crossings, frankincense, ringing at the elevation of the bread and chalice, but there was carefully rejected whatever presented the Lord's Supper as a sacrifice, or accorded with the doctrine of the Roman church, that the mass of the Lord's Supper was made by the priest the unbloody sacrifice of Christ for the sins of the world. It was prescribed, that there should be a distribution of the eucharist among the people *at every mass*, and that this distribution should be of both bread and wine, whereby the popish solitary masses, and the withholding the cup from the laity, were alike condemned.

It is singular that no direction for preaching, or any prescribed place for it, is to be found in the first four editions of the mass-book. As it was ordered by the council of Orebro, that the word of God should be preached in all churches of the kingdom, and that in city churches preaching should take place before mid-day, it is surprising that its place in divine service was not fixed; unless it be borne in mind, that the mass-book of the year 1529, was prescribed for divine service as then held at Stockholm, and that in towns preaching was a part of the morning and afternoon services, when, on the other hand, it was not called for at high mass.

But after this order of the mass by degrees became current in the whole kingdom, the whole order of divine service and the place for preaching were appointed, so as to be included in the service of the mass-book. This took place in 1548.

Previously, there were occasional permissions for the use of the Latin tongue, at first in private confessions to the priest, afterward only in some of the psalms. The edition of 1529 makes no mention of the allowance of Latin in divine service.

As early as 1529, the mass in Swedish was held in Stockholm, and some other towns. Its introduction was not a general ordinance, but took place gradually, where it could be effected by the priests, without creating scandal among the people. As late as the year 1539, when Mans Johansson, who had the castle and fief of Calmar, on occasion of the king's exhortation to the nobles of East Gothland to promote and protect evangelical doctrine, commanded the Swedish mass to be introduced into divine service within his fief, he is reminded by the king, that no improvement would follow the use of the Swedish mass, if the people were not first instructed, and that it was, therefore, of the utmost consequence to procure good and Christian preachers and teachers.

Of the success of a work so important to the Reformation, by acquainting the people with the gospel and its meaning, by introducing true evangelical freedom through a true faith in the Son, who makes us truly free, we cannot expect to procure information from times yet unable to prepare workmen to cultivate the field of the church. The preaching of God's word, the purifying of divine service from superstitious and strange practices, and from a language not understood, together with the reclaiming of the ecclesiastical constitution from being a hinderance, to being a means of furthering the kingdom of God, were important steps, and the commencement of a holy progress to a holy end.

CHAPTER VI.

ELECTION OF A BISHOP—LAURENTIUS PETRI, ARCHBISHOP OF UPSALA —FATE OF THE CHURCH TILL 1539.

THAT influence in the management of the church which the diet of Westeras gave the king, and which was sufficiently indefinite, was used at this time by him, partly to keep under his eye the bishops who were not to be depended upon or were inactive, partly, instead of the chapter, to direct the affairs of any vacant see, and to watch the election to be made by the chapter. As the king, in 1527, had placed the official acts of bishop Brask under inspection, so he appointed the dean of Westeras, Nils Andreæ, as assistant of its bishop, Petrus Magni. The reason assigned was, that the bishop, through age and infirmity, was not able to deal with unruly people, and, therefore, had not in his diocese the due obedience, so that the king had it in contemplation to employ him in another see which was in want of a bishop, there to visit and ordain. Neither the bishop nor Nils Andreæ ventured on any undertaking without the knowledge and consent of the king's officer. The year following, the bishop was restored to the full exercise of his office, but, in 1530, when king Gustavus became dissatisfied with a letter of the bishop to his diocese, on occasion of the edict for taxing bells, Herr Nils was again placed at his side.

The see of Upsala was intrusted to the dean of the chapter, John Laurentius, to be aided and assisted by the cantor, Erik Geting. After the flight of Brask, the care of the see of Linkoping was committed to the succentor, Jons. After bishop Magnus of Skara, in 1529, abandoned his see, it was placed under the care of its provost, master Sven, and any good man of the chapter was also to see to its welfare.

But, in 1529, doctor Jons or John Magni, provost of Linkoping, was elected by the chapter as its bishop, and their election was confirmed by the king, as in Skara was the case with the abovenamed master Sven, whose election was still further fortified by the recognition of the council, which, in 1530, sat at Upsala. By these elections the church of Sweden again broke with the Roman, whose bishops, Brask and Magnus Haraldi, had not resigned their claim. In 1530, Jons Bethius, canon of Wexio, was elected its bishop, as successor of Ingemar, who died some months before, having exercised his office for thirty-five years. But of the consecration of these bishops, as of filling the archiepiscopal chair, there was now no question. The delay appears to have been occasioned by the determination of the king to await the result of the celebrated and, for protestantism, important German diet of Augsburg. It may also have had foundation in the increasing indifference to the episcopal constitution of the church. Laurentius Andreæ, on the contrary, showed himself to be not well content with this procrastination, *and herein were betrayed the first symptoms of the misunderstanding between the king and his chief adviser in matters of church reform.* The dissatisfaction with the long-continued vacancy of the archbishopric spread still further. It was now ten years since it had been held by a consecrated bishop. In 1531, the Helsingers, who were then in a high state of ferment, demanded, among other things, that an archbishop should be called to the cathedral of Upsala, by which they doubtless intended a new election, not a return of Gustav Trolle or John Magnus. The king replied, that he agreed with them, but that in view of the injuries the kingdom had suffered from the bishops of Upsala, it was to be carefully weighed, on whom the honor shonld be conferred. He would very soon confer on the subject with the council of the kingdom. The king had previously given the case his serious thoughts.

During the previous year, 1530, the suffrages of the council of the kingdom and of the chapter, had, at an election held at Upsala, fallen upon the bishop of Abo, John Skytte, whom the king urged to accept the archbishopric. He, however, declined it. In the same year, the chapter of Upsala desired to have bishop Sven of Skara for its archbishop, but he also declined it, unless, probably, as a temporary trust. In the beginning of the summer of 1531, the king called together at Stockholm the bishops and chief clergy of the kingdom to make an election, the chapter of Upsala having neglected, it appears, to exercise its right. The election took place on midsummer day, in the great church of Stockholm. Of the four persons proposed, bishop Magnus of Strängness had four votes, Laurentius Andreæ fourteen, Jons, dean of the chapter of Upsala, three votes. The remaining votes, in number about one hundred and fifty, fell upon Laurentius Petri, who immediately received confirmation from the king to the office.

If the number of voters was as large as represented, protestantism had, among the clergy, a decided preponderance; since of so many votes only seven were withheld from the foremost originators and managers of the Reformation, Laurentius Andreæ, and the brother of Olaus Petri.

Protestants against the Roman church discipline, must *all* those have been, who took part in an election opposed to the practice of the church. It is said to have been the first in that generation effected by any others than members of the chapter.

Chance, or rather a certain providence, prevented Laurentius Andreæ or Olaus Petri from being placed in this the most elevated position in the church. The men who hitherto had been the heads of their party, were not suited to that conciliatory course, which alone could in a peaceful way effect the objects of the Reformation.

Laurentius Petri, thirty-two years old at the time of his election, is scarcely named in history, previous to his appearance on the scene of action, as by the wishes of the clergy and nomination of the king archbishop of the Swedish church, a dignity, whose lustre and importance could not be forgotten by those who a few years before saw it occupied by Jacob Ulfsson, Gustav Trolle, and, though not with full power, by John Magnus. These and their predecessors had rivalled in might the princes of the kingdom, and had not come short of them in pomp and princely retinue. The state of things had indeed been somewhat altered within the last five years, but this short period could not have obliterated the memory of what an archbishop of Upsala had been, and did not suffice to acquaint the occupant of the office with the place which, in the new discipline of the church, he was to hold. Much, if not everything, must depend upon the person who now took the crosier, which had been torn from one or two men yet living, and which could not be fully received from the other, a papal legate though without occupation.

Of the previous life of Laurentius, we know nothing with certainty. That he, as well as his elder brother, received the first rudiments of his education in the Carmelite monastery, at Orebro, is probable. That he accompanied his brother to Wittenberg, no ancient records testify. It is probable that he studied at Strängness, till he became a teacher at Upsala, in which occupation he was engaged, when, without being, it seems, a canon of the cathedral, he was called to be metropolitan of the Swedish church.

The friends of the papal hierarchy spoke of his elevation as an injurious disgrace to the church. Not merely his decided inclination to church reform—not merely his intrusion into the chair legitimately claimed by another—but his youth and inexperience, provoked their malevolent remarks.

During the forty years he exercised his functions, Laurentius Petri justified the confidence which called him to be the foremost guardian of the affairs of the Swedish church, now moulding itself anew. His learning and piety; his behavior, alike meek and serious; his willingness to yield where conscience permitted him; his firm adhesion to what he knew was right; the independence with which he labored for the church's weal, unmoved by the clamor of the zealots for the new, or the obstinacy of the advocates for the old order of things, won a reverence for his name during his lifetime, which the scrutiny of after-ages into his acts, has not been able to diminish. No man could be tried in a severer school, or in a position of more difficulty and embarrassments, than that in which Laurentius Petri was now placed, pressed, on the one hand, within the church's sphere by the encroaching claims of a powerful prince, and, on the other hand, by the opposite parties in religion, one of whom refused to acknowledge him as legitimate occupant of his office, while the other was dissatisfied with the caution he showed in exercising his influence in reforming the church.

Of the bishops who, being present at the diet of Westeras, declared their approbation of the measures there adopted, Magnus Sommar, of Strängness, and Petrus Magni, of Westeras, alone were left. But after the late election of bishops, and influenced by the flattering hopes which the disturbances respecting the bell tax had awakened, of restoring the old order of things in Sweden, they circulated the insurrectionary letters of Trolle, Magnus of Skara, and their coadjutors. They were in expectation also of the approach of Christian II., to recover with the aid of the Cæsar, the three northern crowns; and they either regretted the indecision they had hitherto manifested, or were anxious to make provision for the uncertain future. King Gustavus had summoned the bishops elect of Linkoping, Skara, and Wexio, to appear at Stockholm, on August 13, 1531, for the king's nuptials, and their own consecration. He had also summoned the bishops of Strängness and Westeras to officiate at the consecration of the others and of the archbishop elect. Just before their journey to Stockholm, they prepared, on August 10th, a protestation against all that was now taking place in the land, to the injury of the privileges of the Swedish church, and the advancement of the soul-destroying Lutheran heresy. They protested against the consecration of the intruded bishops and archbishop, which they themselves were necessitated to perform, "under the influence of fears and apprehensions which may well arise even in firm minds." They protested against the use of the Swedish mass, and against the assessment of the clergy. They declared to be invalid and of no effect all that they had done or were compelled to do against the Roman chair and church, which they desired to acknowledge as "their mother, and the mistress of mankind."

This protest was delivered to the well-known doctor Peter Galle, and the canon, Torger Gudlachi, "honor and reverence to the lord Gustavus, king of the kingdom of Sweden, always inviolate." It was not drawn up to be made public, unless under a change of circumstances, which should render it necessary as a self-defence. It was another evidence of the moral laxity in the high places of the church, which we have had more than one occasion to notice. The church, whose sponsors defended themselves by such means, could not count on stability. It is uncertain how far, or when, this protest came to the knowledge of king Gustavus. Bishop Petrus, of Westeras, retained his office, though under some restraints, till his death in 1534, and was succeeded the year after by Henrik Johannes, by birth a northman, who, in 1529, as lector and vicar-general of the Dominican order, signed the decree of the council of Orebro, and soon became one of the most zealous reformers.

Bishop Magnus Sommar, of Strängness, a member of the diet of Westeras, in 1527, was imprisoned by the king, at the time of his second nuptials, in 1536, on account, as is said, of the bishop's adhesion to the Roman church. He was released eight months after, but did not resume his office, retiring to the cloister of Krokek, where, provided with a sufficient support by the king, he ended his days about the year 1543, in undisturbed enjoyment of his faith.

He was succeeded in his diocese, in 1536, by master Bothvid Suneson, who had been for some time, canon of Linkoping, and who was the active ally and intimate friend of Olaus Petri. All these bishops had their appointments by election of the chapter. In the month of August, 1531, the bishops elect were consecrated; the archbishop on September 22d, in the church of the Franciscans, on the island near Stockholm, two days before he married the king to his first consort. Accurate information is wanting of the ceremonies used at this consecration, and how those of former like occasions were observed. The king, however, is said to have delivered the crozier with his own hands, to the archbishop, anointing and robes of office being also used.*

The king assigned to the archbishop a sufficient income to support the dignity of his office, in some degree approaching what it had formerly been. He even assigned him fifty attendants, probably that he might appear with dignity in Upsala, although such a train is certainly inconsistent with the decree of the diet of Westeras, and with the ideas of the office entertained alike by the king and the reformers. The archbishop soon discharged this life-guard, and transferred the expense of them to the support of fifty poor students.

* King John III., declares that the ceremonies he wished used at the consecration of an archbishop, in 1575, should be the same as those used by bishop Lars, of blessed memory.

Two years later, there occurs a contract of the king with the archbishop, which shows the power that, by virtue of the ordinantia of Westeras, the king left to him, in the see whose chief shepherd he was. The archbishop was to have the right of appointment to all vacant benefices within the diocese, but every appointee to the larger benefices was to be first presented to the king. The offences of priests, such as neglect of divine service or unwillingness to preach the word of God, the archbishop was to punish. Full liberty was left him to appoint public confession, and the king permitted the money paid for absolution, and of which account was to be made to him, according to the ordinantia of Westeras, to be turned to the support of schools and poor students. The oversight of the schools of the diocese was especially committed to him, as also of teachers and the course of instruction, in order that fit persons for the service of church and state might be trained. The incomes which teachers hitherto had were confirmed, and the archbishop was to see that these incomes were paid, and if possible increased, and that poor students got what was assigned for their support. But the archbishop was to undertake no reform without acquainting the king, "as hasty reformations were sometimes a scandal."

In 1531, the Swedish church was a complete establishment, with maintenance of the old constitution, but independent of and sundered from the Roman church. It had bishops who labored on the principles of the Reformation. There is nowhere to be found an analogy to the state of things, or the relations here existing. England had not yet broken with Rome. Calvinism had not presented its constitution, which, under an alleged historic testimony, in reality wants that testimony. In Denmark and Norway the hierarchy still contended for Rome, and in Germany neither had the old order been abolished nor the new been established, while the principle adopted at Spire, in 1526, that all electors, princes, and estates of the empire, might, with their subjects, so live and rule as each would answer before God and the emperor, left all in the hands of the administration of the land. The matter was deferred to the next general council or to a national assembly, but such a meeting, in the full sense of the term, never was brought together.

In Sweden the case was, till now, undetermined and vacillating. The church had not settled its doctrine of faith. The confession of faith, published by the German protestants at the diet of Augsburg, in 1530, was not mentioned. The old church law was neither in all respects, nor in any recognized particulars, abolished. Much, if not everything, depended upon the extent to which the king would carry the power that in 1527 was bestowed upon him. By virtue of this decree of Westeras, he decided individual cases without establishing general rules. The king was often consulted in doubtful points, or his judgment was solicited. Thus, in the year 1530, had the peasantry of Kudby, in the diocese of Linkoping, expressed to the king, by a messenger, their doubt how far they ought to tolerate their pastor, who had entered the marriage state. The king advises them to be at peace with what had happened, inasmuch as it was not contrary to the word of God. A woman obtained, in 1531, the king's permission to live separate from her husband. A peasant, whose wife committed adultery, gained the king's license to take another wife. The priest Gunne of Satilla, in the diocese of Skara, begged to know of the king, whether, after losing, by accident, the thumb of one of his hands, he ought to execute his office. The king replied, that, on consultation with men conversant in Scripture, he found there was nothing in such an occurrence, according to God's law, to hinder Gunne from exercising his functions, "however the pope's law might decide otherwise, which we hold in little account when we have God's word for us."

In concert with the bishops and Laurentius Andreæ, the king labored for the settlement of church and state. Olaus Petri continued, though with a less number of writings, his activity as an author. In 1535, there came out two works from his pen. The one is a treatise on the justification of man, in which this question is unfolded with his wonted clearness and strength, conformably to the present teaching of our church. The other, of the same year, is an explanation of the tenth chapter of St. Matthew, de signed as an exhortation to steadfastness under persecution, and that we should not lose our confidence, because many foes of the gospel rejected its truth. They were not to be accounted preachers of the gospel, who could merely talk ill of priests and monks. There was no art in tearing down; a Turk or heathen could do that. *The art was to remove abuses, and give freedom to truth.* With the exception of several editions of his spiritual hymn books, these were the last writings on the subject of the Reformation, which came from Olof during his lifetime. There only came afterward from his pen, that which contributed to lose him the favor and protection of king Gustavus, his "Sermon against the horrible oaths and blasphemy of God, which are now too commonly practised." It was printed in 1539, and awaked the royal displeasure, by the relentless manner in which it denounced the bad habit that was not the least of the king's. It merits also attention as a picture of the times, and was, in Sweden, the first expression of regret that the work of improvement did not bear moral fruit so soon nor of such richness as was hoped and expected, and that the power within the church which was wrested from the pope, there was reason to fear might fall into the hands of a worldly ruler.

The new archbishop appears, in 1538, for the first time, as an ecclesiastical author. This was intended as a blow to the abuses in the church. The use of holy water had been explained at the council of Orebro, in 1529, but had not been forbidden. Some years later, it had been here and there altogether laid aside. The clamor this awakened induced him to publish his work on holy water. His office, he says, admonished him to write on a subject of which no one as yet had treated. After having shown the blasphemies resulting from the abuse of holy water, he concludes with an admonition not to use it or let it be used with consecration or with sprinkling. This little work was the firstling of his public announcement of his principles as a reformer. His time, till now, he had occupied in the exercise of his duties within his diocese, and in a work which was a more conclusive evidence of his energy, his execution of a translation of the Bible into Swedish, of which, probably revised by him, the Psalter made its appearance in 1536, together with the Athanasian creed in Swedish.

From this time much attention was given to edifying the people and clergy in good works, by the publication of books of devotion. Two of these, which came out in 1537, are familiar to us. The one is a lesson of instruction for plain people, based upon the ten commandments, the creed, and Lord's prayer. As usual in books of prayer, it contains, after an exhortation to prayer, a prayer for the grace of the Holy Spirit to teach us to pray, separate prayers on each of the commandments, the articles of faith, and the Lord's prayer, on the sacraments, and sufferings of Christ, with some penitential psalms and litanies. The other, which must have been at the time a most prized and familiar book for edification, since before and during the year 1580 five editions at least were published, is entitled: "The faith and medicine of the soul, useful at all times, but especially at the approach of death." It justifies, by its warm Christian tenor, and its simple and pure representations, the confidence and popularity it obtained among all sorts of people.

The increased demand of the times for the extension, independent examination, and freedom of God's word, by those who were engaged in the promulgation of truth, was often a hinderance to the advancement of that truth. Another hinderance was the uncertain position of the church, and the diminished respect for the sanctity of the priestly office, which threatened a deficiency of clergy and teachers. People became less disposed to offer their sons for the service of the church, when they were to give them up to an uncertain future, uncertain both in regard to an adequate support, and what would be acceptable to God, in an office to be exercised, as it might be, either in the old or the new faith. As early as 1533, the king was obliged to issue a letter, in which he complains that the number of pupils in the schools was lessened. He advises the people to send their sons, that the church might not want men to serve her, and promises to take care of their future. This admonition, "to keep children at school," was afterward frequently renewed, and it was added, that, as a consequence of the people's inclination to curtail their tithes, very few fathers were willing to allow their children to be students. An admonition to the same effect, appeared also in 1571, the year in which the discipline of the church was settled, as will be hereafter narrated.

But the course of instruction necessary for the proper training of priests, or of those destined to the service of church or state, was either incomplete, or sometimes, from the lukewarmness of the administrators, inefficacious. To prepare teachers for their office, many young men were sent to Germany, and were placed, on their return home, in the church, in schools, or in the king's chancery. Laurentius Andreæ advised the bishops to search out and keep about them suitable men, whom they could trust with the charge of the schools in their dioceses. He had also to make provision for the support of those who studied abroad. Many obtained prebends or other sources of income from the king. Many were supported abroad by the bishops. The number of those who pursued and completed their studies in Germany was not small. At the university of Wittenberg alone, from 1527 to 1529, about forty Swedes were matriculated, and this was not the only university frequented, although the civil commotions in Sweden and the quarrel with Lubeck, in 1534 and 1535, were obstacles to travellers.

A great preventive to a high course of scholastic training within the land, was the want of a university. The establishment begun at Upsala in 1477, had stopped at the death of the founders. As early as 1538, king Gustavus conceived himself under an obligation to wipe out the reproach, which he heard was brought against him in Germany, for his neglect to establish a high school. But that man must be ignorant of the full force of the excuse the king offered for himself, the ruin of the kingdom, when he took it as "a lamed and desolated kingdom," the enormous debt of that kingdom, the perpetual insurrections and wars, and the deficiency of men suitable for high schools; that man must be ignorant, that the decree of 1527 did not cast the riches of the church into the king's hand as a booty, to be used at his pleasure, that neither he nor any other could reckon upon how much of these riches would remain for free bestowal, after the right of heirship from the individuals was satisfied, that moreover the abrogation of the existing estab lishments *was not decreed*, but only a slowly maturing fruit of the decree of Westeras and of the adjustment of principles; that man must be ignorant of all this, and of the whole condition of things within Sweden, who does not exonerate the king from all blame at this period. Whether for the subsequent twenty years he is subject to the charge of negligence, we shall, as we proceed, have occasion to determine.

As yet the old church was not condemned, further than the condemnation occasioned by the free preaching of God's word. This preaching and promulgation of the word, required certain changes, but these were not made except when it could be done without scandal. It was acknowledged that truth could make itself known even under the old forms, and that demolition does not evince the presence of God in the strongest light. To watch over the free course of the light of the gospel that it might penetrate and disperse the darkness around, to remove whatever most stood in the way of its activity, constituted the power, the commission, which, in 1527, the king received from his people. He so construed this commission, though by degrees he was led to consider and treat the contending parties, as respectively the opponents of truth and of falsehood. The many plots which endangered the peace of the land and his crown, could not but conduce to embitter his mind against the Roman church.

In Linkoping a certain master Claude had excited attention and disturbance by a Bible-lecture or sermon. The king expressed his surprise, and commanded that they who had anything to say against the word of God or them that preached it, should, within a given time, present themselves before the archbishop. Master Thore, canon of Linkoping, in particular, was summoned, and afterward other zealots of the old order. Two years later, Arvid Trolle, who held the cloister of Wadsten in investiture, was directed to watch carefully the *papistic* party in Wadsten, because the monks there "were begining again to lie and preach their old hypocrisy. The king complains that the monks and nuns of Wadsten, and even the bishop of Linkoping, with some of his old brothers of the chapter, opposed the word of God, although they promised to promote the cause of the gospel.

From this period, the year 1539, a new phase is presented in the history of the Swedish church reformation. It was a breach in the life of the church. Its old order became now abhorred *popery;* and what was previously considered promotion of the gospel seemed now to be the opposite. New men stood forward, and desired in the name of the king to make new views to pass current. He began to lay a heavier hand upon the church, and during the period immediately following, a disorganization began, of which none could say what would be the result, till in time the case assumed a more benignant aspect.

CHAPTER VII.

THE KING'S DISPLEASURE WITH LAURENTIUS ANDREÆ AND OLAUS PETRI—ACCUSATION AND JUDGMENT AGAINST THESE MEN—THE NEW CONDITION OF THE CHURCH UNDER THE INFLUENCE OF PEUTINGER AND NORMAN—VISITATIONS OF THE CHURCHES—PLUNDERING OF CHURCHES—DISSATISFACTION.

THE mind of the king began, in 1539, to be alienated from and embittered against the men who hitherto had been his counsellors and leaders in the affairs of the church. Laurentius Andreæ was a man of too lordly a spirit, to be in immediate contact with his master as soon as the king discovered a greater independence in his views and management of the business of the church. The firmness and boldness which the chancellor displayed toward the old church, was shown, sometimes, perhaps, too indiscreetly, with respect to the king, when he wished to go beyond the path which master Lars had marked out for the improvement of the church in the decrees of 1527 and 1529, in which we have seen his plan of church reform to have been settled. Sustained by his confidence in the justice and utility of this change for the better in the church, he urged the king forward, when the latter considerately or cautiously listened to the progress of the work in Germany, whence as well as from the Netherlands the greatest dangers menaced his throne. But the chancellor wished also to hold back the king, when he threatened the constitution of the Swedish church with the same looseness of discipline, which preceded the stability that protestant Germany, from 1529, subsequently gained.

The tongue and pen of master Olof could, in his youthful ardor, sometimes forget themselves. King Gustavus fancied, that, in Olof's Swedish chronicles, which it is said came out in 1530, he found sundry reproachful hints against himself. Olof, in his preaching, spared not the king. His printed sermon against oaths and blasphemy gave him many sharp cuts, and occasioned a prohibition to the reformers, as before was done to Brask, to print anything without the king's consent.

The king's dissatisfaction with the reformers, extended to the manner in which the Reformation was conducted, and the disturbances which thence arose. The preachers who, according to the decree of the council of Orebro, were sent to the parishes to assist incompetent priests, were not always mature enough to exercise their calling with sense and moderation, and were not always acceptable to the pastors into whose office they intruded. Reform preceded the instruction given of its necessity, and the king seems to have expected from the instruction too rapid results. He had hoped that the new doctrine would be able to exorcise the spirit of insurrection, and the disorders which, in former times, fomented by the church against the rulers of the state, agitated the minds of the people; but he found the reformers themselves not seldom dissatisfied with his course, and with unmerciful freedom expressing their dissatisfaction. He met with resistance on the part of the new bishops, and was reminded, that, by the great diminution of their incomes and those of the cathedrals, by suppressing many canons and prebends, he had, while commanding them to supply the churches with preachers, made it difficult or impossible for them to obey the command. He saw how easily, in 1536, the power of the bishops in Denmark was perfectly broken. His suspicion, nourished by the conduct of many churchmen, caused him to regard every movement of those bishops who did not in all things coincide with his views, as a covert attempt to win back the independence of the hierarchy. The meek archbishop himself received the sharp, but certainly undeserved reproach, of being willing to shear the sheep and use the wool, yet not take care of the flock, while on one occasion he was answered, "Preachers should ye be and not masters." Reform seemed to the king either precipitate and awkwardly begun, or too slow in its progress and incomplete. When the archbishop wrote, that in Upsala there was preaching, not only on the mass in Swedish, marriage, eating of meat, and the like, but on repentance and amendment, the true Christian faith, brotherly love, and a godly and righteous life, the king replied: "Such we do not reprove. But, because this is done in Upsala, it does not follow that it is done over the whole kingdom. Sorrow is to be felt, not for Upsala alone, but for the diocese and the whole land." The king's language, in the same letter, was a harbinger of a new order of things soon to be introduced. "Wherever we hereafter see and learn that God's word is not in a Christian manner and on better grounds announced and promulgated by you and your advisers, than we hear or have heard, we know not what will be our will and pleasure. We must change our mind as God shall give us grace."

The king's dissatisfaction was kept alive, if not originally awakened by the adventurer, Conrad Peutinger, who came to Sweden in August, 1538, and who, in the course of that year, was endowed with the incomes of the cantor of the cathedral of Upsala. For this adventurer the way to the king's favor was to be cleared by the removal of his former adviser. In his projects, respecting church reform, he soon found the aid of another foreigner.

In 1538, master Nicholas Magni, then in Germany, was commissioned by king Gustavus, to look for and send to Sweden some learned man competent to take charge of the education of the young duke Erik. His choice fell on a

Pomeranian noble, George Norman, born in Rygen, and of a family scattered over Denmark. He had studied at Wittenberg. This choice was approved by Luther and Melancthon, with whom Nicholas consulted, and, in 1539, Norman arrived in Sweden, furnished with letters of recommendation from both those learned men of Wittenberg to king Gustavus. He brought with him their testimony, for being a man that feared God, was learned, and of a modest and good behavior.

Norman took part in the consultations regarding the present condition and future prospects of the Swedish church. Both these strangers could only judge of that church by its dissonance from the protestant churches beyond Sweden. For Norman, at least, the electorate of Saxony was the natural exemplar. The king ought in Sweden to have the same power over the church of his land, as the German estates possessed in theirs. Among kings, also, Henry VIII. of England had made himself head of the church in his kingdom. The bishops ought to be removed out of the way; or at least be restrained and limited in the exercise of their office. In the constitution of the church they might be dispensed with. Neither Luther nor Melancthon was bishop. The Reformation in Sweden had not advanced, because the king had not yet in his kingdom instituted the perquisition, which, in the electorate of Saxony, in 1528 and 1529, had, in the name of the elector, been accomplished by ecclesiastical and civil commissioners, in their visitation of the churches. The usages and customs which hitherto had remained in Sweden were stigmatized as unbelief and superstition, which should no longer be tolerated. The king was now transformed into a protestant in the strictest sense of the term, after the pattern of German Lutheranism.

Toward the close of the year 1539, an indictment was brought against Laurentius Andreæ and Olaus Petri, a proof of the use or abuse of the confidence it had been Peutinger's fortune to gain with the king. The articles of accusation, which king Charles IX., from regard to the memory of his father, cashiered from Tegel's history of Gustavus, proved the influence the accused possessed with the king, and how burdensome that influence had now become. That they sometimes abused or made too great use of the confidence reposed in them by the king, is apparent, but it is still more apparent that they acted on principles which the king *now no longer* recognized, or to which he gave a wider scope than the reformers thought justifiable. This is particularly evident from the charges laid against Laurentius Andreæ in regard to church reform. He had, it is said, under promise of fidelity and support, induced the king to undertake this reform, although the king was cautious, regarded himself as not sufficiently provided with the means, and feared the consequences. He had afterward, during the insurrections, not been constant to the king, had precipitated him into difficulties, and left him there, indifferent whether the king swam to land or was drowned. Master Lars had with remissness managed affairs that did not benefit himself, but on the contrary, delighted to be alone the shepherd where he could shear the wool. He had all the senators on his side, and conducted himself insolently toward the king, and thought himself, "with his evangelical crew," as strong as the king, and able to protect himself if the king would not protect him, while the king, having no fit advisers about him, but surrounded by traitors, must disguise his anguish, "which ground his heart like a mill," and must make himself agreeable to master Lars. When the king wished to restrain a dishonest chamberlain, master Lars had winked to him to know "what his majesty wanted with so much money, good friends being better and more profitable than much money." At first the chancellor had declared that the bishops ought not to have greater power than the king would grant them, but afterward had gone backward like a crab, and claimed for the bishops peculiar respect and independent might and power, though he well knew that temporal jurisdiction does not belong to them except as administrators of the people.

Master Lars thus wished, as is evident from this last point of accusation, that the church should not sacrifice its independence, by becoming, in the moment of its deliverance from Roman oppression, subject to the temporal power of the land. Although he did not undertake to carry through his plan in a manner that admitted no alteration in details, he laid the foundation of that admirable form, in which the Swedish church afterward developed itself. That which his successors in the king's favor laid to his charge, distinguishes him as one of the most clear-sighted and deep thinking minds that were ever engaged in the establishment of a protestant church.

Charges were made in common, against master Lars and master Olof,* to the effect, that the latter, through the confessional, became acquainted with the plot of the German burghers of Stockholm against the king's life, that he as well as master Lars, to whom it was communicated, concealed it, that they had taken part with the iconoclasts of Stockholm in 1524, that they plundered churches and monasteries, and pulled down altars, and had done many the like things.

Olof, in particular, was complained of, for his chronicles and sermons. In the former work he appears to the king, as the latter reports, to have too indulgently painted the Romish times, and to have given side cuts to his own contemporaries. The charge against the sermons was partic-

* Master Lars was also accused of having persuaded the king to make the incompetent Olof chancellor, when he himself, from age, could no longer hold the office. Olof became chancellor in 1531, when he resigned the duties of secretary to the council of Stockholm, and was dismissed in 1533.

ularly directed to the one, in which Olof represented certain mock suns that appeared in the heaven, as foreboding punishment for the sins of the sovereign. He had, moreover, perverted the Scripture, to induce the king to spare the lives of traitors, and it seems to have been included in the charges against the sermons, that instead of teaching the people the catechism, they discoursed of the Revelation of St. John.

The court consisted of fifteen of the king's "council and good men," among whom, besides the two foreigners, Peutinger and Norman, may be noticed the three ecclesiastical members, archbishop Laurentius Petri, brother of Olaus, the bishops Bothvid of Strängness, a friend of Olaus, and Henrik of Westeras. After the accused had first denied all intentional offence, but after they had confessed themselves guilty, and on their knees begged mercy, the doom of death was pronounced upon them, at Orebro, on January 2d, 1540. Three commissioners from the court, with two of the spectators, one a Swede and one a German, either the hearers of Olaus at Stockholm or inhabitants of the town of his birth, where he was doomed, went to the king to beg a remission of the sentence. This was finally granted, but with a heavy amercement, which the friends of Olaus at Stockholm paid for him, but which master Lars paid out of his own resources, which by such a disbursement were nearly exhausted.

Laurentius Andreæ withdrew after this tragedy, from the scene of public life. There was no place found for his energy in the times immediately succeeding, and his age entitled him to repose. He retired to Strängness, after participating for nearly seventy years in the public affairs of church and state. He passed peacefully in his retreat the last twelve years of life till his death, on April 29th, 1552, some days after the decease of Olaus Petri. Charles IX., the son of king Gustavus, made, in the face of posterity, an atonement to the memory of Laurentius, when, on examination of it, he would not allow the charges against the brothers to remain in the history of his father. But full justice has scarcely yet been rendered the man who has the merit of having first led the way to a reform of the Swedish church, and led it on the basis of sense and moderation, by which, for the most part, it went forward though amid continual struggles.

The intervention of the king in the affairs of the church, was now for a time chiefly under the influence of his new chancellor, Von Pyhy or Peutinger. But the active measures, through which the king was expected to effect a more complete, and, for the enlightenment and peace of the land, a more decisive improvement, were intrusted to G. Norman. On the 8th of August, 1539, the king made known, "as the supreme defender of the Christian faith over his whole realm," and, in a letter directed to all *his* bishops, prelates, and other spiritual pastors and preachers, that, having with sorrow found, how, in times past, strange schismatical preachers seduced his subjects, under pretext of gospel freedom, into disobedience and carnal liberty against their sovereign, he now appointed George Norman as *his ordinary and superintendent.* This Norman was, with consent of a council and adjunct, appointed for the purpose, to exercise the king's jurisdiction over bishops, prelates, and all other spiritual persons.* He was to take care, that bishops and preachers should set an example in doctrine and life to the king's "poor subjects," who partly wandered in the darkness of simplicity (the friend of truth), and should instruct the people in the ways of charity, peace, and obedience to their temporal prince. Civil and criminal cases he was to remit to the king, and see that nothing was nndertaken to the king's prejudice, by bishops, prelates, or spiritual per-

* The term priest does not occur in the transactions of the king's chancery, during the time of Von Pyhy, but was changed for the correspondent German word for spiritual persons (geistliche).

sons, and that no jurisdiction was exercised by them. All spiritual persons were to be put in office by him with the king's patent, visitations were to be made by him at the places and times named by the king. The doctrine and lives of spiritual persons and preachers were to be examined by him. Those who were incompetent to instruct, were, but with the king's consent, to be removed, and others put in their places. Those who lived lives worthy of punishment, or taught anything contrary to God's word and civil order, were to be sent by him to the king, or left in sure trusty hands.

This regulation was, in conclusion, so modified that, after the visitations of the superintendent, *elders*, probably laymen, were appointed by the king to inspect the places visited by the superintendent or his adjunct, and see that what they were directed to do was effectually put into execution. Over these elders, was also appointed a conservator, who was a layman, and who was to have the oversight of the visitation of these elders. He was to see that the established doctrine and discipline were observed, to punish ecclesiastics, who, either for error of life or doctrine, were complained of by the elders, unless the offence were that of *læsæ majestatis*, high treason. He was to assist the elders on their visitations if requested, to receive visitation reports and transmit them to the superintendent. To the superintendent he was to submit the more difficult cases, respecting ceremonies, divine worship, or marriage, and abide by his judgment. He was to appear before the superintendent and his adjunct, and aid them if they again made a visitation of the places where they had before been. He was to protect ecclesiastics in their office, and see that their stipends were paid, to use the king's jurisdiction and judgment over spiritual persons and their tenants, and inspect the hospitals.

Over the conservator was placed the superintendent,

as exercising the king's highest power over the church. A council of religion of whose meetings, however, nothing was said, were to be his advisers. A council of the church, when occasion required, was to be called together by the king, to deliberate on doctrine, ceremonies, and divine worship, schools, universities, and the support of the poor. At this council were to assemble, the superintendent, his adjunct, the council of religion, and all the conservators. At the council of the church, the church ordinances were to be examined which the king purposed to introduce.

Through this complicated discipline, which the king set up "by virtue of his authority," he actually annulled the treaty and ordinantia of Westeras. Through this, was transferred from the Swedish people to the king, the power to withdraw the wealth and property bestowed on the church by the crown and individuals, and to take the oversight of the administration of the bishops. By these regulations were the bishops so set aside, that no exercise of their office seems to have been left them, except the ordination of priests. All that now seemed wanting to be done was formally to suppress the episcopal office, and declare the government of the church, according to the German pattern, to belong to the temporal ruler of the land, who might decide on Christian faith and worship with the same propriety as in the use of his civil jurisdiction. The king's privileges within the church rested, not on the church's commission, but on his own royal might and power.

In 1540, the king from Orebro had spread over the kingdom his edict, "that by virtue of his high and kingly authority," he desired to remove all kinds of false and perverse doctrines which might be current in the church.*

* In the academy of Upsala were found certain "*articuli ordinantiæ*," among which was the prohibition to use such psalms in Swedish as might "give occasion to carnal liberty;" such as, "The snare is broken and we are delivered."

The regulations of which we have spoken were so immediately carried into execution, that Norman and his adjunct, bishop Henrik of Westeras, commenced their visitation of West Gothland in the autumn of 1539, and finished it before April of the following year. Certain articles respecting doctrine and church usages were proposed to the priests, and answered by them. A visitation of Vermland was made in the course of the same year, as also of East Gothland, which was completed before the end of the month of July. The only information, and it is brief, which we have of these visitations is derived from that which was made of the monastery of Wadsten. The superintendent and his adjunct came there on Whit Sunday, May 16, 1540, performed the mass in Swedish, and forbade all ceremonies in memorial of the saints, except the prayer *pro pace*. On Trinity Sunday, bishop Henrik performed mass and preached in the church of the monastery. The day after, Nicholas Amundi preached there, whom the visitors chose as father-confessor, after compelling the former occupant of that office to lay it down. They finally took an inventory of the chattels of the cloister.

In 1541, when Norman was prevented by engagements relating to the state, bishop Henrik was appointed in connection with Isaac Birgersson for Empteryd, and John Olsson for Asa, to make a visitation over the whole of Smaland. The fief of Calmar was included. The appointment is more limited than that given to the superintendent. They were to impress upon the priests the observance of the church ordinances, respecting doctrine and ceremonies issued by the king through the superintendent. Bishop Henrik was to see that the priests led correct lives, but all the more difficult cases were to be referred to the king.

The visitors who were appointed for Smaland, took also another commission, kindred to that used by superintendent Norman, in the parts he visited, although nothing of this is mentioned in his own commission. They were to take an inventory of all the valuables and silver not needed for public worship. These were to be sealed up and kept safely, till the king should have need of them for "his own necessities and those of the kingdom, and for Christian uses and purposes."

During these visitations, commenced the plundering of churches, which does so little honor to the memory of this great king. The silver tribute, levied in 1523, upon churches and cloisters, was allowed by the estates of the kingdom and by the heads of the church, and had the aspect of a loan or free-will offering. The valuables which, at the dissolution of a cloister, were transferred to the treasury of the king, might be considered as a lapsed inheritance returning to the heir, and even the gifts of individuals be so construed.

But now, the property taken, could in no sense be called a fief, nor was its application a case of necessity, and the surrender of the silver was not with the good will of the parishioners. The king did not apply for the consent of the council or the estates, but merely declares, that "for certain remarkably well-grounded and substantial reasons, he had, considering the necessities of the crown and kingdom, caused to be inventoried and kept, the silver money and other valuables of the churches, to be applied to the service of God, as they had been hitherto misused by these churches to unchristian purposes."

It was left to the judgment of the visitors to determine what, and if anything, should be left to the maintenance of the churches, or as necessary for public worship. The things considered most unnecessary, without taking into account the coined gold and silver, were the images of saints, with their ornaments and shrines. To the list, were added rings, crosses, vessels for frankincense, and the like, not omitting chalices and patens of gold and silver. The amount of the precious metals gathered in masses was not inconsiderable. Master Norman remitted from all the country churches in East and West Gothland seven thousand and ninety-eight marks of pure silver. The tributes levied on cathedrals, town churches, and cloisters, amounted to an enormous sum. From the cathedral of Wexio were taken a gold chalice of two pounds weight, with gilded silver chalices and patens, and many other things of great value. There appears to have been no estimate made of the jewels carried off, but there is no question of their vast amount.

The king was not disposed to abandon the golden mine which was opened to him, when once he had adjudged to the crown whatever the church was thus thought able to spare, in view of the altered state of public worship. The process was continued during almost all the rest of his reign, perhaps interrupted, during the disturbances which soon followed this collection of taxes in Smaland, and, probably, with an observance of greater caution. In 1545, bishop Henrik had negotiated with the peasants, as likely, in his own diocese, to let the king have the superfluous silver, "that it might not be used in the old way." A part of them had offered of their own accord to give it up to the king, with which he declares himself to be "greatly content." From Helsingland, the church silver was sent to the king in 1547, but the messengers made known, that, in the church of Delsbo there was a great deal that could be dispensed with. The king's country steward, Nils Helsing, was accordingly ordered to search into the matter, and send what was there to be found. In 1548, John, the pastor of Bygdea, remitted chalices, patens, crosses, and broken silver, from the southern provostship of Westerbotten. Ten years later, the churches in the fief of Abo were taxed, and very little left them.

The search for whatever of value was to be found in churches, led to the concealment of precious things, till better times.

Thus, the king having obtained information of such a treasure concealed under the high altar of the church of Mora, commands the altar to be taken down, and what was beneath it to be dug up. When churches ceased to be used for divine service, or were pulled down, as was the case with too many in West Gothland, the king declared that the bells and church silver belonged to the crown and ought to be transferred to it. Sometimes he gave away the church silver: he presented, in 1546, Svante Sture and his wife Martha, the sister-in-law of Gustavus, with a crown, two garlands, and all the rest of the silver in the church of Morko, with the exception only of two chalices and what was necessary to the use of the congregation.

This plundering could not but awaken dissatisfaction. It poured oil upon the fire, which, never fully quenched, began to blaze anew. A better acquaintance with the course adopted at the visitations, respecting divine service, priests, and ornaments, would doubtless prove, how greatly this discontent was fostered by the acts of the visitors. At least we know that the shrines and ornaments of the images were carried off. It is probable, that the images themselves were removed or destroyed when the invocation of saints was prohibited, and that the Swedish manual and mass-book of Olaus Petri, of both of which new editions appeared in 1540, were recommended or introduced, without the caution which, in 1539, was required. It is also probable that a stricter inquiry than hitherto, into the abilities and life of the priests, was instituted, and that this is a reason why some of them placed themselves on the side of the malcontents. These probabilities are fortified by the disturbances which, notwithstanding the quiet in other quarters, arose in Smaland and the adjacent province, subjected to the ecclesiastical visitation; disturbances which were the last and fiercest to check and overthrow the new order of things within the church as well as the civil government. As early as the month of April, 1540, when the visitation of West Gothland was threatened, a peasant of that province began to draw followers around him, declaring his intention to slay the knights, and nobles, and all others who held to the Lutheran doctrine. This insurrectionary movement was, however, stifled at its commencement. During the autumn of the same year, there was a hot ferment in East Gothland and Smaland. To this explosion was added, previous to 1542, the insurrection raised by the celebrated peasant Dacke. Among the grievances enumerated by the people against the nobles and stewards of the king, complaint was made, "that the ornaments were taken from the churches and cloisters, and all that their fathers and forefathers had given and designed for the glory of God, so that it would soon be as pleasant to go into an empty wood as into a church." They demanded, that the mass and other church usages should be continued, as hitherto had been customary, "for a child could soon whistle forth a mass." They said that a poor man who fell into danger or misfortune could "enjoy no peace in a church or a cloister," that the principle hitherto, for the most part, pursued, not to press the Reformation forward faster than previous instruction would enable it to avoid scandal, was now forgotten. If the outward magnificence of divine worship were taken away, in order that the people might be taught to worship God in spirit and in truth, and in order that the law might give protection alike to high and low, yet the want was bitterly felt of a sanctuary which, in necessity, might be the refuge of the helpless.

The man, Von Pyhy, who during this period directed the movements of Gustavus, began to lose the confidence of his sovereign. It was altogether withdrawn in the autumn of 1543, at which time he was put in prison, though afterward released. The general ill will toward this councillor, and the measures and steps that were taken during his administration, induced the king to allow the church ordinances, projected by him, in a great degree to fall to the ground. They were never fully carried out, certainly not in the provinces, especially West Gothland, for which they were designed. The king consulted with the "stadtholder," Gustav Olsson, who seems to have been appointed conservator, respecting the hospitals in West Gothland, the care of which belonged to the conservator, and gave him a commission to inquire into the application of a peasant for a divorce. But these cases might seem to belong to the civil administration and courts of justice. The bishops, too, who, under the late regulations, appeared to be superfluous, kept up at least the name. Henrik of Westeras, called himself bishop, and so were called from this time Jons of Wexio, and Sven of Skara. The last named, who, after the regulations made for West Gothland, in 1540, was called the king's under-chancellor, received that year an augmentation of his income; and in 1541, the king issued in favor of *bishops*, prebends, canons, and *church priests*, a letter of protection against the requirement of unreasonable hospitality. The authority of Norman in the church did not cease by any positive and explicit edict. The commissions, however, issued from and after the year 1544, to the heads of the church, do not mention him, though in a letter of 1545, the king commands the chapter of Skara to obey him.

But in order to proceed further in representing the position of the church after the reform of Peutinger, we must fasten attention upon the most important step which, at this time, was taken for the true improvement of the Swedish church.

CHAPTER VIII.

TRANSLATION OF THE BIBLE INTO SWEDISH IN 1541—PROGRESS OF THE REFORMATION—ORDINANTIA OF WESTERAS IN 1544—CHANGE IN CONDITION OF BISHOPS, CHAPTERS, AND PARISH PRIESTS.

TILL KING JOHN III.'S ACCESSION TO THE THRONE IN 1568.)

THE work of inwardly improving the church, of delivering the souls of men from the chains of unbelief and self-righteousness, in which the false and superstitious forms of the church had bound them, was that fruit of the Reformation which does not draw the notice of men, especially at a time when efforts and attention were demanded to remove the hinderances which the church's own institutions presented. Great caution was needed that the wheat might not be rooted up with the weeds. This work is by no means of man, but of the Holy Ghost. Men can, in this respect, do no more than open for every heart an access to the word, which is eternal and can save the soul and cause the life to bear witness to its sanctifying efficacy.

The four years, from 1526 to 1529, had been especially remarkable in the Swedish church, for the efforts used to bring the word of truth and life home to the hearts of the people. The translation of the New Testament; the many writings which treated of the word, and exhibited its meaning, purpose, and doctrine; the decree which paved the way for its free promulgation, and provided for its illustration; and the removal of those temptations which turned the church of Christ into a kingdom of this world, may be numbered among such efforts.

As from this time there was a lively and uninterrupted progress of the principles promulgated as those of the Reformation, it was not forgotten, that hitherto there existed no translation of the whole of the Sacred Volume into the Swedish mother tongue. The preface to the *New* Testament of 1526, had made known that the *Old*, with God's help, might soon be expected. The Psalter appeared ten years later, but the whole Bible for the first time in 1541.

It appears that the multiplicity of business consequent upon the diet of 1527 and its decree, had prevented the two foremost men at that time, engaged in the cause of the Reformation, from taking in hand a translation of the Old Testament. Martin Luther, who, by his example, prompted the work of a Swedish translation, had not in 1534, completed his own in German, of which, however, some portions came out in the following year. We suppose, that as soon as Laurentius Petri was elevated to the archiepiscopal chair, and was able to reduce the business and claims of his office, the work was undertaken and afterward carried on without interruption. It was begun before 1536, when the Psalter was ready and printed. In 1538, it was determined to begin the printing of the Old Testament. This was completed at Upsala, at the close of the year 1540, without the Apocryphal books, but with which and the New Testament, the whole Bible was printed and published in 1541.

The church paid the expenses of this edition of the Bible, out of funds whose management was in the king's hands. The incomes of the archdeaconate of Upsala were used for the printing of the Bible, after Laurentius Andreæ had ceased to receive them. From the tithes of every church also, there was appropriated to this object, the yearly payment of one barrel of pure rich corn, which even to this day is payable, under the denomination of the Bible barrel, although diverted as a crown tax to wholly different purposes. In 1538, bishop Bothvid assigned to Olaus Petri five hundred marks for the purchase of paper on which to print the Old Testament, but whether this was a private gift or drawn from some public fund we do not venture to decide.

Archbishop Laurentius Andreæ was he who took the lead in the work of translation. But he himself reports, that others participated with him in the labor, without, however, giving the names of his coadjutors. Here, as in the translation of the New Testament in 1526, the human instruments are concealed, as if to intimate, that no name of man may mix its empty glory with the work of the Lord. This silence is, doubtless, no small part of the true honor of the translators.

It may be taken for granted, that Olaus Petri was not a stranger to this work. It is probable, also, that Laurentius Andreæ, and bishop Bothvid of Strängness, who seems to have been a man of extensive information and of the reformed principles, both concurred and took part in the undertaking. Although the archbishop seems to intimate that they were engaged in the work of translation at Upsala, yet is there nothing known of the number of those who, in that city, may be supposed to have been the most active workmen. It would be vain to search, with any hope of success, for any one but the archbishop, to whom, for this gift, the Swedish church is under such great obligations—the greater, as this translation is still, with very few changes, the Swedish church Bible.

The translation of the New Testament in the Bible of 1541, is, though not in meaning, yet in words and the position of words, so different from that of 1526, that the former may, with reason, be called a new translation. Beside the means accessible in Upsala, the archbishop borrowed books of George Norman, till he was himself able to procure them.* The language is the purest and most beautiful which has yet appeared in any Swedish book, although here and there places are found which too much remind us of the faithful use of Luther's German translation.

With this translation of the Bible, Laurentius Petri appears on the scene of action, with a more prominent and steadily increasing influence in the momentous concerns of the Swedish church. This, and still more the importance of the subject, require that we call attention to two circumstances, which are in the highest degree significant of the character of the Swedish church. The first is, that the preface to this translation expressly gives notice, that "the Latin Bible is not so much followed as the German of doctor Martin Luther, as well in the preface, glosses, notes, concordances, and order, as in the text itself; because this same German Bible is not only much clearer and better to be understood than the Latin, but because it also more approximates to the Hebrew text." It is the first time that Luther is quoted in a writing, which if it did not go forth in the name of the church, may be regarded as a declaration given in the name of the church. It was the commencement of an evangelical Lutheran church in Sweden. But it is also declared, that this translation of the Bible was undertaken, in order to provide a version more conformable to the original Hebrew Scriptures than the Latin version hitherto used in the western church. That version which the Roman church, five years later, adopted in its own

* Norman had written to the archbishop in Latin or German. The archbishop, who was engaged in clothing the word of everlasting life in a good Swedish dress, answers him in Swedish, and at the end of his letter says: "Because I have observed how you have striven to learn our language, as you cannot well do without it." It was a worthy hint, to the man who, at that time, as the king's superintendent, had the chief direction of the affairs of the Swedish church. But the hint was not regarded by Norman. Till the year 1522, being the year before his death, he made use of the German language in a speech he delivered before the council and bishops of Sweden.

communion, being the Latin vulgate, is here pronounced to be neither of divine inspiration, nor " authentic."

The Swedish church, by an open declaration of the superiority of Luther's translation to the Latin, announced her attachment to the Reformation; but there occurred in the Swedish translation, another circumstance, in which she differed from Luther, and in which she may, with equal reason, be said to have declared that she did not wish so to break with the old church, as to appear to have introduced a new constitution or discipline. In the translation of 1526, the word presbyters, when used of the officers of the Christian church, is agreeably to Luther's judgment rendered, eldermen (ældersmæn); and it is said, in a marginal note, that these " were the same as those now called priests. In 1541, this word, and above all where the meaning is clear, is translated "*priest*," and thus by the same term which in the Old Testament designates the offerer of a sacrifice (offer prester). We cannot interpret this otherwise, than an intimation that these elders were, in the New Testament, what priests were in the old, and that people were not brought by the Reformation into a new church, although the *offering of a victim* in the Lord's supper, was disclaimed, on this idea all the abuses and errors of the old church being in close dependence. This change has much significance, when we reflect, that it was adopted in the Swedish church Bible, and that, in the alterations which emanated from the king's chancery, respecting the management of the church, the terms preachers and spiritual persons were used instead of priest.*

The Bible translation, of which a copy was placed in every church in the kingdom, was in a measure the com-

* The Latin vulgate has the latinized word presbyter, and thereby avoids the idea of sacerdos, although the Roman church transfers the notion of a sacrificer, in the sense of the Old Testament, to the priest of the New. It is observable that king Charles XII.'s Bible has here and there

pletion of the church reform by Laurentius Andreæ, and the commencement of the stricter reform in which the brothers Olaus and Laurentius Petri, at first took but little part, but which the latter afterward carried on, more in the spirit of the original improvements made in church discipline. This stricter reform may be dated from the time when king Gustavus, led by his new counsellor, desired more decisively to settle and alter the church's faith, usages, and constitution, and when the outward means employed, manifested more expressly than before an opposition to the Roman system.

The king's superintendent, Norman, and his assistants, had, at the visitation of churches in Skara, Linkoping, and Wexio, by their instructions and the changes they ordered, made current more rigid protestant views and principles. They were not promulgated and approved by the Swedish church and state, except so far as being followed and put in force by the king and his counsellors. The insurrection of the peasant Dacke, and the ferments which preceded and followed, within the kingdom, somewhat interfered with their being thus enforced, and paved the way to the decay of these novel ecclesiastical measures of the year 1540, although the king was confirmed in his general principles. He made a more complete and desirable breach with the papacy, when it became apparent that the discontents and revolts were connected with the changes in the church, and were fostered by the old hierarchy. Instructionary letters sent to the kingdom by the former bishop Magnus of Skara, fell into the hands of the king, and convinced him there would be no peace as long as in the church there was a foothold for this hierarchy. Such a foothold appeared to him to

restored the word elder, so that in Acts xv., the words priest and elder are used interchangeably in the same chapter and narrative. I acknowledge that the Swedish is the only protestant church which in its translation of the Bible, restores the word priest instead of presbyter.

exist in the old church usages, which themselves originated from false doctrines. From a propensity to these, the changes in which occurred at the same time with those in the civil privileges of the peasant, the people heaped on him bitter reproaches. It was objected that they wanted to rule in matters that they did not understand, to govern the priests, and explain the Latin tongue. They ought to consider, that lately the bishops and priests brought the fatherland well nigh to ruin. "Nay, where the people themselves did not correct the evil, it was to be feared that such would always be the case; so that archbishop Gustav, master Didrik, and others like them, would come with so much papal indulgence, holy water, and frankincense, as would make our nostrils tingle."

From the diet of Westeras, in 1527, which decreed the reform of the church, without which king Gustavus believed himself unable to keep the offered crown, seventeen years had rolled away. Four years after the council of the kingdom did him homage as *Arfking*, as one whose descendants were to inherit the crown, the king appeared before the estates assembled at the same city of Westeras, in 1544, to confirm to him the title of arfking. On this occasion, he reminded them that he aimed to promote sound Christian doctrine, and to procure teachers of it within the kingdom. He was well aware that the basis of this doctrine was trust in the alone availing merits of Jesus Christ. He urged that public worship should be altered into a conformity with this faith, so that whatever was not founded on the Holy Scriptures, should be rejected. This doctrine the old clergy had not enforced in the land by their preaching. He expressed his astonishment, that the people clung to the old bishops and church customs, and recalls to their remembrance the disasters which had grown out of the plots of the archbishops, John Bengtsson against king Charles VIII., Jacob Ulfsson and Gustav Trolle against the regent Sten Sture, and now, from the machinations of bishop Magnus of Skara.

The changes in church customs which resulted from the first diet of Westeras, were confirmed by the *church council*, which, in 1529, was held at Orebro. Those which were now considered necessary, were confirmed at a *council of the kingdom*, by an ordinantia. A new confession of faith was not now proposed, but the old declaration was more forcibly reiterated, "that the word of God and the Holy Gospel shall be more generally used and made known in the Christian congregations here in Sweden." Those abuses, which, in 1529, were merely interpreted to a better meaning, or others which had not hitherto been mentioned, were now *forbidden*. Such were the praying to, or invocation of saints, pilgrimages, holy water, salt, wax, incense, consecration at church gates, or at home in houses, corporation feasts, *masses for souls*, and the so called yearly promissory and mortuary masses. All these were forbidden. The number of saints' days were to be lessened, and some regulations were made respecting church discipline. *The king and all the council of the kingdom, the nobles, bishops, prelates, men of the market towns, and the commons, pledged themselves never to depart from the doctrine now received.*

These decrees are the only ones publicly followed, and carried out during the last twenty years of king Gustavus' reign; but changes took place without any public declaration, took place here and there, till they became by degrees general customs. Among these customs, as a consequence of performing the mass in Swedish, was the delivery of the cup at the Lord's supper, to laymen. In the beginning of the reign of Erik XIV, a council was held at Arboga, in 1561, and at Stockholm the year after, under the presidency of Laurentius Petri, the archbishop, which were in part a carrying out of the decree that in 1544 was passed at Westeras. As a necessary consequence of the prohibition of masses for souls, it was now for the first time, expressly ordered that priests should not perform mass if some communicants were not present to receive; that both the bread and the wine should be delivered to communicants; and that neither mead nor water, nor anything else, should be used instead of wine. As a result of the prohibition of the worship of saints, and of foreign usages within the church, of which we shall speak more hereafter, it was ordered, in 1561, that no images should be allowed in churches, except the crucifix and altar-print. This order, which in many places was not obeyed, was repeated in 1562, with a menace of the king's wrath against those who "like blockheads were not willing to root out images and idolatry;" and the bishops were directed sternly to rebuke the priests "who suffered or consented to such idolatry in their congregations." An application of the interdict against masses and worship of saints, was the order passed at this council, that in each church there should be no more than one altar for the celebration of the holy supper of the Lord, "since more altars led to idolatry, and ought, beyond all contradiction, to be cast out."

The ordinantia of 1544 became prevalent over the whole kingdom. It may be taken for granted, that the Swedish manual and mass were in general use, and that the remaining abrogated church usages were abandoned. It was now considered superfluous to apprehend scandal from the unwise zeal of priests and others. The resistance, as is commonly the case, was sometimes only obstinacy without conviction, and the constraint by which it was removed was not always unwelcome to those who merely lacked *courage* to set themselves free from the old practices and discipline. The change was promoted by the measure adopted of transferring the more qualified priests to congregations whose ignorance or other causes hindered the purification of public worship. A large number of these priests were trained by serving as chaplains in the king's court.

The pastor of Skelleftea, in Westerbotten, Herr Bjorn, who had previously been a prebend of Stockholm, attempted, in 1536, to introduce in his congregation the Swedish mass. "It was not then," he says, "much welcomed." It was probably at once laid aside, since in 1544, the succeeding pastor, who, from being chaplain there, was transferred to the peasant church in Upsala, and now was again transferred to Skelleftea as its pastor, reports, that *up to that time* the Lord's Supper had not been administered under both the elements, but on the contrary, all the popish ceremonies were observed, which afterward were laid aside without noise or scandal. This was not always the case. The scandal was not always avoided.

Pastor Jons Joannis, who, after having been king's chaplain and pastor of Tillinge, was, in 1538, transferred to Ofvansjo, in Gestrickland, was once, for his zeal against popish superstition, well nigh thrown over the church-yard walls by the peasants. When Nils, the pastor of Asby, in East Gothland, introduced the Swedish mass into his church, the indignant peasants would have laid violent hands upon him in the church itself, had not a fear of the king restrained them. From the cloister of Wadsten complaints and imprecations were heard, during the autumn of 1543, against the new bishop of Linkoping, who, at a visitation, had prohibited the offering up of a victim in the Eucharist. The new rulers of the diocese were enjoined to take care that the truth should be preached, all sin and error be removed, and that all *papistic and superstitious worship should be abolished.*

In proportion as the reform of the church acquired consistence, it receded from the popish practices, and took a decidedly hostile attitude. In 1540, *popish* plots began, as we have remarked, to be spoken of as hinderances to the progress of gospel preaching. The transactions of the immediately succeeding years increased the feelings of suspicion and hate, and resulted in a determination to crush such plots. From the year 1543 in particular, after the insurrectionary letter of bishop Magnus came to the knowledge of the king, and many priests had joined the rebellion of Dacke, measures began to be adopted, which were not founded on any express penal statutes against papists, but were expressions of the will of a master, and were instead of law. They were chiefly directed against the priests of Linkoping, Skara, and Wexio, many of whom showed an inclination for the old church, or, perhaps, were not satisfied with the more violent alterations which took place in the discipline and usages of the church. These measures were also pursued against priests in other parts of the kingdom. They reached the cloister of Wadsten, of the stubborn "popery" of whose nuns complaint was made before the king, as Petrus Caroli sadly informs us in his history of king Erik XIV. The officers and stewards of the king were ordered to keep a strict watch over these papistic priests, to remove them from office, to send them prisoners to the king, or to have them punished. To Wadsten, the king sent a competent person to convert the nuns, if he could find any of them so inclined. In conclusion, it does not appear that laymen were tried or punished for popery, unless publicly acknowledged and practised.

The new faith wanted not antagonists who attacked it with the weapons of Scripture. Among these was the before-mentioned master Thore or Thorer, canon of Linkoping, and, as is said, brother of Jons Magni, bishop of that see. He was a most able and undaunted man. He openly declared himself opposed to the novelties introduced into the church at this time. But we are not able to decide whether he, who was as early as 1537, considered to be attached to the old state of things, was now thoroughly a papist, or belonged to that not inconsiderable party, who approved of a change in the relations of the church, but were opposed to the progressive reform. In 1544, master Thure again incurred the king's displeasure, by his open opposition to the new doctrines, and only the bishop's promise of Thure's silence for the future averted serious consequences. Four years later, G. Norman and Claudius Hvit attempted, at Wadsten, to convince and refute him. He was now sent to Stockholm, together with one Andreas Haquin, and was afterward confined in the prison of Gripsholm, where he was kept till 1554, when, after a disputation with M. Agricola and P. Juusten, and a consequent retractation, he was set at liberty, and allowed to pass the remainder of his days in the cloister of Wadsten.

All intercourse with Rome was now broken off. To the church council, which, after the Reformation, was called together at Mantua, in 1537, and then in 1545 at Trent, Sweden was not invited by the pope and Cæsar. But when the council of Trent, after a suspension of nearly ten years, was again opened in 1562, Sweden had advanced into greater importance, and better hopes for the papacy began to be entertained on the death of king Gustavus and the accession of his son Erik to the throne. The papal ambassador, Gianfrancesco Commendone, who, in vain, made a visit to Nuremberg, where the evangelical Lutheran estates of Germany were assembled, had commission to treat with the kings of Sweden and Denmark, and went to Lubeck, whence he solicited for letters of safe conduct to enter this kingdom. In Denmark he was not received. But king Erik answered, on August 24th, 1561, in a letter which was thought to be of good omen to the legate, because it recognized him as the pope's legate, that he willingly granted a safe conduct, which accompanied the letter, but that he designed with the first fair wind to sail for England, and that he proposed to the legate to meet him there. Commendone, though mistrustful of a permission to enter England, went immediately to Flanders, but at last returned with his business unaccomplished, having long waited in vain for Erik, whose journey to England was never accomplished.

The new direction the Reformation began to take, menaced the hitherto existing constitution. We have seen how in the projected constitution, from the years 1539 and 1540, there was no place for bishops, and the reform in church usages was, perhaps, little satisfactory to some of them, of whom there was now none that had not, after 1527, been elected to his office. A consequence of the altered relations was, that many among them left or desired to leave their posts. Bishop Jons Magni of Linkoping, laid down his office in 1543, dissatisfied with the new arrangements. The year following bishop Sven of Skara resigned, having previously obtained as his assistant Erik Svenson Hjort, formerly the king's chaplain, and pastor of Skelleftea. In the same year, or in 1545, Martin Skytte of Abo, begged a dismission, which was granted by the king, on the ground of the bishop's great age, but he continued, nevertheless, the exercise of his office. Skytte is represented as a man of great piety, who was, to a considerable degree, attached to the old forms. He was never married, and had fixed times for the distribution of alms.

King Gustavus appointed as his *ordinarius* in Linkoping, Claudius or Nicholas Hvit, a Dane, previously a Dominican monk of Skeninge, and prior of the cloister of Kalmar. He was, at the commencement of the disputes respecting doctrine, a zealous apologist of the old faith. He went to Wittenberg in the hope, it is said, of converting Martin Luther, but returned home himself converted into a warm protestant. He married a nun of Skeninge, and took care of the see of Linkoping, at the time his two brothers of the Dominican order, M. Skytte and Henrik of Westeras, yet held episcopal chairs in Sweden. The see of Skara was transferred to the afore-named Erik Svensson, and after his death, in 1545, to Erik Falk.

There are no evidences that these nominations were preceded by an election, but they appear to have been made immediately by the king. If this was so, it was the first time the ordinary rulers of a diocese were appointed in such a manner. The thing is in itself probable, as the chapters began to be dissolved, and the king began to convert the right he received from the treaty of Westeras, to have an oversight of the bishops, into the right of directly encroaching upon the relations of the church, by virtue of his kingly vocation.

How far these men were consecrated as bishops, and by bishops, in their office, is not clear, though we regard it as probable that they were so consecrated, because examples of their consecration sometimes occur, and because the superintendents of Denmark were consecrated at least by the German doctor Bugenhagen.

It is more certain, that from this time the king did not allow to these aforesaid inspectors of the diocese the name of *bishop*, but constantly called them ordinaries, inspectors, or superintendents. Of these titles, the last-named was used about the year 400, as a Latin translation of the Greek word *episcopos;* the second was a Swedish translation of the same word, while the first was employed, even by the Roman church, as synonymous with the term bishop. They did not, therefore, constitute a ground of objection to these officials taking a position which might be regarded as churchly, as conformable to the prescription of the church. By the people they were called bishops. But that king Gustavus, although he does not call them *his* ordinaries, as in 1539, he spoke of *his* bishops, had an eye to this change, appears from the circumstance that, *never*, as far as we know, does he apply to them the name of bishop, and during his whole reign *never ceased* giving the name of bishop to the inspectors, who, before 1543, were elected by the chapter. He forbore to address Laurentius Petri as archbishop, and from 1539 only speaks of him as Bishop Lars. He wished to make a distinction between the "great bishops," who claimed "great and unbecoming dignity and honors," and whose office appeared inefficacious for the true life of the church, but on the contrary, promotive of errors, and dangerous to the peaceful and quiet development of the civil government; and those bishops who watched over the discipline and condition of the Swedish church. These last he commonly called ordinaries, and is supposed to have had in view, to let the name bishop expire with the men who then held it, so that with the name the abuses of the office might fall into oblivion.

The alteration was commenced and continued for any length of time only in the dioceses of Linkoping and Skara. The other sees of Sweden were filled by *elected bishops*, until 1556, when the bishop of Westeras died, and the bishop of Strängness was removed from the exercise of his office. These three often consulted together on questions that concerned the interests of the church, as they did on the Interim of the emperor Charles V., and on the third marriage of king Gustavus. In the latter case, they gave an opinion in contrariety to the king's wishes. The bishops Skytte of Abo, and Jons of Wexio, too, took no active part in public affairs.

At the close of the reign of Gustavus, after the occupants of all the Swedish sees were changed in 1550, the archbishop was the only one who still received from the king the name of bishop. After the year 1553, upon the decease of bishop Jons Boson, the see of Wexio was held by Nicholas Canuti. M. Skytte died on December 30, 1550. The see of Abo then remained vacant till the spring of 1554, when it was divided by the king, so that the see of Abo proper was given to M. Agricola, who, from 1548, had assisted Skytte in the management of his office, and the see of Wiborg or Borga was given to P. Juusten. Agricola deserves great commendation with respect to the church of

Finland. He translated and published in the Finnish tongue, in 1542, the New Testament, a large part of the Old, a manual, a mass-book, the psalms, and other religious works.* He died in 1527, and was succeeded by P. Follingius, on whose deposition, P. Juusten was transferred from Wiborg to the see of Abo. At the first nomination of Agricola and Juusten, the king had called to Stockholm the men who might still be considered the chapter of Abo. It seems, therefore, that these two bishops had passed through the form, or at least the pretence of an *election*, so that this process could not have wholly disappeared. They were *consecrated*, on the king's order, to their office, by bishop Bothvid of Strängness. Agricola very soon after excited, though without further consequences, the king's great displeasure, by having worn the old episcopal robes, when he held his first mass or communion service in Abo. In 1556, bishop Bothvid of Strängness also incurred the royal disapprobation, and was forbidden to exercise his office, which, however, he resumed in 1561, after king Gustavus' death. Meanwhile, Erik Svart was ordinarius. After the death of Bothvid, in 1562, king Erik XIV. nominated Nicholaus Olai Helsingus as bishop of Strängness. Bishop Henrik of Westeras departed this life in 1550, and was succeeded by Peter Svart, after whose death, in 1563, Johan Ofeg became bishop. The ordinarius of Linkoping was transferred, in 1558, to the pastoral care of Soderkoping, and after him, Erik Falk, from Skara to Linkoping. The former post of Falk was taken by Erik Hvas, who died in 1560. After him Erik Svart, who filled the place of Bothvid † bishop of Strängness, became bishop of Skara.

* Martin Luther terms him "a youth of erudition, talents, and excellent character."

† This is the bishop, who, when the king once, jestingly, asked him in what chapter of the Bible bishops were permitted to live in elegant stone houses, answered, "In the same chapter where kings are permitted to take tithes of their subjects."

And not only by taking away the name of bishop, but by *dividing dioceses*, the king desired to lessen the hierarchical influence he so much watched and feared. There was another reason for dividing them, which, in 1557, was given by the king himself, that, although the pure word of God had now a free course in his kingdom, there was yet the defect, that the priests were not sufficiently active in their vocation. The bishops and ordinaries could not exercise over them a proper supervision, because the dioceses were too large. He determined, therefore, to divide them. A beginning was made, in 1554, with the diocese of Abo. From that time matters went on actively, so that at the close of Gustavus I.'s reign, and under that of Erik XIV., there were several ordinaries in Stockholm for that city, in Gefle for Norland, in Kalmar for East Smaland and Oeland, in Jonkoping for North Smaland, in Orebro for Nerike, and in Tuna for Dalecarlia. All the sees were thus divided, with the exception of Skara, and the previously diminished diocese of Wexio, which on the contrary, in 1555, was augmented by the districts of Sunnerbo, Eastbo, and Westbo. The pastors or rectors of the above-named headquarters were the ordinaries of the new divisions. The ordinary of Kalmar was put in subjection to the ordinary of Linkoping, and was thus merely his assistant. We suppose that this dependence appertained to the other new ordinaries also, as it is not known that they were consecrated to their office, and as, soon after king Erik's accession to the throne, a distinction was made between bishops or the old occupants of the old dioceses, and the *ordinarii* or occupants of the new divisions. A letter from the king was issued to the "bishops and ordinaries," and in 1556, some of these ordinaries began to write themselves "pastores," pastors. At the commencement of John III.'s reign, this distinction presents itself as settled. The occupants of the old sees call themselves bishops; those of Gefle, Tuna, Orebro, and Jonkoping, ordinaries. This took place in 1569, after which these *ordinarii* are met with no more.

Prelates and canons appeared to the first reformers as offices that might be dispensed with—still less could they be tolerated in the discipline of the church after the year 1540. The king accounted them with the powerful bishops as a papistical party, and about the year 1540 the dissolution of the old chapters was, for the most part, effected. In 1527 the king, exceeding the express grant of the treaty of Westeras, not only settled the incomes of the canons, but how many canons and prebends there should be in each cathedral. At a later period, he stopped not at this diminished number, but suppressed more canonries and prebends as vacancies occurred.

But there was also made, in 1544, an important change in the incomes of bishops, canons, and prebends. They had hitherto received these incomes in the manner usual before the year 1527, and given to the crown the settled annual impost. The king had already, in 1540, appointed a country steward over the tenants attached to the sees and canonries of Skara, and directed bishop Sven to leave the management of these tenants to this steward. When the king, in 1542, called in the ground-rent books, and an accurate list of the taxes on incomes, he is thought to have announced his intention of a change. This change began in 1544, when the ordinarius, canon, and korpriest of Linkoping, petitioned that they, who neither could govern their tenants nor obtain of them their dues, might be allowed to transfer those dues to the crown in exchange for a certain yearly income. This application was well received, and they obtained an assessment on the tithes previously assigned to the crown. The same request was made, the year following, by the bishops, chapters, and prebends of Strängness and Westeras, and it was granted on similar terms. The new arrangement was introduced at the same time within all the dioceses of the kingdom. This, in connection with the power of the king to appoint to the office, imported a complete and significant alteration in the mode of paying salaries, especially when it is considered, that in exchange for the *church goods* they yielded up, they took a compensation out of revenues that were regarded as belonging to the crown.

This reduction, metamorphosis, or change, which was not at all contemplated at the diet of Westeras, in 1527, was extended also to the goods and farms of churches, and the priests attached to churches. The king began, in 1545, to negotiate with the priests, to yield up their farms for a reasonable compensation. During the two succeeding years, this exchange was effected over the whole kingdom. The tenants of the priests became crown tenants, and the priests gained a compensation in tithes and other reserved things, and retained beside, without being obliged to provide entertainment for travellers, the farms that were annexed to their chapels of ease. Even the tenants attached to the churches were transferred to the crown. Nothing was said of a compensation for these. The change awakened dissatisfaction in the land, so that the king found himself under the necessity of offering an excuse. The excuse was, the protection needed for these tenants, and the wretched care taken of the farms. Many priests as well as tenants had made the request.

In another respect also, a change of great importance and influence was made in the position of the pastors or rectors of churches. Bishops, prelates, and canons, especially the first, were regarded, according to the old hierarchical view, as the only representatives of the church. The parish priests represented the bishops, in the care of their congregations, and a large part of the more influential priests were connected with the prelacies and canonries of cathedrals. The suffrage of the church, therefore, in the affairs of the civil government, could only be given by these independent sponsors. The new views occasioned the diminution of the importance of bishops, and a dissolution of the chapters; a consequence of which was, that these could not, with the same reason as before, represent the voice of the parish priests. As the pastors of churches were summoned to the first protestant council of 1529, it was reasonably to be expected they should participate on behalf of the church, in the councils of the kingdom, by their suffrages. And thus it occurred almost simultaneously with the above-mentioned alterations. The pastors of churches appeared for the first time as diet representatives, in 1547, at the diet of Strängness. This diet was sanctioned, and its acts approved by the bishops of Upsala, Strängness, and Westeras, by the chapters or their representatives, and by "some independent persons, from all the clergy of these three dioceses." This change was not established by law, was sometimes neglected or disregarded by king Erik XIV., but was observed with great strictness from the time of John III.

CHAPTER IX.

THE REFORMATION IN DENMARK AND NORWAY.—THE POSITION OF THE SWEDISH CHURCH IN RESPECT TO THE FOREIGN PROTESTANT CHURCHES.

WE have given an account of two very remarkable periods in the history of the reformation of the Swedish church. The one period extends from the diet of Westeras, in 1527, to the council held in 1539. During this period the changes were made on the ground of the treaty and ordinantia of Westeras. The reformation was chiefly a reduction of the riches of the church, a lessening of the number of its officers, the diffusion of the knowledge and preaching of the word of God over the land, and a decadence of conventual establishments, both in wealth and the number of those who made vows within their walls. The second period, from 1539, during which king Gustavus carried on the reformation of the church as a *kingly right*, and went beyond the treaty and ordinantia of Westeras, may with propriety be said to close at the year 1544. But the incidents that then occurred, though vacillating under the reigns of Gustavus I. and Erik XIV., between the royal claims and the independence of the church and estates of the kingdom, extend their influence much further.

The most important changes in king Gustavus' time, except the division of dioceses, were completed in 1546 and 1547, at which period the protestant estates of Germany lay vanquished at the feet of the Cæsar, Charles V., and the

Danish reformation was accomplished. It may throw light upon the picture of the transactions of the Swedish church, to cast a glance upon the other kingdoms of the Scandinavians.

King Christian II., who, during his short dominion within Sweden, chiefly appears as a bloody avenger of the wrongs of the papal church, and by his outrages irremediably injured the church's cause, now steps forth in the history of Denmark, as a zealot for the principles of the Reformation. During his attempts to bend and subdue the hierarchy, the teachers who came over from Wittenberg must have been welcome to him; and he was so much the more induced to notice them, as it was well known that his uncle by the mother's side, Frederick, elector of Saxony, was Luther's friend and protector.

Many of the king's Danish subjects, among whom was the before mentioned Paul Elieson, hailed with joy and hope the movement, when, in 1519, the king wrote to the elector to send him a teacher from Wittenberg, to spread the principles of the Reformation. A certain master Martin Reinhard came, and was installed in the university of Kopenham, and made preacher of the church of St. Nicholas. His labors were short lived and of little fruit in Denmark. As he could not speak Danish, Paul Elieson was employed to interpret what he delivered; but as the latter soon went back to Germany, he could no longer communicate his opinions to those among the people who did not understand the German speech. His gesture and pronunciation also made him ridiculous. He returned in February, 1521, accompanied by one of the king's German secretaries, both being furnished with a commission to induce Martin Luther to take refuge in Denmark, as his freedom and life were now endangered by the approaching diet of Worms. The same offer was made to Carolstad and others. The king had also forbidden the university of Köpenham to write against Luther.

The elector, Frederick, to whom the overture respecting Luther's coming to Denmark was delivered, refused his consent, but Carolstadt and a master Gabler came there in the former part of the year 1521, though they soon returned, for what reason is not known.

In the statutes framed by the king in 1521, for Denmark, and in those laws which he the next year promulgated as modifications of those statutes, there were many particulars, which, after he lost his crown, became, from the year 1527, current law, or silently admitted as law, in portions both of Sweden and Denmark. Every bishop shall, say the statutes, on all high festivals, himself perform high mass, and shall go into the pulpit and preach the gospel, and instruct the people relative to the salvation of their souls. On the downfall of the bishops this duty was enjoined upon the chief prelates. The bishop must not commit the care of souls to any priest who could not preach God's word to the people of the parish. To the bishops was prescribed the dress in which they were to appear before the king, and the train with which prelates and abbots might travel. The archbishop is allowed to have twenty attendants, the other bishops twelve or fourteen. No prelate, priest, or clerk, is allowed to buy real estate, unless he wishes to live in marriage, according to the doctrine of St. Paul, 1 Tim. iii., as their forefathers did. This point in the statutes was altered in the law to a simple prohibition of buying real estate. The laws promulgated, also contain the following ordinances: Spiritual persons or ecclesiastics, must not seek justice out of the kingdom, "in Rome or elsewhere," but in the king's court of chancery, in which doctors and masters should be appointed to give a final decision in spiritual causes. The spiritual court was not to meddle with any causes which were brought before the common courts of the land. Marriage, however, might be treated in the spiritual court. For money dues no one should be excluded from the sacrament. As it would be unjust in a bishop to take all the inheritance of a priest dying without a will, the law provided, that the heir should have three parts, and the fourth was to be appropriated to masses for souls, and to alms. The bishop was to receive from the family of the deceased, "the best jewels and valuables." The gardens and arable lots which the priests had not themselves cultivated, were to be transferred at a fixed rent to the new owners. The monks of cloisters that had rents, were forbidden to beg. Gold, silver, or money, but not real estate, might be given to churches or cloisters.

The force of circumstances, and probably his own unstable temper, soon checked king Christian's zeal for reformation. He had not broken off connection with the pope, whose will he pretended to execute in his bloody deeds in Sweden, whose displeasure with many despotic encroachments on the privileges of the church he wished to soothe, and whose assent to the elevation of his favorites to the sees of Sweden and Denmark, he desired to obtain. Many agents were sent to Rome, especially after Johannes Magni went there as his complainant, but he could not avert the pope's determination, by his own legate John F. de Potentia, sent to Köpenham, to institute an investigation into the massacre of Stockholm. Of this investigation and its consequences we have already treated.

Soon after broke out the rebellion, which, excited by the indignation felt at his outrages, and still further strengthened by his pusillanimity, induced him, in 1523, to abandon both the kingdoms which yet remained to him. The insurrectionists of Denmark brought against him complaints similar to those which, at a later period, were brought against king Gustavus I., by the Dalecarlians of Sweden. They complained of the burdens he had laid on the property and persons of the church; that mass and public worship were unattended; that heretics, who had fallen from the

Christian faith, were allowed to allure others from this faith, "with their Lutheran devices and knavery;" that in the three kingdoms there was no archbishop, and that many dioceses wanted bishops.

King Frederick, Christian's uncle by the father's side, was already pledged to the Reformation, when he received the offer of the crown of Denmark. At the time of his accession he took on him the usual obligations. But the growth of the seed sown, he neither wished nor was able to prevent. The friends of the new principles followed up their work with still greater energy, from the year 1524, at which time Olaus Petri began his career at Stockholm. Hans Tausen, from this period the foremost among the Danish reformers, a priest of the order of St. John, was born in 1494, at Antwerp, in Zealand. He had been sent to the universities of Coln and Louvain, but by reading the writings of Luther, was drawn to Wittenberg. Returning to Antwerp in 1524, or the year after, he began to spread the doctrines of the Reformation. Sent thence to the house of his order at Viborg, in Jutland, he sowed there also the seeds of truth. In 1524, king Frederick began to reform the church in his dukedom of Sleswick and Holstein. Denmark having now no consecrated archbishop, he was crowned that year at Köpenham, by the fugitive Gustav Trolle, but at the same time allowed a priest to perform divine service before him, after the evangelical pattern. It was to no purpose that the bishops now resolved with greater zeal to check the Lutheran heresy, to imprison or in some other way punish its adherents, to forbid thenceforward, the introduction of dangerous and bad books, and allow of no changes, until the general council, which was soon to be called together by Clement VII., should put an end to controversies. The king permitted the friends of reformation to preach their doctrines, but no violence to be committed against the established order. Only by degrees, as he felt his crown more securely settled on his head, did he discover his real principles and views. In 1525, he confirmed the election of John Reffs, as bishop of Opslo, but forbade him to seek confirmation at Rome. The year after, he confirmed, on payment of the usual dues to the crown instead of the pope's treasury, Ake Sparre, elected by the chapter as archbishop of Lund, although the pope had caused George Skotborg to be consecrated for that see.

It was to be expected, that in the kingdom of Denmark, as it then was, the city of Lund should be the corner-stone of the old church, the powerful centre of the archiepiscopate and of the rich chapter. Malmo held this relation, especially after the year 1527, to the Reformation, its citadel and centre for all eastern Denmark. The burgomaster, Hans Mikkelsson, now a Netherland merchantman, whose translation of the New Testament was spread over Denmark, was not the only person who, after leaving the land, desired and endeavored to procure for the truth a free circulation. His successor, Jorgen Kock, put into office by king Christian before his departure, patronized the teachers of the new doctrine. The principal of these was Klas Martensson Tunnbindare, a priest of Malmo, whom even his enemies, while they accused him of ignorance and ambition, acknowledged to be a man of uncommon eloquence. After being ordained a priest of the archdiocese of Lund, he had come to Köpenham to pursue his studies, and there becoming acquainted with the doctrines of the reformers, began openly to propagate them. When the bishop of Roskild, Lage Urne, forbade him to preach there any more, he was invited to Malmo by the burgomaster, Jorgen Kock, by whose permission he preached in a chapel belonging to one of the council, and situated in a meadow outside the city. At the request of the citizens, a chapel was opened for him within the city, and when this did not hold the hearers, the king's permission was obtained to use the church of Sts. Simeon and Jude, where Danish psalms might be sung, and the mass performed in Danish. At length the pastor of St. Peter's church permitted Klas to have preaching there in the afternoon. He seems, as yet, to have cautiously expressed his views, yet so openly, that in 1527 the archbishop banished him from Malmo.

The cause of the Reformation had now become firmly rooted in Denmark. King Frederick therefore determined, that at the diet of Odense, which was opened August 1, 1527, some weeks later than the Swedish diet of Westeras, liberty for its free promulgation should be obtained. In a speech to the bishops, at the opening of the diet, he admonished them to provide for the preaching of the gospel better than had hitherto been done. The old unbelief was abolished in Germany through Luther, and even elsewhere the cheats of papacy were exposed to mankind. In Denmark, too, there was a general complaint that the priests, instead of the pure and unadulterated word of God, propounded to the people human fables, traditions the most absurd, legends and false miracles. The king had, indeed, promised to protect the Roman and Catholic religion, but had not thereby bound himself to defend the fables and errors which had found entrance into the church, and were inconsistent with the word of God. He had promised to defend the order of bishops. This he would do. But, since, in this kingdom, the Christian doctrine, according to the reform of Luther, had taken deep root, so that it could not be suppressed without bloodshed and great danger to the kingdom and people, it was his royal pleasure that, until a general council could be convened, *both religions, the Lutheran and the popish, should be tolerated.*

Notwithstanding all opposition from the spiritual, and from some among the temporal lords, a decree was passed in accordance with the king's speech. Bishops, prelates, and cloisters, were to retain the goods and property they possessed, according to the law of the land, and the tithes were secured to them; but the people were to be free from taxes to the bishop for weddings, the churching of women, and the like. The church was to retain its jurisdiction, except that in causes regarding real estate, the pleas should be made before the temporal court. The crown, nobles, and learned men, were to have cognizance of the fines and suits of their own tenants and servants, except such as concerned murder, and breach of the church's peace, which were to belong to the church. Every man should enjoy liberty of conscience, so that none should call his neighbor to account because he was *a Lutheran or a Catholic*. Every man should have the care of his own soul. The king took Lutherans and Catholics alike under his protection. For some centuries, the officers of the church, canons, monks, and all sorts of spiritual persons, were forbidden to marry; every man might now, as he pleased, marry, or live singly in a pure life. Bishops were not to seek the pallium at Rome, but ask confirmation of the king, after being lawfully elected by the chapter.

It may easily be seen, how unlike was this project of reform in Denmark, to that which simultaneously took place in Sweden. In Sweden a commencement was made by lessening the power of the bishops, with the wealth of the church and her right of pronouncing judgment; all which was preserved in Denmark. The opposite opinions were presented in the light of opposite church parties, while in Sweden it was conceived that there could be but one truth, founded on the word of God, and by its preaching the way was opened to its general examination. No distinction, therefore, was recognized between Lutherans and Catholics, and it was not a question what Martin Luther said or did not say, but what the Scriptures said. The questions concerning the marriage of priests, and the relations of the church to the pope, were in Sweden passed by in silence, as already determined by the gospel, or as to be so determined.

The freedom granted the Lutherans by the decree of the diet of Odense, provoked an open opposition on the part of the old church. Many monks and nuns left their cloisters; many of them married. The marriage of priests, which had commenced before 1527, now became more common. Klas Tunnbindare returned to Malmo, in 1528, with Hans Spandemager, who, with the other, had been obliged to leave that city. It was now proclaimed that from the time of the apostles, no true Christianity had been preached; that no true Christian was found, except among those whom the church declared to be heretics; that the pope was antichrist; that good works were more harmful than beneficial, since they gave occasion to self-righteousness and hypocrisy. Fasts and vows were disapproved, mass was abolished, ornaments were removed from churches, and the holy supper of the Lord was administered not at the high altar, but at a table placed in the church. The pastor was removed, and Klas Martensson put in his place. The war against Catholics was lively and active. Klas once entered the pulpit of the Franciscan church, during afternoon service, and preached against monks. One of these stepped into the pulpit after him to refute him; and so they alternated several times that afternoon. In vain the archbishop of Lund, Ake Sparre, who, being neither confirmed nor consecrated by the pope, wanted full official powers, summoned the reformers before him. The summons was not obeyed. In vain he betook himself to Malmo. His threats and admonitions were without effect. Frans Wormorsen, a Carmelite monk, born in Holland, who, on a promise given to aid in suppressing the tumults, obtained the archbishop's permission to preach in Malmo, proclaimed there the doctrines of the Reformation. In 1529, the Reformation had been fully established in Malmo. In many other towns of Denmark, in Landskrona, Ystad, Trelleborg, the gospel was preached. Only Lund still continued in opposition. Ascer Peterson, a cantor of its church, distinguished himself among the most zealous advocates of the Roman church, and with him was associated one Peter Ivarsson.

In 1529, Wormorsen translated the psalms into Danish, and in the same year appeared a translation of both the psalms and New Testament, by the learned and pious Kristen Petterson, canon of Lund, who, even before the Reformation, was known as an author. He had accompanied king Christian abroad, but returned attached to the cause of the Reformation, and died a rural priest. In 1528, his works, for and against the new doctrines, began to be published. The opposition made in Lund against church reform, combined with the equality of Lutherans and Catholics in the church, produced, in 1529, a resolve to establish, at Malmo, an institution for training the confessors and priests of the Lutheran form of faith. The king approved the application made him, and transferred to this object and the support of an hospital, the property of certain lapsed ecclesiastical establishments in the city. This institution of learning for Lutherans went immediately into operation, under the auspices of Klas Martensson, Wormorson, and others. In 1530, when the Catholics were in expectation that their opponents would be crushed in Germany by the measures adopted at the diet of Augsburg, the bishops of Denmark requested that the protestant teachers of their own country might be summoned to a diet at Köpenham, where controversies of faith should be examined and discussed. Two German theologians were invited from Coln to defend the papal tenets. The protestants appeared in great numbers, and unexpectedly set forth, after a lapse of eight days, a confession of faith, containing forty-three articles, upon distinct portions of which they daily preached, until they were forbidden by the king. A refutation by the papal party, in twenty-seven articles, was again refuted in the like number of articles, with the addition of twelve, energetically remonstrating against the mismanagement of the office of bishops. The publie disputation did not take place, and the diet only conduced to the advancement of the protestant cause.

It advanced from this period with rapid strides. At Köpenham, on July 3, 1530, the church, called that of Our Lady, was stormed, and the ornaments destroyed. A large number of cloisters, especially those of the begging monks, were, in 1530 and 1531, wholly demolished, as was also the case in Gothland and other parts of Scania. In many quarters, as in Halmstad and Ystad, the monks were driven away with violence. Their property was transferred to hospitals, or confiscated to the state, or given away in fief.

After the death of king Frederick, in 1533, the hierarchy endeavored to recover their power, or at least secure what was not yet lost, by means of the resolutions passed at the diet of Köpenham. But the war of the Palatinate, which soon after broke out, left everything unsettled, until Christian III., in 1536, was generally acknowledged as king of the land. Christian was a zealous protestant, and had already resolved on the downfall of the hierarchy. A visit which he paid, in the autumn of 1535, at Stockholm, to king Gustavus I., may have greatly contributed to this resolve. On August 12, 1536, the king framed, with the council of the kingdom, a decree, that all spiritual and temporal power should be taken from the bishops, and that their property should be transferred to the crown. The council pledged itself to the evangelical doctrine, and promised to stake wealth and life for the weal of the church and fatherland. It was also resolved to imprison the bishops, that they might be disabled from opposing effectually the projected changes. The bishops then present in Köpenham were immediately imprisoned. A diet, to which were summoned the nobles, burghers, and farmers, was held in October of that year. On the thirtieth of the month, complaints were laid before the estates, by the king against the bishops, whose acts were minutely criticised. They had been the cause of long continued and bloody contests, had set themselves against an emendation of the church, and persecuted the evangelical teachers. He proposed that the rank and dignity of bishops should be abolished, and their property be transferred to the crown, to pay its debt and lessen the burdens of the people, that the pure evangelical doctrine should be introduced, that superintendents without worldly power should have the management of the church, that tithes and other church property should be converted to the use of learned men, universities, schools, and pious establishments. The estates replied, that they did not wish to have bishops, except in connection with the holy gospel, and that the goods of the church ought to be converted to lessening the burdens of the people.

Thus, within ten years, was religious freedom confirmed to both parties, and the papal church overturned. The bishops were released, but not restored to office, and they took an oath of submission and quiet demeanor. The archbishopric of Lund ceased from this time, having existed from its establishment four hundred and thirty-three years. The last possessor of the office and name, Thorbern Bilde, who was raised to that dignity in 1532, on Ake Sparre's voluntary resignation, was permitted, till his death in 1533, to enjoy the incomes of the deanery of Lund, and of the cloister of Bosjo, on condition of supporting the nuns who were still remaining there. One only of the bishops, Joakim Ronnow, of Roskild, protested against the outrage, and refused to submit. He was held in durance till his death, in 1544; king Gustavus, of Sweden, his relative, having, in vain, for some time, endeavored te procure his release.

The tithes and property of the bishops fell to the crown. Priests and churches were allowed to retain their tithes. The nobles, notwithstanding, appropriated a part of them, and in time a free use of them was obtained by these nobles, for their services to the state. The nobles also obtained, at the diet of 1536, the right of recovering, after the decease of their then owners or holders, such possessions as the nobles themselves, or their forefathers, had given to the church.

Two of the kingdom's seven chapters were immediately suppressed. The remaining five, among them that of Lund, were allowed to continue during the lifetime of their present members. In 1543, they were required to sign certain articles, and a disputation was held with them. Their incomes were afterward, by degrees, transferred to men of learning, priests in the cities, superintendents, and even the holders of civil offices, until, at the time that Scania was attached to Sweden, they generally ceased to exist in Denmark. The cloisters that had rents, which existed till 1536, were suppressed by degrees, and were in part bestowed on nobles, and in part were used for the support of the church, science, the weaker establishments, or for state purposes. The last monastery in Denmark, that of Maribo, in Laland, was a child of Wadsten. It survived its mother, and in 1621 was suppressed.

King Christian III., on the ruins of the old church, which was, it might be said, in the twinkling of an eye to fall, was meditating to erect the structure of the new. For this purpose, doctor John Bugenhagen was invited from Wittenberg, where, as professor and superintendent, he had distinguished himself for learning and a capacity for government and the direction of affairs. By him, who came to Denmark in 1537, the king was crowned, and by him were ordained or consecrated, on the second of September of that year, the superintendents who were now put in the places of the bishops, although the name of bishop was by degrees commonly applied to them also. On the same day with this ordination, was published and set forth a church ordinance, which, composed by the reformers of Denmark and reviewed by the king, was submitted to the scrutiny of the theologians of Wittenberg, and, with their assent, was now brought along with him to Denmark by Bugenhagen. The new church establishment was dependent on the king. Besides the superintendent who was to be chosen by the select men of the city clergy, sergeants of the districts of the see were appointed, who were to have the care of the church goods, and other temporal matters. These, with the superintendent, were also to have the oversight of church incomes, schools, hospitals, the good behavior of priests, and to confirm in office the parish priests who were elected or called and approved by the superintendent.

In Norway, no sign of the reformation movement showed itself before the year 1528, when a monk of Bergen began to preach the new doctrine. King Christian II., when, in 1531, he came forward as defender of the papal church, made his first essay in Norway, and found many to support the views he then entertained. The prop of this church was the archbishop of Trondhem, Olof Engelbrektsson, who, from 1523, represented the holy see, the same man who long protected P. Sunnanvader and master Knut. King Frederick made no attempt to reform the church of Norway, but the decree of the diet of Odense was regarded as applicable also to Norway. After the death of Frederick II., the archbishop kept up a correspondence with the friends of Christian II., while a part of the land did homage to Christian III. After the latter had brought Denmark into subjection, he turned his wrath upon the archbishop, who now in vain desired a compromise, fled Holland, and in 1538 died in exile. Norway was now, by the arbitrary decree of the king and council of Denmark, put in subjection to the latter kingdom, the constitution and ritual of whose church was introduced into the former, and the people, by degrees, imperceptibly, though not wholly without opposition, turned from the popish faith and obedience. The archbishopric of Trondhem ceased, and superintendents were put in the place of bishops. Two of the bishops reconciled themselves to the order of things, and kept their posts; Johan Reff of Opsolo, and Geble Pedersen, of Bergen, the latter of whom, previously elected by the chapter, but not confirmed by the pope, was now ordained or consecrated at Köpenham, by doctor Bugenhagen.

Doctor Bugenhagen returned to Wittenberg, in 1539, the year in which his countryman, master Norman, went thence to Sweden, where a greater task and occupation awaited him than he first supposed.

The introduction of the Reformation into Denmark, had on the condition of the Swedish church an important influence. It was completed just before the time king Gustavus began to manifest dissatisfaction with the manner in which church affairs were conducted in Sweden. In connection with his intercourse with the men who, from 1538, began to win his confidence, and, perhaps, as preparative to that confidence, the Danish reformation stood before the king's eyes as the accomplishment of that which in Sweden he deemed himself to have been able to bring only to a primary development. Laurentius Andreæ had not suffered to lapse the old forms, into which he hoped to infuse new life. The king had not been able to make the church as submissive as it was in Germany and Denmark. But the cases were essentially unlike. In those lands, the civil freedom of the people had long before been prostrated, and by the very greatly superior intelligence of the nobles. Great, too, was the rapacious inclination of the latter to divide the spoil of a rival's power and wealth, so that the Reformation could be effected without difficulty. In Sweden, the suffrage of both the nobles and people was required to break the might of the hierarchy abused with such arrogance. The latter gave their assent, but shared with the crown and nobles the heirship of the property taken back from the church. The necessity of a violent breaking down of the church constitution was obviated in Sweden, by the less degree of power the hierarchy was there at any time able to gain, and by the caution which removed any obstinate resistance to the change. But neither the clergy nor people, nor, at first, a large portion of the nobles, were willing to exchange this power of the hierarchy for another that might still more heavily press on the freedom and improvement of the lower orders of society. The church, as the stay of the people, preserved an independence which gave it an importance even in the public civil transactions of the fatherland. How much the preservation of the people's freedom, and of the civil freedom of Sweden, when threatened by a preponderating aristocracy, was influenced for good by the independence the church retained or recovered, belongs to the history of the sixteenth, and still more that of the seventeenth century. At this time, the most eminent men of the priesthood complained of this aristocracy, that they had become "the tribunes of the people." But this is a subject which rather appertains to the history of the state.

At the same time that a revolution in the church was accomplished in Denmark, king Gustavus removed Laurentius Andreæ from his councils, and began a more thorough reform in the Swedish church. But either from the certainty or the dread of opposition, he did not allow himself to take away bishops from the church except by a change of name. Even this difference of name was not dissonant to ancient usage, and did not resemble the violent overthrow which had taken place in the neighboring kingdom. A change in Gustavus's measures was craved, until they were broken with a strong hand by king John III.

In another respect, also, the Danish church reform worked in Sweden in unison with the more open declaration there made of the approval entertained for the improvements effected by Luther. Sweden had not hitherto stood in connection or correspondence with protestant Germany. The connecting link was furnished by Denmark, which lay nearer to protestant Germany, and was more closely allied with both its church and princes; and the connections of Sweden became correspondently influenced.

Pope Clement VII., warned by the proceeding of a church council, in the beginning of the fifteenth century, had refused to let a council be summoned, to whose judgment the protestants had incessantly appealed. His successor, Paul III., after the papacy recovered itself from the first stunning blow of the Reformation, announced at last the opening, in 1537, of such a church council at Mantua. Called by both the pope and emperor, the protestant estates now refused to participate in this council, because the pope in his bull of summons, by speaking of the extirpation of heretics, was deemed to have stigmatized them under that title, because he was a party and not a judge, and because the place of meeting was too remote. At the diet of Smalcald, where they came to this resolution, they drew up a written defence of their refusal, and put it into the hands of their leaders, the duke of Saxony, and the landgrave of Hesse, to circulate with these princes' own letter. These princes sent both the defence and their letter, with a proffer of alliance, to the kings of Sweden and Denmark.* King Gustavus, with regard to the question of an alliance, declared his readiness to confer with king Christian; but replied to the landgrave, that he with joy heard of that prince's pure and firm faith, assured him of his own intention to hold fast to the same, and his purpose to unite with the protestants of Germany to defend that faith with life and goods against the pope and his followers. After Christian, in 1538, had become a member of the league of Smalcald, king Gustavus bound him-

* According to Theiner, king Gustavus had received from the pope an invitation to send an ambassador and prelates to the council, but he refused. We do not consider this a statement to be relied on.

self, without joining the league, to support it, in case of need, with a body of troops. During the subsequent year, negotiations were continued. When, in 1541, Gustavus was, as appears, again invited to join the league, the German princes employed Luther as the mediator. The king, in his answer, gives him to understand, that he reformed the faith, "according to the doctrine of Luther, but being neglected by the German protestants, he could not renew the already made proffer of a league." In 1542, the king of Denmark was commissioned by the Germans to negotiate with Sweden to join the league of Smalcald. The year following, the German members of the league demanded of king Gustavus the performance of his promise of money and troops. But the disturbances of the times interrupted or broke off the negotiation, till the success of the emperor in the so-called Smalcaldic war, dissolved, in 1546, the league itself.

This was a period gloomy and threatening for the future prospects of the German evangelical Lutheran church. The church council, announced in 1537, had, at last, at the close of 1545, been opened in the city of Trent. The protestants of Germany refused to appear. Sweden was not called. The victory of the Cæsar in the war of Smalcald, seemed to threaten the cause of the Reformation with ruin. Charles V., however, maintained with the pope relations of a doubtful aspect. When the latter removed the council from Trent to Bologna, and thus counteracted the emperor's design of constraining the defeated protestants to appear at the council, he withdrew from the Roman church's obedience, and, by the Interim presented to the estates of the empire, at Augsburg, in 1548, prescribed the rule of faith and ecclesiastical usages, until they should be settled by a general council of the church. This religious ordinance was as little liked by the protestants as by the papists. It was transmitted by the king of Denmark to Gustavus I., who summoned Olaus

Petri and G. Norman to deliberate on its contents. The archbishop of Upsala, bishop Bothvid of Strängness, the two representatives from bishop Henrik of Westeras, Petrus Andreæ Svart, successor of Henrik, and Erik Nicolai, besides Olaus Petri, and the pastor, preacher, and schoolmaster, of the principal church of Upsala, met together, and on March 30, 1549, pronounced their opinion, which was strongly disapprobatory. It contained some things which might be tolerated, if the purpose and intention were good and Christian, but the bad suffocated the good. The Interim was nothing else but an introduction to popery, with its mass-sacrifice for the living and the dead, its worship of saints, its purgatory, and other the like errors, which were now rejected according to God's word. For themselves, they would cleave to the pure and clear word of God, and for this suffer and endure whatever might be allotted them.

As the Swedish church, on the question regarding the Interim, decided against its reception, so did she also decide, about ten years later, in the so-called Synergistic controversy, which was violently agitated in the evangelical Lutheran academies of Germany. She expressly declared herself, through her bishops, against those who regarded the nature of man, fallen through the sin of Adam, still to have strength with God's grace to work out its own conversion. She attributed all to the sole grace of God.

The government of the kingdom of Sweden was charged with an additional duty respecting the church, by the union of Estland and Liffland with Sweden, originated in the reign of king Erik XIV. As early as the year 1561, this king recommends, in his rules for the government of Liffland, the care of the pure word of God, the providing of priests and schools, and the building of churches. But as yet, these countries stood in no near connection with the Swedish church.

In general the Swedish church, although it almost wholly coincided with the Lutheran reformation, had maintained no intimate alliances in matters of faith, with foreigners. Its reform had gone on in its own path, and could not be brought into a full conformity with foreign patterns. The confession of the church was and remained indefinite, except in certain points. The complexity of his political relations justified king Gustavus's caution, in entering too closely into the German protestant league. Nay, within three years after his death, had king Erik already drawn his sword against his nearest fellow in the faith, the king of Denmark and Norway.

Grave proofs would not be wanting of the rational grounds for dreading the intrusion even of Jesuitism. Another little less dangerous foe, Calvinism, awakened contemporaneous disorders and contentions. It is to the imperishable honor of archbishop Laurentius Petri, that he turned aside one of these foes, and armed the church against the other, while he protected her laws against the inroads of external power.

CHAPTER X.

THE LAST WORK IN WHICH OLAUS PETRI WAS ENGAGED. HIS DEATH. LAURENTIUS PETRI AGAINST THE KING, AND AGAINST THE CALVINISTS.

(TO KING JOHN III.'S ELEVATION TO THE SWEDISH THRONE.)

After the suit and trial, which well nigh terminated in the sacrifice of Laurentius Andreæ and Olaus Petri, and wholly removed the former from participation in the public affairs of the church, no trace, for the first three years, is discovered of the renewed or progressive activity of Olof. He appears to have kept himself in voluntary or constrained retirement, while the reformation of the church was zealously conducted under new leaders. He held, by grant of the king, in 1542, the canonry of Alunda, in Upsala, with all its rents. But in the year when the grand insurrection in Southern Sweden was with difficulty suppressed, and the new favorite Von Pyhy was discarded, Olof again steps forth upon the scene of action, nominated by the king, on April 7, 1543, to the pastorship of the church in Stockholm. The king again bestowed on him a portion of the confidence he before enjoyed, listened to his advice, and used his aid. Yet he did not recover his previous degree of influence; nor had his undaunted and incautious zeal been curbed by misfortune. He still continued intrepidly to utter his sentiments and proclaim his opinions. In 1544, he was again in danger of being put upon his trial, probably for indiscreet expressions with regard to the king. The danger, however, stopped at the serious warning he received, to preach among the king's subjects, duty and obedience, and "not so often run a tilt against the buckler of his prince, as was his wont." For the last eight years, he appears to have enjoyed freedom and quiet, until, on April 19, 1552, he closed his active and fruitful life at Stockholm, whose chief church preserves his tomb and epitaph. But a few days intervened between his death and that of Laurentius Andreæ. Both these men, who wrought together in the harmony of Christian faith and knowledge, for the church and their fatherland, went together to their rest.

In little less than eight years from the time of Olaus's return to Stockholm, on January 1, 1553, G. Norman also died. During the fourteen years he resided in Sweden, he steadily enjoyed the favor and confidence of king Gustavus, was elevated by him to the council of the kingdom, in 1544, and was employed in the business of church and state. But the care of ecclesiastical affairs intrusted to him as the king's superintendent, was not, it is said, otherwise exercised by him, after the year 1540, than as adviser of his sovereign. Neither visitations, nor the placing of priests in their cures, are mentioned, as after that time practised by him. To the bishops and priests, he seems not always to have stood in a friendly relation, in consequence of administering or perhaps enforcing the not universally acceptable measures of the king regarding the church. Neither great praise nor blame attends his memory, which his piety protected from stain, and his modest and honorable conduct from reproach.

At the time when these three men, soon after one another, passed to the higher tribunal, at which they were to appear to render an account of their actions, archbishop Laurentius Petri, who shared their labors, and filled the foremost place in the church, had finished the half of his long earthly journey in his important vocation. We have seen him during the first twenty years of that period, step forward, and on each occasion in bold relief, as when, in 1538, he resented the abuses within the church, in 1541, offered a complete translation of the Bible into Swedish, and in 1549, pronounced judgment against the Interim. The year after the publication of the Bible translation he does not appear in any public transaction. But a work which he at this time composed, though not printed till more than forty years after, manifests that he did not disapprove the important measures then pursued for the improvement of public worship. Probably this production was a quiet exercise for his mind in troublous days. It argues, in an easy dialogue, the reasonableness of introducing the mass in Swedish, because the Latin had not a divine origin, and, in its expressions of offering up a sacrifice, was contrary to the word of God. They who took offence at the change had less claim to indulgent regard than those who desired to restore or not to lose the mass in Swedish. A good shepherd, convinced that the Latin mass was not Christian, and that the Swedish was good and right, ought not to give way, but unweariedly teach, exhort, and reprove, and rather hold no mass than return to the Latin.

The activity of Laurentius was quiet and unassuming. He sought not controversy, but did not decline it where it was necessary. He was of that class of men who, in the firm confidence that they are doing the work of the Lord, but also that He alone can give the increase, labor in patience, and without any other ambition than the witness of a good conscience before God, and are therefore yielding and compliant, so long as the sanctuary of truth is not assailed, but firm and ready for the combat, when its protection is demanded. For the last twenty-two years of his life he was the foremost man in the controversies of the church.

The first controversy he had, was with the king and G. Norman. Among the immunities and privileges which, at the time of the Reformation, princes in particular claimed, there were few that required a more nice investigation, were more trying, than those which required the restrictions to be removed that the laws of the church had imposed upon matrimonial engagements. Some of these restrictions were unreasonable and against the law of God. But it was undecided how far the privileges should be extended. The king of England severed the church of his land from Rome, to gain a divorce refused him by the pope. The landgrave Philip, of Hesse, did not wish a divorce from his wife, but constrained Luther and Melancthon to give him permission to add another. This permission was repented by them, and disapproved by the church. In Sweden, king Gustavus, after the death of queen Margaret, demanded the church's approval of his wish to marry Katharina Stenbock, the sister's daughter of his deceased wife. But he could not induce the leading men of the church to give this approval.

The case was laid before bishop Henrik, of Westeras, on the part of the king, when, in the spring of 1552, the latter was on a visit there. The bishop consulted with the archbishop, who, immediately communicating with those who were interested in the question, replied, that, according to his conviction, such a marriage was forbidden by the law of God. Soon after, the archbishop received orders from the king, who gave him to understand that he was determined on the marriage with Katharina, to call together the bishops of Strängness and Westeras, and in connection with them pronounce an opinion on the question. They met at Enkoping in midsummer, and delivered their judgment, in which, though admitting that no express prohibition was to be found in Scripture, they declared that the invalidity of such a marriage was to be inferred from the eighteenth chapter of the third book of Moses, that any respect of persons could have no weight in what concerned the law of God, that a good purpose could not justify the transgression of this law, that examples from the Old Testament did not annul the law, and that scandal ought to be avoided. Dissatisfaction with this judgment brought the king to Wadsten, where, in presence of the council and the dukes Erik and John, the king's cause was pleaded by G. Norman, who attempted to prove, that the degree of consanguinity here existing was no preventive of marriage according to God's law. The bishops, to whom Erik Falk, of Skara, was now added, could not, either by bribes, or by the anger of the king, from whom, in his allowed prerogative, they received hard and reproachful words, be induced to change their judgment. This judgment they averred they could not, for conscience's sake, disavow, but they also averred their inviolable purpose to keep the faith they had sworn to the king, to construe favorably all that was done, and endeavor the prevention of disorders and discontent in the kingdom. Notwithstanding their opposition, the king's marriage took place, on the 22d of August, and the crowning of the new queen followed. Not the archbishop, but the ordinary of Linkoping, Claudius Hvit, who agreed with G. Norman, performed the sacred ceremonies.

It belongs not to us to criticise the reasons which were alleged for and against this marriage on the ground of affinity. But that a king, otherwise so despotic, made such account of the approbation of the clergy, merits observation. The king may have designed to provide against the censure which this marriage might create, but his course shows that the church, at the close of his reign, was still free, and did not suffer her laws to be bowed at the sport of caprice. The king also showed that he respected an opposition which proceeded from pure conscientious scruples. Laurentius Petri acted, not from the love of power, but from conviction of the contrariety of such a marriage to the law of God. About twenty years later, he was alike inflexible in regard to the marriage of first cousins, and allowed himself to be little moved by the sentence of the university of Rostock, which now agreed with the king.

In the case of king Gustavus's marriage, the archbishop, and those of the same opinion, had from the first declared themselves not thoroughly satisfied, inasmuch as the Scriptures were not express on the subject, and they could, therefore, without doing violence to their consciences, give the pledge which they made the king, even after his nuptials, that they would favorably construe what had been done. As this dispute had given warning what the church might fear for the sanctity of its laws, from a power which could throw the sword into the scale opposite to that of truth, so was the archbishop soon summoned to another of great importance to the Swedish church.

The church reformation had been consequent upon the necessity of purifying the church from the abuses to which it had been subjected. The investigation undertaken of the church's doctrine, usages, and constitution, in order to ascertain their agreement or disagreement with Holy Scripture, occasioned different senses to be given to one or other of the doctrines of the church, or a variant toleration for the ecclesiastical customs that in the course of time had become common in the church. There was a greater or less severance from all connection with the past. A separation soon took place between the German and Swiss Reformation. The development of the latter, effected chiefly by Frenchmen, and most of all by Calvin after he removed to Geneva, still further divided them, the more, that an apparent or specious agreement obliged Lutheranism to assume a hostile attitude whenever Calvinism seemed to be going too far. There was still some dissonance between the two bodies, arising from the dissimilarity of their form of government, after Calvinism built for itself a new form of hierarchy divergent from the Roman. But the question respecting the real presence of the body and blood of Christ in the Eucharist, in which question almost all the important differences between Lutheranism and Calvinism are included, together with Calvin's rigid doctrine of predestination, awakened controversies and contentions. Besides this, the gloomy eye of Calvinism saw in the innocent customs and ceremonies of the church retained from former times, a papistic leaven which ought to be removed, and the more zealous Lutherans did not discountenance the removal.

In Sweden, there still existed, even subsequent to the year 1544, much that was unlike what was to be found in other lands. The foreigners who came into the country, and who had more zeal than truth or discretion, interfered with the freedom which was observed with regard to church usages, and which in some places began in consequence to be laid aside; while the Swedes who returned from their travels abroad, not unfrequently brought back with them that spirit of imitation which is wont to present the pretext of a higher cultivation and deeper acquaintance with truth.

Their views were influenced by Calvinistic principles. As early as king Gustavus's time, the professors of those principles had entered Sweden, among whom was Dionysius Beurreus, tutor of duke Erik, of whose origin we have no certain information except that he was a Frenchman. He came to Sweden in 1547. Many others of various shades of opinion came hither, partly to follow up their fortunes, partly to escape persecution in their native lands. Not a few were from France and England. About the time of king Gustavus's third marriage, in Wadsten, occurred there acts of violence originating in an immoderate hatred of popery; at which time the images and pictures which had been left in the churches of the cloisters were mutilated and defaced. It was attributed to "the Calvinists among the king's fiddlers," and it is said that the king did not rebuke the offence, but was more concerned for the scandal than the act itself. To the king, Calvin himself wrote, in 1559, in recommendation of his doctrine. The two older sons of Gustavus, who were among the most accomplished men of their time, were thought to have no disinclination. Erik, it was feared, had drunk of the stream through his tutor Beurreus; and John is said to have become captivated with the writings of Calvin, during his visit, in portions of the years 1559 and 1560, to England, when the works of Calvin became known to him.

On the accession of Erik to the throne, the more rigid protestant party, with which the Calvinists at first took part, were in hope of a still more extended success; since the king, as his father had done before him, invited foreigners to settle in his kingdom. On March 5, 1561, Beurreus, who was that year sent to England, was empowered to issue a charter, by which the invitation was confirmed upon condition that pure Christian doctrine, conformable to Holy Scripture, should be taught by any who came, that no heresies should be sown, and that the religion of the country should not be disturbed, nor the people enticed away from its profession. But, inasmuch as the Swedish church had not yet set forth her confession of faith in all its parts, it could not be accurately determined when these conditions were broken or unfulfilled.

At the diet of Arboga, held in the month of April, 1561, a discussion took place on certain changes which chiefly related to ecclesiastical usages of an indifferent nature, but with regard to which it now became necessary to assert the church's liberty to retain or reject them, or certify their coherence with her confession of faith. The king laid before the clergy orally, and afterward in writing, interrogatories respecting the elevation of the sacrament (that is, of the bread and wine in the Lord's Supper), the use of images, the altar, the mass cloths, and the lighting of candles at the time of divine service. Were these to be retained or rejected? The answer was, that the elevation of the sacrament was an indifferent ceremony, and might be omitted where it could be so done without scandal, but that the worship of it, by which was to be understood the kneeling at its reception, should be retained, because there is the body and blood of the Lord, "which is worthy of all honor and reverence;" that images were not sinful in themselves, but all worship of them should be forbidden; that *one altar was necessary* in every church, but no more; that mass cloths and wax lights were things indifferent, which any congregation might at pleasure retain or reject.

The king appears to have been till now vacillating, and to have been worried by the representations of the foreigners. Somewhat more than a year later, in the summer ot 1562, he shows himself more settled in his views, when he required of the bishops and priests assembled in Stockholm their opinions on certain articles. Different views respecting the holy supper had become current; he therefore asked, in order that the truth might be made manifest, consciences not be troubled, and the quiet of the kingdom put to hazard, that learned men should examine these questions. This was the more necessary, as the "local ordinary," M. Johannes, confessor to the late king Gustavus, was not regarded as orthodox, and ought to be made to give an account of his faith. A decision ought also to be given on the disputed point of dividing the ten commandments, of which some desired four to be put in the first table. It was in conclusion proposed, whether or not the indifferent practices, such as exorcising at the time of baptism, elevation of the sacrament, and the like, should be discontinued.

Any other answer is not known to us, than that of the decrees of a council held at Stockholm, where, however, no doctrinal determinations were promulged. The obscure records of the times, do not even enable us to say with certainty, whether these decrees were passed before or after the propositions, which, on the 7th of July, were presented by the king. However that may be, it appears that the archbishop took upon himself to answer them.

Laurentius Petri found himself, by the circumstances of the times, compelled to come forward in opposition to the party that threatened the freedom of the church and her confession, if such may be termed the Lutheran sentiments respecting the Lord's supper, which were generally prevalent. He was the more induced to pursue the course he adopted, by the sincere and hearty interest he felt for the liberty which called itself evangelical, but manifested its opposition to the papal reverence for the sacrament, by celebrating it with the head covered, or the face turned aside, or in conversation with the bystanders, to exhibit the indifference felt for anything like the real presence.

A challenge to the combat was made in 1562, by two published works of Laurentius Petri. One of these is in defence of exorcism. The other expressly rejects alike the doctrine of the sacramentarians, of a mere spiritual eating and drinking in the eucharist, and the popish doctrine of transubstantiation. It also defends the consecration of the sacrament, and the kneeling at its reception, the allowableness of the use of images, and the liberty of the church in things indifferent. With respect to the elevation of the sacrament in the Lord's supper, which king Gustavus, in 1550, reproached the pastor of Wadsten for voluntarily omitting, the foreigners, it was remarked, had taken offence at the retention of a practice in Sweden, to which they were unaccustomed in their own countries. The archbishop answers, that their judgment might be disregarded, since they who were scandalized at the custom were no less in error than they who considered it essential. In conclusion, the writings of Laurentius, after this time, show that many of the resolutions, adopted in the councils held in the years 1561 and 1562, did not meet his approbation. The better-informed members of the church, he says, had regarded images as to be tolerated in churches. If they were abused by bowing down to them, and the abuse could not otherwise be rectified, they ought to be removed, but quietly, without riot. Abuses have occurred among us, and this was the reason the council of Arboga *permitted* the removal of images. The priests ought to see that the decree was carried into execution *where it was necessary*. With regard to the prohibition of several altars, the church law of 1571 had given notice, that, in towns where congregations were of a greater size, more than one altar in a church might well be allowed.

The gauntlet thrown down was taken up by doctor Beurreus, who felt himself so touched by the remarks of the archbishop against the sacramentarians, as the Calvinists were then called, that he put forth a refutation. In this controversial production, the author undertakes to justify his faith, that is to say, his Calvinism respecting the Lord's supper, by quoting, among other modes of defence, the Augsburg confession and its Apology. This was the first time, if we are not mistaken, that these confessions of faith were quoted in Sweden; but archbishop Lars, in his answer to Beurreus, allows them no special weight and importance; although he observes that between them and the doctrine of the sacramentarians there was no greater conformity than between Christ and Belial. He endeavors, in conclusion, to establish out of the Holy Scriptures and the fathers of the church, his belief of the real presence of the body and blood of Christ in the supper of the Lord.

Beurreus did not hastily give up his case as lost. But with the theological erudition which, from the later days of king Gustavus I.'s reign, was to be found in Sweden, and with the close intercourse kept up between Wittenberg and Rostock, where the most accomplished of the Swedes had studied, it was not to be feared that the archbishop would be left solitary in his combat against Calvinism. Beurreus set forth ten queries, on the orthodoxy of the Athanasian creed, on the Lord's supper, on the participation of the divine properties by the human nature of Christ, and subjects of a like kind; but was answered by Martinus Olai, who, in his turn, put to Beurreus other new queries.*

King Erik soon found the necessity of quieting the commotions which these controversies awakened, and declared his opposition to Calvinism, which, although without mentioning it by name, he stigmatizes as "a distorted doctrine." This he does in an edict issued, Aug. 29, 1563, from his camp, a few days after he went from Stockholm to the war lately undertaken against Denmark. The foreigners were forbidden to propagate their errors among the people, or to engage in disputations with any "but such as are appointed for that purpose," and others were prohibited from entering into dogmatic controversies with them. The foreigners, however, were permitted to hold their opinions, and even to have public worship at fixed times in the churches of the land, probably with a view of converting them from their distorted doctrine.

The schism which occurred between the Lutherans and Calvinists, now crept even into the Swedish church itself. The foreigners seem imprudently to have been desirous of diffusing their opinions, and it is probable, found support from the Lutheran puritans. By this means they roused the Swedish clergy, who applied to the archbishop to preach against them, and warn his flock against their errors. When the church thus appeared to declare against them, the Calvinists of Stockholm were necessitated to appeal to the king's protection. They submitted to him their confession of faith, with very few alterations, the same which,

* Martinus Olai, in a Latin letter to the archbishop, says: "Some set Calvin so high as not to fear asserting that he can err in nothing, because he has the Holy Spirit. *This seems to me redolent of popery.*" Beurreus is said to have accused the archbishop of being a papist. We find no proof of this, though it is probable he deemed the prelate's views to border upon the papal. Of the archbishop he speaks very respectfully, as "an eminent and remarkable man, from whose writings and conversation I much profited."

translated into Latin, was, in 1559, adopted by the reformed church of France at its first national synod, and requested that it might be compared with the word of God, and be printed in Swedish and Latin. They petitioned also to be secured in the free exercise of their religion within their houses, if the king should not think fit to allow them, like the Germans, to have their own churches and public worship.*

The most energetic opponent of the Calvinists in Stockholm, after the year 1562, was Laurentius Olaus Gestricius, pastor of the principal church in the city, and successor of M. Johannes, who had been suspected of Calvinism. As soon as their confession of faith had been submitted to the king, Olaus presented a refutation, accompanied with a letter, in which he avouches that from the pulpit he had warned his hearers of the errors of which he now also wished to notify the king.

We are sufficiently assured from public documents, that these controversies were the occasion of much disorder in Stockholm, but the details have not come down to us. The Calvinists, with whom we suppose that the Lutheran separatists had a common cause,† held their meetings, in which the natives participated, in the northern suburbs of the city. It appears, that, after the king, at the end of June, went to Eastgothland, Laurentius Olaus followed him with complaints of the interruptions experienced in the exercise of his office. He returned, armed with an injunction to the governor of Stockholm that master Lars should be allowed

* These Germans were generally of the Lutheran faith and confession.

† These are they whom archbishop Lars describes in his book written in 1566: "They denounce and decry all others who do not join in their new devices, as papists and hypocrites, and just so did the Novatians and Donatists of old time. God is a God who will have mercy and not sacrifice, as he has himself declared. How much less will he accept the ceremonies of the sacrament in lieu of mercy, that is, in lieu of the peace and concord which Christian congregations should maintain."

to prosecute his labors undisturbed, that the meetings of his adversaries should be suspended, until there could be a more thorough investigation of their doctrine, that no one should speak against the preaching and worship which were in conformity with the principles of Martin Luther, "*which*," says the king, "*we approve and desire to be strenuously maintained*."

King Erik had by this letter expressly declared himself for the Lutheran confession, and it is evident, from its contents, how completely from a state of doubt he had passed to a disapproval of Calvinism and an adherence to the Lutheran tenets. In the public edict, however, he avoids citing the name of Luther. The controversy having continued for some time, and the king having, in 1563, renewed his edict, he, at last, on Dec. 4, 1565, issued a mandate of even a more rigid complexion.

In this mandate he says, that he perceived that some foreigners who had come into the kingdom harbored and endeavored to spread distorted doctrines, denying that the body and blood of Christ were really present and administered in the Lord's supper, and that the humanity of Christ was as omnipotent as his divinity. As such doctrines taught by them are contrary to holy Scripture, from which passages in refutation are quoted, the king in virtue of his royal office admonishes their maintainers to renounce them. If they would not heed this admonition, they must retain their false faith at the peril of their own souls, since the king "would not master any man's conscience." But they were gravely forbidden, by speech or writing, to aim at propagating their errors among the king's subjects. Should they continue faulty as heretofore, the king's officers and governors were to keep them in ward till they promised amendment. Upon a renewal of their fault, they were to be banished the land, unless within fourteen days they made their excuse to the king.

King Erik XIV. was thus determined not to leave Calvinism any influence within his kingdom, notwithstanding he kept his promise of religious freedom to the extent granted in 1561 to immigrant foreigners. That these, especially Beurreus, thought they might venture to attempt the spread of their doctrines is evident; but no sign is to be found, unless at the very beginning of Erik's reign, that they were countenanced by him. At least the church's confession of faith, if we may so speak of its guardians and sponsors, was in such a case strong enough to hold him back; and although among the probable and reasonable causes of his dislike, may be reckoned the treatment shown by Beurreus and Goran Persson to the priests of Upland, whom they moved about at discretion, it was not a single case or words only that awakened fears and complaints of the intention of introducing a new faith into the land.

This doctrinal controversy brought the Swedish church into a clearer consciousness of its close affinity with the evangelical Lutheran confession. It became necessary to prove this affinity, not merely in comparison, as hitherto, with the Roman, but with the Calvinistic church; and as far as the expressions of the king and her theological writers could be considered as those of the church of Sweden, she had expressly announced "her teaching and public worship to be conformable to the principles and views of Martin Luther." Until this period the Swedish church was prottestant as opposed to the Roman; henceforth she was evangelical Lutheran as opposed to the reformed church, as that term was technically applied. But, thirty years were yet to roll away, amid severe trials of faith and controversies, before the work could be graced with full completion.

Simultaneously with the contest against the sacramentarians, arose another cause of agitation, which, though at first view it may appear insignificant, had a close connection with the other, gave rise to a similar train of inquiries, and had the same result of knitting stronger the bond between the Swedish church and the German or Lutheran reformation.

From the year 1544, the laity generally partook of the cup at the administration of the holy communion, and there was, therefore, an increased demand for wine in that sacrament. But the supply not corresponding to the demand, it was proposed, at least from the time that zealous puritanism found fault with the sanctity and reverence entertained for the ordinance and it was probably in some places the practice, to substitute for wine some other element, such as water, mead, or cherry juice. In view of this purpose or practice, it was ordained, at a council held at Stockholm, in 1562, that no other liquid but wine should be used, since there ought not to be a deviation from the institution of Christ. If there was no supply of wine, the Lord's supper should be deferred, and at their visitation the sick should be comforted with God's word. On the breaking out of the war with Denmark, in 1563, and the surrender of Elfsborg to the Danes, the supply of wine was still further diminished, so that commotions and discontents began to arise in Upper Sweden. The archbishop, in consequence, set forth, on February 14, 1564, an address to the clergy of his diocese, to instruct the people that the matter of greatest moment was to put their trust in the merits of Jesus Christ, and that the sacrament, when it could not be enjoyed according to the institution of Christ, might be dispensed with without danger to the soul. The custom of using anything but wine should the less be countenanced and allowed, as such a custom would tend to spread the irreverence which the sacramentarians showed for the holy supper of the Lord. King Erik, who was heedful of these commotions, summoned, during the following month, the archbishop, with the bishops of Strängness and Westeras, to deliberate at Stockholm on the subject. Laurentius Petri maintained the opinion he had already expressed, but allowed that the wine might with propriety be mixed with water. The other view, that the most important consideration was the distribution of the sacrament, in which any element might be used, was maintained by Johan Ofeg, who, the previous year, became bishop of Westeras, after his intimacy with Beurreus, who dedicated to him the above-mentioned work against the archbishop. The king gave on the question the brief order, that the bishops should, on peril of losing their office, take heed that no further complaints were made of the sacrament not being administered.

Hence arose the so-called liquoristic controversy. On his return home from Stockholm, Ofeg published a pamphlet in conformity with the opinions he had expressed at Stockholm, and which he pretended to be generally recognized and acknowledged. The sacrament was not to be administered with water, except in case of the want of wine. This had been sometimes practised in the ancient primitive church. Priests ought not to be deprived of their Christian liberty, which Ofeg did not think consisted in omitting the sacrament, but in the right to give and receive it in other visible elements than those in which it was instituted by Christ. There would otherwise result a dependence upon those who, by denying or hindering access to wine, or stopping its supply, might wish to exclude the inhabitants of Sweden from the use of the sacrament.

Laurentius Petri was not the man to let a cause drop, in which conscience or conviction constrained him to take a decisive stand. When the pastoral letter of Ofeg came to his knowledge, he issued one of a like kind to the priests of Fjerdhundra, or the part of his diocese bordering on that of Ofeg, and warned them not to be led into error. The conclusion at Stockholm had not been such as Ofeg represented. The ancient church had never used water instead of wine. Liberty consisted in the omission of the sacrament. "It is a miserable liberty which binds us to necessity," and "God is wont not to give into the hands of their enemies the people who obey him."

In the answer he gave, Ofeg partly recalled his former expressions. The king made application on this topic to D. Chytræus, of Rostock, and desired his opinion. Before the opinion arrived, the Swedish bishops and priests assembled at the diet of Stockholm, in April, 1565, prepared and subscribed a paper, in which, on the authority of holy Scripture, the church's prescription, and the sense of the Fathers and more modern theologians, the use of anything but wine in the holy communion, is declared inadmissible. Even Johan Ofeg subscribed this declaration, and recanted his former opinion, which seems never afterward to have found a defender.

The archbishop, now near seventy years old, wearied not, by his speech, and writings, and acts, in conducting the church through the perils with which she appeared to him to be menaced. The time was near, when, as he hoped, its discipline should be established by law. He approximated the Swedish church, although always avouching its independence, to the evangelical Lutheran; as it now seemed to him necessary to declare himself openly for one or other of the great leading church parties. The controversies in which he was engaged, and their results, may be briefly described in his own words. "On the first appearance of the reformers, every man was inclined, nay more than inclined, to injure and crush them. One would say, that he could risk on them an old wash-room; another, an old barn; another, so many loads of firewood, so much turf, peat, or birch, with other like expressions of contempt. It was thought much money could not be better bestowed, than in helping to extirpate from the earth such cursed heretics, (that was the expression), and noxious men. It was, as our Lord Christ said to his disciples, the time cometh when whosoever killeth you shall think he doeth God service. This all know and can certify, who are old enough and can remember what occurred six-and-forty years or more agone, when God's pure word was here first proclaimed, through speech and writing, by my blessed brother, master Olof Petri, and those others who were with him in the righteous cause. These things are not now recalled from any vain glory, as God is witness, still less as a reproach to any party. For it is well known, that here, as everywhere else, it has come to pass, rather from foolishness than malice prepense, that they who would advance God's word have before all others suffered, as well in the present time as formerly. For now that the people, through God's grace, have come to some better nnderstanding, and the outcry raised by the papists is thought to be silenced, and the preachers have obtained some little quiet on that side, a new storm arises from another quarter, not less violent than the former, as too often happens in this world. The foe comes again in his wrath, and smites us on the other side. Watchful, as they say, for spirituality and truth, of which they make their boast, these men contemn and decry us as manifest papists, because we cannot approve their new opinions of the sacrament, and because our congregations suffer some of the ceremonies to which they have been accustomed, or which may be used by the papists, to remain undisturbed. In foreign lands, as well with regard to ceremonies as doctrine, there is great dissimilarity, so that the people who have discarded papal errors, are by no means in entire agreement. Each province, each principality, in some places each city, has its peculiar ceremonies and church usages. It is often the case that the same custom is not long preserved, but changes take place almost every month. I know nothing better to say or to advise, than that we assimilate with the congregations who follow the doctrine of doctor Martin. For as we have truly proclaimed that God of his special grace has raised up that man to expose the hideous errors of the pope, and show us the right way, and as we have received his doctrine as the truest, I cannot believe that we shall find any better church usages than they observe who hold the same doctrines as we, that is doctor Martin and doctor Philip, hold. For this the special reason may be assigned, that we can easily and with least offence fall into those customs, because between them and our own, as hitherto practised, there is but little distinction or difference."

CHAPTER XI.

THE KINGS, GUSTAVUS I. AND ERIK XIV.—COMMENCEMENT OF KING JOHN III.'s REIGN—ECCLESIASTICAL LAW—COUNCIL OF UPSALA IN 1572—DAY AND YEAR OF THE DEATH OF ARCHBISHOP LAURENTIUS PETRI.

THE improvement of the church, as exhibited in Scandinavia and Germany, aimed, among other objects, by a nearer union between the church and state, at a removal of the discord which had existed, and which had been the fruitful source of disasters to both. Some members of the church, who saw the need of this improvement, desired also through the temporal power, a release from the strain of that wide-stretched and deep-reaching arm, which would stifle all diversities of opinion. To decide between the contending church parties, really lay in the hands of this power, as far as human might can rule within the realms of truth. It must either unite itself to one of these parties, and suppress the other, or exercise its decision by protecting both alike. This latter course could not long be pursued. A piety at once energetic, and influencing the whole range of human thought, could not possibly penetrate a civil community without some established ecclesiastical confession, and the passions were not always sanctified by the spirit of Christianity, not always checked by the religious element, nor by the interests of the state.

At the beginning of the Reformation, its success could not but be in a great measure dependent upon the personal qualities and disposition of princes. It was sustained in Sweden during the long reign of king Gustavus I., by his powerful hand, which he stretched forth to this work in the full conviction that thereby the victory of the kingdom of Christ was advanced. During that period protestantism developed itself by degrees, till the necessity was apparent of there being established an independent self-existing church. This development was not consummated before the death of Gustavus, at which time the hope was not yet extinct of restoring the unity of the church under the former ecclesiastical relations, by means of the Tridentine decrees, and the devices of the Jesuits to save the tottering papacy. Gustavus I., therefore, did not complete the Swedish reformation. He did not wish, as John III. afterward did, to be himself a reformer; but he was, and continued to be, a disciple of the reformers, and in the different progressive steps he took, and with increased decision on the path of reformation, he manifested a growing confidence in the doctrines of protestantism, which he himself embraced, and caused to be propagated among the people, as the father of his fatherland. The faults which may be observed in the means he employed, and in his actions, find an apology in the character of the era, which was one of great fluctuation, and in the imperfection that attaches to whatever is human, and from which no greatness is exempt. These faults notwithstanding, the Swedish heart shall not cease to bless his memory, while we enjoy the light and freedom for which he fought, and which, in his days, were diffused over our fatherland.

King Gustavus, who died on Sept. 29, 1560, was buried in the cathedral of Upsala, where the cross that had been consecrated to the Virgin Mary became his monument.*

* "During the first three weeks of his illness," says Geijer, "he spoke often, sometimes with wonderful energy, on temporal and spiritual affairs. The three following he passed chiefly in silence, and as it seemed in no

The unhappy reign of king Erik did not interfere with the progress of the church, which now acquired both strength and vigor, on the principles which were followed during the later portions of his father's time.

But, on these principles, it was not yet determined what were the rights of the church, and what the rights of the king, or in what manner the king was to exercise his influence in regard to the former. The church herself had not developed any definite views respecting these questions, and the fluctuating laws of the state had not given a settled or detailed discipline to the church. The general principles, however, may be regarded as explained by archbishop Laurentius Petri in many of his writings, and among them, with a certain degree of authority, in his preface to the ecclesiastical code of 1571. According to this preface, the offices of temporal princes and the servants of the church ought not to be confused or mixed together, "as they had been under the pope." But it is the duty of princes to watch over and provide for the weal of God's everlasting kingdom, as well as their own temporal and perishable dominions. It is the part, therefore, and right of princes to see that the holy word and gospel of God be freely and without hinderance preached and spread, that false and heretical doctrine be removed, that by the establishment of good and Christian schools, furnished with necessary teachers, and properly supported and protected, the way may be

great pain. He was often seen to raise his hands as in prayer. Having received the sacrament, made confession of his faith, and taken an oath of his son to adhere firmly to it, he beckoned for writing materials; but his trembling hand had not power to finish the sentence begun. The confessor continued his exhortations, till, as life was flying, Steno Lejonhufvud interrupted him by saying, 'All that you talk is in vain, for our lord heareth no more.' Thereupon the priest bent down to the ear of the dying man and said, 'If thou believe in Jesus Christ, and hear my voice, give us some sign thereof.' To the amazement of all, the king answered with a loud voice, 'Yes!' This was his last breath, at eight of the clock in the morning."—*Trans.*

prepared for obtaining learned and Christian preachers, and that provision be made for the sick and poor by the founding of almhouses and hospitals. For these objects princes should issue suitable ordinances and make laws.

As yet there was no need, or perhaps no opportunity, to determine and settle these principles, while merely the papal tenets and the abuses of the Roman church were considered as "the false and heretical doctrine." But when, as we have seen, in king Erik's time, variant protestant views began to contend for supremacy, the need became more apparent of a settled and determinate ecclesiastical confession, which the temporal prince was to protect and defend. Then the king and men of the church united in the recognition of the evangelical Lutheran doctrine. But soon the exigence arose, of a dissonance between the king and men of the church, on the question what was the creed of the church, or the confession which should claim support and protection.

This dissonance concerned the very dogmas of faith. A like uncertainty attended the limits of the church's privileges and independence. Bishops and priests were placed or displaced by the kings without election, or verdict of church authority, and after the reduction of the church's property, the incomes of her officers depended on the pleasure of the king. Whether he acted in these matters by virtue of the church's commission, or by virtue of the rights of the civil community; whether the payment of salaries was to be considered as a management of the church's wealth, or as an application of the revenues of the state to church purposes, were points left undetermined. The king appeared to possess within the commonwealth, the rights and duties toward the priestly vocation, which the father of a family has within his own house. The king had, therefore, sometimes in days of yore, addressed words of spiritual admonition and warning to his people, and the long-continued pious custom, for the kings of Sweden to summon their people to the observance of days of penance or thanksgiving, either yearly or on extraordinary occasions, was renewed under the new order of things in the year 1544, a year so significant in regard to church reformation. The custom, however, was ancient, and thus the priestly nature of the royal sentence and decision was a maxim in the Christian church. King Gustavus refers to "the good old and Christian way," and in Sweden it had formerly occurred, that when God's judgments of death visited the land, her kings had summoned their people to mourn for their sins and do penance.

When Erik, eight years after the death of his father, was hurled from the throne, the royal sceptre of Sweden was taken by John III. Like his brother, he had received a careful education. His disposition was peculiarly adapted to quiet meditation. When a youth of twenty, he was admonished by his father for his dreams of solitude. The eyes of mankind were fastened on the church, and circumstances conspired to turn the attention of John on the points of faith which divided the world, and on the means of restoring unity. The question, whether it was unavoidable that the outward unity of the church must be dissolved, pressed heavily on many hearts. At the moment when that unity seemed irretrievably lost, John had seen in England, in 1559, the still fresh tracks of the bloody domination of the Roman church under queen Mary, and the first expiatory movements under Elizabeth. In Sweden, he was a witness to the disorders created by Calvinism, which he could contemplate with the more observant eye, as the storm raged around the walls of his prison. His imprisonment of four years, was shared by his wife,* who belonging to the

* This woman, when offered a princely maintenance on condition of parting from her husband, made answer, by pointing to her wedding-ring with it's Latin inscription: "Naught but death."—*Tr.*

church of Rome had an aversion to the faith and worship of Sweden; and the opportunities for comparing the shades of religion were the oftener presented, as he sometimes was obliged to be his wife's comforter, when her priest was occasionally denied access to the prison. There was also now leisure for study, and now were those plans formed which were productive of well nigh twenty years of strife, during the king's persevering efforts to give the Reformed faith a new shape.

These plans had not come to maturity, nor been put in execution, during the first five years of king John's reign, although the news of them began to be spread. The Roman church was at this time scarcely tolerated. King Erik was not its friend. At the time of his courtship of Mary Stuart of Scotland, it did not escape him, that she was attached to the Roman church. He did not doubt, as he declares, that she would embrace the same faith as he; but his ambassador to Scotland is enjoined to ascertain what queen Mary thought of the ecclesiastical changes that had taken place in Sweden, and ascertain what was the real state and position of the Scottish church. The ambassador replied, that the queen was a papist, and it was not likely she would abandon her creed. A counsellor, whose name is not known, dissuaded the king from proceeding further, because the French kinsmen of Mary would not give their consent, unless in the hope of thereby restoring Sweden to the "papal idolatry." That year, duke John married a Roman Catholic princess. He promised, on that occasion, that he would put no constraint on his wife with regard to her faith; but he also required, on his part, that he should not be obliged to partake of the eucharist according to the Roman usage, at the time of the marriage rite, but be allowed to continue its reception *according to the custom conformable with the Augsburg confession.*

After the breaking out of the civil war in 1568, king

Erik complained of his brother as one who desired to introduce the doctrine of the Calvinists, and was a contemner of the holy word and sacrament of God. But this accusation, which was designed to attract ill will to his adversary during the strifes which the Calvinistic controversy provoked, is deserving of little respect; and the same may be said of another charge, which the same Erik, at the same time, made against his brother, that he was a papist. This charge had then, as subsequently, little foundation.

The power which his father and brother exercised in the church, John had no mind to surrender. In respect to the property of the church, his acts were as arbitrary as those of king Gustavus. At the commencement of his reign, for example, he ordered his steward to transfer to the king's farm at Upsala, the cattle which were found with the priests of Upland. The glebe farms which the priests in the diocese of Skara cultivated were, in 1571, revoked to the crown. The steward of Helsingland was directed to take and register to the king's account the superfluons silver which remained in the churches of that district. In other respects, also, the king proceeded in the same arbitrary manner.

Outwardly, the church retained the same order and constitution in the beginning of king John III.'s reign, as previously, except that the division of dioceses made by king Gustavus ceased to operate, that the sees of Linkoping and Skara were filled by new men, the former by Martinus Olai from 1571, and the latter from 1570, by Jacobus Johannis, previously the ordinarius of Orebro; and that Gottland, Jemtland, and the Herjedalen, were severed from the Swedish church, in 1570, when, at the peace of Stettin, Sweden relinquished all spiritual jurisdiction over those provinces. The church of Gottland, which, from 1527, had been left almost without care, had, in 1572, a superintendent of its own placed there by the king of

Denmark. Jemtland and Herjedalen were attached, as we suppose, to the see of Trondhem.

King Erik had, in the beginning of his reign, proposed changes in the usages of the church, which seemed near enough to the papal. King John published, at his coronation in 1569, some articles, which manifested his determination to maintain discipline and good order among the clergy. The dress of priests ought to be grave and decent; the king would not tolerate in them levity or luxury, but their manners ought to correspond with their doctrine, and their apparel with their office and character. Drunkards, and the unchaste, they who were disobedient to their bishops, they who through dishonest means obtained preferment, they who inflicted too severely the censures of the church for temporal gain, were to be removed from office. Bishops ought not to ordain as priests any but such, as on strict inquiry, were found by their eloquence and intelligence adequate to the office. No priest was to obtain a king's benefice without the recommendation and testimony of his bishop. Other benefices the bishops were to fill. These were admonished not to neglect preaching in cathedrals, and visiting the congregations; and they were authorized to fix, probably out the church tithes, as large a sum for country churches, as was needed to build them and to purchase the communion wine. The widows of priests, were to inherit half the dwelling-house, and the taxes of priests were to be proportioned to their incomes.

The aged archbishop might hope, under this king, to issue the general church regulations by which he had long wished to settle the church's condition. Of the necessity of this measure, he had often reminded Gustavus I., and laid before him a project of the kind; but the matter had come to no result. At the council of Arboga, in 1561, king Erik reminded the clergy of the need of a revision of the chapter of church law; but the clergy, who acknowledged the need, at that time answered, fearing the too strong pressure of Calvinism on the church, that "the time and the hour" were not yet come. The archbishop informs us, that, in the beginning of the year 1563, he submitted to the king his project of church law. It is probable that the influence of Beurreus then prevented the royal acceptance, and the disorders of the following year did not permit the matter to be further considered. The bishops, each in his own diocese, set forth rules of conduct and order, agreeably to the authority committed to them. These rules were in their general features the same, partly because they were based on certain generally recognized principles and decrees, but still more, because of the growing influence of the archbishop with whom they originated, whose age and experience, learning and wisdom, gave additional weight to the official position he held as the foremost man of the church. The church was thus, at the close of king Gustavus's reign, to a great extent united in ecclesiastical customs, as she was harmonious in faith. Amid the confusions with which king Erik's reign began, amid the vociferous clamors for a change in doctrine and discipline which were now raised, and which it was feared would win the king's approbation, the church, beginning to feel herself the stronger after the first shock, drew more closely around Laurentius Petri. She did so with the more affection, in proportion as the need of purity in doctrine, unity in discipline, and agreement in the rights and privileges of the church, was felt.

The church rules and ordinances, composed by Laurentius Petri, were at once diffused by means of pamphlets, and were regarded as current law, until, as was expected, it should receive public confirmation from the authorities of church and state. But while they who deviated from this law were unfavorably regarded as opponents of pure faith, good order, and desirable unity, they had the valid excuse of its defective recognition as a law established; and, as laws should be easily accessible, king John commanded that after it had been sufficiently examined by the bishops and other ecclesiastics, it should be printed, and that afterward, all, under a due penalty, should conform themselves to its requirements in all matters that concerned the church.

The king's pleasure and command, is only known to us, through the archbishop's preface attached to this church code, which in 1571 was put to press. That it was inspected and examined by John III. himself is probable; more so, than what was pretended by its opponents, that he struck out some articles that displeased him, and that he persuaded the archbishop to introduce others which the prelate himself did not approve. Nothing is to be there found, that is not in entire harmony with Laurentius Petri's other writings and acts, and with his known principles and views.

His preface opens with a defence of what he previously advanced respecting the church's freedom and independence of the judgment of foreigners in regulating her own internal relations. That all would be satisfied was not to be hoped, "for where at any time will any man be found so happy as to give satisfaction to all?" He foresaw that the papists would find this church code not to be Catholic, and that the sacramentarians would regard it as popish; but he rejoiced in the conviction that it was conformable to "sound reason and the word of God."

That the holy word of God in the Old and New Testaments was the church's supreme law was pre-supposed, and the preaching of this word was declared to be the most important duty of the church.

Bishops were appointed, and enjoined to watch over the discipline of the church. Their office has not an immediate divine establishment, but was early introduced for the sake of order; and "as this discipline is very useful, and without doubt proceeded from the Holy Ghost, the giver of all good gifts, so was it generally current and received over the whole of Christendom, and thus it has been and must be as long as the world stands; but abuses nevertheless are to be removed. Bishops shall be elected by some of the clergy appointed for that purpose, and others experienced in the subject, who are to present the elect person to receive the confirmation of the prince. He is after that, clothed in a surplice and cope, to be consecrated by a bishop, but without the use of ointment.

Seven cathedrals of the kingdom were to be kept up, and in each of them to be settled, besides the bishop, six persons, the bishop's official or provost, the pastor of the church, a schoolmaster, a reader of theology, a penitentiary, and a proctor. That these, besides their own particular duties, should participate in the bishop's care of the diocese, was not mentioned. To the bishop it appertained, to watch over the doctrine and manners of the priests, over the education and morals of the people, over schools, hospitals, and wards of the sick. He was to visit his diocese yearly, with one or two of the clergy, and if he was himself prevented, to send his provost or official. He might call to his assistance, as was hitherto usual, the provosts of the district, whom he might select from among the most competent priests.

For the settlement of parish priests, the immediate call of the congregation was required; but if the congregation could not find any to take the office, or if he that was called should prove unfit, the bishop was to appoint another.

No one shall exercise the office of a preacher, before being openly, in the congregation, ordained thereto, by the laying on of hands and prayer, "for as the Holy Ghost, without whom this office can in no wise be exercised, is wont, by such means to be given, it would be great temerity in any one to despise those means, especially since it has been customary so to do from the Apostles' times."

The sentence of the church which it was declared should not extend to the life or goods of any man, but only to excommunication or spiritual concerns, might be pronounced and put in force by any pastor of a church. Country priests were to refer the more weighty cases to the bishop, if the case admitted of delay. As prayers, fasts, alms, might be imposed as church penance, it was merely said, that there should be no abuse connected with their imposition. Ignominious punishments, such as standing naked before the church door, or being manacled, should only be used in the case of atrocious criminals. He who audaciously refused to submit to his church penance, was to be punished severely by the temporal arm. He who remained longer than a year under the ban of the church, was to be dealt with according to the chapter of general ecclesiastical law.

This church discipline rested on the same principles with the whole Swedish ecclesiastical reformation, the desire in every possible way to avoid all novelty, and solely by the manifest word of God in holy Scripture to test the doctrine, institutions, and church usages previously existing, rejecting what was inconsistent with that word, but retaining what with a good conscience could be retained.

King John desired this church law to be acknowledged and recognized by the clergy in a church council. This must have been still more the wish of the archbishop; the rather, as according to a contemporaneous author, a report began to be circulated of a threatened alteration of the church customs and usages.

Another reason for this desire, was the controversy that again sprang up respecting the allowableness of the marriage of cousins-german. One of the first nobles of the kingdom, Erik Gustafsson Stenbock, as there was an obstacle in Sweden to his marriage with his cousin-german, had been married by a Danish clergyman within the limits of Halland. But in Sweden, where such a union was generally disapproved, as coming within the prohibited degrees of affinity, the case caused remark and scandal, and it was not to be supposed that archbishop Lars, who would not yield in a similar case which concerned his king, should more easily grant another the liberty which he considered as opposed to the word of God. To no purpose was an opinion procured from the theologians and jurists of Rostock, that such a union was allowable. Of the same opinion were one or more of the Swedish bishops. The commotions which hence arose, were urged as one of the strongest reasons for a council.

King John proclaimed the council, for the assembling of which many obstacles concurred. The first was, that it was to be opened at Upsala, on the 15th of June. But a fire on the 23d of April destroyed the cathedral of that city and part of the city itself, so that Stockholm was then appointed as the place of meeting. But, as there again a plague was prevailing, the king left it to the archbishop, bishops, and heads of the clergy, to call together the council at Upsala, Westeras, or where they would. The 17th of August was named as the day, and the deliberations commenced on the 18th of that month, in Upsala. The king was not present. The assembly was not numerous. Of the bishops, those of Wexio and Abo were absent, though the former was represented. Of provosts, pastors of churches, and administrators of schools, there were thirty in number, as recorded, but many other clergyman made their appearance. For the first time the academy of Upsala is here seen to take part in the public affairs of the church and fatherland, being represented by its rector and two professors, who participated in this council.

After the usual opening with prayer, and an address from the archbishop, who explained the nature of church councils, their various objects, and causes of being assembled, the question of marriage within the degrees of affinity was first discussed. The stricter interpretation of the divine law triumphed, and bishop Marten of Linkoping recanted, and deprecated his inconsiderateness in the case. Ceremonies, church punishments, and the like topics, were then discussed. The need of a fixed and precise confession of faith was acknowledged, but no question appears to have been brought before the meeting, as to the receiving and adopting that of Augsburg, "*although the archbishop promised to give one according to that pattern.*"

The decree of the council was drawn up by bishop Marten, and on the 22d of August was subscribed. It was desired, so runs the document, to abide henceforth, as hitherto, by the pure Christian doctrine contained in the writings of the prophets and apostles, and which has been preached "here in this kingdom for some time." It was desired that what belongs to probity, discipline, and good customs, should be promoted, and what is contrary to them taken away. It was desired that the sanctity of the ties of blood should not be rent in marriage. The union therefore between cousins-german, as contrary to the law of nature and of God, was not to be allowed, notwithstanding that somewhere in foreign lands there was another teaching and practice. It was also decided to abide by the ceremonies and church usages hitherto customary in Swedish congregations, and now settled by the church ordinances set forth in print.

The doctrine and discipline which had been current at the close of king Gustavus's reign, and had continued amid the conflicts of king Erik XIV.'s administration, were now confirmed, and, as was believed, the church was unanimous in her purpose henceforth to guard them. This council was the crowning glory, the lustrous star, in the life of Laurentius Petri, the seal of his labor of forty years. Their father in doctrine, now seventy years old, stood here among his young family,* who, with reverence and confidence, looked up to him, and listened to his words. It was in the hope that the work was now completed, that he cried out: "Lord, now lettest thou thy servant depart in peace." In this hope he received the reward of grace, which God sometimes gives the faithful laborer, to see the glory of the victory, but not the bitterness of strife whereby it shall be won. Or, did he foresee, that within a few years, his work should be again menaced with ruin, and that the very men who now in concord were assembled around him, would be sundered from each other in the hot conflict of human passions, and in doubt of the truth itself; some of them to be displaced from office, imprisoned and exiled, though they now believed that with united hand they had perfected the temple of peace?

There were not wanting prognostics of the coming storm, and anxious forebodings that with the death of the venerated father of the church, troublous times would come. These forebodings were expressed by those present on the touching occasion, when the archbishop, in his sickness, at the close of the council, assembled the clergy at his house, to bid them farewell, and exhort them to steadfastness, for the last time before he was removed from among them. Prognostics in part were connected with the attempts at changes which claimed an antiquity to which they had no title, in part with the audacity whereby the Roman church, which filled the minds of men with awe, on account of its mighty patronage, began to lift its voice, though not by the tongue of Swedish men. Queen Catharine's chaplain, Johan Herbst, from Poland, in defence of the Roman

* It might be literally so spoken of some in this assembly. Laurentius Petri, *Gothus* so called, to distinguish him from the archbishop, Olof Luth, and Andreæ Angerman, famous in the contests of after-times, were at this time, or were afterward, married to the daughters of the aged Laurentius Petri.

church, and in opposition to archbishop Lars, perhaps also to master Erasmus Nicholai, the king's chaplain, composed works, whose object was to show that in that church only were to be found a valid clergy and sanctifying means of grace; that the Lord's supper ought not to be administered under both kinds, and that the invocation of saints was allowable. These writings, which were circulated over the land, and of which some were said to have been submitted to Erasmus Nicholai, were known previous to the council of Upsala, in 1572, when the archbishop promised to answer and confute them. This was done in one or more works written against Herbst.

At the diet of Stockholm, in 1573, the clergy were again assembled, but the archbishop was absent, prevented by the sickness, which in a few months terminated in death. The archbishop's refutation of the writings of Herbst on the Lord's supper, sacrifice of the mass, and power of the priesthood, were on this occasion, adduced by Erasmus Nicholai. The king himself took an interested and observant part in the examination of the doctrinal questions at this council; enjoined it upon Marten, of Linkoping, to dispute with Herbst on the primacy of the pope, the holy Scriptures, and other points; and entered with much zeal into the controversy against the papists opposed to the bishop.

The epoch when these transactions occurred, and their character, must be made to coincide with that period in the life of the Swedish church, when the life also of Laurentius Petri *Nericius* closed. He was taken hence without being a witness of the strife. "Lord, give peace in our days," were his last words, in his last pastoral letter to his diocese, dated April 24, 1573, appointing a day of thanksgiving for the victory won at Liffland. His prayer was heard in another sense than was intended in those words. When he knew that his end drew nigh, he sent, by Erasmus Nicholai, the expression of his gratitude to king John, for that monarch's care of the church, and implored him by that imperishable crown, so much more glorious than his earthly, which he might hope to win, to protect the Swedish church in the purity and stability it now had gained. The good prelate fell asleep in the Lord, on October 25th, 1573, after a life of seventy years, forty of which he had spent in the exercise of his office as archbishop. He was buried by the clergy of his diocese, who mourned him as their father, in the choir of the cathedral of Upsala, where his sepulchre still remains.

His long life had been rich in fruits, but not exempt from trials. Not a few of his troubles resulted from the relations he held towards the royal house, with which, by marriage, he was distantly connected. In addition to the stern and often specious domination of Gustavus, the fraternal hate, and soon fraternal war, between that king's sons, caused the archbishop much disquiet. In 1563, he had probably united with the estates of the kingdom in their sentence pronounced against king John. He was present in Stockholm, when, in 1568, that city was beleaguered by the dukes John and Charles. On that occasion, some of king Erik's officers requested his advice as to what it was best for them to do, so as to answer for it before God. His reply was such as to make a distinction between a defection from the king and a breach of their oath of fidelity. Afterwards he took part in the doom of deposition pronounced on king Erik, and subscribed the sentence which resulted, as the means of obviating revolts and the ruin of the kingdom, in that monarch's death.

At the death of Laurentius Petri, more than half a century had passed away, since the diet of Strängness, which elevated Gustavus Wasa to the Swedish throne, was the occasion of Laurentius Andreæ's influence in the public affairs of church and state, and awakened attention to Olaus

Petri and the preaching of his disciples. The third part of a century had now passed away since the new order of things had become more generally and more firmly established. A new generation had sprung up, and become established under new auspices and relations. In contemplating these new and extraordinary events, we might seek a justification of the changes effected, in the improvement then wrought in the people's manners and intelligence; although the truth and strength of God's word depend not on human wisdom or human agency.

To a perfect picture of the character of the Swedish church, during the last twenty years of king Gustavus's times, and during the year 1573, there is still required the delineation, however rapid, of its constitutional, scientific, and moral position. Such a delineation will constitute a fit introduction to the history of that period, which, with the strength and weapons furnished by the preceding period, witnessed the war of the church for truth, and her gain of a final victory.

BOOK III.

CHAPTER I.

WEDISH CHURCH TO THE YEAR 1573.

THE storms of half a century had shaken the church within our fatherland, when archbishop Laurentius Petri, the man who had deeply impressed on that church the stamp of his own spirit, passed from time into eternity. We wish to collect together, or to present more fully the outlines which seem to us to afford an idea of what it was, when in succeeding years new trials were encountered, when this Protestant church was tried by the attempt to reclaim it again to Rome, or at least reform it to a nearer resemblance to the Roman church.

1.—ADMINISTRATION OF THE CHURCH; BISHOPS AND PRIESTS.

The change introduced by king Gustavus in the church's condition, by the division of dioceses, and the substitution of the name ordinary for bishop, had, as we have already remarked, ceased before the year 1573 to go into operation: so that the old sees, with the exception of Abo, remained the same in compass as at the beginning of the Reformation. The men who filled the new sees were removed by king John, either to some episcopal chair, or to provostships, with the exception of Petrus Caroli of Kalmar, who for a time fell into disgrace, and Andreas Torchilli, who was continued as pastor of Jonkoping.

The bishops possessed an almost unlimited jurisdiction over their sees, subject however to the oversight which the ordinantia of Westeras conferred on the king, and which king Gustavus in 1539 claimed as belonging to his royalty. The limitations of the king's supremacy were not defined, and the rights of the archbishop as primate of the church remained vacillating and uncertain; preserved indeed through the personal qualities of Laurentius Petri, and the respect felt for him, but watched with suspicion by the king. Respecting the mode of managing the common affairs of the church, nothing was yet settled. The church ordinance of 1571, prescribes yearly meetings of the clergy in council within each diocese, and the mode in which those meetings are to be conducted, but makes no mention of a general council for the Swedish church, although such, during the reigns of Gustavus, Erik, and John, were held under the presidency of the archbishop. This church ordinance was itself adopted by the clergy at such a council. The old Laurentius Petri had perhaps intentionally passed over a case which he could not arrange to his satisfaction.

The deliberations and decrees concerning the church, were conducted and passed, sometimes at the diets with all the estates participating in them, as at Westeras in 1527 and 1544, in which case the estate of the clergy was represented by the bishops and other prelates. Sometimes church councils proper were held, as at Orebro in 1529, and at Upsala in 1572, at which only the clergy were present and took part in matters regarding doctrine, discipline and public worship, although the king had there a representative; or as at Stockholm in 1573, where he personally participated in the council. Sometimes the clergy assembled at the diet formed themselves into an ecclesiastical council to deliberate on church affairs, which were sometimes proposed and brought forward by the king himself, or else by one of his secretaries. Sometimes a number of the bishops and clergy were called together by the king, to give their opinions on certain questions laid before them, as in 1549 respecting the Interim, and in 1552 on the subject of Gustavus' third marriage. The form was still indefinite and unsettled, chiefly because of the conflict of principles relating to the church's privileges and independence of the royal power.

King Gustavus's ordinances of 1539 and 1540 were the first attempt to raise for the church a firm government, but as an instrument of the royal power within the church. They were immediately carried into execution, and this king and his two eldest sons exercised this power without law and without legal pretension, though seldom without using the agency of bishops and ordinaries. That there was need of a settled ecclesiastical regimen, appeared in the attempt in the ordinantia of 1575 to create an ecclesiastical consistory. This, however, was never perfected. The third attempt, in the following century, resulted in the well-known project of a consistorium generale.

After those laws lost their force, which, during the papal period, protected the persons and property of the church in privileges which were not always consistent with the weal of the commonwealth and the vigor of its government, the outward discipline of the church lay open to the grasp of every power which gained importance in the state, and could establish its own will, or its peculiar aims, in the place of that fallen order and discipline. The Swedish people had readily and even approvingly, with the consent of a large number of ecclesiastics, transferred to the king the regulation of the church's relations to the state. The limits of his power were, in this respect, as in others, marked out with little accuracy, and were still less defined, inasmuch as neither the regulations nor laws of those who were reforming the church, could claim any validity. The people's content or discontent was the only guide, and king Gustavus had an ample measure of both. He and his sons, however, had a regard for the church, and used their power to uphold ecclesiastical and moral order, and even to protect the persons and property of the church as far as the new state of things allowed.

But the temporal aristocracy, against which the ecclesiastical had in foregone time with difficulty protected itself, desired to enlarge its power at the expense of the now defenceless church. Instead of citing particular cases, we will cite the points with regard to which, in 1575, the clergy prayed the protection of king John against the injuries of the nobles, as they dreaded them, or what is more correct, as current in the times we are describing. In the ordinantia of that year, which was submitted to the king, the clergy petition that the right of patronage should be restrained; that the king would not suffer the nobles to place and displace priests, even if they or their forefathers had paid the costs of the church or glebe; that churches might not "be subjected to their outrages, so as to put their chaplains in them, and seize the rents, for this was to intrude into another man's office," and that no privileges should exempt the nobles from paying tithes to the church and priests. In the same document they petitioned that the clergy should be protected from the demands upon them for entertainment, which, in addition to that given bishops and stewards, whose claims were admitted, was unreasonably exacted from priests by the nobles, who quoted St. Paul's injunction, "that ought to be interpreted only of the poor and needy." They petitioned, moreover, that the nobles' and king's officers should not be allowed forcibly to withdraw scholars from the schools to their own service, a case that often occurred, although the church ordinance of 1571 forbids scholars to be taken from school without the consent of parents. With these demands for redress of grievances, the Swedish church began the contest for its freedom and privileges, which was still more rigorously carried on in the following century.

The edict for reconstructing the chapter, which appeared in the church ordinance of 1571, was not a confirmation of the old relations of that body, but a project for a new arrangement, to take the place of the previous chapter, now wholly dissolved. We do not find the project perfected in any diocese. In 1573, Westeras was the only see which had a reader of theology. In most places a penitentiary, and in Upsala and Viborg a provost, was not to be found, while, in Wexio, the office of provost was connected with that of the pastor of the church in the town where the bishop resided. In 1575, there was proposed a new arrangement, or at least a renewal, with some variations, of many of the old prelatical titles.

The choir priests, who in popish times were placed in cathedrals, and a number of whom were still retained, after 1527, in each cathedral, were now wholly discontinued. The church ordinance, however, regards it as probable that they might again be found useful.

The church ordinance of 1571 speaks of bishops, provosts of a district, and pastors of churches, as members of the clergy. It supposes the existence, though not universally, of chaplains in large congregations, or in benefices which had several churches. These chaplains were known of old in Stockholm, and were supported by the rectors or pastors of churches. In 1561, there were three in the pay of the state. For the most part, except perhaps in large cities, these chaplains were what are now commonly called assistants, and were attached to such rectors as had large benefices or many churches under their care. This was the only reason, according to the church ordinance, which could justify, or oblige the rector to have a chaplain. In case of sickness, by which was meant long-continued, or incurable sickness, or for old age, an assistant was not allowed, but the parish priest was to give up his benefice. He who regularly resigned his benefice, still retained the priestly character, and might, at the request of another parish priest, assist him in his duties.

The chaplains had their domicile and support in the house of the rector of the church, and, by the regulations which the bishops issued for their sees, appear to have been placed under the control and strict inspection of the rector. For the first time, in 1575, is mention made of a settled salary. They who did duty for priests, were to have, at least, four dollars a year, and "any advantages they could get from the parishioners," without violating the rights of the rector.

The bishops are admonished not to ordain more priests than were necessary for their respective dioceses, and there is no mention of the regret felt for the want of young priests, in case of unexpected vacancies, to officiate in public worship, and assume the care of souls. It seems, however, that, according to ancient custom, some such were maintained by the cathedrals. In 1572, king John assured the bishops of the continuance of the prebends and other sources of income, on condition of their supporting "the young persons newly ordained to the priestly office in Skara, until, by benefices, or otherwise, provision could be made for them." In the ordinantia of 1575, which refers to them as previously existing, mention is made, beside the clergy attached to the king's palace, and the parish priests, of another sort of chaplains residing in the houses of the nobility. We know not whether the number of such was large, but of "these chaplains of the nobility," it is ordained, that they should, like other priests, be subject to the bishop, and be obliged to appear at the convocations of the priests, where inquisition was to be had of the learning and lives of the sacerdotal order.

They who wished to enter the priesthood, were to be examined, and afterward ordained. This examination was incumbent for the most part on the bishop; but with whom he might divide the duty, or to whom transfer it, was not determined. In 1575, this duty of examination is assigned to the dean; but in the church ordinance of 1571, it is merely said, that they shall perform the duty to whom it belonged.

The first protestant church ordinance found it necessary, to remedy a bad custom, the obviating of which still appertained to the bishops. This was the removal or translation of priests from one benefice to another. The bishops are admonished not to be precipitate in sending any clerk from one to another, third, or fourth benefice, as has been the injudicious custom; for such a custom gives room to suppose that he who is so ready to change his benefice, seeks not what Christ approves, the care and welfare of the people, but the advancement of his own temporal interests.

The incomes of rectors remained much the same as in former times, except the glebe farms, which, from 1545, were absorbed by the crown, and for which a compensation was not always given. The progress of agriculture made this compensation anything but an equivalent. The appropriations too, which, from this time, were made to the bishops and chapters, after the crown became possessed, not only of their tithes, but their tenants, depended on the good pleasure of the king. The salary was in the nature of an investiture of the crown, and was fixed every year on the register books of investitures. It was not so parsimoniously dealt out by king Gustavus, as one might be led to suppose. In 1556, the archbishop had 625 barrels of corn, besides his palace at Upsala, and a manor near the city. Bishop Bothvid of Strängness, had only 365, but the ordinary of Skara, Erik Falk, had 576 barrels of corn. In 1561, or the year after king Gustavus's death, the bishops and ordinaries had appropriated to them 124 tons, or 5,952 barrels of corn, of which the archbishop had 16 tons, or 768 barrels. The rectors in nineteen towns, besides three chaplains and the preacher of the grey monks' cloister, at Stockholm, had 71 tons, or 3,408 barrels, from 48 to 288 barrels for each. In king John's time, these investitures were augmented, notwithstanding that more ecclesiastical offices were set on foot. At the close of the reign of Gustavus, no other appropriations were made than for bishops and ordinaries, rectors in cities and schoolmasters.

The regulation contained in the above-named ordinance of 1571, that the priest incapacitated from managing his benefice should give it up, was a relict of former times. But the permission to priests to enter into the marriage state, which followed on the reformation of the church, lessened the facility of making any change in their circumstances, and the pity felt for their widows and children occasioned a new legislation. It was a recognized principle, that the vacant benefice should be immediately taken by a new legal occupant, although, as before the Reformation, a portion of the current year's income was to belong to him who resigned the benefice, or to his heirs after death. In 1559, it was ruled that the resigner, or his heirs, should have that portion of the year's income which corresponded with the time of his management of the benefice. The year was divided into quarters, the heirs being entitled to the income of the last quarter, provided they kept up divine service to the close of the year. The widow and children of the deceased had a right to the stock and house-room in the parsonage, for at least the first half year. The same rule is observed in the church ordinance of the year 1571, except that the year is divided into two parts, and that nothing is said of providing for divine service. The afterward often-abused custom, of what was called a whole year of grace, is not mentioned. But both the law and church ordinance of

1559, express, in the same terms, the hope, that the widow will not be removed from the parsonage till otherwise provided for; and the ordinance appeals to the heart of the successor in the Scriptural admonition, not to afflict the widow and fatherless. The hope expressed, that the widow, before being removed from the parsonage, should be provided for by marrying again, or otherwise, became the occasion of the bad practice of patrons inducing unprovided priests to marry the widows and daughters of priests, as the condition of being promoted to benefices. The right to half the house, granted to the widows by king John, in 1569, they were justified in claiming, as is allowed in the ordinantia of 1575, when the clergy begged of the king that after the death of the husband they might be released from this incumbrance.

2.—SCHOOLS AND LITERATURE.

The Reformation which distinguished the fifteenth century, stirred the spirit of inquiry. But when we wish to contemplate its influence on the cultivation of science in Sweden, two distinct questions present themselves; what was done in conformity with the impulse given to literary cultivation at a time when every man was demanded a reason for his faith, and the clergy, in general, were required to possess ability to preach God's word; and, did the absorption and diminution of the church's establishments and property, in any degree, check or lessen the means and opportunities for training up the élèves and scholars of the church?

It has already been remarked, that king Gustavus I., his chief counsellor Laurentius Petri, and the bishops, as soon as they could pay attention to the altered relations that had arisen from the first breach in the church's life and discipline, showed their anxiety respecting the cause of education, for which the new order of things had occasioned a demand. In order to complete the picture we design to draw of the condition of things during and before the year 1573, we must go back to the year 1539, or that period when the more thorough change began to take effect.

The preparative means of education, which the old era left as an inheritance to the new, were the diocesan and state schools, and the cloisters. The former, as far as they were connected with the church, did not suffer by the reduction of the incomes of cathedrals and chapters, because the necessity of maintaining schoolmasters was keenly felt, and the old idea that on cathedrals was imposed the duty of building up diocesan schools, was still dominant. The most important change in the means of instruction, arose out of the dissolution of the monasteries. But in considering the cloisters as a provision for educational purposes, we allude only, or chiefly at the time of the Reformation, to those of the Dominicans and Franciscans. If we inquire where, after these except in Finland were generally dissolved, schools were to be found established, we shall discover, according to the registry of 1561, soon after Gustavus's death, that, in almost all places where these orders existed, there were schools. There were, besides, schools in the diocese of Upsala, at Gefle; in that of Linkoping, at Wadsten; in that of Skara, at Elfsborg and Linkoping; in that of Strängness, at Nykoping and Orebro; in that of Westeras, at Stora Tuna. The Franciscan cloisters of Finland, at Tlokarna and Raumo, had a school at Helsingfors; but, in 1573, Raumo had one of its own. That at St. Tuna was dissolved at the same time with the office of ordinary. The support which was given to students out of the prebends of cathedrals and other considerable incomes of prelates, was withdrawn or diminished, especially after the tithes and other church property, except the thirds of the rectors, were suppressed to the crown.

Out of these, on the other hand, a certain amount was

applied to the support of students in every cathedral. This amount was not parsimonious, and certainly not less than was before given to the same object. In 1561, the whole allotment for the support of students in all the cathedrals amounted to 66 tons, or 3,168 barrels of corn This appropriation might not have been the same every year, but in the later years of king Gustavns, that amount was common. The students of the diocese of Upsala, were rated, in 1561, at 480, and five years before at 470 barrels of corn. Scholars were, besides, supported by alms-begging in parishes, and this method was, in 1571, allowed for the future, by a church ordinance. King Gustavus, thought no scorn to leave in his will a sum of money to schools. It was divided among them the year after his death, and invested for their benefit.

The church ordinance, and the salary project, show that in each school there was but one teacher appointed. The pay of these teachers for twenty-two scholars, was 2,664 barrels of corn; on an average, 121 for each scholar, 144 for the highest, 96 for the lowest. The church ordinance allows them exemption from taxes, and a domicil. In king John's time there began to be appointed, here and there, an additional teacher, or corrector of the school. According to the first school law, occurring in the church ordinance of 1571, it was usual for the pupils of the four lower divisions of schools, to be termed "hearers." It was the practice of old time. This school law limits the instruction in languages, in the four classes, to Latin and Swedish; the latter tongue, "so much as is required for the seasons of the church."

The Latin was the only proper speech of the schools. Not only, as was the case long after this time, were the teachers forbidden to speak to the pupils in any other language, but they who wished to learn Greek or Hebrew, were to question no one in any tongue but Latin; otherwise, preceptors were to look to themselves as liable to be called to account; the reason assigned being, the uselessness of burdening children with a multiplicity of reading. Hence the school was called a Latin school, but its object was to provide fit materials, not only for the priestly office, but for the business of the state, which required a superior literary culture. Within the compass of the Latin, was included what might be termed the humanities. To the reading of the authors of old Rome, were added, in their tongue, the study of grammar, rhetoric, dialectics, and the exercise of the pen in large and small hand, and the strengthening of the memory by repeating certain passages from classic authors and the poets. A deeper wisdom, a training for the wisdom which lies in the life and conduct, was inculcated and effected by the precepts of Christianity; and these were taught out of the Holy Scriptures as the fountain of truth. Singing was a part of the daily exercises of the school. The youth were practised both in choral singing and in what was termed "figurative music," and they were well grounded in the principles of this pleasing science. In the ordinantia of 1575, we find that the acting of plays in Latin and Swedish, both "comedies and tragedies," was customary in schools, and it is spoken of as beneficial to the actors and spectators. That these plays, under the title of "miracles" and "morals," were similar to those performed in other countries, appears from the rule prescribed in the above-named ordinantia, that *after this time* it should not be permissible to introduce in these dramatic performances the persons of the Holy Trinity.

The number of pupils in a school depended on particular circumstances, such as the size of the diocese, and the skill of the teacher, and cannot be given. From a report, that the school at Wadsten had, some years later, or in 1580, one hundred pupils, we may presume that the rest were numerously attended. The age at which lads entered the public schools varied, but it seems that ten was the usual period of life. The time of their remaining at school also varied; depending upon the disposition of the youth, or upon the character of the school, as imparting a complete scientific education, or as merely preparative to a higher course of instruction. They who preferred it, had private tutors for their children.

Among the schools which flourished in the middle of this century and afterward, the most eminent perhaps was that at Gefle, *founded by king Gustavus I.*, in connection, it may be presumed, with the nomination of an ordinary for that town. It is highly prized by its grateful pupils; and these pupils, for the latter half of the sixteenth century, were men eminent in the church and the sciences. The excellent condition and management of this scholastic institution, the only one for all Norrland, but frequented by students from other places, will account for the well-known fact, that most of the men who were foremost in the controversies which arose during the times of Erik and John, were from Gestrikland, Helsingland, and the northern districts. They were zealously attached to the Lutheran reformation, and opposers of Calvinism, popery, and the liturgies of John III.

These schools did not pretend to furnish an education to its full extent. The school ordinance of the year 1571, does not refer to academical studies as a continuance of their labors, but in expressly requiring that the youth of every diocese should be kept to their studies both at home and in *foreign lands*, acknowledges the need of a literary finish, not to be obtained through the ordinary resources of Sweden.

From the diocesan schools the young men were either immediately transferred to the service of the church or State; or, deriving a support from the prebends assigned for that purpose, sometimes from the donations made to students, sometimes from the invested tithes distributed by the bishops, they hastened to foreign academies. A large number of the scholars passed immediately from the schools to the fulfilment of the duties of parish priests. From time to time, king Gustavus demanded that suitable men should be sent him from the schools, to serve in the royal chancery and chamber of accounts. With the schools, however, he was not always satisfied. Thus, in 1559, he complains that the bishops and schoolmasters chose out and sent for the service of king and kingdom unpolished and ignorant pupils, "the vilest trash that one could expect to find."

Schools for special purposes began now to be established. For the advancement of arithmetical knowledge, king Gustavus, in 1538, gave one of the prebends of Strängness to the organist Lars of Stockholm, on condition that he should instruct pupils in keeping accounts. It appears from the ordinantia of 1578, that "writing schools" were established at Stockholm, probably corresponding to what are now called arithmetical schools; and mention is made of schools for teaching to sew, in the place of the nunneries gone to decay.

The extent to which education could be carried in our fatherland, depended, in a great degree, upon the care of the bishops to provide fit teachers for the schools of their dioceses. Such were sought out, and from this time, the men most eminent for learning, were those who had labored in the work of education. It was generally expected that they who had pursued their studies abroad, should, on coming home, offer their services in institutions of learning. This course operated for the present to the less advantage, as almost all the vigor which would have been applied to the church was absorbed in the calling of the schoolmaster; and as the aid of foreigners must be employed in education of a more finished kind, Germany especially was the resource for scientific scholarship. But it was a sacrifice made by a family rich in hope and love, which exposed its deficiencies, in preparation for the spiritual riches which were to follow.

The number of Swedes who sought out foreign universities was not inconsiderable. They received prebends or other means of support, either to pursue their studies in foreign lands, or to perfect themselves in some special walk of science, as theology, jurisprudence, medicine, or to prepare themselves for the higher posts of the government; and they retained these means of support for a definite or indefinite time. Some maintained themselves at their own expense. Schism within the church, was the reason why the protestant universities of Germany were almost exclusively frequented. Among these, Wittenberg and Rostock were the most prominent marks for the travels of science-seeking Swedes. Wittenberg was made illustrious by Luther and Melancthon; and Rostock, in the latter half of the century, by D. Chytræus, who stood in close connection with the learned men and statesmen of Sweden, esteemed and consulted in its ecclesiastical affairs, and the man around whom gathered strangers, especially from the north. On the matriculation register of the academy of Wittenberg are inscribed, from the year 1540 to 1573, the names of more than seventy Swedes and Finns. On the register of Rostock, which might at this time be called with justice the university of Sweden, there are more than a hundred Swedish names; although certainly the names of the same persons are to be found in both places. It is to be considered, that very many went immediately from the schools of our own land into the service of the church and state. If we except archbishop Laurentius Petri, there was scarcely a man of science in Sweden who had not studied abroad. All, however, had the means of support till they reached the higher branches of science; but many after a short stay were obliged to return home. Others remained several years in foreign lands, even after they acquired the master's degree.

This degree was sometimes received by Swedes in one or two years after coming to the university; a circumstance which proves that the schools of our own land were not so low in the higher walks of literature as has been pretended, and as otherwise one might be tempted to suppose. The number of those who, in foreign academies, won the higher titles of learning, has not been clearly ascertained. A catalogue furnishes the names of twenty-five Swedes and Finns, who, from the year 1529 to 1561, were promoted at Wittenberg to the degree of master. But, besides that we have no reports from other universities, even this witness does not fully testify; because it is demonstrable that men who are not there named received these titles of honor at Wittenberg itself during that period, and because the higher attainments in literature were then particularly coveted.

The times of king Gustavus I., however, appear not to have been in general favorable to a learned education. To test the justice of this opinion, as far as regards the blame to be attached to the memory of this great king, those circumstances must be taken into consideration, which did not depend on him, and those for which he is to be censured. Till the first suppression of the monasteries, these institutions, where the love of carnal enjoyment did not interfere, might work beneficially in the cause of education. But the Reformation denied that the influence of the cloisters was beneficial, and in preserving them must have denied its principles. The monks of the sixteenth century were not distinguished for scientific cultivation. The same was the case with the suppression of the chapters, whereby it seemed, because in every diocese they were to a great extent the sponsors of learning, that the influence and regard for learning itself were lessened. But the men of the Reformation and their contemporaries had in general little respect for what did not immediately promote the life of the church and state, and although the chapters were instituted for that purpose, their efficiency had for the most part ceased. To restore them in conformity to the condition of the old church, could not be done by the reformers, who protested against that church and its condition. To build them up in conformity with the new order of things was not the work of a moment, at least not of the Reformation, which had to make provision for its own theories. In Sweden, therefore, the suppression of the chapters was demanded, or they were allowed to expire. But it cannot be proved that the commencement made, in 1571 and 1575, for their reconstruction according to the spirit of the Reformation, was in contrariety to king Gustavus's views and purposes.

The means employed by this king for the promotion of learning, and his defence for the failure of those means, we have, under the year 1539, already made the subject of consideration. Immediately after that period, began the insurrection which more endangered the stability of his throne than any that had preceded, while the increasing breach in the church relations, and the alarms felt for the revenues and dignity of the clergy, militated against the interests of literature. If, after quiet once more returned, there was not immediately a richer bloom, the disregard exhibited for science and the arts was not the fault of the king. Such a disregard cannot be imputed to the man who gave his sons the careful training and educational discipline received by the sons of king Gustavus. For their instruction, the learned foreigners, G. Norman, D. Beurreus, H. Mollerus, the Latin poet, J. Berndes, Tycho Gyllencreutz, were invited into the kingdom, and such men were recalled home as Marten Teit, and Erik Petri, afterward the teacher of the school of Tuna.

It was more perhaps his fault, that with a sparing hand he dealt out the riches of the church that were recovered to the crown, and to which schools might be regarded as the legitimate heir, the claimant by hereditary right. The experience of a great necessity, and want of means to carry out his plans, often tempted him to use parsimoniously the resources painfully acquired; and this temptation continued to operate on the rescuer of his impoverished country, after quiet and plenty had taken the place of disorder and penury. Justice, too, demands that there be taken into consideration the circumstances which pleaded his apology, or in a great measure must soften the censure which might be passed upon him. Among these circumstances, may be enumerated that the king stood in need of ampler means for carrying on the business of the state than were always at hand; that he notwithstanding appropriated no small part of his revenues to the support of schools and students; that the incomes of the chapters were considerably diminished at their suppression; that the prebendal churches, created at the time, acquired pastors for themselves, to whom allotments were made; that the eminent want of men who could manage the dioceses, churches, and schools, in the spirit of the new times, did not always admit the development of his generosity, because he could not always determine how far that want extended. His gifts must be proportioned to the numbers to whom he was to give. At the time when the amount of this want was ascertained, at the end of king Gustavus's reign, there commences the dawn of a brighter day.

That king Gustavus allowed the university of Upsala to decay, we have already shown to be an unfounded accusation. That he pulled down the old cathedral school-house in Upsala, in order to convert its materials to the building of a castle there, is a charge that comes homes to him, only so far as it can be shown that this house was in good condition, and either needed no repairs, or was fit for the purpose to which it was originally destined. Income he could not take away from the academy of Upsala, for it had none. Was it his fault that he did not erect a university out of the temporal and ecclesiastical resources at his command? The former, perhaps, in the later years of his reign, were found sufficient. Of the latter, we have already remarked that they were taken on the pressure of an inevitable and urgent necessity. A university could not be established, except by calling in foreigners to keep it up, and there would thus have existed a foreign university on a Swedish bottom and territory. Gustavus I. preferred the expedient of allowing invited foreigners to instruct the successors to the throne and the princes of the land, while others were sent abroad to receive a liberal education, until his people acquired sufficient science to enable them, from their own bosom, to derive the means of that more liberal education. Different judgments may be formed of the correctness of his course of action; but when viewed in its true light, it must win the approbation of many.

The first traces of the reëstablishment of the academy of Upsala are veiled in darkness. In 1538, there are none found. But within two years after, king Gustavus excused himself for having neglected this important matter; and not long after Peutinger and Norman acquired their influence, the signs of a care for higher literary attainments began, in 1540, to be manifest. An author of the following century reports that king Gustavus, in that year, established the university of Upsala. It is also reported that a Hollander, Jacob Stieger, and one Olaus Magni, were professors at Upsala, the latter in mathematics. But of any statute for the erecting of the academy, or for the pay of these men or their successors, there is no mention. Without positive evidence with regard to persons and particulars, we may presume that the king placed these men in Upsala, and that their being placed in that position, as well as some hints on the subject, were intended as an intimation that the regeneration of the academy was designed. In a subsequent year, the king invited from abroad foreign teachers for special branches of science. Thus, in a letter written in 1547 to some professors at Rostock, he requests them to send him a man skilled in law, to instruct the youth of Sweden.

The need of a university at home was the more perceived and felt, in consequence of the increasing improvement in the manners and habits of the people, and the connection with Germany arising out of the Danish war; king Erik, therefore, on June 8, 1566, made known his determination to found a college or university to be opened in the old chapter house. The king promised "to grant sustenance, privileges, and more than what their necessities required," to its teachers, and he took both teachers and pupils under his royal care and protection. As a beginning, only one teacher was appointed, Laurentius Petri *Gothus*, who was to give instruction in the Greek language, and in what else might be serviceable to youth.

This was a small beginning, but from that time the establishment was without interruption for some years, and was even enlarged. In 1573, the institution had but four teachers, sometimes called professors, sometimes readers, and the high school itself was interchangeably termed a university, academy, and college. There was yet wanting the apparatus and appointments which are regarded as belonging to a university. King John was minded to issue orders for this purpose. The university was to be put upon a more complete foundation, and directions were given for the arrangement of the faculty, or as it is expressed in the edict, for the "four colleges" of which the university was to consist. These were to be directed by a dean, and the whole university to be under the control of a rector. This construction was perhaps the form it took a century after the first institution of the academy. But just at this period, the breaking out of disturbances within the church was the cause of its remaining incomplete, and occasioned for some years an interruption of the progress of the academy, instead of its being amplified as was intended.

The men of the half century between 1523 and 1573, were the last whom the Roman church brought up, and were the first fruits of the Reformation. The latter need not fear comparison with the former. On either side we find authors of the first magnitude, the lights of learning. Improvement in education and manners proceeded slowly; but it cannot be shown that the Reformation was a hinderance, although it counteracted the tendency to pure heathenism to which that improvement at first gave rise. Highest among the learned men of Sweden stand the reformers, at first educated under the discipline of the old times, but by the Reformation made what they were. Among these, archbishop Laurentius Petri is the most illustrious for talents cultivated by extensive reading, but more in the school of life; a bright example of that unassuming conduct which brings to light by their application to the benefit of the commonwealth the results of learned investigation, rather than the labors by which those results are won. He belonged to both the old times and the new. The former expired during his life, but not without shedding some beams of light. From the latter there grew up around him a body of princes, senators, and men of the church, who exhibited in the vigorous measures they pursued no mean degree of culture and science. The men of the times of John III., Sigismund, and Charles IX., were the youths of the days of Gustavus I. and Laurentius Petri.

A probable estimate of the measure of learning required from priests who were not sent to the foreign high schools, may be formed by a reference to the Latin schools, on the supposition that these were a fair exemplification of all the rest. A knowledge of the Holy Scriptures, in the original tongues, was not required; nor was theology taught as a special branch of learning, except as a trial exercise in the church's divine service; an hour every day being also devoted to the reading and explanation of certain portions of the Bible and catechism. The education of priests appertained to the bishops and those who belonged to the chapter, or was conducted by persons specially designated, and was continued at yearly convocations and visitations.

In 1541, it was ordered that youths, after a preparative course of instruction, should be trained in theology, by those who were provided with prebends. The schoolmaster probably also had this duty, where there was no reader of theology. Older statutes, as well as the church ordinance of 1571, refer first and last to the Holy Scriptures, "so that it shall not again come to pass, as under the pope, that so much attention was paid to other things, yes, even to heathenish books, that no time was left for reading the Bible." But an acquaintance with other writings on the part of priests was presupposed. The church ordinance prescribes, as the condition of becoming a priest, only the legal age and some experience in the Holy Scriptures, and says nothing expressly of literary exercises before the convocation.

The Reformation would have denied itself, if it had not sought to promote the cultivation of Christian knowledge among the people. It might be made a question, whether the church, by the suppression of the monastic usages, had not deprived itself of a very useful aid, especially in those monks of the begging orders, whose mission seemed adapted to this object. But even with respect to this object, the reformers condemned that whole body of monks, and we have before remarked in what bad repute the begging orders were then held. The church considered herself able, with great advantage to Christian truth, to dispense with this so lately misused aid.

A long time was to elapse, before an attempt was to be made to enable every man to read a book. One scarcely ventured to imagine such a thing possible. All efforts, therefore, were centred in an oral communication of the knowledge of Christianity. Preaching, therefore, was of the utmost importance, not only that the priest might take his place in the congregation as one who sought for Christian truth, and made it known, not only as one who was to infuse a new spirit into the minds of his hearers, but as one who was even to indoctrinate them into the first principles of the Christian faith. To furnish postils as a guide to the clergy, was, in addition to controversial writing against the Roman church, one of the first things undertaken, in 1528, by the reformers; and from the year 1529, the duties of the pulpit were made obligatory on all priests.

Until 1571, in some country churches, probably the smaller kind, there was no pulpit. The church law, therefore, provides for their erection, and for an alteration in them where they were inconvenient. Whatever interfered with them, altar or image, or anything else, was to be moved out of the way. By preaching and reading from the pulpit, the priest was to be diligent in impressing on the minds of his hearers the truths of Christianity.

There were as yet but few portions of the Holy Scriptures in Swedish, printed in editions accessible to the people. Neither the whole of the Old or New Testament was to be had, exeept in the large and expensive editions of 1526 and 1541. In the year 1530, Olaus Petri expresses his doubt, whether the translation of the New Testament of 1526 was to be found in every priest's hand. The church Bible of 1541, was found at least in every church, but how far it was in common use, is unknown. Its form, its price, and the inability to read, were probably hinderances to its general circulation.

As early as 1530, Olaus Petri proposed that the priest should be required, portion by portion, to read the New Testament from beginning to end, in order to communicate a knowledge of it to the people. He published also, in the same year, a work on Luther's large catechism; and catechetical works appeared from time to time. But the special book of the people, the smaller catechism of Luther, was, as far as known, not yet printed in a Swedish translation. An assiduous attendance on public worship was either pre-supposed or ordered, and the church, even for catechetical instruction, was the peculiar school of the people; a school for all that related to the knowledge of Christianity. Not only an acquaintance with the contents of the Bible, but with the catechism, was there to be acquired. This was a carrying out and an extension of the measures, which, long before the Reformation, were adopted, or at least contemplated.

In 1541, it was proposed, that during Lent sermons on the catechism, should daily be delivered, and four times a year besides. The church law of 1571 prescribes, that there shall be sermons on the catechism in the afternoon, at least twice a year in towns, during the seasons of Advent and Lent. In the country, at morning service, the priest was to spend half an hour in preaching on the catechism, and another half hour on the gospels. The catechism was taught the people by oral instruction, and, as is done by Luther in the preface to his smaller catechism, the clergy are admonished, plainly, clearly, and in the same words, to propound and present its doctrines. It was required that instruction should be received and kept up, and at least, from the year 1540, none were admitted to the Lord's Supper, who could not show their acquaintance with the chief points of Christianity, the ten commandments, creed, and Lord's prayer; or who could not explain why they sought the table of the Lord.

3.—DIVINE SERVICE, MORALS, PURIFYING OF THE PEOPLE'S FAITH.

The public worship had, from 1529, in the towns and other places of the land, and, from 1544, over the whole land, been placed on the same footing in most respects, which it now holds, and, till 1811, with scarcely any difference. There was a strong disposition to promote unity and uniformity in this respect. The bishops prescribed changes or improvements within their own sees, especially their cathedral churches. Many councils, and even the church ordinance of 1571, gave independent directions respecting mass or service books, and manuals generally. The false and superfluous service of the Roman church, was allowed by degrees to die out, but nothing new was added, except the exhortation with which, till 1811, the morning service commenced, and the exhortation which is still used in the mass or service of the Holy Communion.

The most important measure was the publication of a manual to promote the exercise of preaching on every occasion of public worship. Complaint was made, in 1571, that, in popish times, "there was either no preaching, or such preaching as had better be unpreached." The rule for having preaching on every occasion of public worship, was however not absolute. A sermon *might* be delivered, but was especially called for when the Lord's Supper was to be administered.

The whole of divine service was to be in the mother-tongue, especially preaching; and priests are admonished to speak "pure Swedish," and to avoid, in unreasonable measure, foreign words, "since we ourselves have just as good words as any foreign tongue can produce." In 1541, however, it is permitted on high festivals to have the mass or service in Latin. In church music, the use of Latin in conjunction with Swedish, was, till the year 1533, permitted, and even in country churches, it was used on the three high festivals. In 1571, Latin was permitted in singing, on condition that it was understood by some of the congregation. Psalm books, in Swedish, made their appearance from the year 1530, and in 1567, there was published a book of spiritual songs, under the title, "The Swedish Psalm Book," containing ninety-nine psalms, and another, in 1572, with sixty-six psalms. But there was yet no general rule on the subject, prevailing over the whole kingdom.

The centre of the Roman church's divine service, was the Lord's Supper, as involving the sacrifice of Christ, though without the shedding of blood. In 1541, daily mass or service is allowed; but the priests were to admonish the people by catechetical instruction, to celebrate the Lord's Supper. Till 1553, the mass of the Holy Communion might be holden without communicants, although, even then, the priests were enjoined so to instruct the people, that some guests might be obtained for the holy ordinance. For the first time, in 1562, it was expressly forbidden to hold the mass of the Lord's Supper, where no communicants were present. How soon the people, in large numbers, assembled at the table of the Lord, and participated in the sacrament, as a spiritual need, appears from the so-called liquoristic controversy, in king Erik XIV.'s time, and from the church ordinance, which permitted city churches to have several altars, with the reason, that the Lord's Supper might be simultaneously received at them all.

In the use of service-cloths and other outward ornaments, there was a variant practice, according to the variant views of bishops, ordinaries, and priests. The necessity, in the beginning of king Erik's reign, of protecting the church's freedom in these matters, rather increased than diminished their importance; and at length a church ordinance was passed to the effect, that "church attire, such as service-cloths, altar-cloths, pictures, images, lights, candlesticks, crowns, bells, are permissible, where not excessive or abused;" and it is ordered, that the priest "shall clothe himself as was wont." The principles of 1544 and 1529, approached near to each other.

The cathedrals continued to be regarded as the model

churches of the diocese, and the heart and centre of public worship. Divine service was held in them, as generally in the city churches, oftener than in country churches. Absolution, for the more atrocious crimes, could only be obtained at the cathedral, from him who was placed there as the penitentiary for the whole diocese, or from one who supplied his place. Divine service was there more imposing than elsewhere, and after the old canons, vicars, korpriests, and others, that had been employed in church music, disappeared, the duty was performed by the scholars under the direction of the schoolmaster. This duty was imposed on the schools in all towns where schools were to be found, but only on holidays, because on ordinary working days no people were present, and for their sake alone it was now thought divine service should be held.

Of old, each diocese had its own method of singing in divine service, which method it was the part of the bishop to regulate. A priest, who removed from one diocese to another, and they who remained in places transferred from one diocese to another, were to use and observe that method in church music current in the cathedral of the diocese to which they had last become attached.

The decree for diminishing the number of saints' days took effect in 1529, when it was left to the bishops to act in the matter, according to circumstances, and it was repeated in 1544, with more exact details in 1571, when the days of patron saints being no longer observed, the rest were treated as still to be continued, in addition to Sundays and the usual holidays. The visitation of the Virgin Mary and the days of the apostles were also retained in the cathedrals, except St. Peter's day, observed in the Roman church on the 18th of January, in commemoration of that apostle assuming the chair of Rome. In respect to keeping holy the Lord's day, a Christian freedom was allowed. There was, however, enjoined on that day an attendance on divine service, and a rest from labor. During the wild duck and fishing seasons the people were permitted to work in the fields and meadows after divine service was ended.

The old custom of confessing to the priest and receiving absolution was continued. But with the Reformation came also the maxims, that the enumeration of all sins was not necessary, that there need be no fixed time for confession, and that outward penance was not to be required as the condition of absolution. The first of these maxims was absolute. With regard to the third, it was declared to be advisable that the priest should *counsel* the penitent as to his meat, drink, and apparel. The old custom of announcing to every congregation certain times for confession, was allowed to be continued. The country priests were wont on such occasions to assist each other, so that many of them met at the church where confession took place, and the person confessing addressed himself to which priest he chose. But if any important case occurred, it was referred to the pastor of the congregation. Absolution was given with the laying on of hands upon the head of the absolved. The custom, which is now the only one that is common, had already commenced, that many persons confessed themselves at a time. The priest examined one or another, or none, and then delivered to them "a general exhortation from the pulpit," and pronounced a general absolution. Confession was not of necessity immediately to be followed by a participation of the Lord's Supper. It was, however, usual that the guest of the holy table first confessed and received absolution, and the general observance of this custom was the means by which the priest tested the faith and morality of those who came to the holy communion. This test is recommended in repeated directions, as far back as we find any given on such subjects. All were to be able "to pledge themselves," and no one who was in manifest wickedness, or in implacable enmity, was to be admitted to the table of the Lord. The Lord's Supper, for which the rite of confirmation was not requisite, could be administered to children, but not under eight or nine years of age.

We turn our attention to the church's public and charitable care of the poor and sick, a care which from the foundation of the Christian church was regarded as among its first duties. All the church's wealth, after provision had been made for its clergy and those who served at the altar, was considered as belonging to the poor and sick. The bishops, therefore, began to adopt measures that might be lasting for this purpose. Even individuals and the monastic orders provided such establishments, all of which at an early period in the Greek, and from 1311, in the western church, were placed, unless they belonged to the monastic orders, under the inspection and care of the bishops, and they were not to be diverted from their original destination and end. In Sweden, also, by Gustavus I.'s explanation of the recess or treaty of Westeras, the property appropriated to hospitals and almshouses, the abodes of the sick, were exempted from the claims of heirs, and the cloisters of the begging monks were given to that charitable use. How far they were to be regarded as belonging or not to ecclesiastical institutions was a point undetermined.

The views of king Gustavus on the subject corresponded with those he had of the church, and he gives as his reason for regulating the hospitals and almshouses of Stockholm, that it was a part of his kingly office "to know and provide what was best for the poor as well as for others." The king placed them either under the charge of the burgomaster and council, or appointed special persons for the purpose, or intrusted the whole matter to the governor of the district. By the projected ordinance of 1540, it was contemplated to place such institutions nnder a conservator. There seems to have been little or no idea of placing them under the care of the bishops and ordinaries, and the formulary of 1557, conferring full powers on the latter, makes no mention of their oversight of hospitals. In 1571, however, those of them at least which were situated in the towns of a diocese, were considered as in some measure under the care of the church.

The hospitals attached to cathedrals, were to have room and means of support for at least thirty sick persons, and to provide nurses and attendants. They were empowered, as before was usual, to send out collectors of alms furnished with a letter of recommendation from the bishop, and when these bidders, as they were termed, made their appearance in a parish, its priest was to urge upon his flock the duty of giving alms. Every holiday, when the people were assembled in large numbers in church, a collection should be made after divine service. The immediate oversight of them was committed to a proctor or attorney, appointed by the burgomaster and council, in connection with the bishop, or pastor of the church. Over the proctor was placed one of the burghers, chosen for the purpose from the guild, whose members were called guardians. The examination of accounts was intrusted to men chosen by the burgomaster. The pastor of the church was every week to visit the hospital, which was to have also its special chaplain. None capable of work, none who had relatives to take care of them, or had any property, was to be admitted; in the last named case it was understood, that the claim to any inheritance was not to be given up as a condition of admittance.

But when these measures were inadequate to the object, it was advised that every parish should have a few rooms provided for the sick, "so that they who feared God and wished to do what was right and Christian might have an opportunity with their alms and benevolent gifts to prove their faith and brotherly love to their neighbor." This recommendation gave rise to parochial halls for the sick.

In 1561, there were eighteen public hospitals in the kingdom, two of which belonged to Finland. It would hardly be possible to say how the public care of the poor and sick was advanced or retarded in respect to income, when after the state, or church and state together, took the matter in hand, efforts were soon made to place these institutions under strict regulations. It seems, however, that as they either retained their property or received appropriations from the crown, their means of support were not diminished. In 1561, an investiture of tithes was received by the eighteen hospitals of the kingdom, to the amount of 7632 barrels of corn, beside the so-called St. Sigifrid's basket, to the hospital of Wexio. The hospital of Upsala had 480 barrels. Five years before it had received from thirty-five farmers about 206 barrels of corn, beside money and day-labor. The hospital at Westeras, which in 1561 also received 480 barrels, in 1566 had, beside money and day-labor, about 390 barrels, the amount of church tithes from several congregations.

Scarcely had Christianity been able to subdue the minds of the people of the north of Europe to the obedience of gospel faith and precept, an obedience tried by the evils of the papacy and a corrupt church, when the sixteenth century threatened the ruin of the tender plant. There were as yet few traces of what may be called humanizing influences. The habits of the people, retaining something of the old heathenism, weakened the strength of the Christian life, and kept up a looser morality than was consistent with even that to which the Roman church unconsciously paid homage. Nor was the cause of good morals likely to be promoted by a contest respecting the very interpretation of the gospel, or that between a tottering church discipline shaken at its base and another not yet established.

From this condition of things were bred anarchy and a contempt of religion, and in the minds of others a lukewarm indifference. Even the more serious were tempted. From the heat of controversy or defeat sprung hatred, from victory arrogance. During this breach, the old church discipline must of necessity fall with the hierarchy which was its stay. It must fall, not only through the absurdity of many of its penances, which oftener injured than promoted its purpose, but through the false principles on which in later times it was based, when penance was converted from being a proof of amendment and love to God, into a satisfaction for sin.

This abuse or perversion of penance raised the question, whether the discipline of the church might not be altogether resolved into a binding and loosing through the word of God, so that he who sinned, by merely declaring his repentance and desire of absolution, should be entitled to this absolution. In Sweden, there was no intention to abolish all ecclesiastical duty, although the mode and measure of its management were rendered difficult, by the uncertain limits of spiritual authority. It was exposed, on the one hand, to the claims of exemption from it rife among the people, and it was watched, on the other, by the suspicious eye of king Gustavus, who found it either too strong or too weak.

From 1526, submission to the church's discipline was more desired and sought to be maintained, in order to strengthen the use of the temporal sword, rather than from a regard to the word of God. The reason is assigned at a later period, in 1571, when it is plainly said, "The sword does not bite as it ought" the temerity and license with which "men here almost universally commit sin." During the period between those years, as in the ordinantia of Westeras, in 1544, in the admonition to penitence and penance set forth that year by the king to his people, and in various ordinances either of the king or bishops, a variety of offences, such as swearing, perjury, drunkenness, intention to kill, and fornication, were denounced and declared punishable by the civil and ecclesiastical power. There is a vacillation shown in the church ordinance respecting offences. Open public confession and a submission to the ecclesiastical penalty enjoined is required, but only for the grosser crimes, while it is intimated that the general spread of other vices precluded an examination into them.

It was the prevalence of this looseness of morals which in a great measure called forth the Reformation, and, as that gained stability, awakened in the reformers deep thought and apprehension, and at a later period produced what has been termed pietism. Yet do not the delineations made of these times, though the times are dark enough, exhibit a decadence from good morals so deep, but that some, however unreasonably, might deny the breach of the Reformation to be on this account necessary. We do not find an eminent exemplification of improved morals, or any reason for praise, further than is always to be implied from a more diffused and clearer insight into the religious grounds of morality, and the transition from a slavish to a free obedience.

As it is not reasonable to presume an increased degree of ignorance among the clergy, at a time when the cathedral schools remained unaltered, and the foreign universities were frequented more than before, so is there no reason to impute to them a greater degree of immorality. Circumstances might operate disadvantageously. The disinclination of parents to send their children to school, and the chilling effects of the uncertain position of the clergy, might oblige bishops, for the maintenance of public worship, to ordain those who were not ripe for the office. To the usual, and during the strife of opinions, not easily removed obstacles, in the way of an accurate inspection into the conduct of the clergy, was added the inclination to wink at and overlook the transgressions of adherents. Party interest is a merit which covers many offences. Another obstacle existed in the uncertain position of the bishops. It was no settled point how far they could proceed without exciting suspicions of a hierarchical aim, and without being disturbed in their course of action, by the immediate interference of the royal power. King Gustavus, moreover, was not disposed to look with indifference upon the moral qualifications of the clergy, as appears from many of his letters, and the plenary commission to G. Norman as superintendent. The most stern testimony against the clergy of this period, are the articles of king John, in 1569, issued soon after the reign of king Erik, in which he rebukes their ignorance, gambling, love of lucre, loose and gross sensual habits. Similar charges are applicable, at the beginning of the Reformation. The like are reiterated against the clergy who embraced the liturgy of king John, and to follow any practice is to be abused by its opposers.

It cannot be proved that the priests of the first protestant church were worse than those who immediately preceded or succeeded them. That they were better, cannot be shown by witnesses to be cited from a time that cared not to write its own epitaph. Many particular instances occur, that prove the priesthood to have partaken the rudeness of the times, but there is nothing to justify the condemnation of the whole body. In punishing the offences of priests, notwithstanding the decree of 1527 that they were to stand before the civil tribunals as other citizens, it was sometimes regarded as sufficient punishment to deprive them of office, or, according to the view of the Roman church that official character could never be lost, displace them from its exercise.

We have endeavored to show, how, by instruction, admonition, and a Christian-like regulation of public worship, it was essayed to purify by degrees the popular faith from superstition and idolatry. Many customs and usages which the foregoing times approved, or which typified the sanctity of divine service and a holy life, were slowly discontinued, until they could with safety be wholly prohibited, others were allowed to be continued, and of those forbidden many were still kept up, either as mysteries of piety, or as mere popular superstitions, or as harmless customs. The church ordinance of 1571 prohibits many superstitious practices, some of which, it is truly said, were abolished, but of which the very prohibition proves the remembrance still to exist. Such were the covering of church images during a fast, the burning of incense and bowing before them, the taking down of the cross and putting it up again at certain seasons, the carry about of images, and vigils for the dead.

Fasting was still *enjoined* in 1541, so far as to provide for the observance of the usual Friday fast, but the people were to be instructed that it was not necessary to salvation. Subsequently we are not aware of any command or prohibition respecting fasting, except that, according to a church ordinance, it might at confession be enjoined as a beneficial exercise. The practice has been maintained to the latest times.

In connection with fasting, there were repeated admonitions, and even in church ordinances, to the giving of alms. Alms were given by will to the poor, to students, to churches, to hospitals, and to schools. In these wills the cloister of Wadsten was still sometimes remembered. We cannot determine in what manner these testamentary devises to the cloister were connected with the belief in their merit, or the efficacy of the prayers of the nuns. But when we find that men gave money to the cloister for the benefit of their cattle, we may judge how superstition still clung to these institutions.

It ought not to be forgotten that, in 1573, scarce thirty years had passed away since a more rigorous purification had been undertaken of the Roman church's customs and usages. In many hearts was still preserved a secret or less reserved attachment to them, and many still retained an invincible affection for these departed objects. The cloister of Wadsten was still alive. It was richly endowed, and had many nuns. Abbesses were elected, and on king Gustavus's death, in 1560, a still greater freedom was anticipated, because in that year a nun assumed the monastic vows. The nuns, however, were dependent on the uncertain favor of the king and individuals. King John himself, in 1573, took the silver shrine of St. Bridget, to be turned to his own or the kingdom's use, though nine years after he gave a new one. The house and ground which belonged to the cloister were appropriated by him to the castle of Wadsten, and after the town church was, in 1550, destroyed, protestant worship was held in the church of the cloister.

The monks of Wadsten had experienced severer treatment than the nuns. Two priests of seventy years of age were still left in 1570, who did service as father confessors. The one had embraced protestantism, had been promoted by king Gustavus to the pastoral charge of Haradshammar, and been married, but returned to Wadsten after the death of his wife. The other, Johannes Pauli Montigena or Montanus, so called from his home in the Koppar mountain, had entered Wadsten as a monk, but seems to have been also priest of the adjacent church of Hof. During the persecution which befell the monks of Wadsten in 1548, or at the time the canon Thure was imprisoned at Linkoping, Montanus was driven from the cloister, and as he would not submit he was imprisoned in the house called Tavast, in 1554, the same year that Thure on recantation was liberated, and obtained permission to settle himself at Wadsten. By the captain of Tavast and his wife, he was allowed to preach. His books being lost, he borrowed others *from his friends and those of kindred opinions with his own.* He here compiled, in his prison, commentaries in Latin upon the gospels for Sundays. These commentaries, he tell us, were drawn from the writings of the fathers and schoolmen, whose names are given. This, if he had those books in hand, would prove an improbable wealth of books in Finland. He dedicated his work, May 24, 1556, to the Roman archbishop of Upsala, Olaus Magnus, still living in Rome. On the accession of John to the throne, he was allowed to return to Wadsten, where, in 1578, he was accused of superstitious practices and rebaptizing. He reports himself, at a somewhat earlier period, to have been in Kopparberg and in Hedemora, where he practises conjurations over the workers in the mines and other sick persons, and, at the request of the steward, over the huts, when the work of the mines was in disorder.

Beside Wadsten, there were also found some feeble remnants of cloisters at Nadendal, Wreta, and Sko. Nadendal had, in 1578, four nuns, but in the commencement of king John's reign more. Wreta, in 1572, had three nuns, who, in 1580, were still left. In 1579, Sko, according to Possevin, had only two nuns. It is to be suspected, from an investiture given to them that year, that these convents had more tenants. The havoc made with cloisters was a consequence of the warrant of the times, issued against establishments that little corresponded to the purpose for which they were designed.

The few persons left, that belonged to an institution which had been doomed with the old church, were living memorials of the scarcely foregone times, and their thoughts and habits corresponded to those times, and kept up the recollection of them. But others also of the old race had their childhood recollections of those times. The pastor of a church from the diocese of Upsala, declared during the deliberations on the consecration of a bishop for that see, that it would gladden him to see the old abolished ceremonies restored. Almost the same language is used, in 1580, by the papal ambassador Possevin the jesuit. A certain Jons Mansson, who went over to the popish church, sent from Rome, in 1578, a letter and some images of saints to his friends in Sweden. He advises his father to have recourse to the intercessions of saints to God, as his forefathers had done, and recommends his sister Catharine to receive the image of St. Catharine, and take her for a patron, as *our old mother* taught and commanded while she lived.

Possevin relates, that several persons had, on his visit to Sweden, 1758, and the two following years, desired to confess to Roman priests, as their consciences would not suffer them to confess to the priests now in the land; and that an old farmer found his way to him, having, on the news that a Roman priest had come, hastened to the holy father with part of a rosary faithfully kept for a long time. The same Possevin also says, that the people in Gota and Finland were obedient to the old faith. But as he was only a short time in Gota, and never in Finland, he can speak only of what he heard. How little his report is to be relied on will hereafter be shown.

Many popular customs were retained, which had their root in the ideas of the Roman church, or in the heathenism which she admitted into her bosom, giving them merely Christian names. Among these was drinking to the memory of the dead, a practice which the church ordinance of 1571 required to be discontinued among the people; admonishing the priests so to instruct them. Our heathen fathers were wont to drink to the memory of Thor, Oden, Frey, and other of the Asars. The Roman church allowed the custom to be continued, but changed it into draining the feast cup to the memory of God the Father, God the Son, and God the Holy Ghost, and then to that of the Virgin Mary, and the other saints. These cups were followed by verses in honor of the divine persons, or of the saints whose names were mentioned and invoked.

Among the principal resorts of superstition, were the oblation springs. Immediately on his return from the diet of Westeras, in 1544, archbishop Laurentius Petri caused to be taken to Upsala and burnt a crucifix which had been erected at the much frequented spring of Svinegar. More than twenty years afterward, Laurentius Petri relates, that they who oftenest frequented this spring made offerings of money. Olaus Petri had made a catalogue of these springs, and in his treatise sharply rebuked the superstitious rites practised at them; but the archbishop prevented the printing of it, because he was afraid it might produce scandal, and because he hoped that these superstitions would soon be forgotten. But when, in 1568, it became known to him that an Englishman, William Molteke, of a family which, in the middle ages, settled in Sweden, had made offerings at St. Ekil's spring in Strängness, "with much superstition, such as lights, saying of mass, and cross-kissings," the bishops were charged to find out and fill up all such springs, unless necessary for domestic purposes. This had been done by bishop Peter Svart of Westeras, with the spring of St. David at Munktorp. The priests were to instruct the people in their sermons that God was not pleased with such delusions and offerings.

It was natural that Sweden should pay her tribute, also, to the generally current ideas and customs of the times. This remark is applicable to signs and prognostics, which were everywhere seen. Olaus Petri preached, in 1539, upon some mock suns which appeared in the heavens, put up in the church a tablet on which they were painted, and interpreted them as a prognostic of punishment for the sins of the prince. Astrology was, long after this period, still common; and it is known that king Erik busied himself with this art. That the processes of witchcraft, which came into use in the previous century, were not here unknown, appears from the short but sharp order of the ordinantia of Westeras, in 1544, "that idle carls and hags, where they are found, shall be burnt." In 1551, some women in Dalecarlia were accused of witchcraft, whom the king orders to be sent to bishop Henrik of Westeras, who was commissioned to deal with them according to circumstances.

In 1541, there was issued a strict prohibition against the superstitious observance of the Sabbath, or Saturday, which was pertinaciously kept by numbers of people. This prohibition, however, must regard some other than the delusion which, in 1544, was current among some of the inhabitants of Finland, who believed that the hard year and dear times were a punishment from God, because they did not keep Saturday holy, according to the law of Moses, and therefore undertook, according to the Old Testament, to celebrate it as a day of rest. The occasion and extent of this delusion are not known to us. We know it only from a letter of king Gustavus, in which he endeavors to enlighten the deluded, and by admonitions and threats to bring them to reason.

The Swedish church reformation was not the work of a party within the church, but aimed, by a slow and wary change, to alter the whole condition of the Swedish church, and win the consent of the members of all the estates. From the care and attention which the church bestowed on all within the sphere of its efficiency, Laurentius Petri, during this year, excepted those wandering people forming no part of the civil community, who, under the name of Tartars or Zingani, were from this time an object of the legislation of both church and state. In the church ordinance of 1571 they are not mentioned; but, among some articles which, at the wish of the archbishop, were passed at the diet of Stockholm, in 1560, was one that the Tartars shall not have priests, either to baptize their children or bury their corpses. The archbishop abided firmly by this resolution, the reasons of which appear from a letter written by him, at a later period. These people were no other than wanderers from Germany and other regions, and had no Christianity. Pearls are not to be cast before swine—and, therefore, their children were not to be baptized, because they would be destitute of all Christian care. Laurentius Petri, therefore, regards the baptism of children, irrespective of the care of the congregation of believers, and a suretyship for their Christian nurture, to be a superstition and abuse.

The brief view we have taken, shows the plant of church improvement to have been slowly advancing to maturity, as is in general the case with the animal and vegetative life of the north; but the plant was never left without protection and care, sheltered by watchful consideration and love. It was a people's training, under the hand of God, into a full possession of the truth. We see the care bestowed upon the object, but the fruit is not always immediately visible. We must take it as a fact, that this fruit was not wanting. A careful examination of the memorials of these times, leaves us no reason to acquiesce in the oft-repeated opinion that among the people the grossest ignorance prevailed; that a large portion of them knew not, till the beginning of king John III.'s reign, that they were other than catholics, in the sense of the immediately preceding period; and that a crafty policy introduced a change, by the retention of the old forms.

The first is, without doubt, a rash judgment on a people among whom the work of enlightenment was carried on by the persevering vigor and freshness of oral instruction, although book-learning was as yet not common. No less precipitate is the other judgment on a people whose nobles, bishops, priests, merchants, burghers, and commonalty, took part in drawing up the decrees of reform. This judgment cannot affect the nobles, of whom a great portion, from the middle of the century, were remarkable for a high degree of culture; not the clergy, who, in the education they received at home and abroad, imbibed an abhorrence of the papacy, of which their preaching, their learned books, their controversial writings, and their pastoral letters, are a witness; not the burghers, who, by the interests of their professions and trades, and by communication with foreigners, were compelled to become acquainted with the occurrences of the times. With not more propriety can it affect the commonalty, who stood in connection with all these classes of society; who, from the times of the Engelbrects and Stures, awaked to war for their freedom; who now saw the cloisters in their vicinity fall or tumble into ruin, and were a witness to the changed condition of public worship; who more than once were ready to meet with violence every more violent change.

It was not possible that this people, the commonalty of the realm, whose representatives were present in 1527 and 1544 at Westeras, could be ignorant of a change, which only a wilful silence could have hindered their priests from bringing before them, repeatedly admonished as those priests were, by preaching and instruction, to win the consent of the people to the reforms. Even if this were not absurd, the people themselves, under the influence of traditional knowledge, must have made the comparison between now and then. King John III., indeed, says that his people knew not but that they were catholics; but, as he says this as a reason against the change in the mass or public services, which was demanded by Rome, he shows the injustice of supposing that the change had taken place without the eye of the people being opened. The word catholic, too, is ambiguous; to be taken in general opposition to protestant, or as synonymous with Roman catholic.

In conclusion, the judgment passed on the changes made, that they were effected by craft and policy, is the judgment of the men of the Roman church on the Lutheran reformation in general.* They could not apprehend, as opposed to "a rooting up of the tree of Christianity," the principles of the Evangelical Lutheran church, which was to disavow the exclusive right of the Roman church to the old doctrine, customs, and usages of the church; and, in purging away errors and abuses, to assert the privilege of proving all things, and holding fast that which is good.

* Possevin, the Jesuit, says: "They retained in their temples the old rites, in external appearance. *It was a fraud of Luther, by which the people were deceived,* that the name of mass was retained, and parts of it recited, though in the popular tongue, together with surplices, images (except where Calvinism crept in), and things of that kind."

CHAPTER II.

TRANSACTIONS IN THE CHURCH IN EUROPE, BEFORE 1573.—BISHOPS AND OTHER IMPORTANT MEN IN THE CHURCH AT THIS PERIOD.—KING JOHN AND THE ROYAL HOUSE.—FIRST ATTEMPTS OF THE ROMAN CHURCH TO FORM NEW ENGAGEMENTS WITH SWEDEN.

SCARCE had the archbishop, Laurentius Petri, so worthy of reverence, and full of years and honor, passed to the repose of the grave, when, by degrees, flamed forth the contest which for twenty years divided the princes and senators of Sweden, its bishops, priests, and learned writers, into two conflicting parties. To these may be added a third, which consisted of foreigners, who came into the country and drew some of the natives to their side.

Laurentius Petri, at the close of his life, in the conviction that she ought to unite herself with a stronger ecclesiastical society, had approximated the Swedish church to the German evangelical Lutheran. That some genuine and established connection could be effected, was scarcely made a question. This connection, however, was interfered with by the sort of freedom which, in 1526 and 1555, this latter church was allowed—the liberty, on the part of the princes and estates, to choose the confession of faith that was to be proclaimed. All connection had thus the aspect of a state relation; and we have seen, in the foregoing pages, how the negotiations were carried on in king Gustavus's time.

But Lutheranism itself was not long indefinite. Its first written confessions of faith, and chiefly the Augsburg confession, were a project of reform whose adherents, when it was laid before the estates of Germany, in 1530, appealed, if it was not approved, to a general council of the church. The author of this Augsburg confession, Melancthon, in 1540, conceived himself at liberty, on his own motion, to make alterations in it; and in 1545, when the council of Trent was opened, the protestants were prevented from participating in that assembly from objections to its structure. The so-called Interim, which went into operation after the year 1548, was framed on the principle of a future accommodation of differences, by means of an ecclesiastical council. From that time a sterner determination began to manifest itself, and after the decrees of the Tridentine council gave the papal church a confession of faith, which established as the law of the church the errors and abuses censured by protestants, the two ecclesiastical bodies stood poised against each other, and the Augsburg confession became the recognized formula, in contradistinction to both popery and Calvinism.

It was not long that men were generally content with this rigorous antagonism, in which there appeared to many an excess that on either side went beyond the truth. Lovers of moderation have at all times been found, and after the publication of the decrees of the council of Trent, in 1564, there was a Roman catholic party dissatisfied with the rigid maintenance and objectionable structure of the church's doctrine and discipline resulting from that council.

These ideas of moderation began to be diffused, after the middle of the century, through those countries which had been shaken by the Reformation; in most places without fruit; the issue of a mediating policy where the contest is for principles. England, from the accession of queen Elizabeth to the throne, in 1558, was happy in establishing a church government that was neither Roman nor protestant, but might be said to be both combined. In France and Navarre there was, about the year 1560, a moderate party, that recognized the defects of the old, and was on its guard against the extravagances of the new preachers. This party endeavored to find a medium by which, according to the standard of holy Scripture and the primitive church, the church might be made better with the least possible change. In Poland, king Sigismund Augustus II., brother to the first wife of king John III., had, in 1555, requested permission of pope Paul IV. to hold a national council in Poland, for the reconciling of controversies of faith; with a view, also, to the partaking of the Lord's supper in both kinds, the marriage of priests, and the celebration of divine service in the mother-tongue. In protestant Germany, Melancthon and his school, to a great extent, united themselves to this moderate party.

Among those who were dissatisfied with the council of Trent, was the Romish emperor Ferdinand I., the rather that he found himself deceived in the flattering hope that the council and pope would follow out his views respecting Germany. The Cæsar now determined, as his brother and predecessor, Charles V., had done in 1548, to help himself by means of the Interim, and at least for his own land, to endeavor to effect an accommodation between the church parties. Seeking to find a man who could promote an accommodation between the parties, his attention was directed to George Cassander, a Belgian theologian, celebrated for learning and compliant principles. He was called to Vienna, but as sickness prevented his personal appearance, he wrote down his opinions respecting the articles of faith in dispute between catholics and protestants, which, as Ferdinand meanwhile died, were sent to his son, Maximilian II.

In his answer to the letter of invitation, Cassander says: "I find for the church of the present time no other council or help than to explore the mind and judgment of the primitive church, in order that, as far as is practicable, the present, which is propagated from that, may be renovated, in conformity to its constitution and discipline." He believed that thus both parties might be satisfied. In his opinion, therefore, he put the primitive church, anterior to the age of Constantine the great, as the judge between the contending parties. He did not spare the Roman church. He allows that the right of its bishops to precedence in the church was abused, disapproves the withholding of the cup from laymen in the Lord's supper, explains the sacrifice of the mass in a manner to remove or diminish its reproach, speaks cautiously of transubstantiation, condemns solitary masses, urges, in regard to the circumstances of the times, the discontinuance of enforced celibacy, and rejects the worship of saints. In respect to the question of faith and good works, he adopts the moderate views put forth in Charles V.'s Interim.

We shall soon find how this production, which was generally acceptable in Austria, exerted a great influence on the Swedish church. On the same platform with Cassander stood king John and the liturgic party.

In all the important posts within the Swedish church, stood, in 1573, those men who, in purity of life and church activity, were the disciples of the aged Laurentius Petri, and most of them had brought home their learning from the academies of Wittenberg and Rostock. Laurentius Petri, strong in his principles but mild in their application, had during almost his whole life acted upon the conciliatory though energetic policy which his church ordinance displays. At the close of his day he had zealously and successfully contended against the hot puritanism which here, as elsewhere, aimed at currency by a secret or open connection with Calvinism. The university of Wittenberg, through Melancthon and his school, had become suspected in the eyes of the more rigid Lutherans.

In general it may be said, that in the protestant church of Germany many minds became perverted who were not fast rooted in the truth. In the search for a firm confession of faith, the war of controversy flamed forth attended with the bitterest hate. University rose against university; the princes embraced opposite parties; the dukedom of Saxony was arrayed against the electorate; the evangelical Lutheran against the Calvinist; the pure Lutherans against the Melancthonians and cryptocalvinists. On many points, as those of justification, the Lord's supper, and church authority, these strifes made an irruption into the domain of the life of faith, and disturbed its holy peace. The Roman church did not conceal its joy over a discord from which was hoped the self-overthrow and self-destruction of protestantism.

In 1573, on the death of archbishop Laurentius Petri, there was still no provost of Upsala. The pastor of the church was Joachim Olai, who was born in Stockholm and had studied at Wittenberg. More conspicuous, both for learning and firmness of mind, than even this eminent man, were the first professors or readers in the newly established academy, Laurentius Petri *Gothus*, soon called to the post of his namesake and father-in-law as archbishop, Petrus Jonæ, and Olaus Jonæ Luth, both from Helsingland, both students at Rostock, the latter at Wittenberg also, which he visited in 1570, when Petrus had been two years teacher at Upsala, and the fourth the reader Petrus Benedict, from Oeland, who in 1558 began his studies at Rostock. Among the pastors of the diocese, in all respects the foremost was Andreas Laurentii Bjornram of Gefle, son of king Gustavus's faithful and heroical field-marshal, Lars Oloffson. He had studied at Rostock, at whose academy, in 1556, he was matriculated.

In Linkoping the episcopal chair was filled by the learned and valiant Martinus Olai, who had been previously ordinary of Gefle. In the most important post, as pastor at Wadsten, stood Jesper Marci, whose name we find not on the register of either Wittenberg or Rostock.

After Erik Svart resigned his episcopal office at Skara, his place was filled by Jacobus Johannis, who had been previously ordinary of Orebro. Of his youth and studies we know nothing, though he was afterward zealous for the conciliating party. He lived to the following century.

Nicholas Olai held, from 1562, the see of Strängness. A more arduous situation could scarcely be found in the Swedish church; its occupant being required, at the same time, to use his influence in the district that composed his see, for the conflicting interests of the two brothers, the king and duke of the realm. The pastor of the city church was Reinold Ragvaldi, who was born in Strängness, and whose name, in 1555, is found enrolled on the registers of Rostock and Wittenberg.

John Ofeg, known in the church controversies from the time of king Erik, was bishop of Westeras till his death, in 1574. Next him in eminence, was the provost and reader of theology, Erasmus Nicolai, who had studied at Wittenberg until 1562, and was subsequently schoolmaster in his native town of Arboga, pastor of Westeras, ordinary of Stora Tuna, till this office being resigned, he was made provost and court preacher to king John. The schoolmaster of Westeras was Salomo Bergeri, a student of Rostock. Both these men were distinguished, Erasmus as bishop of Westeras, Salomo as provost of that city and court chaplain, and for a short time steward of the church at Stockholm.

The see of Wexio, was worthily occupied by bishop Nicholas Canuti, who died in 1576. The provost and pastor was Nicholas Stephani, named in 1570 as superintendent of Jemtland, but, on Sweden resigning the spiritual jurisdiction of this province to Denmark, he was made bishop of Wexio.

Of the Finnish dioceses, Abo was occupied from 1563 by Paulus Juusten, whom, broken by age and a three years' imprisonment in Russia, king John sent to this see in 1572, where he died four years after. The see of Wiborg was filled by Erik Herkepe. Both these men were disciples of Melancthon.

Of the former ordinaries we have still to mention two, both belonging to the Smaland divisions of the diocese of Linkoping, but unlike in disposition and tone of mind. The one is the quiet and contented Andreas Torchilli, pastor of Jonkoping, who, in 1583, declined the offer of the archbishopric, doubtless from his native modesty, in exchange, on the abolition of the office of ordinary, for that of a bishopric or provostship. The other is the restless and ambitious Petrus Caroli, who, in 1538, eight years before Luther's death, had studied at Wittenberg. In 1540, he is said to have been schoolmaster at Linkoping, and to have aided king Gustavus in the changes made respecting tithes and church property, and in the rooting out of popery, being made pastor of Skeninge and ordinary of Kalmar. As belonging to the dukedom of Erik, he won the confidence and support of that prince and king, and was an intimate friend of Goran Persson, in whose views and secret purposes he was supposed to be well informed and interested. In vain he protested his innocence regarding the murder of Sture, against whom it was believed that he, as newly connected with king Erik, had irritated that prince with false tales.

After the dethronement of king Erik, disgrace and imprisonment overtook him from king John, who now united Kalmar and Oeland to the see of Wexio. But king John, finding him well disposed and useful for his church plans, restored him to favor, and he became bishop of Linkoping. Since his own times, he has been severely faulted for audacity, the love of power, and covetousness. Justice demands that he be commended for what is apparent from his actions when closely examined, his active zeal, for discipline within his diocese, and his fostering care of science and learning.

Laurentius Olai Gestricius, the undaunted champion of Calvinism, being dead, the city of Stockholm had, in 1565, Olaus Petri from Medelpad as pastor of its principal church. He was a man of great respect and influence, and was surrounded and supported by the men of Norland, pupils of the school of Gefle, foremost in opposition to John III.'s plans of reform.

At his side in office, from 1573, and afterward in the controversies in which he was engaged, stood Abraham Andreæ from Angermanland. Of his youth we merely know what he himself tells us, that the reformer Olaus Petri was the first guardian of his youth, that the pastor of Upsala, Erik Petri Helsingus, was his godfather, and the above-named Laurentius Olai his teacher in the school of Gefle. He appears to have studied at Wittenberg, and in 1564, to have stayed at Rostock. A restless and persevering, perhaps somewhat daring energy in gaining a purposed object, is testified by the letters he wrote at this period. It brought him greatness and honor, but at last became his ruin. He was greater in prosperity than in adversity.

We turn from the priests to the laymen, to take a hasty glance at the council and high nobles of the kingdom, who, by their education and the interest they took in the church, which at this time was foreign to no Swede, even as civilians were induced to bend their energies to ecclesiastical inquiries. First of all, comes forward the sister's son of king Gustavus, Peter Brahe, who, with Gabriel Kristersson Oxenstierna, took his seat in behalf of the church among the councillors of the kingdom, at the important diet of Westeras in 1544. He was made chief justice in 1569, and died in 1591, genrally esteemed for learning, wisdom, and moderation. Next, are the illustrious Erik Sparre, a man of learning and great genius, Hogenskild Bjelke, of a highly cultivated understanding, and Nils Gyllenstjerna, for his quickness of contrivance and conciliatory address, admired and caressed by all parties. Many more might be mentioned. A great portion of these appear, however, in church questions to have depended upon the prevailing views of the court. The Frenchman, Pontus De La Gardie, who, in 1565, entered the Swedish service, took an active part as a courtier in matters of faith.

The men who, under the name of secretaries, stood first in the king's chancery, were of special eminence and influence both by their position and their high culture. Of these a large number, if not all, had studied at the foreign academies. The most effective, and one of the leaders in the church during the transactions of the subsequent years, was Petrus Michaelis Fecht, provost and afterward bishop of Westeras, the friend and fellow-student of Erasmus. He was probably born in Stockholm. Supplied with means by the burgomaster and burghers of that city, he went to Wittenberg, where he was enrolled as a student in 1558, on the same day as Erasmus. He became a master in 1561, but was still there three years after. In 1571, he was placed in the chancery by king John, and two years after, he had the oversight of the printing of books in the kingdom committed to him. He was ordained priest, and for some time engaged in matters relating to schools. Abraham Andreæ Angerman, one of his most persevering opponents, bears witness after his death, but while the controversy still burned in the kindling of which Fecht took part, that he was a man of much learning and much respect, and that he showed special zeal for the interests of the church and priesthood. Possevin, who never personally knew him, says that he was in regard to his office quite a learned person.

Not less than any of the men of the church and state, and more than most, the royal house itself is conspicuous in the history of the church, not only on account of the weight of its power, but the part it took in the experiments and decrees that wrought the exhaustion of the church.

Of king Gustavus's four sons, two were removed from the controversy, Erik by his imprisonment after his brother's taking possession of the crown, and Magnus by his mental imbecility, in consequence of which his dukedom of Ostergotland was administered by the king. Mention will be made in the following pages of such of king Gustavus's daughters as participated in these movements. Respecting the two other sons, John and Charles, the church's history of the succeeding period has much to say.

Duke Charles was a child not ten years old at his father's knee, when that father, shortly before his death, took a solemn farewell of his people, and uttered words which then, as always, no Swedish man can hear without emotion. More than any other of the sons the heir of his father's vigor and gravity, he perhaps, also, as is wont with the youngest son who has lost his father, held in deeper reverence and honor that father's memory. When a child of but ten years old, he is said to have often carefully read and meditated on his father's will, which, besides advice as to temporal concerns, admonished him, "not to be drawn from God's pure word, not to be afraid or flinch, but hold to it with firmness." King Erik took great care to carry on and complete the training and education of his youngest brother, to whom, in that king's palace, where Beurreus was staying, and amid the controversies of the period, 1560, strict protestantism, and the nice distinctions between papists, Lutherans, and Calvinists, could not be unfamiliar. When he was about eighteen years of age, at which time he participated in the dethronement of king Erik, he entered upon the charge of his dukedom, which beside the whole of Strängness, included the diocese of Skara with the districts of Vermland, and, from 1571, Vadsbo and Valla in West Gothland.

Respecting the rights of princes over the church within their dukedoms, there was no specific direction in the will of king Gustavus. The priests of the dukedom participated, like others of the kingdom, in ecclesiastical councils, and in the mutual deliberations that concerned the church. This may specially be noticed of the see of Strängness, whose bishop and clerical representatives were present and subscribed the proceedings of the council of Upsala, in 1572, and even those of the following year.

Something has already been said of king John's character and education. It is probable, that even he in early youth received instruction from Beurreus, and that thus the seed of Calvinism was early sown in his mind—sown in a thankless soil. His mind was piously inclined, and once, when he was a child, staying with his parents at Gripsholm, he ran frightened to his mother's arms, exclaiming that he saw the form of the Crucified enter the room and approach him. He was then four years old, and the narrative, which refers to the year 1541 or 1542, may serve to show the turn of mind and impress of his early character. A monk of Wadsten had foretold him when a lad, that he would wear the kingly crown. The fulfilment of the prediction contributed to win for the cloister his royal favor. When, at a later period, the books of Calvin predisposed him to the views of that Genevan, a Lutheran proposed to him, as an antidote, the reading of the works of the church father Cyril of Alexandria, in order to settle the purity of his faith in the Lord's Supper. This study turned his attention and his love to the writings of the church fathers. From Calvinism he was soon fully weaned. The edict he issued at the beginning of his reign, wherein he "gave warning to all the inhabitants of the kingdom who would not unite in God's word and our religion," must have been aimed at the religious patent of king Erik, which spoke especially well of the Calvinists.

How much the divisions in the protestant church of Germany wrought on king John will hereafter appear. In his prison at Gripsholm, where he had time and opportunity "to converse with his books," he continued his reading of the works of the church fathers. On their contents and arguments he discoursed with his wife's chaplains, among whom are mentioned one Albert and Polacken Herbst. These men were not nurtured in jesuitical colleges, or in the principles of the council of Trent. They, therefore, entered into John's views of recognizing the fountain of truth to be, not the church as it then existed under the supposition of its being developed by the immediate inspiration of the Holy Ghost through the episcopate and papal head, but in the Holy Scriptures, as the church fathers set forth its doctrines and bore witness to the faith and worship of the primitive church. The jesuit Possevin, more indoctrinated by the spirit of the new era, therefore remarks, that if these chaplains "had been, as should be carefully attended to in the choice of such persons, better grounded in the doctrines of faith and the church's mode of controversy, it is probable they had long ago been able to bring John over to the Roman church."

The convictions respecting Christian faith and the church which John III. entertained, were the result of his thoughts and studies within the walls of his prison at Gripsholm. They influenced his mind, from the hour he began to operate on the position and relations of the Swedish church till his death, although they sometimes vacillated from side to side. He was, however, for a long time unsettled in his determination, and undecided, until the work and words of one man gave coherence, clearness, and strength, to the thoughts and sympathies of his heart. That work was the opinions given by George Cassander, to which we have before referred. What was there said, gave birth to principles that operated for a time, and were widely spread, but soon disappeared. It did not probably reach the hands of John before his release from prison, and the disturbances of the period immediately succeeding, gave him little leisure for such investigations. His acquaintance with this book was perhaps brought about by a man who had the greatest influence over him. This man was the secretary, Petrus Fecht, a pupil of the school of Melancthon at Wittenberg. Once the king asked him what he thought of the writings and doctrines of the old church fathers and the new authors. Fecht answered, that he found greater satisfaction in reading the fathers. From that hour the bond was tied between the two men. They undertook conjointly to investigate the doctrines, constitution, and ecclesiastical usages of the primitive church. These studies kindled a contest of twenty years within the Swedish church.

King John would certainly have found himself less disposed to seek a medium between the protestant church's claim for the freedom of private judgment, and the Roman church's demand of blind obedience, had not the claim of the latter been strongly impressed on his mind by his Roman catholic wife, Catharine. Not being at first zealous for her faith, but sliding into zeal for *his* conversion and instruction, though a truly pious and godly woman, she had a legitimate claim to his attention, from the proved love she had shown him in the day of his calamities. Through her the Roman priests obtained access to her husband. On her, and the consequences resulting from her influence, the Roman church built the hope thus awakened to a new life, of restoring king John, and with him his people, to the obedience of the papacy.

At first, by degrees, and during the menacing progress of protestantism, the Roman church began to meditate upon what concerned its peace. It had acted under an illusion, which is the doom of human judgment that has lost its way. It had let loose, or not essayed to restrain the newly awakened propensity for science and investigation, without turning it to the service of the church, without seeking to bend it to the obedience of faith. It had allowed those calling themselves servants of God to pay tribute to infidelity, and audacious vice had sat uncovered in holy places. It had struggled to subject to itself princes and people, but had relied for support on the weapons of violence. It found, therefore, its foes and vanquishers in the spirit of inquiry, in the knowledge brought to life of faith and good works, in a living piety, in a temporal power professing a true faith, all of which were turned *against* the then existing faith and confession of the church. A reaction against the church's corrupt principles of action had commenced, too, within its own bosom, and in Italy itself; and it is remarkable that, after the death of Marcellus III. and of Paul IV. in the same year, 1555, men of great morality were elevated to the papal chair.

But it may be said of a hierarchy, be it a popish, episcopal, or presbyterian church, that its inner mission can only be regenerated by its peculiar priesthood, or those who fill the active post of doctrinal teachers. Such a class was to be found in the Roman church, in its monkish orders. The begging monks were not adapted to the change of times, and had not fulfilled their original destination. Upon the contrary, the newly-established order of Jesuits became the preservers of this church, because they understood its wants. With the deepest piety, according to the forms of his church, Ignatius Loyola learned to read its heart, and out of that piety grew the system of his order—by the science of faith to bend science to the obedience of faith, by austerity and devotion in their bringing up, to bend the rising generation into a reverence for the church; by the strength of self-mortification and sacrifice, the immeasurable power of suffering, to bend princes and people to the ecclesiastical rule and sway. The obedience of the members of the order to their chief, was to bend the world to the obedience of the church.

An institution, called forth by the deep necessities of the time, stands nearly full fledged in the hour of its appearance. The order of the Jesuits obtained its first confirmation from the pope, in 1540, to the number of sixty members. Three years later, this limitation was removed. Nearly twelve years after, Ignatius, himself the first general of the order, who died in 1555, counted in his order more than a thousand members, in a hundred colleges, houses, and residences. This number was soon multiplied. The order stood as an outpost in those parts of Europe which had not yet wholly thrown off the yoke of the papacy. Behind it protestantism made no progress, and lost a part of what it had won, while the waxing courage of the order began to act on the offensive, in order to win back the people who had discarded the obedience of the papacy. The nature of its piety, the deep inroad which, in many cases, it made upon the sanctity of Christian morals, and even its success, made this order to be regarded in relation to the Christian life, as was the council of Trent in relation to the church's faith and constitution. Its "holy craft" substituted for violence, soon rendered it an object of the most lively abhorrence and hatred to protestants.

The hottest zealot for the full re-establishment of the Roman church in Poland, the fatherland of the Swedish queen Catherine, and a warm friend of the Jesuits, was Hosius, the bishop of Kulm and Ermeland, who, in 1561, was made a cardinal, and lived eighteen years after that elevation. He was a pattern of jesuitical piety, was put in the high posts of the church, and is much commended for good works and learning. In 1571 he composed, at the request of the Polish bishops, a confession of faith, in opposition to that of Augsburg, and endeavored, by letters and representations, to harden the lenient heart of king Sigismund, against any toleration of heretics. He was in hope, on occasion of the theological disputes in the Lutheran church, to win over the duke of Saxony and his land, for which purpose he sent the Jesuits there, and exhorted duke Albert of Berne to assist him, which that prince, however, declined to do. When, after the death of Sigismund Augustus, in 1572, the Polish estates established freedom of faith for the protestants, the *pax dissidentium*, he used all his efforts to prevent the newly-elected king, Henry of Anjou, from acquiescing in this arrangement, and when that monarch had confirmed it, to induce him to break his oath as by no means binding. This is an exemplification of the moral worth of Hosius. The Lutherans, in his view, could not be considered as Christians; their priests were, in his opinion, servants of Satan.

It does not appear that, immediately after his marriage, any connection with Rome was kept up by king John's wife. But, from the commencement of the year 1540, a stir began to be noticed both for and against the Roman church. The training of the young successor to the throne was first intrusted to a Roman catholic teacher, not on the ground of any resolution to educate him in this faith, but partly to please the mother, and partly in conformity with John's idea that he should be devoted to neither church until he could make his own choice between them. This view resulted, not only from John's persuasion that there was a middle path, but also from the reflection that young Sigismund must not be excluded from the future possession of either of the kingly crowns, that of Sweden by right of his father, or that of Poland by right of his mother's brother or mother's family. This hope was centred in this son of John's imprisonment. The popish teacher, Nicholas Mylonius, was, however, in 1572 or 1573, removed from this trust, because the estates of Sweden were dissatisfied that the education of the crown prince should be committed to such a man. It was at this period that the controversial writings of Herbst roused attention to the enterprize of the papists and the care of the Jesuits, stretching even to tight little Sweden.

The reaction which awakened the Roman church to renewed activity, extended even to Sweden. The reanimation had, by degrees, affected all the adherents of this church; and a more zealous interest in what relates to the church began in our own land to be felt. We have before noticed a change in the mind of queen Catherine, proceeding either from the influence of the spirit of the times in general, or from her increasing intimacy with men of more decided views. It appears probable, but we cannot determine to what degree, that the above-named Mylonius had a share in the change. We have more certainty of the influence over her exerted by a priest, whose name is not known, that came from Rome, and seems to have accurately inquired into the state of the queen's mind, and to have excited her zeal for the church. Through him or some other, attention had been attracted at Rome to the means of reknitting the connection with Sweden, of which the queen was to be the link; and cardinal Hosius made use of his intimate relationship with the royal house of Jagellon to put himself into immediate communication with her. His first letter to queen Catherine, written in May or the beginning of June, 1572, is the commencement of a correspondence carried on for some years. It commends her steadfastness in faith, and unity with the church, her zeal for her husband's salvation, in requesting that some Jesuits might be sent to Sweden, by whose aid she might restore to the right path those who had been led astray by the servants of Satan. The whole city—Hosius was then at Rome—was talking about it. The cardinal could not forbear expressing to her his pleasure and congratulations at the report that her husband too was not far from the kingdom of God. He supplicates God's favor on her efforts to restore her husband and people from damnation, offers his assistance, and assures her of the pope's benediction.*

Doubtless the cardinal gives the queen's wishes and purposes a stronger import than they really deserved. We cannot regard this desire of having Jesuits sent hither, otherwise than as a loose expression heard in Sweden from those who supposed that such must be the wish of the queen—and so it was made a reality. We find no means adopted; and when at last Jesuits came here, there is no hint of their having been earlier called.

The queen, brought up in a Polish family, in more liberal views than those now current, must, if by her king John and his people were to be won, be herself first reclaimed to that unity with the Roman church, for which the cardinal had already commended her. Rome could no longer be satis fied with an imperfect connection. Catherine, who was commonly regarded as possessing so much power over her husband, had been induced *by him* to partake of the Lord's Supper in both kinds, without a papal dispensation, and her catholic chaplain had in this manner administered it to her. A priest, that had lately come hither, informed the pope and Hosius of this, and the consequence was a prohibition to the queen so to receive, and to the priests so to administer the Lord's Supper. This awakened dissatisfaction. The queen now addressed the cardinal in a letter, dated Nov. 12, 1572, with a request that he would obtain for her the pope's pardon, and also his permission to continue receiving the eucharist in both kinds. King John ordered his ambassador in Poland, A. Lorich, to endeavor, through the papal legate in that country, to gain this permission. The king expressed himself in strong terms against Rome, and accuses Hosius of having prevented the grant of the

* Gregory XIII., the same who celebrated with a *Te Deum* the horrid murder of the Huguenots, and had a medal struck in honor of the event.

queen's request. The refusal had afflicted the sick queen, who could not be induced to take the Lord's Supper from Swedish priests, or be disobedient to the pope, but only wished, by participating in both kinds, to win the favor of her subjects. The pope had often absolved from this command, and from another *which is against God and nature.*

Hosius replied to the queen's letter, in March, 1573, and expresses a wish to do her service, but represents how wrong she had acted, since it was better to obey God than men. The priest who permitted her to take wine in the sacrament had been in great error, when he said that Christ himself so instituted it. He had indeed given the apostles both bread and wine, but it did not follow that laymen had the same right. If the king still required this mode of reception from her, she was to answer in words that the cardinal puts into her mouth, that she would willingly comply with the king's wish, if he would grant a little prayer of hers, to restore his people to the obedience of the Roman see, himself to take his departure, and humbly beg pardon for the fifty years' separation between Sweden and Rome. The cardinal assured her that the use of the cup would readily be allowed, if thereby Sweden's kingdom could be won.

The withheld dispensation was used as a spur to the queen's zeal for conversion. But the royal house of Sweden had also for its negotiations with Rome a worldly motive. Queen Catherine had, in conjunction with her sister, after the death of their mother, Bona Sforza, who was buried at Naples, a considerable inheritance, the principality of Bar, with some ready money. As the Spanish government raised difficulties in giving it up, the pope's intervention was requested. Even this was promised, if any inclination was manifested on the part of Sweden to a reconciliation with Rome. Hosius became adviser to the conscience of the queen, and at this time held a frequent correspondence with her by letters. She was urged to endeavor to gain her husband to the papal church. "It was," says the cardinal, "a good sign that he allowed his wife to negotiate at Rome respecting the use of the cup in the Lord's Supper." "Gregory VII.," he proceeds, "seems to have been the pope through whom Sweden first received the gospel, that from and with him the present Gregory XIII. was the seventh, a number peculiar to the Holy Ghost, whose gifts also are seven." He promises the intercessions the queen had requested of him, and sends in his letter, prayers to Christ and the saints of Sweden for its conversion.

This letter, from which we have made these extracts, appears to have been written in June, 1573. At the same time the cardinal attempts to bring himself in connection with king John, who had hitherto avoided all open communication with the men of the Roman church. He wrote him a letter, but uncertain how it would be received, sent it to the queen, whom he left to decide whether its delivery would be prudent or not. It was produced, and the cardinal was happy enough to receive an answer, though not in accordance with his wishes. The king appears to have merely justified himself in regard to the cardinal's allusion to the allowing the queen the religious liberty guaranteed at her marriage. The queen having in one of her letters spoken of the threat of the Swedish people, that they would not endure her popish priests, as the reason for her taking the cup of the Lord's Supper, the cardinal replies to the king, that he could not believe the king would allow his sceptre to be wrenched from him by his subjects. "Is this, in God's name, the gospel, that subjects shall not submit to their princes, but princes must submit to their subjects?" But when king John alludes in his letter to the matter of the inheritance, as desirous of using the assistance of the Roman court, the cardinal gives him to understand that a greater disposition for a church communion with Rome would be attended with a more lively participation in that cause. To the Roman chair, from the times of the apostles, all disputes had been referred, as the king might learn from Hosius's confession of faith, of which a copy accompanied the letter. The divisions in Germany ought also to admonish him that the act which was now most concerning to a king was the reclaiming of his people to the unity of the church.

To the crown prince, Sigismund, now eight years old, the cardinal at the same time wrote a letter, in which he expresses the hope, that Sigismund, through his mother's piety, would be preserved from the confusion of tongues which had already arisen in the tower of Babel begun to be built in Saxony. That he might understand what the catholic church is, books are sent him, out of which his teacher, whom Hosius supposes to be a catholic, might read for his struction. Other small presents and prayer books were sent him and his sister Ann, then a child of six years of age.

In this correspondence from Rome the queen was not forgotten, but received letters from both the pope and Hosius. She had, in a letter to the former, thanked him for the receipt of absolution for her fault in taking the cup in the Lord's Supper, assured him she had not harbored and did not harbor the design of being disobedient to the church, expressed her wish for her husband's and his people's return to the bosom of the church, and begged permission to continue the use of the cup. Gregory declares, in his answer, his delight with her church principles, promises, in the question of using the cup, to determine what God directed him as consistent with his own honor and the church's welfare, sends her two hundred guilders for the nuns of Wadsten, whom she had recommended to him, with some *Agnus Deis* for herself and children, and refers her, in conclusion, to a letter she would receive from Hosius.

This letter of the cardinal was, on the contrary, less

gracious. He had expected, what a letter from Herbst allowed him to hope, that the queen would have already refrained from the use of the cup in the Lord's Supper. As long as this was not the case, she must not hope for permission to be allowed its use. He had already written to her, that the condition of the permission would be the queen's endeavor "that some sign should appear in the kingdom of a return to the church, and a reëstablishment of the sacrifice of the mass with its ceremonies." With respect to the threat of the Swedes not to endure Romish priests and the mass, the cardinal repeats what he expresses in the letter to the king.

It was now considered at Rome that a step further might be taken. The letter of Hosius to the queen ends with the notice that a Jesuit priest, Stanislaus Warsewitz, from Poland, would soon arrive in Sweden, and that the pope desired six noble youths to be sent to Rome to be trained in Christian piety.

The further progress of the matter will be related after we have described the measures for a change in the church, which after 1573 were adopted.

Meanwhile the intercourse which was now opened between Sweden and Rome, had awakened anxiety over Europe, as to king John's purpose of returning to the obedience of the Roman church, provided the pope would permit laymen to partake the Lord's Supper in both kinds, and grant marriage to the clergy. There was, however, a general conviction that the transactions of the year 1573, chiefly regarded the pope's recommendation for obtaining the queen's maternal inheritance at Naples, and that after the recent vacancy of the Polish throne, in 1574, John desired to win the pope's co-operation in the suit for the crown of Poland.

CHAPTER III.

THE CHURCH COUNCIL AT STOCKHOLM IN 1574—ELECTION OF AN ARCHBISHOP—CHURCH ORDINANCE OF 1575—CONSECRATION OF BISHOPS IN 1575.

MORE than seven months went by after the death of archbishop Laurentius Petri, before his successor was named. This space of time was devoted by king John and his friend Fecht to the studies which might give their judgment and measures respecting the church both character and stability. A scheme was concerted for sundry changes and additions to the church ordinance of Laurentius Petri, and the king desired, before the election of an archbishop, to assemble the bishops and priests in order to ask their confirmation of this scheme, possibly, also, to ascertain beforehand how far they might be disposed to any further alterations. Before the meeting of the council, negotiations were carried on with the newly-elected bishop of Westeras, Erasmus Nicolai; and the scheme was previously communicated to him through Fecht, with the king's injunction that he should endeavor to gain for it the consent of the clergy of his diocese.

It is said that the delay in filling the archiepiscopal chair was occasioned by another plan of king John, to elevate to that post his cousin-german, John of Hoya, bishop of Munster in Westphalia, count Per Brahe's half-brother. It may be that king John spoke of it without reflection, and that while a general attention was drawn to the popish scheme, suspicions were raised and conjectures formed as to such a step and its consequences. It is not probable, however, that it was seriously contemplated, as the man belonged to the Roman church. However this may be, the whole matter came to nothing by the death of the bishop, which occurred at this time.

The ecclesiastical council, with which commence, within the Swedish church, the movements called liturgic, was opened on June 6, 1574, at Stockholm, the day and city appointed also for the meeting of the diet. The bishops were summoned, and were to bring with them certain members of their chapters, and principal priests of each district. There are one hundred and four names of the clergy recorded as present, in which number, the representatives of the see of Linkoping are not counted.

The king sometimes appeared in person at the council, sometimes took part in it through the agency of Fecht. He had found it necessary to clear himself from the suspicion of being attached to the Roman church. It was, he said, "a Jewish lie." For his part he was desirous of maintaining, protecting, and propagating the doctrines *of the old church.* It was well known, how many heresies were spread over all the countries of Europe, what disunion and disorders prevailed even among the theologians of the Augsburg confession, of whom those of Wittenberg and Leipsig wished to adapt themselves to the primitive church of the fathers, which the others presumptuously assailed. Yes, doubtful of their own doctrine, as not uninterruptedly derived from the apostles, they had, this very year, sent ambassadors to Constantinople to seek a union of protestants with the Greek church. Amid such doctrinal discords, it would be well to close with *the apostolic and Christian verity of the primitive church,* evidenced alike by holy Scripture and the writings of the holy fathers of the church. There had been in many respects a deviation from those old paths, especially in the order of divine service, and a beginning ought to be made by a return in that office of the mass to the primitive purity.

The ten points which were proposed to the clergy by Fecht, related either to the proper address of the priests in the time of divine service, and the administration of the Lord's Supper, or to some church usages. They had for their object the maintenance of the sanctity of worship and the sacrament, for which king John, as did the old Laurentius Petri before him, showed himself solicitous. Both of them referred in the same terms to the Calvinistic and puritan mischief which had prevailed in the times just past.

The first point having confirmed the order of the mass which had been settled in the year 1571, the priests were exhorted to prepare themselves carefully for divine service. They often made no preparation for their sermons before the hour of delivery. They ought to call to mind the holiness of the cause in which they were engaged, especially the mass. During singing, while they stood before the altar, they ought both for themselves and the congregation to offer up holy and Christian prayers, especially those the fathers and teachers of the church had used, which had been composed with great piety. The people should be admonished to approach with the greatest reverence the Supper of the Lord. There should then be the same mind, thoughts and gestures, as in prayer to God. A preparation should be made, by both those who administered and those who partook of the sacrament, with fasting, mortification, and frequent prayers. The priest who was drunk the afternoon before he administered the Lord's Supper was to be degraded. At the mass they ought to demean themselves with outward reverence, and respect the service cloths, and not, as some were wont to do, lay their old hats or dirty gloves upon the altar. If the offered bread and wine at the time of the eucharist was not enough, the priest was to consecrate more. He should see that none remained, but if any of the wine remained, he was to drink it at the altar, and afterward rinse the cup with unconsecrated wine, which he was also to drink. The "lauds," which the old church was wont to sing as an introduction to the mass, were again to be used. The priests should in their lives and vocation conduct themselves with propriety. The layman who seduced a priest into drunkenness, or otherwise put a constraint upon the liberty his office requires, was himself to be subjected to punishment.

These proposed points, which were thought to appertain to a bishop to be presented to a convocation of his clergy rather than to a king in the presence of the clergy of the kingdom, produced sundry objections, when the clergy came to consider them. Of these objections, in the answer and criticism afterward given by the king, *who thus concluded the matter*, one only, regarding a change in the formula of prayer, was respected; the rest were disapproved. The clergy had objected to a repetition of the words of consecration, when fresh bread and wine were placed upon the altar, because it seemed to sanction the popish doctrine of transubstantiation. The direction was retained, but it was added, that it was not meant that on these words depended the real presence of the body and blood of Christ. In respect to the consumption at the altar by the priest of the bread and wine that were left, the clergy declared that they would treat them reverentially, but that they by no means considered that there was in what was left any such presence of Christ as in the participation of the sacrament.

The king gave his judgment respecting the objections of the clergy, but after they were made known, he called the bishops to the castle, and made them a speech, which is an exposition of his whole course. They must not be surprised that he meddled with theological matters. It resulted from his zeal for the house of God. He had seen how carelessly the sacrament was treated. They must not suppose him unskilled in these subjects. During his imprisonment he had thoroughly perused many works of the best fathers of the church. He wished both to guard the clergy against the intricate meanings of the new theologians, and to arm them against the papists. He inveighed against the theologians of Wittenberg and Rostock. Among the German theologians were as diverse opinions as there were members in their body. No two agreed together. Their writings, therefore, were to be cautiously used, or not be read at all by the Swedish priests, who should rather devote themselves to the church fathers, whose works contained on one page more matter than the thickest books of the new theologians. He would, therefore, no longer permit Swedes to study in Germany, but would take care that there should be sufficient instruction for them in the academy of Upsala.

After the king had subscribed the decree of the council, the election of an archbishop was at last taken in hand. The bishops, priests, and teachers of schools, gave their votes. The greater number of these votes were divided between bishop Marten of Linkoping, and the professor at Upsala, Laurentius Petri. The former had a majority, as a man of stricter protestant principles, bnt the king's vote gave Laurentius the office.

Laurentius Petri thus took, after his namesake and father-in-law, the foremost place in the Swedish church. His elevation was the result, not of a treacherous surrender of the claims of duty, not merely of the royal favor, or his connection with the family of his predecessor, but also from his known talents for business. In learning he surpassed most, and was inferior to none of his countrymen of that time. The man who, in 1566, was before all others chosen for the first chair in the newly-established university of Upsala, and soon became its chief pilot, could not want respect. But when he took the archiepiscopal chair, the post was for its occupant no less perilous if not more so than when the old Laurentius Petri entered on the path, in which, with honor and success, he cheerfully passed through so many rough and thorny places.

King John's self-confidence in his own theological acumen, and his lofty ideas of the width and weight of his kingly episcopal rights, was for the leader of the church no less dangerous than the terrible power of his father had proved. The Roman church also, after it began through the order of Jesuits to comprehend its own relations to the times, had opened a more insidious mode of controversy than its former reliance upon measures of violence. The new archbishop was not deceived. If he yielded to the king's plans, it was not from courtly pliancy, but because he would give the weight of the royal approbation to those plans and views, in many of which from perfect conviction, he coincided with the king. A conviction which is not perfect but vacillates, can find no limits to compliance, when tried by a demand for concessions. Laurentius Petri was led farther than he expected or wished.

It must be supposed, either that king John and his friend Fecht, had not yet, in the middle of the year 1574, during their investigations, clearly determined upon their measures, or that their design of bringing the Swedish church into those measures met with so much opposition, so many objections, that they were compelled to delay for some time carrying them into execution. Otherwise it is unaccountable why those changes were not at once brought forward, which, four months later, were proposed and adopted. Although to the changes which took place in 1574, the clergy gave, not without great caution, their consent, there is no evidence that the king and Fecht deferred them longer than they could. On the contrary, the proceedings of the council of June, 1574, must have contributed to enlighten these men of a middle way, as to the path they were to pursue, and we cannot be mistaken in regarding an occurrence that happened during this summer, a few weeks after the close of the council, and while the impression of its transactions was still fresh, as having greatly contributed to complete the king's and Fecht's consciousness of their position as theologians and church reformers.

On the 16th of July, there came to Stockholm, heralded by a letter from Hosius to queen Catherine, Stanislaus Warsewitz, the first Jesuit known to have reached the shores of Sweden. During the time he stayed here, which did not exceed a month, he had four conferences with the king, and many with Fecht on faith and the church. King John, of whom Warsewitz remarks, that he was ingenuous and eloquent, more willing to teach than be taught, could not be won from the principles he had already embraced. Every one, however, who has experienced how, in the struggle of the human spirit from its dim depths to extract a firm and clear conviction, each word, especially of objection and contradiction, is a spark that fires and enlightens, may understand what influence, even in those few conferences, Warsewitz's manner, piety, culture, and ductility, must have had on the king, seeking for truth, and not unallied to the Jesuit in his views. If we may credit Warsewitz's own report, his influence was still greater with Fecht, whose star of life his own resembled. Like Fecht, he had been a pupil of Melancthon at Wittenberg, and in Poland held the same relation to king Sigismund II. as Fecht now held to John III., the brother-in-law of that king. Each was secretary to the prince he served.

To Warsewitz, John had declared, that, above all, he designed to re-establish the primitive church usages; and they consulted together upon ceremonies valid and invalid, with regard to which, the king held fast to the stand-point of the testimony of the church fathers. Warsewitz is fond of representing this determination of re-establishing the usages of the primitive church, as a fruit of his conference with the king. That this determination was not now first formed in John's mind, appears from the foregoing transactions, especially from the council of 1574; but that it now presented itself to him in all its importance, is clear from the measures which were taken in the course of two years from this time, and through which John's reformation nearly attained the limits by which he firmly abided during the rest of his life.

Warsewitz left Sweden in the middle of the month of August, and soon after, the plan was developed into a church ordinantia, adopted the following spring. The new archbishop, who did not yet hold a full commission from the king, was summoned to Stockholm, in December, and here were presented for his approval seventeen articles, which are manifestly a programme of the ordinantia, such as it was designed to be. Assurance might thus be had of his assent to the changes to be proposed for general acceptance.

That it was in contemplation to go further than had yet been attempted, will soon be made manifest. After the archbishop had approved these articles, he was confirmed in his office, and he pledged himself to maintain the pure doctrine of the church, according to the writings of the apostles and prophets, and not allow any opinions that conflicted with "the unanimous faith of the true, universal (catholic) church," to be spread in the kingdom. Many false doctrines had sprung up, or been revived, such as the physical presence everywhere of the body and blood of Christ, and the profanation of the Virgin Mary, instead of the former extravagant reverence and adoration of her, contrary to God's word. The reason was, that men contemned or neglected the witness which the primitive church bore to truth.

The archbishop, therefore, promised to maintain and defend the right doctrine, according to the Nicene, Apostles', and Athanasian creeds, and the witness of pious antiquity, and to engage as well the professors of Upsala, especially those of theology, as the priests of the diocese, to read "the writings of the purer church." He bound himself to pay attention to the lectures delivered in academies, and for the theological, to furnish materials from the writings of the church fathers. Over the doctrine and lives of priests he would keep a watchful eye, and see that they were regardful of their studies, pious exercises, fasts, sobriety, chastity, and prayer, and observed the church's ceremonies and holy days. His jurisdiction he would not abuse, and would, in other respects, comport himself in conformity with the law which was or should be adopted, and not introduce anything that was not sanctioned *by a church council, and the king.*

Soon after the archbishop had given this pledge, the archbishop, the bishops of Linkoping, Skara, Strängness, and Westeras, with the priests of Stockholm, the provosts Sveno Benedicti, of Skara, and Salomo Birgeri, of Westeras, the pastor of Strängness, Reinhold Ragvaldi, and the schoolmaster of Skara, Olaus Laurentiæ, were, on Feb. 1, 1575, assembled in Stockholm by the king's summons. Possibly, there were more present, though their names are not given. Before these, when assembled, were now laid the proposed changes or additions to the church ordinance of 1571, in conformity to the articles accepted by the archbishop elect. The proceedings were conducted under the leading of Fecht, and occupied an unusually long time. On the sixteenth of March, the new ordinantia was ready, which the above named persons subscribed, "in their own behalf," and pledged themselves to hold and comply with, as far as could be done, and it won general consent.

This church ordinantia was framed, not to be substituted for the lately adopted one of 1571, but as an *interpretation* or explication of it, and has the merit of accuracy and precision in many cases which were passed over in the former. It is worthy of note, as an exemplification of the discipline current in Sweden for nearly twenty years after, but it is no less so on another account.

It has been remarked, that the aversion of king John, and those of like sentiments, toward the contemporaneous German Lutheranism, was based on the many variant opinions and the controversies thereby provoked, which well nigh caused Melancthon to be pronounced a heretic, and threatened to overthrow the peace and unity of the church. The same year that the plan for the ordinantia, which, in most respects, is a confession of faith, was concerted in Sweden, there took place the first attempt of a serious kind to effect a union among Lutherans, so as to exclude all open or secret Calvinism from the doctrine respecting the Lord's Supper.

The year after the ordinantia was adopted, when a liturgy was established in Sweden, there was effected among the Lutherans of Germany a union, which, in 1577, by the so-called Form of Concord, more strictly severed the Lutherans, as well from the Roman church, as in especial from Calvinism. Thus was abandoned the old archbishop Laurentius Petri's plan of uniting the Swedish church with that of the evangelical Lutheran, of Germany, just at the point of time when the latter began to attain a more complete stability and unity; and men were willing to go back from a settled confession of faith into the momentous disputes of the times, at the very moment they were terminated in Germany. The German "form of concord," a child of nearly the same age with John III.'s ordinantia, became, at last, after the lapse of ninety years, and when John's building of union had fallen, the rule of faith, even for the Swedish church.

The principles of both these writings are the same. Almost in the same terms as the form of concord, the Swedish ordinantia declares, that "the Scriptures are the standard and the test of all writings." But here commences a difference. The German form of concord adopts, as its symbol, the Augsburg confession, its apology, the articles of Smalcald, and Luther's catechism, terming them the "layman's bible," and still further developed and determined the doctrines then in dispute

In Sweden, on the contrary, no mention is made of these writings. It is declared, that men are to be satisfied with "the 'simplicity of learning,' which so clearly places before us what we believe and hope, and how we ought to live." In controverted points, the confession of the primitive church should be maintained, as that is testified by the writings of the church fathers. These, therefore, ought to be diligently read and carefully studied. The authors were mentioned who were regarded as the best, from the apostles' times till the death of Gregory the great, in 604; Ignatius, Justin Martyr, Irenæus, and many others, the chief writers of the Greek and Latin church.

But, as even among the church fathers, different views present themselves; it was remarked, that in their writings the subject matter is twofold. They either treat of doctrines of faith, in which they all agree, and "of which there has never been, is, or can be, among the godly, any disunion or difference of belief," or they treat of questions on which men may think differently without injury to salvation, or at least, shaking its foundations.

"As the Scripture is not of human origin, but God's own strength and wisdom, which God has spoken and given through men, so the right understanding and interpretation of Scripture is not of every man's judgment and strength, but is God's special gift and the work of the Holy Ghost." This gift ought to be highly esteemed. This gift was possessed by the "old sound godly doctors of the church, especially those who lived next the apostles' times, and in the beginnings of Christianity." Tertullian also says, that the first and oldest is the surest, but that which is new and of later origin is uncertain and false. This is the reason that men ought to abide by the writings of the fathers, and after that, to compare Scripture with Scripture, and seek the meaning of Scripture from the interpretation of the fathers.

Individual interpretation of Scripture was hereby expressly rejected. "By individual interpretation is meant that which each man, in regard to Scripture and Christian learning, after his own opinion and will does, contrary to the principles of Scripture and the quality of faith, when he casts away what other godly men aforetime have in the matter rightly thought and taught."* This had God designed to obviate, by the office of preaching and the oral interpretation of God's word, in order that the word, which in itself is clear, might in us be clear and comprehended.

In regard to modern writings, the advice is given, that simple people read them sparingly, but if they are to be read, let the choice rest on those of Luther, Brent, or Melancthon. It will be best to follow the elucidations already given in the church discipline, and now given respecting faith and ceremonies. Priests are dissuaded from reading the many postils which are now written in foreign lands, as such reading would interfere with their perusal of the Scriptures and the postils of their own land. For the purpose of obtaining access to the sort of reading recommended, and to put a check upon that which it was desired to lessen, it was resolved to petition the king, that libraries might be established in all cathedrals, that presses and paper works might be encouraged, that books imported should be examined by the bishops before they were offered for sale, and that the printing of Swedish books abroad should be forbidden. Within the land, no book should be allowed to be printed till it was examined by a bishop. For this, the reason was given, good in itself, but probably with other motives, and not very much to the point, " that we might for us and our

* The archbishop, in a programme, thus defines private interpretation: "Private interpretation is exercised when any one follows, in the explication of Scripture and doctrine, his own spirit and not the sense of the church." This question has been lately, in England, one of the most urgent controversies of a system which, allowing for times and circumstances, is as near as possible like the liturgism of Sweden

successors keep pure and right our Swedish mother-tongue, unmixed with foreign tongues, either Latin or German."

Protestant in relation to the form of faith, church usages, and constitution, as they had been exhibited for the last thousand years within the church of Rome, this ordinantia was tottering and vacillating when it referred to the writings of the first centuries, for the finding of truth. It was the more so, as the very doctrines now in dispute were in the first ages not developed; and when it acknowledged no other judge than the church fathers, whose evidence was plenteously quoted, it was compelled to shun, as irrelevant and over curious, every doctrinal question which went beyond the old church's confession.

It defines the doctrine of man's original sin as chiefly evil concupiscence, the forgiveness of sins as derived solely from God's grace and mercy, "apart from all human aid," and received through faith; but the root of sin remains. Man, therefore, must always acknowledge himself an unprofitable servant, though works of faith are not unprofitable.

On the sacraments, it is remarked, that the term means all that God in his holy word has commanded, with a glorious promise attached, such as penance, amendment, prayer, temperance, alms, marriage, God's word and gospel, and its ordinances, *the office of prince*, and the like. But the things peculiarly sacraments are, baptism and the Lord's Supper, to which might be added absolution as a third. They have their completeness from God's word, and depend not upon the worthiness of him who administers them, work not *ex opere operato*, but require intelligence and faith, are not indispensable, but may not be used contrary to the institution of Christ, such as the baptism of bells, the putting of the bread after consecration "into a box to be carried through the streets in procession, like a play, and worshipping it as God himself." *Ceremonies are declared to be adventitious things.*

In treating of the questions at this time agitated, the ordinantia is especially diffusive on the Holy Supper of the Lord. We are to be careful of the errors which are found, not only among the papists, but among those who claim for themselves evangelical faith. We are to abide by the words of institution, and hold our judgment imprisoned. "Were human judgment to be decisive in the case, then the Turk has as good a religion as we; so have the sacramentarians and the anabaptists." "If any old customs and human decrees are to prevail over God's word, our case is no better than that of the papists. The body and blood of Christ are really present in their natural and corporeal essence, not merely in their power to be participated and received; but an over curiosity pretends that the humanity of Christ, as well as his godhead, is always in all creatures, and in all places, therefore, also in the Lord's Supper.* But as little to be accepted is the popish transubstantiation. The words of the fathers do not imply that the natural essence of the bread disappears after consecration."

It is an abuse, practised by the papists, to consecrate the sacrament not to be received, but shut up. So, also, to take away the cup, which, *contrary* to the order of Christ, they have reserved to the clergy alone. That of the sacrament is made a sin offering for the living and the dead, "is not only unreasonable and a plain error, but is to be regarded with extreme disapprobation and abhorrence." Some of the fathers had called it *sacrificium*, an offering, but because of Christ's true body and blood therein present, for its fruit, as an application of the offering of Christ, as a remembrance of this offering, and as a thank-offering. In regard to confession, was expressly rejected the popish claim to an enumeration of all sins, which was declared to be contrary to

* An express disclaimer of the doctrine of ubiquity, which, by the form of concord, became current in the Lutheran church. It was objected to as a laying of false principles, *now* done in some foreign lands.

God's word, and the writings of the fathers. *The priest was not a judge, but a servant.*

It was acknowledged that confirmation of the young had not been properly attended to, and a new form for its reception was adopted. That the instruction of the young in Christianity might be duly cared for by pastors, parents, and sponsors, the bishop, or if he could not, the provost, or some others, appointed by the bishop in every parish, should examine the youth, previously instructed by the pastor before such examination. After examination, the visitor should, with exhortation and prayer, confer the benediction of the laying on of hands upon each candidate.

The ordinantia condemns, in many words, the invocation and worship of saints. If it be that they pray for us, we ought not to pray to them. They ought, however, to be held in reverence, especially the Virgin Mary, who doubtless was chosen by God to a holy office before she was conceived, and, therefore, sanctified and purified by the Holy Ghost in the womb, and afterward ruled by the same Spirit all her days. Care must be taken "not to condemn all those, and hold them as castaways, who from human infirmity have erred in this article, by having invoked the saints." From the number of saints' days previously observed, were now withdrawn the festivals of Magdalen, Laurentius, Corpus Christi, the assumption and nativity of the Virgin Mary.

One of the principal objects of the ecclesiastical legislation of this period, was the restoration of church discipline from the uncertainty of the limits for its application, caused by the Reformation. The ordinantia is in this respect very decided. It takes note of twenty-nine "grievous sins," commonly called notorious crimes (*crimina notoria*), which formerly were subjected to the punishment of the church, and to punish which was still her right. The things accounted crimes are such as militate against Christian and moral order. There are also enumerated fifteen sorts of church punishments, afterward made the subjects of church legislation; and it was declared that some of them had Christ, others of them had his apostles, the fathers, and the congregation of the faithful, prescribed, and that they ought to be respected as necessary and useful church punishments.

This jurisdiction, it belonged to the priests, the servants of God's word, to use and exercise. But the servant of God's word, *be he who he may*, has no godly right or license to use, as the expression is, both swords; for the Scripture speaks clearly to the contrary. But where some bishops and men of the church have worldly right and authority, there have they them as a donation, gift, and grant, given and granted by human authority and permission.

The ordinantia thus puts aside all the claims of the popish hierarchy. But it does not define the limits of the rights of the prince within the church. In respect only to the election of a bishop, it settles this right according to the church ordinance of the year 1571. The chapter was to announce an occurring episcopal vacancy, to the prince, who thereupon should call in the votes of the other bishops, and most influential priests of the diocese, for a successor, according to custom. After these votes were given, the prince ought to investigate which of those voted for was the most fit person, and nominate him, *so that the prince has the chief vote.* For the valid consecration of a bishop, prayer, and the laying on of hands, are declared to be sufficient. It was regarded as proper to use the episcopal bonnet and staff, the mitre, and crosier, which had been customary since the time of Constantine; but they were not essential to the office, or to consecration.

The chapter was to consist of a provost, who was to be the bishop's assistant, a dean, who was to have the oversight of schools, and examine matters relating to the priesthood, and as notary keep the chapter's records; an archdeacon, who was also to be reader of theology and public penitentiary, and besides these, the pastor, schoolmaster, and proctor.

On account of the many and difficult cases which fell to the jurisdiction of the church, and that a good ecclesiastical order as well in doctrine as in church discipline might be kept up, it was proposed to erect in Stockholm an ecclesiastical consistory (*ecclesiasticum consistorium*), which should consist of the bishops, and of " old, godly, learned, and experienced men." They were to meet together twice a year, or oftener if it was necessary, and deliberate, consult, and give their opinions upon the cases respecting doctrine, or other topics laid before them by civilians or ecclesiastics.

The ordinantia expresses also the wish, that there should be appointed, at Stockholm, a reader of theology, as well for the sake of young men who were there in the priesthood, or at court, as of the strangers who understood Latin, but not the language in which divine service was performed in churches.

It concludes with lamenting that cloister edifices were for the most part destroyed. It allows that the cloistral life had occasioned great abuses, but the buildings might have been turned to Christian purposes. The cloisters that still remained, or could be repaired, might be converted into a refuge for priests advanced in years, or decayed, and others who have no appetite for the world; or for aged matrons and young women "who have no desire for marriage or are not adapted to it," who there may live in quiet, and in spiritual exercises. The occupants of cloisters, as well those for men as women, should be obligated to train up fatherless and motherless children, and instruct them in reading, writing, singing, and sewing. These children were to be recommended by the prince. There was to be no lifetime vow. Such cloisters, it is added, would be properly schools, and it would be an honor to the kingdom, if at least one such, with a yearly income, were found in every diocese

We have been prolix in presenting the different points of this ordinantia, because it, more clearly than anything else, exhibits the character and importance of the often misconceived reform which king John III. aimed to introduce into the Swedish church. It opposed itself, on the one hand, to the Roman church, and on the other, not merely to Calvinism, but to what soon after was current as the sole pure Lutheranism. It was now, however, accepted by all the men, who, afterward, for their opposition to this ordinantia and the liturgy, hazarded their office and personal liberty. But it was accepted, not without opposition and many scruples. The transactions, which, for the most part, were held before the king himself, were unusually prolonged. On the 16th of March, it was subscribed by those present.

After it was ready, an opinion upon it was demanded from the readers at the college of Upsala summoned thence to Stockholm. They found the church's recognized doctrine to be in this document, *provided it be rightly understood*, unfalsified, and presented in a clear light. They approved of what was prescribed respecting ceremonies, as far it did not create scandal, and referred, in conclusion, to the further explanation of the bishops and the consent of the estates of the kingdom.

Everything shows that these, and a large number of those present at the proceedings, rather yielded an acceptance and acknowledgment, in order to avert what seemed a danger, than actively promoted the cause. Questions had been mooted on some other points than those comprised in the ordinantia. Two at least of the articles previously exhibited by the archbishop were omitted in the ordinantia, extreme unction, and prayers for the dead at their burial. Anointing at the consecration of bishops had been proposed, but was rejected. Fecht was the active man in carrying through the ordinantia, exercised the greatest influence on the proceedings and decrees, and was arbitrary enough in drawing it up in writing. His signature, in which he promises that nothing shall be added, altered, or taken away in this ordinantia, from the hour it was subscribed, shows the impatient dread lest any zealously urged addition should steal in, lest the terms in which truth was expressed, or the exact limits of concession, should be changed.

After the ordinantia had thus been recognized by most of the bishops, and by the most noted men of the church, and thereby even the ceremonies of the episcopal consecrations were settled, it was resolved that the ordinations of the yet unconsecrated archbishop, and bishops of Linkoping and Westeras, should take place. Bishop Marten had already for many years filled his see. The consecration of Erasmus had been contemplated the previous year, but at the desire of the king had been deferred. Previously to the ordinantia it had been stipulated, that it should be conducted with greater splendor than had of late years been usual. For this consecration, all the bishops and a portion of the priests of Upsala were assembled, in the beginning of the month of July. The king, who was not himself present, to heighten the external splendor of the solemnity sent thither four of the principal men of the kingdom, the lord chief justice Per Brahe, and the senators Hogensk Bjelke, Erik Sparre, and Erik Stenbock, together with his secretary, Fecht.

The impatience which already betrays itself in those who had consented to the ordinantia, was here put to a new trial, when Fecht unexpectedly came forward with a command from the king, that anointing with oil should be used in the consecration of the bishop. This custom, which had been retained in Sweden even after the commencement of the Reformation, and we suppose until ordinaries were put in the place of bishops, was afterward eschewed as papistic, and had, in 1571, been omitted from the church ordinance.

Disturbance and dissatisfaction were now awakened by the bitter experience so constantly repeated in human life, that concessions only provoke new claims. The bishops had entered the same middle passage to the church of Rome with the king himself. A correspondence by letters was carried on between the king and archbishop. The former reminded the latter of his engagement respecting ceremonies, wondered why he disdained the ceremonies which both in the Old and New Testament were used, which had been employed by his predecessor, the old Laurentius Petri, and by which many still living priests had been consecrated to their office. In conclusion, he declared that the archbishop as well as the bishop of Linkoping *must* submit to the anointing, if they would retain their office.

The archbishop appealed to the deliberations before the king at Stockholm in regard to anointing, to the tenor of his pledge, in which the mitre and crosier were mentioned, but not anointing. This custom was in the Roman church attended with more superstition than any other. Apart from all superstition, he could for his part accept it, if the resulting dissatisfaction among the priests did not grow to such a height as to make a separation in the church to be apprehended. The clergy present, chiefly from the diocese of Upsala, declared their disapprobation. Such ceremonies would be agreeable to the partisans of the old church, who said that the old church usages were about to be restored; would be the cause of many defections, and rouse against the clergy the just reproach of levity.

King John, for the first time, exhibits in this matter the obstinacy with which he afterward handled the affairs of the church. We are unacquainted with the progress of the negotiations, but the end was that his will conquered. The archbishop was anointed with oil, at the splendid consecration, which took place on the 14th of July, in the cathedral of Upsala, and at which the dress of the old times, with the mitre and crosier, was borne by all the bishops. He was ordained by the old bishop of Abo, P. Juusten, at whose consecration, by bishop Bothvid of Strängness, these ceremonies were, probably, used. The archbishop afterward consecrated the two bishops.

During the gathering together at Upsala, Fecht was active in recruiting consentents to the ordinantia. He engaged a large number of the clergy to go with him thence to Stockholm, where the subject was again discussed; but these debaters seemed willing to pull with the times, and they were vanquished by a desire to get home, accepting the ordinantia conditionally, with a reserve of further examination some time hence. It was accepted as an exposition of the church ordinance of which we have before spoken. A protestation too was made, that they by no means designed by such acceptance to give room in doctrine, church usage, or any indifferent thing, to the errors contrary to God's word and the faith of the congregation, which the papists and others harbored and entertained. The superstitions, the wrong meanings, *on account of which these ceremonies had been once laid aside*, they hereby had no intention to recognize.

The new regulations were regarded as adopted, in consequence of the subscriptions of the bishops, although they were not sanctioned by a church council. Such a council it was desirable to avoid, in order that increased strength might not be given to the opposition. Hence, there was no effort to circulate the ordinantia by means of the press. It was left to the zeal and good will of the bishops to apply its directions, and by pastoral letters, visitations, and clerical meetings, to carry its various points into practice. It therefore proceeded slowly and uncertainly, and might almost be considered as not issued.

The most energetic among the churchmen for the regeneration it was desired to effect in the church's character and outward order, were the archbishop and bishop Erasmus of Westeras. The latter informs the king, in the spring of 1575, that he had partly introduced, and by degrees would introduce, into his diocese, the order and ceremonies now recognized. His zeal soon began to cool, and in the following year the king complains that this bishop, as well as many others, began to draw back. The energy of the former was more comprehensive, as proceeding from a higher position.

On the first of February, 1576, he issued, in conformity with his promise to promote in academies the study of the church fathers, a well-written programme, in which he expresses himself to the same effect as in the ordinantia respecting the writings of the fathers and the reading of them, and gives it to be understood that an hour every day should be spent in that line of study. He urges all who are in the priesthood to devote their attention to such reading. The same year he put to press a catechism, whose contents may be judged from his general principles. For the solemnity of church music, he directed, by a circular through the archdiocese, that youths should assist in it; and for the musicians a place was to be provided in the choir, or in a part of the church built specially for that purpose.

The determination to circulate the works that breathed the spirit with which it was desired to animate the church, was not without effect. In 1576, for the first time in Sweden, was printed an edition of the celebrated work of Vincentius Lerinensis, who died in the year 450, which by pronouncing that to be Christian truth, which had always, everywhere, and by all, been received as such, proclaimed the very principles which the Swedish church now appeared to adopt. In the following year a translation was made into Swedish of the opinions of G. Cassander, of which we have before spoken.

The king had before this time bestowed his attention on

the re-establishment or rebuilding of the dilapidated cathedrals and other churches in the towns and country, and continued to do so during the whole of his reign. Priests and congregations never in vain for this purpose invoked his helping hand. The cloisteral edifices, and churches also, were an object of his attention. The restoration of Alvastra was already contemplated in 1573, when count Per Brahe was accused of having demolished the buildings there and removed the materials to Wisingsborg.

Duke Charles shared, at least at first, this care of the king for the cloister edifices. In 1574, he called the attention of the king to Warnhem, situated in his dukedom, and to the question of its and its church's restoration. From 1575 the king's care of this matter became still more active. He received this year information that the church of Alvastra was in good preservation, that the cloister-house might be rebuilt, but that the other buildings were more in ruins, and that the park should be enclosed and provided with a keeper. The year after he gives order that the church should be put in complete repair, and divine service be there held. This was at once commenced, at the same time with the restoration of the cloisters of Nadendals, Askaby, Arno, and Stockholm. Of the establishment of cloisters as a proposed object of the ordinantia, we have no information.

The concern previously felt for the king's inclination to popish doctrines, was, by these changes, still more increased. It proved how little participation was to be expected on the part of the people in such a return. It was employed as a fertile accusation against the king, in their plans for setting free the imprisoned king Erik, and elevating him again to the throne. These imputations made no noise till 1574, when the people of Upland showed an inclination to release the unhappy prisoner from the castle of Orby. But they became more rife, when, during the two following years, plots were formed in West Gothland and Smaland by a priest, one Mauritz of Bone, in the diocese of Skara. The movements in behalf of king Erik provoked, on March 10, 1575, from the council and the "bishops and prelates" assembled at Stockholm for setting up the ordinantia, a motion for that prince's death. This death is rendered more melancholy by its connection, at least in point of time, with the changes that were designed for the church's improvement.

The separation within the Swedish church which the archbishop apprehended, began already to be manifested not only in the disinclination to the projects of the king and Fecht, but also in the threatened defection from the new order of things, of the church in the dukedom of Charles. The duke, who, in 1574, became attentive to the direction which the effort to improve the church began to take, or apprized of the purpose of the council of Stockholm in 1575, immediately wrote a letter to the bishop of Strängness, acquainting him with the position which the church of his principality would assume, as far as depended on the duke himself. He reminded the bishop of the character and nature of the church during his father's reign and to this hour, and how he doubted not that Almighty God would henceforward avert all heretical doctrines, "the pope's fables and tricks." He would also admonish the bishop to hold fast to the pure doctrine, which in the time of the duke's father had been generally preached and acknowledged in the kingdom, and also to keep his clergy steadfast in the true confession of faith. As the Swedish church had for the most part conformed to the church of Wittenberg, in harmony with the writings of Luther and Melancthon, so it was advisable she should continue in the same course. The duke, therefore, transmitted to him the confession respecting the Lord's Supper, which the theologians of the dukedom of Saxony had, in 1574, drawn up at Torgau.

The duke appointed the bishop to meet him at Orebro,

while the latter was busy with the transactions at Stockholm. At this meeting Charles expressly declared, what he soon after, Feb. 19, repeated in a letter to the bishop, that he designed on his part "to make no new unnecessary changes in religion whatever, whether in points of moment or in ceremonies, for this could not be done without danger and scandal to many men. * * * And you may," concludes the duke, "communicate these our views to whom you please, for so we are persuaded."

Bishop Nils, who was now placed between two fires, but, as is shown by his subsequent course, more inclined to John's than Charles's views, took part in the council of Stockholm, in the spring of 1575, and subscribed and recognized the ordinantia. When the question arose of its introduction into the diocese of Strängness, the duke professed that he feared that this church ordinance, although seeming to have a good sense, would not bear good fruit, but would produce, by the change in public worship, scandal among the people. His opinion, therefore, was, that it ought not precipitately to be introduced into the churches. In his cathedral of Strängness, the bishop could introduce such ceremonies as he pleased, or as were usual in other cathedrals. "Nothing, however, might be allowed in ceremonies, which has any savor of popery, even if a specious pretext might be offered for the same."

Upon this very point, in the following years, were opinions divided, whether the projected changes had a savor of popery, or of the Christian church, which Lutheran protestantism, turning to the purer times of the church, considered to be its own type. When the reform in Sweden, by the publication of the new liturgy, proceeded a step further, a large part of the clergy and men of the church found themselves compelled to draw back, and the dreaded separation occurred.

CHAPTER IV.

THE LITURGY.

THE principal object of the change king John and Fecht wished to effect in the church was the divine service, and especially the mode of celebrating the Lord's Supper. It seemed to them, that by the Reformation the reverence for the most holy thing in the worship of Christianity had either disappeared, or been diminished. It had disappeared in Calvinism, which denied the real presence of the body and blood of Christ in the Lord's Supper, a denial which too often coincided with a scorn of the pious worship of the papist. This reverence again seemed diminished even in the Lutheran church, which, till now, had been unable by convincing proofs to secure its confession against the assaults of Calvinism, and had become too much infected with a slight regard for the sacrament. The service of the mass by Olaus Petri, which, till now, was used in the Swedish church, appeared too meagre and cold, and moved neither priest nor layman to a deeper piety.

Subsequently to the few changes which were proposed by king John and Fecht, and which passed at the council of Stockholm, in 1574, and subsequently to the short visit of Warsewitz, which gave clearness to the views of these men, they began at the same time with the plan of the ordinantia, which was adopted the following year, to work upon a new order for the mass in the church of Sweden.

The fruit of this labor was the traduced liturgy, or the

red book, as it was wont to be called, from the color of the binding of the printed volume. They had collated with it many liturgies, which were respectable for their antiquity, or, at least, laid claim to such respect. They based their own upon the Roman missal, but examined and altered this, according to the principles which before the liturgy was completed, were publicly, in 1575, set forth in the ordinantia. The first difference it at once betrays from the mass of Olaus Petri, is, that the title is given only in Latin, the preface in Latin, the liturgy itself not merely in Swedish, but also in Latin, while all the directions for the priests, with the marginal remarks and notes, are only in Latin.

The Swedish mass of Olaus Petri, on the one hand, in the length of the service, and in many particulars as to the contents, resembled the Roman mass, although from the former was rejected whatever in the latter militated against God's word in Scripture, together with superfluous prayers and practices. John III.'s liturgy, on the other hand, did not want all similitude to the mass hitherto customary in the Swedish church. But, while from this it retained the exhortation and confession at the beginning of divine service, and the preface for the mass of the Lord's Supper, there was added a declaration, that the former might be sometimes used, the latter when deemed useful and necessary.* Upon the contrary, the liturgy took many, or properly speaking, all the parts of the Roman mass, but omitted the crossings, bowings, and altar kissings, and changed its offensive expressions. It retained also the prayers and psalms, which the Roman mass prescribes to the priest when putting on the mass-dress and washing his hands.

It may be proper to present some points of comparison, which were most commented on during the succeeding con-

* In the notes the words of institution were quoted from six different liturgies, from the so-called apostolic, St. James's, that of Basil, Chrysostom, Ambrose, and Gregory the Great or the Roman.

troversies. The Roman mass has the words, "We beseech thee * * * that thou wouldst accept and bless these gifts, these things presented, these holy and pure offerings, especially those which we present before thee for thy holy universal church,* which thou vouchsafest to deliver, to protect, * * * and with thy servant our pope, and our spiritual rulers [their names are recited], as well as all the faithful in Christ." The Swedish liturgy has, "We beseech thee * * * that thou wouldest accept and graciously hear our prayers which we present before thee for thy holy universal Christian church, which thou vouchsafest to deliver, to protect, * * * and with all princes, spiritual and temporal, of whatsoever dignity, rank, and name they be, as well as all the faithful in Christ." Instead of the remaining prayers (*memento*), and remembrance of the saints, in the Roman mass, the liturgy has a prayer, that the bread and wine might, "by righteous use," become to us the body and blood of Christ. The most offensive passage was the following: "Thy same Son, the same offering, which is a pure, holy, and undefiled offering, for our expiation, shield, screen, and shelter from thy wrath, from the terrors of sin and death, presented for us, we embrace and receive with faith, and with our humble prayers *present* before thy glorious Majesty." The order of the prayers and actions were sometimes transposed. The words of holy Scripture are quoted in the Latin, from the so-called Vulgate version, but are altered in some places according to the original text. The words of the Swedish Bible are in correspondence, and independent of the translation made in the year 1541. The annotations partly explain the expressions that occur, or refute erroneous meanings.

That which is not the least remarkable in the liturgy, is the preface given by the archbishop, which contains a strong

* "Catholic." This word John's liturgy translates into "Universal."

censure of the preceding times. Mankind, he says, are tossed between two extremes, superstition and irreverence. Our predecessors had to contend against superstition; but it was to be feared they had gone too far, and thereby left their flocks a prey to the too cruel wild beasts of irreverence and unbelief. They had thoughtlessly loosened the bonds of order and church discipline, and opened a door to dissoluteness, against which the battle was now to be waged. There need be no fear, that by restoring exercises of piety and useful regulations, the people would again fall into superstition. Piety should not merely be found in the heart, but manifest itself in the life of the whole man, in the speech and behavior. In order that beginning with the priests, especially in the administration of the Lord's Supper, these acts of piety might be restored, since by neglect of them piety itself had greatly decayed, a more spiritual order for the mass had been re-established; and this attempt to resist the contagion of a contempt of holy things, which the sacramentarians were spreading, ought to be thankfully welcomed.

From the spring of 1576, the liturgy having been printed, began to be circulated throughout the land. It was published in the name of the archbishop, who, however, had taken no part in its composition. It was the work of Fecht and the king. That Herbst lent his assistance, is a supposition that wholly wants proof. He was thought to have more of the king's confidence than he really possessed. Equally groundless is the supposition that the Jesuits either wrote or were concerned in its preparation. No Jesuit was in the land when this liturgy was compiled. But the preface seems, for good reasons, to have been written rather by the archbishop than any one else. It was at the close of the year 1576, that this preface was added. Laurentius Petri showed a compliance which the promoters of the liturgy too well understood how to use, and which he soon had cause bitterly to repent. This easiness had its basis in a congruity of views, but he went beyond the limits of what a man is required to do for his friends, when he was ready, more than once, to lend his name and the influence of his office to the writings laid before him for subscription. The first promulgation of the liturgy was not followed by any command that it should be used. It was expected that this would by degrees take place through the bishops, in their dioceses, and that they would make it known by formally bringing it into use in the congregations; an acquiescence in it was also sought by separate negotiations. The issue of these attempts would certainly have deterred any less capricious man than king John, or one less persuaded of the truth and righteousness of his cause.

In the month of March, 1576, it was brought to duke Charles by Goran Gera, Erik Sparre, and secretary Henrik Mattsson, who for divers purposes were sent to Nykoping, from the king. He requested that the liturgy should be used in the dukedom, as in the rest of the kingdom. The duke answered evasively, and half reproachfully, "What the new church customs require he could not so quickly and easily conform to, calling to remembrance that he, and his brothers and sisters, had been solemnly counselled and admonished, in their father's will, to beware of human devices and double doctrines."

Continued negotiations, during the summer and autumn, could not win from the duke a more favorable answer. The duke, and the clergy of his dukedom, forthwith took a position from which they could neither be allured nor driven. Mindful of his rights, he previously caused extracts to be collected from the records, on which he grounded his claim to spiritual and temporal jurisdiction within his duchy. He finally assembled, at Nykoping, the representatives of his dukedom, who, on September 26, 1576, pledged themselves to steadfastly protect the true faith and doctrine, and not to accept other ceremonies than those, which from the time of king Gustavus to the present, were in Christian use. No express mention was made of the ordinantia or liturgy; but the reception that these, and especially the latter, had to expect in the diocese, was plainly signified.

Within the dukedom, disposition was already apparent still further to lessen and remove all novelties. We have before noticed in what manner even bishop Erasmus, of Westeras, began to look about him. But the signs of a more active opposition commenced at Stockholm, from its pastor master Olof, and its schoolmaster master Abraham. Although the priests of that city subscribed the ordinantia of 1575, they yet refused to execute its prescriptions, as soon as it was manifest by the liturgy into what measures they might be led, if they went forward in the path they had begun to take. They refused to celebrate the festival of Corpus Christi, which occurred in June, and was prescribed in the ordinantia, but might reasonably give birth to their hesitancy, from its near connection, in the Roman church, with the doctrine of transubstantiation. When, in autumn, the festival of the Virgin Mary, September 8, was approaching, they refused to celebrate it, and expressly declared their purpose not to acknowledge the liturgy, the commencement of whose use, at Stockholm, was appointed for that day. This open repugnance was more than king John could bear, especially as it might become a dangerous example, from the respect entertained for the men who thus opposed the new order of things.

On the 7th of September, the day before the festival of the birth of the Virgin Mary, the two chaplains, Erik Petri, and Petrns Erici, together with master Olof, and master Abraham, were, as repugnants, deprived of their office and kept prisoners in their houses. The king accused them, not only of disregard of the church ordinance, but of disobedience to the command of the temporal prince.

When the noise of the increasing storm began to wax

louder, Fecht left the country, but introduced another man, who exerted no inconsiderable influence on succeeding transactions.

King John had at last overcome his repugnance to enter into open correspondence with Rome, and determined to send Pontus de la Gardie, and Fecht, into Italy. The avowed reason for their journey was to obtain Gregory XIII.'s support in persuading the emperor to enter into a confederacy against Russia, and if necessary, against Denmark. The embassy was also to receive from Spain the maternal inheritance of the Swedish queen, and for that purpose to negotiate at Naples with the Spanish vice-king, Ignatius Mendoza. The secret commission was to enter into a negotiation with Rome respecting a church union, which John proposed on the conditions he soon after again set forth. The king seems now, especially, to have laid great weight on obtaining bishops that were not sundered from the unity of the church. We can, from the king's and Fecht's stand-point, very easily comprehend their scruples on the validity and efficacy of an episcopate severed from the church's outward unity, and their wish to remove those scruples by a new inoculation of bishops from Rome, of whose bishop they thus acknowledge the rights of a patriarch over the Swedish church. But the king did not venture, and, indeed, did not wish to allow such bishops to be nominated abroad, or that foreigners should fill the office, or even that the consecration should be performed by Roman catholics. He therefore requested of the pope to permit him to nominate them himself, and to allow them to be consecrated in Sweden by some man previously ordained for that purpose. Fecht was the man selected to be consecrated at Rome, and afterward to propagate a purer episcopacy in his fatherland.

This project sufficiently shows how little the king and Fecht understood the Roman church, and as little the decided direction in which, after the council of Trent, it resolved to renew its youth. The judgment of this church, on the whole reform of king John, was based on Possevin's judgment of Fecht, to whose efforts he found three reasons to object. The first was, that though Fecht had some inclination for catholic truth, he wanted the necessary training for the cause he had taken in hand. He had, therefore, compounded a sort of "mixed theology," without distinguishing times and circumstances, when some things, such as the reception of the Eucharist in both kinds, and the marriage of priests, may be tolerated, allowed, or enjoined, according as the church has occasion *to declare the sense of the Holy Ghost.* The second objection was, that although Fecht perceived, and even told the king that the composing of mass books and the like belonged not to laymen, yet he, himself, was concerned in what he disapproved. The third objection was, that although married, he hoped to hold from the pope the office of priest and bishop, without violating the required vow of chastity.

Although Fecht came to Rome, he was not able to gain the object for which he came. Perhaps he would not have remained in his former stand-point without either becoming wholly converted to Rome, or by this nearness to the focus of papacy recoiling to protestantism. Perhaps, had he returned to Sweden, he would have entered more deeply into the interests of his king, his fatherland, and its church.

A higher power had otherwise ordained. The vessel which, in November of 1576, was to have carried him and De la Gardie to Germany, was wrecked near Bornholm. De la Gardie was saved, and pursued his journey to Rome. Fecht, who depended on his skill in swimming, cast himself into the water to swim to land, and perished in the waves. His body was found, and buried at Bornholm.

King John was probably the only person who experienced a great loss in this unexpected death of his faithful friend, just when he was about to finish the full arrangement of their plans. Few, or none of his party appear fully to have comprehended them, and both protestants and papists saw in his removal by death the righteous judgment of God; the former, for what they termed his defection; the latter, for his presumption in being willing to advise in the affairs of the church.

But when Fecht for the last time left Sweden, he had introduced to the king's favor a man, who for a time possessed his confidence, and no doubt had great influence in promoting the plans and views for which Fecht took his journey. This man was the Jesuit Laurentius Nicolai, born in Norway, won to the Roman church during his travels, and made a Jesuit at Louvain. He came to Stockholm in April, 1576, concealed his real belief, which was not suspected by the Norwegians, and won, by his learning and insinuating manners, the confidence of even the clergy of Stockholm.

The wish expressed in the ordinantia, that a reader of theology might be established in Stockholm, had not yet been accomplished. It was, however, in contemplation; and previously to the coming of Laurentius it had been resolved to set up a literary institution in the former convent of grey-friars, now called the holme of the knights. In Laurentius, who was well versed in the language of the country, a suitable man was thought to be found for a teacher, and he was accordingly appointed to the post. The new institution was opened in August, 1576, under the usual name of a college. From his domicil and activity, Laurentius acquired the well known name of Klosterlasse, or the man loaded with a cloister.

The disguise under which he appeared, allowed him to enter into the king's and Fecht's views of catholicism, in which they flattered themselves that they were joined by the men of the Roman church, but in which these latter saw only the beginning of a complete conversion. It was natural that he, as long as the mask was not removed, should be a zealous advocate of the liturgy, especially as this was a means of getting rid of the very dangerous opponents of his schemes, master Olof and master Abraham, the pastor and schoolmaster at Stockholm, who already began to penetrate his real character. He must therefore rise in the king's favor, in proportion as it was lost by those men.

The imprisoned priests of Stockholm were not subdued. When the question of the liturgy came up, they and the two chaplains produced a declaration of principles, which opened a challenge of war against the liturgy; the firstling of a great host of controversial writings, which on that subject marched forward from that hour till the close of the contest. They presented, with firmness, dignity, and vigor, their objections, for the most part the same as those afterward urged. Their reasons for refusing to accept the liturgy were as follows:

As no just complaint could be brought against the order of the mass hitherto used in Sweden, there was no reason for a change, especially as a change would be attended with scandal, which God's word forbids us to provoke. Their forefathers had, at Upsala, in 1549, upon the question of the Interim, for themselves and their successors, promised to abide by the doctrine and usages of the evangelical church. To this, the reverence due their forefathers obliged their posterity to adhere. The ceremonies which it was now desired to append to those hitherto customary, changed the Lord's Supper into a sacrifice. By this means, the papal doctrine was encouraged, and men were drawn into the same yoke with those who held false opinions. The sacrifice of the mass thus became accepted, and there seemed an express avowal of the papal errors, as there was also a prayer for the pope, under a shadowy disguise. The liturgy laid great stress upon the dress and attire of the priest, as if there was in them some special sanctity; made the sacrament dependent on the piety and prayers of the priest, and enjoined canonical times and fasts, as if they were commanded by God.

They meant not, by their refusal to acknowledge the liturgy, to deny the obedience and duty they owed their lawful prince. They had every reverence for the king when he commanded what concerned the peace of the true church, and the maintenance of good order. But, as the liturgy disquieted God's congregation, and called down God's wrath, by the recognition of false doctrines, they prayed God to change the king's mind, so that he might not wish to command the observance of this order of the mass in his kingdom.

This opposition was regarded as the individual conviction of these men, and to be vanquished. The king resolved merely to remove them from Stockholm, but to situations, the taking of which could not be considered as a detriment. Master Olof was nominated to be provost of Upsala, master Abraham was offered the professorship in that city, and when he declined, it was proposed to make him pastor of Oregrund. But, as he was reluctant to supersede the then incumbent, he was appointed preacher at Oregrund, with the perquisites and pay of the schoolmaster, the duties of which he performed. They were both obliged, before leaving Stockholm, which they did in July, 1576, to pledge themselves not to dissuade those who were willing to accept the liturgy, but to attend solely to the duties of their vocation. The archbishop was enjoined to watch their conduct.

Of the two chaplains, the one, Petrus Erici, took refuge with duke Charles; the first of the opposers of the liturgy who was received in the dukedom of Charles, and exercised his office there. The other, in respect to his great age, was allowed to remain at Stockholm, and did duty for a time in master Abraham's school, in which, however, instruction was chiefly carried on by Klosterlasse, and his companion to Sweden, the popish priest Florentius Feyt, until the latter, in the year following, left the land.

The king called the provost Salomo Birgeri from Westeras to Stockholm, to manage the office which master Olof had left, until a successor could be procured. Birgeri, after manifesting a dislike, at first, of the liturgy, suffered himself to be persuaded into its acceptance.

A more general dissatisfaction with the liturgy began to spread wherever it became known; and it is worthy of remark, that as its chief opposers among the priests and theologians were natives of Norrland, so, too, we have evidence that the discontent among the people was greatest in that part of the kingdom. Many in Norrland, says the king, in December, 1576, had put a wrong construction upon the liturgy. He was, therefore, minded to have a translation made of its preface into Swedish, and sent to the provosts of that region.

The disturbances began to be more active in the city, which was considered the chief seat of the Swedish church, and the second capital of the kingdom. Master Olof had received at Upsala an honorable office, but his removal was looked upon as a persecution of the truth, and the professors at Upsala, especially Petrus Jonæ, and Olof Luth, participated in his and master Abraham's indignant sense of their treatment. Olof Luth was of a quiet and peaceable temperament, but Petrus was more impetuous, was a man of great learning, of inflexible and undaunted resolution, and deeply attached to Lutheranism.

Immediately after the coming of master Olof from Stockholm to Upsala, the archbishop performed, on the morning of Christmas day, the service in Latin, according to the new liturgy, in the cathedral of Upsala. Under the impulse of his first astonishment at this novelty, Petrus Jonæ preached the day after, or during Christmas-tide, in the cathedral, a sermon on the persecution of pious teachers. The fourth day after Christmas, the provost, master Olof, preached on the murder of the babes of Bethlehem, and the cruelty of tyrants. Perhaps these sermons did not contain an express reference to the character of the times, but the novelty of this mass, which was disliked as popish, and the persecution of the priests of Stockholm, gave them a meaning which was of no advantage to the archbishop. Provoked, he immediately summoned both these men before him, and forbade them the exercise of the priesthood. He himself preached on the following Sunday, justifying himself from the charge of heresy, and inveighing with great warmth against both the preceding preachers.

As soon as information of these disturbances reached the ears of the king, Petrus Jonæ and Olof Luth, the latter of whom declared himself against the liturgy, were summoned to Stockholm, where, on January 10, 1577, they made their appearance. On the following day, a disputation was held between them and Klosterlasse and Feyt, on the regard due to the Holy Scriptures, and the interpretation of them. On the 14th of January there was a meeting at the house of count Per Brahe, and under his presidentship, in the presence of the king's secretary and court preacher, with many others. The chief subject of controversy was now on the sacrifice of the mass. Klosterlasse drew his proofs from the testimony of the church and the writings of the fathers; but, as the reporters say, went no farther than to maintain that the mass of the holy communion was an offering of praise and thanksgiving. Upon the contrary, when questioned as to his own meaning, he declared that the sacrifice was that which the priest with his hands offered up and presented before God. The Upsalians, who excused themselves as not having paid sufficient attention to the contents of the liturgy, requested and obtained eight days' indulgence, in order to present their opinions in writing.

Their written reflections, disapproving the liturgy, were delivered in upon the 22d of January, and after that day fruitless negotiations were carried on with them.

The next fruit of the disputation at the house of Per Brahe was, that the provost, Salomo Birgeri, newly called to serve in Stockholm, went over to the side of the opposers of the liturgy. It had anew stirred up controversies and doubts, and he accused himself of dissimulation, which never gave peace to his soul, after he declared himself for the liturgy. When, soon after, he performed the liturgic mass in church, he fancied, in a vision, that he saw a burning flame on the altar, and in the flame many whom he knew as dissemblers. Struck with terror, he was compelled to break off the service, went weeping home to the house of his brother-in-law, where he abode, and sent a message to the king with a renunciation of his office.*

The king had determined to call together the bishops and clergy for a public recognition of the liturgy. The priests of Stockholm had not appealed to a church council. But meanwhile, before this was done, the king negotiated with the clergy and people by persons sent into various parts of the land, probably to prepare business for the approaching diet, in addition to what was to be brought before the church council. With bishop Sven of Skara, and the clergy of his diocese, Erik Gyllenstjerna negotiated, and they promised to accept the liturgy. Agents were sent to Helsingland and Dalecarlia, and the archbishop, and bishop Erasmus, were to attend the fair at Enkoping. The archbishop was directed to treat not only with the senators of the kingdom, but with the people, at the fair of Upsala. At the same time the provost Olof was banished from

* On a certain occasion, after he was won to the liturgy, he stepped forward to the altar, when the bishop sent him the liturgy with a request that he would follow it in the service. The provost took the book, but immediately cast it from him, in the sight of the congregation, down into the body of the church.

Upsala to a property he had on the coast, and the preacher at Oregrund, master Abraham, was put in ward at Rydboholm, an estate of Per Brahe.

There came to the king, or, perhaps, were procured by these agents, written complaints from city and country congregations respecting the immoral lives of their priests, and written petitions for a change in divine service and church customs. If not now first presented, a use was now made of them. At the time for opening the council, Olof and Abraham were recalled to Stockholm. But when they and the three others persisted in their refusal to acknowledge the liturgy, they were all put under ward, Olof, Abraham, and Salomo, at the king's farm in Sodertorn, the Upsalians at Svartsjo.

The estates were, on February 8th, called together. The king opened the diet three days after. After speaking of the condition of the kingdom and the prospects of peace and quiet, he turned to the affairs of the church. He drew a dark picture of its condition, or rather of that of the clergy; a picture which awakens a double interest, if compared with that which fifty years earlier his father gave of the same subject. John complained that the priests neither in knowledge nor life rightly corresponded to their holy vocation. They allowed the churches to tumble down, and especially he complained that they treated the Lord's Supper in an unworthy manner, attending it with unwashed hands, in dirty clothes, and often in riding-slippers and spurs. Not seldom they administered the holy repast from trenchers and from cups of tin or clay, while to entertain guests in their own houses they used silver goblets. One or another introduced new practices according to his own whim. The king, therefore, alike from his own impulse, as from the written petitions of many of his subjects, and with the aid of the archbishop and bishop of Westeras, had drawn up an order for divine service and for the worthy administration of the sacrament, in order that priests might guide their hearers to the true fruits of godliness. They ought not to give credit to the false report which was circulated, that the king wished to introduce heresy and unsound doctrine, wished to restore divine service in Latin, wished to separate priests from their wives, and that he had invited into the kingdom monks by thousands.

The king then asked the estates if they would accept the published liturgy. They who gave an answer, answered yes.

It seems the clergy were not present on this occasion. But, however that was, their consent was considered as not having been given with the other estates. On the following day was opened the church council, if one may call it so, under the king's own presidency. He ordered the votes to be immediately collected. Those in favor of the liturgy were to take the right hand, the others the left. On the right hand they gathered about the archbishop. On the left, the less number joined bishop Martinus Gestricius of Linkoping, who now took the leadership of those opposed to the liturgy.

The king and Klosterlasse now endeavored to persuade the dissentients. The liturgy was surely not contrary to God's word, and corresponded with the usages of the primitive church, excited the mind to piety, and promoted outward decency in divine worship. The archbishop, to whom, as head of the church, the rest owed obedience, was in favor of it. It was acknowledged by the other bishops, and was used in many places. The senators of the kingdom and estates had also, on their part, accepted it.

The king caused the above-mentioned written complaints and petitions to be read, and said that the peasants threatened that they would not pay tithes to their priests, if the latter did not accept the liturgy. For his own part, he would abide by it, and he who, by his opposition, awaked dissatisfaction and disturbance in the land, should answer for the offence before him and the council of the kingdom.

A disputation was carried on between the archbishop and bishop Marten, in presence of the king, who himself went into an explanation of the meaning and design of the liturgy. When the day appointed for a meeting of the clergy in the castle of Stockholm had arrived, bishop Marten stood alone. Those who shared his opinions had deserted him. The day passed in fruitless negotiations.

Bishop Marten was a man whose reputation for learning and an uncorrupted mind gave his judgment the greatest weight. His observations upon the liturgy made a deep impression upon the assembly, although during the disputation there was none who ventured to stand up by his side. All, or many, admitted that he was right. In the confirmation, therefore, of the liturgy which was subscribed, a declaration was added, which referred to the very observations he had presented.

The explanation which the king gave of the liturgy was found to have a soothing effect, and was taken down in writing by the archbishop, after which, translated into Swedish, in a fuller form, it was, February 16, 1577, accepted and subscribed. The liturgy composed by the archbishop, it says, had been critically examined, and that liturgy, *according to the declaration now made and soon to follow*, being found to be in agreement with God's word and the Holy Scripture, promotive of godliness and reverence for the Lord's Supper, was welcomed and accepted. "Be it, however, understood, that it must be rightly and not wrongly sensed and interpreted." There were also appended observations upon the cloths for the service of the mass, upon the accompanying prayers and supplications before and after the consecration of the sacrament, upon the true meaning of consecration, and upon the expression presenting God's Son and his merits. It was also added, that they coincided with the doctrine which the "catholic church" had always from the apostles' time embraced, shunning the rocks alike of superstition and irreverence. They, therefore, humbly prayed that all, "both in and out of the kingdom," would interpret their meaning for the best. They had, according to the king's pleasure, and that of the council of the kingdom, of the nobles, burghers, and peasants, consented and resolved to hold fast to, introduce, and afterward follow, the ceremonies of this order of public worship. The resolution was subscribed by the bishops and ninety-six priests.

There is no need to weigh in the balance of a rigid criticism the expressions used by the clergy in their resolutions of February 16, 1577, in order to discover that men do not speak thus, who with a free conviction pledge themselves to that to which they subscribed their names, and with such terms of consent, are not contented where their hearts approve. It was one of those thousand cases recorded in history, of an attempt at adjustment, when parties who are really opposed to each other meet in a territory which unwise mediators call that of peace and moderation, but which is for both parties, or one of them, a territory of lying and dissimulation. They meet for an hour, but are soon sundered, with increased bitterness, still farther from each other.

It required the capricious blindness of king John to believe, that he could build the concord of the church on this sandy foundation. But he foresaw that disturbances would be excited by the proposed changes. As just at this period he allowed his unhappy brother Erik to suffer, on February 26, the violent death to which he had been for some time adjudged, it is not improbable that the design of preventing dissatisfaction with the changes in the church from being used as a pretext for political plots, may have contributed to this sad event.

Negotiations in the council proceeded till almost the close of the month, partly to induce the opponents to give way, or the hesitating to take a firm position, partly by conferences and explanations to influence the clergy in favor of the principles which it was desired should be ingrafted into the church.

As soon as the liturgy was accepted, the prisoners that were in ward at Svartsjo and Haringe, were restored to Stockholm, in the hope that the explanations given and the example of numbers might induce them to yield. But the efforts of the archbishop and even the king proved fruitless. Both the professors of Upsala obtained leave to return home, but it seems that at first they were forbidden to lecture. Master Abraham was transferred to the pastorship of Saltvik in Aland, where it was believed he would be prevented from exerting any influence upon the clergy and theologians. Master Olof was permitted to settle on his estate at Roslagen, with the grant of a yearly stipend. Master Salomo was for some time kept prisoner at Wentholmen, but was subsequently released and allowed to return to Westeras, where, in 1585, he met the summons of death.

With what other business the council was occupied, appears from the questions which the king, on the 23d of February, laid before the bishops, respecting the Holy Scriptures, the church's authority, the value of her judgment in the interpretation of Scripture, and the testimony of the catholic church and the fathers. Their answers may be conjectured from what has been already narrated. They modified and explained, with the usual caution, that what they said was not to be received in a wrong sense. A more candid and explicit answer was given from his prison, by provost Salomo Bergeri. He notices the mistrust which any constraint must create against the liturgy; refers to the oft-repeated complaint that there was a design to coerce priests by means of the obedience claimed for bishops, and avows that he acknowledged no other spiritual prince in the congregation of Christ, who had a right to rule our faith, than Jesus Christ alone.

The bishops left Stockholm on the 27th of February, each for his own diocese, to promote, or to waive compliance with the new arrangements. The archbishop endeavored, in his diocese of Upsala, to prevail on the clergy to introduce the liturgy. The priests, however, were slow in obeying his command. He, therefore, on the 20th of April, issued a cogent letter, in which he complains that a large number of them avoided the use of the liturgy, although its difference from the former order of the mass was satisfactorily explained. He would not tolerate disobedience in matters of religion. The pastor, therefore, who would not, before the feast of St. Erik, the 18th of May, accept the liturgy, must present himself at Upsala, and resign his benefice.

Even this vigorous proceeding could not fully answer his purpose. At a meeting of the clergy, in Upsala, in July, the subject of the liturgy was again canvassed, and the option of being deposed, or of acceptance, was laid before them anew. Two of those present, stood up, and declared that they could not, against their conscience, acquiesce in this order of the mass. They were immediately deprived of their benefices, which were at once bestowed upon others. The peaceable Olof Luth, who respectfully begged the archbishop to act with more lenity, was ejected from the meeting.

The bishop of the diocese of Skara was, together with his clergy, in favor of the liturgy. The bishop of Westeras did not actually oppose it, although his zeal for the changes seems to have come to a sudden stop. Of what was done for the liturgy in Finland, which contained the diocese of Abo, we have no information. In the diocese of Wexio, of which its former superintendent, Andreas Bjornram, was, in 1577, appointed bishop, and whose priests were not summoned to the council, because the king wished to spare the pockets of those who lived so remote, the liturgy was, at the king's command, made public, and by the clergy was accepted.

Only in the dioceses of Linkoping and Strängness, the cause encountered great difficulties, especially on the part of the pastors of the parishes. Bishop Marten, after his return home, did nothing to promote the acceptance of the liturgy, but with his chapter set forth a manifesto, in which was to be found no command or obligation for its diffusion. This tergiversation was reported to the king by Hogensk Bjelke, the prefect of Eastgothland, to whom the bishop assigns as a reason, that he could not persuade the clergy to accept the liturgy before the explanation came out, which the archbishop had undertaken to publish. How far this was justified by the convocation which, on the 3d of May, was held at Linkoping, is unknown to us. The bishop seems to have thus, in a considerable degree, declined compliance with the requirements of the king; either because he could not persuade himself of the compatibility of the liturgy with protestant truth, or as his enemies supposed, consideration for his wife and ten children quieted the claims of conscience.

During the session of the council of Stockholm, bishop Nils, of Strängness, who was there present, sent a message to his prince, duke Charles, to inquire what he thought of the new mass service. The duke answered, that he wist not of any other church service or mass service than that which had been a long time used in the land, and that he could not be "desirous of accepting a new one, under whatsoever fair pretext offered, until it had been reasonably proved that the old was wrong, and unjustifiably adopted." He therefore bid the bishop to take heed, and at the same time sending a copy of it, reminded him of the resolution passed by the clergy of the dukedom. The 16th of February is the date of the duke's letter, on the same day the liturgy was subscribed by bishop Nils, but with a reserve very wide of his uncertain pledge.

Within the dukedom, nothing was done toward the recognition of the liturgy. The attitude, however, of this diocese, was less offensive than defensive, as long as bishop Nils was its leader.

Duke Charles was as immovable in his determination as king John in his, and when, in August, 1577, he was about to undertake a foreign journey, he advised his still unmarried sister, Elizabeth, to hold fast to the doctrine which in their father's time had been acknowledged. During this journey, he reminded the bishop, more than once, not to allow any change to be introduced into divine service while he was absent. He recalled the students belonging to the diocese of Strängness, from Upsala, as they could "there," he said, "gain no further improvement." He would place them as assistants in the schools of the diocese until he could, the following spring, find them an opportunity for pursuing their studies in foreign institutions of learning. Duke Charles stood forth as the prop of the opposers of the liturgy, and began, as before remarked, to open, in 1576, a refuge within the dukedom for those priests and teachers who had lost their places. This, however, was done with great caution, as the king's loudly expressed discontent with his brother's measures, had not yet reached that brother's ears.

In the measures and steps taken, the king was supported by many of the council of the kingdom, and by his secretaries. Among his supporters, the principal names in the controversies of the church were those of John Henriksson, Henrik Mattson Huggut, and Olof Sverkersson Elfkarl, of whom the last named, at least, had studied at Rostock. In the execution of their master's pleasure these men did not always ask themselves what a king's dignity and clemency required. The king labored for the spread of the liturgy, and the maintenance of church discipline, and often himself drew up rules for the ecclesiastical punishments to be inflicted on offenders, and for the external sanctity and dignity of divine worship.

Much attention began to be paid, in 1577, after the liturgy had been accepted, to the books coming from abroad; a subject to which reference had been made in the ordinantia. The king's officers, in all the maritime towns, were notified that as errors were here spread, especially from Germany, imported books were not to be sold until a catalogue of them was sent to the king, who would, with the bishops, decide whether they might be sold or not. When a catalogue from Eastgothland contained the names of some unknown books, the king ordered that the books should be sent to Stockholm; and when a bookseller of Stockholm imported not the books for which he had got an order, but others injurious to God, and not conformable "to the writings of the fathers of holy church," the king doomed him to be deprived of the whole stock.

Most of the bishops had declared in favor of the liturgy; but their zeal was not ardent for its introduction, as they either winked at disobedience, or allowed the priests to use merely a part of the liturgy, with an alteration of the passages which the performer of the service considered most scandalous. Thus it cannot be said to have been at any time generally and fully in use.

The chief assistant of the king in his plans, though with wider aims, was Klosterlasse, whose mask began to fall off quite rapidly, until at length he stood forth an uncovered Jesuit and papist. The leaning which the king showed to the side of Rome, allowed this man to keep his disguise, and venture a long time. On the 6th of October, 1577, being the eighteenth Sunday after Trinity, he preached in the cloister church of the grey monk's holm, on the gospel for the day. Among the Pharisees, he counted those who believe themselves to have the Holy Ghost more than others, and in this persuasion interpret Scripture, such as Melancthon, Luther, Brentius, and others of a kindred faith. Soon after, he was present at Upsala, when the king deposited the bones of St. Erik in the silver chest in which they are still preserved, and allowed it to be borne from the castle of Upsala to the cathedral, by Roman priests, and placed in its present position on the high altar. On this occasion, being All Saints' day, Klosterlasse preached on the invocation of the saints and prayers to them, and gave great offence to his hearers. Petrus Jonæ, Olof Luth, Henrik Gadolenus, pastor Joachim, and the schoolmaster at Upsala, Olaus Andreæ, were commanded by the king to express in writing their opinions of this sermon. They, therefore, drew up and submitted a paper against the invocation of saints, which inflamed the king's wrath against these men, of whom the first named was suspended from the exercise of his office, and lost his benefice.

The coming of the Jesuit Possevin to Stockholm, at the close of 1577, contributed to increase the discontent, so that the king was induced, the following year, publicly to contradict the reports spread through the land respecting imputed changes of doctrine. The king justifies himself, by the consent of the bishops and priests to the changes that had been made. They had, without constraint, acquiesced in these changes, and promised to abide by them. This was at a time when the king was most zealously pressed by the missionaries of Rome, and furnishes a remarkable comparison with the position of his father when he was pressed by the friends of the Reformation.

Klosterlasse and Possevin hastened the breach by the imprudence with which they acted. The archbishop, Laurentius Petri, who, even before the council of Stockholm, was charged with having said that the new mass service was forced upon him, began to be concerned for the consequences of his own conceptions, which brought him into a nearer connection with and dependence on the papists than he himself either wished or expected. He refused, even before the king himself, to promote any further the liturgical cause, and declared that it could not proceed without danger of bloodshed. An occurrence which created general scandal, induced him afterward altogether to break with Klosterlasse, and more closely to examine into his own position in the controversies of the church. The result of his inquiry was an explanation of the principles of the ordinantia and liturgy, which, in 1578, he published to the world. In this production he professes his conviction of the great value of the writings of the fathers, as the oldest witnesses of the church, and of their importance in determining the faith of the church, but at the same time he finds that the uncertainty as to the genuineness of these writings, and the contradictions contained in them, occasion great difficulties in their use.

It is not improbable that the intricate and disagreeable position in which he was placed by the increasing hatred of the anti-liturgical party, and by his dependence on the king, who seems still more to have attached himself to the Jesuits, became humiliating to the archbishop. His bodily health became affected by the agitation of his mind, and on February 12, 1579, he bade adieu to the cares of earth. He left the affairs of the church in the greatest confusion, and it was not permitted him to see the feeble light which shone through the more decided separation of the liturgic cause from that of the Roman church and Jesuitism. Yet was he spared from being a witness, perhaps a partaker, of the persecution which overtook the opposers of the liturgy, perhaps from being necessitated openly to appear against the cause he had himself promoted.

The liturgic movement was at first intimately connected with the attempt of the Roman church to use it for its own advantage. This scene of the same drama and of the same period we are now to present.

CHAPTER V.

ROME'S ATTEMPT TO RECOVER THE SWEDISH CHURCH, FROM THE YEAR 1574 TO 1580

THE correspondence which it chanced to cardinal Hosius to open with queen Catharine, and thereby with king John III., led to a determination to send a Jesuit to Sweden to ascertain if the king might be reclaimed to the Roman church, to which it was believed he was well-disposed. The Jesuit, Stanislaus Warsewitz, rector of the Jesuit college, which, in 1569, had been founded at Wilna, was considered by Hosius the most suitable man for this purpose, and received, September 1, 1573, the pope's order to turn his attention to Sweden. His journey was delayed till the following summer. Hosius had previously given notice of his coming. Concealing that he was a Jesuit, he merely announced himself as a Roman priest, and made his appearance in Stockholm as ambassador from queen Catharine's sister, the princess Anna, the wife of king Stephen Bathori.

The avowed errand of the Jesuit was to negotiate respecting the maternal inheritance of the princesses of the house of Jagellon. Queen Catharine, in order that his presence might attract as little notice as possible, had provided him a residence in one of the royal castles. The king, when he understood that Warsewitz was a Jesuit, was at first displeased that such a man had been sent him, and apprehended trouble from the hatred which the reputed character of this order had already awakened in Sweden against its members, before the arrival here of any of them. The king himself assured Warsewitz he was the first Jesuit he ever saw. With king John, whose fears made him impatiently to wish for the Jesuit's speedy departure, Warsewitz had four conferences. In these, he succeeded in removing John's repugnance to the members of his order, and opened the door to a consideration at least of a return of the Swedish church to a union with the Roman.

John was not disinclined to acknowledge the pope as being St. Peter's successor, to be primate of the church, but required that his authority should be confined within certain limits, so that if the pope should become an enemy of the gospel, he might be deposed. He was offended when Warsewitz remarked, that the Swedish bishops had no power to consecrate the sacrament, after the Reformation had broken their succession from the apostles, and their unity with the apostolic church. We have already observed how much this remark wrought upon the king, and induced him to wish Fecht consecrated a bishop at Rome.

The king disapproved the worship of relics, but thought prayers for the dead allowable, and declared that he himself daily prayed for his father's soul. When, at last, Warsewitz asked what hope he could give the pope of the king's and the kingdom's return to the obedience of the Roman chair, the king gave him the decisive answer, that no union could be contemplated, as long as the pope refused to allow the peoples' participation of both the bread and wine in the eucharist, and the marriage of the clergy. The king also wished that permission should be conceded to hold divine service in the Swedish language. Meanwhile he was desirous of restoring the former usages and regulations of the church, a resolution probably not now first formed, but one of which the ordinantia of 1575, and the liturgy of 1576, were the fruits. After a stay of little more than forty days in Stockholm, Warsewitz returned, having secured for his cause the good will of some prominent men, and received from queen Catharine the precious gift of St. Bridget's arm.

All the king's movements were watched at Rome with great attention, and after the ordinantia was published, cardinal Hosius wrote him a letter, which, although with a wary use of terms, plainly presents its author's principles. Every day information more and more gladdening came to Rome of the measures the king was adopting to restore the old faith and the former customs and usages. God was thanked that the king was reclaimed to the obedience of Christ, but thereby was meant not merely of Christ the head, but of the church his body. The king ought not to believe himself wiser than the fathers, that is to say, the fathers *assembled in council to declare the meaning of Holy Scripture.* The king was said to doubt if the use of the cup in the Lord's Supper was rightly forbidden to laymen. The church had for one hundred and fifty years, at the councils of Constance, Basle, Rome, and Trent, settled the question. The divisions among the protestants of Germany showed how the heretics lacerated Christ. Rome was the centre of unity. The king was purposed, as the cardinal hoped, to acknowledge *one* shepherd of the church, as the holy fathers and his own forefathers had done. He ought, therefore, to send some of his court to certify his affection, and on his own part to promise that he would be the church's leal son. Pope Gregory VII. had manifested great care of this matter, when Sweden was newly converted to Christianity, as appears from his letters to the kings of the Swedes and Goths, of which letters a copy was sent to king John. The cardinal advises him to send clerks to Rome, to be there trained in Christian faith and culture. Gregory XIII. would watch over these lands, whose condition seemed to be now better than then. If, therefore, the king would send some young men to Rome, to be trained in the sciences, in morals, and in piety, the pope would cheerfully defray the expenses, until they returned to their fatherland. The king ought without delay, by sending an ambassador to Rome, to meet the affectionate advances of the pope, so full of love.

A report had gone abroad that count Per Brahe materially seconded the king in carrying out his plans. The cardinal, therefore, began to spin around that nobleman the same net in which he endeavored to imprison John III. On the same day with the above-named letter to the king, he wrote to Brahe, expressing joy at having heard that he was not far from the kingdom of God. If the king's wholesome measures were prompted by him, he deserved great praise. But there could be no sheepfold where there was no recognition of the shepherd. He ought, therefore, to induce the king to recognize this shepherd, and would, if he succeeded, render his name deathless, and win everlasting honor in the kingdom of heaven.

These letters were written January 8th, 1576. Not long after, Hosius appears to have had the liturgy sent him, and was little satisfied in seeing that the king obstinately stuck at the same point. It rejoiced him, he wrote to Herbst, on the 8th of July, that Herbst strove by degrees to bring the king into a resolve for the re-establishment of the former church customs. "But to what purpose would be this service, as long as there was no acknowledgment of a shepherd, or of a sheepfold? Who can approve of the king's conducting himself as if he were the pope, and governing the congregations after his own discretion? The bishops of Sweden themselves did not approve of this. * * * To this purpose the words of St. Ambrose should be impressed on the mind of the king, 'Beware of believing that you have an imperial right over what belongs to God. * * * Palaces belong to the Cæsar, churches to the priest.' * * * The king ought to be persuaded, that it appertained to him to be the son of the church and not over the church. The obedience he owes her he should exhibit to her as his mother." It was now the mournful lot of kings, that from fear of their people they did not venture openly to acknowledge Christ. The people had assumed an authority even over the consciences of their princes. The queen ought to be advised not to be so much concerned for the use of the cup in the Lord's Supper, and to endeavor to *discourage* the king from pressing the point. They had neither the body nor blood of Christ who were out of the bosom of the church.

The jesuit Warsewitz had, in the report of his first mission, remarked, that if the king or the queen asked for more Jesuits for Sweden, one of them should be a Pole, the other able to speak Swedish, or to learn that language. But as such an invitation did not come, the pope directed the general of the order to look for and send immediately to Sweden a member of the order who understood Swedish. The choice fell upon the Northman Laurentius Nicholai, the before mentioned Klosterlasse, who, in the autumn of 1575, was summoned from Louvain to Braunsberg, in Prussia, there to await the orders of cardinal Hosius. Compelled to remain here over the winter, at the close of April, 1576, he arrived at Stockholm, in order, while he disguised his character as a jesuit, "to comfort the queen, and endeavor cautiously to open a door for the catholic faith." He brought with him the aforenamed letters to the queen and Per Brahe.

As soon as Klosterlasse and the companions of his journey, a priest from Belgium whose name was Florentius Feyt, and a surgeon who was a layman, had reached Stockholm, they were desired by the queen, through Herbst, to observe the greatest caution, and Klosterlasse in particular, not to betray their character of Jesuits. This disguise was approved also by king John, who at this time was fearful of giving nourishment to the plots which were centering about the imprisoned Erik XIV. He therefore counselled Klosterlasse to endeavor to win the confidence of the Germans residing in Stockholm, as well as of the clergy, so that the king might cover his course under their approval.

After Klosterlasse had without difficulty obtained, by following this advice, letters of recommendation from the Germans, he applied himself with every art of persuasion to the priests. He had, he said, long studied abroad at Louvain, Douay, and Cologne. After he had heard of the king's intention to found a college at Stockholm, he resolved to come and offer his services, because he wished to benefit his fatherland, or its neighborhood, rather than countries more remote and foreign. He, therefore, solicited the clergy for their recommendation to the king.

Captivated by the dexterity and grace with which he spoke Latin, in which they were themselves very unskilled, they proposed Klosterlasse as head of the college it was in contemplation to establish. It was resolved that he should there lecture on theology, and Per Brahe was directed to put the cloister and cloister-house of the grey monks' holm in order, for the opening of the new institution.

During the preparations for opening the college at Stockholm, cardinal Hosius, apprized of Klosterlasse's favorable reception, gave him the following directions for his conduct: He must, before all things, procure a church in which he should be allowed to preach: as the *Lutherans* were allowed to have their churches in Poland, Germany, and France, the king of Sweden ought to allow the *Christians* of his country to have theirs. But a missionary ought to avoid giving offence; "He might exalt faith to the skies, profess Christ to be the only mediator, and that the sacrifice offered upon the cross is the only one whereby we can be saved." After he had in general taught this, he might then rightly explain what he taught, and make it plain to all that nothing else was preached in the realms of the pope.

In August, 1576, Klosterlasse began to give instructions in the college, and to preach in the church of the monastery. King John collected there young priests and candidates for the ministry, in no inconsiderable number, and they had a free support or assistance in some other form.

Klosterlasse began to lecture with great approbation. Well versed in the writings of Luther and Calvin, he had them always at hand, and from them he proved his assertions, which either covered a protestant sense or were designed to bring to light the disagreement between the reformers and the church fathers. The enchantment was of no long continuance. Klosterlasse was sufficiently openhearted toward his scholars, because he believed himself to have won them more than he actually had, and he roused their dissatisfaction and suspicions.

The pastor of Stockholm, master Olof, and the schoolmaster master Abraham, now began to discern foul play. Klosterlasse seems to have avoided any close connection with them. Master Abraham, in particular, who was a favorite with the courtiers, burghers, and teachers, sounded the note of alarm, and gave warning of Klosterlasse's doctrines. Both those men soon became his decided opponents; but they were also opponents of the king in his plans for the church, and they were removed from Stockholm. On the contrary, Klosterlasse took the liturgy under his protection, as he hoped it might contribute to introduce by degrees the Roman faith.

The prospects were at first promising. King John still dreamed of the possibility of a union with Rome on the principles he had himself concerted; queen Catherine exulted over the good work; duke Charles' love schemes turned his attention from the affairs of the church; many of the foremost men of the kingdom sustained the church politics of the court; and it was believed that the opposition to the liturgy, which was at first weak and hesitating, would soon be stifled. The friends of that liturgy did not yet compre hend the differences which divided them from the new Roman church.

Under these circumstances, Klosterlasse could work all the more openly. His conferences with the king removed many of his unfavorable sentiments of the pope and Roman church. The number of his pupils increased. He reported, in the spring of 1577, that he had already converted thirty to the Roman faith, and laborers alone seemed wanting to win back Sweden. He could now send the first fruits of the Swedish youth to be brought up at Rome as priests This was done, as Hosius, in 1574, had desired, with consent of the king, who gave the young men money for their journey. Six in number, led by a nephew of bishop Brask, a youth of nineteen, they *clandestinely* left their fatherland, in the summer of 1577, to enter the German college at Rome, enlarged by pope Gregory XIII.

Klosterlasse mourned over the want of laborers in the field; of this he complained to the queens Catharine of Sweden and Anna of Poland. Feyt, who in 1577 returned to the Netherlands, was commissioned to bring back with him priests, books, and a press, for which object he received money from the king. He had found, as participants of his travels, two priests, a physician, and a printer. Books had been *given* in great number by the students of Louvain, who sent to Klosterlasse the writings of the church fathers, and the later Roman catholic authors, as well as the old Greek and Latin classics. But before the return of Feyt and his companions, the man had already made his appearance in Sweden who, in personal energy, takes the foremost rank among the missionaries of Rome to that land.

In Rome, the case was regarded in a light somewhat different from that in which it was viewed by Klosterlasse. He sought, by moderate measures and concessions, to gain an entrance for the Roman church and professors of its faith, and expected to carry the king in the current, if he was fortunate enough to build up a strong Romish party. Hosius, and the pope, were not satisfied with half popery, and laid great weight on gaining over the king, who they believed would carry his people along with him. This was also the aim of Klosterlasse, and he used every opportunity to impress the king with more favorable sentiments of the leaders of the Roman church, and he succeeded in giving him an esteem and love for pope Gregory, whose beneficence and other virtues he highly extolled. In conformity with these attempts, and by the express desire of Hosius, in a letter dated January 8, 1576, but also in conformity with his own principles and aims, the king sent Pontus de la Gardie and Fecht to Rome. The death of the latter we have already related. De la Gardie delivered his message respecting the church, as well as he could according to oral instructions and Fecht's rescued papers. The pope ordered a congregation of cardinals and theologians to take the matter into consideration. But there was one point of John's demands to which they were willing immediately to accede, the rather with the hope of thereby avoiding the unpleasantness of giving an answer to the rest. This was to send to Sweden a man with whom John could personally treat.

On the choice of this man, the success of the work of conversion in Sweden seemed to depend. The pope regarded this mission as so important, that he declared he would be willing himself to go to Sweden did not the care of the whole church compel him to forbear. The choice fell upon the jesuit Possevin, who, after some entreaty, submitted to the pope's command.

Antonio Possevino was born in Italy, at Mantua, in 1534, had studied at Rome, and had long fixed his eye on the learning and piety of the Jesuits, the two objects of his own life, when, in 1559, he became a member of the order.

He was soon after sent to Piedmont, to engage the duke of Savoy in the interests of the Roman church. He wished to convert the protestants of Piedmont, and penetrated its valleys, either alone or with the soldiery who were to coerce the conversion of its inhabitants. From 1562 he began to operate in France; at first by visits from Savoy, afterward by a continued abode there. Here, as in Savoy, he at first concealed his being a Jesuit. He labored at Lyons by preaching, writing, and personal influence, to convert the protestants. He was sent on important embassies, and with success to the French court, contributed to open France to the Jesuits, was rector of their college first at Avignon, and afterward at Lyons. In 1572, soon after the massacre of the Huguenots in France, of which mournful tragedy he must have been a spectator if not a participator, he was sent to Rome to attend the election which made Eberhard Mercurianus general of his order. He was retained by its chief as secretary of the order. He familiarized himself with Sweden, by reading the historic work of Olaus Magni, long before he foreboded any personal acquaintance with this land.

The commission he now received from the pope was to effect king John's entire restoration to the Roman church. But there was another to be won, if even the chief purpose failed. During the contest which William of Orange commenced against Spain for the liberties of his church and country, it was feared that the fleets of the north would come to his assistance, and Possevin was to prevent a fleet being sent from Sweden to Belgium. He was enjoined, on coming to Sweden, to change his ecclesiastical attire for that of a civilian.

The embassage from John III., which occasioned the departure of Possevin, could not but be welcome to the Roman chair and create many hopes. Gregory XIII. not only showed his satisfaction by furnishing De la Gardie with a letter of recommendation to the vice-king of Naples, and by speaking in his favor in the matter of inheritance that first gave occasion to the intercourse between Sweden and Rome, but both he and Possevin were furnished with letters from the pope to the king, queen, duke Charles, and count Brahe.

The letters to the king expressed great content, but exhort him, laying aside all human considerations, wholly and entirely and without delay to return to the bosom of the church and there find rest. The letters to duke Charles, and especially that of introduction, which Possevin brought along with him, show that as yet that prince was not mistrusted. Gregory expresses the hope, that the duke would not be among those foes that met the pope with unrighteous hate, and he endeavors from the words of Augustin to prove, that out of the catholic church there was no salvation, and that the catholic church was that which was then so called. Even Hosius now wrote to the king, expressing his joy, and dilating upon the necessity of the church's unity opposition to many-headed heresy. It seems to have been the last letter to Sweden from the man who first opened an intercourse between John and the pope. He foresaw not that this intercourse was already nearer its end than its beginning.

Possevin left Rome in September. At Prague he received a commission from the dowager empress Maria as her ambassador, to acquaint the king of Sweden with the death, on October 12th, of her husband, the emperor Maximilian. He disembarked at Kalmar, and continued his route by land for eighteen days to Stockholm, where he arrived on December 19, 1577, in company with two jesuit priests, an Irishman, W. Good, and a Frenchman, J. Fornier, who followed him from Rome.

He appeared as the imperial ambassador in civil attire, with a sword by his side, and was received by the king in great state. In private he presented himself to the king as the papal nuncio, delivered the letters he had brought with him from Rome, and, after learning from the queen and Klosterlasse the state of affairs, he commenced his negotiations with the king, which were daily carried on, either by oral conferences or written communications. The investigation was, on the king's part, rigorous and earnest, and Possevin was obliged to employ all his learning and practice in theological controversy, in the endeavor to overcome his doubts.

John contended for his privileges, and while both were agreed in their disapproval of protestantism, and in arraying against it the catholic church, the nuncio claimed that he only was to be acknowledged a true catholic, who was in visible connection with the Roman church, and was its and the peope's leal son. The king presented written questions, which were answered in writing by Possevin, and they show how the former endeavored to avoid being driven into the only refuge the latter opened to him. Could not they, asked the king, who avouch their faith in the Scriptures and hate sin be saved, even if they do not accept all the articles of faith of the catholic church? Could not they who are sundered from the church's outward unity be saved, if they hold all that belongs to faith? Have not the Lutherans, bishops and priests, or is not the church there where true bishops and priests are not? There were other similar questions.

All these questions revolve around a centre, which it was all important to the Jesuit carefully to defend—obedience to the Roman church. But while he rejoiced to see the king daily approximate to his views, he experienced what Klosterlasse said to him upon coming to Sweden, that the king was inflexible on certain points, and would not be persuaded that the pope should not on these give way. Even on these points there was an earnest discussion, and the king believed that he had satisfied Possevin of the reasonableness of his propositions, in conformity with the holy Scriptures, the institutions of the apostles, and writings of the fathers, and even the edicts of popes and decrees of councils. Possevin, when he found the king's obstinacy in these points was invincible, was obliged in part to yield, and appear to deem it not impossible that the pope would consent to the use of the cup in the Lord's Supper and the marriage of the clergy. He, therefore, sent the king's demands to Rome, to be submitted to the pope's examination and final decision.

Meanwhile the Jesuit and John continued to interchange arguments with each other, and what Possevin could not gain from John's convictions, he hoped to effect by means of his deep piety, his facile imagination, and his sensative heart. No one was more suited to the task of obtaining an influence over king John than Possevin, whose grave and self-denying life, manifested in bodily mortifications and fasts, whose eloquence, great learning, and acquaintance with the Scriptnres, which was peculiarly estimable in the king's eyes, made him in all respects a man after John's own heart. Drawn to him by this similarity of character, the soul of John was bowed under the stronger will and fascinating powers of his companion.

One day, while they were conversing on the catholic church, and, it seems, on the death of Peter Fecht on his journey to Rome, and the king was in an agitated frame of mind, Possevin remarked what a difference there was between the Peter who went on the sea and when he began to sink was rescued by the hand of the Lord, and him who, because he was not called of the Lord, perished in the waves. The king ought to imitate the former, to deny himself, to take up his cross and follow Christ. Then would he be able to save his people. The cross and its suffering would by God's help disappear. He ought,—the Jesuit was proceeding, when John burst into tears, abjured all heresy, made a general confession of his whole previous life, received absolution, and professed his determination to be guided by his counsels who occupied the place of Christ upon earth. When John had avowed his purpose, Possevin put into his hand the creed of pope Pius IV., or that of the so-called council of Trent, for his examination and acknowledgment, and appointed him three days for reflection, after which he was to confess and obtain absolution.

Hardly was the second day at an end before John again summoned Possevin, and declared himself ready. On his knees, the king confessed all his foregoing life, and after promising obedience in all things, received absolution from the papal nuncio.

The nuncio now kneeled down, thanked God for the king's conversion, and prayed that the good work which had been begun, might be brought to completion. The king stood up in great agitation, and embracing Possevin, exclaimed, "I embrace you and the catholic church for ever!"

The following day, which was the 6th of May, 1578, the king requested Possevin to perform mass in his presence. This was done the same day in the king's parlor, in which he and his two secretaries, Nils Brask, the nephew of bishop Brask, and John Henriksson, received the sacrament from Possevin.

Such, in brief, is the narrative of the only man who has left it us, respecting king John's return to the Roman church. Possevin himself would willingly have it as he represents it, but his own representation and conduct create mistrust. He was too much inclined to mistake a hasty transport of feeling for a serious conviction. The king certainly thought himself in connection with the Roman catholic church, even if the words he uttered in an hour of great excitement, do not assure us of this sentiment. It would be more to the purpose, if, as reported, he acknowledged the Trindentine creed, which, in many points, is at war with John's views, expressed before and after this time. But John had an idea of the Roman church other than its then condition justified. He had *never* ceased to believe in the possibility of the concession of what he required from the pope. He could not have acknowledged his belief in the creed of Trent, unless he either dissembled, for which there was in that hour no call, or, mastered by his feelings, spoke unconsciously, which is not probable; or, if he did so speak, believed himself able to explain that creed consistently with his own views, or, if that were too much for even John's blind egotism, regarded his union with Rome, not as a full conversion, but as embracing it with the reserve of perfect freedom.

This last supposition seems the most probable; and Possevin either did not understand the king, or would not understand him. Before the king received absolution after confession, he must have promised to submit to the pope's determination in regard to the required concessions. The following day, immediately after the administration of the Lord's Supper by Possevin, the king conferred with him respecting these concessions, without which he regarded a reunion of the Swedish church with the Roman to be difficult or impossible. When Possevin said he did not believe the pope would grant them, the king was amazed. *He had*, he said, *during the whole time presupposed this mode of pacification.*

There is not the slightest evidence that John III. partook of the Lord's Supper *even once* after the 6th of May, 1578, at the hands of Possevin, during the three weeks the latter subsequently remained in Stockholm, or from the hands of any Roman priest. This, according to the custom of the times, he doubtless should have done, if he considered himself to stand in full ecclesiastical communion with those priests. When he empowered Possevin, under promise of certain advantages, to engage Roman catholic families to immigrate to Sweden, he added a half permission that they might bring their own priests and open a church. But the condition was attached that they should perform mass in their native language, and, at least when they first came, twice a week in Swedish. This proves that he did not consider his liturgy incompatible with the Roman catholic confession.

Possevin, himself, found the success of his cause very uncertain ; an uncertainty which equally affected the king, as to the possibility of converting his people. The cause of the catholic religion, he writes, has as yet *no* firm foundation in this kingdom, and "I am in great distress of mind when I know what our hinderances are; an extraordinary mercy from on high and a watchful attention are needed in this undertaking; otherwise, the whole of this frail web will either be broken or illy continued, and so there will be a separation." Even at Rome, according to Possevin's own representation, it was found that the king was agitated by a variety of opinions, wishes, and fears, and that the cause "was far from being as prosperous as was hoped."

Possevin thought it best to go to Rome, not only because he was afraid of a further explanation with the king and hoped that time would furnish opportunity, but to reflect upon the measures and steps to be adopted, how the denial of the king's demands might be given in the mildest manner.

Possevin left Stockholm on the 28th of May, 1578, after more than five months' stay. The king expressed to him the wish that the house of St. Britas, or Bridget, at Rome, should be converted into a Swedish seminary for priests, and gave him reason to expect a project for the support of that seminary out of the Neapolitan inheritance, giving him at the same time an instalment out of that resource for the purchase of books and church ornaments. He was conveyed by a royal ship to Dantzic, accompanied by five Swedish youths who were to be placed in the German college at Rome, and then to Braunsberg, accompanied by the secretary John Henriksson. This last person soon returned to Stockholm with four Jesuits, of whom two, A. Wisowsky, and the Warsewitz who was here in 1574, became chaplains to the queen, the other two being assistants to Klosterlasse in the college.

Possevin took with him many commissions, one of which was to propose the marriage of young Sigismund with a member of the Romish imperial family. He sent to Rome an account of his embassage, and a project for carrying on successfully the missionary work in Sweden, together with a most important scheme for educating Swedish young men. Possevin proposed the extension of the jesuit colleges established in 1565 and 1566 at Braunsberg and Olmutz. The former, instituted by cardinal Hosius, was peculiarly adapted to the purpose, because it lay near the coast of the Eastern sea, not far from Dantzic, so much frequented by Swedes, and between that city and Konigsberg. For youths either leaving Sweden or returning, as well as circulating books in that country, this place was exceedingly convenient. Toward the close of 1578, these institutions obtained the pope's confirmation, according to Possevin's project.

These seminaries were to pay special attention to the work of conversion in Sweden, Denmark, Norway, and Russia. The pope appropriated a sum of money for the support of a hundred youths, fifty in each place, together with their teachers and those who were to superintend the work of missions in northern lands. The young men were to have everything free, except clothes. Some time after their entrance they were to pledge themselves always to maintain the Roman catholic faith, but if they renounced or apostatized from this faith, they were to refund all expenses. They were not obliged to become priests, but each was at liberty to choose his calling. In their studies they were to confine themselves to such a course as corresponded to the character and needs of the people among whom they were to live. If for the Swedes or Finns who were at Braunsberg, there was danger, from proximity to their fatherland, of falling into heresy, or being recalled by their parents or relations, they were to be removed to Olmutz, which, as more inland, was considered more secure. After Possevin had put everything in order for opening the seminaries, young men were at once admitted, and of these Olmutz, in 1580, had ten Swedes and Finns, whose names were enrolled the preceding year, and Braunsberg probably still more.

Some time before Possevin left Sweden, he had received, in March, 1578, and immediately sent to Rome, king John's conditions, which not being granted, that prince declared a reunion of the Swedish church with Rome impossible. These conditions were twelve, and were regarded in Rome as a demonstrative proof how little the result of Possevin's mission corresponded to the hopes entertained from an easily won victory. The pope caused them to be examined by a congregation appointed for the purpose. The most important were, that the pope should allow that the mass should be celebrated in Swedish, that the Lord's Supper should be received in both kinds, that priests might marry, that catholic priests should refrain at their mass from reading with a loud voice the invocation to saints and prayers for the dead, and that the use of holy water and some other ceremonies might be abrogated. All these were refused by the pope.* With some hesitation, he was willing to grant the

* On the question of administering in both kinds, it was answered, that the church thereby distinguished her children and confessors from heretics so that when these received only the bread, the church required the Lord's Supper to be administered under bread and wine, and vice versa.

king the right he claimed of judging bishops in cases of life and death and high treason, and to take their oath of allegiance. The latter was only granted on condition that the oath was in a suitable form, which the pope was to draw up. The king's request that the church property recovered by heirs should not be restored, the pope would grant, and give its possessors absolution, but on condition that they were converted to the catholic faith. His request to have preachers and some ceremonies of the Lutherans, could only be granted as to the preachers, if the king for a good purpose wished to hear them. That the cloister of the Franciscans at Stockholm should not be re-established, but continue in use as a college, was conceded, with the proviso that catholic teachers were placed there.

King John had made it one of his conditions, that the grave of his father, in the cathedral of Upsala, should not be disturbed; to this it was answered, that certainly it was contrary to the holy rules and order of the church that a heretic should have his grave in a catholic church, and in a chapel of the virgin Mary, but the pope would respect the king's filial reverence, and therefore leave king Gustavus' body in quiet where it was laid. Doubtless king John's request was approved that God should be entreated, by general prayers, to give a happy issue to the negotiation. The pope ordered these prayers, but without naming the king or his kingdom.

The determination of the pope was, on July 25, 1578, communicated to Possevin, in a letter from the cardinal of Como. An Italian nobleman, L. Cagnoli, who lived at Stockholm, had, in 1577, been sent to Rome with a letter from the queen. He was on the eve of returning to Sweden with the answer to John's demands, when Laurentius Magnus, a nephew of the archbishops Johannes and Olaus Magnus, himself designed for a high place in the contemplated new Roman church, came with the information that

Possevin had left this land and was on his way to Rome. According to Possevin's plan, Herbst and Good, who with Possevin's other companion remained behind in Sweden, were empowered to receive the pope's answer and communicate its contents to the king. Cagnoli came to Stockholm in October, 1578, bringing with him, besides this answer, letters from the pope to the king, queen, Per Brahe, Nils Brask, and a lord of the council not named.

When this answer came to Stockholm, events had occurred which in part already changed, in part threatened to change, the state of the case. The principal cause of them was Klosterlasse, whose indiscretion fixed suspicion and censure on the college he supported. This indiscretion probably, too, gave nourishment to the grudge felt for the favored foreigner, and gathered over his head the hate and disdain which were naturally excited, when, notwithstanding his disguise, his double-dealing and art began to be manifest.

King John's secretary and favorite, Johan Henriksson, lived with the wife of a man who, after a false report of his death reached Sweden, unexpectedly came home. This connection the archbishop Laurentius Petri pronounced unlawful. The husband, after his return, was murdered by Henriksson's servant, who was punished with death for his deed. His master, who was suspected of having instigated the crime, was obliged to pay a fine. Henriksson wished afterward to marry the woman, but the archbishop refused to allow him to do so. He now applied to Klosterlasse to obtain the papal dispensation, which, under existing relations, might be considered valid. Klosterlasse referred the case to the general of his order before the first coming of Possevin, and laid great stress upon Henriksson's being much in favor with the king, who wished his favorite to be gratified. He was, moreover, a man of great influence, the torment of the Lutheran priests, a zealous patron of the cause of the Jesuits, and Klosterlasse's particular friend. When Possevin subsequently arrived, the marriage suit was submitted to him, and, as the result, Klosterlasse, on February 6, 1578, "by the authority given him from almighty God," and by the plenary power which the imperial legate Possevin held of the apostolic chair, and now imparted to Klosterlasse, declared that he gave Henriksson and the woman absolution of their sins, and allowed them to marry.

This letter of license soon came to the knowledge of the archbishop, and could not but awaken his suspicions and dislike of the man whom, till now, he seems to have thought really attached to the Lutheran church. But that he should attempt, by virtue of the papal authority, to attack the discipline and order of the church, was more than the duty he owed his office and his conscience would allow the archbishop to tolerate. In a letter of the 20th of March, to Klosterlasse, he declared the displeasure with which he had seen a dispensation grounded on false authority, and, "by the authority given him by God and the congregation of God," he pronounced the dispensation of no effect, and Klosterlasse unworthy the priestly office, from the exercise of which he was to be suspended until the archbishop, repentance and amendment being manifested, should again reinstate him.

This took place while Possevin was still at Stockholm. The hate entertained for Klosterlasse and his college preceded the sentence of excommunication pronounced by the archbishop, and aroused the king's fears. He, too, had become so dissatisfied with Klosterlasse that he required Possevin to remove him, and recalled the commission given him as rector of the college. Possevin hesitated, but after the doom of suspension by the archbishop was pronounced, and the priests of Stockholm began to preach more decidedly than usual, he was obliged to take some steps for quieting the commotion. What these steps were has not been reported, but probably the ingress of more Roman priests from Poland, to assist in the college, left Klosterlasse more unnoticed.

The eyes of the archbishop had become opened. His zeal for the liturgy had cooled, and he was of opinion that it was impossible to go further without disturbing the peace of the land. He began to ally himself more closely to his former friends, and came forward as an author against the liturgical cause and popery, as soon as he became aware of the jesuitical plots. His reply, aimed against the plots of the papists, was circulated through the land, and must, as coming from a man suspected of being their secret friend, have excited attention and raised the courage of the party which was averse to liturgism and popery; the rather that a report soon followed the circulation of this reply, that his qualms of conscience had hastened his death.

It was about this time that master Abraham came to Upsala from his exile in Aland, and preached a sermon, such that "a heart not of granite or steel must surely have wept." He spoke of the public worship of papists and Lutherans, and showed that the former was framed on false principles, and having prayed for true preachers of God's word, denounced Klosterlasse and his party as betrayers and murderers of souls, beseeching God to protect fatherland from this voracious wolf.

The king could not avoid seeing that the cause of the ordinantia and liturgy was signally hazarded by being thrown into the vortex of the lively abhorrence of popery and Jesuitism. As the opposition derived its strength chiefly from the hatred of the latter being transferred to the former, it might be hoped that opposition would be weakened by separating the two from each other.

Among the council of the kingdom and high nobility, there were many who, having at first favored the king's plans, began to reflect with dread, that if a union with

Rome was effected, the valuable investitures they held of the church property suppressed to the crown, might be taken from them. One of these was the king's favorite, Pontus de la Gardie, who "sailed with all winds."

By his alliance, in 1578, with the family of one of the German protestant princes, duke Charles stood forth mightier than before, and became a centre and rallying point to the dissatisfied. The eyes of Europe were turned on Sweden, and state policy struggled for king John's conscience and ecclesiastical faith. The protestant princes feared to have behind them a popish king in Sweden, and strained every effort to avert John from a union with Rome. On the other hand, the pope exhorted the Roman catholic princes to take part with him, and the proud and powerful Philip of Spain kept, in 1578, his own ambassador at Stockholm, to prevent the apprehended union between king John and prince William of Orange.

D. Chytræus, of Rostock, who at an earlier period stood in intimate connection with king John, and in 1574 had addressed him in praise of the Swedes who were in the university, requesting him to send more there, was among the most indefatigable in the work of protestantism in Sweden. Chytræus either did not mistrust, or hoped to win over the king.

Under these circumstances, came the letter which contained the pope's answer to the requests John had presented. Impatient when he heard of its arrival, he summoned Warsewitz and Good, and desired to know its contents. When Warsewitz orally communicated them to him, he did not believe him, and when he read the letter himself, he seemed astonished and disturbed, and frequently exclaimed: "I obtain not all and can do nothing; it is then done with altogether." When Warsewitz requested to know his pleasure respecting the wish contained in the same letter, that a church might be opened for papists, the king answered that he could not grant anything, since the pope denied his requests.

The words of the king just quoted, were in themselves, in reality, a termination of the question as to a union with the Roman church. The errors, in consequence of which he believed himself able to execute anything as a mediator, began to be dissipated. But his heart still clung to Rome, and the inflexible conviction of the correctness of his own views, which is a remarkable feature in John's attempts at reform, prevented his believing in a like inflexibility in others. He declared his purpose of accomplishing his intention to re-establish cloisters, but asked permission of the pope to convert them, for a time, into schools and hospitals. He wrote anew to Rome by his secretary, J. Typotius, to see if it were possible to obtain the required concessions.

The language of this letter shows that *he* had no intention to yield. Possevin, it says, was convinced of the reasonableness of the king's demands; he would bear procrastination no longer. He therefore desires a positive answer from the pope, and desires that the cardinals would modify their views to the promotion of peace. The queen, also, sent information to Rome of the critical situation of affairs in Sweden. While the letter by Typotius was on the way, Possevin, who early in 1579 left Rome for Poland, received the pope's command to return *with all speed* to Sweden, where the hope of success was declining, in order to induce the king not to press the conditions he persisted in with such stubbornness.

Possevin went to Stockholm in a vessel sent for the purpose, where he arrived at the close of July, 1579, accompanied by Laurentius Magnus, who was ordained priest in Prussia, by the Jesuit Ardulf, and by N. Mylonius, already known in Sweden. He now appeared in the dress of his order, because it seemed a time to act openly, so as to give courage to those whom he well knew as concealed papists.

The day after Possevin landed, duke Charles returned to Sweden, accompanied by his bride of sixteen, with the animated spirits and joyous hopes that follow on the marriage of a youthful pair. The duchess Maria, granddaughter of the landgrave Philip of Hesse, renowned in the history of the German Reformation, and the daughter of that Louis VI. of the Palatinate who established in his land the Lutheran confession, though it both before and after his reign yielded to Calvinism, became the protectress of the protestants, as the queen was of the papists.

On his arrival in Sweden, Possevin found his cause in a worse condition than he expected. The king was alarmed by the menacing attitude of the protestants, both within and without the land. The revolt of the Belgians against king Philip's religious persecution, appeared to him a fearful warning. His disquiet was kept alive by many of the lords of his council. Chytræus had, it is probable with an object in view rather than inconsiderately, dedicated to the king a new edition of his history of the Augsburg confession, and in this dedication had praised king Gustavus I., who early embraced and faithfully protected the pure doctrine, and had expressed his hope and satisfaction that the son was like the father. This book was circulated over all Sweden, as was also the discourse of the same author on the state of the Greek church, which awakened the deepest attention from its assertion, that this church had no sacrificial offering, no invocation of saints, that the Lord's Supper was administered there in both kinds, and priests allowed to marry.

Possevin confessed in the writings of Chytræus and his followers, his own most dangerous foes, who withered the fruits of his former efforts. He made fruitless attempts to gain over this man. Klosterlasse had not been able to recover the king's confidence. The Spanish king's ambassador, F. Erasso, who entered Stockholm in great splendor, distributed alms, gave largely to the college of the grey monks' holm, and whose house and Romish chapel were frequented by many of the nobility, also lost the royal favor, if he was not even put under arrest. The cause of this, was the suspicion that he had an eye to the Swedish crown. Some Swedes who openly professed themselves papists, were imprisoned, and the king attended the Lutheran churches as assiduously as he did at any time before.

When Possevin came to Stockholm, the king was staying at Upsala, where the former was soon summoned. Here he appeared as ambassador from the emperor and many other princes. From Philip of Spain he tendered a considerable sum of money, to aid in the work of conversion of Sweden. The king had till now hoped for some concession from the pope, but when he found himself deceived in his expectation, he let Possevin understand that nothing further could be done.

Possevin with his coadjutors remained a year in Sweden. Their object was to recruit as many youths as possible for the jesuit seminaries, to strengthen in their faith those who belonged to the Roman church or were converted, to sow the seed of future conversion, and by perseverance endeavor to overcome John's obstinacy and fears.

Immediately on the arrival of Possevin, his drag-nets were put out to catch éleves for the seminaries, for which purpose any express condition of their becoming converts to the Roman church was avoided. The good condition of the jesuit institutions made it a desirable thing to many parents to find there situations for their sons. The success was such, that in the autumn twenty young men were sent off. The nuns of Wadsten were encouraged by Possevin to procure from among their relatives four or six pupils of noble birth, to be sent out as managers of a seminary at Braunsberg. Many were sent afterward. Possevin carried fifteen with him on his second return, and without counting those who had previously gone to Rome, the whole number amounted to fifty.

Of these young persons, many from sickness or other causes, and with permission of the Jesuits, returned to their native country. Others came home at a later period of life, but attached themselves to the new order of things. A large number lost for ever their fatherland. Among those who soon returned, were the aforenamed Per Brask, who, in 1579, had been sent to Rome, and Erik Falk, són of the deceased bishop of Linkoping. Another, Lars Eriksson, who accompanied the first exportation made by Klosterlasse, returned in 1579, openly denounced the infidelity of the Roman church and its management of the German college, and occasioned Possevin and his coadjutors much annoyance and vexation, when they endeavored, though in vain, to silence him.

An important object of the Roman mission was to strengthen in their faith those who belonged to the Roman church. The centre of these cares was queen Catharine, through whom this missionary field was opened. Now, surrounded by Jesuits, she became herself more active. But when her term of life, worn by sickness, seemed near its close, and she herself was, therefore, not to be taken into the account, her own zeal and that of herself and missionaries, failing in the hope of gaining the husband, was directed to her children, especially the heir to the crown. To save them to the Roman church was a prime object of that zeal. The looseness of religious principles in which king John had thought this heir, now thirteen years of age, should be brought up, aided the work of turning his youthful mind in favor of his mother's views. When the father required him to attend the liturgic service, Sigismund refused with a firmness which provoked the king to inflict corporeal punishment on his obstinate son. John's displeasure extended to the Jesuits, whose success in the case became, through God's wonderful providence, the means of rescuing protestantism, when a way was opened for Gustavus Adolphus the great to the Swedish throne.

Possevin was at this time active in Sweden, furnished with extensive powers and with briefs of indulgence for those who believed and those who should be converted to the papal faith. After confession, the Lord's Supperwas administered to those who openly or secretly professed their attachment to the Roman church. Among the latter were Nils Brask, now burgomaster of Stockholm, and count Per Brahe. Of the latter it may be observed, that his inclinations undoubtedly leaned to the faith of Rome, which he regarded as consonant with the catholicism expressed in the ordinantia and liturgy. But that he formally joined the ranks of Rome wants proof, unless his making confession, in 1579, before the court chaplains of the queen, and receiving the eucharist from their hands, may be so considered.

This is said to have been done by many of the chief persons of the court, though without the king's knowledge, and without their being therefore considered as having lapsed to Rome, the king himself having in the previous year acted in the same manner without being a decided convert. The manner in which the Lord's Supper was administered prevented attention from being fastened on the difference between the faith of the two churches. Possevin, for example, and we presume the other Jesuits also, employed under the name of ablution, and as an old custom, the trifling trick of giving the communicants immediately after administering the bread, wine mixed with water thereby to rinse the bread. This was not given from the same cup out of which the priest received the wine, and it is probable that a great number of the recipients wist not but that they were taking the body and blood of Christ under both bread and wine.

A special object of Possevin's cares was the cloister of Wadsten, "that blooming garden inclosed in a forest of heresies." The other remnants of the monastic institutions were of no account. Nadendal was not again to bloom, although the king furnished a project for the support of the buildings and nuns, and queen Catharine encouraged the nuns that remained, by virtue of the decree of the bishops in 1575 for restoring cloisters, to adopt as many young girls as possible, to be nurtured in good works and charity, in the faith of the apostolic and catholic church, according to the institutes and rules of their predecessors and abbesses. The queen promised to provide for the expenses.

The eyes of Possevin were particularly directed to Wadsten, whose nuns, when compelled to attend the Lutheran service, protected themselves from its effects by the precaution recommended to them by the abbess, of stopping their ears with wax. This institution seemed to him wonderfully preserved by God, as the only Noah's ark in the north, to restore the seed of catholicism, well-nigh drowned by the flood of heresy. He directed that the number of nuns should be augmented, and himself consecrated some new ones, even against the will of their kinsfolk. They were incited to adopt girls, to be trained in letters, and be indoctrinated in the Roman faith.

But even here the old faith was recast in the spirit of the new times. The nuns and the priests were in future to be pledged to the creed of Trent. The catechism of Canisius and a book of devotion were left, of which every nun was to write out a copy. It was expected that the priests of the cloister would, by manœuvring, be able to found the like establishments for the new popish church in Sweden, or be themselves of the number who were to go as missionaries into other lands. The much frequented school of Wadsten, where the teacher was a secret papist, was taken into account. Wadsten, in a word, was to be the centre of the work of conversion in the land, especially as the prospect of establishing a Jesuit college in Stockholm became more dark. This monastery was the more deserving of watchful and tender attention, as the institution and its abbess at this time enjoyed the special favor of both the king and the queen.*

The more the hope of king John's decided conversion disappeared, with the more unreservedness did the Jesuits address themselves to his people, to sow at least the seed of a future harvest. Mylonius preached in Germany, in the chapel which the king allowed Possevin to open in his house, and Possevin administered the Lord's Supper. At Upsala, where Possevin with his company stayed some weeks, there was less opening for the activity of the Jesuits, which, however, called forth the opposition of its professors and priests. A severe pestilence which raged at Stockholm, in the autumn of 1579, promoted their plans, as the king with the court and queen's chaplains removed to Westeras, and the clergy were less mindful of watching the steps of the Roman missionaries, to whom the burgomaster Brask was a friend and patron. It was at this time that Sigismund was, while staying at Westeras, completely fixed by Warsewitz in his attachment to the Roman church.

A portion of the Jesuits, among whom was Possevin himself, left Stockholm, and took up their abode at Lindo in the parish of Lofo, at which place the king gave them a college, and afterward the queen her property at Torfve-

* The abbess, from the year 1553, was Catherine Gylta, descended from one of the most illustrious families in the land. King John and she were walking in the garden of the convent, in an avenue shaded by trees. The king asked her, if a longing for marriage and the world's life did not sometimes arise in the hearts of the sisters. She answered, that as they could not hinder the birds flying over their garden, but could prevent them building their nests—so they could not prevent such thoughts from hovering over their hearts, but they could prevent those thoughts from nestling there.

sund, the present Drottningholm, where they greatly enlarged their house, as a protection from the pestilence. During their stay at Lindo, they instructed, by means of an interpreter, the peasants in the catechism, and read the litany and prayers, which sentence by sentence were translated into Swedish. They endeavored to give while there consolation to the dying, probably using an interpreter, or in houses where their foreign speech was understood. When they withdrew from this place Klosterlasse was left behind, on whose great eloquence and knowledge of the tongue of the country much hope was built. The catechism of the Jesuit Canisius had been translated into Swedish, and fifteen hundred copies of it were dispersed, with a great number of German prayer books. In February, 1580, Possevin and his followers were summoned to Wadsten, where the king and the court had gone to attend a diet that was to assemble in that town. They remained in East Gothland, Wadsten, Linkoping, and parts adjacent, and labored to spread the popish doctrines until they left Sweden, the same year, in the month of August.

But their success corresponded not with their expectations or their efforts. Possevin had, he writes to Warsewitz on November 29, 1579, received information of the missions of the Jesuits in Brazil. They had in one year converted five thousand men, "and what have we effected here? We are in truth their antipodes."

Possevin comforts himself, that the jubilee which the Jesuits held at Westeras, November 1, 1579, had borne good fruit. This fruit, which was confined to the court alone, appears only in the entire conversion and first communion of Sigismund. In Stockholm nineteen persons, who were previously numbered among the papists, had, at the time of the jubilee, received the Roman church sacrament. During the devastation made by the epidemical disease, the dying applied chiefly to the Lutheran priests. The Jesuits could assign no better reason for this, than that it was done for the sake of being buried and having preaching over the dead body.

Success was at this time expected from Klosterlasse's labors. Some came to hear him preach, but though he admonished them to come to the sacrament of confession, not one confessed to him. "So deeply," exclaims Possevin in his astonishment, "have the roots of heretical insensibility struck." In Wadsten, on Easter, 1580, there were eighteen communicants, in which number the court, members of the cloister, and the Jesuits, are, probably, to be counted. In Linkoping they had some women to communicate with them, and it was resolved that these were no more to seek absolution or the Lord's Supper at the hands of Lutheran priests.

The activity of Klosterlasse had a different result from what was expected. The hatred, which, from the beginning almost of his career, was felt toward the disguised Jesuit and his college, was exalted to its height, when he threw off his mask; and in the spring of 1580 there took place a riot, directed against the college, whose buildings were well-nigh being set on fire, and whose occupants were driven out. Order was restored and the rioters were punished, but the king forbade Klosterlasse to have any concern with the school, banished him from Stockholm, and ordered him to confine himself to Lindo or Torfvesund. He remained in a state of inaction, till he with Possevin left Sweden. His double dealing with the king deprived him of even this degree of protection, when he began to abuse in speech and writing the liturgy he had before so warmly defended.

In Stockholm the zeal for conversion on the part of the Jesuits had the same result. Possibly also the influence of duke Charles or his court, where there were Calvinists, and the death of pastor Nils Olai, approximated the Lutherans and Calvinists to each other, so that on Easter, 1580, they partook of the Lord's Supper together. Possevin regards this union as the cause of the riot which drove away Klosterlasse, for which, however, reasons enough before that were to be found.

The illusion would be unaccountable by which the Jesuits believed that they could effect anything in Sweden, where almost all were against them, did not their whole history, with the exception of their first exertions and the long-continued consequences, testify that their fate was—it was the curse of their false principles—to live in illusory and deceitful hope, and to destroy their own work by precipitate measures. They speak of the Swedish people's inclination for their faith, without understanding and comprehending the good fruits preserved and rendered firm by the storms of the warily-conducted Reformation, and they must acknowledge that among this people they could make but a very small number of proselytes. They speak of the leaning of Sweden's priests to the Roman faith and public worship, without comprehending the many national characteristics here maintained, without comprehending, as foreigners cannot, the old Swedish simplicity and modesty, which, for a while, give way before conceited disapproval of home customs and relations, until sense and after-thought again restore to the mind its elasticity. They speak of many friends within the senatorial council of the kingdom, that same council which at this very time, and *during* the riot of Stockholm, made to king John serious remonstrances, assuring him that both within and without the land he was suspected of desiring to introduce old and new errors. They then advised him, to declare that he merely aimed at a general union, to reinstate the priests who had been removed on account of their religion, to take heed that the crown prince of Sweden, Sigismund, was nurtured in the pure faith. In these remonstrances the very men took part, who are most claimed by the Jesuits from among the council of the kingdom, Per Brahe, Nils Gyllenstjerna, Hogenskild Bjelke, and Erik Sparre. The Jesuits speak of the great advances they made with king John, but they soon give him up as the *sole* cause of the miscarriage of their projects, a judgment as little reliable as that which made them believe the king himself an easy or a possible conquest.

On Possevin's second coming to Sweden, he found king John determinately unwilling to deviate from the explanations he had already given. Possevin's influence, and the esteem entertained for him, much softened the mind of the king. But Possevin's representations could not bend the king, nor could Warsewitz effect anything. The latter, during the king's stay at Westeras, received from the former written directions how he could best work on the king's mind, even the words, which for that purpose he was to put into the mouth of the queen, A. Lorich, and others to be depended on, including, though with less assurance, Per Brahe, Erik Sparre, and the secretary Henrik Mattson.* In vain had Possevin more than once begged that a church might be allowed the confessors of the Roman faith. The almost scornful answer was, that this could not be granted unless the pope would grant the required dispensation, or in Rome grant a church to the Lutherans.

During the time of the pestilence some of the youths belonging to the college, who had turned Romanists, died. But the confessors of the Roman church had no place of burial, and it was not permitted them to bury their dead according to the usages of their church in any of the usual graveyards. They were, therefore, buried by Klosterlasse in the grey monks' holm, secretly, at midnight.

King John, already dissatisfied with the pope, was still

* As one of the means of working on the mind of the king, Possevin recommended to impress on him that his fears would render him the laughing stock of the protestant princes.

further irritated in consequence of Sigismund's conversion by the Jesuits to the church of Rome, and his refusal to take part in the liturgic service, and they experienced not only hard words, but threats of scourging, imprisonment, and exile. The king's wrath was quieted, but not his dissatisfaction, and when he summoned Possevin and his coadjutors to East Gothland, his intention was to allow the visitation of Wadsten by the papal legate, but no less to prevent the Jesuits in his absence from having free play in the rest of the land, and thus creating scandal. The king, who hoped to constrain Rome into granting the desired dispensations. could not wish to be convinced that the work of conversion could go on without them. This Possevin perceived. "I find," he writes to Warsewitz, on November 14, 1579, "that if the king is grieved for anything, it is that he sees the cause has great success." That the king harbored a special fear of their success is not likely. Possevin finds proof of this, for he warns them not to trust in Per Brahe and Erik Sparre, of whom he had before spoken very well. A law of the council at Wadsten, in 1580, shows that the king more rightly estimated these men than did the Jesuits.

The king dissuaded persons who professed themselves inclined to go over to the church of Rome. They ought, at least, to wait till it was seen whether the use of the cup in the Lord's Supper would be allowed. Sigismund's first communion must have taken place without his father's knowledge. At Wadsten, the king, in presence of the papal legate, permitted the marriage according to the Lutheran liturgy, of Pontus de la Gardie, with his natural daughter Sophia Gyllenjelm. The ceremony was performed in the cloistral church restored to the nuns in 1577, and created no little scandal to the papists, who regarded it as a profanation of that church, and therefore considered a misfortune which happened during the service, by the falling down of the gallery, as a judgment from heaven.

The hope of the Jesuits to lay Sweden at the feet of the Roman pope, miscarried, and all the blame was laid on the king. Had he, as they fancied, possessed a resolute will, and left them free hands, Sweden would have been converted, for, "it is a simple and good people, which, enough to make one weep, follows in life and death its leaders and teachers, just as they happen to come." The Swedish people have indeed accounted this fidelity their commendation, but in a higher sense, as directed *of free will* to those high and noble aims for which the heart of a people ought to beat. That their fidelity was so directed, just such a case as the present shows. The same John III. could, *notwithstanding* his resolute will, as little bring his liturgical reform into operation, as could the Jesuits establish the Roman church, and Sigismund, who gave the Jesuits free hands and wished their success, was obliged in the attempt to sacrifice the royal crown of Sweden.

The attempt which was now made, had called forth in many minds the remembrance of their fathers' faith. The old were reminded of the customs and usages of their youth; the younger generation could recall but little of what in the homes of their childhood was acknowledged and practised. This faith showed itself not to be dead, but alive, ingrained, and strong. From this remembrance, the Jesuits hoped a future harvest out of the seed now sown.

Meanwhile, there was for the present nothing more to perform. King John was content to be free of the missionaries who seemed to hate the peace of his kingdom, and were a hinderance to his own plans. He wished, if he did not order, their departure, and they themselves regarded further attempts as fruitless. On the 10th of August, 1580, Possevin departed from Stegeborg, and left Sweden for the second and last time, carrying with him Klosterlasse, who was summoned to Rome before the general of his order, to clear himself from the not unfounded accusation of having by his double dealing ruined the cause. Mylonius, who afterward obtained, through Sigismund, a priest's charge at Dantzic, and all the other Roman priests, took their departure at the same time, with the exception of five, Warsewitz, Wisowsky, J. Ardulf, who stayed with queen Catherine, and an unnamed individual who remained at Stockholm to attend upon the papists there. The aged Laurentius Magnus also remained in Sweden, having a pension of two hundred ducats from the pope, and as it seems, was now admitted into the cloister of Wadsten.

The attempt, then, to recover the Swedish church to the obedience of Rome, had failed, although begun with brilliant hopes. At first, after king John's death these hopes for a short hour revived.

CHAPTER VI.

THE COMPLETE BREACH BETWEEN THE LITURGIC, LUTHERAN AND ROMAN CATHOLIC PARTIES.

(UNTIL THE DEATH, 1585, OF BISHOP NILS OLAI, OF STRANGNESS.)

At the beginning of the connection between king John and the men of the Roman church, each party calculated on an easy victory; just in proportion as they fancied themselves to be near each other, could neither understand the other. The king could imagine nothing else than that the papists should be ready to extend to him the hand of brotherly union, if not wholly turn to him where he stood on a stand point which he conceived that church to have never denied or rejected. He let slip from his memory two important circumstances. One of them, which the papal church soon learned, was, that she could, during the ferment of the Reformation, only save herself by holding fast to the position she had at the time of the outbreak; purifying herself from the worst abuses, and quickening her life by pietism. The other was, that the *papal* church never actually stood where John stood. At the period, about the fourth century, which for John was to be the ecclesiastical pattern, he could find nothing of popery in the modern sense, and he would not receive it as developed by the continued influence of the Holy Ghost. At that period, too, there was found no supreme prince within the church, and he therefore could not comprehend the preaching of the Jesuits respecting the kind of obedience he owed as a son of the church.

On the other hand, the Jesuits deemed incomprehensible

the obstinate opposition to them of a man whose views seemed so nearly allied to their own. Some believed that he broke off the connection from fear; others, that he acted with the dishonest cunning of a selfish man, merely to obtain the good will of Rome in gaining possession of his wife's inheritance. Some, more clear-sighted, discovered the true reason that the king, "who esteemed himself wiser than all others, had built up a religious reform little differing from the Roman, and therefore published his liturgy, and conceived he could not wholly cast aside the pope's authority."

The Jesuits, who received from the king the assurance which abated their sorrows, that he never could become a Lutheran or Calvinist, but at the same time the distressing information that he contemplated seeking a union with the Greek church, must have seen how perseveringly, even under their watchful eyes, he labored for the reception of the liturgy. This labor became the more earnest as he saw more clearly the hopelessness of a union with Rome. Meeting the views of the Jesuits, he had allowed them to believe that he regarded their views as preparative to a union with Rome, and that he "was practising a device to gain over his people.". But the Rome he sought was, as we have often remarked, not the Rome of the Jesuits and papists of the latter half of the sixteenth century.

His doubt whether the Swedish church had a legitimate priesthood, induced him, when Klosterlasse left Sweden, to try if the latter, who was thought to be a temporizing man, might not be drawn into the views of the king. He proposed to Klosterlasse to remain here, on condition he did not attempt to spread the doctrines the king disapproved. Although this proposal miscarried, the king persevered in avoiding a nearer relation with the priests of the Swedish church. His father confessor was one Martinus, who had been a Roman and afterward a Lutheran priest, but now was attached to the liturgy. The king wished this man, who lived in separation from his wife, to receive absolution from Possevin for defection from popery; but when it was refused by the legate, the king caused Martinus to be absolved by a priest of the cloister of Wadsten.

After the project of union had come to the ground, the parties stood completely sundered from each other. The papists soon had no public worship in the land, except in queen Catherine's court, where preaching was held only in the Polish language. The priest who remained at Stockholm, at Possevin's departure, was obliged soon after to leave the country in consequence of a riot in Stockholm; so that of the Jesuits, Warsewitz and Ardulf alone were left.

The Roman confession was embraced by the young heir to the throne, and by king Gustavus' daughter, the margravine Cecilia, who for a while lived a widow in Sweden, but in 1579 left it altogether. The chief men of Sweden who approximated to the views of Possevin, stopped short within the liturgical church. Per Brahe, Nils Gyllenstjerna, Goran Gera, Hogenskild Bjelke, and Erik Sparre, subscribed on the 9th of February, 1580, all the deliberations of the council. Brahe, who died in 1591, and Gera, who died in 1588, were regarded as having breathed their last in the bosom of the evangelical church. Of the three others, neither was among those whose defection to Rome was, in 1595, avowed. Bjelke declared, in his last confession, that he had not intended the introduction of popery. Possevin wrote, some time before his departure from Sweden, to Sparre, of his having once *expected* that Sparre would aid in restoring in Sweden the old truth. Sparre, therefore, was not a papist.

When the pope, in 1581, was endeavoring to save some threads of the connection with Sweden, which were now breaking asunder, he wrote to Nils Gyllenstjerna, and praised his steadfast faith, and urged him to activity in its diffusion. He did the same to Pontus De La Gardie, adding his thanks for the great and important services rendered Possevin, and reminding him of his promise to assist king John in his plans for the catholic religion. There is some hesitancy in deciding whether this language is a reproach, or really meant, or pretended ignorance. It is the same Gyllenstjerna, whom, in 1596, a Jesuit calls "a thorough biting foe of the catholics," and the same De La Gardie, of whom Possevin himself complains that he, of all others, except Typotius, caused the work of conversion to miscarry, and to the latest hour labored against the legate's plans.

It may, in conclusion, be remarked, that the lords who were accused at Linkoping in 1600, were regarded as faulty in having promoted the liturgy, "which is an entrance to popery," and circulated it in the land, and with both threats and good words constrained the clergy and people, but these lords were not accused of having fallen into popery, which certainly would not fail to have been laid on Erik Sparre's head, if there had been reason found to do so.

The very strong opposition to the papal church moulded the Lutheran such as it existed at the court of duke Charles, with a leaning to Calvinism, to which the duke himself began to be inclined. Calvinists were staying at his court, and exorcism began to be laid aside there, a change contemplated in the Swedish church in king Erik XIV.'s time, but not at that time acceptable. The Calvinistic public worship was not used there or at Stockholm, except in private conventicles, whose worshippers were publicly regarded as belonging to the Lutheran church. Pure Lutheranism was professed by the princess Elizabeth, who, in 1581, was married to duke Christopher of Mecklenburg. The Lutheran public worship was scrupulously maintained in the duchy of Charles, as it existed in the time of Gustavus; and the largest part of the Swedish people embraced it with a seriousness of heart, which by the trial it was now passing through, made them more and more to appreciate its depth and strength.

Between popery and Lutheranism, but with a preponderating inclination to the former, and on the same basis with it stood "*the king's religion,*" founded on the ordinantia and liturgy of 1575. This religion had in favor of it the outward show of piety, and the license which often covers itself under the abused name of protestant freedom. It had also in its favor, a pretended agreement with the doctrine of the fathers, and presented all the fascination of royal favor, with its rich rewards on the one hand, and the discouragements attached to the threats of power on the other.

To such an extent had men in Sweden become divorced from the Roman church, that a likeness to it became the liturgy's most dangerous foe. The council of the kingdom at Wadsten, drew the king's attention to this circumstance, at the same time that their deliberations gave support to his zeal for introducing the liturgy, which now under a wider separation of the two other parties was more eagerly pressed than ever.

The next sacrifice to this zeal was bishop Marten of Linkoping. In what manner his opposition made difficult the first recognition of the liturgy by the clergy in 1577, has already been narrated, and how he and his chapter afterward declared themselves against its introduction. The appearance of the Jesuits at Wadsten and Linkoping in 1580 increased the ill will. Admonished by duty and conscience, the bishop preached publicly against the pope's primacy, called him anti-christ, watched the steps of the Jesuits and endeavored to counteract their attempts.

This open enmity to the Roman church awaked the displeasure of the king, to whom Possevin complained, and who still wished peace with that church, if no outward unity could be effected. His displeasure was still more increased, when the bishop included the liturgy in the same category of condemnation. He opposed it in speech and writing. He declared that his consent had been extorted. He had not willingly, but with great regret and pain, subscribed the liturgy with an explanation. It was not enough at the council of Stockholm, in 1577, to be willing to resign office, but whoever did not subscribe was threatened with being accused as a traitor and insurgent.

The king, while staying in East Gothland and four months in Linkoping, perceived how little the liturgy had in that diocese come into use. He, therefore, while on his visit at Linkoping, issued from Wadsten a letter, which menaced the bishop and his clergy, that unless they kept to the liturgy, they should be looked upon as traitors and lose their support. We suppose that this letter was issued at a later date than that of the explanation to which the bishop alludes. But when, during the negotiations respecting the liturgy, the criticisms of an unfavorable kind written by Abraham Angerman from a protestant point of view, and by Klosterlasse and his friends from a papistic, made their appearance, the king found it advisable more openly than hitherto had been done to express his disapproval of these men and their views. This was done in a stringent edict, which, from that time, and while the Jesuits were still going over the matter with the king, was issued against the opposers of the liturgy.

The king had, it is there said, with dissatisfaction perceived that, although bishops and prelates by their promise and their subscriptions had pledged themselves to introduce the use of the liturgy into divine service within the congregations of the kingdom, this pledge had been by many neglected. The priests ought to be constrained strictly to follow this liturgy, and not merely, to save appearances, the preface be read, and the rest left out. The disobedient should lose all investitures and tithes, and be punished as perjurers. The provosts were on their court days to take a sworn assurance from the priests to observe the liturgy in all its parts. If any one excused himself, because master Lars of Stockholm (Klosterlasse) had spread and caused to be spread writings which were contrary to God's word and the truth, the king would give such a one to understand that he did not approve of these writings, whose author had been forbidden to read in the college and to preach. He had purged out false doctrines, and this liturgy had no alliance with the Roman mass-book. Master Abraham of Saltvik had also written against the liturgy, "with silly arguments and little correctness." As the king approved neither the writings which master Abraham and his party, nor those which master Lars and his followers, had put forth, they and such ought all to be collected and burnt in the king's chancery. Whoever concealed them or spread them should be punished as a traitor.

Some weeks later, when the king had called together the clergy of the diocese of Linkoping in the city of that name, bishop Marten was declared unworthy of his office, and its robes were taken off him before the altar of the cathedral. Hogenskild Bjelke was commissioned to give the people an account, at the fair of Linkoping, of the reasons for displacing the bishop, and to let them know that Klosterlasse and the schoolmasters at Stockholm and Wadsten who had caused scandal should not only be displaced, but banished the kingdom.

Before the assembled priesthood of Linkoping the king repeated his disapproval of Klosterlasse and Abraham, and his prohibition of their writings. They ought not to believe, he said to the clergy, that the Holy Ghost was confined to Wittenberg, or Geneva, or *to Rome only;* truth could be but one, and must be sought for in the writings of the church fathers.

Although our information of this meeting is but partial,

it shows that even here the king's will met with contradiction. Separate assurances and subscriptions were not taken of those present, perhaps in order not to provoke a stronger opposition. But the king's competency to regulate and give order in these matters had been questioned. On this point, he said, they touched him both as a Christian and as a king. He had been bidden to stand by the faith his father held. The king objected, that his father might have been misled. Not his father's faith but that of *the fathers* was to be followed.

In the year 1580 commences that point of time in the history of the liturgic controversy, which was marked by more rigid measures. As in 1577, so now, the king adopted the expedient of sending agents into various parts of the land, either to treat with the people and present the king's views, or to ascertain how the liturgy was received. H. Bjelke labored in East Gothland. But the king's principal assistant at this time was his secretary Henrik Mattson, who was directed this year to provide a new edition of the liturgy, from which the Latin annotations were to be removed. Erik Stenbock and the bishop of Skara, were ordered to treat with the priests in West Gothland, Knut Lilje with those of Smaland, and he and John Henriksson with the people assembled in 1581 at the fair of Upsala. It was a visitation which, with many and great differences, may be compared to that king Gustavus appointed in 1540 through G. Norman and his assistants. As king Gustavus was led to adopt this course, because he thought the bishops did not go forward with the work of reformation, so now king John III. complains, that in his reform "nothing was smoothly done," and he resolved that the cause should, on the part of the bishops, be pressed forward with activity and determination.

Besides the persecution which overtook the leaders of the opposition, and of which more will be said, John adopted a measure which shows to what width he thought his royal rights within the church to extend. But he pronounced beforehand judgment on the vanity of his own attempts; because all history witnesses that he who thinks meanly of men, never executes for humanity a work that lasts. It is love that wins fruit-bearing victory, but not disdain. The measure to which we have referred, was an attempt, by the prohibition of tithes, to overcome the dislike of the clergy to the liturgy. The suppression in 1527, and especially in 1544, of two thirds of the tithes to the crown, was connected with the principle, that what was restored to the church was to be considered an investiture from the crown, and not only was a compensation given for the suppressed glebe, but two thirds of the tithes of the rent of the soil belonging to the priests was regarded as an investiture of the crown. Not only then was the holder dependent on him who had recovered the property, but the king was obligated to protect the rights of the priest against the tithe-payers of the thirds. According to a decree of the year 1527, the right of the clergy to tithes was so secured as not to be called in question. But this security was not operative against the principle that knew of no right but the king's will.

This payment, therefore, became for the priests, a question of privilege; and John's self-will permitted him not to slight the exercise of power which the state of the case offered him, as to the affairs of the church; since for their temporal incomes, all parish priests were dependent on the king. The entire incomes of bishops, professors, and teachers, were investitures of the crown. Promises of privileges were the bait for every change to which the consent of the clergy was to be won. Fecht first gained their confidence, according to Abraham Angerman's report, by promising, among other things, to procure greater privileges for them from the king. But the opposition made to the king's views, was followed by the recall of such privileges. This revocation was, from 1580, extended by king John to the tithes of the parish priests.

A royal edict came out, which threatened the withdrawal of tithes and all investitures, from the priests who did not follow the liturgy in public worship. No longer relying upon the good will of the bishops, or mistrusting their ability to overcome the ill will of the parish priests, the king applied himself to his stewards. They were ordered to stop the compensation, or other means of support from the crown, and to sequester the tithe of unthreshed corn brought into the barns of the priests, who refused to follow the liturgy in divine service.

The bishops and clergy, it is said at the commencement of this edict, had not abided by what they had promised respecting the liturgy, or, as the king expresses himself, had been "disobedient to him in matters of religion." Their support, therefore, and the composition made with them, was recalled, and the parsons or pastors were forbidden to take from the people, tithes of unthreshed corn, as long as they would not abide by the liturgy, or take an oath at the court of assize that they used it, and give a written pledge to that effect.

The king did not take into account the people's selfishness. The tithes of unthreshed corn were always to be delivered, and the stewards were to permit its being threshed, but not to let the priests have any before they took the prescribed oath. If the stewards did not obey this command, they were themselves to repay the tithes they allowed to the disobedient priests. The prohibition was renewed over the whole kingdom, or in special parts of it, and was declared void for particular districts, as soon as obedience was shown to the king's will. From Gestrickland and Medelpad, petitions were sent in for their priests, but were rejected by the king, who expressed his astonishment that they should petition for those who would not accept the order and ritual of the mass.

The king's inflexible determination to enforce the general acceptance of the liturgy, necessarily brought him into unwonted collision with his brother, duke Charles, and made the spirit of the chief persons opposed to the liturgy more unrelaxing than before. The duke, who was not of a disposition to trouble himself with cloisters and monks, and thought that things more important and necessary for fatherland might be undertaken, was as firm in his opposition to reform as the king was to carry it through. The mind of the king was particularly embittered, when, from 1584, the duke not only received into his duchy and protection, the men who, by their repugnance to the liturgy, drew upon them the king's displeasure, but *invited* to him many among the most eminent of these men.

The courage of the enemies to the liturgy increased with the prospect of security for their temporal support, and within the duchy raised up an opposition party, which was animated and led by the most cultivated theologians and priests of the land, made the more eminent by the lustre of the persecution they suffered. *All the men* who were prominent in the contest which duke Charles now commenced against the liturgy of John, were those who had previously held places *not* in his duchy. Charles, therefore, stood in this contest, not in the strength which the church already possessed within his dukedom, and which might have sufficed to sustain him, but he formed a band of warriors out of the forces John himself supplied. One only of these men, Henrik Gadolenus, who a short time before had been reader at the college in Upsala, appears to have taken the pastoral charge of Balinge, in Sodermanland, in the duchy, previous to the open breach.

A part of Charles's dukedom, the districts of Vermland and Valla, and Vadsbo, lay in the diocese of Skara, whose bishop was favorable to the liturgy. There could not fail being a contest between the spiritual ruler, who in his jurisdiction enforced the reception of the liturgy, and the temporal, who would permit no change. Dissatisfaction with bishop Jacob, determined the duke to separate his portions from the diocese of Skara. He then offered, in 1581, Jesper Marci, who had been for two years deposed from the pastoral cure of Wadsten, to become superintendent of those portions, and appointed him accordingly, on condition that he would watch over the church's doctrine and ceremonies, so that nothing should be introduced contrary to God's word in holy Scripture rightly interpreted and understood, or contrary to the usages of king Gustavus's time, and that he would abolish all abuses.

Jesper held the pastorate of Ullarva, and from 1583, the newly settled Mariestad, as his place of residence. In Carlstad and Mariestad, schools were founded, and for the latter, collections made in the parishes which before had contributed to support the school in the diocese of Skara.

Bishop Marten, who had been displaced in 1580, remained in Linkoping nine months, without office or salary, until duke Charles, soon after the coming of Jesper, gave an invitation to the bishop also, took him under his protection, and appointed him to be pastor of the congregation of St. Nicholas, at Nykoping, the capital of the duchy. Master Marten wrote to the king, and solicited his favorable consideration. He deemed that he had done no wrong, but he could not draw in the yoke with sophists and papists. The duke, too, made application to the king, though in vain, that what was left of the bishop's sequestered property at Linkoping, might be restored to him as a free gift.

The men who previously refused to acknowledge the liturgy, could not avoid acknowledging the pressure of the king's renewed severity. The provost, Olof, was permitted, on his promise of silence, to enjoy the freedom of private life. Peter Joachim was persuaded to accept the liturgy. More immoveable were the two readers, Petrus Jonæ, and Olof Luth, whom neither persuasion nor loss of salary could bend. The latter was, in the beginning of 1580, removed from trouble by death.

Master Petrus, truly named, became now a rock on which the opposition founded itself, together with Olof, who had been allowed to continue teaching at Upsala, until in consequence of the plague's breaking out, the king closed the college. His salary had been withdrawn, and he asked the king for the benefice of Funbo, situated near Upsala. The answer was, that it would be granted him on condition that he allowed divine service to be performed by a chaplain of the king. At first he refused, but removed at last to Funbo, to escape the contagion of the plague. Unvanquished by the persuasions of Knut Liljes, and Henrik Mattsson, at Upsala, he was called in 1581 to Stockholm, and, when neither threats nor promises availed, he was cast into prison. Still inflexible, he was banished by the king's order, to a place within the Russian territories; but in the autumn of 1581, he found an opportunity to escape, and went to Nykoping.*

He was soon met there by the third of the more noted refugees, Abraham Andreæ. The latter had remained un-

* While under arrest at Stockholm, his wife and children were supported by alms, in the glebe at Funbo. His wife was a brisk woman, who coincided in her husband's views. She made application to the king for her husband, and was in treaty with his secretaries. She called on Henrik Mattsson, who gave her to understand, that her husband's obstinacy would cost him his life. She gives an account of the interview: "I answered him, 'I thank you, Henrik Mattsson, for your comforting answer. I have not before been aware of your plots and purposes, for the tongue readily speaks what the heart dictates.' Then I said to him, 'Henrik Mattsson, as this is a serious matter, and may cost a neck, I would be over curious with you, and know whether it is to cost me mine with his, for he and I are of one faith.

disturbed in Aland, until his activity against the liturgy occasioned his being, in 1580, imprisoned at Abo. After some time, he gained an opportunity of laying his case before Pontus de la Gardie, who, on the ground of his present enlightenment repenting his participation in the church's disturbances, of his own motion, released Abraham. Abraham was then sent to Saltvik, there to remain till his wife and de la Gardie should go to Stockholm, and obtain for him the king's grace. The attempt miscarried, because he who now managed the diocese of Abo, declared that all order would be lost if Abraham again got at liberty. The order was given that he should be returned to Abo, and thence to a life imprisonment in some castle on the confines of Russia.

In vain he begged, that with his sick wife, and children, he might reside in some remote corner of fatherland. But when they who were to seize him had already come, he flung himself into a boat, and fled to the coast of Sweden, and there found refuge with duke Charles. This prince, at the request of the exiled Abraham, and Petrus Jonæ, petitioned the king and council of the kingdom for them both, and as he was aware that the king was averse to them because they could not conscientiously comply with some religious points, he expressly declares the reason of his peti-

But which is the true faith, that which my husband maintains, or that which hereafter you will put forward? Shall I hold to the former, or with the latter? Which is better for me?' To this he replied: 'The king's is the true faith.' 'If God will so have it,' was my answer. Then he replied again, with asperity: 'Is the king against God?' Said I, 'I am not his judge; God searches the heart.' The longer we talked together the more we disagreed. So I went from Pilate to Herod, (Nils Hansson). He poured out to me from the same bottle, all sour and no sweet," &c., &c.

Advised by her husband of his flight from Stockholm, she also fled, and after many adventures, came to Nykoping. Her children, whom she left at the glebe, were driven out, and after some months came to their parents.

tion in the words, "we, too, acknowledge the same religion that they maintain."

It could not escape king John, how fruitless his severity was likely to prove, as long as Charles confessed himself to have a common cause with the opposers of the liturgy, and kept his duchy open to them. He called together a diet in 1582, and summoned to it about eight hundred of the clergy. Of these he required a new subscription, which, also, by the exertions of Henrik Mattsson, was brought to pass. The church ordinance of 1575, (that of 1571 was not mentioned) and the liturgy, were to be the rule of *all* congregations in Sweden. Whoever would not submit to this decree, they would reject and esteem them to be unreasonable and disobedient men. They avowed their recognition of all the king's privileges within the duchies, of but "one public worship in the kingdom, of but one king and one law."

What these privileges were, in relation to the church, was set forth in an ordinance of the king, published some days later. The church customs which, in other parts of the kingdom were received, were agreed to by the bishops, prelates, and many clergy, and which were in conformity to God's pure and clear word, should be also received within the duchies. No one but the king and archbishop had authority to settle bishops anywhere in the kingdom. He who was guilty of an offence against the king, and removed into the duchies, should not, against the king's will, be protected and harbored by their princes, but every man be compelled to obey the king's warrant.

The duke could not be induced to give his assent to some of these points. The king soon after issued a warrant to the three refugees, to appear in Stockholm, and make answer to the charges the king had against them; but the warrant was not obeyed. Master Marten declared that he could not appear, because he had been displaced without examination or trial, and was now the duke's servant, and thus could not be righted out of the duchy. The king's anger against this man was not abated. He was, in 1583, proclaimed a perjurer and infamous, and his breach of oath to maintain the liturgy, was proclaimed worthy of the pillory. The old man remained, till his death in 1585, undisturbed in his benefice.

The king's wrath did not permit the two others to remain quiet in the dukedom; but they removed to the fief of Bohus, which was subject to the crown of Denmark. Fearing that the protection and countenance there afforded them might occasion a strife between the king of Sweden and Denmark, and that thus they might seem to rely upon the arm of flesh, they passed over, at the close of 1582, into Germany, furnished with a recommendation by duke Charles to his sister Elizabeth, the dutchess of Meklenburg. When at the same time, duke Charles took himself a journey to Germany, he was followed to Lubeck by Petrus Jonæ with his wife and children, for whom there seemed no safety in Sweden. Petrus Jonæ and his family, however, returned in August of the same year, with the duke, to Nykoping, of which, after the death of Marten, he became the pastor. Master Abraham, to whose restless impetuosity the duke did not wish to be in too close proximity, and whom it was thought advisable to remove from the king's wrath, kept himself in the north of Germany, till, in 1593, he was recalled home to take the archiepiscopal chair of Upsala.

Bishop Nils of Strängness, who, from 1577, took no further part in the injunctions of the king, was not now more able to endure the still greater and energetic requirements of the duke. It seems that the duke, on a visit of the bishop to Nykoping, in 1582, presented a project, from the approval of which the bishop endeavored to escape by hastily leaving the town. He soon after requested permission to resign his office, as being too old for its duties.

Charles, who, after the publication of the edict of

1583, could not be desirous of a vacancy in the see, expressed a wish to confer with the bishop. He ex-excused himself on the plea of sickness from coming, and Henrik Gadolenus was appointed, in conjunction with the chapter, to manage the episcopal office, which he continued to do till the death of his father-in-law. This master Henrik also drew upon himself the displeasure of the king; being accused by Bjelke and Baner, of having, in a sermon, inveighed against the king. Duke Charles took him under his protection, declared him innocent, and refused to permit him to be tried beyond the duchy.

During these commotions there was, from the commencement of the year 1579, no archbishop of Upsala. While the negotiations with Rome were going on, the king did not wish to fetter himself by a nomination, whose validity, in case of a union, might be called in question. In conducting, moreover, his compulsive measures within the church, a vacancy in that office left the king more at liberty. The choice of a proper person was not easy. King John was favorably inclined to the before-named Laurentius Magnus, recommended by his relationship to the last of the papal bishops. Bothvid of Nerike, celebrated for his learning, was also proposed. These, probably, were the candidates of the Jesuits. But after the breach of the purposed union with Rome had rendered these men, who had gone over to that church, ineligible, the king fixed upon Andreas Torchilli, pastor of Jonkoping, who, notwithstanding his refusal, was, in 1583, summoned to Stockholm, with the bishops who were to consecrate him. His persistent refusal probably rendered the choice of him ineffectual, and Andreas Laurentii Bjornram, bishop of Wexio, was looked to as a suitable person for that high post. This man, who for his father's services, and his own zeal in the liturgic cause, had won the king's favor, and been promoted to the bishopric of Wexio, seems to have become sufficiently lukewarm; so that his own chapter did not, until 1580, accept the liturgy, and that through Lilje's and Henrik Mattsson's exertions. He had, beside reputation for learning, acquired much esteem as a man of pure character and sound faith, so that the anti-liturgical party considered him as one of them. Now upon the contrary, he declared himself expressly in favor of the ordinantia and liturgy, and was suspected of having sacrificed his convictions for the hope of elevation and the royal favor.

The provost Nicolaus Stephani succeeded him as bishop of Wexio. After bishop Marten's displacement, in 1580, he was succeeded by provost Petrus Michaelis, who was then eighty years of age and died the same year. The diocese was administered for two years by superintendents Klap Petri, penitentiary of Linkoping, and Nils Petri, school-master of that city, until the father of the latter, Petrus Caroli of Kalmar, now a zealous liturgist, was, in 1582, appointed bishop, who, in the following year, acquired the addition to his diocese of Oeland, Kalmar, and More, which, for a time, had been attached to the see of Wexio.

A few weeks before bishop Marten's displacement, Fecht's former friend, and for a time the promoter of John III.'s reform plans, bishop Erasmus of Westeras, departed this life, not without self-reproach for the aid he furnished in a cause which menaced the church's stability and freedom. As his successor, Petrus Benedicti was nominated, who, being reader at Upsala, had subscribed the church ordinances of 1572 and 1575, but was transferred to the pastoral care of Soderkoping, before the men of Upsala opened the contest against the liturgy, which he in 1577 accepted.

After the death of P. Juusten, in 1576, Abo had, during the insecurity of the following years, remained vacant. In 1579, the provost Henrik Knutsson was appointed its superintendent. In 1583, Erik Erici, born in Finland, at that time school-master of Gefle, eminent for suavity and learning, was nominated as its bishop. The diocese of Viborg, vacant by the death of E. Herkiepes, in 1580, was re-united to Abo.

The new bishops of Linkoping, Westeras, and Wexio, had, soon after their nomination, been consecrated. They were now summoned, in September, 1583, with all the other bishops, to attend the consecration of the archbishop, which took place on the fourth of that month. The archbishop then consecrated the bishop of Abo. There is no doubt that the ceremonies were now used which nine years before created so much disturbance.

On this occasion there were assembled, beside the bishop from Srängness, all the bishops of Sweden, to whom was now added the bishop of Revel, Christian Agricola, son of the bishop of Abo. Certain resolutions were adopted in presence of the king, to confirm and perfect the liturgical reform. It was not a question of doctrine, but of church usages of which they treated. The principle they professed was, that although they acknowledged that without the guidance of the Holy Ghost, whom they must seek by prayer, they could not rightly fulfil the work of their office, yet for this purpose some certain regulations and rites were necessary as a means. They would, in their dioceses, follow accurately as a pattern the ordinantia of 1575, and for the culture of priests in the doctrines of the church fathers, they would import and circulate the necessary books. At the mass the liturgy should be accurately followed, and they would have an eye to the church music, such as had been wont to be practised in each diocese.

The bishops promised that on high festivals they would perform the mass themselves, and on all occasions, as well as festivals, use their appropriate dress. The priests should be obligated, when going to administer the Lord's Supper to the sick, to use their canonical attire, and on other official occasions, at least the dress called roklin. Care was to be taken that the proper garments were to be found in all churches.

Uncomely images, which might bring the saints into contempt, should be removed from the churches. In cathedrals and the towns, where a part of the congregation understood Latin, there should, on high festivals at least, one mass be performed in Latin, but at the same time, at one or two of the other altars, in Swedish, especially if guests for the Lord's Supper were found. The bishops were to be careful that suitable persons were called to the priests' office. They would, at the ordination of priests, adopt the old custom of anointing with oil, provided *it could be done without scandal*, an exception which reminds us of the question of the foregoing times respecting the removal of unnecessary or injurious church usages. The same exception was now made, when they were to be taken up again.

One of the resolutions underwent a separate investigation, the bishops either wishing to avoid attracting general attention to the subject, or taking it up, for the first time, at a late period. This was their engagement to instruct the clergy that they were to anoint the sick with oil.

The resolutions of the bishops, passed on the 10th of September, 1583, mark an important point in liturgical reform. King John had now found for the church, leaders who, in union, and unconditionally it was thought, would enter into his views, and be ready and willing to promote them. This, in connection with the conciliar decree of 1582, and the compulsive measures taken since 1580, seems to announce that the work was now complete; and yet it was near its dissolution.

The church was now by no means fully reformed. The first to rebel was Charles' duchy, which, under the guidance of the duke's firmness and strength, and the decided faith of the men whom John's zeal had driven thither, was more and more alienated from liturgism. We must also, at this time, take into account, what is usually found to be the case, that where good will is wanting, edicts and decrees are slowly and inertly, or not at all operative. After the strong measure of forbidding the payment of tithes had been carried into operation, and after the decree of 1582, and under a bishop favorable to the liturgy, the priests of the chapter of the cathedral of Westeras itself were not unanimous respecting the use of the new order of the mass; and it was neglected in many places of the diocese, both in the towns and in the country.

Even after the pledge made by the bishops, the archbishop himself is reproached by the king for giving the charge of congregations and parishes to men who were opposers of the liturgy and the king. We conclude, therefore, that the change was not carried through. The bishops winked at a disobedience which they did not always disapprove. It may be supposed, what is not unusual, that the measures pursued with the priests had different effects. Many contented themselves in their straitened circumstances, or with the good will of their congregations, on which they depended for support when the tithes were withdrawn. Many who could not see into the dangers which the better informed apprehended from the liturgy, its origin, its relations, and aims, or who could not show where lay its false doctrines and superstitious usages, followed the judgment of those on whom their confidence rested. Doubtless there were not wanting those who could find good reasons, such as might cover their personal interests with the cloak of a zeal for truth—men who consulted only their temporal advantages.

Many were removed from their offices, or laid them down of their own accord. But when it is said that priests were often put into places, whose only credit was their avowed attachment to the liturgy, men who not only were unlearned, but adulterers, thieves, murderers, perjurers, drunkards, and libidinous persons, it must be borne in mind that these charges brought by each party against the other have no great weight, in a time which constantly so painted the character of foes. These charges only show that no period and no party can boast of perfection. But while on the one hand we allow that party interest could blind the eyes to manifest vices, we must on the other hand give credit to the sincerity of the assertions of the friends of the liturgy, that their efforts were directed to the promotion of Christian piety and virtue.

The rigorous measures by which king John now desired to press the reception of the liturgy, were the trial that purified the Swedish church into a clear consciousness of its protestant principles. Beside what we have already told, many cases are mentioned of the perturbations produced by this war of opinions, and the mental conflicts which agitated individual priests, upon the question whether conscience would allow the reception of this liturgy or not. The names of many are on record, who either in their last moments deplored in deep repentance their being seduced into an acknowledgment of the liturgy, or terminated their anguish in madness; and the reports of these particulars were carefully taken down and witnessed under the hands of members of the congregation who allowed their names to appear in print.

Of the people's inclination *for* the liturgy, there is no testimony offered, other than the requests made to king John in 1577, and what is reported by Possevin. No dissatisfaction, such as was expressed in king Gustavus's time at the removal of superfluous ceremonies, betrays itself now against the priests who refused introduction. Upon the contrary, it is asserted, though not by unexceptionable witnesses, that very many kept away from public worship in the churches where it was conducted according to the liturgy, and frequented those only where the liturgy was not used; that many refused in their last hours to receive the sacrament when they could only receive it from the hands of the liturgical priests, and that parents recalled their sons from their schools and studies, to save them from the storms of the future.

During the active contests between the more rigid protestants and the friends of the king's religion, the prospects of the Roman church became more and more dark. John and his party were reluctant to admit that the projected union had failed, had, as so often is the case, been converted into a more bitter hate, and that the courtesy toward Rome, on the part of the philoliturgists, had become a scandal in the eyes of the misoliturgists. The former did not permit those bitter sallies against the pope and his adherents of which the protestants were not sparing. Even those must sometimes speak against the papists; but, as master Abraham remarks, they spoke of the pope as at present not in his natural condition. They said: "So thought *formerly* some passionate papists; * * * but of antichrist, the wolf and devil who harrows and ravages the fold of Christ in the kingdom of the Swedes and Goths, they whisper not a word." But there was cause for remark, even among those not the most zealous, when the archbishop, in a sermon on the virtues which adorned queen Catharine, preached at the cathedral of Upsala in 1584, praised her even for her steadfast adherence to the catholic faith which she inherited from her forefathers and out of whose pale no one can be saved. The expression does not expressly imply praise of the Roman faith; but he was censured by the protestants, to whom the only excuse of the archbishop was the obedience he considered himself to owe the king's will. In the Swedish psalm-book were contained many energetic psalms against the pope. These were regarded as offensive, and were either removed from the edition of 1585, or altered into milder effusions.

Rome, on her side, was still willing to hope for a change, and pope Gregory wrote in 1581 to the king a letter, in which he commends his good purposes, and exculpates his own refusal to assent to the king's demands, especially with respect to the Lord's Supper. The Tridentine council had passed its decree on this subject, but he would willingly allow the question to be examined anew by a church council, if one could be assembled. He would take it into further consideration. The chief point seems to be the overture made by the pope, that as the king had no valid priests in his kingdom, he should appoint a popish bishop only in some remote parts of Finland, to effect the restoration of the church.

This letter was brought from Rome by Possevin, who was at this time dispatched on an embassage to Russia, undertaken with the like flattering hopes as that to Sweden, but with the same fruitless results. Once, when pressed by a war with Sweden, Poland and the Crim Tartars, the Russian czar, Ivan Vasiljevitsch, determined, by an advantage proffered to the Roman church within his dominions, to win the pope's mediation for peace with Poland. The business was undertaken by Possevin, who was fortunate enough to re-establish peace between Russia and Poland, on the 15th of January, 1582. But there had not been taken into account what impression this interference to bring about such a peace would make on the king of Sweden, who alone continued the war. Dissatisfaction with the peace might recoil upon the peace-maker.

Soon after, on September 16, 1583, the bond was broken on the death of queen Catharine, by which Rome first gained an opportunity of approaching king John. She had, during the last years of her life, remained under the influence of the Jesuits, who, through her had access to the king. The queen's death raised in the foes of the Roman church the hope that its advance in Sweden was now at an end, and so audible were the threats, that Warsewitz and Ardulf prepared immediately to leave the land. Nothing but the king's promise of protection induced them to remain for some time. Warsewitz, however, in the spring of 1584, took his departure, taking with him five Swedish youths for the seminary at Braunsberg, to which the queen bequeathed a large sum of money.

Of the two children of Catharine who survived their mother, the princess Ann was lost to the Roman church. There seems to have been no special attempt to win her who was not heir to the throne. She was considered as having followed the faith of her mother, but had, according to king John's assurance, already, before her mother's death, "altogether abandoned" the Roman faith and doctrine. There is a report that Ann, without being observed, was present when the queen, near her end, made known to Warsewitz her fear of purgatory, and asked if she could hope that the troubles she now suffered would contribute to shorten its pains. Warsewitz answered, that there was no purgatory, but that the doctrine thereof was fabled to keep the simple in check, an answer which occasioned his own dismissal from the queen, and in the princess an unchangeable abhorrence of Roman doctrine.

Upon the other hand, Sigismund was, and remained, attached to the Roman church, one of the most obedient sons, after the Reformation, she had among the princes of Europe. In vain the king and council of the kingdom sought to detach him. Their representations, that by his attachment to popery he hazarded the crown he was to inherit, merely called forth the answer, that he did not so much value an earthly crown as to be willing to throw away a heavenly. Notwithstanding this firmness, he now more than before took part with his father in the liturgic worship and service. There was, however, held for him a special popish mass, and the Jesuits were constantly found about the person of the prince.

When the illusory hope of concessions on the part of the church of Rome, which hope was the offspring of John's own imagination, had dwindled away, he was brought no nearer to the protestant church; but, driven by necessity to look for a strong ecclesiastical body, he turned his thoughts to a union with the Greek church, with which, though sundered from the Roman, the Lutherans of Germany had not the good fortune to connect themselves. Bishop Erik, of Abo, such was the king's scheme, was to translate the liturgy into the Greek language, and with it journey to Constantinople to open negotiations with its patriarch. The king, however, abandoned this project.

The disguised attacks which the papists and their near of kin, the liturgists, among whom were many who unreservedly confessed the popish faith, made upon protestantism in their sermons, awakened a dissatisfaction that was loudly expressed. Protestantism was the object of the popular belief and affection, and when, about a year and a half after queen Catharine's death, king John married Gunila Bjelke, who by education and inclination belonged to the protestant church, the dissatisfied began to hope a nearer access to the king's ear and heart.

At the time of the marriage festivities at Westeras, in February and March, 1585, the assembled council and bishops availed themselves of the opportunity to offer the king their serious remonstrances. The councillors complained of the insolence with which the faith and church of the Swedish people were assailed. The king ought to adopt in time measures and means to put a stop to it. They urged that such mischievous persons should either be banished the land, or punished in some other way, and they said that it was currently reported that the populace and soldiery threatened at any rate, if they did it themselves, to get rid of such weeds. Prince Sigismund's Polish priest preached openly and in Swedish against the religion of the country, and circulated books and tracts to the same purport. The council required that a stop should be put to this, that the prince should follow his father's faith, or that at least his priests should be forbidden to preach in any language but that of the Poles.

The bishops complained that the preacher at Stockholm, Lars Forsius, or Franne, had fallen off to the jesuitical faith; that another "Jesuit," Johannes Finne, had in their presence, and at other times, declared that in Sweden there were no bishops or priests, but soul-murderers, who had no power in matters relating to salvation. The bishops, including the otherwise compliant bishop of Linkoping, remonstrated against the king's interference with the discipline of the church. If a priest, for viciousness of doctrine or life was displaced, he was without trial reinstated by the king. The king allowed the chapter to continue either incomplete in numbers, or to melt away, whereby bishops were shorn of their strength, since one man is no man. This was an effort to regain the church's lost independence, made by the very men whose power king John wished to elevate, but only on the supposition of their submissiveness to him. They were to be catholic bishops, but likewise, merely as the king's working gear, superintendents of the districts around them.

This struggle for freedom had at this time no consequences. But the outcry against papists had an easier success. Forsius, who openly renounced the faith he was pledged to preach, could not be patronized. He was cited to Westeras and stripped of his clerical robes, on a festival, before the altar of the cathedral of Westeras; a publicity similar to that with which bishop Marten, of Linkoping, five years before, was displaced. Johannes Finne, then present in Westeras, challenged the bishops to a disputation, a challenge which they did not accept.

It was natural that the city whose teachers were discovered to have fallen away, should attract to itself general observation, and the conduct of the papists was resented. In Stockholm, notwithstanding the riots of 1580, a Roman catholic congregation had been kept up, which celebrated divine service in a private house. Now, or soon after this time, their service was prohibited, and the free exercise of their religion was permitted the papists only in Wadsten, until Sigismund, after his mother's death, took up his abode at Drottiningholm, to which place those of them who by engagements or occupations were not confined to Stockholm seem to have resorted.

At the same time, and for the same reason, a more stringent course was adopted with the then existing college at grey monks' holm, near Stockholm. After the opening of the year 1580, when the work of instruction was laid waste by the scourge of pestilence and the king's persecution of the teachers at Stockholm, the college at the holm was the only institution for the higher kinds of literature in the land, and was shielded by the king's special favor. As the first Swedish principal of the institution, John Billius, was a secret papist, he was removed from his office.

Qualified teachers, most of them afterward the chief ornaments of the church and of the academy of Upsala, such as Lars Lælius, Erik Skinner, and Paul Kennicius, were forthwith installed. Books of instruction and science, theses and disputations, bear witness to a lively energy, and among the most eminent men of the following period, are to be found those who received their literary training in this institution. These instructors, who entered on their office about the year 1585, were all of a protestant mind, but at first undetermined or reserved. If they did not side with the liturgy, they were at least not against it, until the transactions of subsequent years compelled them to take a more decisive part.

The commencement of 1585 was a moment in which

the hope of victory dawned on the friends of protestantism. The archbishop and bishops undertook, upon inquiry, to exonerate from the use of the liturgy, those persons whose consciences it wounded. The judgment passed on Forsius, whose inclination to popery the Lutheran puritans could not separate from the cause of the liturgy, was thought, after the sufferings of some years, to afford them freer scope. The old master Olof, formerly pastor of Stockholm, hastened back, by the archbishop's permission, to his flock, and began to preach in the large church of Stockholm, certainly not in the spirit of a philoliturgist. In like manner acted other priests, whom the king forbade the pulpit. The clergy of the cloister church appear to have laid aside the liturgy. But this was not king John's intention. The archbishop was severely reproached. Master Olof was banished the city, and for a time deprived of his support. Another clergyman, master Brynolf, was even sent abroad, and the priests of the cloister church were threatened with displacement. In this respect the year 1585 was a picture of the year 1580. As when Klosterlasse and master Abraham were at the same time condemned by the king, so now at the same time with the above-named persons, the chaplain at Stockholm, Johannes Salhmontanus, who followed the footsteps of Forsius, was forbidden to perform divine service. The king kept with impartiality the middle path of the liturgy, between the opposing parties.

For the Roman church there remained little more than the hope of better times, through Sigismund. To save him was the object of their most solicitous cares. To him pope Gregory, a little before his death, wrote a letter, exhorting him to steadfastness. The new pope, Sixtus V., soon after his own accession to the papal chair, implored Sigismund's aunt, queen Anna of Poland, to watch over her nephew, whom he wished to be separated from his father and put under her care. Sixtus wrote also to John and Sigismund, thanking God for the catholicism of the former, and warning the latter to shun the rocks of heresy.

Gregory had resolved on another Jesuit mission to Sweden. He informed Sigismund, that, hearing of his love for church music, he had selected three qualified youths, who were moreover versed in the Holy Scriptures, and from whose musical talents and conversation, the prince in his domestic hours might be edified. They were Jesuits, chosen by Possevin, who also drew up instructions for their guidance. They were carefully to conceal what they really were, to hide their dresses and books from sight, and during their journey, only in private to perform their devotions. They were to announce themselves as sent by queen Anna to her nephew. On their arrival in Stockholm they were to put themselves in communication with Nils Brask and one father Vandeler, but in all things to be guided by the Jesuit Simon Nicovius. To the king they were to make known and assure him of the pope's good will, although weighty reasons did not suffer him to enter into the king's wishes for a council. If they did not gain access to the king, they were to put down the purpose of their errand in writing, in a handsome chirography, in which the king took great delight.

How these young men were received we know not. But, a few years later, the king's mind became so averse to the Jesuits, that he warned Sigismund to beware of them. They were the worst of priests, and were wont to have one foot in the pulpit, and the other in the council, and were ready to perpetrate any evil, if only their purposes could be thereby promoted. He could not, without repentance and grief, reflect upon the trouble they brought upon him, what time they were in Sweden. Sigismund ought to drive them from him, and thereby obviate the suspicions which the Swedes would otherwise harbor of the heir to the throne.

During the course of these transactions, the episcopal chair of Strängness became, in 1585, vacant by bishop Nils Olai's death. The events which followed, prepared the ripened fruit of the decrees of the council of Upsala, which were the basis of the present Swedish church.

CHAPTER VII.

CONTESTS RESPECTING THE ELECTION OF A BISHOP FOR STRÄNGNESS —SIGISMUND'S ELECTION TO BE KING OF POLAND—REMONSTRANCE OF THE CLERGY IN CHARLES'S DUCHY AGAINST THE LITURGY—THE BEGINNING OF THE DEFECTION.

(TILL KING JOHN III.'S DEATH IN 1592.)

AMONG the indefinite parts of king Gustavus I.'s will was this, who was the church's guardian within the duchies apportioned to his younger sons? Was it a right invented by the king, or had Gustavus thought the church and its discipline so merely and purely a separate part of the state, that the rights of the dukes in this respect must be the same as the other powers they possessed in their lands?

But if he borrowed this principle from the neighboring protestant countries, it cannot be supposed that he wished to annex the right of establishing or abrogating within their duchies the faith and worship of their subjects at pleasure, as was sometimes done in the German states. He did not foresee the divisions which began to appear in the realms of protestantism even before he went to his rest, and if he regarded the royal authority as carrying along with it the rights which he, from 1539, allowed himself to claim, he had little idea that they would be used otherwise than for the protection of his own work. The matter was now brought to that pass, that his successor to the crown regarded the royal right to consist in making ordinances other or in addition to those which marked the church's condition in his father's time, while the only one of his sons who retained the duchy left him by his father's will, considered it his princely right and duty to uphold his father's work in opposition to the king himself.

The point about which, in the existing relations and posture of the church's constitution, the question specially revolved, was the right to nominate bishops, a right which king Erik had enforced against his brother. Between John and Charles the discord in this respect began to manifest itself in connection with the demand of the former, that the decree respecting the liturgy and other matters passed in a council called for the whole kingdom, should be obligatory on the church of the dukedom. The ordinance of 1582 was answered, by Charles's removal, without consulting the king, of Nils of Strängness from the exercise of his office, and by putting another in the place on his own ducal authority. He had previously placed a styresman or administrator, independent of the bishop of Skara, over that part of the diocese which was subject to his duchy. But when, by the death of the occupant, the see of Skara became vacant for a nomination, the case was rendered more pressing and intricate.

Charles, after the death of bishop Nils, allowed an election to take place, according to the church ordinance of 1571, and confirmed the election. Not only was no respect paid to the ordinance of 1582, but scarcely, bishop Marten of Linkoping being now dead, could a man more unacceptable to John be pitched upon than he who was now chosen, the former professor at Upsala, the now pastor of Nykoping, the opposer of the liturgy, the refugee from the vengeance of the king, the protégé of the duke, in a word, *Petrus Jonæ.* The choice of this man was an open defiance of the king and his darling liturgy. It was not wonderful that king John's wrath was roused. He declared the election invalid, made without consulting him, and an infraction of his royal rights. He threatened the people of the duchy with outlawry if they sustained the election.

Charles, and the priests and people of his duchy, remained unmoved. Petrus Jonæ, however, was not episcopally consecrated, a matter on which probably he and the duke laid little stress, but which, if the consecration was to be performed by bishops, could not be brought to pass, while the controversy with the king was unsettled, since the elected would be acknowledged neither by the king nor by the bishops. He did not remove to Strängness, but retained his pastorate of Nykoping, and abode there. But from the hour he was placed at the head of the clergy of the duchy, he made their views, struggles, and dangers, his own, and chiefly through him and other men of note, united to him by the persecution against the anti-liturgists, the passive was converted into an offensive opposition. The strong position they were able to assume by virtue of the case itself, together with the learning and suffering of its supporters, caused the numbers of the opponents of the liturgy to increase. One by one of its friends fell off, so that at the death of king John, scarce a voice was raised in defence of his most dear and cherished work.

Soon after the election of Petrus for bishop, there was held at Orebro a council, whose decree, issued in the name of king John, decidedly announced the position tahen by the duchy. It began to be perceived that the Reformation had, in many points, degenerated from its first plan and direction in 1527, and in others had taken a direction whose consequences were now regarded as pernicious. A reform of all this was to be essayed. He who railed at "the Christian doctrine and our *Swedish customs*" was to be instructed and admonished by the priests, and if he did not amend, was to be given up to the prince. The ceremonies at divine service, were, without alteration, to be observed, as was customary a long time after the Reformation, and as by a decree of the council of Upsala in 1572, they had been generally practised.

The ordinantia and liturgy indeed were not expressly named, but a cut is evidently aimed at them in the clause, that the people should be instructed in the difference between God's word and "these church usages and gestures, which are established only on human authority." A protest against the king's intrusion into the management of the church's discipline, is apparent, in the covert language of the direction, that as the recess of Westeras allows it, in an action between a priest and layman judgment should be administered according to the law of Sweden, but in what concerns the doctrine and conduct of priests, and in cases of conscience, the heads of the church should have the free and independent exercise of judgment, without any interference of the temporal power.

We connect this ordinance with the troubles, represented the same year by the bishops, as caused by the king's interference with the affairs of the church; and we find a general effort on the part of the church, in consequence of John's oppressive measures, to recover itself from an unsettled condition, to a law-established freedom. The principles of the year 1539 had been learned by experience. A return to the ordinantia of Westeras was the resolution, that the heads of the church (the name bishop was avoided) should give judgment in cases of marriage, which the king had been in the habit of deciding.

In regard to the bestowal of benefices, it was prescribed that the applicants should first be strictly examined by the heads of the church, and afterward referred to the prince for letters of confirmation. The purpose of this evidently was to obviate a bad practice in the time of John, and also before and after, of sending priests from the governing temporal authorities to the bishops, with a command to provide the priests so sent with benefices, irrespective of a trial of their competency. This was also a rectification of the abuse, which had arisen from the right of inspection and oversight given by the ordinantia of Westeras to the king.

The recess of Westeras had declared it to be the duty of the priests to have a care and make an inventory of the two thirds of the tithes withdrawn to the crown. That declaration was now interpreted to mean, that those clergy should consider themselves bound to do this, "inasmuch as churches, pastors, schoolmasters, and hospitals, were to be supported from such resources." The transfer of these tithes to any other purpose was disapproved.

The articles were not calculated to diminish king John's dissatisfaction with the duke, which many other causes raised to a degree that threatened the breaking out of a war between the brothers. In vain did the duke, by a messenger, represent to the king that the clergy, in the election, acted in conformity with the church ordinances printed and acknowledged by the king, who had prescribed no investigation into the case before the election was made, while the king's right of confirmation could only be valid for the person whom the duke had previously accepted. The king avowed his unwillingness to accept Petrus Jonæ, because he disturbed the kingdom, and moreover had treated his sovereign with disrespect.

The diet of Wadsten, in February, 1587, was designed to settle these as well as other contested points between John and Charles. With respect to the election of a bishop, it was resolved that the archbishop and his chapter, together with the clergy of the see of Strängness, should nominate three of the clergy of that see, with the exception of any who had fallen under the king's displeasure. Out of these three the king should nominate the bishop. The nominated should take the customary oath of allegiance to the king, and with a due correspondence of obligation, also to the prince. The nominated should have the same powers of office as other bishops of the kingdom.

The schools of Marienholm and Carlstadt, established by the duke, were to be continued, and twelve benefices were appropriated, in which to collect parochial alms for the support of the scholars. These alms the duke had, by his own authority, withdrawn from the schools of Skara, to be applied to those portions of Skara contained within his duchy.

On some few points an agreement could not be effected. Among these, was that of the ordinantia and liturgy. On this point, it is said, in treating of an arrangement that as the church ordinance of 1571 was not annulled by the ordinantia of 1575, and as, to the order of the mass, nothing was added by the liturgy, except some godly prayers and songs of praise, and as the smaller congregations in the duchy ought not to oppose themselves to what the greater number and the most distinguished, such as the archbishop, had recognized, so ought this book, even within the duchy, to be received and accepted. But as the duke could not pledge himself by any promise for the clergy of his duchy now absent, the subject should be postponed to a church council, which the king, sometime hence, would cause to be called together.

The fixedness of purpose with which duke Charles now came forward as the head of the misoliturgists, and the reference of the decision of the liturgical question to the clergy of the duchy and a church council, warned Charles to arm himself and his priests for the contest which could not longer be avoided.

He hastened to summon the exiled master Abraham to the assistance of the cause of protestantism. With him the duke does not appear, after he left him, in 1583, in Germany, to have established any correspondence. But now, on Charles's summons, he came forward as the foremost warrior against the liturgy, although remote from fatherland. He was desired by the duke, soon after the diet of Wadsten, to visit the universities of Leipsig, Wittenberg, and Helmsted, and send home their written opinions of the liturgy; and the duke sent him letters of recommendation, with money for his journey, and soon after a copy of the liturgy, which did not reach its destination.

He fulfilled the commission: and opinions from those academies, and from the theological faculty of Frankfort on the Oder, arrived. They find in the liturgy the same faults which had been, and continued to be, in the controversial writings of the day, the subject of criticism in Sweden. Wittenberg remarks, moreover, that as the Jesuits had spread the report, that by their means Sweden would be recovered to the obedience of the Roman church, there was abundant reason for going forth entirely from Babylon, and not halting between two opinions. Leipsig compares the liturgy to a whitened sepulchre, outwardly beautiful, but inwardly full of dead men's bones, and all uncleanness; and accuses it of ascribing the work of the devil to the Holy Ghost. The most passionate of these opinions was that of Helmsted, which observes, that when the archbishop speaks in the preface, of the wild beasts of superstition and profanity, he was himself a third, the devouring wolf in sheep's clothing.

But the zeal of master Abraham, praised, salaried, and incited by the duke, did not cease with the procuring of these documents. In the autumn of the same year, he published a collection of the opinions of the German divines and theologians on church usages, and how far there might be similarity in them to the church of Rome. The work was dedicated to the preachers, shepherds, and servants of the gospel, in all the Swedish dioceses who truly taught God's word, and guarded the faith that sanctifies.

He now, also, undertook an edition of the writings of Laurentius Petri the elder, those to which we have before alluded, and those which had not yet appeared in print.

They commanded respect from the name of the author, were applicable to the church's present relations, and were rendered still more so by a preface and dedication. This latter was made to the qneen Gunilla, the princess Ann, and the archbishop and bishops of Sweden. In it, the author very respectfully addresses the king and bishops, severely scourges the liturgy, "the Herbestic, Possevinic practices," and its underwriters.

These books were imported into Swedish ports, in defiance of the prohibition against Swedish books printed abroad, and were dispersed by the misoliturgists all over the kingdom. A bitter controversial tract, by Abraham, against the Archbishop and his party, was, in 1587, sent to the friends of the author in the duchy, and circulated by them, through copies of it, within the dominions of the king.

But while these firebrands from the exiled master Abraham were being cast into his fatherland, the war of opinions had burst into a full flame. Immediately after the diet of Wadsten, the duke sent to Petrus Jonæ and the chapter of Strängness, his court preacher, Matthias, to consult with them what was now to be done. It was proposed to call together the clergy of the diocese, for common consultation. The priests and theologians of the diocese should, each one for himself, be prepared to speak his sentim ents of the liturgy. This council of priests was opened on the fourth of May. Its members were all assembled in about a week's time, and each individual pronounced his opinion, which, agreeably to the spirit that reigned in the body, was a disapproval.

The most learned and eminent remained behind, and supported by the duke for a month's time, either singly or by pairs, wrought out in form their reflections. The writings published against the liturgy, at the commencement of the controversy, by Petrus Jonæ, Olof Luth, and Martinus Olai, were accurately examined. The most complete and argumentative opinion at this time produced, was that jointly composed by Olaus Marten, bishop Marten's son, and the learned Matthias Marci Molinæus. It was welcomed for the most part, as the general sentiment of the clergy of the diocese. The clergy in the districts of Vermland and Valla, and Wadsbo, had not participated in the transactions at Strängness. The duke sent the document to the superintendent Jesper Marci for their opinion, which was furnished in accordance with that given by the members that met at Strängness.

This opinion disapproves of the liturgy. It was regarded as unnecessary, because the former order of the mass was conformable to God's word, because scandal should be avoided, and the liturgy warred with the pledge given at Westeras, in 1544, with the confession of the Interim in 1549, and with the church ordinance, which, in 1571, had been accepted. The clergy of the diocese of Strängness had also pledged themselves at Nykoping, in 1576, not to introduce new ceremonies. It was regarded as an attempt to darken the light of truth, and open a door to popery. Soon after the death of Laurentius Petri the elder, there began to be an approximation to popery; "until the book called the multiplication of church ordinances, and that written in the year 1575, under the pretext of extraordinary, but false piety, and with crafty forms of expression, came out;" and afterwards, "in an evil hour," followed the liturgy. Attention had not been paid to God's command, that we should not be unequally yoked together with unbelievers. It was held to be filled with errors and false ceremonies, and it used phrases liable to misinterpretation. An illustration whereof was afforded by Possevin's assertion in his answer to Chytræus, that the word "oblation," which appears in the Swedish liturgy, was precisely that which signified the offer ing in the Roman mass. It had occasioned much evil in the kingdom. Under this head were enumerated the ruin of the college at Upsala, the establishment of a popish school at Stockholm, under Klosterlasse, "who was very dexterous in deluding simple youth;" the sending youths to Jesuit academies, from which coming home they circulated false opinions, and yet were held in honor while others were despised and persecuted; the qualms of conscience in those who accepted the liturgy, and lastly, the sale of popish books translated into Swedish.

With papists, sacramentarians, and anabaptists, they wished to have nothing in common. They hoped that neither the king nor any other would require them to introduce the liturgy into their congregations, and by so doing, prove the truth of the union or agreement to which the diet of Wadsten had referred.

The opinion was distributed to all the priests of the duchy, through the medium of copies, which, by order of the duke, were made by the teacher's dictation to the scholars. It was also circulated throughout the dominions of the king, with proper precautions for the personal security of the messengers.

These things occurred at the time Sigismund went over to Poland, to receive the crown vacated, on December 12, 1586, by the death of Stephen Bathoris. King John and the council of the kingdom were anxious to secure for the Swedes in Poland ecclesiastical and religious freedom; the council looking to the exercise of their own authority in relation to the latter, and both they and the king, to the liturgic services in relation to the former. On the same days that the clergy of the duchy, under duke Charles's protection, were seeking at Strängness to ward off the liturgy, as the entering wedge of popery and the occasion of much evil in the kingdom, the king and council at Wadsten were devising means for guarding this service, king John's church constitution, against his son's papistry.

Sigismund should, when in his father's life-time, visiting Sweden, not have more priests in his court than hitherto. He should afterwards not bring with him more than ten, and take them again with him when he left the land, and not allow them, while staying here, any service in churches and schools, or suffer them to revile the religion of the land. The free exercise of religion should not be allowed those who were of another faith, unless the king, on some special occasions, saw reason to give his assent. The Swedes who followed him to Poland should there enjoy religious freedom. They who did not embrace the faith recognized in the cathedrals of the land, and by the mass of the people, should not be employed in the public service, or be supported out of the public revenues. The cloisters and hospitals should be maintained in a condition correspondent to the religion now prevalent in Sweden. Wadsten might maintain a popish priest, but the nuns who wished so to do, should be permitted to take the Lord's supper in both kinds. The church ceremonies which were already accepted, or should be introduced in king John's life-time, were not to be altered. The Gregorian calendar should not be adopted. The incomes paid to the archbishop, bishops, and priests, by king John, were not to be taken from them by his successors. For the first time, because these incomes were considered an investiture of the crown, it was now purposed to secure them from the change apprehended from a popish king.

While the king was endeavoring to secure the stability of his work against his own son, he wished also to guard that son against too great a submission to the Roman chair. He ought not, when at his coronation he addressed the pope by letter, to use the word *obedience* (obedientia), because it encroached too much upon the kingly dignity, but to use the word *obligation*, (obsequium). Thus had John acted towards Gregory XIII. Pope Sixtus V., who opposed Sigismund's election, deserved not greater honor. He was not to speak of foot-kissing, (the common expression, cum devota osculatione pedum) since it would stir the ill blood of Swedish men, who from Sigismund's too great reverence for the pope, might apprehend the bringing in of the inquisition.

If the king and father was disturbed by these partly grave and partly trifling considerations, it may readily be supposed what anxiety the power of Sigismund, augmented by the Polish kingdom, awakened in the protestant people of Sweden. Precisely at the period of these apprehensions and fears, appeared the declaration of the clergy of the diocese of Strängness against the liturgy. Charles sent a copy of it, but without his subscription, to the king.

Any audacious attempt to wrest from him or to dishonor his crown, would probably have less embittered king John, than this onslaught made upon his darling work: an attack made on one side, while he was busily engaged in guarding it from danger on another and an opposite. One only of the more eminent men who were banished for the sake of the liturgy, had found a rest in the grave. The others again came forward, not alone and unsupported, but in combination with the whole clergy of Charles's dukedom, and the king could not avoid foreboding that this open declaration would now, more than ever, find an echo in the rest of the Swedish church.

His wrath was without bounds. He issued a patent against these traitors, grand-liars, faith-breakers, blasphemers, ignorant, good-for-nothing assheads, and every other nickname his anger could invent. They ought to know that the word *offereimus* does not signify we sacrifice, but we present Christ, which is done in the heart, in belief, in prayer. They appealed to the council of Westeras in 1544, but they neither kept its decrees, nor were there many of them left by whom it was comprehended. They ought, by the doom of displacement against Forstius in 1585, to have perceived that the king did not approve the management of the popish priests. They called the king and his faithful men papists. They should call themselves Satanists; "since they obeyed the devil, who is the father of lies." They excused themselves on the plea that they must follow God rather than men; the same plea common in the mouth "of Nils Dacke, when he engaged in his treasonable practices against king Gustavus." Having now, these many years, provoked the king to wrath, he could no longer endure such limbs of Satan, but proclaimed the priests of the districts of Sodermanland, Norike, Vermland, Wadsbo, and Valla, *outlawed.* If any of them showed himself outside the duchy, he should be seized and held in custody, until he became converted or convinced, by God's pure and clear word. All their goods and inheritance not in the duchy, should be sequestered. The priests and teachers within the king's domains, who participated in the like opinions, should be treated in the same manner.

In the first century of the Reformation, it was not uncommon with any party, to utter, in the name of the Holy One, the most violent language of human passion. If the king could forget himself to the degree which this patent testifies, it is not to be expected that the crowd of after-speakers would weigh their words. A lampoon, containing the most virulent sallies against Luther, the Reformation, and clergy of the duchy, was circulated through the land, and was particularly remarkable and influential, from being regarded as the composition of one or more of the king's secretaries. It called forth from Petrus Jonæ and Olaus Martini, a calm and dignified answer, which by the side of this cruel scorn of the work of the Reformation and its foremost man, from the adherents of the liturgy, could not but operate advantageously for the cause it defended. The answer was circulated over the dominions of the king.

But the king stopped not at the point of issuing the

patent. His bailiffs were enjoined to keep a watchful eye upon the priests of the duchy. The extreme men on either side were to be checked. The castellan of Stockholm was directed to summon L. Forsius, who was still to be found in the city, and "roundly reprove him" for spreading popish errors, whereby the king and his true men were exposed to the suspicion of being papists. Both he and Hans Kantor, whom the king accuses of contemning God's word, and calumniating the sacrament, should be threatened with severe punishment. The bishops and chapters were written to on the subject of the treason of the clergy of the duchy. The patent was read aloud in the churches. On the 28th of April, there were assembled at Borgholm, the clergy of Oeland, and a part of Smaland, with the bishop of Wexio; and the king made them a speech. This speech, which is entirely in harmony with his other expressions, specially testifies to his conceited blindness, which made him believe himself the only wise man. He boasts of his erudition and learning, and he considered deviation from his views of faith, as rebellion and treason against his kingly authority. A like meeting was held at Stegeborg, with the clergy of Eastgotha, who signed, as before, a declaration against the clergy of the duchy, but only a part of them, constrained by the king's secretary, without knowing what they signed.

The king's patent was spread even within the dukedom. In Strängness, it had already been made known at the fair gathering, and the chapter applied, with anxiety to the duke, inquiring what they ought to do. They inquired of him, whether, in order to avoid the king's accusations, an investigation ought not to be instituted in every benefice, so that every one might legally testify to the life and doctrine of the priests. This was virtually a project of appeal from the king to the people. They proposed, further, to submit their confession of faith to be tried by the council of the kingdom, and to publish a justification of themselves in answer to the king's letter. They petitioned, lastly, for protection of their property lying beyond the duchy, and for liberty to go to it when they pleased. The duke answered them calmly, and promises protection, but advises circumspection and "a gentle answer," that their silence might not be misconstrued. To his bailiffs he wrote to watch over the safety of the priests, so that they should suffer no violence, as long as they resided within the limits of the dukedom.

In conformity with what had been agreed upon, the clergy convened at Orebro, and thence sent out letters to the king and others, but more full to the council of the kingdom, to the bishops and inferior clergy of Sweden, remarkable for the calm and temperate, but at the same time, firm tone in which they are written. They transmitted also to the king, a Latin confession, reiterating the reasons which hindered their acceptance of the liturgy. The time was now come, when the Swedish protestant churches were to seek safety in confessions of faith of more general validity, and more widely known. The clergy, therefore, of the duchy, who now came forward in the cause of the church, in order to defend themselves against the charge of being betrayers of the faith, expressly appealed to the confession of Augsburg, of the year 1530, and to doctor Luther's smaller catechism, translated into Swedish, as embodying a summary of the truth contained in the writings of the prophets and apostles.

They repelled the charge of treason. What they spoke and wrote against the liturgy, did not militate against the obedience they owed their lord and king. "The weapons of our warfare," they said, in the words of St. Paul, "are not carnal, but mighty before God to the breaking down of strongholds, with which we demolish projects and every high thing that exalteth itself against the science of God, and bring into captivity every thought to the obedience of Christ." The king had doubtless, "in a hasty manner and in wrath," suffered his letter to be published. Tehy prayed for some means of averting his displeasure. The letter to the bishops and inferior clergy, was met by a letter from the king, in which he required, that at a council to be assembled, each and every priest should express his opinion of the writings of the priests of the duchy against the liturgy, renounce all fellowship with that body of clergy, and condemn their conduct as ungodly and rebellious, and affirm this written declaration with their names subscribed.

Matters had now reached the crisis, when this very liturgy, which was designed to be a medium of union for the divided church parties, menaced a schism within the Swedish church. No diocese, however, appears to have unreservedly placed itself on the side of the clergy of the duchy; but either a declaration such as the king asked for was given, as had been done at Borgholm and Stegeborg by the assembled clergy, or a temporizing and more pacific position was taken. In the former line of action, the clergy of the diocese of Wexio, whose bishop favored the liturgy, chiefly and zealously distinguished themselves. They declared that as the priests of the duchy had opposed themselves to Almighty God, to his word rightly understood, to the accepted order of the mass, and to the king, they would consider them as outlawed. They disapproved their opinions, and would hold no fellowship with them.

Others again condemned this declaration of the priests of Wexio, as rash and well nigh ungodly. The priests of the duchy had acted unreasonably, when, instead of awaiting the church council which had been determined on at Wadsten, they had, by their writings against the liturgy, aggravated the difficulties of reconciliation and peace. It could not be denied that in the liturgy there was one or another particular that needed to be altered, that there occurred superstitious usages and objectionable forms of expression. But one ought not, therefore, to pronounce damnation on his brother, who had the same foundation of faith, and administered the sacrament in the same manner as other priests of the congregations in the kingdom. A sin would thereby be committed against God's prohibition, to judge another's servant, the old Swedish order of the mass, would thereby be condemned, and indeed the whole Swedish church, by which, for forty years, it had been used. It would also be bearing false witness, if, as the clergy of the see of Wexio had done, it was said that the priests of the duchy erred against God and the right understanding of his word by refusing to accept of some ceremonies, whose dissimilarity, like dissimilar forms of expression, should in their view sever the unity of faith and charity.

If, moreover, in despite of the king's own assurances, they accused him of a design to introduce popery, or if they plotted rebellion, all intercourse with them should be withholden. But on the question of the liturgy, there should be nothing further done, till a request had been made the king to call together a provincial council of the Swedish church. Possibly, by mutual conference, the controversy might be laid to rest, if, the first preface and notes upon the liturgy being removed, a new preface and notes explained what in the mass book or liturgy, had given occasion to scandal.

The project for conciliation, noble and cheering by its aims, and by the probability of its being effected, was made public in a series of reflections from the pen of the schoolmaster at Upsala, Petrus Petri, at the time when a council of the clergy of the archdiocese was to be opened, at which it was feared the archbishop would press the recognition of the king's demands. These reflections sufficiently well expressed the general sense of the diocese, to which Petrus Jonæ and Abraham Andreæ by birth belonged, and in which they both began their war against the liturgy. The priests of the diocese of Upsala, also declared their acquiescence in this project. They admitted that the clergy of the duchy had occasioned much discord and skeptical confusion, by disapproving of the order of the mass, and crying out against those who followed it as men papistically inclined. They had done as the king had done, "gone too far." For themselves, they would neither digress from the faith and duty becoming subjects, nor from the liturgy. But they did not denounce fellowship with those clergy, and desired the calling together of a church council, to re-establish concord and unanimity. This desire foreboded the approximation of the council of Upsala.

On the other hand, the letter from the clergy of the diocese of Strängness, was answered, in a less friendly spirit, by the archbishop and chapter of Upsala. A correspondence by letters, was carried on, with repeated accusations on the one hand, and apologies on the other, respecting the liturgy and the clergy of the duchy, to whom was imputed a contempt of the royal authority, together with mutual charges of papistic and Calvinistic tendencies. From Strängness, it was proposed that the dispute should be decided by impartial and unexceptionable arbitrators, and this proposition was accepted at Upsala, on condition it was approved by the king, who it was well known would allow the cause to be determined in favor neither of Rome nor Wittenberg. The conclusion of the correspondence was, that the archbishop and chapter of Upsala declared all intercourse forbidden between the clergy of Upsala and those of Strängness.

Meanwhile, the books of master Abraham had been circulated through the land, and sustained or increased the scruples and dislike of the liturgy, which the clergy of Charles's duchy awaked to new life. King John, in vain, endeavored to hinder the spread of these books, which against him addressed themselves to his people, to the clergy and bishops of the church, to his own daughter and his wife. He wrote to the princess Anna, exhorting her not to be seduced by the writings Abraham dedicated to her. He ordered inquiry to be made of such as imported or sold them, and all the copies to be seized. Whoever concealed them should lose his property, and be indicted as guilty of a capital crime.

It might be supposed, that the last years of king John's life and reign, from 1588, would have brought with them a change in his views and measures, as to the church. But this was not the case. Dissatisfied with himself and his renewed efforts, wearied with the opposition that encountered him on all sides, longing for his son absent in Poland, and troubled about him, he complained of Brahe, Nils Gyllenstjerna, Erik Sparre, and others, who were now out of favor, that while they abetted their king in his efforts for the liturgy, they would themselves not tolerate a priest who used this order of the mass. The king became reconciled to duke Charles, who now even took part in the management of the kingdom. The duke excused himself on the score of the liturgic controversies, inasmuch as he had neither himself written against the liturgy, nor incited others to do so, and of the clergy of the duchy only some few "who would gladly be wiser than all others," had raised up an opposition.

The council, in view of the prevailing contentions, had urged an accommodation at Wadsten, and the clergy of Upsala in their declaration against the diocese of Strängness, had also desired a church council; while the duke himself had said, that if at the beginning a *free* Christian council could have been called together, the difficulties would have been overcome, or at least the violence of the strife been obviated. There was, therefore, in 1590, an accommodation effected between John and Charles, on the condition, that a church council should be held, in which every member should have a free vote and voice; but if an agreement could not be attained between the two parties of the clergy, neither should put a restraint upon the conscience of the other, and no contentions or contumelious writings should pass between them, but all should live with each other in peace and quiet, so long as they were at unity in the true principles of God's word, however they might differ in church usages. It might from this be supposed, that John was wavering; but that very year, 1590, he directed, in his last will and testament, that the confession of Christian faith and worship, which were accustomed to be held and observed in the later years of his reign, and especially at court, should be held and observed in his kingdom after his death.

It was now, from 1590, agreed on all sides, to refer the subject to a church council. But in the complicated state of the case, this measure was more an expedient for getting rid of it for the present, than with any expectation of its being thereby immediately and finally settled. Still did king John, before his death, design to renew his vain attempt to enforce obedience by severity, and he was to witness the commencement of that decadence and downfall that waited on his work.

About the middle of the year 1580, men were put in office at the college in Stockholm, who were already acquiring eminence for their learning and cultivation. Now, and at a later period, disputes were engendered by the preference shown by many of these teachers to the philosophy of Ramus, in opposition to that of Aristotle. Ramus had been a martyr for protestantism, being murdered in the massacre of St. Bartholomew. His theological tenets, it is said, had been introduced into the universities of Leipzig, Wittenberg, and Rostock. These universities were still frequented not only by the subjects of duke Charles, but also and chiefly by students from Norrland and Stockholm, which were the birthplaces of those teachers. Their coming back hither presaged no friendship for the liturgy.

They avoided for some time all interference with the controversy, until the open declaration of the clergy of the duchy and still more master Abraham's writings, induced them to take part with the anti-liturgists, while on the other hand the king demanded a decided acceptance of the liturgy. The option was left them, in 1589, of subscription to the liturgy or banishment. Three of them, Nicolaus Olai, Petrus Kenesius, and Ericius J. Schinnerus, refused subscription, and when in strong terms they condemned the liturgy for the same reasons as those of master Abraham and the clergy of the duchy, they were thrown into prison.

The same fate awaited Erik Olai Schepper of Angermanland, who became from this period very conspicuous in the controversy. He was a man of restless and impetuous spirit, was from 1583 schoolmaster and then preacher at Stockholm, had been a warm admirer of the liturgy, and wrote in its defence. He acknowledged the difficulties connected with its use and introduction, but remained vacillating, until his friend, Erik Schinner, one day met him at the gate of Stockholm, took him by the coat, and besought him to change his mind. From this hour he became a most zealous anti-liturgist, thereby acquiring the king's displeasure, and from his former friends the nickname Turncoat. King John endeavored to win him back, but failing, turned him into ridicule, with the exclamation "To the lion and adder shalt thou go." Even the chaplains of Stockholm, Erik Petri and Englebert, were imprisoned, as was also the pastor of Taby in the archdiocese, Johannes Johannis, who wrote against the liturgy.

Complaint was made that the case was now rendered more complicated, since the rejection of the liturgy was regarded as a breach of loyalty, while it was not settled whether this breach consisted in mere disobedience to the king's will, or in the reasons offered for refusing the mass-book as an entering wedge for popery. Now, as before, those who protested, denied the king's power to decide what confession of faith his people should adopt, but repelled the accusation that they meant any wrong to the king's person. They demanded freedom of conscience, and appealed to a council of the church. The three lecturers at the college of Stockholm in vain implored the archbishop's intercession. A paper laid before them, by which they were to acknowledge that they had been misled, they refused to sign, because they would thus condemn their own and the church's cause. The question now was that of banishment. But they were kept in prison until the death of king John.

The point of time was approaching, when the words of freedom that had been spoken, and which hitherto had slumbered in many minds, or were silenced by prudence and hesitation, were to find a general echo. At the commencement of 1591, departed this life archbishop Andreas Laurentii Bjornram, who had been the king's most faithful ally in the contest for the liturgy. That he sacrificed his convictions to the royal favor, in the zeal he displayed for promoting the king's plans, cannot with full assurance be maintained. But he is obnoxious to the charge of being willing, by means of the royal favor, to force forward the establishment of a church discipline, since he was disposed to stigmatize the refusal of that discipline as a breach of loyalty. His place remained vacant till the council of Upsala. In 1587, the zealous liturgist, bishop Petrus Caroli of Linkoping, had died. To that see Petrus Benedicti of Westeras was, in 1589, translated, and in his fidelity the king had great confidence. Olaus Stephani Bellinus, pastor of Gefle, was chosen bishop of Westeras. Of these changes the vacancy only of the archbishopric could be of importance, or give occasion to fear any disturbance of the discipline that had been set up. There was, however, given a sign of defection from a quarter whence it could least have been expected.

King John had begun to give the city of Stockholm a more perfect ecclesiastical organization and division than it had before, by the appointment of pastors to the churches of Riddarholm and St. Clara. But, by the imprisonment of Schepper and the two chaplains, a priest was wanting for the congregation of the large church or Storkyrk, the rather, as Petrus Pauli, its pastor, by his open zeal for the liturgy and the suspicion of his inclination for popery, had lost the confidence of his flock. The king adopted the measure he had previously taken, of calling from the dioceses priests to perform divine service for a short time in the city. In 1592, the bishop of Wexio received an order to send up two priests. At a convocation of priests at Wexio, on the 20th of May, of that year, this matter was brought under consideration, in connection with the king's inquiry how the liturgy was observed in the diocese, of which these clergymen were to give him information. On this occasion the clergy prepared themselves for the consequences of not accepting the liturgy. They drew up in form their reasons against it, and these sufficiently testify to the influence of the confession set forth by the clergy of Strängness, and particularly of the writings of master Abraham; and as they had formerly been among the most zealous to condemn the clergy of Charles's duchy, so were they now the most forward, under the leading of their bishop, to make amends for this uncharitable precipitation, by a resolution to present their objections to the king, and refuse the use of the liturgy. They pictured, in a missive to the king, the unhappy effects of the liturgy, which occasioned disturbance to the conscience, doubts of the truth of religion, suspicions and controversies. Their consciences were wounded and made sore by the use of the liturgy, and they, therefore, begged to be delivered from it, begged not to be tied in religion by human ordinances, but to be allowed Christian freedom, which they would not abuse to a carnal self-will. They begged to be allowed to return to the church practices, which, before 1560, had been in use. But in order that unity might be restored to the church of fatherland, they requested the calling together of a church council, whose decree in respect to the order of the mass, they promised to respect and obey.

The two priests, who were selected by the bishop to be sent to Stockholm according to the order of the king, Steno Magni and Jonas Andreæ, pastors respectively of Wexio and Moheda, brought along with them the document and delivered it.

King John was now sick, and awaiting the approach of death; but he did not falter in his resolution respecting the liturgy. His answer was severe and reproachful. Pardon for their request to be allowed to break their promise, was all that the petitioners obtained of the king. To particularize, however, the king said to the messengers, that he allowed them, on the subject of the order of the mass, to act as they believed they could conscientiously answer to God and the king. They both refused to return with such an answer to their brethren They received at last one, more gentle but oral, and accompanied with a promise that the king would overlook a neglect of the use of the liturgy.

The steps taken by the bishop and clergy of the diocese of Wexio, could not but awaken joy and hope, in proportion as the hearts of the people and clergy were attached to the order which was to yield to the liturgic. The men especially, who led the opposition to the liturgy, must have hailed the dawn of the day of freedom and release. The two messengers from Wexio, received congratulatory letters from the imprisoned lecturers and chaplains of Stockholm, testifying their true faith and fellowship with them. Master Abraham exulted at the news of their success, and the gentle reception they had experienced from the king. Soon after, bishop Olof, of Westeras, also, in the name of his clergy assembled in September, 1592, forwarded a petition to the king for release from the liturgy, whose inconsiderate acceptance grieved and harassed their consciences. It is uncertain whether this petition ever reached the king during his last protracted sickness. By the opposition he experienced, and especially by the defection of the diocese of Wexio from the liturgy, he had become doubtful, not of the truth of his cause, but of the possibility of its now acquiring a lasting stability. For himself, he remained faithful; renounced all fellowship with the pope; excused his interference with the affairs of the church, by its condition at the commencement of his reign, and by the judgment of the kings of the Old Testament; and while he expressed his disapproval of the recall, by the priests of Wexio, of their given promise, added that he was not "the king of their consciences." This bitter controversy had afflicted his mind; and for four years, until a few weeks before his death, he had withdrawn from the partaking the Lord's supper. Its reception implied forgiveness of those who had offended and opposed him; and he ordered the release of those who had been imprisoned on account of the liturgy; which release, however, did not take place before his death. This occurred on the 17th of November, 1592.

CHAPTER VIII.

COUNCIL OF UPSALA.

THE death of king John foreboded vehement contentions and agitations, not only in the ecclesiastical, but in the other relations of fatherland. The last years of his reign were, for Sweden, one of those periods in a people's life, when a determined and dominant will, which puts itself above law or the public opinion which is stronger than law, thereby awakens opposition, and brings everything into disorder. The measure of the people's dissatisfaction was full. In the church, the liturgy which had been forced upon them, had already begun to be abandoned; and the increasing opposition which foreboded its approaching death, gained from the king the order for release of the men who had been imprisoned on account of that liturgy. One woe had come; another was soon to follow. The estates had already done homage to John's successor in the papistic Sigismund. From his blind attachment to jesuitism, whose great power was at his command, and from his obstinacy, which, if possible, was greater than his father's, the most alarming dangers menaced the church's freedom. But the last twenty years had taught the church what was due to its freedom, and wherein it consisted. The sympathy or acquiescence which was found for John's liturgy, was not to be calculated on for Sigismund's popery. The priests and people of Sweden had proved what they were, and now swore allegiance to protestantism. To preserve their most sacred inheritance, they must secure, against their powerful foe, a surer foothold than that which could be won on the smooth and slippery ground of the liturgic middle-way. This necessity was the doom of the liturgy.

All were of one mind, that the freedom of the evangelical confession must be guaranteed and made sure, if power was left in king Sigismund's hands. If the liturgy were not set aside before he returned from Poland, where, from 1587, he had been residing, and where complaints were made of his assaults upon the liberties of protestants, there would be danger and risk to the freedom of God's word and the pure preaching of it, not less than when one carries a light in a furious storm. But if the king would not guarantee to the land the freedom of the Gospel, he had lost all just claim to the inheritance of the Swedish crown, which had been granted to the race of king Gustavus I.; because this grant was based on the twofold service rendered by Gustavus, in having delivered his fatherland from foreign foes, and from the darkness of popery.

Of the sons of king Gustavus, there only now remained, since the demented Magnus was out of the question, duke Charles, in whose eyes the reformation, carried through in his father's time, was sacred, and to whom it was precious as a condition of the claim of his race to the Swedish throne. General attention was now directed to him, and his position in the commonwealth, as well as his resolute character, made him its chief. Immediately after king John's death, he presented to the consideration of the council, the project so often urged since 1587, and from so many quarters, of a church council, in which it might be settled whether the liturgy was to be retained or not. He soon after called home Abraham Andreæ from Germany. The king had pardoned all who were out of favor; and the duke thought that the sooner master Abraham came the better. He left also, with consent of the council, supplies of money for Erik Schepper and the professors who had been released from prison, and who, for some time, had been deprived of their incomes.

The duke then had already agitated the question of a church council. It was urged soon after by a portion of the clergy, who, on the 30th of December, 1592, were assembled at Stockholm on occasion of the solemn interment of the body of king John. It had been promised by the deceased king, as a means of reconciling all schisms in the church of fatherland. The duke purposed to lay before the council of the kingdom, his views on many points connected with this question. One was, how far it was admissible to announce the meeting of this council, without the king's knowledge, and before his return. It seems to have been concluded, that the council ought to be held, because its object was not merely unity respecting the liturgy, but still more to provide a defence for the protestant confession against the popish church favored by the king. Another subject of consideration was, whether the clergy only should be called together, or the estates of the kingdom. The former was urged by the council; the latter by the duke, who remarked, that as it was desired to provide a safeguard against popery, its practice ought not to be followed by holding only a council of priests. There was no difference of opinion upon the point, that the clergy, principally, were the persons to deliberate and decide at the council; but it was made a question, how far the liberty of decision, respecting the reform of the church, should be extended. The council advised that all alterations should be limited to a return to the condition of the church at the close of king Gustavus's and beginning of king John's reign, until the meeting of the council of Upsala, in 1572; an advice which seems to discover a dread of the influence of the duke's Calvinistic tendencies. The duke and council, on the 8th of January, 1593, gave each mutual pledges, to maintain in unison the government of the kingdom during the absence of king Sigismund, and to protect every man in the true religion, in the clear and pure word of God, *according to the Augsburgh Confession.* The duke, on the following day, issued, in his own and the name of the council, a summons to the administrators of the dioceses, to meet in a council of the church, agreeably to the request of the clergy assembled at the funeral of king John. The council was to be opened at Upsala, on the 25th of February next, in order to establish unity in doctrine and ceremonies, as had been purposed for some time; to make decrees regarding these matters and church discipline, and to elect an archbishop and suffragan bishops. The bishops should be attended by members of their respective chapters, by the provosts, and some of the most learned and qualified persons of each district.

King Sigismund's permission for holding the council, was neither asked nor waited for. The right of calling it together, was founded upon the commission which the king, on being advised of his father's sickness, gave his uncle, to watch over the affairs of the kingdom, in case of that father's death, and upon a subsequent authorization for the duke and council. Information thereof was sent to the king, by the secretary Olof Sverkersson; and the duke expressed his hope, that the king would both sanction the calling of the council, and the decrees it should pass. The king's assurance, that he would maintain religious freedom, and show neither hate nor love on account of any man's faith, was not trusted.

The experience of seventy years lay between the time of opening this council, and the time when the teachers of the Reformation began to preach in Sweden. The hierarchy had been shattered, and the errors were by degrees cast off, which for five hundred years had grown and been rooted in the church. King Gustavus had carried for his people, who willingly followed him, the work of reformation to its summit, and after the insurrection of Dacke, not an arm was lifted in defence of the old order of things, and only a few, who were pitied, remained attached to that cause. While the king and people sought a common goal, the principles which led each man to it were not accurately triticised. King Gustavus had, in the last twenty years of his life, acted on principles which prejudiced the people's freedom in matters ecclesiastical. But when, by their vigorous application, John first wounded the love and affections of his people, and when Sigismund's religious convictions and faith threatened to wound them still deeper, it was thought necessary, and that the time had come, when opposition should be made to those principles. The decree of the council of Upsala was a solemn protest against the principles of 1539, that there was a right in the king to determine what the religion of the land should be, and the council itself, indeed, was still more a protest.

This protest, whose consequences for the promotion of external quiet and freedom were incalculable, was attended by a grave and deep toning of the popular mind. But if there was a general inclination to follow duke Charles and the clergy of his duchy, in the contest against the Roman church, and to a great extent against the liturgy, there was also a dread of their too great influence, because they were suspected of Calvinism, which was not at all acceptable to the majority. Against this, too, must the freedom of the church be maintained. The favorers and defenders of the liturgy could not anticipate an acquiescence in their views and measures, but there was no certainty beforehand that a favorable turn might not give preponderance to their opinions and movements.

The clergy assembled at the appointed time in large numbers at Upsala. There are reported as present, four bishops, Petrus Benedicti of Linkoping, Olaus Bellinus of Westeras, Petrus Jonæ of Strängness, and Erik Erici of Abo. The bishops Jacob of Skara, and Nicolaus of Wexio, were, in consequence of their great age, absent. There were present, also, the four professors who belonged to the college of Stockholm, but who, after king John's death, were removed by permission of duke Charles and the council, to Upsala, to the re-establishment of whose academy king John, before his death, had given his assent. There were, as reported, also present at the council, twenty-two masters, and other priests, to the number of three hundred and six or three hundred and eight, without counting those who without a special summons were there. Duke Charles and nine of the council of the kingdom, together with many of the nobles and some representatives from the towns and the country were also present, but without taking part in the transactions and decrees, with the exception of the council of the kingdom who did so participate.

The day on which the council was called was the 25th of February, being the first Sunday in Lent. On this day, after evening service, the clergy of the archdiocese of Upsala assembled in the large audience-room of the college or academy, where, afterward, the meetings were held. The pastor of Upsala, Joakim Olai, made the opening address of welcome, and spoke of the reasons for calling the council, and of the propriety of electing a prolocutor or president.

The day after there was a general gathering of the members, although the order of proceedings was not yet settled, and they seemed to have waited for the coming of duke Charles, who, on Tuesday, February 27, made his appearance. On the previous day, February 26, bishop Bellinus of Westeras delivered a long address, setting forth the objects of the council, to establish a confession of faith, church ceremonies, and discipline, as well as to elect an archbishop, and bishops also, in place of those shepherds of the flock who were now well stricken in years. He exhorted to unity and peace, and implored the members each to regard his brother in the spirit of gentleness and love.

As yet nothing, after the opening of the council, had clearly manifested the tone which it would assume. This was sufficiently indicated the next day. Professor Erik Schepper delivered a discourse on the Holy Scriptures, and the studies proper to a theologian. He commended Luther and king Gustavus's merits toward the church, enlarged against the liturgists, and especially against the bishops, who, though they ought to have discovered the mischievousness of the liturgy, in the spirit of court adulation supported king John, who, with good intentions only, promoted its cause. The pastor, Petrus Paulinus, was severely reproved for one of his writings in favor of the altered litany. The church councils meanwhile had been of no use, since the questions discussed regarded only subscription to the liturgy. The bishops, professors, and the most eminent among the clergy, convened to deliberate on the rules of order and the course of proceeding in the council. On the subject of a prolocutor, the bishops urged the deferring of the election of an archbishop, until the council had passed its resolutions on other questions. The professors of Upsala, and the clergy of the archdiocese, demanded that an archbishop should immediately be chosen, because they could not take part in the council as long as there was no archbishop, nor any one instead of an archbishop to preserve order. It cannot be supposed, that a paltry impatience of the archdiocese's right of precedence operated in this objection. But as the archbishop, as long as the church's freedom was respected, was always regarded by natural right to be the prolocutor of a church council, or as at the first council of the reformed church in 1529, a prolocutor had been appointed *pro hac vice*, while the archbishopric was vacant, the wish to elect an archbishop before taking up other business probably proceeded from an anxious care for the church's freedom. The term president (præses), was avoided as a term of worldly power, or a Calvinistic form of expression, implying a free election for the time being. Probably, too, the fear operated, that some one of the priests suspected of Calvinism might be chosen. Therefore, after the duke had come, he was, on February 28th, waited upon by three of the prominent clergy, the pastors of Gefle, Tierp, and Ljùsdal, who on behalf of the diocese requested leave to proceed immediately to the election of an archbishop. The duke promised that after consultation with the council of the kingdom, he would on the following day give an answer. When the bishops also appeared before the duke, bishop Petrus of Linkoping was received with severe reproaches for his unwise zeal in promoting the cause of the liturgy. The bishop confessed and deprecated his fault. At a meeting together of the priests, Joachim, pastor of Upsala, met with similar reproofs from the chancellor, Nils Gyllenstjerna. Reproofs and apologies were received and offered by several other clergymen.

All things being now ready for the opening of the council and proceeding to business, the council of the kingdom, headed by chancellor Nils Gyllenstjerna, entered the hall where the clergy were assembled. There the chancellor, in behalf of the duke and council, respectfully saluted the clergy, and then announced that what king John had promised and what the clergy had requested was now to be accomplished, and a *free* church council be holden. Unity in faith and church usages, was necessary for even the temporal quiet and welfare of fatherland, as was too manifest from the ravaging wars that were raging in France and the Netherlands. Every member should be allowed freely and openly to utter his opinions, and give his reasons for them. In his own, and the name of the council of the kingdom, he declared that they desired to be rooted and grounded on the Augsburgh Confession of the year 1530, and on the church ordinance of archbishop Laurentius Petri the elder. He asked the clergy if they could promise and give assurance that they who were absent would approve and adhere to the decrees passed by those now present. This was unanimously affirmed. The king, continued the chancellor, shall not be, on his return, lord over our faith and our consciences. A confession of faith ought, therefore, to be drawn up and subscribed by all and every one, to be laid before the king, for his recognition and assent. That the election of an archbishop should precede any other acts of the council was not necessary, since an individual might be chosen, who instead of an archbishop could preserve order and act as prolocutor, and the priests of Wexio and Skara were here present without their bishops. He concluded by invoking God's blessing on the council.

The chancellor's speech was answered, in behalf of the clergy, by the bishop of Linkoping. The poor man, who, the day before, had been reprimanded by the duke, now brought down upon himself a storm of indignation from his fellow-members, by requesting directions from the duke and council of the kingdom, how the proceedings of the church council should be conducted. Schepper and the professors accused him of being always a court flatterer. This was a free church council, and directions were improper and unnecessary.

The question respecting a prolocutor, was still undetermined. The majority, and especially the priests of the see of Upsala, pressed the immediate election of an archbishop. The others, among whom were the bishops, wished the election deferred. A church must be built, was one of the arguments, before a priest was required. In this agreed those who loved not the freedom of the church, and did not do homage to its episcopal constitution. The result was a reference to the duke, and a request for his opinion. Two councillors, therefore, went up to the castle, to lay the case before him. The duke, who often expressed himself in a manner that showed he was disposed to find the right in what was opposed to the usages of the Roman church, answered, that one ought not to ape the pope in thinking it necessary to have an archbishop or bishop, as prolocutor of the council. They ought to elect from among themselves a suitable man, who, however, when the council was closed, should have no authority.

The election of a prolocutor was appointed for the following day, which was the 2nd of March. The session was opened, as were all that followed, with prayers and singing of the Veni Creator Spiritus. Professor Ericus Jacobi, and the schoolmaster of Nykoping, Olaus Martini, were chosen for secretaries. The votes were then taken, of which 196 fell to professor Nicolaus Olai Bothniensis; 56 to bishop Petrus Jonæ, of Strängness, and 5 to the bishop of Linkoping. The election was confirmed by the duke, in favor of master Nils, who, notwithstanding his endeavors to decline the trust, was at last persuaded to take it upon him. The result of the election satisfied both those who wished to regard the prolocutor as merely acting in place of the archbishop, and those who dreaded the strong influence of Calvinism, with which the duke and priests of Strängness were supposed to be infected. As the person elected had suffered persecution for his inflexible opposition to the liturgy, the views of the council seemed thus beforehand ascertained. On the proposition of master Ericus Jacobi, it was resolved to choose twelve assessors, who, together with the bishops, should act as counsellors and assistants to the prolocutor. The election of them, however, was put off to the following day.

On that day, the seventh from the day on which the council had been called together, being the 3rd of March, the proceedings were opened at 8 o'clock in the morning, in presence of the council of the kingdom, and a large number of nobles. The twelve assessors were first chosen; being men selected from all the dioceses. The first chosen was the old master Olof Medelpadius, formerly pastor of Stockholm, and a leader of the opposition to the liturgy. From the see of Upsala were chosen professor Kenicius, and pastor Olof of Gefle, and Schepper, the newly made pastor of the great church of Stockholm; from Linkoping, pastor Clemens of Wadsten; from Skara, pastor Gunnar, of Nylodose; from Strängness, pastor Reinold, of Strängness, and the reader of theology there, Paul Melartopæus; from Westeras, pastor Petrus Jonæ, of Arboga; from Wexio, provost Petrus Svenonis; from Abo, Gregory, the rector of the school at Abo; from Mariestad, in the diocese of Skara, superintendent Matthias Marci, who had been removed from that office.

After the prolocutor had delivered a short speech, thanking the council of the kingdom for permitting the church council to be held, and recommending to the members unity and prayer for the divine blessing, the first and most important point was, to settle the church's faith and confession of doctrine. Olaus Martini read seven theses, presented by the prolocutor on the Holy Scripture, enforcing its divine origin, its sufficiency for human faith and practice, its perspicuity and power to explain itself, its exclusive honor as the only rule for faith and works. Apart from this Holy Scripture, the writings of the fathers and the old doctors, could only be of value where the doctrine of the apostles and prophets was believed and acknowledged. The Apostles', Nicene, and Athanasian creeds, were acknowledged and confessed as expressions of the doctrine of Holy Scripture.

These theses and opinions were further explained and enlarged upon by the prolocutor, and by bishop Petrus Jonæ. They were considered as the basis of the deliberations of the council; as they expressed contrary views to those put forth in the ordinantia of 1575, and the liturgy. They corresponded with the German form of concord, in 1577, which, at the council of Upsala, was not mentioned. But as these conclusions were wanting in the Augsburgh Confession, they were offered as an introduction to it. Master Nils, after going through these theses, declared, that beside the three creeds, the Augsburgh Confession was an expression of the truth contained in the Holy Scripture; and the reading of its articles was immediately commenced.

They were proposed, in succession, by Olaus Martini, both in Latin and Swedish. After the reading of each article, it was explained by the prolocutor or some other; and the prolocutor recommended every member who was not satisfied with the explanation given, or harbored a doubt of the article itself, to present openly his thoughts and opinions, that he might not complain either of misconceiving the truth, or that the council was not conducted with full freedom. By noon the first four articles were gone through; and in the afternoon, between 3 and 6 o'clock, the five following. Pastor Joakim, of Upsala, who wished to defend an expression applying the word oblation to man's faith and prayer, was attacked by the prolocutor and the bishops, and obliged to recall it.

On Sunday, the 4th of March, there was no meeting. But when it is observed that pastor Joakim performed mass according to the old manual, we may thence conclude, that the previous Sunday the liturgy of John was still used at divine service in the cathedral. Bishop Petrus Jonæ preached at high mass or morning service, and in the afternoon the chaplain, Engelbert of Stockholm, who had suffered for the liturgy.

On Monday morning, March 5th, between 7 and 10 o'clock, the reading of the Augsburgh Confession was continued, with explanations and remarks upon the papistic and calvinistic errors which lay on each side of the truth. In proof of the article of the Lord's Supper, bishop Petrus Jonæ of Strängness, stood up, delivered a long address on the error of the sacramentarians, and complained of the suspicion which had been fastened upon him, but which he repelled, of being a secret favorer of Calvinism. On the article respecting the office of a preacher, the bishops were reminded by the council of the kingdom, not to ordain more priests than need required. The prolocutor hereupon was somewhat warm, and used a proverbial expression, that if one struck on a bush immediately ten priests came forward. Mention was made of a prescription of the canon law, that whoever ordains more priests than necessary must himself support them. On the following article, concerning ceremonies, there was complaint laid before the council; of a treatise in defence of the liturgy, composed by Petrus Paulinus, formerly pastor of Stockholm, as a work peculiarly obnoxious to censure. Twelve clergymen were selected to examine the production. The nineteenth article being reached in the forenoon, they assembled again in the afternoon at 2 o'clock, and concluded the examination of the Augsburgh confession. Then E. Schepper, addressing the body, complained, of the conduct of the jesuits and papists in Stockholm. A burgher of the city, Tideman Cornelii, had allowed them a room in his house, where they held public worship. The same thing was done in Drottningholm. The clergy generally objected to the cloister at Wadsten, its suppression was demanded, and the transfer of its incomes to the support of poor students. It was further urged, that no papist, Calvinist, or anabaptist, should be permitted to serve in the work of education in the national schools, or in the chancery; and that the Swedes who studied in jesuit seminaries should be forbidden to return to their native land. The council of the kingdom promised, in concert with the duke, to take the necessary measures and steps in all these respects.

After the reading of the Augsburgh confession, and the examination of it, were completed, bishop Petrus Jonæ rose up and asked the council of the kingdom and the rest of the assembly, if they received the confession which had been now critically examined and approved, and would hold fast to it, even if it should be God's will that they should on that account somewhat suffer. All arose and declared unanimously that they would not deviate therefrom, but be ready for it to stake their life and blood. Then the prolocutor exclaimed with a loud voice, "*Now is Sweden become one man, and we all have one Lord and God!*"

This hour, June 24, 1527, was, of all others, the most important and conclusive for the Swedish church Reformation, and thereby for the future of fatherland. On the principles of the decree now passed, rest the religious culture and character of our people, though more than two hundred years have rolled away. Not merely the future of Sweden, but of Europe, was determined by this decree, in the strength of which Sweden soon after came forward to war and conquer in the cause of religious freedom.

On the following day, March 6, Schepper preached in the morning at the cathedral, after which the men who had been selected for the purpose, met together at noon, to examine Petrus Paulini's treatise in defence of the liturgy.

The council assembled at 1 o'clock in the afternoon. The liturgy was now brought forward, and whoever would, was invited to come forth in its defence. But it found not a warrior in its cause, not a voice was raised in behalf of that order of the mass which for seventeen years had occasioned such convulsions in the Swedish church. When it thus was doomed, the prolocutor turned to the bishops with the reproachful inquiry, how they had brought themselves to accept it. There now took place a renunciation of the liturgy by acclamation. The three bishops present, who had been friends of the liturgy, stepped forward. Bishop Petrus of Linkoping declared, he had accepted the liturgy partly from ignorance, partly from constraint, or led on by those who then managed the church. He acknowledged himself to have done wrong, and prayed God's and the church's forgiveness. Bishop Bellinus of Westeras said, that he had been imposed upon by the explanations given of the liturgy, and offered as an apology that, before king John's death, he had already recalled the approval he had given. Bishop Erik of Abo professed that he had only acquiesced in the liturgy because he regarded it as compatible with pure doctrine. After this the priests of the city, the teachers, king John's court preacher, and lastly, the clergy of the dioceses, came forward, and, without an exception, recalled their consent to the liturgy. It became the cause of many abusive terms and nicknames. Strict inquiry was made of the course pursued by those who had more actively labored for the liturgy, or who had declared themselves in its favor. Many priests, who, without any other merit than accepting the liturgy had been promoted to good benefices, were displaced. Pastor Joakim of Upsala, was again attacked. He said that if all the rest abandoned the liturgy he was willing to do so. Master Nils was not satisfied with this, but wished a plain answer to the question, whether in accepting the liturgy he was conscious of having done good or evll. Joakim made no reply, and the matter dropped. Schepper thanked master Erik Jacobi, who had recovered him from error. Many of the priests of the archdiocese acknowledged individually their fault in having shown a zeal for the liturgy. This was done in the name of the bishop of Skara and the diocese, by the bishop's son, Olaus Columbus, who was dean of the chapter and pastor of Larf.

An inquiry was now set on foot respecting the writings, which, by king John's direction, were issued in 1588, in the name of the diocese of Linkoping, Westeras, and Wexio, against the clergy of Charles's duchy. Pastor Olof of Linkoping, exculpated himself and the brethren of his diocese, on the plea, that the king's secretaries, Olof Sverkersson and Henrik Mattsson, laid before them at Stegeborg a paper without any writing, on which they were compelled to underwrite their names. The bishop of Westeras declared, that to this lampoon he had never given his assent. In behalf of the diocese of Wexio, the provost of Wexio professed their sorrow at having been the occasion of scandal in the church, and offered the apology, that before king John's death they had withdrawn their support from the obnoxious liturgy.

Hereupon, the chancellor rose and thanked bishop Petrus Jonæ, and the priests of Strängness for the firmness with which they had striven and suffered for the truth. The councillor, Gustaf Bauer, admonished the priests to be warned how they signed obligations without reflection. They might be sure that it would bring ruin on their heads to be again tempted to defection. When Hogenskild Bjelke spoke in the same strain, he was spared, by his rank in the commonwealth, from hearing what was whispered among the clergy, that he ought to ask himself what he was thinking of, and what were his opinions, when, some years before, he forced the liturgy upon the priests of East Goth land.

Mutual reconciliations took place among the clergy, and promises to bury the past in oblivion. The question being then put by the prolocutor, whether they would abandon the liturgy, and the answer being unanimously in the affirmative, the session was closed by reading the confession of the diocese of Strängness on the liturgy.

When they were assembled in the morning of March 7th, from 6 to 1 o'clock, the prolocutor summed up the reasons on which the liturgy must be regarded as worthy of condemnation, and there were read the opinions on it of certain German universities.

Petrus Paulinus was then cited to answer for his treatise, to which allusion has before been made, and other charges were brought against him. He had, in that treatise, made use of contemptuous expressions toward the opposers of the liturgy, had defended the doctrine of the change in the eucharistic bread in a manner jejeune and tending to superstition, and in relation to ceremonies, had said, that man was to be instructed in religion by two processes, in his youth by ceremonies, at a later period of life by the word of God. He endeavored to defend himself, but was overwhelmed with replies. He excused himself by saying, that this treatise was composed by king John's direction; but one of the councillors testified, that the king had expressed dissatisfaction with Petrus and his book. There were now other accusations brought against him; but the case was deferred to the following day.

In the afternoon, at three o'clock, another session was held, in which there were brought under review the church customs and usages, that as a consequence of rejecting the liturgy, ought to be removed. Such were the saints' days introduced by the ordinantia of 1575, the white roklin of the priest, the episcopal robes and crosier, prayers for the dead, ringing at the elevation of the sacrament, chiming bells in the morning and afternoon in praise of the virgin Mary, the so called ciboria or tabernacle for the consecrated elements in churches, the washing of the hands of the priests at the altar, the removal of the mass book from one corner of the altar to the other, the having more altars than one in the same church, the shrines of St. Erik and other saints Resolutions were not passed in respect to these several points, with the exception of abolishing the newly introduced saints' days.

On the 8th of March, after a sermon by the German

preacher at Stockholm, the general subject of church ordinances and church usages, was introduced by the prolocutor. He reproached the bishops with having surrendered a great part of their jurisdiction to the chancery of the king, and reproached the officers of that court, with having intruded on the episcopal office. The whole question embraced the principles that, in 1586, were promulgated in the church of Charles's duchy, by the articles of Orebro. On the question of what mass or service book should be adopted in place of the liturgy, it was generally desired to return to that which was in use before the introduction of the liturgy. Thus was the old manual confirmed.

The case of Petrus Paulinus was afterward again brought up. There now came forward, as his accusers, Schepper, Engelbrecht, chaplain at Stockholm, and the representative whom the burghers of Stockholm had elected and sent to Upsala for this very purpose. He had forbidden the use of the Latin catechism of Chytræus in the school of Stockholm; he had, to an indiscreet excess, carried the doctrine of faith and good works, as presented in John's ordinantia and liturgy; had, in a funeral sermon at the burial of the burgomaster, N. Brask, who died in the popish faith, praised him as blessed; in a word, both in his preaching and his life, had manifested pride, ambition, and covetousness. A general dislike seems to have been accumulated on his head; and the council doomed him, as unworthy of his office, to have his official robes publicly taken off him by the bishop of Linkoping.*

On the next day's session, being the 9th of March, from eight to one o'clock, the subject of the mass book and man-

* Only one young man, an eye witness of his deposition, at the council of Upsala, shed tears over his ruin. This was his younger brother, Laurentius, newly come home master from his studies in Germany, who in after years, became archbishop of Upsala.

ual was taken up, in order to decide what ceremonies ought to be laid aside or retained. On motion of the prolocutor, the principle was recognized, that ceremonies were in the class of indifferent things, and could with Christian freedom be retained, but ought to be abolished when they were misunderstood or abused. This was the old principle of the Swedish reformation. Hereupon arose a question, respecting the use of exorcism in baptism, which had been, at an early period, debated in Sweden, and which Laurentius Petri, the elder, defended against the Calvinists of his time. It was now determined to retain the practice, as a declaration to the people of the child's condition before baptism. But as the usual words in this ceremony, "begone thou foul spirit," were thought to be hard and susceptible of an ill sense, the milder expression, "may he depart hence," was substituted. More easily than in the case of exorcism, which, as before remarked, had been abolished in the court of Charles, was there an agreement respecting the uselessness and superstition of certain other customs,—such were the lighting of candles on the altar when the gospel was read, and which were held behind the priest at the elevation of the sacrament; the carrying of a light in the hand at the churching of women, and the giving an offering to the church at the time; the bearing of a cross and standard before the dead body at burials; the consecration of the dead body and of graves; the use of frankincense; the practice of having lights at weddings; the marching with a train of the bridegroom around the church or churchyard. On this day, however, as on the 8th of March, the topics were canvassed, but no decree was passed.

The afternoon session began at three o'clock, with an examination of some priests, complained of for too great zeal for liturgism, but whose case was not till now settled. These were, Petrus, pastor of Skeptuna, in the archdiocese;

Hakan, of Stockholm, Thomas, of Abo, and Amured, of Stockholm. They were now received into fellowship.

As on the previous days, the council had drawn up its decrees, regarding matters of faith, divine worship, and church usages, the question of church ordinances and church discipline was discussed at this session. The church ordinance of 1571, was accepted and adopted, having been read and criticised in those portions, which, in the deliberations on ceremonies had not already been examined. Here, too, the views of the council were manifested, although they were not put in the form of decrees. To the conduct of priests especial reference was made. They ought to be examined before being ordained, and undergo a new examination when they were promoted to benefices. An elderly priest, who relinquished his benefice to his son, or son-in-law, should be allowed to take it again, if he experienced from him either ingratitude or disrespect.

The same subjects were canvassed on the following day, being the 10th of March. Mention was made of a church ordinance, that preaching and prayers should not last more than one hour. Complaint was made of the claim of the nobles to the right of patronage. The bishops and chapter ought, in conjunction, to have the right of conferring benefices. None should be transferred from one benefice to another, without passing through a fresh examination. Priests were admonished to take heed to themselves, and not to become "gadabouts." They should always bear in mind that they stood in the stead and place of God.

On this day, the council had concluded its deliberations and decrees, on all the topics whereof they considered themselves to have freedom of decision. But, while it was in session, much had occurred, and much was still to be desired, for the church's weal, that could not be perfected without recourse to the civil authority. Sixty-three points were therefore presented to the duke and council of the kingdom, containing the demands of this council of the church.

The first part contains the demands of the council in regard to the exercise of religion. The duke and council are requested to acknowledge, confirm, and subscribe the decrees of the ecclesiastical body, and to take care that they were approved and confirmed by the other estates. King Sigismund, before entering on his reign and being crowned, should confirm them. No alteration should take place through the constraining or persuasive influence of individuals, but through the joint action of the clergy and laity; and this action should not be accounted as an offence against the prince. The king should not have more than three popish priests, natives of Sweden; and these, as well as those from abroad, should be allowed to preach only in the king's court, and were to be carried with him when he left the land. The exercise of the popish or any foreign religon, should not be allowed, save in the king's chapel. No native, or foreigner, of another faith than that now adopted, should obtain office or service in the kingdom, should enter into marriage with a Swedish maid or widow, stand godfather, or receive public burial; and if there was no change of opinion within a night and a year, should be banished the land. Frequenting of jesuit or calvinistic schools should be prohibited. Clergymen who sought those schools, should be deposed; fathers who sent their children there be fined.

The second part contains the demands of the council for the church's freedom, in relation to the temporal power. Bishops should not be intruded, but be legally elected, and within three months after the coronation, be confirmed by the king. They should be allowed to exercise their office according to the laws of Sweden, the ordinantia of Westeras, and the printed church ordinances; by advice and consent of their chapters should place and displace priests and teachers, according to their merit or demerit; should exercise in the church the power of binding and loosing; have judgment in all marriage cases; hold visitations and convocations; and decide on disputed cases between those who were entering upon and those leaving a benefice. The bishops and their chapters should be at liberty to call together diocesan councils; and the archbishop, with the consent of the other bishops, to hold a general and free church council, if need were. The bishop or his official may see that the parsonage is kept in repair, and the priest must not be made to build beyond the legal requirement, but the parish must keep up the repairs. Except in the more weighty cases, such as high treason and capital offences, accusations against a priest may be brought before the provost of the district, from whom there shall be an appeal to the bishop and chapter, and from these to a council of bishops; and in like manner, if any one had a complaint against the bishop and chapter, in a matter that involved punishment. The bishops were critically to inquire into false doctrine, admonish, put under ban, and if there were no amendment, inflict banishment. When the bishops were summoned to court, one was not to be summoned to answer for the rest, but all were to be present at once. The lagmen, justices of the district, and stewards, were to encourage the people in reverence for the clergy, and in freely giving the salary to which they are entitled, on the principles and by the command of Holy Scripture.

The third part treats of the sanctity of divine service; and prescribes punishment to those who make a noise in or do not to go to church. The assize should not be holden in Advent, contrary to Swedish law, nor in Lent, Passion Week, nor on Saturday. The sergeants of the district and stewards, at their meetings in the church tower, "must not fall to wrangling." Proctors of cathedrals must always be priests.

The council now proceeded to pass resolutions respecting the incomes of the church and clergy. The wine and corn levied for building churches, should be maintained without diminution, and the tax laid where it did not already exist. Settled and established rates of salaries should be drawn up for bishops, chapters, priests in towns, and teachers, so that they might not, from their straitened resources, be necessitated to tread court stairs, and become the poor, mean, door-watchers of the great. Amelioration was desired of the heavy tax of entertaining guests from the wayside, and writing certificates for them ; since the priests excused the neglect of the proper duties of their office, by the hindrances and cares required by such calls upon their time. Release, especially was asked, from borough law meetings; instead of which, it would be preferable to pay a yearly tax. It was also requested that the compensation which king Gustavus gave to the support of the domestic establishment of each priest, might be affirmed, and they who had none, as yet, might obtain it out of the tithes of river and other fish ; so that poor priests, and the widows of priests, might have the old support.

In respect to the work of education, the council urged, that the regulations which it was now in contemplation to establish, might be applied to the college and schools. In every cathedral there should be a reader of theology, to have the oversight of schools. From every diocese some students should be supported at such foreign academies as acknowledged the Augsburgh Confession. Teachers should be allowed a yearly income. The professors of the college should be twelve in number, "double that number being found in the smallest foreign academies, and there could not be fewer, if things were to be conducted as they ought to be." A fellowship for students should be instituted; the libraries at Stockholm and Upsala inventoried and kept in order ; and no man be allowed to send his children to study abroad, till they had been previously taught at Upsala.

It was further requested, that the printing press should be removed from Stockholm to Upsala, whose chapter and professors were to take care that no popish or calvinistic books were printed there. A new edition of the Bible ought to be then printed, and the writings of Olaus and Laurentius Petri the elder, be collected and put to press, as also the Swedish Psalm-Book, with the excluded psalms reintroduced and all the newer ones left out.

The clergy requested that no vows on entering upon their office should hereafter be taken by priests, other than such as were publicly known and prepared in a form common to all, and that the duke and council of the kingdom would aid in restoring the written pledges to the liturgy, that they might be destroyed.

Finally, with regard to the cloister of Wadsten, whose dissolution was urged on the 5th of March, the council limited itself to requiring, that the nuns should be obliged to listen to a sermon on the Augsburgh Confession.

These demands, picturing the position of the church and the judgment of the clergy respecting that position, and constituting a programme of the Swedish church's history from 1593 for the succeeding century, were not separately deliberated upon by the council. There is no mention of a decree passed for their being made a rule of action, nor of the time of its being done.

After the session of the 10th of March, and a rest on the following day, which was Sunday, when bishop Petrus Jonæ preached in the cathedral, no meeting was held, either on the 12th or 13th of the month, those days being occupied in writing out clean copies of the decrees that had been passed. It is highly probable, as a manuscript gives us reason to believe, that during the examination of the previous proceedings, these "postulata" or demands, were arranged into divisions, and collected into a whole, and were then, with the addition of some new points, transmitted, on March the 13th, together with the decrees, to the duke and council of the kingdom. The consent of the duke to the decrees of the council, and his answer and that of the council of the kingdom to the "postulata" were anxiously expected, but in vain.

The council again assembled in session on March 14th, after hearing a sermon; and the hitherto deferred subject of the election of an archbishop occupied the attention of the members. The council had come together without the king's knowledge and assent. They had, independently of him, passed decrees, which they foresaw would prove unacceptable to him, and had expressed the determination of making his acknowledgment of these decrees a condition of admitting him to take possession of the throne. It now concerned them, to find a man sufficiently tried for courage and firmness, to be put in the chief seat of the church, amid those struggles and dangers with which the maintenance of the decrees of the council threatened the occupant of that seat, and the church itself. Master Abraham Andreæ, who had not yet returned to his fatherland, was looked upon as the most worthy of that dangerous honor; and he was called by an almost unanimous vote from his banishment to the highest honor and office in the church.

On the following day, being the 15th of March, an election was ordered for the sees of Skara and Wexio, the great age of whose occupants seemed to require a release, and for the see of Wiborg, which was to be again sundered from Abo. In these votes, only the masters of arts and the city pastors of the respective dioceses participated. To Skara, Henricus Gadolenus was elected; to Wexio, Olaus Martini; to Wiborg, Petrus Melartopœus. At the intercession of their dioceses, however, the two first-named bishops were afterward retained in office, although their former compliance with the liturgy, no less than their age, was regarded as a fault by the council. The see of Abo remained unmutilated.

The council had, with perfect unanimity, cast out the

papacy, and provided defences against it for the church. They had also, without difficulty, vanquished liturgism, and won its general rejection. But from the termination of the proper proceedings of the council, on the 10th of March, there began to rise a storm, which threatened to destroy the not yet perfected building of a sole church in fatherland.

The decrees of the council yet wanted confirmation of the civil government of the land, which was exercised by the duke and council of the kingdom. That council had been present and followed the course of the ecclesiastical synod; and as we have seen, one or more of the members of the former had given expression to his opinions before the latter. The duke, upon the contrary, had abstained from all interference with the movements of the church council. Both the council of the kingdom and the clergy construed this as a proof of his care for the church's freedom, and deliberated and decreed without applying to him for advice. There was also an anxiety to guard against the influence of Calvinism, of which there was something to be feared from the duke. His favorite bishop, Petrus of Strängness, had, as we have remarked, thought himself obliged to exonerate himself before the council from the suspicion of that error. But, after the transactions of the council, on the 10th of March, were terminated, the duke, who in all other things was in harmony with the council of the kingdom and the clergy, began to make known his dissatisfaction, that diverse church customs offensive to him were retained. From that day forward, there was a private altercation on the subject. But the synod neither would nor could retreat. And the decrees, notwithstanding the duke's known displeasure, were recorded, and on the 13th of March forwarded to him. When still, on the 16th of March, the answer of the government to the request for confirming the decrees was not received, the bishops, and some of the priests, waited on the duke, who was residing at the castle, formally to solicit his approbation and assent. The duke addressed them in harsh terms. They had, shutting him out, of their own pleasure prepared the meat for the dish, but they ought to bear in mind that the lid was not closed. His wrath was moderated, when the bishops excused themselves, on the plea that they believed the council of the kingdom to have acquainted him with the progress of matters. But they could not induce him to yield the points, in regard to which he required the council to alter its decrees. These were chiefly three, that exorcism should be removed from the baptismal service; that the use of salt and candles should be dispensed with, and that there should be no elevation of the sacrament in the mass or service of the Lord's Sup per. The duke refused to subscribe the decrees as long as these changes were not made. When he could not be induced to yield, the council held a new session in the afternoon of the 16th of March, to deliberate on his requisitions. It was fully expected by the duke that the council, which in concert with him had assumed the right of assembling, and by its decrees had well-nigh put at defiance the king of the land, would be tamely submissive. The council resolved to abide by what had been done, both to preserve the church's freedom in indifferent things, and because it was thought that these church customs could not be laid aside without creating disturbance and scandal. This was the very principle, which, about thirty years before, Laurentius Petri the elder, in quite the same form, maintained and pressed against king Erik and D. Burræus.

The council so far yielded, as to deem that an alteration might be made in drawing up the decrees, by the use of a moderated form of expression, and the decrees were, therefore, on the 17th of March engrossed, and they were in those points couched in the sense they afterward retained.

On Sunday, March 18th, there was a meeting at the close

of high mass; and the recent modifications of the decrees of the church council in the disputed points were read and approved. They were also approved by the duke. But a number of the clergy, at the head of whom were the bishops of Westeras and Abo, and the professors at Upsala, were dissatisfied with the alterations made, and by duke Charles's obstinacy they had been put still more on their guard against the dreaded secret influence of Calvinism. The decrees contained a rejection of heresies, among which was also specified the doctrine of the sacramentaries. It was urged that the name Calvinists should expressly be introduced. Hereupon arose the most vehement debates in the assembly.

Many, perhaps cautiously, wished to avoid a word which in their secret sentiments betokened nothing damnable. In vain the prolocutor reminded them that the Calvinists were included in the general term sacramentaries, and that after an accommodation with the duke had been brought to a happy close, he ought not to be again troubled and provoked. The opposition party were not to be moved from their demands, and the prolocutor, in an angry mood, left the assembly, without any decree on that point being passed. A portion of the clergy immediately left the city, without waiting for a decision on the case. But after evening service of the same day, the peace-loving and mediating bishop of Linkoping, with a number of the clergy, met together, and the decree was accepted and acknowledged in the form in which it had been last drawn up. It was agreed that they would assemble the following day, to subscribe it. At that meeting, which was on Monday, March 19th, a large part of the members of the council refused to subscribe the decree unless the Calvinists were in it expressly condemned. The moderate party were now obliged to yield, and the bishops of Linkoping and Strängness, with the prolocutor of the council, went to duke Charles, to obtain his consent to the required addition. Displeased with this demand, and with what he suspected to be its reason, the duke objected that the decree ought to contain the condemnation of others who were equally heretics with Calvin, but finally said, "If you put in all whom you know to be of that sort, you must include the devil himself, in hell; for he, too, is my foe." There was now added to the decree a condemnation of the Zwinglians and Calvinists.

After this was done, the clergy assembled the same day, being March 19, 1593, in the castle of Upsala, in presence of the duke, the council of the kingdom, and the rest of the laity, and delivered up the decrees as recited. The duke, council of the kingdom, and those present, acknowledged, received, and promised to subscribe them. The duke declared the council at an end, and dismissed the members to their homes.

The decrees of the council are a convincing proof that, as in recent times, discord and disunion, in matters of religion, within the realm of Sweden, had been the cause of divisions and scandal, and experience had shown that nothing is more mischievous in a kingdom than discord and disunion, and nothing more beneficial, or more calculated to bind hearts together, than concord and unity in religion; this unity was to be best won by a Christian general free national council. Such had been common from the apostles' times; and as King John had, some years before his death, consented that a council should be held, so had this assembly, by universal consent and approbation, been brought together at Upsala. Here, in the name of the Holy Trinity, after an earnest calling upon God, and after a godly and close investigation, had the following points been conciliarly settled.

1. All desire and will to continue and abide in the pure and saving word of God, contained in the writings of the holy prophets, evangelists and apostles. They acknowledge this holy Scripture to have its origin from the Holy Ghost; to contain fully all Christian doctrine; to be the basis and

stay of the true Christian faith, and judge in all religious controversies, and needs no additional light either from the holy fathers or any else.

2. The council further recognizes the unity and agreement of the Swedish with the church of the first ages, by acceptance of the Apostles', Nicene, and Athanasian creeds, with the reformed evangelical church, by acceptance of the Augsburgh confession of 1530; with the previous reformation of the Swedish church, by acceptance of the church ordinance of 1572, as the expression and exhibit of that religion which, at the close of king Gustavus's reign, and the life of archbishop Laurentius Petri *Nericius*, was here received and professed in this kingdom.

3. In respect to certain ceremonies at baptism and the Lord's supper, such as the use of salt, candles, and the elevation of the sacrament, the moving of the mass book from one end of the altar to the other, which ceremonies, from their abuse, had been rejected by most congregations; the council ordered that as well the parish priests as the bishops, at their visitations, should endeavor to remove the abuses from the minds of the people. But if this could not be done without rejecting and casting off the ceremonies themselves, the bishops, with their chapters, and the most learned of the clergy, should meet together and deliberate upon the most suitable means of getting rid of the evil, without scandal or noise. In regard to exorcism in the baptismal rite, the council declared that it was not necessary, but that, as it corresponded with the effect of baptism, it might be retained in congregations with Christian freedom; the words, "may he depart" being substituted for "begone hence." In retaining exorcism, there was no intention to condemn "high persons here in the kingdom," with whom it was not in use.

4. As the liturgy, which some of the clergy here in the kingdom had adopted, was superstitious and promotive of

scandal, and in its principles, altogether resembling the popish mass, so was it disapproved, together with all its evil train of doctrine, ceremonies, and discipline. The errors, moreover, were rejected, of the Zwinglians, Calvinists, Anabaptists, and all other heretics.

5. The church discipline, so it was said, was principally made known by the printed church ordinances; but as its exercise had been for some time neglected, all now promised to put it in force, and what was wanting in written prescriptions, the care of the bishops and chapters was to supply.

6. Although the council considered that foreign modes of faith could not be allowed to become established in the kingdom, yet, as they could not well be hindered, it was resolved that the professors of such modes of faith should not be allowed to hold any public meetings, in houses or elsewhere; and the council threatened those with punishment, who were convicted of the same, or who spoke injuriously of the religion of the land.

7. Whatever else was agreed upon and resolved in this council, should be forthwith made known in print. This promise, however, remained, by the circumstances of the times, unfulfiled.

In conclusion, they all, with great unanimity, pledged themselves, by God's help, to hold fast, and maintain the decrees that had been passed, committing themselves and their cause into the hands of Almighty God, "His Divine Majesty," as they express themselves, "being to us a gracious defence, and ever-ready shield."

The decrees of the council of Upsala, the fundamental principles of the Swedish church unto this day, were published and proclaimed in the name of Charles, the chief feudatory noble of the kingdom of Sweden, and in the name of the council of the kingdom, and of the bishops and numerous clergy, who had been present. They were subscribed by the duke, council of the kingdom, knights, nobles, clergy, and men of the market towns, for themselves and their successors, on the 20th of March, on which day the subscribers, though a small number only of the members of the council, first enrolled their names. The decrees, however, were sent around the dioceses, in copies which were subscribed by those who had been present at the council. Nor was this done by them only, but as the synod had desired, by all others, by the council of the kingdom, the bishops, knights and nobles, priests and crown officers, individually, and by the burgomasters and councils of towns, in the name, and with the seals of their corporations. The vow was appended, that this document should be for them and their posterity perpetual.

These subscriptions were continued during the following spring and summer. Many of the councillors and others travelled about in various parts of the land, to make the people acquainted with the decrees. A century later, when the Swedish church, in 1693, celebrated the jubilee of the council of Upsala, a copy of the decrees of the council, with the names of all the subscribers collected together and in order, was issued to each diocese. The names appended are those of duke Charles, duke Gustavus of Saxony and Westphalia, the nephew of king Gustavus I., fourteen councillors, seven bishops, 218 knights and nobles, 137 holders of court offices, 1,556 priests, of whom 250 were of the diocese of Abo; making a sum total of 1,934 persons. To these are to be added the subscriptions of the burgomasters and councils of 36 towns, and that of an agent who came from Narva, for the purpose of signing in behalf of the burghers of that town, both Swedes and Finns. The list is closed with 197 names from the remoter provinces and districts.

The Swedish people rose up as one man, publicly and unanimously to confess and acknowledge the faith in which alone they found unity and peace.

The cause was won, and the descendants of the men who, by an honest war against that cause, had in reality promoted and perfected the victory, now by subscribing the decrees at the council of Upsala, gave up the formularies of their fathers. Among those who subscribed, are to be found a nephew of bishop Brask, and a son of Dionysius Burræus.

The recognition of the council by king Sigismund was still wanting, and it was uncertain if this could be won from him. In vain did Thure Bjelke the councillor, who was sent in the summer of 1593 to Poland, use all his efforts for that purpose. But the dread entertained of the king's obstinacy, was one of the causes that roused the Swedish people to enter warmly into the the contest for the freedom of their church. When, therefore, king Sigismund, on disembarking at Stockholm, on September 30, 1593, was met at the castle bridge, not only by duke Charles and the council of the kingdom, with others, but by the clergy, headed by the newly elected and newly returned archbishop Abraham Andreæ, the token of respect was an expressive sign, that there was no intention of neglecting the council of Upsala, or of slighting its decrees.

The autumn slipped by in fruitless negotiations and a suspicious; apprehension and occasional malign occurrences increased the bitter feeling toward papists. In the churches E. Schepper, and the Jesuits who came in the train of the king, preached against each other. Scenes of violence occurred, and only under protection of Polish weapons could the bodies of the popish priests who died be buried in the churchyards. It was demanded, that the king should banish from the country the papal legate, Malaspina, who had accompanied him hither. Although that Jesuit, in defiance of the prohibition of the council of the kingdom, attended the funeral obsequies of king John at Upsala, the alarming menaces he received forced him and his compeers to abstain from burying in the cathedral of Upsala. On the occasion to which we have just referred, being February 1, 1594, the sermon delivered over the body of the deceased king was preached by the man he most hated, Abraham Andreæ.

When king Sigismund had come to Upsala, where, after his father's obsequies, his own coronation was to take place, and where the estates of the kingdom were summoned to meet him, the subject of giving his sanction to the council of Upsala was brought before him. The king who, soon after his return to Sweden, had stopped the printing of the decrees of the council of Upsala, finding there was no hope for its entire suppression, endeavored to obtain such a modification, as respect for the faith he professed might authorize him to demand and expect from the estates of the kingdom. He offered to confirm the religion which was current and received at the close of his grandfather's and beginning of his father's reign. He required merely the suppression of the points which related to free exercise of any other faith than the evangelical Lutheran confessions. He promised to give his sanction to the council of Upsala on condition that the estates of the kingdom should re-examine its decrees. He finally shrunk his demands to the single request, that the yet unfinished church of Sodermalm, in the suburbs of Stockholm, might be opened for the exercises of his religion. All was in vain; nothing was conceded beyond what had already been conceded—the right of the king to have the papal service performed in his own court.

When the negotiations had for some time been carried on, under a growing impatience on the part of the estates, and an attempt to divide them on the part of the king's faction, and to gain over at least the peasantry, the estates assembled, on the 11th of February, at the college, in the same room where the church council had met. The archbishop read the decrees of that council, and asked if the estates were willing to abide by them. The four estates now entered on an examination of the several parts of those decrees. Soon after, the priests and burghers individually made known to the archbishop, who filled the place of prolocutor, their resolve not to deviate from the evangelical doctrine, but for it to venture life and goods. So also did the commons, and finally the knights and nobles, who all pledged themselves as willing for that faith to live and die. They declared, that whoever apostatized from this faith should lose all their inheritance, and if their children forsook it they should be disinherited by the parents. The same punishment was to be meted to those who allowed their children to be brought up in any other faith. All this was confirmed by all the estates, with the addition, that whoever refused to subscribe the decrees of the council of Upsala, should be incapacitated from holding any spiritual or temporal office in the kingdom, and that the exercise of no foreign religion should be allowed, except in the king's chapel. After this solemn confirmation of the council of Upsala had been given, the whole asssembly fell on their knees, while thanksgiving and prayers to God were read by the archbishop.

Two days after, on February 13th, the declaration that had passed and been engrossed was read. The commander of the military forces, who had not been present on the 11th of February, was now called up, and on the archbishop's putting the question, declared his hearty assent to the decrees of the council. A member of the assembly was appointed to inform the king of what had been done.

Finally, on the 16th of February, the king promised unconditionally to accept the decrees of the council; on occasion whereof, the following day, being the first Sunday in Lent, the *Te Deum* was sung in the cathedral of Upsala. The archbishop elect of the council, who preached that day, and himself raised that *Te Deum*, had not yet received the king's confirmation to office. It was not surprising that Sigismund should withhold it to the last moment, from the avowed foe, not only of his own, but his father's doctrinal views. It was given, however, at the last hour, on the evening of February 18th, and on the following morning he was consecrated, by the bishops of Linkoping, Westeras, Strängness and Abo. On the same day took place the coronation of the king. The king was spared the humiliation of being compelled to allow the archbishop to place the crown on his head, and put on him the other regalia. But even in this transaction was marked the victory gained by protestantism. The bishop of Linkoping, who was preferred by the king, was not allowed to perform the act, but the archbishop drew back, only on condition that Petrus Jonæ, bishop of Strängness, scarce less odious than himself, should take his place.

The king, on this occasion, pledged himself to protect and preserve his subjects in their religion according to the Augsburgh confession of faith of the year 1530, such as it was at the close of king Gustavus's and beginning of king John's reign, and as it had been settled by the council of Upsala in 1593, and that none should suffer let or molestation for the profession of that faith. Some weeks later, he confirmed and certified the demands presented by the clergy at the council of Upsala, and which had, though in a mitigated form, been offered the king for his recognition. The king obligated himself to nominate as bishop, one of three persons presented to him "by the clergy, chapter, and diocese." Of the privileges reserved to the bishops by the council of Upsala, those only were confirmed which gave them the power to appoint and displace priests and scholars according to the ecclesiastical ordinance of 1571 and the ordinantia of Westeras. The right of the chapter to give its assent, and the *jus patronatus*, were protected, as also the king's right to confirm in office the pastors of cities, and those of the royal benefices. A church council was not to be called without the king's consent; but the archbishop, who, by virtue of his office, "ought to have honor and authority above other bishops," was to possess the right, aided by the different chapters, of holding a general visitation throughout the kingdom. Bishops were to have the right of pronouncing sentence of excommunication. If the excommunication was not regarded, the case was to be referred to the king. The academy of Upsala was to be well supported, and kept up in strength. The king, by advice of duke Charles and the council of the kingdom, was to settle the incomes of churches, priests, schools and chapters. The tertial tithes were confirmed. In all disputes that concerned temporal matters, the clergy were to plead before the assize of the district, in spiritual causes before the bishop and chapter.

We have already begun to trespass on that circle of time, in which the eye, looking forward, contemplates that development of the church for the enjoyment and possession of which the Swedish people endured a struggle of seventy years.

Blessed be the memory of the fathers who bequeathed to posterity the good inheritance. *Amen.*

APPENDICES.

THE CONVERSION OF THE SWEDES TO CHRISTIANITY.

UNDER the kings and queens of the Yngling race, the darkness of heathenism reigned over the land of the Swedes. Some knowledge, however, of Christianity was, in all probability, acquired by its inhabitants through the commerce which, in the third and fourth centuries, was carried on, to a greater or less extent, with Constantinople, where, even before its change of name from Byzantium, the gospel had gained a permanent settlement. But the conversion of Sweden to the faith of Christ was not undertaken by missionary zeal, till the earlier part of the ninth century. In the year of our Lord 817, Louis, the son of Charlemagne, conferred with certain bishops on the most advisable means of converting the northern regions to Christianity, and induced Pope Paschal to appoint Ebbo, at that time archbishop of Rheims, as apostle of all the North. But Ebbo, although not contemning the papal bull and order, preferred the quiet of his see to the risk of a journey to Sweden, and the probable crown of martyrdom. The coldness, however, of the archbishop did not wholly defeat the purpose of the emperor. Solicited by a message from the then king of Sweden, he sent, in 829, a Benedictine monk named Anscar or Ansgarius, who afterward became the first archbishop of Hamburgh, with directions to use his zeal in converting the nations of the North, and bringing them into obedience to the chair of Rome. After a year spent with some success, Anscar returned to the emperor; but as neither the king, Biorn III., nor his people, were converted, it cannot be said that Sweden was yet Christianized

That the spark kindled by Anscar might not be wholly extinguished, Pope Gregory IV. deputed, in 836, Gautbert, or Simon, as he is sometimes called, to carry on the work of conversion; and with this object in view, conferred on him the episcopal dignity. But the rashness of this missionary and his fellow-laborer Nitard, caused them to be driven from the land; and they left no favorable impression behind them. This event distressed the pious heart of Anscar, who not only, in 837, sent the eremite Ardgar to king Biorn, but urged on bishop Gautbert to return once more to Sweden, fortified with a papal bull and the archiepiscopal authority. This prelate, however, excused himself, on the plea of being too distasteful to the Swedes, and proposed his relative Erimbert as worthy the commission of a missionary to that people. At length, and because no other would, without him, undertake the office, Anscar himself, in 860, commenced a second journey to Sweden, accompanied by Erimbert, with a letter of recommendation from the emperor Louis to king Olof. In this latter journey Anscar obtained, before returning to his see of Hamburgh, a free permission to preach the gospel throughout the land; and converts were made. But a hundred years were yet to elapse, before Sweden could properly be said to have embraced Christianity. And although Anscar, who died at Hamburgh in 869, did not neglect the seed which he had sown, but sent two able missionaries, Ragimbert and Rimbert, to strengthen the things that remained; and, although the archbishops of Bremen, where the see of Hamburgh was removed, either themselves, as in the case of archbishop Unno, went to Sweden or sent others to labor in that field, yet, during the whole of the ninth and tenth centuries, the gospel and heathenism were still in conflict for the mastery. The Swedish writers themselves attribute this slow progress of divine truth, partly to the greater interest shown by the missionaries in winning the people and their kings to an obedience to the Roman chair than to a knowledge of the gospel, and partly to the policy of the rulers, who feared openly to avow themselves in favor of a new religion which admitted no compromise with the old.

Not till a thousand years after the birth of our Lord, did *Suithiod*, the kingdom of Sweden and the Goths, become obedient to the faith. At this time Olof Skötkonung, or the lap-king (so called because he was made king when yet an infant in his mother's lap), was ruler of the land, and inherited from his father Erik the throne of Upsala. The king of Norway, Olof Trygasson, whose people had been already converted to the gospel, had received from England a bishop named Sigurd or Sigfrid, who, together with his prince, had become offensive to the Norwegians. The bishop fled to Upsala, to king Olof Skötkonung, who kindly welcomed him, and when sufficiently instructed, received from him, A. D. 1001, the rite of baptism, at a place still called, from the event, the spring of Sigfrid. This memorable baptism, which gives to Olof Skötkonung the honor of being the first Swedish monarch that openly professed the Christian faith, was followed by commotions excited on the part of those who still adhered to heathenism, except in Westgothland, where the rite had taken place, and where Christianity had been most widely diffused. To this diffusion king Olof Trygasson, of Norway, had in no small degree contributed, by the introduction of English priests, especially after the intermarriage of his sister Ingeborg with Olof Skötkonung's cousin-german, Ragwald Ulfsson, jarl or earl of Westgotha, who himself received baptism, with many of his courtiers, relatives, and people. This example was soon followed by men of every rank; and the zeal of Sigfrid was not without abundant fruit in the soil which before him king Trygasson had caused to be sown.

The work of conversion was ably, zealously, and with success, carried on during the reign of Skötkonung, to whom the archbishops of Bremen had sent Odinkar, the elder and younger, Gothbald, an Englishman, Folgard, a German, and others, to assist and strengthen the pious purposes of the monarch. Among these missionaries should not be omitted the mention of Torgoth, a learned man, devoted to his work of evangelizing the North. He came, in 1010, to Sweden, to whose queen and infant princes he administered baptism, and became the first bishop of the diocese of Skara, established by his exertions.

King Olof Skötkonung had so long welcomed the teachers sent him by the archbishops of Bremen, and submitted himself in whatever concerned religion to their guidance, that archbishop Unvan, as papal legate, conferred on him the title of *Most Christian King*, a title which his son and other successors to the throne of Sweden long retained, and of which the kings of France also, for many ages, made their boast. But King Olof soon had reason to hold such flatteries in suspicion, and to observe, that those prelates had in view to subject his kingdom, under pretences of religion, to the authority and dominion of the Roman see. He began, therefore, to look for teachers from another quarter. The neighborhood of England, especially to Westgothland, where the teachers of the gospel had found the most ready welcome, naturally attracted his attention; and accordingly we find that many of the missionaries in this king's reign were sent to Sweden from the British isle. Among them the most conspicuous is St. Sigfrid, who, actuated by a like zeal with his predecessor of the same name, left his archdeaconry of York in England, and passing through Norway, came, in 1020, accompanied by his three nephews, to preach and plant the everlasting gospel in the kingdom of the Goths. His steps were soon followed by other teachers, as Eskil and David, from the same shores. These men at first established themselves in no particular locality, but, like the apostles of old, journeyed wherever time and circumstances seemed most to require their presence for the preaching and proclaiming grace and salvation through Jesus Christ. In process of time, however, they found it necessary to imitate the other parts of Christendom, in establishing centres of action, which were to constitute the future sees of Sweden. Thus, St. Sigfrid, after having long preached the gospel over almost every part of the land, settled at Wexio, as the first bishop of that diocese, where he died in 1067. St. Eskil organized, after many labors in the work and duty of a missionary, the diocese of Strängness, where, in 1076, he received the crown of martyrdom from the hands of those who still retained their adhesion to the old idolatry; while St. David, at an extreme old age, died, in 1080, in the see which he had established in Westeras.

These, together with Skara, are the oldest dioceses of Sweden; and it is not without reason, that her historians attribute to the reign of Skötkonung the first firm establishment of Christianity in the land of their fathers, and the commencement of all that can claim the clear light of history in her civil or ecclesiastical annals.

II.

TRANSLATION OF A LETTER, FROM STOCKHOLM, WRITTEN IN LATIN, BY A. G. KNOS, DOCTOR AND PROFESSOR OF THEOLOGY IN THE UNIVERSITY OF UPSALA.

To the Reverend Dr. Henry M. Mason.

Reverend Sir: I seem to myself at liberty, with propriety, to count it among the pleasant and honorable events which have occurred to me, that the book which I published on the constitution of the Swedish church, has become known to you, reverend sir, and that you have sought more accurate information on a subject which has appeared worthy of a further explanation. Your letter, Reverend Sir, dated the 19th January, of this year, in reference to this subject, and which is an evidence alike of your courtesy, learning, and piety, I have received with the grateful feelings which it merits; and in carefully replying to it, will endeavor, to the best of my power, to explain the matter in question, concerning the succession which is called apostolic, of the bishops of Sweden. The evangelical Lutheran Swedish church, does not, indeed, make this question of such importance as does the reformed episcopal Anglican and American church, but that we do not altogether neglect it, appears from my book just mentioned.

In treating this subject, the first point to be considered is, on what authorities rest the constant opinion and declaration of our historians that Petrus Magni, bishop of Arovia,* received episcopal consecration at Rome. It will readily be agreed between you and me, Reverend Sir, that the testimony of Roman catholics themselves, who lived at the same time with Petrus Magni, and were intimately connected with him, must be of great weight in proof of that point. Two such testimonies I am able to present. *In the first place* (and this is most worthy of regard, and would, if nothing else could be shown, put it beyond doubt, that this was so done), it is read in the diary of Wadsten, as written down in their diary, by the monks of that monastery (whose brother, that is a presbyter monk, Petrus Magni, had been), from the time, when returning from Rome to his country, he took up his abode with the monks of Wadsten, and informed them of his consecration received at Rome. In that great work, which is entitled "Writers of the Swedish Affairs of the Middle Ages," edited in folio, tom. i, at Upsala, 1818, there is extant, a very recent and accurate edition of the annals of Wadsten, from which the following particulars are very accurately transcribed. At the year 1524 (l. 4, page 218), it is said "on the eve of the separation of the apostles, came our brother Petrus Magni, consecrated at Rome, as bishop of Arovia; received in the hall of the proctor, he then spent two days in the infirmary of the monastery, entertained with collations† among us. He afterward retired to the diet of Joncopia."‡ In the same diary, for the year 1499 (l. c. page 204), it is written: "that the lord Petrus Magni was consecrated for a brother priest;" and again, for the year 1508 (l. c., page 209), "Brothers Petrus Ingemar and Petrus Magni, went forth for the recovery of the house of our mother St. Bridget"‖

* From ancient times, even to our age, that city (and therefore diocese) is called, in Latin, Arovia, which poetically is termed Westeras. For, the first and most ancient name of this city was Westra Aros, i. e. Western Arovia (wester, westra, is poetically the same as in English west); but because, from the twelfth century, the name of Eastern Arovia was become obsolete; (previously the port and suburbs of Upsala were so called), Arovia is always the same as Westeras.

† Collacionando, a barbarous term whose nearest primitive we must probably deem to be *Collatio*. We suppose that by this is signified, that the monks of Wadsten received and honored Petrus Magni with a somewhat more generous entertainment, which surely was done on account of his episcopal dignity.

‡ The diet is the same as the comitia of the realm. This year it seems the Comitia of the realm was held at Joncopia. At that time, as is now the case, by law the bishops were obliged to be present at the comitia of the realm.

‖ The monastery of Wadsten was of the order of St. Bridget. Of this order and monastery, St. Bridget was the founder (St. Brigetta), a noble Swedish woman, [died at Rome, 1373] who spent some time in Rome, and there obtained a house appropriated to herself. This house was afterward considered as belonging in some sort to the monastery of Wadsten; on which account some monk of Wadsten almost always dwelt at Rome, and had care of the house of St. Bridget. This house was at that time the hospitium of the Swedes who were staying at Rome.

Another proof of this point is found in the epitaph of Petrus Magni which was most certainly composed by some Roman catholic, and, indeed, not long after the death of Petrus Magni, who departed life 1534. This epitaph is to be found in the great work of J. Messenius which is entitled, "Scandia Illustrated," tom. ix., page 49. This work was printed at Stockholm in 1700. It is proper, by the way, to mention that this Messenius was enrolled among the holy persons of the papists. This is the epitaph:

"Stranger, pausing awhile, learn something of me and my complaints, which, perhaps, it will do you no harm to know.

"I was Petrus Magni, called so after the manner of the Swedes;* a monk of Wadsten, and thence am I created a doctor.

"For being sent to Rome, I learned not without quickness, the arts, and chiefly those which relate to sacred things; which gave me my degree.

"In the mean time, our farm was put under my care, and the house itself, of Chloris,† in addition to the field.

"Being elected bishop by the fathers of Arovia, I am there‡ consecrated. At length, I return home to my chair. I repented of my return, because the king, about to introduce the doctrine of Luther in the country, was making there everything new. It is not allowed me to return to my cloister, as I often desired; nor am I permitted to have care of the faith, as I ought to have.‖ Not a few bishops remain consecrated by me, some of whom have left the faith.§ Thence to the Lutherans sprung a clergy in the land of the Swedes, and that wounds my mind.

"Worn out for the work of religion, by these and other evils, which were more than the stars, I commend my weary soul to the powers above, but they my body to the ground. And now, stranger, you may take your departure."

Notes by me [Knös] added:

* Petrus Magni, to wit the son, poetically Magnusson, so also in English, Anderson, &c.

† Under a poetic title St. Bridget is thus not obscurely indicated. See note ‖ preceding page.

‡ i. e. at Rome, which clearly appears from the context. ' The ancient chronicle of the bishops of Arovia, written in the Swedish tongue, adds, that this was done by a certain cardinal.

‖ History informs us, that Petrus Magni, even to the close of his life, favored the form of the religion of the papists, though cautiously and timidly.

§ Petrus Magni, on the 5th of January, 1528, consecrated at Strängness, as bishops, Magnus Haralds for Skara, Magnus Sommar for Strängness, and Martin Skytte for Abo. The two former did not leave the form of the pontifical religion. One of them, namely, Magnus Haralds, left his country, as an exile, in 1529; the other, namely, Magnus Sommar, abdicated his bishopric in 1537, and being endowed by king Gustavus I. with an annual stipend, passed the last part of his life in the monastery of Krokok. See also below.

If you ask further evidence, by which the consecration of bishop Petrus Magni may be proved, it may well be alleged that after his return from Rome to his own country, he always wrote himself bishop of Arovia, never elect. Many documents, in proof of this, are extant. Those which follow, I adduce from the great collection of diplomas edited by Hiernman, the keeper of the archives of the kingdom. And the autographs of the diplomas, are kept in the archives of the kingdom. The title of Hiernman's book is, "Riksdagors och Motens Beslut," *i. e.*, "Decrees of the Diets and Councils of Sweden;" and this work is edited in 4to, at Stockholm, 1728, seq. In tom. i., page 40, of this work, is read a diploma, given January 24, 1526, written in the German language, which begins thus: "Ni Nachgeschrifwene, Johannes des Erstifts Upsala electus, Johannes der kirken zu Linkoping, Petrus zu Westeras Bischof, Magnus zu Skara, und Magnus zu Strengnäs electi," &c., *i. e.*, rendered word for word: "We, the underwritten, John of the archdiocese of Upsala elect, John and Peter, bishops of the churches of Linkopa and Arovia, Magnus of Skara, and Magnus of Strängness, elect,"* &c. Another diploma, dated at Arovia, on the day of John the Baptist, 1527, written in Swedish, and cited by you, Reverend Sir, in your letter to me, in exhibiting the consent of the bishops, on the aforesaid day, to an Arovian recess, begins thus: "Thy Hans, med Gudz nad, biscop i Linkoping, Pader, med Samma nad, biscop Vesteras, Magnus Scara och Magnus Strängnas, med somma nad electi," &c., *i. e.*, rendered into Latin: "We, John, by the grace of God, bishop of Lincopa, Petrus, by the same grace, bishop of Arovia, Magnus of Skara and Magnus of Strängness, by the same grace, elect," &c. I wish you to observe, that John Brask and Petrus Magni, in both diplomas, are called in exactly the same manner, bishops; and that both are distinguished by the same mark of dignity from the other two, elect. We must also attend to the order in which their names are in this place recited. For the old order of the dioceses of Sweden, from the first propagation of Christianity through Sweden, to the present day, has been uncorruptedly preserved.

* *John*, who is named in the first place in this diploma, is John Magni, born 1488, legate of the pope to king Gustavus, 1522, elect archbishop of Upsala, 1524. At first a refugee to Poland, in the month of October, 1526. He afterward went to Rome, where he died, 1544. *John*, who is here named in the second place, is John, [poetically Hans, according to a common Swedish abbreviation of the name John. See inf. dip. seq.] *Brask*, born 1464; bishop of Lincopa, 1513. He left the kingdom of Sweden, August 1527, and died in the monastery of Olivæ, near Dantsick, in Poland, 1538. Petrus is that Petrus Magni of whom we now chiefly treat, whose name, in the following diploma, is written Pader, according to the old common Swedish pronunciation of his name, which in our daily talk is now so contracted as to be written Pär, Per, Petri.—Of these two here named *Magnus*, see above note §.

1, Upsala, an archdiocese, however; 2, Lincopa; 3, Skara; 4, Strängness; 5, Arovia; 6. Wexio; 7, Abo; 8, Lund, from the year 1658, when the province of Scania was subjected to the dominion of the Swedes; 9, Gothoborg, from the year 1655; 10, Calmar, from the year 1678; 11, Carlstadt; 12, Hernoland; 13, Wisby, from the year 1772. Abo is now subject to the empire of Russia. It easily appears, that Petrus Magni, whose diocese was the fifth in order, obtained in these diplomas, the place in which his name appears, on no other account, than because he, equally as John Brask, was a consecrated bishop; and therefore his name was placed before the names of Magnus of Skara and Magnus of Strängness, although the episcopal sees of both these, otherwise always preceded that of Arovia. This argument is shown to be of great force, from the circumstance, that as soon as, at Strängness, 1528, Magnus Harald and Magnus Sommar were consecrated, another order of their names makes its appearance. Thus, the decree of the council of Orebro, held in the year 1529 begins (Hiernman, l. c. page 92): "Ny efterscreffne, Laurentius Andreæ eirkideken Upsala, frä erkiebiskops sätes vagner presidens, och Hogmechtigh Furstes konung Gustaffs fullmindighi sendebudh; Magnus Haralds i Scara; Magnus Sommar i ; och Petrus Magni i Westeras, biscopa;" in Latin: "We the under written, Laurence Andreæ, archdeacon of Upsal, presiding in the place and name of the archiepiscopal see, and sent plenary legate of the most potent prince, king Gustavus; Magnus Haralds, of Skara; Magnus Sommar, of Strängness, and Petrus Magni, of Arovia, bishops." In this diploma, the true order of dioceses and bishops, used even to our time, is preserved. So it is in other acts. Lastly, I might produce the unanimous consent of the historians of Sweden, the cotemporaries of this Petrus Magni, and those more recent. But let us forbear their testimony. We hold it for certain, that the above evidence sufficiently, and more, attests to all, even the most critical, the historic faith of a matter so transacted.

Let us pass then to the other part of this question, viz., that the first evangelical Lutheran bishops of the Swedish church were consecrated by Petrus Magni. Proofs of this exist in the epitaph above cited, and in the chronicles of Sweden, written at the very time. In these chronicles it is recorded, that king Gustavus I., was anxious concerning the apostolic succession of the bishops of Sweden, and that for this reason, Petrus Magni, by order and admonition of the king, received consecration at Rome, with the very object, that by him this succession might be preserved and propagated; moreover, that Petrus Magni, by order of the king, on January 5, 1528, at Strängness, consecrated as bishops, Magnus Haralds for Skara, and Magnus Sommar for Strängness, also Marten Skytte for Abo; moreover, that at Stockholm, in the same year, on the Sunday next before the feast of St. Michael (September 22), in the church of the Franciscans, (at this time Ridathholm), Laurentius Petri elect, archbishop of Upsala, was consecrated by the same Petrus Magni, and Magnus Sommar; all those three, then very lately consecrated bishops, also assisting, as some annalists assert. Thus it is proved, that the thing was done, even with reclamation (we may say protest or reservation, though less properly in Latin), by the bishops Petrus Magni, and Magnus Sommar. Two well-known canons, adherents of the papal church were present, when this reclamation was drawn up and confirmed, with the subscribed names of these four. In this writing, these bishops declare, that not of their own accord, but yielding to the powerful authority of the king, and salvo jure of the Roman pontiff, they had willed the episcopal consecration conferred on the other bishops and the elect archbishop. This reclamation, which they certainly thought not of making public, unless a changed order of ecclesiastical affairs in the country, should perhaps require it, to defend themselves by it before the papists, was found after their death, and is preserved in the archives of the kingdom. Written in the Swedish tongue, it is too long to be now transcribed by me and turned into Latin. This reclamation was printed in a collection of acts upon the history of the Reformation of Sweden, by P. E. Thyfelius, doctor of theology, edited at Stockholm, 1841, f. 99, under the title, "Handlingar till Noriges Reformations och kyrkohistoria.' There is also read in vol. 2, page 21, f 99: "The archbishop Laurence Petri, lived to the year 1573, and through the whole of this time, the space, therefore, of 45 years, executed the archiepiscopal office. There can be no doubt, that all the bishops of Sweden, who were at this time elected and confirmed by the king, were consecrated by him, though the place and day of consecration we cannot indicate in all cases. This is proved chiefly by three arguments. 1. The apostolic succession of bishops, was, from the very beginning of the Reformation, a subject of great regard with king Gustavus I. 2. A law, to this day incorruptly observed, orders that no bishop, before he be consecrated, shall enter on the episcopal office, or preside in a diocesan chapter, or perform in any manner, the duties of the episcopal office, or enjoy the returns and emoluments of his office. Wherefore, from the times of which we speak, to our own age, the custom has prevailed, that every bishop, immediately after he has been elected and confirmed, and so, in the space of one or another week, at the most of one or another month, has been consecrated. 3. When in the reign of John III., who too much favored popery, bishops were to be consecrated, a great dispute, indeed, arose concerning the rites and ceremonies with which this consecration should be performed; because the king wished all the ceremonies of the papists introduced in these acts, while the clergy admonished him that certain of these ceremonies, as redolent of superstition, had not for some time been observed in the consecration of the bishops of Sweden. Yet, not a word was said of the bishops themselves, to wit, whether they should be considered to have received legitimate consecration, and were able to impart it to others. This was not doubted, either by the king, or by the legate of the Roman pontiff, the well-known cardinal Possevin, who then treated with the king in Sweden. I am not ignorant that some of the papists, in later times, have been unwilling to admit this apostolic succession of the bishops of Sweden. But they have been able to bring none at all, or very foolish arguments to sustain this opinion. Some, indeed, have said, that we ought to prove the consecration of Petrus Magni, performed at Rome, by documents drawn from the archives of the Roman pontiff. But how could that be done? since, to these archives access is given to no protestant, and the papists themselves, by no means wish to publish any such testimony. Moreover, they pretend that if it be granted that Petrus Magni was legitimately consecrated, it does not thence follow that the consecration he imparted to others is legitimate; since it was both done without the assent of the Roman pontiff, and Petrus Magni himself wrote a secret reclamation of this act. But it cannot escape you, Reverend Sir, that such a kind of argument, openly contradicts the doctrine of the papists themselves, concerning the force and efficacy of the opus operatum. In the same manner, perhaps, they might call in question the apostolic succession of the protestant bishops of England and America.

The matter being thus explained, I hope that the act itself may be considered worthy of acceptation. Most surely I seem able to contend, that no historian, who should examine a thing proved by so many and important documents, would refuse his belief in it.

To you, Reverend Sir, I give and entertain the greatest gratitude, that you have been pleased to write to me. Surely the time has come, when it is necessary that Europeans and Americans should more and more be united in a literary commerce. I cannot but grieve, that the theological and ecclesiastical literature which at this time flourishes under happy auspices in the republic of North America, with the exception of a few names is almost wholly unknown in Sweden. I am ashamed to confess this; but I promise, with all my heart, that I will labor with all zeal as far as in me lies, that this evil or disadvantage may be removed.

Farewell. God be with you, wishes, with sincere prayer,

Your most devoted,

A. G. KNOS.

Given at Stockholm, on the 14*th day of May, in the year* 1857.

III.

TRANSLATION, MADE IN SWEDEN, OF A ROYAL RESCRIPT, RELATIVE TO ENGLISH CANDIDATES FOR CONFIRMATION.

CARL JOHN BY THE GRACE OF GOD, &c.

By our royal grace and favor, &c., &c.

WHEREAS, on the 21st of March last, you have represented, * * that frequent applications may now be made in the city of Gothenberg for the rite of confirmation; that although the English Factory there existing is furnished with a special minister, he, the aforesaid minister, is not empowered to perform the act of confirmation, which, according to the statutes of the English episcopal church, can only be done by a bishop: AND WHEREAS, the bishop of London, under whose authority the aforesaid minister is placed, having denied him the right to confirm, has yet found a Swedish bishop competent so to do: AND WHEREAS, moreover, a Mr. Nonnen, merchant of the city of Gothenberg, being of the English nation and church, has made application to you for the confirmation of his daughter: AND WHEREAS, you desire that we would graciously allow Swedish bishops to confirm children belonging to the church of England, according to the rules of the ritual of the Swedish church, provided the aforesaid children possess sufficient knowledge of the doctrine of salvation, together with the first rudiments in the Swedish language; by which gracious permission these our subjects would be spared the great inconvenience of taking their children to England for confirmation, without which the right of entering into the state of matrimony and other privileges cannot be obtained: AND WHEREAS. you finally, humbly advance, that you, for your own part, would not scruple to fulfil such desire on the part of brethren in faith, the more so, as evangelical tenets are daily becoming more and more united, and that you consider that the act of confirmation might be performed in such wise that the English minister having let candidates either in presence of the congregation (which, however, is not customary in England) or of the bishop, give proof of possessing the requisite knowledge of the parts prescribed; the examination might be conducted in the English tongue, the bishop performing the act of confirmation, according to the prescriptions of the Swedish ritual, reading the "Our Father," and using the laying on of hands, in England considered essential: AND WHEREAS, you desire that this confirmation, in order to avoid attracting public attention, or causing disturbing assemblages of people, might be performed in the English Factory church: THEREFORE, in view of these things, We have found good to grant you the right of confirming members of the church of England in the manner humbly proposed, whenever application shall be made to you to that effect. We therefore graciously give you these in answer for your guidance.

We graciously recommend you to the Almighty God.

CARL JOHAN,
A. C., OF SKULBERG.

Stockholm Castle, 4th May, 1837.
To the Bishop of Gothenberg,
C. F. WINGARD.

In witness whereof,
Ex-officio,
OSCAR ED. RAHE,
Cons't Not'r.

IV.

FROM THE PRESENT CHURCH MANUAL; OR, BOOK OF COMMON PRAYER OF THE SWEDISH CHURCH.

CONTENTS OF THE WHOLE VOLUME:

CHAP. I.—Of the Public Divine Service.
1. Morning worship.
2. Noon divine service.
3. Afternoon worship.

Week preachings.

CHAPTER I.

OF THE PUBLIC DIVINE SERVICE.

ON SUNDAYS AND HOLIDAYS.

1.—*Morning Worship.*

It is to begin with a morning psalm or some other suitable psalm. After a verse in the pulpit is to be read the usual morning prayer.

I thank thee heavenly Father, through Jesus Christ thy well beloved Son, that thou hast preserved me this night from all hurt and danger; and beseech thee to forgive me all my sins, and mercifully to preserve me this day from sin, misfortune, and all evil, so that my thoughts and all my actions may be acceptable to thee. I commit myself in body and soul into thy hands. May thy fatherly care be my protection. Amen.

Our Father who art in heaven, &c.

Then are explained, on fast-days, the texts appointed therefor, and on high fast-days texts suitable therefor, but on Sundays a portion from the Catechism. After the sermon is to be read, on Sundays, the prayer, "Praised be God and blessed forever," &c., (See p.); but in its place, on festivals, that compiled for the day and the prayer introduced in chap. 2. Afterward the prayers for princes, and the sick; lastly, the Our Father, &c., and the blessing; then divine service is closed with a short psalm.

2.—*Noon Divine Service*

Is begun, according to the nature of circumstances and places, with a short psalm. After the priest meanwhile has gone before the altar, he continues, turned to the people, to say the begun divine service, thus:

Holy, Holy, Holy, Lord God Almighty! The heavens and the earth are full of thy glory. We praise thee, we honor thee, we worship thee, we give thanks to thee for thy great glory, O Lord God, heavenly King, God the Father Almighty! O Lord the only begotten Son of the All Highest, Jesus Christ! O holy Spirit, Spirit of peace, truth and grace.

O eternal God, all thy works praise thee. Eternal as thou art is thy power: unchangeable thy Godhead. Look, O eternal Father, with clemency upon a people assembled in thy sanctuary, to adore thee, to give thee thanks for thy blessings, and to invoke thy grace for their spiritual and bodily welfare. Enlighten our understanding by thy wisdom, and make our hearts to lay before thee a holy offering of a true obedience. Loaded with the weight of our sins, we fall down before thee in the dust. and beg of thee forgiveness and grace, O God our Saviour! Merciful and good art thou: great in grace, and pitiful. Hear graciously the united sighs which are here lifted up to thy throne!

Here the priest, together with the congregation, falls on his knees and prays:

I, poor, sinful man, who, born in sin, afterward also, through all my life in manifold ways, have trespassed against thee, confess with all my heart, before thee, holy and righteous God, O Father, fountain of love, that I have not loved thee above all things, nor my neighbor as myself. Against thee and thy holy commandment have I sinned in thought, word, and deed, and to me, therefore, would there be an eternal condemnation, if thou shouldst condemn me as thy justice demands and as my sins have deserved. But now hast thou, beloved, heavenly Father, promised with mercy and grace to embrace all penitent sinners, who turn themselves to thee, and with a lively faith fly to thy fatherly mercy, and the merit of the Redeemer Jesus Christ. In him thou wilt overlook what they have trespassed against thee, and never more impute to them their sins. On this do I poor sinner depend, and trustingly pray, that thou, according to the same thy promise, wouldst be compassionate and gracious to me, and forgive me all my sins, to the praise and glory of thy holy name.

May the Almighty God, for his great unfathomable mercy, and the merit of the Redeemer, Jesus Christ, forgive us all our sins and give us grace to amend our life, and to obtain with him the life, everlasting! Amen.

Then the priest reads:

Lord, have mercy upon us.

Christ, have mercy upon us.

Lord, have mercy upon us.

Then, after he has stood up:

Glory be to God on high: and peace on earth, to men a good will!

Or also the congregation sings, after the priest has stood up:

Lord, have mercy upon us.

Christ, have mercy upon us.

Lord, have mercy upon us.

Whereupon, the priest standing, and turned to the altar sings:

Glory be to God on high!

Afterward is sung a psalm.

Then the priest turns himself to the congregation and sings:

The Lord be with you!

The congregation answers:

The Lord also be with you!

Or the priest reads (when the congregation does not answer):

The Lord be with you!

The priest turns himself again to the altar and reads or sings; on fast-days and occasional high festivals, the prayer which hereafter follows; but on Sundays and other holy days, that which stands before the epistle.

Let us pray!

We beseech thee, Almighty God, heavenly Father, that thou grant us a true faith, a steadfast hope in thy mercy, and a just love to our neighbor, through Jesus Christ our Lord! Amen.

Afterward are read or sung the texts of the day, on which there is no preaching, and they may be thus prefaced:

The following words writes the prophet N., or evangelist N., or apostle N.

Then is to be read or sung the creed, during which, in the former case, the priest stands turned to the congregation. If it is sung, it is customary to introduce the creed rhymed in the psalm-book.

When the creed is read, the apostles' creed may be used.

We believe in God the Father Almighty, maker of heaven and earth. We believe also in Jesus Christ, his only son, our Lord, who was conceived by the Holy Ghost; born of the Virgin Mary; suffered under Pontius Pilate, crucified, dead, and buried; descended into hell; risen again on the third day from the dead; ascended into heaven; sitting on the right hand of God the Father Almighty; thence coming to judge the quick and dead.

We believe also in the Holy Ghost; a holy Christian Church, the communion of saints; the forgiveness of sins; the resurrection of the dead and a life everlasting.

Afterward is sung a suitable short psalm or verse in the pulpit; after which preaching is held, on the subject either of the ordinary texts, or on those proclaimed for days set apart.

On high festivals, fast days, New-Year's day, Good Friday, Holy Trinity, and Advent Sunday, is sung an appropriate psalm for the Memoriæ. After preaching, follows, on common Sundays, the prayer, "Praised be God," &c., and then "Merciful God," &c.; but on Fast days, the Litany; on Lent Sundays, on passion preachings, on Good Fridays, the passion prayer; and on the high festivals, the select prayers appointed therefor; and then follow, the prayer for princes, the prayers for certain occasions (e. g. Diet prayers during the session of the Diet), for the fruits of the earth (that for the common season), intercessions for the sick, thanksgivings for the recovered and for the dead, the bidding of*

* *The mode of thanksgiving for the dead*

A new remembrance of our mortality is left us to day, when before this Christian congregation is made known, that the Most High has willed, after his all-wise counsel, to call from hence N. N., after a life of — years, — months, — days: N. N., after a life of — y., — m., — d.

After all are named in one and united thanksgiving, it is added

In submission to God's will, we revere his providence, and desire grace so to think on our own understood departure, that when death calls us we may be prepared for a happy decease (*here a necessary caution in distinct cases is to be observed.*

banns, the Lord's Supper prayer (when the Lord's Supper is celebrated), and finally the Our Father, &c.*

Then are to be recited the king's orders, and the respective notices of colleges and office men, (which ought to be left with the clergy before divine service is begun), and finally closing good wishes over the congregation.

Prayer after preaching:

Praised be God and blessed forever, who has comforted, taught, advised, and warned us with his word. May his good Spirit maintain the same in our hearts, that we may not be forgetful hearers of his word, but daily increase in faith, hope, love, and patience to the end, and be saved through Jesus Christ our Lord. Amen.

Merciful God, Father of all good, whose mercy endureth from generation to generation! Thou art patient, long-suffering, and forgivest all those who repent of their misdeeds and sins! Look pitifully on thy people, and hear thy children's sighs! We have sinned: we have been ungodly, and thereby become unworthy thy goodness and love; against thee have we sinned, and have done evil before thee; but remember not our transgressions. Have mercy upon us. Help us, O God, our Saviour, for thy name's sake. Save us and forgive us all our sins, and give us the grace of thy Holy Spirit to amend our sinful life, and to obtain an eternal life through Jesus Christ our Lord. Amen.

We call upon thee, O eternal and almighty God, the creator and preserver of all things. Have mercy upon us for Jesus Christ's sake, whom thou, after thy wonderful counsel, hast ordained as a mediator and for a propitiatory offering for our sins, that thou mightest manifest both thy justice and thy mercy. Sanctify and govern us with thy Holy Spirit. Gather, strengthen, and preserve thy Christian people through the word and holy sacraments. Give us grace, according to this word, to pass with a right faith to a holy life. Preserve and bless our beloved king (*here to be introduced, according to circumstances, the rest of the royal family*), the kinsmen of the royal family, all trusty officials, all the land and sea forces, and all the other inhabitants of the kingdom, to the honor of thy holy name and the mutual welfare of us all. Bless the administration of the kingdom, give peaceful and happy social intercourse, good and suitable

* *The bidding of banns takes place thus:*
A Christian agreement to marry is published in this congregation the first, (second, third) time, between N. N. and N. N.; the first (second third) time, between N. N. and N. N. (*and so on, and to the end, till all publications are recited*). And there is wished them, to this important union, happiness and the blessing of God, who has instituted marriage.

weather, equitable and Christian counsel to all that we undertake, and after this life, an eternal salvation, through thy Son Jesus Christ our Lord. Amen.

Another:

We thank thee, Almighty, heavenly Father, for all the grace and all the blessings which we, through thy fatherly care, daily enjoy—for all the good things our souls possess—for every blessed hour when we delivered ourselves up to the contemplation of thine infinite love—for all the good purposes which thou hast awakened in us, and for every deed good and acceptable to thee, which we have been able to perform through thy grace.

We thank thee for the patience, wherewith thou hast borne with us—for thy fatherly long suffering, wherewith thou hast overlooked our faults, which we confess and repent in heart—for every glad hour thou hast bestowed upon us, which we have been permitted to enjoy in thy blessed fear, with our neighbors and friends—for all the help and care which we even in the things of the body have experienced when we, under thy blessing, have undisturbed and with success been able to pursue the business of our calling—that no good thing has been wanting to us—that we have possessed health and strength, and in the sweat of our faces could gain and enjoy our daily bread.

O Lord, we know that all thy works are goodness, and that thy love to us extends as wide as are the heavens. Who then should not, with humility and a child's submission to thy will, bear the cross thou imposest! Oh, that in our society no one were himself the cause of his own trouble and destruction. Father! thy will, thy righteousness and good pleasure come to pass always among us.

With love and confidence of heart we trust to thee our future days. Be thou for all time to come our God and Father! Strengthen thou our endeavors for the quality of a true Christian, after the exemplar of thy Son, to live justly, chastely, and godly. Quicken us hereafter through hope to an eternal salvation, and let us in all conditions of life enjoy thy divine aid and presence.

Fill our beloved king's heart with the spirit of thy wisdom, that it may be easy to him to guard his important duties, so that by his wise, mild, and just reign, thy pure worship may be promoted, and righteousness and peace kiss each other. Protect and bless the king's dearly beloved consort the queen (*here is added, according to circumstances, the rest of the royal house*), the kinsmen of the royal family, all trusty officials, all the land and sea forces, and all the other inhabitants of the kingdom, to the praise and honor of thy holy name and the mutual welfare of us all. Thou art a Father for all men, for the glad and the sorrowful, for the rich and the poor, for the happy and the neglected, for the widows and the fatherless—help and comfort all who put their trust in thee.

If thou wert not, O Lord! what were we without thee? But thou art—thou art our hope, our refuge, our salvation's God, the Father of the human race! Humble and trustful we cast ourselves before thee. We laud to-day and forever thy name, for thou art our God. Amen.

Prayer for those who shall go to the Lord's Supper.

O Lord Jesus Christ, who in this holy supper givest us thy precious body and blood, under bread and wine! Grant those who now design to be partakers thereof, that they worthily receive it, to strengthen and assure their faith in the forgiveness of sins. Give grace, that they with right hearts call to mind thy bitter pains and death, renew the covenant which they entered into in baptism, and seriously purpose by thy help to persevere in a true faith, godliness, love, firm hope and Christian patience, and so not wilfully violate what they with absolution have vowed in thy holy sight; that thus they may at last, with all the faithful, be partakers of the great supper in heaven. Amen.

Our Father, &c.

After all is ended in the pulpit, there is to be sung a short psalm, or some verses, during which the priest goes before the altar. When the Lord's Supper is celebrated, and the singing is ended, the priest, turned to the people, begins with this form:

Blessed Christians! Let us open devout hearts! Let us contemplate with veneration the Supper of the Lord, in which God's pitying love comforts penitent and burdened souls. Here is celebrated to-day the Supper of Jesus. Here is distributed and received under bread and wine, his body and blood, in a supernatural and inscrutable manner, according to God's own wisdom, truth, and omnipotence, who has himself ordained the Holy Supper. How we should be qualified to become partakers of this precious treasure, the apostle Paul teaches us, when he admonishes that we, each for himself, examine ourselves, and so eat of this bread and drink of this cup. And we have examined ourselves properly, when, having called to mind our trespasses and sins, we hunger and thirst after righteousness and reconciliation in Christ for all that which repented of in this Sacrament shall be forsaken; and when we conceive an earnest purpose to do better in future, to forsake sin, and lead a godly life. So also has our Lord commanded us to use this Sacrament in remembrance, that is, that we therewith call to mind his death and the shedding of his blood, and think and believe that it is set apart for the forgiveness of our sins. Therefore if we, with sincere repentance of heart and reliance on our precious Saviour, eat of this bread and drink of this cup, in a firm faith in the word we here listen to, that Christ died for us, and that his blood was shed for our sins; so shall we also be assured of the forgiveness of sins, be delivered from the death which is the wages of sin, and obtain eternal life with Christ. But he who unworthily, that is with an impenitent heart, without faith in God's promise, without placableness, and without purpose of amendment, eats of this bread and drinks of this cup, becomes guilty of the body and blood of the Lord, and attracts to himself thereby condemnation. Therefrom may God the Father, and Son, and Holy Ghost, mercifully preserve us. Amen.

Afterward the priest sings or says, still turned to the people:

The Lord be with you!

When the priest says this, he is not answered, but when he sings it, the congregation answers:

The Lord also be with you!

The priest further sings or says:

Lift up your hearts to God!

In this case the congregation answers:

God lift up our hearts!

Afterward the priest says or sings, turned to the altar:

Our Lord Jesus Christ, in the night when he was betrayed, took the bread, gave thanks, broke it and gave his disciples, and said: Take and eat! This is my body which is given for you. Do this in remembrance of me.

Likewise took he also the cup, gave thanks, and gave his disciples, and said: Take and drink all ye of this! This cup is the New Testament in my blood, which for you and for many is shed for the forgiveness of sins. As often as this ye do, do it in remembrance of me.

Then is said or sung:

Holy, Holy, Holy, Lord God Almighty! Heaven and earth are full of Thy glory. Give salvation from on high! Blessed be he who cometh in the name of the Lord! Give salvation from on high!

The priest continues:

Let us now all pray, as our Lord Jesus Christ himself has taught us:

Our Father, &c.

Afterward the priest says, turned to the people:

The peace of the Lord be with you!

The communicants now approach, and the congregation intones:

O Lamb of God, that takest away the sins of the world, save us, merciful Lord God!

O Lamb of God, that takest away the sins of the world, hear us, merciful Lord God!

O Lamb of God, that takest away the sins of the world, give us Thy peace and blessing!

Then is sung by the congregation, some Lord's Supper Psalm.

During the singing is distributed, to each communicant, first the bread, wherewith to each and every one is said:

Jesus Christ, whose body thou partakest, preserve thee to everlasting life. Amen.

Afterward the cup, wherewith to each and every one is said:

Jesus Christ, whose blood thou partakest, preserve thee to everlasting life! Amen.

After the singing is ended, the priest says, turned to the congregation:

The Lord be with you!

Let us give thanks and pray!

The priest turns himself to the altar:

We thank Thee, Almighty Father, who hast instituted this holy Supper of the Lord, through Thy Son, Jesus Christ, for our comfort and salvation, and we beseech thee, grant us grace so to celebrate the remembrance of Jesus on earth, that we may also partake of the great Supper of the Lord in heaven! Amen.

Or,

We thank Thee, Almighty God, that thou hast comforted and refreshed us with this precious banquet of grace, and we beseech thee, that it may serve to strengthen our faith, and advance us in all Christian graces, through thy Son, Jesus Christ, our Lord! Amen.

* * * * * * * * *

Then the priest turns himself to the people, and sings:

Let us thank and praise the Lord!

Hallelujah, Hallelujah, Hallelujah!

The congregation answers:

Thanks and praise be to the Lord:

Hallelujah, Hallelujah, Hallelujah !

Or also the priest says :

Let us thank and praise the Lord !

Thanks and praise be to the Lord !

At length the priest says :

Incline your hearts to God, and receive the blessing :

The Lord bless you, and keep you ; the Lord lift up his countenance upon you, and be gracious to you ; the Lord turn his countenance upon you, and give you an everlasting peace, in the name of God the Father and Son and Holy Ghost ! Amen.

After the blessing, is sung a short psalm or verse.

When the Lord's Supper is not celebrated, and all is concluded in the pulpit, a psalm or verse is sung, after which, the priest, turned to the congregation, sings or says :

The Lord be with you !

When the priest says this there is no answer, but when he sings it the congreagtion answers :

The Lord be with you also !

Then the priest says or sings the prayer after the gospel for the day, but on prayer days the following prayer :

O Lord, Lord God, pitiful, long suffering, of great grace and mercy ! again to-day hast Thou called us to amendment ; again to-day, dost Thou offer us Thy grace. May none among us still harden his heart ! Enlighten Thou us, that our repentance may be sincere, our amendment solemn and enduring. Let us never break the vow which we to-day have made thee ; and grant us grace always to be a people that under all circumstances, trust in Thy mighty aid, through Jesus Christ, our Lord ! Amen.

Then the priest sings :

Let us thank and praise the Lord !

Hallelujah, Hallelujah, Hallelujah !

The congregation answers :

Thanks and praise be to the Lord !

Hallelujah, Hallelujah, Hallelujah !

Or the priest also says :

Let us thank and praise the Lord !

Thanks and praise be to the Lord !

The priest at length says :

Incline your hearts to God, and receive the blessing !

The Lord bless you and keep you ; the Lord lift up his countenance upon you, and be gracious to you ; the Lord turn his countenance upon you, and give you an everlasting peace, in the name of God the Father and Son and Holy Ghost! Amen.

The divine service is ended with a psalm or verse.

V.

AN OUTLINE OF THE SWEDISH CHURCH CONSTITUTION.

FROM the time of the council of Upsala, in 1593, as described in Mr. Anjou's History of the Reformation, the faith of the Swedish Church has reposed on the Apostle's, Nicene, and Athanasian creeds, in connection with the Augsburgh Confession. She is therefore catholic, by avouching the Nicene creed as the faith of Christendom through all time, and protestant in the usual sense of that term, as rejecting the added corruptions of the church of Rome. At the commencement of the sixteenth century, there was no known community of Christians that did not recognize and acknowledge the visible church of Christ as the depository of the faith once delivered to the saints, to be framed on the principle, that there was an order of men divinely commissioned to administer to the people in holy things; that of this order one class, who from the days of the apostles had been termed bishops, had alone received, and therefore possessed the power of perpetuating their line and power, always, even to the end of the world. This principle was then known, as it is now, as the apostolic succession. When determining, as in the foregoing history has been shown, to root out of his kingdom the corrupt practices, and intolerable tyranny of the Roman court, Gustavus Wasa was not the less anxious to preserve the rule, which he was aware had been observed before and in his time through all christendom. With this object in view, he caused to be consecrated as bishop, at Rome, one of the learned presbyters of Sweden, and through this man, Petrus Magni, as has been seen in the foregoing pages, the "apostolical and canonical succession," to use the words of one of Sweden's most eminent ecclesiastical historians and bishops, "has been in truth obtained among the Swedes." On these foundations of doctrine and discipline, the Swedish church has built up an external organization, which, like that in other lands, though more intimately the case in Sweden than elsewhere, has been deeply influenced by the national peculiarities.

At the entrance of Christianity into Sweden, the constitution of the country was a federative headship. Each province had its own king; and in time these petty kings became in a degree subject to the great king at Upsala, who was there the administrator of the religious rites and pagan worship. The people were represented in a general assembly by freeholders, among whom there was of course a diversity of influence; the man of law or lagman, being considered the most important personage, especially after the disappearance from the scene, of the petty kings. The Roman church accommodated herself to the condition and character of the people on the introduction of the new order of things. The dioceses were made to correspond with the old division of provinces, and an archbishop was established at Upsala, who, as well as the other bishops, in many particulars filled the rank of the ancient lagman. The parallel, indeed, between the bishop and that officer of the old Swedish people, is traced in many of the institutions and laws of the kingdom, and the popular reverence, combined with traditionary recollections, withstood even the strength of Gustavus I. in many of his attempts to weaken the episcopal power.

The hierarchy, on the other hand, were unable to introduce the canon law into Sweden; and so utterly opposed were the nation to whatever resembled arbitrary rule, or an infringement of the freedom which had descended from their forefathers, that in reference to the jurisdiction of the secular courts and other particulars which still existed in active operation in Sweden, pope Innocent III. complains, that "in no part of the world is the church so subject to the people as in the northern realm." The church of Sweden was in a greater state of freedom before the Reformation than that of almost any other land. It may well be supposed that this great event did not diminish or impair this freedom, or the spirit of that liberty wherewith Christ has made his people free. The Reformation, therefore, found in the liberties of the church and in the old spirit and freedom-loving character of the Swedish people, a soil in which it could easily take root, and the Swedish church may be said to retain its ancient features and characteristics to the present time, with the exception of those corruptions which the middle ages had introduced, and such changes as circumstances may have required, without affecting the essentials of either truth or order. We shall proceed, then, to consider the present constitution of the Swedish church in relation to—

1. The privileges of separate congregations.

2. The royal supremacy and popular representation.
3. The diocesan consistory and clergy.

1.—OF THE PRIVILEGES OF SEPARATE CONGREGATIONS.

The democratic feature—to use a familiar term—in the Swedish church constitution, is the more or less frequent meetings of the parishioners for various purposes. They are held twice, sometimes oftener, in the course of the year; are presided over by the pastor; and are summoned, either by their president, by the consistory, of whom we are hereafter to treat, or, when the congregation requires it, by the provincial governor. Though in some parishes the voices of the majority prevail, the general rule is, that the determination of any measure, at these meetings, depends on the votes of the land-holders, according to the amount of their taxable property. The sphere of business extends to whatever concerns the interest and advancement of the parish: the building and repair of the church, parsonage, and school-house; the election or dismission of the school-master, sexton, organist, and other inferior officers, such as the sixmen, or keepers of order in the parish; the rating of parochial contributions; the contract for the salary of the clergymen; and, indeed, not a few of those matters, which would seem to belong to the civil jurisdiction, and of which the burden is felt and regretted by many in the church of Sweden;—a burden, however, in part resulting from the union of church and state. At these parish meetings, are chosen delegates to the consistory, or council of advice, attached to every congregation, consisting of the pastor as president, with his assistant ministers, if there be such, and four, or at most eight, respectable inhabitants. Before this consistory, are tried any members of the congregation accused of immorality, non-attendance on divine service, matrimonial discord, neglect of children, and like offences. If the accused be found guilty, he is first to be privately admonished by the pastor, and in case of non-amendment, to be brought again before the consistory to be excluded from the holy communion. In every congregation, two of its members are annually chosen, who, in conjunction with the pastor, are to have the care of the church edifice, to keep the accounts of the parish, provide the alms-chest, and supervise in general all the outlays of money. To these, are joined two assessors, who, also under direction of the pastor, are chiefly to attend to the wants of the poor; while a third class, who may be termed school directors, are to watch over the interests of education in the parish, and see that in their districts proper schools are established, and that the pupils are religiously trained.

The synodal decree, introduced in the seventeenth century by bishops Rubeck and Gezelius, has become the general law of the land, that none should be married who could not read, or had not learned the catechism. The schools, indeed, of Sweden, are to be considered as a church communal institution, under the direction of the pastors and their congregations. The sexton of the parish is very often the schoolmaster; the election being made by the congregation; but the voice of the pastor is reckoned as equal to half the other votes. The clergy are expected or required to visit these schools, and to have the oversight of the morals and religious acquirements both of the teachers and pupils.

Upon the school instruction follows a preparation for the rite of confirmation, which in Sweden is made with great conscientiousness, on the part of parents. Nor does the religious instruction close with the rite of confirmation. Preparatory to the first communion, catechetical examinations are held before the whole congregation; the bishop, or provost, on general visitations, taking part in questioning those, the bans of whose marriage have been published, on their spiritual fitness for such an engagement, the young on their moral condition of mind, and other members of the parish, in their respective spheres, on their growth or decline in grace. To these means of advancing the life of Christianity in parishes, may be added what are called house visitations, which, originally due to the zeal of the clergy themselves, and subsequently sanctioned by law, embrace, in each district of 150 persons, the examination from house to house of the spiritual and moral estate of the occupants.

2.—THE ROYAL SUPREMACY AND POPULAR REPRESENTATION.

It is not possible for the safety of a state otherwise to exist, than by its having only one sovereignty, whether that be sustained by one person, as in a monarchy, or by many, as in an aristocracy or a democracy; for in them, also, there is but one supreme power. It will follow, that the supreme authority in a Christian State belongs to him or them in whom is that sovereignty. The church and state are two bodies, each of which, in things properly pertaining to it, has received a plenary power from Christ, the former subject to the latter in this world, and expecting its kingdom hereafter; the latter having a temporal dominion begun and to end in this world. There may be a conflict, as before the age of Constantine, between the two, or a union in which it is possible for both to move harmoniously without interfering with the other; the state culminating in that union to a high degree of eminence as in England; or, as in our own land, the severance of church and state may exist without danger to either. It is not, however, the part of this brief outline of the Swedish church constitution, to reflect upon the abstract blessings or evils of a union of church and state, but to consider, in relation to it, the organization of the church of Sweden, in which that union exists, and where that union is deeply fixed in the affections of the people.

To king Gustavus I., and his cotemporaries, it seemed as a necessary consequence of the Reformation, that the king should be, as in the neighboring kingdom of England, the head of the church. This great event had taken place under his guidance, and though a few dissatisfied prelates had left the realm, the rejection of the Roman yoke was welcomed in the hearts of the large majority of his people. There is no doubt that in practice, as was the case with Henry VIII., Gustavus stretched the power of his authority in the church to undue limits; but he asserted for his title nothing of supreme episcopal authority, or of purely spiritual jurisdiction; and, to use his own words, claimed to be only "the chief protector of Christian belief in his realm," an expression almost identical with that of his grandson, Gustavus Adolphus, who claimed the title of "*Defensor et Nutricius Ecclesiæ.*" There was danger, however, of the encroachment of the title and power of the king, as head of the church, on her spiritual jurisdiction, and the Swedish church apprehended, and sometimes experienced what that danger involved

It was a principal object of Gustavus I. and all the princes of the house of Wasa, to promote and fortify the union between the church and state; but in prosecuting that object, the first prince of that line desired to take the work of Reformation into his own hands. The protestant bishops retained no small share of the reputation and power of their predecessors of the church of Rome; and Gustavus, in order to break that power, which he believed fraught with peril to the interests of his realm, adopted measures, which, rivalling those of Henry VIII., of England, in the appointment of Cromwell, subjected in a great degree, as we have seen in the foregoing pages, the spiritual to the lay element in church and state—measures obnoxious to the sentiments of the leading reformers, such as the archbishop Laurentius and his brother, as they were to the people in general. His whole system, however, in its oppressive relation to the bishops, soon came to decay. The short reign of his eldest son, the unfortunate Erik XIV., had little significance in the affairs of the church. John the third, and Charles IX., the former with Roman, and the latter with presbyterian tendencies, were, like their great father, anxious to maintain that supremacy in the church which might aid their own views in the changes she was undergoing.

The shrewdness, however, and watchful care of archbishop Laurentius Petri, had provided a church ordinance, to which he gained the consent of the king, and, in 1572, the acceptance of the clergy. This ordinance contains the rudiments of all the Swedish church constitutions of the present day. It became a strong bulwark against the attempts of Charles IX., to use the royal supremacy for the introduction of his Calvinistic dogmas and presbyterian usages. Against these attempts, also, he found arrayed the strong and vigorous hand of Olaus Martini, the then archbishop, as well as the general voice of the clergy and people. The result of the contest, in which the unusual spectacle was exhibited of the king and archbishop writing books against each other, was, as it affected the power of the prince in the church, the full recognition, by even that imperious monarch, of the principle, that the royal claims were simply *jura circa sacra*, and not *jura in sacra*, terms, which in that age, as now, were known to involve a material distinction.

This prince left behind him a new source of contest on behalf of the church. At the close of his life, he had made mention of the establishment of a high consistory. His illustrious son, Gustavus Adolphus, bequeathed the idea to his friend and chancellor, Oxenstiern. This celebrated statesman devised a plan for a *Consistorium ecclesiasticum generale.* The presidency of this college was to be held alternately by the chancellor of the kingdom and the archbishop. To these were to be added certain assessors of the laity, two senators, and three judges of the then highest court of justice; of the clergy, the bishops of Strängness and Westeras, and the court preacher, the professor of theology at Upsala, and the pastor of the cathedral at Stockholm. The sphere of activity of this consistory was to embrace the whole range of ecclesiastical and scholastic discipline. It was to have the oversight of the bishops, of the diocesan consistories, of the clergy, of the schools, of the unity of doctrine and worship, and the appointment of suitable pastors, and be a court of appeals in all questionable cases.

Against the establishment of such a *Consistorium generale* arose a vigorous remonstrance, under the guidance, on the part of the church, of Rudbeckius, bishop of Westeras, a man to whom the church of Sweden owes many obligations. It was not questioned that the church, in outward things, should be dependent on the state. There was no desire to restore the old hierarchy in its tyrannical practices. A correspondence to the presbyterian form of government was regarded as ruinous to the church of the Swedes; and he who advanced the mere congregational or voluntary principle, would have been considered as the promoter of the spirit of indifferentism. It was readily acknowledged, that "the church should be under the care and protection of the king." But it was feared that such a Consistorium would reduce the church to become a part only of the civil administration; that she would thus, in worship, discipline, and the care of souls, be made subject to the state; and. as a consequence, lose more and more of her spiritual character, while, as was maintained on the part of the objectors, the diet of the kingdom was itself the proper Consistorium generale, since, in that the clerical estate was properly and fitly represented.

It appears from the controversy thus elicited, that such a Consis torium was regarded by all the clergy as unnecessary, unnational, and dangerous. Of the result of this conflict, in the church law of 1686, we shall have further occasion to treat. Returning, however, from this brief but necessary historical digression, it may in general be remarked that, in Sweden, a state church without an episcopate, or an episcopate without a state church, is regarded as a thing incompatible with the national weal. The privileges of the clergy and the freedom of the church, though culminating in a royal supremacy, kindred in many respects to that in England, are secured by the coronation oath of the kings, and by various laws extending from the earliest times to the present.

The Swedish church is closely united, but is not amalgamated with the state, and has assigned guarantees for its rights and freedom. The first of these guarantees is that by which the pure evangelical Lutheranism in faith and worship is secured. No other doctrine is permitted to be openly promulgated, and other forms of religion are only tolerated under certain restrictions. The king and royal house, officers of government, and members of the diet, must be professors of that faith according to the confession of Augsburg and the decrees of the council of Upsala, in 1593. To the king, as visible head of the church, appertain indeed high prerogatives; but he may force no man's conscience, if there be no disturbance of the public peace. In all important church questions, the people, by their representatives, take a part.

The freedom of the press is under mild restrictions, offences against which are tried before a jury; blasphemy, denying the existence of God or a future state, deriding public worship, the word, or the sacraments, being subjects of punishment. No proselytism from the faith of the national church is allowed; and the law yet exists which punishes with banishment apostacy from the pure evangelical doctrine; although Sweden, from the rooted attachment of the people to their faith, among other causes, has been free from the evils of persecution. The peasantry, which constitutes the most numerous and powerful class of its people, have remained almost untouched by the rationalism of modern times; the Bible, the writings of Luther, and the symbolical books, being familiar in their households.

In the church law of 1686, to which reference has been made, it is said, "that the oversight, care, and protection of the church and commonalty, are intrusted by God to the king." It is not understood in Sweden, that by these expressions, the king has authority over faith, or worship, or matters purely spiritual; but only over such things as concern the church in her outward relations, and in reference to her union with the state. The "oversight" denotes only what has been termed the *jus inspectionis sæcularis*, the right of taking precautions against a collision between the church and state, The "protection" includes the obligation of the king to guard the church in her rights and freedom. What the term "care" must signify, it is hard to say; but, since the last political revolution of Sweden, in 1809, limits have been set to the meaning, of which the indefiniteness was, at least by one of the kings, Charles XI., abused.

Every year, oftener when necessity requires, there is held, in Sweden, a diet, which consists of the four estates, of the nobles. clergy, burghers, and peasants. The representatives of the clergy are the archbishop as speaker, all the bishops, and the pastor of the cathedral at Stockholm, by virtue of their office, together with a certain number of pastors, chosen by the diocese, and a representative from each of the two universities. The king, or any member of the diet, including the clerical estate, has the right of presenting propositions, which are to have a formal enunciation in one diet, and be decided at the next. The decision is made by a majority of voices in each one of the four estates, by a simple yes or no, without admitting an alteration in the proposition considered in the former diet. The king possesses an absolute veto. In this construction of the national diet, therefore, is seen the influence of the popular representation upon the church legislation.

It may readily be supposed that the rights of the king, as head of the church, under the limitations of that term to which we have referred, have an administrative direction. All changes of the limits of a provostry or of a parish, whether to enlarge, as was formerly, or to diminish, as is now more often the case, and the questions not of a purely spiritual kind that occur in diocesan Synods, such as the salaries of the pastors, and the gravamina brought before the consistories for adjudication, are finally submitted to the decision of the king. His right to appoint the archbishop and bishops, as also the pastors of the so-called royal benefices, he exercises under many limitations. It is ruled by law, and the king always chooses one of the three persons presented to him as elected by the majority of voices among the clergy, a choice to which he is limited also in the case of the pastors of congregations, except in the royal benefices.

In Sweden, the church has no public protection but that of the state, so that the representation of the people acts not only as a state, but church representation, or general synod. The idea of a state church is therein carried to its extreme point, but not without counterbalances to preserve the freedom of the church. The holding of church councils was practised in Sweden, as elsewhere, before the Reformation, and at that era also. But, because, at that time, there were important church questions which affected also the interests of the state, they were brought under consideration and subjected to the action of the diet of the kingdom. Thus the groundwork of the Reformation was laid at Westeras in 1527, at Orebro in 1529, and, finally, at Upsala in 1593; in which last famous assembly, not only the clerical, but the other estates were present, and when the transactions gave it the character of a spiritual synod, the decrees were accepted and signed by all the estates.

Questions of a purely ecclesiastical character are previously considered by the clerical estate, and it is seldom, or never, known that in these questions the other estates decide contrary to the will of the clerical. As in England, however, the acts of convocation do not, *proprio vigore*, bind the laity without the consent of parliament; neither in Sweden is the action of the clergy a law without the assent of the estates in diet assembled. It is proper to add, that, in 1846, a project for a general synod appeared, which may result in fortifying the strength of the church. It is a prevalent opinion in Sweden, that a church representation mixed with that of the state, as is there the case, can hardly be the proper tribunal to decide, in the last resort upon such questions as the liturgical formulary of the church book of hymns, and the national catechism. The necessary changes in such matters have always been intrusted by the king to eminent churchmen, before being presented to the diet for final ratification; and sometimes a clause is added, which makes the introduction of a liturgical change dependent upon the consent of the individual congregation. It may also be remarked, that in many cases, not only the opinions of the popular representation and the clerical estate, but also of the diocesan consistories, are demanded before the king passes his verdict on church questions; these consistories being indeed, as we shall explain hereafter, a central organ for the affairs of the church. When a church question is special, it is referred to the diocesan consistory to which it properly belongs; when general, the united consistories decide the point. When a a church question is presented by the king to the popular representation, or to the clerical estate, the opinions of the consistories are at the same time presented; when it is primarily brought by either of those bodies to the notice of the king, he lays it before the consistories.

The royal supremacy is in many ways restrained by legal regulations, and is made subservient to the popular representation and the ecclesiastical jurisdiction. To the royal rescript, is required the countersign of the proper minister to whom the ecclesiastical matter belongs, to which that rescript refers. But while there is a check upon the king, in this responsibility of the minister, there has arisen, in Sweden an apprehension, lest this very responsibility should, in case of a conflict between church and state, result in a dominancy of the former over the latter; a result, however, of which, as no such conflict has yet occurred, prudence forbids the anticipation. Out of this union between the two, says professor Knös, grows "the principle of the church legislation and administration, not according to the presbyterian theory of a self-ruling of the church, so that only a veto is reserved to the state, but according to the principles of Lutheran protestantism, or, so to speak, the protestant episcopal system managed conjointly by the state and church in all weighty questions. We here find the popular element acting in a higher and lower sphere: in the latter, in the single congregation; in the former, as embracing and uniting the whole. The union of the two," concludes this author, "not interfering with each other, but promoting each other's aims in the temporal and, above all, spiritual welfare of the people, is perhaps the highest reach of humanity. The dangers we do not deny; but in what that is human are there not difficulties, for the conquest of which we must rely on the Eye that watches and the Arm that protects his church."

3.—OF THE DIOCESAN CONSISTORIAL CONSTITUTION AND THE DIOCESAN CLERGY.

The division of the country into dioceses, the episcopacy, the chapters, with the whole organization of congregations and the clergy placed in them, the Reformation found already existing, and the popular resistance was effectually raised against attempted changes, except such as protestantism made unavoidable in liturgical forms, the election of bishops, and the limitation of spiritual jurisdiction. The memorable council of Upsala was succeeded by the attempt, as we have seen, on the part of the state, to establish a consistory general as a central board for the whole church administration, a project defeated by the concurrent disapprobation of the clergy. In opposition to this plan of beurocratic centralization, and, indeed, before its appearance, there had arisen in the church itself its own conception of advancing protestant knowledge and the Christian life, in a diocesan organization resulting in that which is at this day a distinguishing feature of the Swedish church.

That which was chiefly designed was the regeneration of the visible through the invisible church, and by the true means, the efforts of the clergy themselves. The purpose of these synods, thus restored to their annual assembling, was at the same time to obtain a deeper insight into the fundamentals of faith, and an examination into the pastoral fidelity of ministers. To further the objects of these synods, there was, in 1620, created a gymnasium in every town where there was a bishopric. This was not only a preparatory school for preachers, but designed for the promotion of learning in general, and supplied the place of the former cathedral school. In these gymnasia, the heads of chapters acted as readers, and thus raised the credit of the chapters themselves; while the controversy on the proposed Consistorium generale proved how unjust was the charge that the opposition of the bishops originated from ambition, since at that time much of the authority of the bishops passed over to the chapters. In the establishment of the consistory, whatever was not of a purely spiritual character became gradually transferred to the proper state office and the secular courts. Thus was the foundation of the present diocesan organizaton laid, which, combining the episcopal and consistorial constitution with the establishment of synods and academical preparation, resulted in the law of 1687, from which there has been little change. The whole system aims at the promotion of divine life and Christian knowledge, and not the least promotive of these aims was the establishment of synods.

In the first place stands the bishop, whose title, "venerable father," sufficiently indicates the relation he is held to bear to his clergy. Next to him stand the most eminent men of the diocese, sharing his cares and accountability, who form a consistory, a diocesan concentration of Christian ministers, including all the clergy in the wider sense of the term, and the greater part pastors of distinct congregations, the sphere of the consistory being centred in purely church objects, such as the learning and behavior of the clergy, and through the gymnasium, for the formation of suitable preachers of the divine word. The young candidates were nominated to office by these their ghostly fathers, who afterward, as members of the consistory, examined the official rectitude of their former pupils. With these their overseers, was the diocesan clergy strictly bound together; the younger by the remembrance of former relations as pupils, the older by the esteem they gave these honored and young companions, to assist them in the duties of love and office. On the yearly visitations of the bishop, accompanied by some members of the consistory, these counsels had a public organ in the synods. Through these synods was the bond of unity still closer knit, and a wide field opened to pious zeal and Christian experience. Thus was the diocese constituted as an organic whole in a wider sphere, as the single congregation in a narrower one; while in the deputies of the clergy assembled at the imperial diet came the united dioceses in combination with one another.

This organization yet subsists in substance, though within the last few years it has undergone some changes. The diocesan synods are less frequently held. The Latin disputations have ceased. The more important church questions are determined in the imperial diet, and the synods are chiefly confined to local regulations, while the pastoral conferences are much neglected. Efforts, however, are being renewed to restore their weight and importance in the church. Episcopal addresses, like the charges of the English bishops, have again been restored, through the praiseworthy zeal of bishop Wingard; and annual synods have been again re-established in the diocese of Skara. The position of the gymnasium and university for forming candidates for the pulpit, has also been somewhat varied. Even after the great Gustavus II. had devoted his own patrimony to the revival of the university of Upsala, the formation of the clergy remained attached to the gymnasia. But as the university rose in scholarly rank, the gymnasia were more or less reduced to the class of preparatory schools; and, in 1831, a complete theological census, at present under the direction of the learned and accomplished Knös, affords the clerical students of that institution advantages equal to the highest schools of Europe. In consequence of an address from the representatives of the people (against which the clerical order protested), the whole school discipline has become changed, in so far that every gymnasium is now joined with the elementary schools, theological training being comparatively disregarded to make room for other scientific studies. The effect on the church, it is feared, will not be favorable, although the royal rescript, in 1849, is in general terms. Yearly free diocesan pastoral conferences, and the reintroduction of general synods, are demanded by the almost universal voice of the Swedish churchmen.

Each diocese of Sweden is to be considered as an independent member of the church of the land, co-ordinate with other dioceses, and subordinate to the king, in the manner which has been described. No metropolitical power belongs to the archbishop. He is only as *primus inter pares*, and the other bishops are not subject to him as suffragans. He acts, however, as their speaker at the diet, and the right belongs to him of consecrating the other bishops—this right being transferable in particular cases to others of the episcopal order. The old dioceses of Sweden were in number seven, but by the division of the larger dioceses there are now twelve. The capital, though belonging to the archdiocese of Upsala, is almost a separate diocese, and is governed by a special consistory.

At the head of each diocese is the bishop, whom the king, after election, as has been said, by the clergy, appoints to the office. The yet current church law of the kingdom requires, that consecration not only to the episcopal but the clerical office, must be altogether performed by a bishop. He has, in his diocese, the general supervision over sound doctrine and discipline, holds visitations either in person or by a delegate, announces the meeting of diocesan synods, and, with the provincial governor, superintends the conduct of schools and the due administration of church property. He also presides in the consistory, where the voice of the majority decides many points of church discipline and ecclesiastical jurisdiction.

The diocesan consistories, or as it is yet usual, according to old custom, to name them, the chapters, were formed of the bishop as president, the provost as secretary, and six gymnasial teachers as assessors. The assessors were named, partly by the king, partly by the consistories. The majority were to be always of the clerical order, having a right there to sit. By the consistories matrimonial causes and the offences of the clergy are tried and adjudged, but there is an appeal to the civil court, which, however, only declares what is the punishment assigned to the offence by law, the consistory itself carrying that punishment into execution.

The peculiar position of the Swedish consistories may perhaps be conceived, by considering them partly as a diocesan representation of the church, partly as a diocesan church bureau. In the former capacity, when they proceed to censure, and the warnings are fruitless, excommunication is pronounced. In regard to the clerical office, to the consistory, in connection with the bishop, appertain the two examinations required for the assumption by the candidate of the pastoral charge, as also the appointment to vacant congregations, except in some special instances, as where the rights of the patron or the crown are concerned. So intimate in Sweden is the alliance between the church and schools, that the office of schoolmaster is considered kindred to the clerical, and he has, when ordained, a title to promotion through the consistory, the bishop, as Ephorus of the school, having a double voice. In its capacity as a clerical bureau, the consistory carries the sentences of the diocesan synods to the king, in cases which require his sanction, and has, in general, the management of funds for pious purposes, of local church ordinances, and such matters of even a civil complexion, as the tables of nativities and deaths.

The diocesan clergy are under the inspection of the bishop and consistory, exercised in every provostship by the provost, who makes visitations according to a rotation ruled by the bishop, and who almost always conducts the installation of parsons in their parishes. He presides at the elections of bishops and in those of the clergy to the imperial diet.

The division of Sweden into benefices and parishes is of early origin, and, from the sparseness of population, the jurisdiction of the parson or pastor varied from 1700 to 400 souls. A law of 1851 has sought to remedy the evil of too widely extended parishes, but soon after the Reformation it was found necessary to appoint in the larger benefices comministers or capellans, sometimes called deacons, who, by the law of 1633, were to live in the sexton's house, and have a fixed salary from the parson and congregation. Here they learned and were exercised, after ordination, in the various duties of the pastoral office, till they were fitted to fill the benefices to which they were sure to be appointed.

The right of vocation to the preacher's office, belongs, in every diocese, to the consistory, but of ordination to the bishop only, as is explicitly said in the ordination formulary, "by virtue of the authority which is committed to him by God." The person ordained, at the time of laying on of hands, solemnly declares, that he will preach no other doctrine than that contained in Holy Scripture, as expressed in the Apostles', Nicene, and Athanasian creeds, and in the Augsburgh confession of 1530, as it was received by the council of Upsala, in 1593, and as it is explained in the Book of Concord.

The revenues of the clergy are derived from the parsonage and tithes. At the Reformation the parsons retained a third of the tithes, the other two thirds being diverted to the uses of the crown. This tertial tithe is still the chief revenue of the clergy, and is of all species of grain, and cattle, and produce of the mines. In towns the salaries are raised from free gifts, and from subscriptions by means of books circulated among the congregations. The duty of residence is enforced, and pluralities are not allowed. The parson enters his benefice on the first of May, and his heirs keep the revenues till the May ensuing.

From this brief, and it is to be confessed, bald outline of the Swedish church constitution, its principal features may, however, be easily discerned. Did we not know the contrary, we might be led to suppose that the Church of England and the Protestant Episcopal Church of the United States had combinedly furnished the leading characteristics of this church of the north. Government, in church and state, being both of divine origin, may exist in either, with or without connection. In connection, the one may overbear the other, as, during the culminating power of the papacy, the church usurped many of the prerogatives of the state, and as in the earlier periods of the Reformation, and subsequently, the state, both in England and Sweden, has intrenched on the rights of the church. In neither of these countries, however, has what is termed the royal supremacy assailed the purely spiritual jurisdiction of the church. It has never, in Sweden, adventured into the realm of the sacramental ordinances, or assumed to itself the ordination, the spiritual commission of the ministers of the church, in any of their sacerdotal functions. This power is reserved to the bishop, who, in Sweden, as in the far larger portion of Christendom, since, and without exception in all parts of the world professing the name of Christ, before the Reformation, derives that power from those who possessed it by succession from the days of the Apostles. This principle is maintained as a matter of fact, though the church of Sweden has not authoritatively pronounced on the invalidity of orders otherwise derived, or on the schismatical character of Christian bodies whose sacraments are by other channels administered; and it must be confessed that the sentiment and feeling both of clergy and laity is loose and comparatively indifferent to the doctrinal view, in regard to a possession, which they have, however, in reality strictly observed. The clerical order in Sweden retains much of its ancient weight, by forming a special estate at the imperial diet, more in accordance with the principle devised by the first Edward of England, than that of the British parliament, where the bishops form, as barons, a part of the house of lords, and where the restrained voice of the church speaks through her convocations. The consistories of Sweden may be compared to the standing committees of the church in the United States, and her parochial organization resembles that of parishes in our land, while the intimate alliance between the scholastic and academical system is far greater in Sweden than either here or in Great Britain. A liturgy, compiled from the most ancient, as is our own, with the addition of like offices for special occasions, protects the Swedish church from innovations upon faith, of the individual mind. In a word, the claims of the church of Sweden, as a legitimate branch of the catholic church of Christ, repose on her full acceptance and maintenance of the catholic creeds acknowledged always, everywhere, and by all, as expressed in the Nicene, and in her possession of the sacerdotal power, as bequeathed from the apostolic times, in the commission of our Lord. Her faith in the Augsburgh confession, avouches her protestant character in the modern sense of the term—for the catholic church is necessarily protestant against all error—as disclaiming the mediæval corruptions of the church of Rome; while the debt of gratitude is yet to be repaid to her gallant people, for the martyr blood, shed by the bravest of her sons and the noblest of her kings, on the plains of Germany and the field of Lutzen, in the cause of evangelical truth.

FINIS.

www.ingramcontent.com/pod-product-compliance
Lightning Source LLC
LaVergne TN
LVHW021050110826
845150LV00001B/32

* 9 7 8 1 4 2 5 5 6 7 9 3 4 *